The

New Vegetable Growers Handbook

The
New Vegetable Growers Handbook

By

Frank Tozer

Green Man Publishing

Santa Cruz

ISBN: 978-0-9773489-9-2

Library of Congress Control Number: 2013943611

Green Man Publishing

Santa Cruz

P.O. Box 1546

Felton

CA 95018

Visit us online @ Greenmanpublishing.com

Printed in the U.S.A.

Contents

Introduction

Up until the twentieth century, people in rural areas commonly produced a significant proportion of their own food in their gardens. This was what people had always done this and no one would pay for vegetables with scarce money when they could grow their own. The garden provided a margin of comfort and economic security, supplying its inhabitants with a better and more varied diet and making their lives easier. Indeed often the only difference between a comfortable family and an impoverished one was whether they had access to land for a vegetable garden. It was also the most secure and reliable source of food and if a crisis occurred, it could became a matter of life or death; providing the food that kept people alive.

The industrialization of the twentieth century not only brought greater affluence, it also broke the old bonds with the land. People moved to the cities and suburbs and the big, productive vegetable garden largely became a thing of the past. To most people food became just another commercial product, like shampoo or detergent, produced on factory-like farms and available year round, ready packaged from the supermarket. It ceased to be the most vital link between humans and the earth and as a result our view of nature became distorted. We now see ourselves as somehow separate from nature and are easily convinced that the health of the economy is more important than the health of the planet.

We have been encouraged to look at our food production system solely from the viewpoint of how much food costs at the checkout. The fact that Americans spend a smaller proportion of their income on food than any other country is considered proof of our success; that we must be doing it right. Unfortunately this simplistic viewpoint ignores the fact that our cheap food is totally dependent on cheap energy and actually has a very high ecological price tag.

We are told that modern agriculture is the most efficient the world has ever seen, but it is really only efficient in terms of the amount of food produced relative to the amount of human labor expended. This has been made possible because we have replaced human energy with massive amounts of cheap fossil fuel energy (as much as 10 calories of fossil fuel energy are expended to produce 1 calorie of food energy). Vast quantities of oil, electricity and natural gas are used to run machinery, produce fertilizers, pesticides and other chemicals, to pump irrigation water, for refrigeration and for fuel to transport the food an average of 1500 of miles to the table. It also uses vast quantities of water and in many places this is being pumped from underground sources much more rapidly than it is being replenished (basically it is being mined).

Chemical farming also burns up so much topsoil that it's been said that we are already past the point of peak soil. In parts of the plains over 50% of the topsoil has disappeared in less than 100 years because of the way we grow food. Not only does the loss of soil threaten future food production, but it also has another, more immediately damaging effect. The part of the soil that disappears is organic matter and it is converted into huge quantities of greenhouse gases. When a tonne of soil is burned up it liberates about three tonnes of carbon dioxide, along with nitrous oxide (an even more powerful greenhouse gas). Together these are the equivalent of about 33 tonnes of carbon dioxide. Many farms are losing several tonnes of soil per acre annually, so it's no surprise to learn that our system of industrial agriculture may produce 40% of all greenhouse gases.

Cheap food has also cheapened the essentially noble human activity of growing food and made it into a menial task. The people who do the work of actually growing our food are near the bottom of the heap in terms of status and wages. This is why they are often immigrants, doing work Americans consider to be beneath them. We live in a strange world when the activity that is most essential to human life is considered to be demeaning.

It is quite obvious to anyone who wishes to see, that the industrial methods we have been using to produce food won't work for much longer. There is no alternative to eating, so how will our food be grown in the future? Do we increase our reliance on a brave new world of technology, machines, ever increasing chemical use, genetically engineered organisms and multi-national corporations (whose primary responsibility is to make money for their shareholders), or do we look to more sustainable and self reliant ways of producing food?

There isn't a single answer to this question, but part of the solution is as close as your backyard. If you look at food production per acre (or in relation to the amount of energy, water and other inputs), home gardens are the most productive way of growing food that humans have ever devised. If every house had its own productive food garden, it could revolutionize the way food is grown in this country. The United States is in a unique position to be at the forefront of a new green revolution, because it has a benevolent climate and plenty of space for anyone who wants to have a garden. In recent decades suburban sprawl has swallowed up vast tracts of prime farmland, so fertile land is often right where people live. Some estimates say there are 30 million acres of irrigated suburban lawn in this country. If a proportion of this land were devoted to home food production, the changes could be dramatic.

If we ever succeed in building a truly sustainable "green economy", the organic food producing garden will no doubt become a central part of every home and people will look upon a house with no garden as they would one with no kitchen. As Christopher Alexander wrote "In a healthy town every family can grow vegetables for itself. The time is past to think of this as a hobby for enthusiasts; it is a fundamental part of human life". There will also be a need for a new kind of urban and suburban farmer, growing food intensively on small plots of land, in and around our cities. Some imaginative pioneers have already done this successfully in various cities, as did our ancestors around all major cities, before cheap transportation became available. For a couple of real world glimpses of what can be achieved with a little imagination search online: "cuba organic food" and also "incredible edible todmorden".

I don't want to give the impression that I think everyone should have a food producing garden out of duty to the earth, or that it is some kind of sacrifice. You actually get a lot more out of your vegetable garden than you put into it and far from being a chore, it becomes a wonderful source of satisfaction and pleasure. Working in it becomes a part of everyday life, something you do without thinking and as natural as going to the market to buy food, or spending time in the kitchen cooking it. You look forward to going into the garden to see how things are progressing. Often you find yourself going straight to the garden when you get home from work, before you even go into the house. You also find yourself getting up a half hour early, so you have time to walk around your garden, before you do anything else.

The benefits of a vegetable garden

The vegetable garden can improve your life in many ways, here are a few of them.

Fine food

I love great food and have found that the best way to get it is to grow it myself. One of the great pleasures of the vegetable garden is in eating the best food that can be obtained anywhere. With a little effort you can grow foods that are of exceptional flavor and quality and often simply aren't available commercially at any price. All serious home gardeners are familiar with the superior flavor of homegrown food, often it is so much better it doesn't even taste like the same thing. This may be due to the use of superior tasting varieties, because the plant receives better nutrition, because it is a lot fresher, or even occasionally just because you have grown it with your own muscles (which is still perfectly valid).

Health

Organic food, fresh from your own garden, is the most nutritious there is and it can improve your health significantly. It's been noticed that domestic animals will usually choose organic food in preference to that grown with chemicals, which suggests they can sense something that we don't. Organic foods may have more protein, vitamins and minerals to begin with, largely because they aren't bloated with water to make them bigger (the much vaunted high yields of chemically dependent agriculture are often simply extra water). When you are harvesting from your own garden the food can also be eaten within minutes of picking, before any of their vitamins and other nutrients have started to break down.

Of course organic foods don't contain any pesticide residues, which is significant because we really don't know the long-term effects of multiple pesticides in the body (As I write this the EPA is trying to raise the allowable residue of glyphosphate in food). This is particularly important for children, as they consume larger quantities of pesticides in relation to their body weight. Many conventional farmers have an organic garden for their own consumption.

Health is more than just good food of course and the garden helps here too. It is both a pleasant way to relax and one of the best forms of exercise, as it alternates between gentle and fairly vigorous activity (your body functions best when it is used). Working in the fresh air, at your own pace, at a satisfying meaningful activity (growing the food that sustains you), also contributes to psychological health too. Any stress I have soon evaporates when I get out in the garden and among my plants. It's actually been suggested that a persons stress level is directly related to how close they are to plants; that plants are actually a biological need for humans.

Environmental

A home vegetable garden can help to lessen your impact on the earth, by reducing your consumption of resources. The food is produced with only a fraction of the energy and water used by commercial agriculture and there are no transportation costs. It also has an impact on the amount of stuff you throw away. You can eliminate the packaging that comes with purchased foods and you can compost your food waste and any soiled paper packaging. You can use rainwater catchment and gray water to reduce the amount of water needed to grow food. An even bigger step would be to recycle human waste though the garden, though this still needs some refining. A system to do this safely would be a momentous step forward in reducing water use and pollution, and in recycling valuable nutrients back to where they can be an asset.

Financial

A vegetable garden can save you money. It is said that the average American family spends only 10% of their income on food, so it would seem that growing your own won't save a great deal. However statistics can be deceptive and at least one third of Americans spend 20% of their income on food. Those statistics are only talking about average food too; if you want to eat high quality, organic food growing it yourself may be the only way to make it economically feasible. Incomes have actually declined for most people in recent years, while vegetable prices have increased, making organic vegetable gardening even more cost effective.

The vegetable garden can also teach you a significant lesson in how money and the good life aren't synonymous; that you don't always have to spend money to enjoy yourself. When you get down to the fundamentals, life can actually become richer and more satisfying when you consume less and live more. It can also teach you that physical labor can be rewarding and that life isn't just about finding ways to avoid working up a sweat (your garden can even replace the gym).

Security

The ability to produce your own food also gives you a measure of psychological security. The number of Americans who remember the last serious economic upheaval is diminishing rapidly, but many will testify that their vegetable garden was an invaluable buffer against economic crisis. Americans have rarely lived with the threat of not having anything to eat, but in other parts of the world it is an all too frequent reality. I recently read an account of how many city dwelling Russians survived the demise of communism and the resulting economic collapse, by growing food in community gardens. Without this lifeline they would have been in dire circumstances. It is comforting to know that if food ever becomes scarce or very expensive you could always grow your own.

I am not pessimistic by nature, but any thinking person has to have some concern about the future. The economic situation of most Americans has declined since I wrote the first edition of this book and shows little prospect for real improvement. Humans continue to multiply and devour the earths resources at an ever increasing rate. A few large corporations maneuver to take control of the whole worlds food supply. Global warming continues to accelerate much faster than anyone predicted and may be starting to affect food production. All of this leads to the feeling that the future may not be as easy as the recent past and that the ability to feed yourself may one day prove to be an important skill.

Spiritual

I think everyone should be involved in growing some of their own food, simply because it is a part of being a complete human. Going though life with no real connection to one of the things that keeps you alive is quite perverse, but sadly so commonplace that we don't even think about it. It's been said that "gardening is the natural activity of man" and for me that pretty much sums it up. Most people will get interested in growing food if they have the opportunity, because it is real in a way that most everyday activities aren't. The fact that a small area of soil can keep you alive and well fed is quite astounding and can completely alter your worldview (think about molecules from the soil in your garden becoming molecules of you!) It brings you back to the reality that we are totally and absolutely dependent on the earth (our mother) for our well being, and that we should look after her a little more carefully.

On a higher plane gardening is about using human energy to make a place more productive, more diverse, and biologically richer than it would be otherwise. I find it to be one of the most gratifying and fulfilling activities I do. I love to be out in the garden, nurturing the land and bringing crops to fruition. If you garden long enough you will even begin to understand what is meant by the expression "the garden cultivates the gardener".

Making the garden work for you

Of course the vegetable garden is only a source of all of the good things mentioned above if it is successful. If it isn't then it is simply a waste of time and an embarrassment you will want to forget about. I want you to get as much out of vegetable gardening as I do and discover that all of the benefits I talk about are real (and not something I'm making up to sell books). The purpose of this book (and its companion The Organic Gardeners Handbook) is to give you the essential information you need to make it work, so it is pretty well packed with facts, figures and suggestions. The book is a reflection of my experiences in the garden (along with some research to plug a few gaps) and I hope you will find it useful. I don't want all of this information to give you the impression that vegetable gardening is difficult or complicated, because it really is simple enough that pretty much anyone can do it successfully.

I give fairly specific instructions for what you need to do, what, when, why, where, etc. When you first start gardening your best chance of success is to follow these fairly closely. They are only guidelines though, not hard and fast rules and as you gain experience you may find other ways that work just as well. Gardens are such variable places (climate, season, soil, pests, variety, weeds, etc) that as soon as you formulate a rule you will inevitably find exceptions to it. Time and time again I think I have something figured out, only to have something new pop up that contradicts what I thought I knew. This isn't a bad thing (it helps to keep it interesting), it just means you have to use your own brain and eyes before you do anything.

As someone who has lived a life of mostly voluntary (though occasionally involuntary) simplicity, I know what it is like to live with little money and I have tried to bring that experience into this book. Organic vegetable gardening is a very democratic activity, open to anyone who is physically capable of lifting a few pounds and has access to a patch of soil; it doesn't require very much money. In fact poorer people will benefit from growing their own delicious organic food more than anyone else (being poor doesn't mean you have to eat badly). I actually enjoy the challenge of working without money and there are lots of ways you can reduce your costs. Your kitchen and garden (and your body) can provide most of the fertilizer you need and with a little initiative the rest can be obtained for free, as they are often someone else's unwanted waste. Water can come from rainfall, your roof or gray water. You can save seed from most crops and you if you want to try new varieties you can swap seed with other gardeners. Tools can be obtained from yard sales. You can even make money from your garden by selling surplus food, seedlings or even seed.

I don't imagine many people will sit down and read this book from cover to cover (as excellent and informative as I imagine it to be). It is intended to be a practical handbook, to be taken out into the garden with you and referred to as questions arise. The more dirt you get on the pages, the more successful I will have been. You should definitely read through the whole section on a plant before you start to grow it though, as there may be information that pertains to your situation right at the end. I also highly recommend keeping a journal, where you can make notes on all of your gardening activities (especially what you planted and where and when you planted it). Also make note of extreme weather (first and last frosts, lowest temperatures, highest temperatures, rainfall patterns) and anything else you think is relevant. This information will be a big help in understanding the climate of your garden and in planning future gardens.

This new edition

It has been five years since I wrote the original Vegetable Growers Handbook. It was the gardening book I always wanted to find, but as no one else wrote it, I had to do it myself. I was very happy with the book when I finished it, but five years is a long time in the garden and I eventually started to see deficiencies that had to be fixed. To remedy them I have created this expanded, updated, revised and much improved version, which is essentially a new book. It isn't as pretty as most other gardening books and I have no illusions that it will grace many coffee tables. That is okay though, because it is intended for the tool shed, rather than the coffee table. When you are out in your garden and need information, you don't need to look at pictures, you need practical information.

Smartgardener.com

A new development since the first edition has been my involvement with smartgardener.com. I have been working with them to create a website that helps you in the planning, planting and maintenance of your garden. This free website helps you to plan your garden on-line (right down to ordering seeds) and then helps you with a weekly emailed list of things you need to do. It simplifies the most difficult part of growing vegetables, which is planting things at the right time, by gently reminding you each week until you do them. If you find this book useful I think you will also enjoy the site (they really complement each other).

Amaranth

Amaranthus ssp

Introduction: In North America the amaranths are most familiar as weeds of disturbed places and are particularly common in the rich soil of vegetable gardens (is there an American vegetable garden that doesn't have at least one kind of pigweed?) We really should pay a bit more attention to them though, as amaranth can provide not one, but two valuable crops; it can be grown either for its seed or for its leaves. In other parts of the world they are important crop plants and they could be here too.

It is estimated that amaranth has been cultivated for at least 9000 years, which would make it one of the oldest crops in the world. It reached its greatest popularity in its native South and Central America and up until the arrival of the Spanish in the 15th century it was a staple grain crop. Due to its use in various religious rituals the Spaniards considering it a symbol of pre-Christian culture and actively suppressed its cultivation.

The use of amaranth as a leaf crop slowly spread to other parts of the world and it was adopted by subsistence farmers in Africa, Asia and Europe. In recent years it has been rediscovered as a grain crop and cultivation is increasing around the world.

Amaranths even find their way into the ornamental garden and some varieties (notably Love-Lies-Bleeding) are grown purely for their beauty (these too are edible). The appearance of the various species ranges from bizarre to quite attractive to downright spectacular and the latter are certainly very ornamental.

About Amaranth

Seed facts
Germ temp: 50 (60 - 80) 90˚F
Germ time: 5 - 14 days
Seeds per ounce: 30,000
Viability: 7 yrs
Germination percentage: 70%+
Weeks to grow transplants: 4

Planning facts
Hardiness: Tender
Temp for growth: 60 (70 - 85) 95˚F
Plants per person: 10
Plants per sq ft: 1 grain
1 - 4 leaf

Transplants:
Start: 2 wks before last frost
Plant out: 2 wks after last frost
Direct sow: 2 wks after last frost
Succession sow: every 6 weeks
Plant height: 2 - 8 ft
Plant diameter: 1 - 2 ft

Harvest facts
Harvest: 95 - 150 days seed
30 to 60 days for greens
Harvest period: 4 weeks seed
4 - 12 wks leaf
Yield: Grain 1 oz / sq ft
Leaf 1 lb / sq ft.
Yield per plant: 2 oz (seed)
4 - 16 oz (leaf)

Crop value: Amaranth is sometimes referred to as a pseudo-cereal (as are buckwheat and quinoa), as it is grown as a grain crop, but isn't a member of the grass family. It produces a nutritious, high protein grain that has considerable potential as a garden scale grain crop. It is one of the most practical home grain crops, as it is nutritious, tasty, easy to grow and requires minimal processing to make it edible.

In warmer parts of the world (especially in the tropics) the amaranths are very important as a heat tolerant, easy to grow leaf crop. This is known variously as Chinese spinach, hinn choy, tampala, calaloo and by many more local names.

This is a rather neglected leaf crop for American growers and really deserves to be more widely used. If you are looking for a warm weather substitute for spinach, this is your best bet in most places. It is tasty, tender, easy to grow, very productive, fast growing and requires almost no work. I got into it because my garden was full of volunteers from a previous grain crop and I had to do something with them.

Ease of growing: Plants don't come much easier to grow than amaranth, both as a grain and a leaf crop. It is an outstanding summer green vegetable, which naturally takes over as the cooler season crops fade. In recent years it has become my default summer potherb, as it is pretty much always available.

Nutritional content

Leaves: These are high in vitamins A and C, as well as protein, iron and calcium. They are significantly more nutritious than spinach, to which they are often compared

As with spinach, amaranth leaves contain oxalic acid (though in smaller amounts), which can react with calcium and make it less available to the body. It may also contribute to the formation of kidney stones, so anyone prone to them should probably avoid the leaves (and spinach). Fortunately this is not a significant problem to anyone with a reasonable intake of calcium. If used as a potherb, a lot of the oxalic acid will be leached out in the cooking water.

Wild pigweed often ends up in books on poisonous wild plants, not only because of the aforementioned oxalic acid, but because of its habit of accumulating nitrates when growing in fields where nitrate fertilizer has been used. This can cause it to become mildly toxic. The cultivated crop can accumulate nitrate too (as can spinach), so be careful not to give them too much nitrogen.

This compulsion to classify everything as poisonous (even one of the most important wild edible greens) is a good example of how disconnected we have become from the natural world and where our food comes from.

Seeds: These are rich (up to 16%) in high quality protein and have a better amino acid balance than almost any other common vegetable protein. They even contain the lysine and methionine so often lacking in grain proteins. They also contain about 20% oil, along with the minerals calcium, iron, phosphorus, potassium and zinc.

Amaranth seed is an outstanding source of energy, with around 1700 calories per pound.

The seed also contains squalene, a powerful antioxidant which is also found in olive oil. It has been suggested that this substance might be the reason for the low cancer rates in those who eat Mediterranean diets.

Climate: Amaranth is a tropical plant and likes warm, moist, sunny weather (ideally 70˚F - 85˚F). Like corn and sunflower it uses C4 photosynthesis, which makes it particularly efficient in hot, sunny climates.

When grown as a grain crop amaranth doesn't need a lot of water and it is often grown commercially in warm dry climates. It has been grown in desert areas with as little as 8″ of water. In some cases drought may induce early flowering, which means an earlier crop.

Soil
pH 5.5 (6.4) 7.0

Leaf Amaranth can be grown almost anywhere, even soils that are too poor and dry for most crops, but will be most productive on a rich, moisture retentive, well-drained soil. It doesn't mind acid soil.

Leaf crops need a good supply of nitrogen (and respond by getting bigger), but too much can be a problem as the leaves can accumulate nitrates and become mildly toxic.

Grain Amaranth needs a well-drained and fertile soil (similar to that for corn) to produce a good crop.

Soil preparation: Amaranth doesn't need a great deal of nitrogen or phosphorus, though it does like potassium. The plants respond to extra nitrogen by growing bigger, though this doesn't always mean more grain.

Planning

Where: Amaranth thrives in warm sunny weather, so if your garden isn't very warm you need to plant it in a sunny sheltered spot. It doesn't do very well in the shade. In summer I often use amaranth to fill in any vacant spots, or interplant it between widely spaced crops (it's so easy to just scatter a few seeds.) Amaranth is such an independent plant, it is worth trying as a grain crop anywhere that is warm enough.

When: I find my garden tells me when it is time to plant amaranth because volunteers (and amaranth weeds) start to appear all over the place.

Amaranth needs warm weather to get started, ideally 70˚F or higher in the day and no lower than 60˚F at night. Don't plant it until at least two weeks after the last frost date. If your growing season is short, don't wait too long to plant a grain crop, otherwise it may flower prematurely when the days get shorter (see **Day length** below). Also fall frosts may arrive before it is fully mature. This is one situation where you might want to start it inside.

Day length: Amaranth originated in the tropics and is short day length sensitive. It is important to keep this in mind and plant by June at the latest. These plants will be the most productive because they won't flower and produce seed until they have accumulated enough food reserves.

If you plant too late in the summer, the short day length will cause the plants to flower while they are still quite small and you won't get much of a harvest (of grain or leaves).

Succession sowing: In the early part of the growing season you can make plantings of leaf amaranth, every 3 - 4 weeks.

Planting

Using transplants: In warm weather amaranth germinates and grows so vigorously that there is little to be gained from starting it inside. However if the growing season is very short, you might start a grain crop indoors. It does best when planted in cell packs, soil blocks or plug trays. Plant it out when the transplants are about 3″ high and the soil has warmed up.

Direct sowing: Amaranth is normally direct sown, by broadcasting or planting in rows. The seed is small and it is easy to sow a lot of plants at one time, but you usually don't need many. If you are sowing a large area you might want to mix the small seed with sand to make sowing easier.

The seed is ideally planted ¼ - ½″ deep, which means either covering the broadcast seed with a thin layer of cover soil, planting in shallow furrows or raking the soil after planting.

The seeds are small and the newly emerged seedlings are quite delicate initially. Crusting or capping of the soil can make it difficult for the seedlings to emerge.

Spacing

Grain: If you are growing amaranth for grain you will probably want to plant a fairly large area and will usually plant in rows. The spacing will vary depending upon what you want to achieve.

Typically you want the plants to be spaced 12 - 18″ apart in offset rows. If you want to minimize the amount of seed you plant, you can plant them 12″ apart, in rows 30″ apart. This will result in fewer, but larger and more productive plants.

In large mechanized operations, plants may be grown in densely packed beds as close as 4″ apart. Apparently this makes for more uniform head size and ripening, which is good for machine harvesting.

Leaf: If you are growing in a bed you can broadcast the seeds and then harvest thin (eat the thinnings) until the plants stand 6 - 8″ apart. You can also plant in rows, spacing the plants ½″ apart in the row, with 18″ between the rows. The plant rows are then gradually harvest thinned to a final spacing of about 6″ apart (eat the plants as you remove them).

Care

Amaranths are very independent plants with a lot of wild vigor and they don't usually require much care. Just put the seed in the soil and stand back; they will do the rest.

Weed: Amaranth is essentially a weed itself, so doesn't generally have much of a problem with weeds. You should keep the bed free of weeds until the plants have all emerged and keep weeded until they get to 8 - 10 inches in height. After this they can compete against almost anything.

Weeding a direct sown crop can present a problem because crop amaranth looks the same as weed amaranth. The best solution to this is to plant in rows, so you can safely remove any plant that isn't in a clearly defined row.

Many cultivated types have purple tinted leaves when young and these are usually quite easy to identify.

Fertilizing: If leaf amaranth plants are being harvested repeatedly they will benefit from an occasional dose of compost tea. Not too much nitrogen though, as you don't want them to accumulate toxic nitrates.

Water: Grain amaranth is relatively drought tolerant (it wilts readily to save water, but also recovers rapidly). However don't let it get too dry as this may reduce the final harvest. Too much water can also be a problem, as it can cause the roots to rot.

Leaf amaranth should always have moist soil to maximize productivity.

Mulch: If water is limited you should mulch the plants to conserve moisture and deter moisture robbing weeds.

Pests: The succulent leaf amaranths are a favorite of slugs and snails and young seedlings may be destroyed if not protected. Flea beetles will often chew tiny holes in the leaves of young plants. Generally they are pretty resilient though and can tolerate quite a lot of leaf damage with minimal effect on yield.

I have encountered leaf miners on grain amaranth, while commercial farmers sometimes have to deal with army worms, blister beetles and tarnished plant bugs.

Diseases: Amaranth is not very susceptible to disease problems and the worst I have seen has been damping off (which hardly counts). Apparently curly top virus can also be a problem in commercial plantings (it is commonly transmitted by leafhoppers).

Lodging: Plants loaded down with a heavy seed head will sometimes fall over (especially after heavy rain or wind), in which case you may need to support them. If you plant them fairly plant close together, they will keep each other fairly uniform in size and will mutually support each other.

Pollination: Amaranth is monoecious, with separate male and female flowers on the same plant. It is self-fertile and wind pollinated, so you don't have to even think about this.

Harvesting

Grain:

When: It takes from 3 - 5 months from planting the seed to fully ripe seed heads. As harvest time approaches, examine the flower heads regularly for ripe seed by rubbing the flowers between your fingers or palms to loosen any ripe seed. You can tell if seed is ripe by biting it; a fully ripe seed will be firm rather than chewy. This is important because it will start to drop soon afterward.

Often the plants will keep on ripening more seed until they are killed by frost (so you may be able to harvest more than once). If the plants begin to wither, or frost threatens, gather the whole heads.

How: If you only have a few plants you can bend the heads over a bucket and rub them to loosen the seed.

If you have a lot of plants, cut the whole heads and lay them on a tarp in the shade to dry. Then lay another sheet on top of the dry heads and beat, crush or walk on them to loosen the seeds. The bristly flower/ seed heads can be hard on the hands so it's a good idea to wear gloves.

Other than winnowing to remove debris, the seed needs no other preparation for eating. It is very important that it be dried thoroughly for storage, otherwise it may mold. Small quantities of seed can be dried in a paper grocery bag.

Vegetable: You can harvest the leaves any time they are big enough to be worthwhile (anywhere from 3 - 6 weeks after sowing). Start by harvest thinning extra plants when they are about 8″ tall, to get them out of the bed and leave the remaining plants at the desired spacing.

Once the plants are growing strongly, you can harvest individual leaves or whole growing tips. The plants have strong apical dominance, so pinching out the top makes the plant branch out and get bushier with new growth.

In some tropical home gardens, harvesting of leaves doesn't start until the plants are 4 - 5 feet high. Then the tops are pinched out and eaten. After this the side shoots are harvested, as they reach useful size (you can harvest every week or two). Any flower buds are removed promptly and eaten with their surrounding leaves. By harvesting frequently and preventing them flowering, the plants can be made to produce edible shoots for months.

When the plants eventually bolt, you can save the seed for planting next year. You might also scatter some around the garden to encourage volunteers (don't overdo it though, or it may become a real weed).

Storage: The leaves wilt quickly once cut, so it is best to harvest them fresh and use promptly. They can be kept in a plastic bag in the fridge for a few days. If you have a large harvest you can cook the leaves like spinach and freeze them.

The grain should be dried to 11% moisture before storing in a rodent proof container.

After harvest: Heavily cropped leaf plants will benefit from a liquid feed of seaweed, applied to their roots. Don't use compost or manure tea, as you will be harvesting again fairly soon and don't want pathogenic bacteria on the leaves.

Seed saving: This is pretty simple, just treat it like a grain crop and take seed from the best plants. Amaranth is monoecious, with separate male and female flowers on the same plant. They cross-pollinate easily, so it's best to have only one variety flowering at a time (in theory they should be separated by 1000 feet). Take seed from at least 5 plants to maintain some genetic variability.

The grain types produce a ton of seed, but the leaf varieties can be very variable. I have grown types that produced a lot and others that produced a mere sprinkle.

Unusual growing ideas

Volunteers: Amaranth commonly self-sows and can become a weed (or useful bonus crop, depending upon your perspective). One year I let an entire bed get taken over by volunteer grain amaranth. The only thing I did was to thin out the stand, by harvesting many of the plants for greens. Some plants reached 8 feet in height and gave me as good a grain crop as if I had sown it deliberately.

Usually I use my amaranth volunteers as a mixed green leaf crop, as there isn't enough seed to make a worthwhile grain crop.

Wild garden: You can take the volunteer idea one step further and deliberately sow the seed in patches of disturbed soil. These should be in full sun for maximum growth. I do this quite a lot and it really can be productive.

Using the weeds: If you don't want to grow the cultivated amaranth you might think about using the weedy amaranth that is probably growing in your garden. See **Pigweed** in the section on edible weeds at the end of this book.

Animal feed: Amaranth is widely grown as animal feed in China and it's said that over 100,000 acres are devoted to it.

Ornamentals: Some amaranth varieties (Love–Lies-Bleeding and Josephs Coat) are usually grown as ornamentals, but are also perfectly edible. Some of the grain varieties are positively spectacular when flowering, especially the gold and purplish red types and make lovely (but tall) specimen plants.

The leaf varieties tend to have less attractive flowers, though they often make up for this by having interesting variegated leaves.

You could use amaranth as an ornamental grain producer. Just plant it en masse for visual effect.

Varieties:

There are about 60 species of *Amaranthus*, but only a handful have been cultivated to any extent. There are quite a few grain varieties available, but less leaf types.

Some botanists consider all of the varieties below to be variations of *A. hybridus*. Others separate them into several species (*A. caudatus, A, cruentus, A. gangeticus, A, hypochondriacus, A. tricolor*)

Grain Amaranths:

These have mostly been bred to be determinate, with one large seedhead and few side branches. I have found all of the grain varieties to be very productive. The pale colored seed types tend to have a better flavor than the black seeded ones. Their leaves are often just as good as those of the leaf varieties.

Elephant Head - Big purple seed heads.

Chinese Giant Orange - Tall (8 ft) with bright orange flowers.

Hartmans Giant - Tall plants with black seed.

Hopi Red - Also used for red dye.

Leaf Amaranths:

The flowers of these varieties are smaller and less conspicuous than those of grain types and don't produce as much seed. Some are occasionally grown as an ornamental.

Hinn Choy - An old Chinese variety.

Red Leaf Amaranth - Red and green leaves.

Tiger Leaf - Red and green leaves

These three leaf types are all quite similar and may actually be the same thing!

Kitchen use

Grain

Amaranth differs from most cereal grains in that the seed needs no preparation (hulling, husking, threshing, etc). All you have to do is separate it from the seed head and clean it to remove debris.

The flavor of the seed can be improved by toasting, which causes it to pop like popcorn. This can be done in a hot pan in the same way as for popcorn (if it won't pop try sprinkling a little water onto the seed).

If you have a large quantity of seed, you could try popping it in the oven. Spread it a half inch deep in a covered pan and roast it at 350°F for a half-hour. Stir occasionally to prevent it burning.

The toasted seed can be added whole to baked goods, ground to flour for baking (it's usually mixed with wheat flour), or boiled as a kind of porridge.

The whole raw seed can be sprouted like alfalfa until about ¼″ long and used in salads and sandwiches.

The seed can also be boiled like millet in salt water. Some people soak it in water overnight before cooking.

In Mexico the popped grain is mixed with honey or molasses to make various sweet treats.

Leaf

Amaranth leaves are tender and mildly flavored and can be very good. They can be steamed, or boiled in a small amount of water (the latter may be better as it can reduce the amount of oxalic acid they contain). Don't cook them for more than a few minutes or they will get mushy. In Asia they are often stir-fried or used in soups. The very young leaves can be added to salads.

A good way to cook the leaves is to sauté some onion and garlic in a pan and then add the washed greens. The water sticking to the leaves is enough to cook them.

Try using the recipes described under chard and spinach. They are just as good when made with amaranth.

Horta

Horta translates as weeds or wild greens and is a traditional spring peasant food in Greece. It is traditionally made from a mix of wild greens, but you can use a wide variety of greens and weeds from the garden.

2 lb greens (these might be amaranth, chard, chicory, dandelion, kale, komatsuna, spinach, stinging nettle or any other edible greens).
1 lemon
1 cup water
2 tbsp olive oil
Salt
Pepper

Wash the greens to remove any soil or debris, then chop into pieces (discard any tough bits) and cook with a cup of water to your taste (don't over-cook). Drain off the water and add 2 tablespoons of olive oil, the juice of the lemon and salt and pepper. It is good eaten warm immediately, or cold the next day.

Artichoke, Globe

Cynara scolymus

Introduction: Artichoke is native to the Mediterranean, where its flower buds have been a favored food since the time of ancient Greece. They are quite a unique vegetable, in that the part eaten is actually a part of the flower (the scales and swollen base). They are also relatively unusual in being a perennial.

Artichoke is considered to be one of the finest of all vegetable foods. I think it fully lives up to its reputation, no other vegetable is quite as decadently delicious when cooked fresh from the garden. This is somewhat ironic, when you consider that it is a kind of thistle.

Artichokes are quite nutritious, but you don't usually eat them in sufficient quantity for them to be an important food source. Also the sprawling plants need a lot of space, so the yield per square foot is low.

Nutritional content: Artichokes are a fair source of vitamins A and C, as well as niacin and folate (the natural form of folic acid). They also contain a variety of valuable anti-cancer and immune-boosting phytonutrients, including cynarin and luteolin. They are one of the highest rated foods for antioxidant content, though of course they are not usually eat in quantity.

Cynarin is not only a useful antioxidant, it also stimulates taste bud receptors and actually makes food taste better.

Crop value: You don't generally eat a lot of artichoke, so it tends to be more of a treat than a substantial food. It is actually a highly nutritious food though and there is a lot of room for us to increase our consumption of these delicious and nutritious buds. Grow them yourself and you can live like a Roman emperor, stuffing yourself with artichokes every few days (well a little bit like one),

Ease of growing: In the right climate artichokes are pretty low maintenance and need almost no attention. They are perennial and can yield for up to 7 years, though the best hearts are usually produced in their second and third years. This is why they are usually replaced with new offsets every 3 years.

When growing as a perennial, artichoke needs a lengthy rest period of cool weather (anywhere from 10 - 50 days under 50˚F, depending upon the variety). It doesn't do well if it is too mild, too cold, or too hot and dry in summer (though it may survive the latter by going dormant).

In very mild or very cold climates it can be quite difficult to grow as a perennial, but don't despair, you can still grow it as an annual. This is more work and the harvest won't be as big, but it can work out,

Climate: Artichokes grow best in a mild, damp, maritime climate, such as is found in coastal California. The cool growing weather means slower growth and higher quality buds.

If the climate isn't suitable they won't produce very large (or high quality) flower buds. The best approach to growing them is determined by your climate. In the ideal cool and mild climate they are planted in spring and harvested in fall and through the winter.

Though artichokes prefer cool weather they are not very frost hardy and won't survive in areas with cold winters. Even relatively mild temperatures (28˚F) will kill the flower buds, while lower temperatures (especially when combined with wet soil) will kill the whole plant. In colder areas artichokes must either be grown as annuals, or the roots must be protected over the winter in some way.

About Globe Artichoke

Seed facts
Perennial in zones 7 - 11 (though may need some protection)
Germ temp: 50 (65 - 70) 75˚F
Germ time: 7 - 21 days
Seed viability: 6 - 10 yrs
Germination percentage: 60 +
Weeks to grow transplants: 10 - 12

Planning facts
Growing temp: 50 (60 - 65) 75˚F
Plants per person: 3
Plants per sq ft: 1 plant needs 9 sq ft
Transplants
Start: 6 weeks before last frost
Plant out: 2 weeks after last frost
Days to harvest: 6 - 12 months
Plant height: 3 - 5 ft
Plant diameter: 4 - 6 ft

Harvest facts
Harvest period: 8 - 12 weeks
Yield per sq ft: 1 head
Yield per plant: 24 - 48 heads
Plants per person: 1 - 2

Soil

pH 6.0-7.0
The best soil for growing artichokes is deep, rich, well-drained, sandy and slightly acidic. Good drainage is particularly important in cooler climates, because if the roots stay cold and wet for long periods they will often rot (this is the commonest reason plants don't survive through the winter).

Soil preparation: Artichokes are a short term perennial, so you won't be able to dig the soil again without disturbing them. Amend the soil generously before planting and if you are feeling energetic you might even double dig.

Because the plants are so widely spaced, you could amend the individual planting holes, rather than fertilizing the whole bed. Dig a large planting hole and replace half of the soil with compost or aged manure. You should also give them some greensand (for potassium), colloidal phosphate (for phosphorus) and kelp (for trace elements), or an organic fertilizer mix.

If your soil isn't well-drained you should grow your artichokes on raised beds or mounds.

Planning

Where: These large plants need a lot of space for the amount of food they produce and this is probably the main reason they aren't more popular. They are just too big for the intensive vegetable garden beds and are best planted individually in any odd vacant corner. You want to put them somewhere they can get as big as they want, without causing any problems. They work well as a border or low hedge for the ornamental garden.

In the ideal climate artichokes should be placed in full sun, but in hot dry ones they may do better with some light shade during the hottest part of the day. They should also be sheltered from strong winds, as they are also somewhat vulnerable to being blown over.

Don't plant artichokes close to established trees or shrubs, as they won't be able to compete. This is particularly important in dry climates.

When: In suitably mild climates the roots can be planted while they are dormant in late winter or early spring. In colder climates they should be planted 2 - 3 weeks before the last frost date (the soil temperature should be at least 50˚F).

To grow artichokes from seed you usually start them indoors in late winter, six weeks before the last frost date, An early start is particularly important if you are growing them as an annual, as this allows them to grow for longer and get bigger. This is important if you want to harvest flower buds before the plant is killed by frost (which you do).

Planting

Artichokes are usually propagated vegetatively from offsets. They can be started from seed quite easily, but this doesn't breed very true, which means there will be a lot of variation in the offspring. If you must use seed, choose the best seedlings to grow on and discard the rest. In future years you can propagate your chosen plants vegetatively.

Growing from seed:
Indoors: Start the seed indoors in cell packs, soil blocks or individual 3″ pots. If you don't have many seeds, put one in each cell / pot; if you have lots put 2 - 3 in each one and thin to the best plant when

all have germinated. Artichoke seedlings grow quickly, so be prepared to transplant them into larger pots if necessary.

Plant the seedlings out in their permanent position after all danger of frost is past and they have at least two sets of true leaves. The plants will grow rapidly once they get established in rich soil.

If any buds appear during the first year, they should be nipped off to encourage strong root growth. Obviously if you are growing it as an annual, you don't do this.

Outdoors: If your climate is suitable you can sow the seed directly outdoors (½″ deep). The best way to do this is to start them in a nursery bed and transplant them when they are big enough.

Vegetative propagation

What: Artichokes are normally grown from the suckers (offsets) that emerge from the old plant in spring. These work much better than growing from seed, as you can select suckers from the best plants. These are the plants that grow most vigorously, produce the best quality buds, yield earlier and are most productive. All of the suckers from the same plant will be genetically identical of course.

If you don't have any plants to propagate from, you can buy them, or look around for a friend or neighbor to beg, steal or borrow from. Alternatively you can start from seed and then use the best plants for propagation in future years.

How: Suckers are removed from the parent plant as they emerge in spring. The normal practice is to dig down the side of the plant and cut off the emerging sucker (it may be up to 10″ tall) with a heel of old root attached. Trim off most of the leaves (the minimal roots can't support them) and plant it immediately in a well-prepared site, with the growing point at surface level. Alternatively you could plant it in a one gallon pot, or in nursery bed, until well rooted and then plant out.

These suckers are pretty tough and even if they appear to die, don't give up on them straight away. I had a batch of plants that appeared to die, but they actually lay dormant all summer. When cool moist fall weather arrived they burst into life.

Buying plants: Artichoke plants may be found for sale in garden centers as either seedlings or dormant roots. You need to plant these whenever they are available (which is early spring in colder areas and all winter in milder ones). They should go in the ground at the same level they were in the nursery.

Spacing: A single artichoke plant will get bigger and bigger over the years and can easily grow to be 4 ft tall and 4 ft (or even 6 ft) wide. Obviously you need to give a plant this size plenty of room. The exact spacing may vary quite a bit, but usually you will grow them in rows.

Space them 36 - 48″ apart within the rows, with 48 - 72″ between the rows.

Growing as an annual: If your climate is too cold for artichokes to grow in the ground year round, you may still be able to grow them as annuals. You just have to use the right varieties and start them indoors early enough. You won't get the big buds and big harvest of a mature perennial (and it will start later), but something is generally considered to be better than nothing.

Choose a variety that is adapted for annual growing and start the seed indoors 6 - 8 weeks before the last frost date, as described above. Plant out the seedlings 2 weeks after the last frost date. You want the plants to grow rapidly so you should pamper them with a regular feed (every 2 - 3 weeks) of compost tea or liquid kelp. The first buds should start to appear towards the end of the summer.

You don't necessarily have to let the plants die over the winter, you can try any of the several ways of overwintering them. See **Frost** below for ways to do this.

Care

True to its thistly nature, the artichoke is a vigorous and robust plant that needs little attention once established. Its only real weakness is its minimal tolerance of cold.

Water: Though the artichoke is quite drought tolerant, it is important that the plants have evenly moist soil (at least an inch of water per week), particularly when the buds are developing. Water is essential to produce succulent buds and those produced by drought stressed plants may be tough and poorly flavored.

Don't keep the soil wet all the time, as too much water can cause crown rot. Allow the surface to dry out between watering.

Fertilization: Artichokes are hungry plants and yield best when grown without any check in their growth. To achieve this they must get all the nutrients they need.

The plants are usually fed annually with a mulch of compost or aged manure. If the soil isn't very fertile you can also side dress them with an organic fertilizer mix (in spring in colder areas, in fall in milder ones). You can also give them a liquid feed of compost tea occasionally (they particularly like nitrogen).

Mulch: These widely spaced plants benefit from a layer of mulch during the growing season, especially when newly planted and there is a lot of bare soil between them. A mulch of compost is not only the main source of nutrients for these perennial plants, but it also helps to retain moisture, keeps down weeds and keeps the soil cool in summer.

Mulch is even more important in cold climates as it is used to prevent the ground from freezing in winter and so protects the tender crowns (see **Frost protection** below).

Support: Artichokes are fairly tall plants and can get quite top heavy, which makes them vulnerable to being blown over by strong wind. On a windy site you may have to stake them firmly to prevent this.

Thinning plants: After a couple of years of growth a plant may end up producing a dense cluster of 10 or more shoots. If all of these were allowed to mature they would get very crowded and would have to compete against each other. It is common practice to allow only 3 or 4 shoots (offsets) to develop on each plant. The rest are removed in spring and used for propagation. These should be removed even if you don't want them for propagation.

Pruning flower buds: It isn't good to allow too many buds develop on a plant at once, as they won't all reach full size. There should only be 3 - 5 buds (depending upon the size of the plant) maturing at one time. This ensures that each bud will grow to a good size.

Sometimes all of the lateral shoots and buds are cut off to leave only one main bud (known as the "king head"). This will then reach maximum size (in Italy these are very highly prized and fetch a premium price).

Renewal: Commercial growers usually replace the plants after 2 or 3 harvests as their vigor begins to gradually decline after that. Home growers may do this too, replacing a portion (20% - 33%) of their artichoke plants each year. In this way you will always have vigorous young plants and will replace them all every 3 - 5 years. However if you prize low maintenance more than high yield, you don't have to do this.

Frost protection: In cold climates artichokes will be killed by hard frost if not well protected. If you want your plants to survive the winter where the soil freezes hard, then you will have to protect them in some way.

The usual way to protect them is to cut off the tops, leaving about a foot of leaf (you can tie these together to protect the crown). You then cover the plant with a thick 24″ deep mulch and then cover this with a cold frame or cloche. The latter is important as it keeps them dry (they often rot from too much moisture). If protected in this way they may survive down to 20˚F.

This protection should be removed after the danger of hard frost has ended in spring, but before the plants start growing again. This allows the soil to warm up.

In very cold climates, you could try digging the roots in fall and storing them inside for the winter (what have you got to lose?) This is no more difficult than it is for Dahlias, simply lift the root as the leaves die back, cut off all but a couple of inches of stem and brush off loose soil. The best place to store them is in a burlap sack in a root cellar at 35 - 40˚F. Alternatively you could plant them in 5 gallon pots and keep them in a cold (but not freezing) garage.

Weeding: The plants should be weeded regularly when young and occasionally thereafter, as weeds may compete for water and nutrients. Of course the mulch will also help to suppress weed growth.

Pests: I haven't found artichokes to be seriously bothered by disease or pests, but in some areas they can be severely affected. Slugs and snails appreciate the damp shade and numerous hiding around the plants and sometimes damage the buds. The larvae of the artichoke plume moth can ruin the buds. Aphids can also be a problem (watch for lots of telltale ants), but are easily washed off.

Disease: Crown rot (*Botrytis*) fungus can be a problem in warm wet weather.

Artichoke curly dwarf virus: This disease shows itself as curled leaves and small or misshapen flower buds. It is usually passed through infected offsets, rather than seed. If this becomes a problem remove all plants and start again from seed in a different location.

Harvesting:

When: Perennial plants aren't harvested until the spring of their second year. Then the terminal bud is harvested as soon as it reaches full size (2 - 4″ in diameter) and while the bracts are still tight against the bud. Don't wait until they start to open up or they won't be as good.

If you miss the right harvest time, you should still cut the over-mature buds, as this stimulates the plant to produce useful secondary buds. If a bud is left to mature it will cause the plant to waste energy making unwanted seed. After the terminal flower buds are removed, more will be produced on side shoots. In this way a single plant will produce a whole series of buds for several months (these will gradually get smaller as food reserves are diminished).

You should remove all of the flower buds as they are produced, even if they are not usable. If you leave any on the plant, it will waste energy making seeds and may even die.

How: The buds are cut with a knife, leaving at least an inch of stem. Handle them carefully after harvest as they are easily damaged. In Italy they commonly cut artichokes with longer stems as the interior is edible too.

Storage: The buds are best used fresh and start to deteriorate in flavor as soon as they are picked. They can be stored in the fridge in a plastic bag for up to two weeks. A fresh artichoke is squeaky when squeezed.

If you are suddenly overwhelmed with artichokes you can freeze the prepared hearts (or can them).

After harvest care: After the last buds have been cut in early fall, the plant may be cut down to ground level and fertilized and mulched (compost does both at once). This will encourage it to regenerate itself and produce new buds for next year.

Seed saving: Saving artichoke seed is easy enough, but it is rarely done because they are normally propagated vegetatively. Allowing a plant to produce seed will weaken it, by causing it to divert energy away from vegetative growth.

Artichokes produce seed readily, as one flower can pollinate another on the same plant (though not itself). They will often self-sow if given the opportunity and volunteers can even become a pest.

If you live in an area where it is classified as a noxious weed, don't let the seeds fly away.

Unusual growing ideas

Ornamental: If room in the intensive vegetable garden is limited you could put these space hogging plants in the ornamental garden. Their blue/purple flowers are quite spectacular, though of course they are rarely allowed to appear.

Containers: It is possible to grow artichokes in large containers and they can make striking ornamentals.

Wild garden: The artichoke is independent enough to be planted in a vacant corner and left to grow itself. You just have to give it enough care to keep it productive.

Varieties:

These can be divided into those that are used for perennial growing and those that are suited to growing as an annual.

Perennial artichokes

These can be divided into the large globe types and the smaller spiny types.

Globe types - These are the familiar artichokes we see in markets.

Green Globe - The most important commercial American variety.
Imperial Star

Kiss of Burgundy - Tolerates more heat and cold than other varieties. It isn't easy to find.

Spiny types - In Italy they eat a lot of spiny artichokes, which produce smaller buds and are often purple tinged. They look more like wild plants and are more tender and better flavored.

Violetta di Albenga - Produces purple buds.

Annual artichokes - These varieties will produce useful buds in their first year. They need less exposure to cold weather (for vernalization) to trigger flowering.

Imperial Star - The most commonly grown annual type.

Grande Beurre - Very large heads, but isn't easy to find.

Kitchen use

If insects get in between the bracts soak the bud in salt water for 10 minutes to get them out before cooking.

Artichokes are cooked and eaten in different ways in different parts of theworld.

The traditional American way to cook an artichoke is to cut off the stem and the top of the head and then trim back the points of the scales. The heads are then boiled in salt water for about 30 minutes (don't overcook them). They are then left upside down to drain and are served with butter or other dressing. They can also be steamed or fried.

The traditional American way to eat an artichoke begins by pulling off the individual bracts and stripping off the tender end with your teeth. When you have finished with these, you remove the fuzzy choke from the top, leaving the best part for last. This is the heart, which is one of the most delicious foods in the whole vegetable kingdom. It was almost inevitable that such a sensuous food as an artichoke heart would be considered an aphrodisiac.

Any cut artichoke surface will quickly turn gray, so they are often dipped in cold water and lemon juice to prevent this. You should also avoid cooking artichokes in aluminum or iron pans as it will discolor them.

Cardoon

Cynara cardunculus **var** *altilis*

Cardoon is has been popular in Greece, Italy and around the Mediterranean since ancient times. They are still very popular in that area, but are very much overlooked in this country (in fact they are pretty much invisible). This is probably because it requires blanching and some rather fussy preparation to make it edible. This is worthwhile though as the cardoon is a special food (and has its devoted following).

This plant is a close relative of the artichoke, in fact it is probably its ancestor. Not surprisingly it likes the same growing conditions and is grown in pretty much the same way. It is easier to grow however, because you only want the big fleshy leaf stalks, you don't have to worry about flowering.

The cardoon looks a lot like an artichoke and is equally useful as an edible ornamental. The flowers aren't as big as those of artichoke, but as you should remove any buds that appear (so the plant doesn't waste energy on flowering and seeding) it's pretty academic anyway.

Climate: Cardoon isn't very hardy and is only a true perennial from zone 7 and up. In colder areas it must be grown as an annual.

Propagation: Cardoon is easily grown from seed, in fact it does this so readily that in the milder parts of California it has become a pernicious weed, under the name artichoke thistle. The airborne seeds are very mobile so don't let the seed escape and become a problem.

If you are growing cardoon as an annual you should start early, at least 8 weeks before the last frost date. It won't grow very fast until the weather warms up though.

Once you have some established plants, cardoon can be grown from suckers like an artichoke.

Spacing: The plants can get quite big and need plenty of room. Space them 3 feet apart each way.

Blanching: The leaf stalks are much better when blanched to reduce their natural bitterness and make them more tender. This is done by tying the leaves together in a bundle (make sure they are dry). Often the plant is then tied to a stake to prevent them falling over, though you can also earth them up. You then wrap each bundle in brown paper to exclude light for 2 - 3 weeks. The normal process is to blanch a few plants at a time to extend the harvest.

An alternative way to blanche them is to bend the plant over and cover it with soil.

Harvest;
When: In mild climates cardoons can be harvested all winter. In warm weather the leaves become bitter and unpleasant.

How: Gather the leaf stems by cutting them down at the base. Be careful when handling them as some types have very small spines that can be painful.

Varieties: There aren't many varieties out there and still less that are easy to find. Usually you find a generic "Cardoon".

Gigante

Porto spineless

Tenderheart

I mention the names of these varieties, but good luck finding them.

Kitchen use: Cardoons have to be prepared properly to be good. This means trimming off the leaves, thorns and any tough stems. They are then peeled to remove the stringy skin. The remaining parts are cut into 3″ pieces and rubbed with lemon juice to prevent them discoloring. The prepared stems can then be kept in the fridge for several days, though they are best used immediately. They are usually boiled for 20 - 40 minutes until tender.

Cheese making: The purple stamens of the cardoon flower contain one of the best vegetable rennets (cynarase) and are used for making cheese from sheep and goat milk (they don't work well with cows milk). They are widely used in Italy, Spain and Portugal and are responsible for some of the flavor of their unique cheeses.

You might try using the stamens to make curds from fresh milk.

Artichoke, Jerusalem

Helianthus tuberosus

Introduction: Jerusalem Artichoke is a tall perennial sunflower that produces edible tuberous roots. It is now often called the sunchoke when sold in stores, no doubt part of a marketing effort to popularize it with consumers. It is the only common (if you could really call it that) vegetable crop that is native to North America.

Crop value: Jerusalem artichoke is a very productive and easily grown plant and can be a very useful food for self sufficiency.

It was widely cultivated by Native Americans, or more accurately encouraged by them, as it doesn't really need much cultivation.

Nutritional content: Like most members of the daisy family (*Asteraceae)* Jerusalem Artichokes store their food in the form of inulin, rather than starch. Humans tend to have problems with inulin as we lack the enzymes to digest it in the small intestine, so (like beans) it passes into the colon where it is broken down by bacteria. As with beans this can result in the production of malodorous gas (flatulence) and sometimes also stomach pains or even diarrhea. Apparently this is worse when the plant is eaten raw. The severity of this effect varies between individuals, in some people it is bad enough that they never try it again, while for others it isn't an issue at all.

The tubers contain useful quantities of B vitamins, as well as iron. calcium and potassium. Their energy content is about 300 calories per pound, but how much of that you are able to digest depends upon the individual.

Inulin is considered beneficial as it can increase the absorption of calcium and magnesium. It may also encourage the growth of beneficial intestinal flora.

Ease of growing: Jerusalem artichoke is very easy to grow, in fact sometimes most of the work comes in preventing unwanted plants coming back again the following year.

Climate: This plant can be grown almost anywhere in the country, but does best in areas with cold winters and warm summers. It is very hardy while dormant and can take hard frosts and even completely frozen ground. It doesn't like very cool summers and does best with a warm growing season of at least 125 days.

About Jerusalem Artichoke

Planning facts

Perennial
Hardiness zones: 2 - 9
Growing temp: 55 (65 - 85) 95°F
Plant out: 2 - 4 wks before last frost
Plants per person: 5
Plant height: 5 - 10 ft
Plant diameter: 12 - 24″

Harvest facts

Yield per plant: 2 lb
Yield per sq ft: 1 - 3 lb
Days to harvest: 6 months
Harvest period: Up to 5 months

Soil

pH 6.0 to 7.0

Jerusalem Artichoke can do well on almost any soil, but it will be most productive when growing in a rich, moisture retentive one. Like many root crops it does better on sandy soils than clay ones (and the tubers are easier to dig).

Soil preparation: Though this plant will grow well almost anywhere, it is fairly hungry and will be more productive if given additional fertilization. If your soil isn't very rich you should incorporate lots (3″) of compost or aged manure into the top 12″ of soil.

Like most root crops it doesn't need a lot of nitrogen, though it does like phosphorus and potassium. To provide this you might want to give it greensand and colloidal phosphate. Some kelp powder would also be good (or a good organic fertilizer mix).

Planning

When: The tubers are very hardy and can be planted any time from late winter to early spring. If growing as an annual it is good to get them in the ground early (2 - 4 weeks before the last frost date) so they have as long a growing season as possible. They can go in the ground even earlier than this, but if the soil is too cold (below 45°F) they will just sit there until the ground warms up. You can also plant them later, but the harvest may be smaller if they have less time to grow.

Where: Jerusalem artichoke can be grown as an annual in the intensive beds, but it is a big plant and takes up quite a bit of space. I prefer to give it a permanent bed, where it can grow for several years without interruption (except for harvesting). The tall growing plants can be quite ornamental and work well as a deciduous summer screen.

These plants will be most productive when growing in full sun, but they will tolerate some shade for part of the day. They can grow up to 12 feet in height (and become quite dense), so don't put them where they will cast shade on other sun loving plants.

Planting

Vegetative: Jerusalem artichokes are not grown from seed, they are propagated vegetatively from tubers (or pieces of tuber).

If you don't have many tubers, you can cut them into several pieces, so long as each piece is about 2 ounces in weight and has at least one bud (preferably 2 or 3) on it. Plant them soon after cutting so they don't dry out. I use a bulb planter to make 4 - 6″ deep holes for planting.

Spacing: A plant can easily get 8 - 10 feet tall and 2 ft in diameter, so it needs lots of growing room. If the plants don't have enough room they can get overcrowded, which may result in lots of small tubers (which are more inconvenient to use). More space equals bigger tubers.

Bed: Space the plants 15 - 24″ apart in offset rows.

Row: Space the plants 12 - 18″ apart in the row, with 36″ between the rows.

You can also grow them in double rows, with plants spaced 12″ apart in the rows, with 18″ between the rows. The advantage of this is that it is easier to earth them up and to give them support. The entire row soon becomes a temporary screen and can even be used for decorative effect.

Care

Once these plants are established and growing well you don't need to pay much attention to them. They are close to wild plants in their nature and will take care of themselves.

Watering: Jerusalem Artichoke is fairly drought tolerant, but tuber production suffers if they don't get enough water. For maximum yields you should keep the soil evenly moist at all times, which means regular irrigation in dry climates. If water is in short supply then save most of it for when the tubers are forming.

Weeding: The plants should be weeded when young, but they can soon handle any weeds that come along. In fact they handle weeds so well they have been used as a smother crop to eradicate them.

Earthing up: If you find your plants start to fall over, you should earth them up, by piling soil against the stems. Ideally you should do this when the stems are about a foot high. This makes them more stable and less likely to be blown over by strong winds.

Earthing up has other benefits too; it gets rid of weeds, it may increase the number of tubers produced and it makes them easier to harvest.

Mulch: This helps to make these independent plants even more independent, by conserving moisture and feeding the soil. Put it down once the plants are up and growing strongly (too soon and it may keep the soil cold). In cold climates you might add more mulch in fall to keep the ground from freezing (so you can dig the tubers).

Fertilization: If you are growing Jerusalem artichoke in a permanent bed, you should fertilize it annually. The best way to do this is with a top dressing of aged manure or compost to supply nitrogen, and some wood ashes to supply potassium (or use an organic fertilizer mix).

Support: These plants can get very tall and in wind prone areas you may need to support them. Do this by putting strong 6 foot stakes in the ground at 6 foot intervals. Run string along these and tie the stems to the strings. Plants supported like this can make a useful windbreak.

You can also make the plants less top heavy by cutting off the top three feet of growth. This shouldn't affect the resulting crop too much.

Pests: This crop is just too tough to die. When I planted it in my garden in Western Washington, slugs ate the emerging spring shoots repeatedly for about two months. Every time they sent up new shoots they would get eaten, yet by the end of the summer the plants were about nine feet high and produced well.

A few other pests may occasionally eat some of the leaves, but the plants are so vigorous this is rarely a problem.

Gophers will eat the tubers (though they aren't a favorite), so if they are a problem you may have to grow it in an underwired bed, or wire baskets. The latter can even make harvesting easier, just pull up the basket and empty it out.

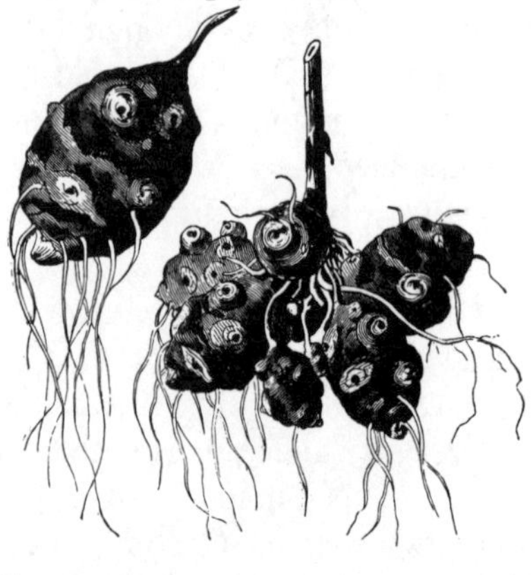

Disease: Very few disease problems occur with this plant. Sclerotina (white mold) is occasionally a problem, as are downy mildew, rust and southern blight.

Eradication: Some people say that this plant doesn't need any pests, because it is one. If any fragment of the persistent tubers is left in the ground, it will sprout and grow. I haven't found this to be a big problem however, as in spring the emerging shoots give away the location of the tubers and can easily be pulled up. If you neglect to remove them all, the plant will come back as strong as ever, so be warned.

Harvesting

The plants flower in late summer and fall and can be quite attractive at this time. The tubers start to develop at the same time and mature about a month after the flowers have finished and the plant starts to die back. They can be harvested from this point on, right through the winter, until they start to grow again the following spring,

The flavor of the tubers actually gets better as the winter progresses. This happens because exposure to low temperatures causes some of the inulin to be converted into sugar, which makes them sweeter and more digestible.

It is a good idea to cut down the stems after the plants die back, leaving about a foot sticking out of the ground (these make it easier to locate the tubers later on).

Harvest the tubers as needed, by digging with a fork as you would potatoes (though some of the tubers may be further away from the plant). They have thin skin which is easily damaged by rough treatment, so handle them gently. If you have a perennial bed you can just harvest the large tubers and leave the small ones behind.

Storage: The tubers have thin skin and lose moisture rapidly after harvest, so it is better to dig them as you need them and store the rest in the ground. If the ground tends to freeze, cover them with a thick mulch so digging will be easier.

If you must dig them all, they can also be stored in damp sand like carrots.

For short term storage keep the tubers in the fridge in a perforated plastic bag (to keep humidity high).

Seed saving: Jerusalem artichoke doesn't usually produce viable seed (though just today I found someone who says he has some), so it is always propagated vegetatively. You don't usually have to consciously save tubers for this, as some will remain in the ground after harvest and grow themselves. However they can be stored just like those you keep for food.

Unusual growing ideas

Screen: These tall plants have been planted in double or triple rows as a deciduous screen (in windy areas they will need support).

Cut flowers: The clusters of small yellow sunflowers can be used for cut flowers. Taking them won't affect tuber formation.

Support plants: You can use the plant as a living trellis for pole beans (plant these on the south side).

Wild garden: This plant is very independent and really can be grown with no attention at all. I grew it in my garden beds for a couple of years and then decided to stop growing it. Being soft hearted and not wanting to kill it, I transplanted the remaining tubers out into one of the wilder parts of my garden. With no watering and no protection from gophers I forgot about them for a couple of years. They managed to hang on though, and I recently rediscovered a couple of plants and brought them back into cultivation.

Emergency food: This plant could be grown as an ever-multiplying source of emergency food by those who worry about the future. As a perennial it would naturally grow in the same place for years anyway, so doesn't suffer much from pests or disease (unlike the potato).

Compost crop: This fast growing plant can also be grown as a perennial compost material crop. It can be cut several times in a season and will regenerate itself without replanting. Of course this will have an adverse effect on tuber production.

Energy crop: This plant can be very productive (as much as 20 tons per acre) and has potential for use as a source of alcohol for fuel. In Germany it has also used for brewing recreational alcohol in the form of schnapps

Ornamental: With its small sunflowers, this plant is actually quite ornamental when grown en masse. Some varieties produce flowers very freely and make good cut flowers.

Varieties

This isn't a very widely grown crop so there aren't many varieties (and still less are easily available). If you want to grow a specific variety, you will probably have to buy the tubers from a mail order company. If you don't care it's easier and cheaper to buy them in a produce market. It doesn't hurt to use locally grown tubers where possible as they are more likely to be adapted to the area.

Improved Mammoth French (American: More uniform and heavier yielding, it is the commonest commercial variety.

Boston Red: Large red, knobby tubers.

Fuseau: Has long, straight, knobless roots, that somewhat resemble sweet potatoes.

Golden Nugget: Also has straight, smooth tubers.

Red Fuseau: Similar to Fuseau, but red (obviously).

Stampede: This very early variety matures in as little as 90 days.

Dwarf Sunray: A smaller plant than most, it flowers well and is quite ornamental.

Kitchen use

Apparently Jerusalem Artichokes have become fashionable in recent years and are appearing in various guises in expensive restaurants (just in case you wanted to know).

The tubers can be cooked in the same ways as potatoes, though they are sweeter. Peeling is optional. They are good cooked for 10 minutes and then sauteed with chopped onions. If you cook them for too long they can become mushy and not very pleasant.

Very slow baking converts some of the inulin into fructose and makes them more digestible.

Unlike potatoes they can also be eaten raw in salads and some people claim they resemble water chestnuts (though raw tubers are much more likely to cause digestive problems).

The tubers have also been used to make wine.

Arugala / Rocket

Eruca vesicaria ssp *sativa*
Syn E. sativa

Introduction: This plant has its own distinctive pungent flavor and has been in and out of fashion since Roman times. It is a plant that people tend to have strong opinions about, they either love or hate it. I'm not a big fan, but I know people who find it almost irresistible.

At the moment arugala is quite fashionable again and is a key ingredient in many commercially grown salad mixes.

About Arugala

Seed facts
Germ temp: 35 (45 - 70) 75°F
Germ time: 2 - 7 days
Seed viability: 2 - 5 yrs
Germination percentage: 80%+
Weeks to grow transplants: 3 - 4
Plant height 12 - 24″
Plant diameter: 12″

Planning facts
Hardiness: Hardy
Growing temp: 45 (60 - 65) 75°F
Plants per person: 10
Plants per sq ft: 2 - 4
Direct sow: 4 - 6 wks before last frost
Days to harvest: 25 - 40
Harvest period: 1 - 4 wks

Climate: Arugala is native to the Mediterranean, but grows naturally as a late winter or spring flower, so it is fairly hardy plant. It needs cool weather for best growth, being able to germinate and grow in cold soil and tolerating light frost. It bolts quickly when growing in hot weather (often within weeks of planting).

Nutritional value: Arugala is rich in vitamins A and C as well as calcium, iron, magnesium, zing and folate.

Soil

pH: 6.00 (6.5) 7.00

This hardy plant can grow almost anywhere, but does best in a fertile, moisture retentive, well-drained soil. If the soil is very poor they may bolt quickly.

Soil preparation: I don't consider arugala to be a very important crop and just plant it in any convenient vacant space, without doing any special soil preparation. However for maximum productivity this fast growing plant needs nutrients that are readily available. It needs quite a bit of nitrogen and slightly less phosphorus and potassium. Add 2″ of compost to the soil and perhaps some organic fertilizer mix.

Ease of growing: Arugala is little changed from a wild plant and is pretty easy to grow. The only real problem is the short harvest season before it bolts (flowers). I have read that in an ideal cool, moist situation it can get up to 3 ft tall, but mine usually bolt before they get anywhere near this size.

Planning

Where: This fast maturing and compact plant doesn't take up much space, so is often interplanted between slower growing crops, rather than being given space of its own.

Arugala needs full sun for best growth, though like most leafy greens it will tolerate some shade (and may prefer it in warmer weather).

When: This hardy member of the Mustard family grows best in the cool weather of spring and fall. In hot weather it gets very pungent and bolts as soon as it has produced a few leaves. In mild climates it can be grown all summer and if winters are mild it can be grown through the winter too.

Spring outdoors: Rocket germinates well in soil as cool as 45˚F and can be sown 4 - 6 weeks before the last spring frost. For an even earlier crop warm the soil with cloches for a week or two before planting.

Fall crop: Arugala also does well as a fall crop. Start sowing whenever the weather starts to cool down sufficiently (the seed doesn't germinate well above 75˚F).

Winter crop: Arugala is well suited for growing in cool weather and in areas with mild winters it can be an important winter crop. It can also do well in colder areas if grown under cloches or tunnels (or in the greenhouse).

Succession sowing: Rocket is a fast crop at the best of times, but especially as the weather warms up. If you want a continuous supply, you should make succession sowings every 2 - 3 weeks until it gets too warm.

Planting

This annual is usually grown from seed, sown directly into the garden at a depth of ¼ - ½″.

Spring indoors: In spring arugala is sometimes started indoors 4 - 6 weeks before the last frost date and planted out 3 - 4 weeks later.

Spacing:
Beds: If you grow it in beds you can sow the seed 2″ apart and thin the plants to a final spacing of 6″.

Rows: Sow the seeds 2″ apart in the row, with 6″ between the rows. As the plants get bigger you harvest thin to the desired spacing of 6″ apart. If you give it more room (up to 12″) the plants will get bigger, but you will have less of them.

Arugala if often grown as a cut and come again crop, in which case you sow the seeds about 1″ apart.

Care

Weeds: This plant competes against weeds quite well, because it practically is a weed. It will need weeding while young though.

Watering: Arugala is fairly drought tolerant, but needs moist soil for best growth and flavour. This is especially important in warm weather as dry plants get pungent and bolt quickly.

Feeding: If your soil isn't very good you might want to boost growth with a feed of liquid kelp or compost tea. You will probably only need to do this once before it is ready to harvest.

Frost protection: Though this is a hardy plant, a fall crop will usually grow faster and be more productive if given the protection of cloches or tunnels.

Pests: Many of the pests that attack the related Brassicas will also eat arugala. Flea beetles are the commonest problem in my garden, peppering the plants with tiny holes. I don't normally do anything about them though, because these fast growing plants usually recover quickly.

Diseases: Though these are not usually a big problem, arugala is sometimes bothered by damping off, mildew and various bacterial infections.

Problems: Unpleasantly pungent and bitter leaves are usually the result of hot weather and / or a lack of water.

Harvesting

You can start harvesting individual leaves as soon as they are of sufficient size (2 - 3″), which may be only 2 weeks after transplanting. You can also harvest the whole plants up until they start to flower. Cut them off a couple of inches above ground level and the remaining plant will usually re-grow.

The leaves are best when harvested immediately before use. If necessary you can store them in a plastic bag in the fridge for a few days,

Seed saving: Rocket bolts readily so saving seed is easy. The perfect flowers are cross-pollinated by insects, but since there are few varieties available (and you are unlikely to have more than one type flowering any a time), this isn't usually a problem.

When the seedpods begin to ripen, cut the whole plants and put them in a paper grocery bag to dry. When they are fully dry, crush them to free the seeds. Arugala produces seed abundantly and you can get a lot of seed from a few plants. I always have far more than I have use for.

Unusual growing ideas

Salad mix: Rocket is commonly grown for use in salad mixes. It may either be grown in a mixed bed, or in a section by itself. I prefer the latter approach, as it is more vigorous than most salad mix plants and can take over. It does well when grown in this way, as its ever present tendency to bolt is less of a problem. See **Salad mix** for more on this.

Micro-greens: This is just a smaller version of the above. You plant the seeds ¼″ apart and start harvesting when the first true leaves appear. This can be within 2 weeks. See **Microgreens** for more on this.

Containers: Arugala does well as a container plant, so long as the container is at least 6″ deep and you keep the soil moist. It will even do well inside.

Wild garden: Arugala self-sows readily and can become a minor weed. Because of this I rarely plant it in its own bed. I just encourage it by scattering seed in suitable spots. As I write this it looks as good now as it has all year and it is almost Christmas.

Varieties: There are a few, mostly claiming to be slower to bolt, but I can't say I've noticed much difference in any of those I have tried.

Kitchen use: If you don't like it raw, try it in soups, or steamed as a potherb, as this changes the flavor a lot (this is a good way to use older leaves too).

The white flowers can be added to salads.

The abundantly produced seeds can be ground into a condiment like mustard (see **Mustard** for how to do this).

The seed can also be sprouted for salad greens.

Perennial arugala / Sylvetta *(Diplotaxis tenuifolia and D. muralis)*

Since I wrote the above about arugala I have discovered this intriguing perennial and have been very impressed with it. The main reason I like it is because it doesn't bolt to seed at the first opportunity (as ordinary arugala is inclined to do).

When I grew it the plants didn't flower for several months after planting. When they did finally do so, I collected seed for sowing next year. Actually this wasn't even necessary as it is a perennial. If you cut off the flowering heads early, it will put on more vegetative growth.

I have found that it tastes pretty much the same, though some people claim it is stronger flavored.

Asparagus

Asparagus officinalis

Introduction: This native of coastal areas of Eurasia has been prized as a gourmet food since the ancient Greeks. The newly emerging spring shoots are regarded as one of the great delicacies of the vegetable garden.

Crop value: Asparagus is a great perennial crop. It's low maintenance, easy to grow, expensive to buy and better when home grown. As an added bonus it's available early in the growing season, when few other crops are producing.

Asparagus does have some significant drawbacks as well. It takes a long time from planting to first harvest. The harvest season itself is pretty short, usually only 6 weeks or so. Perhaps most importantly for the intensive gardener, a good sized planting takes up a lot of space. When you consider all of these factors, it's not surprising that asparagus is one of the most expensive vegetables to buy.

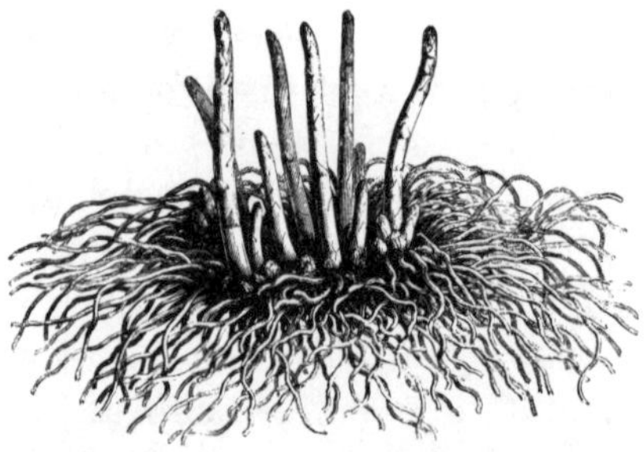

Ease of growing: Asparagus is a pretty independent plant and doesn't require much care. It isn't very productive for the space it occupies, so isn't a good crop for small gardens, or intensive beds in general. It is quite attractive though and can be planted in any spare corner of the garden, or even grown as an ornamental. Birds eat the berries and sow the seeds, so given the right conditions it may escape from your garden and naturalize.

Nutritional content: Asparagus has been called a superfood for its nutritional content. It is rich in vitamins A, B6 and C, as well as soluble fiber, selenium, folate, rutin and various antioxidants. It is low in energy, with only about 90 calories per pound.

About Asparagus

Seed facts

Germ temp: 50 (60 - 85) 95°F
" time: 7 - 21 days
53 days / 50°F
24 days / 59°F
15 days / 68°F
10 days / 77°F * Optimum
12 days / 86°F
Seed viability: 2 - 5 years
Weeks to grow transplants: 10 - 12
Plant height: 3 - 5 ft
Plant diameter: 2 - 3 ft

Planning facts

Perennial
Hardiness zones: 4 - 9
Growing temp: 45 (60 - 75) 85°F
Plants per person: 5
Plants per sq ft: 1 plant needs 2 - 4 sq ft
Transplants
Start: 11 wks before last frost
Plant out: 1 wk after last frost
Direct sow: 2 wks after last frost
Days to harvest: Seed - 3 years
Root - 2 years

Harvest facts

Harvest period: 6 weeks
Yield per plant: ½ - 1 lb (20 shoots)
Yield per sq ft: 12 oz sq ft

Climate: Asparagus prefers mild temperatures, not too hot and not too cold. It doesn't like very hot humid areas, or very mild winters (it needs a significant rest period).

Soil

pH 6.5 (6.8-7.0) 7.5

Asparagus isn't a particularly fussy plant, but it will produce more food if given ideal soil. This is deep, rich, well-drained and fairly neutral (not acidic) with lots of organic matter to help it retain water. Originally a coastal plant, it is very tolerant of saline soil.

Plants growing on very light and sandy soil should be monitored carefully to ensure they don't dry out.

Asparagus will also do okay on heavy soil, so long as it is well-drained. It can tolerate short term flooding, but prolonged wet soil can cause the fleshy roots to rot over the winter. If you want to grow asparagus in soil that gets wet in winter, you should plant it in raised beds.

Soil preparation: It's important to amend an asparagus bed thoroughly (and lime if necessary), prior to planting. Once the plants are in the ground, you can't incorporate anything else and any further fertilization must be as a top dressing or mulch.

If your soil is heavy or compacted it is a good idea to double dig an asparagus bed before planting. This allows you to cultivate the soil to a depth of 20 - 24″ and enables you to remove perennial weeds (very important), tree roots and other debris.

Deep cultivation also allows you to incorporate organic matter and amendments evenly throughout the soil. Incorporate as much compost, or weed free aged manure as you can spare, along with liberal quantities of colloidal phosphate (it loves phosphorus), greensand (for potassium) and kelp (for trace elements). Of course you could also just use an organic fertilizer mix.

Planning

Where: An asparagus bed may last 15, 20, 30, even 50 years (100 year old beds have been known), which is longer than many fruit trees. Consequently it is important to choose the growing site carefully.

The first criterion is that it should be in full sun. It will take some light shade, but won't be as productive. The bed should be sheltered from strong winds and well away from large trees or shrubs, with their vigorous feeder roots. Lastly it should be placed where it won't cast unwanted shade, compete with other crops, or interfere with other everyday garden operations.

An asparagus bed takes a lot of space. Each plant sends out roots several feet in all directions and they must be spaced far enough apart to prevent competition. In addition the individual plants aren't particularly productive, so you need quite a few to get a reasonable harvest (ideally at least 5 plants per person). Taken together these factors can make for a pretty good size growing bed.

If you don't have the space for a full sized bed of asparagus, you might be able to fit a dozen or so plants in various spots around the garden. You won't get a huge harvest, but it's better than nothing. Asparagus is quite pretty with its ferny foliage and can blend into the ornamental garden pretty well.

Planting

Planting options: Asparagus is most often grown from 1 or 2 year old roots. If you have more time than money you can grow your own roots from seed, instead of buying them.

Seed

Raising transplants

If you are patient, you can raise asparagus from seed and plant it out when a year old. This is the least expensive way to go, though of course the drawback is having to wait 3 - 4 years to get a worthwhile harvest. However this isn't such a big deal if you consider that they may live for 20 or 30 years.

Growing from seed can be somewhat unpredictable as some seed may be more vigorous than others (small seed is often inferior and is sometimes discarded). Some authorities recommend treating the seed with bleach to control fungus disease. Pre-soaking seed (at 60 - 80°F for 2 - 4 days) can be useful to speed germination.

Starting indoors: Seeds are usually started indoors in late winter, about 3 months before the last frost date. This gives them the maximum growing time in their first year.

Start the seed in individual 4″ pots, cell packs or 1 ½″ speedling trays. Normally you plant two seeds to a pot / cell and remove the weakest one when both have germinated. They can also be grown in 4″ deep flats, just sow the seed 2″ apart and ½″ deep.

Keep the containers at 75 - 85°F until all seed has germinated and then reduce it to 70 -75°F (60 - 65°F at night). Better seedlings result if it isn't too warm.

The seedlings grow quite vigorously and in 3 months may be 9 - 12″ tall and big enough to be planted outside in a temporary nursery bed, or even planted in their permanent position (See **Using 12 week old transplants**). By next spring the one year old roots will be ready to go out into their permanent position (only use the most vigorous plants).

Starting outside: The seed may also be started outside in a nursery bed, when the soil has warmed up a little (to at least 50°F) or about 2 weeks after the last frost date). Plant the soaked seeds 3″ apart and 1 - 2″ deep. You might also plant a few radish seeds to mark the row, as the asparagus may take a while to germinate.

Weed the newly emerged seedlings carefully and when they are 6″ tall thin them out (you could try transplanting the thinnings) to stand 6″ apart. They are then left to grow for one year and dug the following spring. They can put on a surprising amount of growth in this time.

Direct sowing: It is possible to sow directly into the prepared asparagus bed (it is certainly vigorous and fast growing enough). However it isn't very practical to plant a seed every 24″ and then wait for a couple of years. Planting in a nursery bed makes a lot more sense.

Using 12 week old transplants

This is a recently developed alternative method of growing asparagus from seed. The seedlings are grown as described above and planted out in their permanent position after all frost danger is past. They go in a small ridge (3″ high) at the bottom of a 8″ deep trench. Space them 10 - 18″ apart in the row, with 4 - 6 ft between rows (trenches). You might want to plant something else in between the rows to temporarily make use of the empty space.

Roots

Asparagus is usually grown from one or two year old roots. The two year old plants produce earlier, but one year old plants are generally better. These are not only cheaper, but can eventually out-produce the older plants because they suffer less from transplant shock (asparagus doesn't really like transplanting). They are also less troubled by disease, probably because of their more vigorous root system.

If you can't plant the crowns as soon as you get them, they should be stored in a cool place in the shade (ideally at 40˚F and 90% humidity).

Planting roots:
Asparagus can be planted out in early spring, as soon as the soil is in workable condition (and at least 50˚F). However there is no rush, as it will take up to three years before you get a good harvest. Some people say late spring is actually better, as the plants will start growing faster in the warmer soil. This means there is less danger of loss to rot. Transplant only the best individuals and discard any weak or inferior roots (or plant them in the ornamental garden).

Planting: Both one and two year old crowns are planted in the same way. The traditional procedure is to dig a hole or trench 18″ wide and 12″ deep. Put a small mound of compost in the trench, along with a source of phosphorus and spread the roots out over the mound. Cover the root with a 2″ layer of a soil mix (3 parts soil to 1 part compost) and water thoroughly. As the plants grow, slowly fill up the trench with more of the same mix.

Recent opinion is that you don't have to be quite so careful in your planting. It is now thought that gradual burial isn't necessary and that you can just fill the hole loosely with soil up to the original level. Careful spreading of the roots probably isn't necessary either.

Shallow planting: Researchers have found that asparagus yields more and earlier, if planted at a depth of only 6″, rather than the traditional 12″. This fact can also be used to give you more flexibility in harvesting, as you can have some early yielding (shallow planted) plants and some later yielding (deep planted) plants.

Spacing:
Rows: The recommended row spacing is 18 - 24″ (depending upon the fertility of the soil) between plants, with 5 ft between the rows. This gives the plants plenty of room to fill in as they grow, but also provides for good air circulation.

It has been found that wider spacing produces more shoots and they also tend to be larger. In tests it was found that plants spaced 24″ apart, produced twice as many spears as plants that were closer together. This can give you the same harvest while using less plants.

Beds: In a 5 foot wide bed you might plant three rows, with 18″ between the rows and 18″ between the plants.

Care

Asparagus is an independent plant, but if given even a moderate amount of care, it will be much more productive. A well cared for asparagus bed should last for thirty years or more, but it can deteriorate quickly if neglected or over-harvested.

Weeds: If you conscientiously removed all perennial weeds before planting your asparagus bed and apply a thick mulch, then weeds should not be a big problem. They will need occasional weeding in their first year, but these vigorous perennials get tall and soon outgrow most weeds.

You should give the established bed an occasional maintenance weeding to stop new weeds getting established or seeding. Hand weeding is recommended, so as not to disturb the shallow feeder roots. Traditionally weeds were killed with salt water, as asparagus is very salt tolerant, but this is no longer recommended as it is bad for the soil (and everything else).

Volunteer asparagus seedlings can become weeds themselves.

Watering: It is important to keep the soil moist (not wet) while the plants are young. Older plants are quite drought tolerant and rarely need watering in areas with summer rainfall. The amount of water they get in summer is important because it determines how much food they can store and how many shoots they will produce in the following spring.

In very dry areas they should receive an occasional deep watering to keep the plants growing vigorously. If they get too dry they may go dormant in summer, which is not good because it means they are not storing food for next year.

Automated drip irrigation works best as it means you can forget about these low maintenance plants altogether.

Generally the plants don't need much watering while they are producing spears in spring, because there is usually plenty of moisture in the soil and they aren't photosynthesizing very much. Once the ferns start to unfurl they require more water.

Plants are often allowed to dry out in September so they will stop growing and start to store food for the winter.

Fertilization: Asparagus isn't a very hungry plant and doesn't need a lot of fertilization, but you have to think about this carefully because it is a perennial. Most nutrients will be supplied by mulching (see below), but to encourage maximum production you can also give them a foliar feed of compost tea or liquid kelp, once or twice in the season. In poor soil you might also apply a side dressing of fertilizer mix either before emergence or after you finish harvesting.

Renewal: If a plant starts to decline you can dig it up in winter and divide it. Separate the plant into separate pieces, each with several growing buds. Replant them as if they were new crowns.

Mulch: The best way to fertilize asparagus is with a nitrogen rich mulch of compost, aged manure or seaweed (asparagus loves seaweed), applied in fall. This works well because asparagus is shallow rooted and most of its feeder roots are near the surface.

Newly planted beds have a lot of bare soil, which should be covered with mulch to prevent soil degradation.

Pests: Asparagus beetles, cucumber beetles, aphids, leafhoppers, asparagus miners, Japanese beetles, tarnished plant bugs, thrips and cutworms all attack asparagus, but their damage isn't usually too serious. Just keep an eye on the foliage to make sure the damage doesn't get out of hand.

Slugs can be devastating to the young plants. I once had a whole planting wiped out by slugs. Every time the plants re-sprouted they were cut down again.

I once had another problem where whole fronds were disappearing, leaving just a stub. This perplexed me, I just couldn't figure out what would do that kind of localized damage. It turned out my girlfriend was taking the pretty ferns for use in flower arrangements.

Disease:
Fusarium wilt, **Verticillium wilt**: These diseases may be seed borne so if in doubt you should treat seed with hot water (122˚F for 25 minutes) or dilute bleach solution (be careful with this as you can damage the seed). Some varieties are resistant / tolerant.

Crown rot (*Fusarium moniliforme*) and **Asparagus rust** (*Puccinia asparagi*) can also be serious problems and can survive in soil for years. Many newer varieties are resistant to rust.

Gophers: These creatures love asparagus as much as humans. If these are a problem, you will have to protect each individual plant with a good sized basket of gopher wire. There is nothing more discouraging than finally having your plants start to produce after several years, and then see them disappear down a gopher hole (except maybe never seeing them again and not knowing why).

Control: Asparagus often self-sows all over the place and can become a minor weed problem. I don't mind though as they can be a good source of plants for transplanting, bartering or giving away.

Self sown seedlings can be a significant problem for commercial growers however. They often stop the plants from self-seeding by cutting the tops in fall, when the foliage begins to turn yellow. If you only have a few plants you could simply remove the berries.

Harvesting

When: The year after planting the roots you can get your first small harvest. Do this quite sparingly and only harvest for 2 - 3 weeks. This cutting can actually stimulate the plants to create more buds.

The second year you might harvest for a month (or longer if the plants are very healthy).

From the third year onward you can harvest for 6 weeks or more. The state of the plants will tell you when to stop harvesting. If most of the shoots are less than 3/8″ in diameter then it's time to stop picking.

The emergence of the first spears is dependent on soil temperature and starts when it gets up to 50˚F. You can start gathering the shoots when they reach 6 - 8″ in height and are still tightly closed. As the temperature rises the shoots will start to emerge more rapidly and you may have to harvest daily to keep up. Once the tightly curled tops start to loosen, the shoot starts to toughen and eventually becomes inedible, so pick them before this happens.

The growth of the spears varies according to the weather and can be slow in cool temperatures or very rapid in favorable conditions (in some situations it may be necessary to harvest twice daily).

You may be surprised to find that the small spears are often tougher than large ones. This happens when they grow more slowly and so contain more lignin.

If you are harvesting for personal use you don't care if the spears are crooked or bent.

How: The best way to harvest is to snap the shoot off down at ground level (any remaining stub will dry up and disappear). This also has the advantage that it breaks where it gets tender. The traditional method is to cut them with a knife just above the crown, but there is a danger that you will damage emerging buds. Keep them cold after harvest for best flavor.

Don't harvest too many spears from a single root in one season, as you can weaken it.

Storage: The spears can be stored in a plastic bag in the fridge for 7 - 10 days. For longer-term storage freezing works best.

After harvest: The beds must be treated properly after harvest because it is the summers growth that provides energy for the following years crop. The larger the ferns get, the more food they produce and the bigger the future harvest. Keep the plants well watered and watch for signs of pests or disease.

If you must cut back the plants in fall, don't do it while they are green, wait until they die off. Actually it's best not to cut back the tops at all, as they help to protect the crown and can hold snow in place over the winter.

Unusual growing methods

Ornamental use: With its feathery, light green foliage asparagus is undeniably an attractive plant. As it can take up a lot of room for relatively low return, there is a good argument to be made for putting it in the ornamental garden instead of the vegetable garden.

Male plants: Asparagus plants are dioecious, which means there are separate male and female plants. It has been found that male plants produce up to 25% more spears than females, though they tend to be slightly smaller. Another benefit of male plants (for commercial growers at least) is that they don't self-seed. There are now a number of cultivars that produce all male plants.

Forcing: To get an earlier crop the roots can be forced in spring, as described under **Rhubarb**.

Delayed harvest: One way to get a longer asparagus harvest is to initially harvest from only half of your bed. When this half begins to slow down, after 6 weeks, cut down all the new growth on the other half and it will send up a fresh crop of shoots. You can then cut from this for a further 4 - 6 weeks.

It is also possible to get shoots later in the year, by cutting the plants right down to the ground, which forces them to send up more. This practice runs the risk of weakening the plants however.

Wild garden: Asparagus is a long lived perennial and is often found on the sites of abandoned gardens. If it can do this then it can also grow in your non-abandoned garden with equal ease. It does well as a border for the vegetable garden, or at the edge of a forest garden (it does need plenty of sun though).

Propagation: You can propagate asparagus vegetatively be dividing the crowns. Just make sure each piece has several buds. This is useful if you want to multiply a small number of special plants (or any of the hybrids).

Seed saving: You don't really need to save asparagus seed as it is a perennial, but it is easy enough to do. The plants are insect pollinated, so to keep a variety pure there should be no other asparagus varieties (or wild plants) within a mile. The plants are dioecious and only the female plants produce the red berries, each containing 6 seeds.

Varieties

Choosing the right variety is particularly important with asparagus because you will be living with it for many years. You can't change to a different variety without starting all over again.

If you buy your asparagus plants locally you will only have a limited choice of varieties. If you want an unusual variety you will probably have to mail order it.

Connovers Colossal - An old variety, good for growing from seed.

Argenteuil - Rust resistant French variety.

Martha Washington - An old standard.

Mary Washington - Another time tested classic.

Purple Passion - Has purple spears that are supposed to be sweeter.

Hybrids: There are now quite a few hybrids that produce very vigorous all male plants. These don't waste energy producing seeds, so are more productive than female plants. Generally I hesitate to grow hybrids, because I like to save my own seed, but in this case you only need to plant it once, so it isn't really an issue. If you do want to multiply them you can always divide the plants

I have read that the hybrids can start to lose vigor after a few years and don't last as long as the older varieties (I don't know how true this is, but it wouldn't surprise me).

All males: These include
Jersey Giant - Prolific and rust resistant

Jersey Knight - Prolific and rust resistant

Supermale - Are supposed to produce twice as many spears as other types.

Kitchen use

The traditional way to cook asparagus is to tie the spears together in a bundle and boil them upright. The tender tip is out of the water and is cooked by the rising steam (if under water it would be overcooked). They need about 10 minutes to cook sufficiently. Gourmets with too much disposable income can buy special tall asparagus pans, specifically designed for cooking it to perfection.

The problem with boiling asparagus is that it leaches out some of the valuable nutrients. It is better to steam or roast it.

Asparagus soup

This is a great way to use an over-abundance of asparagus.

1 lb asparagus
1 medium onion
1 ½ cups vegetable stock
1 cup soy milk
1 tbsp butter
2 tbsp flour
1 tsp salt
½ tsp black pepper

Simmer the asparagus and chopped onion with a ½ cup of vegetable stock until tender.

Put it in a blender and puree until completely smooth. Melt the butter in a pan, with the flour and salt and pepper and cook for 2 minutes, stirring to prevent it turning brown or burning. Add the rest of the stock and bring to the boil, stirring to make it smooth. Then add the soy milk and the asparagus puree and heat up thoroughly, stirring occasionally.

Basil

Ocimum basilicum

Introduction: Basil is a native of southern Asia and many kinds are grown there. The name comes from the Greek word "basileus" meaning "king" as it is often considered the king of herbs.

Basil is without doubt the most important culinary herb in my kitchen, In fact I think of it more as a vegetable than as a flavoring herb and grow it like spinach. I can use as much as I can grow, because I make any surplus into pesto and freeze it for winter use. Pesto is always quite expensive to buy, so this can be a very valuable crop.

Nutritional content:
Basil contains some powerful antioxidants that give it anti-cancer activity. It may also help to lower cholesterol. It contains about 130 calories per pound.

Crop value: Basil is easily grown, very flavorful and I love it. Consequently I rate it as one of the most essential crops and grow it in vegetable sized (as opposed to herb sized) quantities.

Ease of growing: Basil isn't a very demanding crop so long as it gets warm weather. In the right circumstances it will often grow like a weed. If it doesn't get warm weather it is not so easy; it really doesn't like the cold.

Climate: Basil is a short lived perennial in tropical climates, but anywhere the temperature drops below 60°F it has to be grown as an annual.

About Basil

Seed facts
Growing temp: 60 (75 - 85) 90˚F
Germ time: 5 - 10 days
Seed viability: 8 years
Weeks to grow transplant: 4 - 8

Planning facts
Hardiness: tender
Germ temp: 60 (70 - 85) 90˚F
Plants per person: 4
Plants sq ft: 3 - 4
Start in: 4 - 6 wks before last frost
Plant out: 2 wks after last frost
Direct sow: 2 - 4 wks after last frost
Plant height: 6 - 18:
Plant diameter: 6 - 12″

Harvest facts
Days to harvest: 60 days
Harvest period: 1 - 3 months
Yield per plant: 4 oz

Soil

pH 5.0 (6.0-7.5) 8.0

Basil prefers a rich, light, well-drained soil.

Soil preparation: Basil can produce a lot of foliage in the course of a summer, but needs plenty of nutrients to do so. Incorporate 2″ of compost or aged manure into the top 6″ of soil before planting.

Planning

Where: Basil will be unhappy if it isn't warm, so in cooler areas it should be put in the warmest and sunniest spot in the garden (and sheltered from cold wind). If even this isn't warm enough, then grow it under cloches.

As you are only growing basil for its leaves, it can be grown in part shade. However it won't be as productive as when in full sun.

When: Basil is slow to get established if the weather is not warm, so the first plants of spring are usually started indoors, about 6 weeks before the last frost date. Don't plant it out until at least 2 weeks after the last frost, when the soil has warmed up (to at least 60˚F and preferably 70˚F). If you are in a hurry you could hasten this process with cloches or plastic mulch.

Succession sowing: Basil can be harvested for quite a while if you use the right technique, Nevertheless it is common to make several sowings over the course of the summer, perhaps every 4 - 6 weeks or so (these later plantings are usually direct sown). This will give you a continuous and abundant supply of new plants and will ensure you never run out of pesto.

Planting

Indoors: The first basil is usually started indoors, in flats, cell packs, soil blocks or plug trays. Sow the seed in ¼″ deep furrows or scatter it on the surface and then covering with a ¼″ of sowing mix. When the plants have at least 2 (and up to 4) pairs of true leaves you can transplant them into the garden (they transplant quite easily).

While the plants are indoors you should go easy on the watering and keep them well ventilated to avoid damping off fungi.

Outdoors: If the weather is warm enough it's better not to mess with starting indoors, just sow directly into the garden. Plant the seed ¼″ deep and keep moist and well weeded until the plants are growing well. The seedlings are easy to recognize by the pair of distinctive D shaped cotyledons (seed leaves).

Direct sowing is a lot less work than raising transplants, but you won't get a crop until a little later. I use both methods, growing my earliest plants from transplants and later ones by direct sowing. Try sowing some seed when you transplant your first basil seedlings into the garden.

Spacing: The spacing for basil varies from 6″ - 8″ - 12″ apart, depending on the variety and how big you want the plants to get. If you want the plants to grow into 24″ tall bushes you may even plant them 18″ apart. I find the closer spacing works well because I harvest prune by pinching the shoots off frequently.

Care

Warmth: The biggest problem with basil is its dislike of cold weather. It just won't thrive if the summer isn't warm. Fortunately this isn't a problem in most of North America.

Weed: Keep the plants weeded at all times, but especially while they are young.

Water: Basil must have evenly moist soil for maximum productivity and best flavor, so water whenever it gets dry. Plants sometimes respond to drought by bolting.

Fertilization: If you are repeatedly harvesting from the same plants, you should give them a liquid feed (compost tea or liquid kelp) every couple of weeks. It's probably best to use this as a soil drench, rather than as a foliar feed, as you want to keep the leaves as clean as possible.

Mulch: This is beneficial in hot weather as it conserves moisture and suppresses weeds.

Pruning: The growing tips should be pinched out when the plants are 6 - 8″ tall (this is actually the first harvest). This causes them to send up two growing tips, making the plants bushier and larger. It may also delay flowering. If you carefully harvest prune the plants, you can harvest from them for weeks, or even months.

Frost: If frost threatens you can try protecting the plants, but they are very sensitive to cold. If it is late in the year and it's getting cold anyway, you should just harvest everything you can and freeze it. You might also try potting up some plants and putting them in the greenhouse, but it must be warm.

Pests: Basil growing in the garden isn't much bothered by pests, though snails and slugs may eat it when young. Aphids and leafhoppers might show up occasionally too.

Disease: Fusarium wilt can be a problem when it is grown on a larger scale.

Harvesting

When: The leaves are at their best before the flowers appear, though they are still worth gathering even if the plants are actually blooming. It pays to remove any flower stems as they appear, as this encourages more leafy growth.

If done carefully you can get 3, 4 or even 5 harvests from one planting (and make them last for a good part of the summer).

How: Harvest by pinching off the growing tops just above a pair of leaves. You can start doing this when the plants are only 6″ tall. Always leave plenty of foliage on the bottom of the plant (at least 4 sets of leaves), so it can regenerate and give you another harvest later on.

You can also harvest whole plants, but that only makes sense if you are selling the plants and want to make nice bunches. You will get a lot more leaves by repeated harvest pruning.

Storage: Basil has thin leaves and wilts quickly once cut. It will keep for a few days in a plastic bag in the fridge. You can extend the life of whole plants by keeping them in water like cut flowers.

The easiest way to store basil is to dry it in a warm shady place. This alters its flavor considerably, but it is still very good. It must be dried quickly though, if it takes too long, it will deteriorate and turn black.

It is possible to store the fresh leaves by packing them in a jar and covering with olive oil.

You can freeze the leaves whole in a plastic bag, but a better idea is to put the chopped leaves in ice cube trays and cover them with water. Once they are frozen you can transfer them to a plastic bag.

I usually make pesto (see below) and freeze it in meal-sized portions (so I don't have to saw up large frozen chunks). You can also put it in a plastic bag (flatten it so that it will break easily when frozen).

Unusual growing ideas

Cuttings: You can root soft cuttings of basil in water and get new plants faster than growing them from seed.

Companion planting: Basil works well with tomatoes. Just plant it all around the tomato bed, to fill in any empty space.

Container growing: Basil grows well in containers and this is the best way to grow it if you live in a cool climate (this is much easier than trying to coax it along outside). Put 3 plants in a 12 inch pot and give it a warm, sunny window sill. Be sure to keep it well supplied with water.

You can also try digging up plants at the end of the growing season and bringing them inside (they won't last indefinitely though).

Micro-greens: Growing basil in this way allows you to have the nice fresh basil flavor in winter. See **Micro-greens**.

Multi-plant blocks: Multi-planting works well with basil. Sow 4 - 5 seeds in a block or cell pack and thin to the best 3 seedlings. These are planted out in a clump and grow together.

Harvest the largest plant when it gets to be a suitable size, leaving the others with more room to grow. When the biggest of the remaining plants gets to a suitable size, harvest it too (you may have to do some judicious pruning to keep both plants growing well). Then harvest the last plant when it reaches a suitable size.

Alternatively you could allow all three plants to grow and just keep harvesting the growing tips.

Seed saving: Bees love basil flowers and will cross-pollinate any plants within 150 feet of each other. For this reason you should only have one variety flowering at one time. Basil sets seed very readily; all you have to do is leave it alone. Don't collect seeds from the first plants to flower (remove them), as you don't want to select an early bolting strain.

Varieties

If you thought basil was just basil, you are somewhat mistaken, there are actually around 150 types of basil, each with its own unique properties and distinct flavors. The most common include

Sweet: This is the standard basil you were thinking about. I have tried quite a few types of basil, but still come back to these deliciously aromatic, large leaved types:
Genovese
Lettuce Leaved Basil
Superbo

Bush: Sometimes said to be a separate species (*O. minimum*), It has smaller leaves and is more compact, but tastes like the above.

Cinnamon / Mexican: This has a mixed cinnamon / basil flavor.

Lemon: This has a distinct lemon / basil flavor and is often used for tea. It is popular in Indonesia.

Licorice: This has a hint of anise to go along with the basil flavor

Opal: Has small purple or purple / green variegated leaves.

Purple: Small purple leaves.

Sacred: This is a different species (*O. sanctum*). It is popular in India.

Thai: Has a lemon / basil flavor. It is popular in Thailand.

Kitchen use

Basil is traditionally used to flavor tomatoes and eggs and is an essential ingredient of Italian cooking. It is probably best known for its use in making pesto (or the French equivalent pistou).

The seeds of basil are not commonly used as food in the west, but they have their own unique properties. They are coated with a substance that swells up into jelly when they get wet (no doubt to provide moisture for germination). In parts of Asia they are commonly used to thicken and flavor a variety of drinks (nam manglak, falooda). Whether you like these drinks is very much a matter of taste, some find the unusual texture and delicate flavor delightful, and some find the texture to be slimy and revolting.

The seeds work well with cold fruit juices, herb teas and milk to make cooling summer drinks. Go light on the seed (at most 2 tsp per pint), otherwise you may end up eating your drink with a spoon.

Pesto

1 clove garlic
1 cup basil
3 tbsp pine nuts (or almonds or sunflower seeds)
½ tsp salt
Pepper
½ cup olive oil
2 oz Romano or Parmesan cheese

Blend the oil and basil together in a food processor, then add the garlic, pine nuts and salt and pepper. It can then be frozen for storage. I think it tastes better if it is cooked for a few minutes, but it isn't essential. It is traditional to add 2 oz grated Parmesan, or Romano, cheese just before serving (though it isn't essential).

Beans, Bush and Pole

Phaseolus vulgaris

Introduction: The bean was first domesticated over 6000 years in Central and South America and its use had spread over much of North America before Europeans arrived. It is now a very important crop around the world, as beans are the most important source of protein for many people on earth (black beans, kidney beans, pinto beans and others). A number of other species also yield important beans crops (in the Ph*aseolus, Vigna, Vicia* and *Glycine* genera), but this is the most important.

Beans are important to gardeners for another reason too, they (like most members of the *Fabaceae*) have a symbiotic relationship with nitrogen fixing bacteria. This means that beans can actually add nitrogen to the soil they grow in.

Crop value: When gardeners talk about beans in the garden they usually mean green beans, but these plants have a lot more to offer than a green vegetable. From a self-sufficiency standpoint few crops can match the dry beans. They are tasty, easy to grow, drought tolerant, need little attention, enrich the soil they grow in, are easy to process and prepare and can be stored for several years. What more could you ask for in one crop?

A large bean patch enables you to produce a nutritious high protein food with relatively little effort, and give you one of the best ways to increase your self-reliance.

Ease of growing: Beans are an undemanding crop and do well almost everywhere, so long as it isn't too cool. You have to really work at it to fail with beans.

About Beans

Seed facts
Germ temp: 60 (80) 85°F
Germ time: 6 - 18 days
16 days / 59°F
11 days / 68°F
8 days / 77°F * Optimum
6 days / 86°F
Seed viability: 3 years
Germination percentage: 75+
Weeks to grow transplants: 3 - 4

Planning facts
Hardiness: Tender
Growing temp: 60 (70 - 75) 85°F
Plants per person: 10 - 20
Plants per sq ft: 9
Start inside: on the last frost date
Plant out: 4 wks after last frost
Direct sow: 4 wks after last frost
Succession sow: every 3 weeks

Harvest facts
Days to harvest:
Dry beans: 85 - 115 days
Green beans: 60 days
Harvest period: 4 - 8 wks
Yield per plant: 1 oz
Yield per sq ft: ¾ lb green
1 oz dry

Nutritional content: Green beans are rich in iron, potassium and silicon and well as a multitude of antioxidants. They contain about 140 calories per pound.

Dry beans are rich in protein, soluble fiber (which can lower blood cholesterol levels), complex carbohydrates, thiamine, niacin, folate, calcium, iron, magnesium, phosphorus and potassium. They contain about 1400 calories per pound.

Beans are somewhat deficient in the amino acid methionine, which is why they were traditionally eaten with methionine rich corn (2 parts corn to one part beans).

Beans also contain a trypsin inhibitor, but this is destroyed by heat (which is why beans must be cooked to make them fully edible).

Climate: Beans are very much a warm weather crop and prefer a growing temperature between 70°F - 85°F. They grow poorly below 60°F (cool wet weather also encourages various diseases). On the other hand they don't like intense heat. Temperatures above 85°F can slow growth and cause flowers to drop rather than setting pods (especially if they are stressed by lack of water too).

Soil

pH 6.0 (6.5-7.0) 7.5

Beans grow best in a light, well-drained loamy soil (not too heavy), with lots of organic matter. It should be fairly fertile for best growth, and also fairly neutral.

The soil doesn't have to be very rich in nitrogen as they can fix their own. In fact they won't do this if nitrogen is already abundant in the soil. However it should have good quantities of potassium, phosphorus and other nutrients.

Beans are sometimes planted after a crop that was heavily manured, or after a winter cover crop.

Soil preparation: Incorporate any amendments into the top 6 - 8″ of soil, as this is where most of the plants feeder roots are located. Beans dislike acid soil, so add lime if necessary, or wood ashes (beans love wood ashes).

Inoculation: It is important to understand that the bean plants themselves don't fix nitrogen. They simply play host to nitrogen fixing *Rhizobium* bacteria that live in nodules on their roots. If the right strain of bacteria isn't present in the soil, no nitrogen will be fixed and the bean plants will take it out of the soil for their own use, just like any other plant.

If you have grown beans in the past 3 - 5 years, there are probably enough bacteria already in the soil for good root nodulation and you don't need to inoculate. If you haven't grown them recently, you can ensure it is available by inoculating the seeds with the appropriate bacteria. This greatly increases nitrogen fixation and can boost yields by as much as 60%.

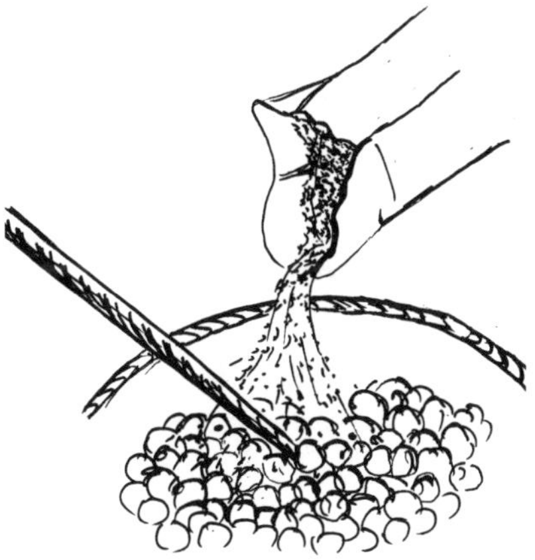

Inoculant is a living organism and doesn't last indefinitely. For best results keep the packet in a cool dark place and use it before its expiration date.

How: The simplest way to inoculate the beans is to moisten them with water (some people add a little molasses to the water to help the inoculant adhere) and then roll them in the inoculant powder. Some gardeners then roll the inoculated seeds in colloidal phosphate to supply phosphorus and to protect the inoculant.

Planning

Where: Beans are fairly tender plants and prefer a warm sunny spot. Tall pole beans are vulnerable to being blown over, so should be sheltered from high winds. Bush beans are less demanding and are often interplanted between slower growing, but more space hungry crops.

When: Beans originated in the tropics and can't stand cold weather. If the seeds are planted in cold soil they will often rot before they get around to germinating. Don't plant them out until all frost danger is past and the soil is warm (60˚F is a minimum and 80˚F is better). This may be 4 weeks after the last frost date.

If you want to get an early crop, you can warm the soil beforehand, with cloches or plastic mulch (and possibly start them inside). Raised beds also help because they warm up faster than flat ground.

Succession sowing: Beans can produce a lot of food in a short time, especially the bush types. This is fine for dry beans, or if you plan on freezing them for later use, but can also be a problem. For fresh eating you really want a modest and continuous harvest, preferably over a long period of time. The way to get this sustained yield is to sow small quantities of plants in succession every 2 - 3 weeks, until mid summer. Pole beans bear for a longer period than bush beans, so can be sown less frequently.

To grow dry beans you plant them all at once, as soon as the soil is warm enough. They need a longer period of warm weather for the green pods to mature into dry beans. They are not at all hardy and any frost will kill them.

Planting

Starting indoors

You usually only start beans inside if you need to get them started early, or if you want to avoid hungry early birds. Growing beans from transplants is a lot more work than direct sowing and they dislike the root disturbance involved, If the soil is warm enough the large seeds germinate and grow so fast outdoors that direct sown plants often catch up to transplanted ones. It always surprises me to see six packs of bean plants for sale in the garden center when it is better, cheaper and just as easy to direct sow.

How: Start the seed indoors in soil blocks or cell packs (they don't like root disturbance so avoid flats). If the germination percentage of the seeds is high, sow one seed in each cell. If germination is not so good, plant two seeds and thin to the best one after they have both germinated. Don't forget to inoculate them.

Direct sowing

Beans are usually direct sown as it is a lot less work than transplanting. This is particularly important if you are sowing a large area for dry beans.

Pre-planting treatment: In warm weather some people soak the seed overnight prior to planting (this is not a good idea if the soil is cool). The best way to do this is put the seed on a wet paper towel, so they can absorb the moisture at their leisure. Submerging them in water may cause them to absorb water too quickly and can apparently cause problems.

A good way to improve germination in cool conditions is to pre-sprout the seeds indoors. The seed can then germinate in optimally warm conditions and could save you 10 days or more. You then plant out the already germinated seeds, being very careful not to damage the tender roots. Don't forget to inoculate them.

How: Pole beans are best sown in long rows down the bed, as it's easier to support them. Simply make a furrow at the required depth, lay your seeds evenly in the bottom and pull the soil back into the furrow. Of course you can also plant them around whatever supports you have provided, using a similar method.

Bush beans are usually planted in offset rows across the bed, an equal distance apart. I start by placing the seeds on top of the prepared seedbed, at the correct spacing. When I am satisfied that they are all correctly spaced, I simply push them down into the soil with my finger and close up the small hole. Of course the seeds should be inoculated as described above.

Depth: The depth of planting varies according to the soil temperature and moisture content. They should be planted 1″ deep in cold, moist soil and 2″ (or even 3″) deep in warm, dry soil. The deeper planting ensures they get enough moisture.

Thinning: It is common to sow roughly twice as many seeds as you need plants and thin to the approximate spacing after they have all emerged. The best way to remove the extra plants is by pinching them out as this doesn't disturb those remaining. Always remove the inferior plants and leave the best ones (obviously!).

Spacing: The biggest factor in determining spacing is whether they are bush or pole varieties.
I have given a range of planting distances because it varies with circumstances (variety, soil fertility, moisture availability). A close spacing means more plants, but each one will be less productive than when growing with more room. Beware of overcrowding which can result in poor air circulation and possible disease problems. You need to experiment a little to find the ideal spacing for your plants.

Bush: Space the plants 3 - 5″ apart both ways in the beds. If you want to grow in rows then put them 4 - 6″ apart, with 18″ between the rows.

Pole: These are best grown in rows, down the middle of the bed, as this makes it easier to support them (you can interplant a low growing crop in the vacant space). You want the plants to be 3 - 6″ apart, with 18″ between the rows. You could also space them like bush beans, 6 - 8″ apart in offset rows across the beds, but this makes them harder to support.

If you plan on using a teepee of poles for support, then plant 4 - 6 seeds around each pole. When these have germinated, thin to leave the best 3 - 4 plants at each pole.

Care

Beans are pretty easy plants to grow and most of the care they need is in watering and weeding when young. Native Americans sometimes used to leave their plants for weeks at a time to pretty much grow themselves.

Weeds: Young bean plants can't compete with weeds very well, so it's important to keep down weeds initially. They are quite shallow rooted, so be careful not to damage them if you use a hoe. Widely spaced pole beans may benefit from a mulch to keep weeds down, but bush beans cover the soil pretty well by themselves.

Water: A lack of water in hot weather will affect the set of the pods, so make sure they are well watered at this time. The most critical time is when they are flowering and sizing up their pods.

Keep the soil evenly moist, but don't over water as this can lead to disease problems.

Try and avoid wetting the leaves when watering, as mildew and fungus diseases can be spread in this way. The best way to irrigate is with drip or soaker hose.

Dry beans are quite drought tolerant and do well as a dry farmed crop, (grown with no irrigation), though yields will be slightly lower. The plants should be spaced further apart, to lessen competition between plants and to give their roots more soil to extract water from. Try spacing them 9 - 12″ apart and see how it works.

Fertilization: Bush beans don't usually need feeding, as they aren't in the ground for very long. Pole beans may benefit from a feed of compost tea or liquid seaweed, every 3 - 4 weeks. This is particularly helpful when they start to flower.

Pollination: Beans are generally self-pollinated, so it usually happens pretty much automatically. However if the temperature is much above 85°F the flowers may drop off instead of being fertilized.

Mulch: This is often used to cover the soil under widely spaced pole beans, as it conserves moisture and keeps down weeds. Don't apply it until the soil is warm though. Bush beans tend to cover the ground pretty effectively and don't really need it.

Supports

Pole beans often reach 8 feet or more in height so need a sturdy support. This should be put in place when planting, so you don't damage the growing seedlings.

A good support is a teepee of tall sturdy wooden or bamboo poles. Use poles at least 8 ft long and tie them together at a height of about 5 ft, so the tops spread out and the plants don't get so congested. Their height really depends on how vigorous your beans are.

Another good trellis can be made with pairs of tall poles, 2 ft apart at the base. A row of these is connected at the top to a long crossbar. I'm not sure I'm explaining this very well, but look at the picture.

An arch can be made by planting two rows of supple poles (willow is good) and bending over and tying the tops. These are then connected with long crosspieces to tie the whole thing together.

One of the easiest field scale supports (for large plantings) consists of 8 ft metal T posts, with a ¼″ nylon rope at the top, supporting horticultural netting (or chicken wire netting).

Many other kinds of supports can be devised for supporting pole beans. chicken wire, bamboo canes, hog fencing and string have all been used. I like to use wire fencing, simply because its less work than most other arrangements.

Whatever you use should have a fairly rough texture so the plants can get a grip and twine around (if it is too smooth they may slip down). It is also important that the support is strong enough, as the total mass of vegetation can get quite heavy.

Pea sticks (see **Peas**) are another easy solution that doesn't require you to buy anything.

The traditional Native American support for beans was corn or sunflowers. This was a good solution for a pre-industrial people who didn't have access to string, wire or metal tools to cut poles. They simply grew the supports they needed and obtained food from them at the same time.

If you want to try this, you must make sure the corn has made enough growth, so that the beans don't overwhelm it. They also planted squash to cover and make use of the open ground between the corn hills. This very efficient growing system was known as the three sisters and was widely practiced by many tribes. See **Corn** for more on this.

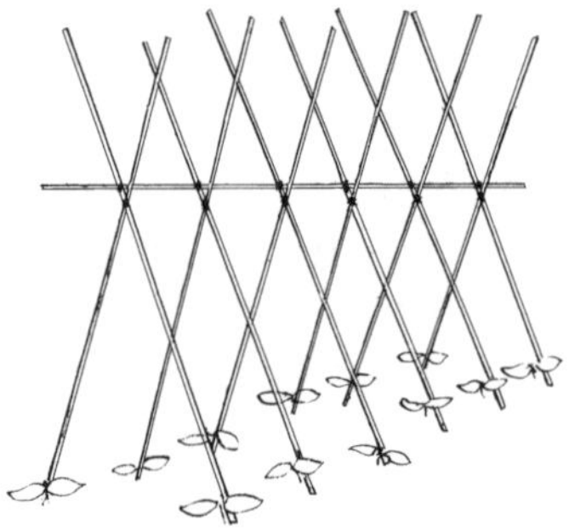

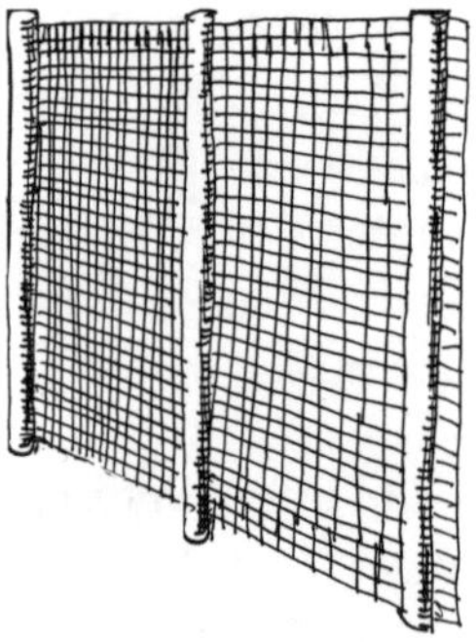

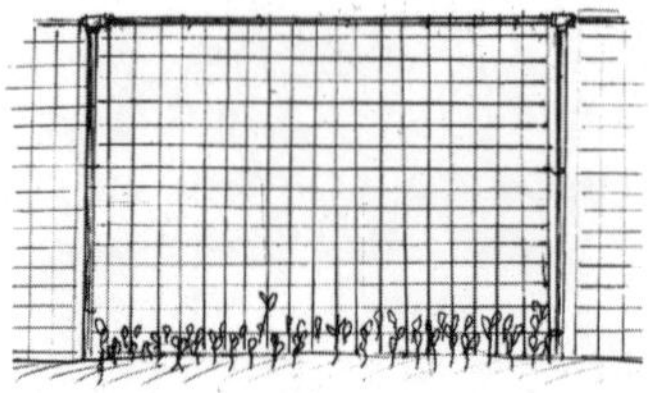

Pests: Though beans are an attractive food source for many creatures (especially in warm weather), they are pretty vigorous plants and are rarely seriously affected by most pests. A young plant can lose as much as 50% of its leaves and still recover completely.

Mexican Bean Beetles: These are a potentially serious pest and can quickly get out of control (watch for their yellow eggs). A traditional remedy was to interplant with potatoes, garlic or nasturtium, but I can't vouch for their effectiveness. Hand picking works well for small numbers of plants.

Cutworms: Will often go for the emerging seedlings. See **Cabbage** for ways to deal with them.

Aphids: If these are a problem, blast them with a jet of water.

Other pests: Bean leaf beetle, bean weevils, wireworms, leafhoppers, tarnished plant bugs, leaf miners, flea beetles, mites, cucumber beetles, green stink bugs, whiteflies and caterpillars.

Birds and mice will often go for the newly planted seed, or seedlings, especially in spring. Net the beds and / or get a cat or dog.

Disease: Beans are prone to a number of bacterial, fungal and viral diseases, especially in areas with lots of summer rain.

You can reduce the incidence of disease problems by careful rotation and by cleaning up crop debris after harvest (or incorporating it into the soil). Avoid poorly drained soil, give the plants good air circulation and watch for disease vectors such as aphids and leafhoppers. Also choose resistant varieties when available.

Anthracnose, halo blight and bean mosaic are serious diseases and may be seed borne, so watch out where your seed comes from and discard any unhealthy looking seed.

Bacterial blight, leaf spot, curly top virus, downy mildew powdery mildew, white mold and rust can all be a problem under certain conditions. It is important to keep the foliage dry and don't work around the wet plants.

Frost: Bean plants are very tender and are usually killed by frost. Don't plant until after frost danger is past and harvest before frost kills the plants (or cover to protect).

Harvesting

Snap beans (Haricot Vert)

When: The pods take 18 - 21 days to go from pollination to full size. They are best gathered just as they are reaching full size, but before the beans start to swell. They should still snap in half easily. Many people prefer them when they are just slightly smaller in diameter than a pencil. You might try harvesting the pods at different sizes to see which you like best.

If you get them early enough, you can eat the immature pods of many dry bean varieties as snap beans, (they may have strings though).

How: The best time to harvest is in the early morning when it is still cool. Gather the pods carefully so you don't damage the plants. Hold on to the vine and pull down on the pod, so there is no danger of pulling the plant out of the ground.

The best way to harvest older beans is to break off the bean just below its stem and then break sideways and pull, leaving any strings attached to the plant. In humid areas it's not good to harvest while the foliage is wet, as this can transmit disease.

You must gather the green beans conscientiously whether you want them or not, as the plants may stop producing when seed starts to ripen. If you harvest pole beans every 2 - 3 days, it is possible to keep the plants producing for weeks.

The key to large harvests is early and regular picking (just like life, the more you take the more you get).

If the harvest gets away from you, remove all the pods of any size. With luck this will encourage a new growth of pods.

Shell Beans

These are harvested as soon as the beans reach full size (4 - 8 days after the pods reach full size), but before they toughen up.

Dry Beans

After the green pods and shell beans we get to the dry beans, which is the final stage. All beans can be used as dry beans, but those grown for their pods tend to be smaller than those grown specifically for dry beans.

When: If you live in a warm and dry climate the beans can be left to dry completely on the vine. They are gathered after the pods are dry and leathery and you can hear the seeds rattle inside. Farmers start harvesting when the moisture content drops to 18%.

How: You can gather small quantities of pods individually, but this is a little too time consuming to be practical for larger harvests. If you have a large area of beans pick the whole plants and lay them on a tarp to dry before threshing them.

If the climate is uncooperatively wet and cool you may have to cut whole plants and hang them in a warm dry place to mature and dry out. Slightly immature beans will ripen fully even after picking (and turn the right color).

Threshing: If you have a large quantity of beans they can be threshed (freed from the pods) by walking on the dry plants, by using your hands (you may need gloves for protection), or by banging the plants inside a barrel. You then need to separate the beans from the chaff (pod debris). Traditionally you would do this on a windy day, but you could also use a blower or compressor to blow away the chaff and leave you with clean beans, ready for use.

Dry means dry: The threshed seeds must be dried thoroughly (until they have 15% moisture or less) before storage. A completely dry bean is so hard it will shatter when crushed. If you can make a mark with your fingernail it isn't dry enough. A simple way to see if the beans are dry enough is to put a few in a closed jar for a few days. If condensation forms on the inside of the jar, they still contain too much moisture.

If there is any possibility that weevils may have got to your beans, you should freeze them for a couple of days (24 hours is probably long enough) to kill any eggs, larvae or adults. After this treatment they should probably be dried again (they may pick up moisture) before long term storage.

Storage: Green beans may be stored in plastic bags in the fridge for a few days (this may be necessary if your plants are producing less or more than you can use at one time). For longer term storage they can be dried, pickled or frozen. Shell beans can also be frozen.

Fully dry beans store well in a cool airtight container and will stay edible for several years (thought they are best when eaten within 12 months).

Seed saving: Beans are among the easiest crops to save seed, you just grow them like dry beans. They are mostly self-pollinating, though insects may cause some cross-pollination. For this reason it is best to have only one variety flowering at a time. If this isn't possible you should separate them as much as is practical (put at either end of the garden). It is often easy to tell when they have crossed because the beans will have different colors or patterns.

Be aware that some viruses may be transmitted through the seed and try not to gather from diseased plants.

If you choose seed from the best yielding and earliest plants you can create your own specially adapted strain for your garden.

Unusual growing ideas

Field scale: Henry Thoreaus' account of growing beans as a cash crop at Walden pond has some interesting observations on growing dry beans and other things.

Varieties

Beans are commonly divided into green (snap), shell and dry beans, with both bush and pole types for all of these. This somewhat arbitrary division is somewhat complicated by the fact that many varieties can be used in more than one way. For example some dry beans can be used as shell or green beans and vice versa.

Pole Beans: These are the original beans and are generally more productive than bush beans because there is more photosynthetic area for food production (some may grow to 10 ft or more in height). They are also more interesting visually and take up less horizontal space in the garden. They also bear for a longer period and there is less damage from pests such as slugs. They are easier to harvest too, as the pods are off the ground. All of these features makes pole beans more useful for the home gardener than bush beans.

The big drawback to pole beans is that you have to give them something to climb up, which means an extra step (more work) in growing them.

Bush Beans: These were developed for commercial growers who didn't want to have to support the plants. They tend to bear earlier than the pole types, though not so abundantly. They are more compact as a crop (only to 3 ft maximum) and easier to deal with.

Other differences mainly involve the final use of the beans, whether they will be used as dry beans, shell beans or green beans.

Snap Beans: Also known as string beans, French beans or green beans, they are a mainstay of the traditional vegetable garden. Most modern varieties don't have strings, which is why they are now referred to as snap beans, rather than string beans. Good varieties include:

Bush: **Golden Wax, Jade, Provider, Romano, Royal Burgundy, Tendergreen.**

Pole: **Blue Lake Pole, Kentucky Wonder, Romano**

French Filet beans (Haricot Verts): These are some of the best quality varieties of snap bean. The pods are harvested when very small (¼″ diameter or less) and tender. These varieties are all outstanding:

Bush: **Fin De Bagnol, Nickel, Royalnel, Triomphe de Farcy, Vernandon.**

Pole: **Emerite, Fortex**

Shell Beans Flageolets): Sometimes called shelly beans, these are gathered when the beans reach full size, but before they start to harden and mature. The soft beans are shelled out and cooked.

Bush: Lows Champion, Vernel, Tongue of Fire, Dwarf Horticultural.

Pole: Good Mother Stallard

Dry Beans (Haricots)

These are unsurpassed from a nutritional and self-sufficiency viewpoint, as they are a major source of easily stored protein, as well as a great low work crop. Of course dry beans are also relatively cheap to buy (they lend themselves to mechanization), so may not be worthwhile to grow unless you have a lot of space (or really need the food).

Kidney beans, pinto beans, black bean, Swedish beans and navy beans are all simply different varieties of the same species. There is a mind boggling number of bean varieties out there and I won't even try and recommend any varieties. I will just say the following have all worked well for me.

Bush: **Anasazi, Black Turtle, Borlotto, Hutterite Soup Bean, Tigers Eye.**

Pole: Cherokee Trail of Tears, Hidatsa Shield Figure

Kitchen use

Green beans: Trim the tops and bottoms off the pods and steam (or boil) them for a few minutes.

Flatulence: You can't really talk about using dry beans without mentioning their unfortunate tendency to cause flatulence. This occurs because they contain various polysaccharides (complex sugars) that aren't easily digested in the small intestine because we lack the appropriate enzymes. Consequently they pass through into the colon, where they are broken down by various types of bacteria. In the process these organisms produce the smelly gas (a mix of hydrogen and methane).

This tendency can be reduced by soaking beans and discarding the water before cooking. You can also change the water once or twice during cooking. Fresh beans are less of a problem than old ones. Also don't add salt until they are cooked (this makes them tougher anyway). If you eat beans a lot your body may become more adapted to eating them, so this becomes less of a problem.

The fungus *Aspergillus niger* contains the enzyme alpha-galactosidase, which breaks down these polysaccharide sugars in the small intestine. This is available commercially under the name "Beano". I can't say I've ever felt the need to try this though.

The fastest way to soak beans is to bring to boil for a few minutes and then leave to soak for an hour (it would take at least 4 hours in cold water). Then rinse and cook in fresh water,

When using beans in a recipe it is best to cook them separately and then add other ingredients. Don't cook everything together from the start.

Refried Beans

Refried beans aren't really fried twice (or even once), it is simply a mistranslation of reheated beans.

1 ½ cups cooked beans
2 tablespoons olive oil
Salt
Lime juice
1 teaspoon oregano

There isn't much preparation, you simply mash the beans and add the rest of the ingredients and heat. The prepared beans will keep in a container in the fridge for up to a week.

Bean, Fava

Vicia faba

Introduction: The fava bean originated in the Middle East, but has been grown in the colder parts of Europe as far back as the Iron Age. It has long been (no pun intended) a staple of Northern European peasants and was actually their only bean until the discovery of the Americas and their various beans. They are also popular in parts of Asia, South America and North Africa.

Crop value: Fava bean isn't closely related to any other bean and is actually a kind of vetch (*Vicia*). It does resemble other beans in being very rich in protein (it has been called the soybean of the north) and because it is a nitrogen fixer. It is quite easy to grow and is often recommended as a good crop for beginning gardeners.

The fava bean has great potential as a self-sufficiency crop. It isn't highly productive for the space it takes up, but because of its ability to grow in cool weather, it can often be planted as a winter / early spring crop, using space that would otherwise be vacant.

Ease of growing: Fava bean is a fairly easy crop to grow so long as it gets suitably cool weather (warm weather brings problems). It doesn't need very fertile soil as it fixes its own nitrogen.

Nutritional content: Fava beans are very nutritious with 24% protein, 2% fat and 50% carbohydrate. A comparison of protein quality shows soybean 68, fava bean 67, kidney bean 55 and peanut 52. They also contain soluble fiber (which can lower cholesterol) and complex carbohydrates. They contain about 1530 calories per pound.

It has recently been found that fava beans contain a substance called levodopa which is used in commercial medications to control Parkinson's disease. Some people have been using fava beans instead of the commercial drugs, apparently with some success.

Caution: Some people, particularly males of Mediterranean (and sometimes Asian) descent are allergic to fava beans. It causes a serious (sometimes even fatal) allergic reaction known as favism. Favism occurs in people with a deficiency of a blood enzyme called G6PD and destroys red blood cells. If you have any reason to think you might be allergic then it is usually recommended, that you eat only a couple of beans initially (the first symptom is urinary bleeding).

Some people are even allergic to the foliage or pollen and get a rash when they come in contact with it.

Soil

pH 6.0 - 7.0

Fava beans do well in most soil types, so long as they aren't too acidic. Their preference is for a fertile, fairly heavy soil, with lots of organic matter to retain moisture.

It is important that the soil be well-drained, especially for an over-wintering crop, as their roots may rot if they sit in cold wet soil. The large seeds are also prone to rot if they sit in cold wet soil for a long time without germinating (some seed is pre-treated with a fungicide to try and prevent this). If your soil tends to stay wet in winter then raised beds are a good idea.

Soil preparation: Fava beans like organic matter, so incorporate 2″ of compost, or aged manure, into the top 6″ of soil. If they are following a crop that was heavily fertilized, you don't need to do this. They don't need a lot of nitrogen, because they host nitrogen-fixing bacteria in nodules on their roots. If the pH is low, add lime, as they don't like acid soil.

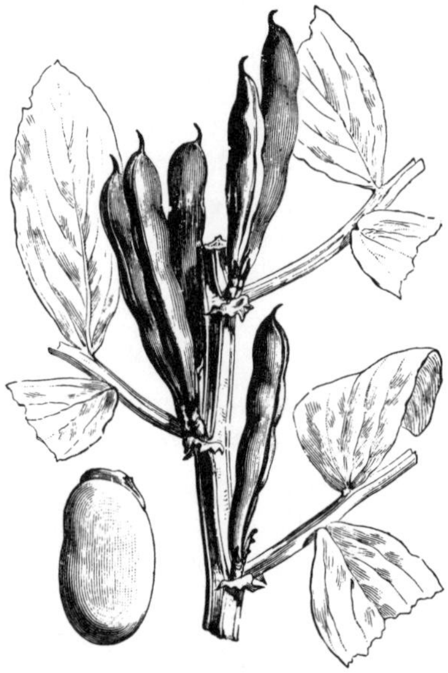

Climate: This species is unique among commonly cultivated beans in that it actually dislikes heat. It is a cool weather crop, with requirements more akin to the pea than other beans. If your climate is too cold for other beans, this is the one to try.

Most of the United States is too warm for fava beans in summer, so it is grown in spring or fall (at the same time as peas). It is grown as a summer crop in colder climates like Britain and as an over wintering crop in areas with mild winters like Italy. In the tropics it is only grown in high mountains.

Fava bean grows best at a temperature of 60 - 65°F. It won't really work if it gets much above 70°F, because the flowers will fall off instead of setting pods. It is very hardy (down to 20°F) and doesn't mind cold soil so long as it isn't actually frozen.

About Fava Bean

Seed facts
Germ temp: 40 (40 - 75) 75°F
Germ time: 7 - 14 days
Viability: 2 - 6 yrs
Germination percentage: 75%+

Planning facts
Hardiness: Hardy
Growing temp: 40 (60 - 65) 75°F
Plants per person: 10
Plants per sq ft: 3
Direct sow: 4 wks before last frost
Fall crop: sow 4 - 8 wks before first fall frost
Succession sow: every 2 - 3 wks
Days to harvest:
70 - 90 shell beans
90 - 150 days dry beans
Plant height: 3 - 5 ft
Plant diameter: 12 - 18″

Harvest facts
Harvest period: 6 - 8 wks
Yield per plant: 2 oz beans
Plants per person: 5
Yield per sq ft:
¼ - 1 lb sq ft (green beans)
1 oz sq ft (dry beans)

Planning

Where: Like most plants that grow in cool weather, fava beans need full sun for best growth. When growing in hotter weather they may benefit from light shade during the hottest part of the day. They can get quite tall (5 ft), so don't put them where they might cast shade on other crops.

When: Fava beans like the same growing conditions as peas, with 2 - 3 months of fairly cool weather being ideal. The best time to plant them depends on the climate, there are several options.

Spring: In areas with many weeks of cool spring weather, they are often grown as a spring crop. They are planted out as early as the soil can be worked, which may be 4 weeks before the last frost (or even earlier if sown under cloches). These plants should be out of the ground by the end of June, leaving plenty of time for another crop.

Summer: In areas with cool summers, they can be succession sown every few weeks, to give a continuous harvest all summer.

Fall: You can plant them in late summer / early fall for a fall crop.

Winter: In areas with mild winters they can be sown in fall, to grow right through the winter and mature in early spring. The trick is to use a suitably hardy variety and for the plants to be advanced enough when cold weather comes that they keep growing. If they are too small they may never really get started.

Early spring: If winter isn't mild enough for continuous growth, you can sow them in mid winter for an early spring crop. In England some particularly hardy varieties (the long pod types) are sown in winter, to emerge in early spring. These plants bear a few weeks before spring planted ones. Much of North America is too cold for this however.

Germination problems:

When fava beans are planted in cool, wet soil they are prone to rotting and may not have a very high germination rate. If this is a problem wait until the soil has warmed up a bit more. If you have continued problems with poor germination you might want to try pre-germinating the seed.

Planting

Inoculation: If you haven't grown this crop before, it will fix more nitrogen if inoculated with the appropriate nitrogen-fixing bacteria (one suitable for vetches). By enhancing the health of the plants it may also increase yields. See **Bush and Pole Beans** for how to do this.

Indoors: Fava beans aren't usually started inside, because they do so well when direct sown. The large seeds can germinate at low temperatures and grow quickly once they have germinated. I suppose you might want to start them inside to get a very early start, or if birds or rodents are a big problem. They can be started in flats, but (like most legumes) they dislike root disturbance, so it is better to start them in large soil blocks or cell packs. The seedlings grow quickly and won't need to be inside for very long.

Outdoors: The seeds can germinate at temperatures as low as 40˚F, so they can be direct sown into cold soil. You can hasten germination by pre-sprouting the seeds, though you have to be careful not to damage the delicate shoots.

The seeds are planted 1″ (small seeds) to 2 ½″ (large seed) deep, using a dibber. It is a good idea to plant a few extra seeds at the end of the row, to fill in vacant spots where seeds fail to germinate.

You can speed up germination and growth of your earliest planting by starting it under a cloche or poly tunnel.

Succession sowing: To get a continuous harvest, you can make succession sowings every 2 - 3 weeks.

Spacing: This varies according to the fertility of the soil and the size of the variety. Dwarf varieties are planted closer together than the larger types.

Beds: Plant 6 - 8″ apart in offset rows across the bed.

Rows: Taller varieties do best when planted in two rows, down the center of the bed. Space the plants 4 - 6″ apart in the rows, with 18 - 24″ between the rows.

It is possible to plant 2 double rows in a bed. Space the rows 9″ apart, with 6″ between plants in the row. Separate the 2 double rows by 24″.

Care

Weed: Fava beans are pretty robust plants and can handle almost any weeds when full grown. The young plants will need to be kept free of weeds though.

Watering: Water regularly in dry weather, as lack of water can affect the number and quality of the pods. Fortunately dry soil is not usually a big problem in the cool weather they prefer.

Water is most critical when the flowers appear and they are setting pods. If water is in short supply, just give it when the flowers open and again when the pods begin to swell.

Fertilization: This isn't usually necessary if they are growing in reasonable soil, especially as they fix their own nitrogen.

Support: Though these beans don't climb, they may get quite tall, to 4 feet or more. When they get a heavy load of pods they can become top heavy and fall over (especially in windy areas). Consequently they may benefit from some kind of support. The simplest approach is to earth up the stems to stop them falling over. You might also use a network of bamboo canes and garden twine.

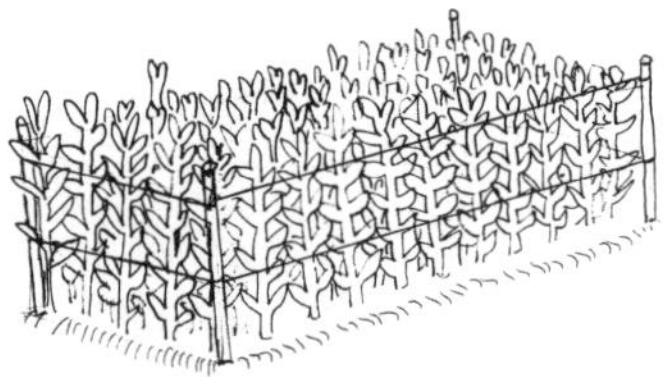

If they are grown in a dense stand the plants tend to be mutually self-supporting (corner stakes and twine can stop the plants at the edges from falling over).

Pruning: It is a common practice to pinch out the top 4 - 6″ of the plant after it has set three sets of pods. This not only helps the pods to develop, but also discourages bean aphids (these are attracted to the succulent new growth and can be a major pest). If the tops aren't infested with aphids, they can be used as a potherb. If they are infested they should be removed from the garden.

Companions: It is said that fava beans don't like garlic or onions, which is ironic as they go together so well in the kitchen.

Pests: Most pests and diseases aren't very active in the cool weather when fava beans are doing most of their growth, so they are relatively pest free. Cutworms may destroy the young seedlings as they appear. Slugs and snails can also be troublesome.

Other pests include bean beetles, broad bean weevil, flea beetles, leafhoppers and mites.

Aphids: Bean aphids are the common problem and as soon as it gets warm enough their appearance is almost inevitable. They tend to cluster on the growing tip of the plant, which is why this is often removed after enough pods have set. You can also try washing them off of the plants with a strong jet of water from a hose.

Diseases: Diseases include anthracnose, chocolate spot, mosaic and blight.

Harvesting

The plants are indeterminate, so the lower pods ripen first and then those above. If temperatures get much above 70°F, the flowers will usually drop off instead of setting pods.

Pods: The very young (2″) pods can be used like green beans. They should be harvested before the beans start to enlarge and the interior of the pod gets cottony.

Shell Beans: Fava beans are most often harvested in the green shell stage. They should have reached full size, but the skins shouldn't have started to toughen. At this time the pod will still be quite soft and the seed will be not much bigger than a penny. Gathered at this time, the seeds are tender and delicious.

Dry beans: These are gathered after the pods turn crisp and almost black (don't wait too long or the seeds may start to mold in the pod).

Greens: The succulent growing tips can be harvested for use like spinach.

The flowers are not only edible, but also taste pretty good.

After harvest: Don't pull the plants out of the ground after the harvest is over, cut them off at ground level instead. This leaves the nitrogen rich roots to decompose directly into the soil.

Storage: The pods can be stored in a plastic bag in the refrigerator, for up to 2 weeks. Shell beans can be canned or frozen. The dry beans (they must be really dry) can be stored in a cool dry, aerated place, where rodents can't get them (though they can be frozen too).

Seed saving: Fava beans are usually self- pollinated, but may occasionally be cross-pollinated by bees, so to ensure purity you should only grow one variety at a time. Allow the pods to ripen fully and dry out on the plant. Take seeds from at least 5 of the best plants and dry thoroughly for storage. Don't keep any seed that has gone moldy or has black spots on it.

If you want to grow fava beans as a cover crop you will need quite a lot of seed. The best way to get this is to save it from your own plants.

Unusual growing ideas

Second harvest: If you cut the plants down to the ground after harvest they will sometimes send up new suckers. These may actually produce more pods (not a lot, but some). Even if they don't, they will provide biomass for composting or green manure.

Greens: Fava beans can also be grown as a super hardy, low maintenance edible leaf crop for spring or fall (or you can eat some of your green manure). Simply sow the seeds and when the plants appear you can start harvesting the tender young greens, If you cut them at a node when 4 - 6″tall they will grow back with two stems instead of one. Do this several times and you get a bushier plant that can then be allowed to produce flowers and pods.

Cover crop / green manure: Fava bean is commonly used as a green manure or cover crop. In mild areas it will grow right through the winter and reach a height of 5 feet or more. It not only fixes more nitrogen than most other crops (it's been estimated that 100 lb of green material contains ½ lb of nitrogen), but also produces a lot of biomass for compost material, Their roots are good for loosening compacted soil and generally improving tilth.

Fava beans are a useful crop for re-establishing a garden on a neglected site, either as a winter cover crop or a summer green manure (in cooler areas). When used as a green manure, the plants are dug into the soil when they start to flower.

For a cover crop the beans should be planted 6 - 9" apart, which means you need quite a lot of seed to plant a large area.

As a bonus you can eat the tender parts of the green manure plants as greens.

Insect food: The plants are an important source of food for insects in winter or early spring. They are also a good source of pollen for honey bees.

Survival crop: Fava beans are an excellent survival crop: high in protein and calories, easy to grow, they fix a lot of nitrogen, produce a lot of biomass and grow in the colder part of the year (leaving the warmer part for another crop. The only drawback is that they take a lot of space (but in winter it probably isn't used anyway).

Containers: Fava beans can do quite well in containers, though you probably won't get much of a harvest.

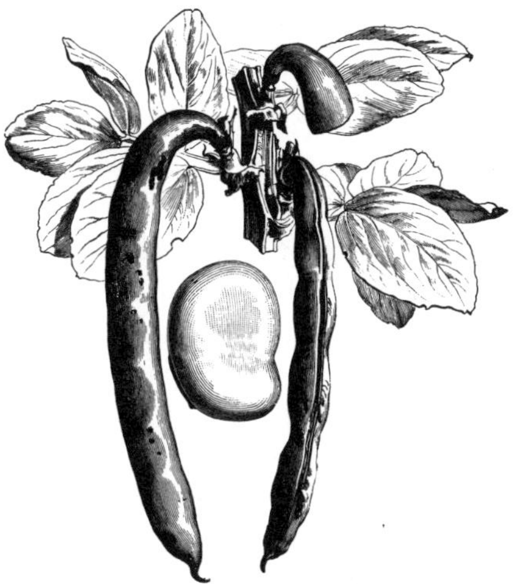

Varieties

The larger seeded types are usually used as shell beans. There are distinct varieties for autumn and spring sowing and its important to choose the right one. Fava bean isn't a very popular crop in this country and the choice of varieties is limited (mostly to imported European varieties).

Longpods: The pods on these varieties may be over a foot in length, with as many as 8 large kidney shaped seeds. They are very hardy and are often sown in fall, as a winter or early spring crop.

Aquadulce - A classic early variety.

Extra Preoce Violetto - A hardy Italian

Ianto's return - Very cold hardy variety.

Windsors: These varieties produce short pods with only 4 smallish round seeds per pod. They are not as hardy as the longpods and so are usually sown in spring. Some people say these are the best-flavored types.

Broad Windsor - An old English variety.

Express - Not easy to find.

The Sutton- Not easy to find.

Bell beans: These are the small seeded fava beans that are commonly used for green manure and animal feed (which could be why they are sometimes called horse beans). They are also good for humans to eat however.

Sweet Lorane: This variety can be used as a edible cover crop, as it produces tasty, small seeds.

Foul (Ful) Masri This small seeded Egyptian variety does well in warm weather. In this country it is most often used as a green manure for warmer areas, but the seeds are also edible. In Egypt it is commonly used for making hummus.

Kitchen use

Fava beans are usually eaten as shell beans, either steamed, stir fried, or boiled for 5 minutes. If you are using older beans you might want to remove the tough skins before eating (though you don't have to and it is tedious). This is done by snipping off the end with scissors and squeezing out the bean.

The dry beans may be used like kidney beans, though they take longer to cook. They are often used in soups, stews and other dishes. I've read that they can also be popped like popcorn, though I have never tried it.

The tender young growing tips are edible, as are the flowers.

Falafel

Falafel is usually made with chickpeas in this country, but in the Middle East (where it originated) it is usually made with fava beans.

1 lb dry fava beans
½ cup flat leaf parsley (chopped)
½ cup cilantro
8 green onions (chopped)
6 cloves of garlic
2 tsp ground coriander
2 tsp ground cumin
1 tsp baking powder
Salt
Black pepper

Soak the beans for 24 hours and then boil them until tender (about an hour). Puree them in a food processor (or mash to a paste) and then add the chopped parsley and onion and the rest of the seasonings. Leave for about an hour, then mold into 1½″ balls, coat in sesame seeds and fry. They are normally deep fried, but you can also saute them.

The balls are eaten with pita bread, tomatoes, lettuce, cucumber and a sauce made from tahini, lemon juice and garlic. Of course you can use them in any other way you can think of too.

Bean, Lima

Phaseolus lunatus

Introduction: It is believed that this South American bean was first cultivated almost 8000 years ago. It was brought to Europe from Peru, hence its common name and spread from there to other warm areas around the world.

Lima bean is very much a tropical plant and needs a warm climate to grow successfully. It is cultivated in much the same way as the bush and pole beans described above. The main difference is its preference for warmer growing conditions.

Crop value: Lima beans are a nutritious and useful crop for warmer areas.

Nutrients. The beans contain protein, soluble fiber and complex carbohydrates. It is also rich in folate, thiamin, tryptophan, iron, manganese, molybdenum, phosphorus and potassium.

The dry beans contain over 1500 calories per pound.

Caution: The early lima beans contained poisonous cyanogenic glycosides and had to be soaked before cooking to leach these out. Modern varieties don't contain these toxins, but some individuals are sensitive to lima beans and have problems after eating them.

Ease of growing: I haven't had a great deal of success with lima bean since I lived on the west coast. My gardens have always been too cool for these heat loving plants. If you give it a suitable climate it is pretty easy to grow however. I don't pretend to be an expert on lima beans, so this section will be fairly short.

About Lima Beans

Seed facts
Germ temp: 65 (75 - 85) 90˚F
Germ time: 7 - 18 days
31 days / 59˚F
18 days / 68˚F
7 days / 77˚F * Optimum
7 days / 86˚F
Germination percentage: 70+
Viability: 3 - 5 yrs
Weeks to grow transplants: 4 - 6

Planning facts
Hardiness: Very tender
Growing temp: 65 (70 - 80) 90˚F
Plants per sq ft: 2 - 3
Transplants
Start: On the last frost date
Plant out: 4 wks after last frost
Direct sow: 4 wks after last frost
Days to harvest: 60 - 80 Bush
80 - 90 Pole

Harvest facts
Harvest period: up to 10 weeks
Yield per sq ft: 2 - 3 oz
Yield per plant: 1 oz

Soil

pH 5.0 - 6.0
Lima Beans are like most beans in that they like a rich, well-drained loamy soil, with lots of organic matter. They like phosphorus and potassium (especially wood ashes), but don't need a lot of nitrogen. If this is readily available they won't bother to fix any. Too much nitrogen can cause lush growth at the expense of pod production.

Soil preparation: Incorporate 2″ of compost or aged manure into the top 6″ of soil, where most of the plants feeder roots are located. They dislike acid soil, so add lime if necessary. They are sometimes planted after a crop that was heavily manured.

Climate: Lima beans need warm weather (ideally 70 - 80˚F) and can't stand any frost. They don't do well in my garden because it gets too cold at night even in summer. Very hot and dry conditions are not good either, as they can result in flowers dropping without setting pods.

Planning

Where: Lima beans need a warm, sunny sheltered spot for best growth.

When: This is a tropical plant and shouldn't be planted out until the soil is fairly warm (65°F is a minimum, 75 - 80°F is better). In short season areas you can warm the soil with black plastic or cloches to enable earlier planting.

Planting

Inoculation: If you haven't grown this crop before, it will fix more nitrogen if inoculated with the appropriate nitrogen-fixing bacteria. See **Beans** for how to do this.

Transplants: The plants need warm weather, but take quite a long time to mature, so they are often started indoors. Sow the seeds on the last frost date and plant the seedlings out 4 weeks later.

Lima beans dislike transplanting, so use cell packs or soil blocks. If germination is good, plant one seed per cell, or block. If it is poor then plant two and thin to one later.

Direct sowing: Lima beans shouldn't be planted out until all frost danger is past and the soil is warm (a minimum of 65°F and preferably closer to 70 - 75°F.) If planted in soil that is too cold they may rot, so wait until at least 4 weeks after the last frost date. If you want to plant them earlier, you could warm the soil with plastic mulch or cloches. Plant them 1 - 2″ deep, depending on how warm the soil is.

Spacing: The climbing types are usually planted 4″ apart, in rows (10″ apart) (or around a teepee of poles).

Beds: Bush varieties can be planted in offset rows across the bed, with 8″ between plants (the smaller baby lima varieties can be planted as close as 3 - 4″).

Rows: If you want to plant in rows, space them 2 - 4″ between plants (later thinned to 4 - 6″), with 24″ between rows.

Care

Watering: Lima beans need a steady supply of water (1″ per week) and may not set pods if the soil is too dry.

Support: The pole varieties are vigorous climbers and need something to climb up. See **Bush and Pole Beans** for suggestions.

Pests: These are pretty much the same as pole beans.

Harvest: Shell beans are harvested when they have swollen in the pod and are plump and shiny. The pods turn a pale whitish green at this time.

Dry beans are harvested after the pods turn crisp and the seeds rattle inside.

Storage: You can keep shell beans in their pods in the refrigerator for several days, but they are best used fresh.

Seed saving: Lima beans are mostly self-pollinated, but the nectar rich flowers are very attractive to bees, so they do get cross-pollinated to some extent. For this reason it is best to have only one variety flowering at a time (otherwise it needs isolating by one mile or caging.) Gather and prepare the seed as for other beans.

Varieties

Lima bean needs a long, hot summer for best production, so does best in the southern States. If you want to grow it in a more northerly location, you will need to use a fast maturing variety.

Like other beans this crop can be divided into the bush types and the pole types.

Bush

Fordhook 242 - An old favorite.

Jackson Wonder - Fairly cold tolerant for a lima bean.

Pole

Christmas - Tall and productive.

King of the Garden - Big plants and big beans, very productive.

Baby limas: These are simply small seeded varieties that mature earlier than other types.

Henderson - An old favorite from 1888.

Kitchen use

Fresh lima beans are one of the great treats of the summer garden. They shouldn't be eaten raw though, as they may contain toxins.

Shell beans: Bring water to a boil, add the shelled beans and simmer until tender. This will only take about 5 - 7 minutes.

Dry beans: Pre-soak the rinsed beans overnight before cooking. Discard this water, cover with fresh water and simmer until cooked (usually about 45 minutes). Add your seasonings after they are cooked.

Bean, Mung

Phaseolus mungo
Syn P. aureus

Introduction: Mung beans are almost unknown by name to most Americans, yet they are often familiar as "Chinese" bean sprouts. The plants are as easy to grow as any other beans.

Nutritional content: The bean sprouts are high in protein, vitamins B1 and C, pantothenic acid, folate and several amino acids.

Dry mung beans are high in protein and contain about 1560 calories per pound. They have less tendency to cause flatulence than other beans, as they are low in the polysaccharides that cause this problem.

About Mung Beans

Seed facts
Germ temp: 60 (80) 85°F
Germ time: 3 - 12 days
Seed viability: 4 years
Germination percentage: 75+

Planning facts
Hardiness: Tender
Growing temp: 50 (60 - 70) 80°F
Plants per sq ft: 3 - 4
Direct sow: 3 wks after last frost
Days to harvest: 70 - 100 days
Height 24 - 30″

Crop value: This nutritious crop is fairly easy to grow and has a variety of uses. It is best known for its use as bean sprouts though.

Ease of growing: Mung bean is a vigorous and fairly weedy plant and in suitably warm and humid conditions it is pretty straightforward to grow.

Soil: Any good garden soil will work for mung beans. The plants fix their own nitrogen, especially if inoculated.

Planning

When: Mung beans dislike cold weather, so are not planted out until the soil has warmed up to at least 60°F and preferably 70°F.

Where: A warm, sunny, sheltered spot works best.

Inoculation: If you haven't grown this crop before, it will fix more nitrogen if inoculated with the appropriate nitrogen-fixing bacteria. By enhancing the health of the plants it may also increase yields. See **Bush and Pole Beans** for how to do this.

Planting

Direct sowing: There is little point in starting mung beans inside, because they germinate and grow, rapidly when the weather suits them. Plant the seeds ½″ deep once the soil has warmed up. If any seeds don't germinate within 12 days, sow more seed in the gaps (or transplant seedlings from denser spots. (Or the edges)

Spacing:
Beds: Space the plants 4″ apart in beds.

Rows: Space the rows 24″ apart, with the plants 3 - 4″ apart in the rows.

Care

Watering: For best production keep the soil evenly moist.

Weeding: The young plants need regular weeding.

Mulch: This keeps the soil moist and keeps down annual weeds.

Support: Mung beans are bushy, vigorous twining plants that can be grown with or without support. Their stems are firm enough that they can climb up each other. Keep them away from other small plants though, or they may smother them. They could be allowed to grow up tall plants such as sunflowers or corn.

Harvesting

When: The green immature pods are small, but can be eaten like snap beans. They should be harvested when the beans first start to swell in the pod.

To get dry beans simply leave the pods to dry on the vine. Don't wait too long to harvest though, because when fully dry they split open quite energetically and disperse their seeds.

How: If you only have a few plants, you can gather the dry, pods individually. If you have a lot then cut down the whole plants and dry them on a tarp.

Storage: Make sure the seeds are thoroughly dry and store like any other dry beans.

Seed saving: Just save some of the dry seed.

Varieties

I have never seen any mung bean varieties for sale anywhere, except for use as sprouting seed. so that's what I used.

Kitchen use

You can cook the green pods like snap beans and the dry beans like adzuki beans.

Bean Sprouts: Mung Beans are most often sprouted to make the familiar bean sprouts. See **Sprouting seeds** for more on this.

Bean, Adzuki

Phaseolus angularis

I wanted to mention this valuable Asian bean because it is one of the most useful of the lesser known beans. However it is grown in pretty much the same way as the mung bean, so I'm not going to say much about it (just look at the previous page).

Adzuki beans prefer warm days, cool nights and fairly neutral soil. They don't like wet soil.

Plant the seed 1½″ deep and 4 - 6″ apart, in rows 18″ apart. They are generally small bush plants and grow up to about 24" in height.

The young plants don't compete against weeds very well, so must be kept weeded until they get going.

They take up to 4 months to produce dry beans, though the pods can be used for snap beans earlier.

The seeds can be sprouted (this takes 2 - 4 days) or cooked like other beans. They cook more rapidly than most other beans and are more digestible.

Adzuki beans are sweeter in flavor than most beans and in Asia they are commonly eaten with sugar in candies, baked goods and desserts (including a popular ice cream). Beans as dessert can be a difficult concept for Westerners to accept, but of course it is just what you are used to.

Bean, Scarlet Runner

Phaseolus coccineus

Introduction: This Central American bean has been grown as a crop for over 4000 years. It is a vigorous and easy to grow plant that is as ornamental as it is useful. It is the most commonly grown green bean in Britain, where it is more popular than bush or pole beans (which don't grow so well in the cool climate).

Crop value: The scarlet runner bean can be eaten as green snap beans or as nutritious dry beans and tolerates cooler temperatures than most beans. It also produces beautiful red (or white) flowers that are very popular with hummingbirds and bees. All of these things make this a very useful crop for those aiming for more food self reliance.

Scarlet runner bean isn't very popular in this country, simply because most people don't realize its potential. However when they get to know it, they tend to get very enthusiastic.

Nutritional content: The beans are rich in protein, soluble fiber (which can lower blood cholesterol) and complex carbohydrates.

Climate: Though a tropical plant, the scarlet runner is happy to grow in cooler conditions than most beans. It is very popular in the Pacific Northwest and Northern Europe, where other dry beans don't do so well. They produce a lot more pods in cool weather and don't actually like very high temperatures. Above 90˚F the flowers may drop off instead of setting pods.

Ease of growing: The scarlet runner bean really is one of the easiest beans (or any other plant for that matter) to grow. It's large seeds quickly produce a vigorous plant and it doesn't even need to be particularly warm.

Soil

pH 6.0 - 7.5

This plant prefers a well-drained, moisture retentive loam, with lots of organic matter. It can be grown in light soils if you add plenty of compost.

Soil preparation: Like most beans it doesn't need a lot of nitrogen, but it should have good quantities of potassium, phosphorus and other nutrients. Dig 2″ of compost into the top 10″ of soil. You might also add a source of phosphorus, such as colloidal phosphate.

Planning

Where: Though this species is a perennial in the tropics, it is usually grown as an annual in northern climates, as it can't survive cold winters. In cool climates it should be planted in a warm sheltered place (it is a tall sprawling plant and will suffer in windy locations). In hotter climates it may do better with light shade during the hottest part of the day.

A trellis covered in these plants will eventually turn into a solid wall of dense vegetation that casts a lot of shade. Obviously you should only put it where this won't be a problem for other plants. It makes a good temporary screen.

When: The seed won't germinate in cold soil (below 60˚F), so don't plant out until 2 - 4 weeks after the last frost date. If you are in a hurry you can start them inside on the last frost date (the seedlings grow rapidly with all of the food in that big seed).

About Scarlet Runner Bean

Seed facts
Germ temp: 60 (80) 85°F
Germ time: 6 - 14 days
Seed viability: 4 years
Germination percentage: 75+
Weeks to grow transplants: 3 - 4

Planning facts
Perennial
Hardiness: Half hardy
Growing temp: 50 (60 - 70) 80°F
Plants per person: 10
Plants per sq ft: 3 - 4
Transplants:
Start: on last frost date
Plant out: 3 - 4 wks after last frost
Direct sow: 2 - 4 wks after last frost
Days to harvest: 70 - 100 days
Plant height: 4 - 10 ft
Plant diameter: 12″

Harvest facts
Harvest period: 4 - 8 wks
Yield per plant: 1 - 2 lb
Yield per sq ft: 6 lb

Support: I already talked about various support structures for pole beans in **Beans, Bush and Pole** and the same structures can be used here. The only difference is that the structure may have to be taller and stronger, to cope with the larger vines. Scarlet runner beans are very vigorous climbers and a mass of plants can grow tall and heavy.

Its best to install the supports before you plant the seeds. Don't wait until the plants are growing (for obvious reasons - there is a danger of damaging the young plants).

When covered in flowering vines the support structure becomes a thing of beauty and you should take advantage of its ornamental value.

A few plants can be grown up tall existing plants, to add productivity and beauty.

I read somewhere that scarlet runner beans climb counterclockwise, whereas other beans climb clockwise. I don't know whether this has any great significance, or whether it is even true for that matter (you shouldn't believe everything you read in books).

Planting

Inoculation: If you haven't grown this crop before, it will fix more nitrogen if inoculated with the appropriate nitrogen-fixing bacteria. See **Beans** for how to do this.

Transplants: Scarlet runner bean is sometimes started indoors in cell packs or soil blocks, to get an early start and to minimize bird and rodent damage.

The seeds germinate easily and grow rapidly in warm conditions, so often only need 3 weeks before they are ready to go outside. These should be started on the last frost date and planted out 3 - 4 weeks later.

Direct sowing: These plants don't like cold weather and are not started outdoors until the soil has warmed up, 2 - 4 weeks after the last frost. Planted 2″ deep, the large seeds germinate readily and quickly grow into vigorous seedlings. It is a good idea to plant a few extra seeds at the end of a row, to fill in any gaps where seeds don't germinate.

Spacing: These tall plants are usually grown in rows because it is easier to erect a support structure for them. Sow the seeds 2″ deep and 6 - 9″ apart. Double rows (12″ apart) also work well. They can also be planted in a circle (6″ apart) to grow up a teepee of poles.

Care

Watering: For best production the plants need constant moisture. This is especially important when the pods are forming and in hot weather. Don't allow the soil to dry out at these times.

Fertilization: These plants put on a lot of growth in a short time and will benefit from an occasional feed of compost tea or liquid kelp.

Mulch: This is helpful to keep the soil evenly moist and keep weeds down (which is important while they are young). Don't apply it until the soil has warmed up.

Pruning: Some gardeners pinch out the tops of the plants when they get to the top of their supports. This is said to encourage the production of new side shoots lower down.

Pests: I have never had any problems when I have grown this crop, but it can be attacked by any of the pests that afflict pole beans. Gophers and groundhogs love the thick, nutritious roots.

Harvesting

Harvest the pods for baby green beans when they are a few inches long. You can also wait until they reach full size, but before the seeds start to swell inside. As with pole beans, you need to harvest regularly to keep them producing well, so go over the plants every 2 - 3 days. If you find any old pods that you previously overlooked, remove them, as they can slow down flowering and pod production.

The immature full sized beans can be used like shell beans.

If you want dry beans just let the pod develop fully and turn crisp and brown on the plant.

Storage: Ideally the pods should be picked in the cool of morning or evening. You can store them in a plastic bag in the fridge, for a week or so (or until you have enough for a meal). For longer term storage freezing works best.

Seed saving: This is pretty much the same as with other beans. The flowers are very attractive to bees and hummingbirds and the former are the main pollinators. The seeds can also self-pollinate, but they still need to be visited by insects to trip them.

Because of their popularity with bees it is best to have only one variety flowering at a time within a half-mile. This essentially means only having one variety in your garden in a season, because they will keep flowering until frost cuts them down. Of course if you don't care whether they cross you can have more than one. Have a red and a white flowered variety and you may see interesting differences in their offspring.

Unusual growing ideas

Ornamental: In this country these attractive vines are commonly grown purely as ornamentals. Often by people who don't even realize that they are edible.

No support: This crop is occasionally grown without support, being allowed to sprawl and run along the ground.

Perennial roots: In mild winter areas the roots may survive the winter and sprout anew the following spring (then again they might not - I haven't found them to be very reliable). In a suitably tropical climate they can grow for years and become a useful perennial crop (they were once commonly known as seven year beans).

They are sometimes kept going as ornamentals for more than one year. Some cold climate gardeners dig the roots and store them like dahlias over the winter, for replanting the following spring.

In temperate areas they aren't usually worth growing as a crop for a second year, as the plants are so easy to grow from seed and so productive.

Varieties

Most varieties have red flowers, but some have white, red and white, or even pink ones. The white types are considered to have the best flavored dry beans. In this country not many improved edible cultivars are available, though more are now appearing.

Scarlet Emperor - Red flowers.

Painted Lady - Red and white flowers.

Sunset - Pink flowers.

Jack In The Beanstalk - White flowers, to 20 ft tall.

Kitchen use

This is quite a versatile food plant, with a variety of uses.

In England the immature pods are very widely used as green beans and many people say their flavor is superior to snap beans.

Older pods can be good too, but you have to cut off the strings on each side with a knife (they are so big this isn't difficult).

The dry beans are good when cooked like pinto beans. The white types are a classic ingredient in Greek cooking and are known as gigantes.

The flowers are edible too and are often used to decorate salads.

Gigantes

1 lb beans (soaked overnight)
¼ cup olive oil
3 cups chopped onions
1 cup chopped celery
3 garlic cloves, minced
2 quarts water
2 cups chopped tomatoes
8 tbsp tomato paste
3 bay leaves
2 tbsp fresh Greek oregano
2 tbsp fresh thyme
1 tsp red pepper
Black pepper
Salt

Sauté the onions and garlic in the olive oil for 5 minutes, then add the water, beans, tomatoes herb and red pepper and bring to a boil. Then simmer until the beans are tender (don't overcook or they go mushy). The length of time this takes will depend upon the beans, but start checking them after 30 minutes.

Bean, Soy

Glycine max

Introduction: Soybeans have the highest protein content of any common crop and have been cultivated in China for over 5000 years. They are a major crop in North America, for human and animal food and for their oil (which has many industrial and food uses).

Soybeans can also be an important crop for people working towards control of their own food supply. Add potatoes, kale and amaranth or quinoa and you could have a pretty nutritious (if not particularly interesting) diet.

Probably the main drawback with soybeans is that they don't taste as good as most other beans. You should always beware of growing something you do not actually like to eat.

Nutritional content: Soybeans are rich in all necessary amino acids, which makes them one of the best vegetable sources of protein (they are 35 - 45% protein). They are also rich in oil (15 - 20%) and contain omega-3 fatty acids, tryptophan, iron, fiber a whole range of valuable phytochemicals, with antioxidant and anti-cancer properties.

Depending upon who you listen to soybeans may be praised for their high nutritional value or condemned as the source of various toxins and allergens.

Crop value: The soybean is justly famous as a source of protein rich beans, though it needs a fairly warm climate to live up to its potential. It is also a good source of fat, which is almost as important as the protein from a self sufficiency standpoint.

Ease of growing: When I lived on the east coast with its warm summer days and nights, I found soybean to be pretty easy to grow. Where I live now the nights are cooler and I haven't had as much success with it. Admittedly I haven't made much effort though. I'm sure I could get it to work if I found the right variety.

About Soybean

Seed facts
Germ temp: 65 - 75˚F
Germ time: 7 - 14 days
Viability: 4 yrs
Germination percentage: 75 +

Planning facts
Hardiness: Tender
Growing temp: 60 (70 - 80) 90˚F
Plants per sq ft: 3 - 4
Direct sow: 2 - 4 wks after last frost
Days to harvest: 70 - 120 days

Harvest facts
Yield per plant: ⅛ oz
Yield per sq ft: ½ oz

Soil

pH 6.5 - 7.0
A light, well-drained soil is ideal for soybeans. It doesn't need to be very rich in nitrogen, as it fixes its own.

Soil preparation: Soybeans need phosphorus, potassium and trace elements, so add colloidal phosphate, greensand (or wood ashes) and kelp. They dislike acid soil so add lime if necessary.

Planning

Where: The more sun the plants receive, the faster they will grow and the higher the yield. They need warm growing conditions to perform well.

When: Soybeans love heat (they will tolerate temperatures up to 100˚F) and must have warm weather for good growth.

Don't plant soybeans until the soil has warmed up in spring (60˚F minimum), which is usually 2 - 4 weeks after the last frost. If you plant them too early they may well rot and certainly won't grow very much until the soil warms up. You can hasten the warming of the soil prior to planting, with cloches or black plastic mulch. The young plants are quite frost tender, so watch out for late frost and cover if necessary.

How much: Soybeans aren't very productive, so you will have to plant quite a large area if you want to grow a significant quantity of the dry beans.

Planting

Inoculation: If you haven't grown soybeans recently, the seeds should be inoculated with their specific inoculant (*Rhizobium japonicum*). A garden bean inoculant probably won't work very well.

Transplants: Like most legumes, soybeans resent transplanting, so are usually direct sown. They could be started indoors if you use cell packs, or soil blocks, to minimize root disturbance. However this isn't really very practical if you are growing dry beans, as you would need a lot of plants to make it worthwhile. You might do it for growing early shell beans however. Start them inside on the last frost date and plant them out a month later.

Direct sowing: Plant the seeds 1 - 4″ deep, depending upon the temperature of the soil. The warmer and drier the soil, the greater the planting depth.

If the temperature of the soil is marginal for germination, you can pre-germinate the seed indoors before planting. Just plant out very carefully to avoid damaging the delicate sprouts.

Succession sowing: If you are growing them for shell beans, you should make a succession sowing every 3 weeks to ensure a continuous harvest.

Spacing:
Rows: If you want to grow in rows space the plants 4″ apart in the row, with 12 - 15″ between the rows.

Beds: For maximum production soybeans are usually planted in wide beds, as close together as they can tolerate. This is quite close as they don't branch very much. Space them 6 - 8″ apart in offset rows across the bed.

Care

Once established soybeans need very little attention.

Weeds: The plants need weeding while young, but once they are well established their foliage makes a dense canopy that suppresses weeds and shades the soil.

Watering: In dry weather they need regular watering to ensure maximum productivity.

Support: Soybeans don't climb and don't usually need support. However some of the taller varieties may reach 36″ in height and are prone to lodging (falling over). These may benefit from a few strategically placed stakes and string.

Pests: Soybeans may be affected by many of the same pests as bush and pole beans. The biggest pest I have encountered was the Japanese beetle, though the damage wasn't too serious (I hand picked them off).

Disease: Several fungus diseases may affect soybeans, so the plants should be rotated annually.

You may need to protect the seeds and young seedlings from birds and rodents. Larger animals such as rabbits may get a taste for the green beans if given the chance.

Harvesting

When:
Shell beans: Gather the immature green beans as soon as they reach full size, but before they color up (and turn yellow or black). The harvest period is only about 2 - 3 weeks.

Dry beans: It takes another month for shell beans to turn into dry beans. By this time the whole plant is dying back and the dry pods shatter easily.

How: Gather dry beans by cutting the plants off at ground level and then hang them upside down to dry.

The easiest way to deal with large quantities of plants is to lay them on a tarp to dry. Walk on the dry plants to thresh out the ripe seeds.

Storage: Dry beans should have a moisture content of about 14% and should shatter when hit with a hammer. Store them in a cool dry place at 32 - 40°F. See **Beans** for more on drying and storage.

Seed saving: This is exactly the same as saving the dry seed for food. Soybeans are self-pollinated, in fact pollination usually occurs before the flower even open.

Unusual growing ideas

Green manure: Soybeans have often been grown as a summer green manure crop to improve the soil. They could profitably be planted on land that will lie fallow for a full season. Don't buy special seed for this, just plant some bulk soybeans from a food market. You don't care what variety they are, or even if they have time to mature. Remember to inoculate them of course.

Vacation planting: Soybeans are a good crop to plant if you are going to be away from your garden for any length of time during the summer. As I already mentioned they need almost no attention once established. Simply weed when young to help them get established, then mulch and forget. They are quite drought tolerant, but in dry areas they will be more productive if you put them on a drip irrigation system with a timer.

Varieties

Soybeans are day length sensitive, so you need to plant a variety that is adapted for growing in your area. Ideally you will choose the longest season variety you can grow, as earliness comes at the expense of productivity. Like other beans, they can be divided into those grown for dry beans and those for use as shell beans (Edamame).

Dry beans:
Chico - Small seeds.

Panther - Fine flavor

Fiskeby V - Very early

Shell beans:
Envy - Early and quite productive.

Fledderjohn - Brown seeds.

Kuromame - Tall, productive plants.

Black Pearl - Large sweet seeds.

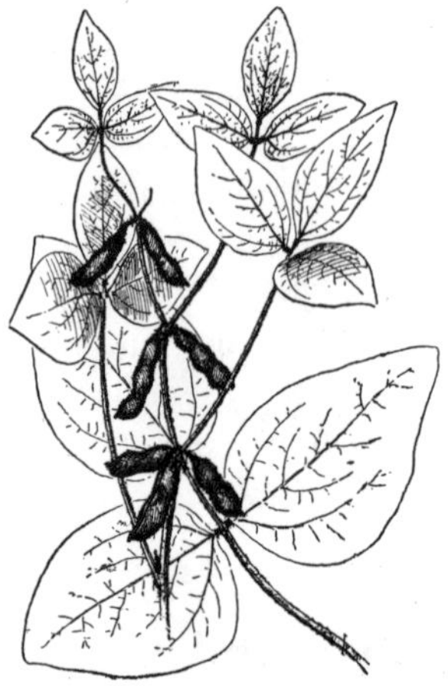

Kitchen use:

Soybeans are very good when prepared as green shell beans (these are known as edamame in Japan). Boil the pods for 5 - 10 minutes, then shell out the green beans and cook for another 15 - 30 minutes. You can also cook them in the pods and shell them as you eat. The shelled cooked beans can be frozen for later use.

Soybeans take longer to cook than most beans and generally don't taste as good (which is probably why they are disguised in so many ways). The cooked beans have been used in a variety of ways: soups, burgers, or made into tofu or tempeh (if you are ambitious).

The dry beans can be sprouted (and then cooked - they are not eaten raw).

Making tofu

In its homeland the soybean is often used to make tofu, which is more digestible than the whole soybean. It is also richer in calcium

Making tofu is a fairly straightforward project, though quite time consuming (it lends itself to a bigger scale than a single home). I am going to give a brief outline on the procedure, but I don't have the room (or the expertise for that matter) to go into much detail. There are some good websites that explain it all in much greater detail.

To make tofu the dry beans are soaked for 12 hours and then ground to a paste and mixed with water to make a slurry. This is brought to a boil and simmered for about 10 minutes and then the milk is drained off. The remaining pulp (called okara) can be eaten in various ways or fed to livestock.

A coagulating agent is then added to the soy milk to curdle it. Nigari (a naturally occurring calcium sulphate) is the traditional agent, but Epsom salts, apple cider vinegar or lemon juice can also be used)

The solids are then separated out, put in a cloth and pressed to make tofu (the longer and harder it is pressed the firmer the tofu).

Beet

Beta vulgaris

Introduction: Beet still grows wild around the coasts of Western Europe and is still sometimes gathered for use as a green vegetable. It is an old crop and has been used as food for humans and livestock since the time of the Romans.

Crop value: Over the years beet has been bred to produce several quite different crops. It is important for its leaves (see **Chard**) and for its edible root, which is either eaten as a root vegetable or refined to make sugar. In Northern Europe the root is also commonly used for winter animal feed.

If you are aiming for food self-sufficiency then sugar beet could be an important source of sweetener (and calories)

Ease of growing: Beet is a fairly easy crop to grow, so long as you give it a suitably moist soil, a cool sunny climate and you thin and weed properly. If you don't give it these things, you may end up with lots of top growth and spindly little roots (if this happens you can always eat the leaves).

Nutritional content
Leaves: These are actually more nutritious than the roots, containing large amounts of vitamins A and C, as well as calcium, phosphorus, potassium and iron. They also contain oxalic acid, but this is no more of a problem than it is with spinach.

Roots: These are rich in carbohydrates and many beneficial phytochemicals, including folate, betacyanin and betaine. The contain about 200 calories per pound. Sugar beet may contain up to 20% sugar.

About Beet

Seed facts
Germ temp: 50 (70 - 80) 85˚F
Germ time: 5 - 21 days
42 days / 41˚F
16 days / 50˚F
9 days / 59˚F
6 days / 68˚F
5 days / 77˚F * Optimum
5 days / 86˚F
Viability: 5 years
Germination percentage: 60%+
Weeks to grow transplant: 3 - 4

Planning facts
Fertility needs: High
Hardiness: Half hardy
Growing temp: 45 (60 - 70) 75˚F
Plants per person: 10 - 20
Plants per sq ft: 12
Transplants
Start in: 3 - 4 wks before last frost
Plant out: On last frost date
Direct sow: 2 - 4 wks before last frost.
Fall crop: 8 weeks before first frost
Days to harvest: 50 - 100 days
Plant height: 12″
Plant width: 6 - 12″

Harvest facts
Yield per plant: 4 - 8 oz
Yield per square foot: 3 lb sq ft

Climate: Beets are a moderately hardy cool season crop that will tolerate some frost. They grow well enough in warmer weather, but higher temperatures (above 75˚F) produce poor quality roots. These tend to be tougher, unevenly colored (zoned) and often somewhat bitter or lacking sweetness. This occurs because on warm nights they use the sugar they produce for further growth, rather than storing it in their roots.

Soil

pH 6.0 (6.5-7.0) 8.0

Beets do well in most soils, but the ideal is loose, sandy, well-drained and close to neutral. It should be quite fertile to get the continuous uninterrupted growth that is necessary to produce good roots. If the soil is poor, growth will be irregular and the roots may show concentric growth rings (zoning).

Like most root crops, they don't like rocky soil (or wet or acidic ones).

Soil preparation: Beets are quite heavy feeders, though they don't need a lot of nitrogen. Too much of this encourages top growth at the expense of root growth and retards sugar storage. Like most root crops, they like phosphorus (colloidal phosphate) and potassium (greensand or wood ashes).

Kelp meal can be used to supply essential boron (they need more of this than most plants because they don't use it very well) as well as other trace elements.

Fork 2 - 4″ of compost or aged manure (not fresh) into the top 6 - 8″ of soil. This is where most of the plants feeder roots are found, though these deep rooted plants may go down to 24″ or more.

If the soil is heavy clay you should loosen it by cultivating deeply and adding organic matter. If this isn't possible you can dig a trench (at least 6″ deep and preferably 12″ deep) and fill it with a mix of compost (or aged manure), sifted soil and sand.

If the soil is acidic add lime to bring the pH up above 6.0.

Planning

Where: Beets need full sun for best growth, especially when growing as a fall or winter crop. However in warmer climates they can also do okay in light shade.

When: Beets are quite fast growing, taking 50 - 80 days to maturity. They like cool weather and grow best with warm days (60 - 70˚F) and cool nights. In most of the United States this means growing them as a spring or fall crop.

Succession sowing: You won't need many plants at one time, unless you really love beets. For a continuous supply of small, tender roots you should plant in succession every 2 - 4 weeks.

Spring: Beets are quite hardy and can be started 3 - 4 weeks before the last frost date. The soil should be at least 50˚F for good germination. They don't like waterlogged soil, so don't plant if it is too wet.

Fall: Beets can also be planted in late summer as a fall crop (6 - 10 weeks before first fall frost date). This is the crop to store for winter.

Winter: In mild winter areas you can plant beets in late summer, to mature in fall. They will continue to grow slowly over the winter and can be harvested as needed.

Vernalization: Beets are biennial and theoretically shouldn't flower until their second year. However if your spring plants grow too big (have stems ¼″ in diameter), too early, then exposure to cool temperatures (below 50˚F for 2 weeks) can vernalize them. When this happens they think they have already been through one year and bolt as soon as the weather warms up. These plants will use up all of their energy in producing seeds and will never produce useful roots.

Planting

Each beet "seed" is actually a cluster of flowers fused together, each one containing a single seed. This is why you end up with several plants from one seed. It is possible to gently break up these clusters and get individual seeds to plant.

The seed clusters also contain a water-soluble germination inhibitor. This can be leached out by soaking them overnight prior to planting. Don't simply soak them in a bowl of water overnight however, as they can absorb so much water they can be damaged. Instead they should be put on a damp paper towel, so they can absorb moisture slowly. Pre-soaking is most useful in hot dry weather.

You could take this one step further and actually pre-germinate the seed.

Transplants

Starting inside: Beets can be grown from transplants, but they are very tolerant of cool temperatures, so this doesn't give you much advantage for the extra work involved (at best they would just be a little earlier). There is also a danger they will be vernalized if it gets cold again after you plant them out.

Beets don't like root disturbance, so cell packs or soil blocks work best for starting seed indoors. Sow the seed ½″ deep, with one seed capsule in each cavity (this will produce more than one plant).

Transplanting beets may retard them by a couple of weeks.

Hardening off: In cold weather the transplants should be hardened off before they go out. You do this by putting the plants outside for 2 hours on the first day, then 4 hours on the second day. Add 2 hours every day for a week, until they are outside all day. Alternatively you can put them in a cold frame for a week. Then you simply open the lid during the day and close it at night (this is certainly less work).

Planting out: Plant out the transplants no earlier than the last frost date, as they aren't very hardy. To get an earlier start you could warm the soil with cloches before planting and cover the seedlings with cloches.

Direct sowing: Beets are usually direct sown at a depth of ¼ - ¾″. The appropriate depth depends upon the warmth and dryness of soil; the cooler or wetter it is, the shallower you should plant.

Broadcasting: Scatter the seeds so they are evenly spaced about 2″ apart across the bed. It's easier to get the proper spacing with these large seeds, than it is with smaller ones such as carrot. The scattered seed is then covered with a layer of soil. If the soil in the bed has a tendency to crust, use a mixture of topsoil and compost to cover them.

Rows: The seed can also be sown in rows. Simply make shallow furrows 12 - 18″ apart across the bed, drop a seed every 2″ and re-fill the furrow (use cover soil if necessary).

Spacing: The distance between plants has a direct effect on the final size of the root, the closer the spacing, the smaller the root. Spacing also affects the time they take to mature, the more room they have, the faster they will mature.

Suggested spacing

5″ spacing: Large roots or poor soil.

4″ spacing: Main summer planting.

3″ spacing: Small roots for pickling.

Seedling thinning: If germination is good, you will have a little clump of seedlings every 2″ (remember every "seed" actually contains several seeds). These clumps thin themselves to some extent, the largest and most vigorous ones eventually crowding out the others. However it may be better to do it yourself so they don't compete. Just pinch them off at ground level when the tallest seedling is about an inch high.

Care

Beets need to grow quickly, so they can produce plenty of sugar to store in their roots. They can only do this if they get everything they need, when they need it.

Thinning:

When all of the plants are growing well you need to start thinning, so they are spaced properly. I can't emphasize the importance of this enough (**It is very important!**) Insufficient thinning is one of the commonest causes of failure to grow good beets. If the plants are overcrowded the roots will be small and stunted and they may suffer from disease problems caused by poor air circulation.

First thinning: Thin the growing plants when they are 3 - 4 inches tall. Do this at the same time you are weeding them, ideally in cool cloudy weather. The first thinning should give you a single plant every 1 ½ - 2″. Don't thin them to the final spacing at this time, as some might not survive.

Second thinning: When the roots have swollen to an inch in diameter, thin them again. This time to the desired final spacing. The thinnings from this round are big enough to eat in salads or stir-fries.

Feeding: The plants need a moderate amount of nitrogen when they are young (until the leaves are 4″ tall). If you soil isn't very fertile, you may want to give them a feed of compost tea or liquid kelp every 2 - 3 weeks. Don't give a high nitrogen fertilizer as it can encourage too much leaf growth.

Weeding: Beets grow slowly when first planted and can't compete with weeds very well, so it is important that they are weeded properly. It is best to hand weed, as their shallow roots and raised shoulders are easily damaged by weeding tools.

Water: Consistent watering (at least 1″ per week) is essential for good root production. Beets grown without sufficient water may have tough, woody roots, may show concentric whitish zoning, may crack and may bolt prematurely.

Regular watering is particularly important in warm weather, as it can help to prevent them getting woody and poorly flavored. Don't over-water your beets however, it is possible to give them too much. This can result in bushy, luxuriant tops and small roots.

If water supplies are limited, keep the soil evenly moist while the plants are young. Then give them extra water when the roots are sizing up, to boost their final size. Be careful though, as irregular watering can cause splitting.

Mulch: This helps to keep down weeds, conserves moisture and keeps the soil cool (which is important for beets). In spring wait until the soil has warmed up to near 60˚F before applying it however.

Problems

Cracked shoulders: The rounded shoulders of the root commonly stick out of the soil, exposed to the elements and this can result in cracking and woodiness. Cylindrical varieties are particularly prone to this. It can be prevented by earthing up with soil, or using mulch. A good leaf canopy also helps.

Bolting: Though beets are biennial, they sometimes bolt if planted very early in the year. As I explained earlier this is caused by them being vernalized by low temperatures. Once this occurs there isn't anything you can do about it, so you need to prevent it happening by planting at the right time. Some varieties are more resistant to bolting than others.

Forking: Forked roots are most often caused by rocky soil or fresh manure, but careless transplanting can also be a cause (they don't like it).

Pests: The only significant pests I have encountered have been leaf miners. As you don't normally grow them for their leaves, this is only a problem if they get out of hand and start to destroy entire leaves. You can crush them in the leaf and scrape off the white egg clusters, but it's easier to use row covers.

Beets may also suffer from aphids, flea beetles and caterpillars. You can use row covers for all of these too.

Diseases: These include cercospora leaf spot, downy mildew, curly top virus and scab. You control these in the usual ways, by keeping foliage dry, controlling sucking insects and giving good air circulation.

Boron deficiency This results in corky black areas in the root and is known as black heart. Boron is only needed in minute amounts and too much is toxic to plants. The best quick source is liquid kelp or compost tea. If you have a problem with this, add plenty of compost to your soil as it is the best source of boron.

Harvesting

When: You can start harvesting the roots as soon as they are large enough to be worthwhile (1½ - 2″), which should be in about 60 days or so. Scrape some soil from the base of the plant to get a good look at the root.

Young beets are nice and tender, but not very sweet. The roots get sweeter as they get bigger, but also more fibrous and less tender. Generally they are good until they reach 3 - 4″ in diameter, but when they get bigger than this they have a tendency to become woody. To some extent this depends on the variety, growing methods and time of year, so it's not always the case. In winter they will stay in good condition for much longer.

How: Usually you can simply pull up the roots by the tops (if these are tender they can be used for greens, so don't waste them). If you are going to store the roots be very careful when harvesting, as the slightest injury can lead to premature decay. To prevent moisture loss from the root, cut off the leaves to within an inch or two of the root. Don't cut too close to the crown as this may cause them to bleed. If you want to store them, leave the long stringy root tips in place and don't wash them.

Storage: Beets store well and in Europe they were once an important winter crop for peasants and their livestock.

The roots can be stored in a plastic bag in the fridge for several weeks.

In mild climates the roots are best left in the ground where they will continue to grow slowly all winter.

In colder climates they can also be stored in the ground, though they will have stopped growing. They should be covered with a thick mulch to keep the ground from freezing.

In very cold climates they don't keep very well in the ground, so are usually dug and stored in a root cellar (or something similar). They are usually packed in a box filled with damp sand or sawdust. If stored at 32 - 40˚F and 90%+ humidity, they will last for 4 - 6 months. On the farm they were once regularly stored in a clamp (see **Potatoes**). They shouldn't be allowed to freeze however.

Beets can also be canned, pickled, frozen or dried.

Seed saving: Beets are cross-pollinated by the wind, so must be isolated from other varieties (and from chard). This means having only one variety flowering at one time within a distance of two miles (that's the theory - if not very practical).

Beet is a biennial, which means the root has to survive the winter before it can produce seed. In mild climates, you can simply leave them in the ground (cover with mulch if necessary). In colder climates you may have to lift the roots and store them in a root cellar, as described above. Replant the best roots in a convenient spot in spring and the seed will ripen by midsummer.

A flowering beet plant may get to be 8 feet tall and can be quite top heavy, so may need staking to prevent it falling over. You will get a lot of seed from one plant, let alone 5 plants, which is the minimum number required to maintain some genetic variability.

Unusual growing ideas

Multi-planting: This works well with beets. Simply sow two seed capsules per soil block (or plug tray) and thin to leave the best 3 or 4 plants in each block. You then plant out the whole thing and let them all grow to the desired size.

Varieties

Newer varieties may be sweeter than older ones and resistant to diseases such as downy mildew.

Bulls Blood: Has deep red leaves that are popular for use in salad mixes.

Lutz Green Leaf - A great all around variety.

Monogerm: Has only one seed per capsule.

Detroit Dark Red: Perhaps the commonest variety.

Chioggia: This Italian heirloom has red and white striations. It is very pretty, but not particularly tasty.

Burpees Golden: This species is very sweet because it contains some genes from sugar beet.

Formanova: A cylindrical beet with tasty tops and roots.

Sugar beet

As a commercial crop the sugar beet is far more important than beet roots. I have never seen specific varieties of sugar beet for the home gardener, just a generic "Sugar Beet" (and that isn't easy to find).

Kitchen use

The roots can be eaten raw in salads, cooked as a vegetable (especially in soup), or pickled. It is also very good when roasted.

Don't forget about the leaves, as they are the most nutritious part. The young leaves may not be as good as those of chard, but they are still useful as a potherb, or a colorful minor addition to salads.

The roots can be used as a pink food coloring.

Grated sugar beet is sometimes used as a sweetener for cakes and other baked goods. You can also make your own sugar fairly easily, though this is of dubious health benefits.

Beets have also been fermented to produce alcohol for drinking (wine, beer, vodka, brandy) and fuel.

Making sugar

Begin by shredding or finely chopping the roots and put them in a pot. Add just enough water to cover them and cook for an hour until soft. Then strain off the liquid and press the mix to extract as much liquid as possible.

The next step is to boil off the water to make a thick syrup. Be very careful towards the end of this process, as when it starts to thicken as it can burn very easily. The stuff remaining at the end is sugar, or some close approximation thereof.

Broccoli

Brassica oleracea var *alboglabra*

Introduction: Broccoli originated somewhere in Eastern Europe and has been grown there for at least 2000 years. Its use spread throughout Europe via Italy, hence it is generally known by its Italian name (apparently when first grown in England it was known as Italian asparagus).

In the past 25 years broccoli has come from relative obscurity, to become one of the most popular garden vegetables in America. This is a good thing because it is not only delicious, but also one of the most nutritious of all common vegetables.

Much of what was written about cabbage also applies to broccoli, which is a close relative.

Crop value: Broccoli is one of the most nutritious and useful of all of the Brassicas and is highly recommended for all cool weather gardens.

Ease of growing: I had a hard time growing broccoli when I first started gardening. It would either bolt before the head got large enough to be useful, or it just kept growing in fall and never produced a head before it was eventually killed by frost. I have since learned that success with broccoli is all about timing. It is actually pretty easy to grow, if you plant it at the right time (and give it plenty of water and nutrients).

Nutritional content: Broccoli heads are rich in vitamins A and C, calcium, iron, potassium and folate. It is considered one of the very best anti-cancer vegetables, as it contains a whole range of beneficial phytochemicals, glucosinolates, luteine sulfuraphane, myrosinase and isothiocyanin. The heads contain about 150 calories per pound.

About Broccoli

Seed facts
Germ temp: 45 (60 - 75) 85°F
Germ time: 4 - 20 days
20 days / 50°F
9 days / 59°F
6 days / 68°F
5 days / 77°F * Optimum
4 days / 86°F
Seed viability: 3 - 4 yrs
Germination percentage: 75+
Weeks to grow transplants: 4 - 5

Planning facts
Hardiness: Half hardy
Growing temp: 60 - 65°F
Plants per person: 5
Plants per sq ft: 1
Spring transplants:
Start: 6 - 7 wks before last frost
Plant out: 2 wks before last frost date
Fall crop: Direct sow 10 - 14 wks before first frost
Days to harvest: 80 - 120 days
45 to 70 days from transplanting
Plant size: 24 - 30″ tall.
12 - 18″ width

Harvest facts
Harvest period: 2 - 6 wks
Yield per plant: 1 lb
Yield per sq ft: ¼ - ½ lb sq ft

Soil

pH 6.0 - 7.5

Broccoli needs to grow fast for best quality. To do this it needs a rich, moist, well-drained soil with lots of organic matter and available nutrients. It is quite salt tolerant.

Soil preparation: Prepare the soil by incorporating 2 - 3″ of aged manure, or compost, into the top 6 - 8″ of soil (which is where most of the plants feeder roots are found). You might also add a handful of organic fertilizer mix (or a mix of colloidal phosphate, wood ashes, kelp and dolomitic limestone).

Broccoli likes lots of calcium and magnesium and doesn't like acid soil.

Planning

Climate: Like most of the Brassicas broccoli is a cool weather plant and prefers fairly mild growing conditions (55 - 75°F), so in warmer areas it is grown in spring and fall. It is a hardy plant and tolerates quite hard frost (some varieties more than others). It doesn't like hot weather and tends to bolt above 75°F, though some newer varieties are slightly more heat tolerant.

Where: Broccoli likes full sun, especially when growing in cool weather. It will tolerate some shade, but this delays maturation. It takes up quite a bit of space, but this usually isn't an issue in cooler weather, as the winter garden is often half empty anyway.

Crop rotation: Ideally broccoli should not be planted where another Brassica has been grown in the past 3 years.

When:
Spring: The earliest spring transplants are usually set out in the garden about 2 weeks before the last frost date.

Fall: Broccoli does best as a fall crop, as it prefers cooler temperatures, growing and heading up best at about 65°F. It is also less bothered by pests in cool weather and the heads stay in peak condition for longer. Mature plants can sit in the garden, ready to harvest for weeks. They are quite hardy and can survive frost as low as 20°F.

Autumn broccoli should be sown 2 - 3 months before the first fall frost date, so it is close to maturity by the time cold weather hits.

If you plan on growing a lot of broccoli for freezing, you should plant it at the optimal time, which is late summer. This also means you will need to keep it frozen for a shorter time.

Winter: In very mild climates broccoli can be sown in autumn, as a late winter / early spring crop. In harsher climates it won't usually survive the winter.

Succession sowing: You generally don't want a large amount of broccoli to mature at one time (unless you are going to freeze it). For this reason it is usually sown in succession, every 3 - 4 weeks.

Repeat harvesting: Broccoli can yield for quite a while, as most types will produce side shoots after the main head is harvested. These can be cut and will regrow several times. This characteristic is dependent on the variety however, some are bred for commercial harvesting and only produce one big head.

Planting

Transplants

Starting inside: Like most Brassicas, it doesn't mind transplanting, so is commonly started indoors (especially in spring, when time is of the essence). It can be sown in flats, cell packs, soil blocks or plug trays.

Start the seeds indoors 4 - 5 weeks before you want to plant out. Sow them in a flat, 1″ apart and ⅛ - ¼″ deep, When they have all germinated prick out the best ones into another flat, spacing them 2″ apart. By the time they go outside, the plants should be 3 - 4″ high, with 3 - 5 leaves and a stem diameter of less that ¼″.

Hardening off: If transplants are to go outside while it is still cold, the seedlings must be hardened off. They will then tolerate temperatures as low as 25°F. You do this by putting the plants outside for 2 hours on the first day, then 4 hours on the second day. Add 2 hours every day for a week.

A simpler alternative is to put them in a cold frame, which is opened for longer periods each day and closed at night.

Planting out: Set out transplants slightly deeper than they grew in the flats, up to the depth of their first true leaves.

Transplants

Starting outside: Fall broccoli transplants can be started outdoors in a nursery bed. The seeds are sown in a small, protected area, pricked out into a slightly larger area and finally transplanted to their permanent position. This is a much more efficient use of space than direct sowing at their final spacing, as they don't take up much bed space for the first month or two of their lives.

Direct sowing: Though broccoli is often transplanted, it can also be direct sown. This works out best for an autumn crop, as the soil is warm in late summer so germination will be rapid. Direct sowing doesn't work very well in spring.

Sow twice as many seeds as you need plants, at a depth of ¼ - ½″. Thin to the required spacing when they have their first set of true leaves. Of course you will probably have problems with pests when direct sowing in warm weather, so be vigilant.

Vernalization: Spring broccoli is somewhat prone to premature bolting, which means producing a very small head while the plant is still small. This is usually the result of vernalization, which occurs when transplants are allowed to get too big before they go outside.

If the stem of a transplant is over ¼″ in diameter it will be vernalized by exposure to temperatures below 50°F for two weeks. This causes it to sense that it has been though the winter and it will bolt soon after it warms up again. This is another reason broccoli does better as a fall crop.

Other transplant problems: Broccoli transplants are quite sensitive and need careful treatment. They mustn't be allowed to get too big and they shouldn't sit in the container for too long before being planted out. They also need to be hardened off carefully before planting out. The shock of low temperatures combined with transplanting can be too much for them. They will then just sit in the ground without growing, until you get frustrated and pull them up. Avoid this by making sure your plants are still growing vigorously when they go out and are hardened off properly.

Spacing: The spacing you use depends on the fertility of the soil and how large you want the heads to grow. The wider the spacing, the larger the individual plants (and their heads) can get. At 18″ spacing, the heads may grow to be 10″ in diameter. At 6″ spacing they may only grow to 5″. Closely spaced plants don't produce as many side shoots either.

Rows: When planting in rows give them 12 - 18″ between plants and 36″ between rows.

Beds: The spacing in beds will depend upon the soil and how big you want the heads to get.

12″: Excellent soil, small heads

15″: Good soil, medium heads

18″: Poor soil, large heads

Care

The plants need looking after carefully. If there is a check in growth, they may never recover and can bolt prematurely.

Weed: Competition from weeds may also cause bolting, so keep them well weeded (especially when small).

Water: Broccoli transpires quite a lot of water and for optimal growth the soil must be moist at all times (but especially when the heads are developing). Fortunately it is generally grown in fairly cool weather, so watering isn't usually a problem. In hot weather it is critical that they receive sufficient moisture, as a lack of water may cause premature bolting.

Fertilization: If your soil is less than ideal, give your transplants a feed of compost tea, or liquid seaweed 2 weeks after planting out. This will encourage early vegetative growth. You might also give them another feed a couple of weeks before harvest time, to encourage maximum growth and production of side shoots.

Mulch: This is helpful to keep down weeds. Plastic mulch is sometimes used in spring, to warm the soil before planting. Organic mulch should be used in summer, to cool the soil and keep it moist (warm soil can cause broccoli to bolt). Broccoli likes seaweed mulch.

Pests: Broccoli is a member of the cabbage family and is prone to the same multitude of pests and diseases. These include aphids, cabbage worms, loopers, diamondback moths, root maggots, flea beetles and more (see **Cabbage** for more on these). You can avoid many of these problems by covering the young plants with row covers.

Aphids are a particular problem in warm weather and will often infest the heads as well as the leaves.

Disease: Possible diseases include alternaria blight, black Leg, black rot, downy mildew, fusarium wilt and wirestem.

Clubroot is the most serious diseases of Brassicas (see **Cabbage** for more on this).

Bolting: I already mentioned how cold spring weather may cause broccoli to bolt, but it can do so for other reasons too. Bolting is a natural reaction to any kind of stress (poor soil, lack of water, poor transplanting, hot weather). The plant senses it is living in a precarious world, so tries to make seed to carry on its genes.

Harvesting

When: Harvest the mature heads as soon as they reach full size, which may be anywhere from 3 - 6″ in diameter. You can eat them before this time, but you won't get as much food. This may not matter if you have a lot of plants and doing this can help to spread out the harvest.

The right time to harvest broccoli is when the flower buds are visible individually, are somewhat swollen and the head is dark. As the head develops the individual florets start to separate and the yellow petals become visible. Broccoli is edible at this stage (and even after the florets have separated and some of the flowers have opened) but it's not as good. If you miss the optimal harvest time you should still cut off the heads, as this will stimulate the plants to produce new side shoots

How: Cut the head off with a sharp knife. The standard for commercial harvesting is to leave 5 - 6″ of stem on the head, as they want the extra weight. However if you leave more stem on the plant, you may get more useful side shoots.

Side shoots: After the main head is cut, the plants will send out side shoots in the axils of the leaves. On large healthy plants these can be 5″ in diameter (though more often they are 1 - 3″), so don't remove the plants after harvesting the first heads. After you cut the side shoots, the plant will send out yet more shoots and may continue to do this for several weeks (it really wants to flower and set seed). Keep on cutting the side shoots until they get too small to be worthwhile.

In warm weather it can produce side shoots in only a few days, so keep on top of harvesting.

These side shoots greatly increase the size and duration of the harvest and make broccoli a much more productive crop.

After the side shoots are finished, you might try cutting the plant right back, almost to the ground. This sometimes stimulates it to send up a new stem.

If a hard frost threatens, you should harvest any remaining heads and eat or freeze them. They won't survive a hard freeze.

Storage: Broccoli is quite perishable so is best used immediately. It will keep for up to a week in a plastic bag in the fridge (don't wash it), but won't be as good as when it was fresh (this isn't supermarket food). For longer term storage broccoli freezes well.

Seed saving: Broccoli is cross-pollinated by insects and will cross with any member of the cabbage family. To keep the seed pure, it must be the only variety (of any *Brassica oleracea* species) flowering nearby (theoretically within a mile!) Otherwise it is fairly easy to save the seed (see **Cabbage** for more on this). To maintain some genetic variability, you should save seed from at least 6 plants.

Varieties

The choice of broccoli varieties has increased quite a lot in recent years. Most of the new varieties are hybrids and have a high degree of uniformity in size and maturation date.

These traits may be desirable for commercial growers, but are not good for the home gardener. Unless you are growing for freezing, you don't want plants that all mature at the same time. You want plants that mature at different rates, over a long period and that produce lots of side shoots. Look for these traits in the variety descriptions.

Hybrids:
These have significant advantages.

Early Dividend F1: Very early, produces lots of side shoots.

Green Comet F1: Early (55 days) and bred for heat resistance.

Packman F1: Early, uniform, fairly heat tolerant.

Open pollinated:

De Cicco - Fine old Italian heirloom

Italian Green Sprouting - Heavy producer.

Umpqua - Produces over a long period, ideal for home gardeners.

Calabrese - Produces lots of side shoots.

Green Goliath - Produces a large main head and some side shoots.

Romanesco Broccoli
This plant is somewhat confusing because it looks a lot like broccoli and is often called broccoli, but it is actually a type of cauliflower.

Kitchen use

Fresh broccoli is much superior to that you buy in the store. It is best when cooked for just a few minutes, until it is tender but still bright green and firm. If it turns olive green and flaccid you have cooked it for too long.

Broccoli is also good raw and this is the way to get the maximum benefit from all of those phytonutrients.

If you find the heads are infested with aphids, try dipping them in a mix of warm water and vinegar. Don't soak them for too long though, or you may have vinegar flavored broccoli (and broccoli flavored vinegar).

The interior of the stem can be eaten like kohlrabi.

If you need a good reason to eat lots of broccoli, then you should know about its potent anti-cancer effects. In particular it has been found to reduce the risk of prostate cancer.

Sprouting Broccoli

When British gardening books talk about broccoli, they often mean sprouting broccoli (they often use the name calabrese for what we think of as broccoli.)

This plant is different from broccoli in that it produces many small heads or shoots, rather than a single large one. These are cut with a long (5″) stem attached. The plants may continue to send up new small heads for weeks.

The big advantage of this plant is that it is an early spring crop, appearing weeks before asparagus and often when there is little else available from the garden. It isn't broccoli, but it is just as good.

Sprouting broccoli is hardier than broccoli and is sown in the fall, for a spring crop. It doesn't work well if planted in spring, because it needs exposure to cold weather (below 50°F) before it will head up. It is otherwise grown and used in the same ways as broccoli.

The biggest problem with growing this plant is probably finding seed to plant. Varieties include

Purple Sprouting

White Sprouting

Chinese Broccoli
Gai Lohn

Introduction: This is the same species as the above and may have been developed from plants introduced into China by the Portuguese, some time in the sixteenth century. It differs from broccoli in that the flower stems are quite slender, only ½ - ¾″ in diameter.

This fast growing plant is cultivated in much the same way as broccoli, but is easier and more forgiving. It deserves to be more widely grown in the West

When: This is a fairly easy crop to grow, tolerating cold and heat better than other broccoli. In cool climates it can be grown in succession all summer, though late summer tends to give the best results as it is less likely to bolt prematurely. In warm climates it is usually grown as a fall and winter, crop. It may also do well in spring, if you get it going early enough.

Spacing: This varies from 6 - 12″ depending upon the size of plants required. Larger spacing gives larger plants.

Harvest: The first flower shoots are followed by lots of side shoots, so the plants can be harvested 3 or 4 times. Check the plants every couple of days and cut all mature shoots. Don't let the flowers open.

Varieties: Green Lance is the most readily available variety.

Kitchen use: In China the shoots are usually stir fried or steamed.

Brussels Sprout
Brassica oleracea var *gemmifera*

Introduction: As the name suggests this crop originated in Belgium, sometime in the eighteenth century. It is a crop you either love (some people adore them) or hate, but don't be too quick to judge until you have tried them fresh from your own garden. I have always disliked them, but with a little effort they have started growing on me recently.

Nutritional content: The sprouts are rich in protein (for a green vegetable), vitamins A and C (much more than cabbage), as well as potassium, iron, folate, riboflavin and various antioxidants. As an energy source they contain abut 200 calories per pound.

Crop value: Brussels sprouts are a nutritious crop, but not very easy to grow, not particularly productive and they take a long time to grow.

Climate: Brussels sprout is quite specialized in its growth requirements and doesn't grow well everywhere. It needs a long period of suitably cool conditions 40 (60 - 65) 75°F for growth and (particularly for) maturation and in most of the country it can only be grown as a fall crop. It is a very hardy plant and tolerates hard frost.

Ease of growing: Brussels sprout isn't the easiest of crops to grow well. It is somewhat temperamental, with fairly narrow climate requirements and it needs to be planted at the right time to take advantage of suitably cool weather. It is also fairly slow growing and is in the ground for a long time, which means there is lots of time for things to go wrong.

About Brussels Sprout

Seed facts
Germ temp: 45 - 85°F
Germ time: 4 - 20 days
20 days / 50°F
9 days / 59°F
6 days / 68°F
5 days / 77°F * Optimum
4 days / 86°F
Seed viability: 3 - 10 years
Germination percentage: 75+
Weeks to grow transplants: 4 - 6

Planning facts
Hardiness: Hardy
Growing temp 40 (60 - 65) 75°F
Plants per person: 5
Plants per sq ft: ½
Transplants
Start: 2 - 3 wks before last frost date
Plant out: 2 wks after last frost date
Fall crop: Plant out in midsummer
Direct sow: 2 wks after last frost
Days to harvest: 140 - 250 days

Harvest facts
Harvest period: 8 - 10 weeks
Yield per plant: 1 lb per plant
Yield per sq ft: ½ lb

Soil
pH. (6.0 to 6.5) to 7.5

Brussels sprout likes a heavy, moisture retentive soil. It should be rich in organic matter and all nutrients for well balanced growth. It likes lots of potassium and phosphorus, but doesn't need too much nitrogen, as this can adversely affect the flavor of the sprouts.

Soil preparation: Prepare the soil by incorporating 2 - 3″ of compost or aged manure, along with colloidal phosphate, wood ashes, kelp and dolomitic limestone. Work all of this into the top 6 - 8″ of soil, which is where most of the plants feeder roots are found.

Planning

Where: These plants get quite big and are in the ground for a long time, so you want to put them in the right place. Make sure they are in a warm sunny spot (not a frost pocket) and that the soil is well-drained. They should not be planted where another Brassica has grown in the last three years.

When: Proper timing is absolutely essential if your Brussels sprouts are to do well. They need cool weather for growth and cooler weather for maturation. They don't work as a spring crop because the sprouts would mature in warmer weather, which would seriously impair their flavor and quality.

They are also a very slow maturing crop (some varieties may take eight months), so are in the ground for a long time. This means that a fall crop might have to go into the ground in early to mid summer (depending upon the climate and variety). In cool summer areas it is sometimes planted in the middle of spring.

Fall: Brussels sprouts are planted some time in summer to mature in fall and early winter. They can be direct sown, or grown from transplants (in Britain they are a traditional Christmas "treat").

Planting

Raising transplants: Like other Brassicas, they don't mind transplanting and may even like it.

Starting inside: The plants can be started indoors in flats, cell packs, soil blocks or plug trays. Sow the seeds 1″ apart and ⅛ - ¼″ deep, 4 - 5 weeks before you want to plant out. When they are big enough prick out into another flat, leaving 2″ between the plants.

Starting outside: If Brussels sprouts are started during warm weather there is no need to start them in a greenhouse. An outdoor nursery bed will suit them just fine. Sow the seeds in a small protected area, prick the seedlings out into a slightly larger area and finally transplant the young plants into their permanent position. This saves bed space until it is really needed.

Planting out: The seedlings should be transplanted outside when they are 4 - 5″ high and have 5 - 6 true leaves. Don't wait too long to plant them out, or they may get stressed. Plant them a little deeper than they were in the flat, up to the first true leaves.

Direct sowing: There is no reason why you can't sow directly into the garden, except for the fact that they will be taking up a lot of bed space. Plant the seeds ½″ deep and keep well watered.

You must take precautions to prevent them getting eaten though, otherwise there is a very good chance they will end up as a snack for some of the many hungry pests that love Brassicas.

Spacing: The plants need a lot of space, so plant in two rows down the bed, with 18 - 24″ between the plants. Of course you could also plant them in a single row too. Another crop can be interplanted with them, to take advantage of the large areas of vacant space between the plants.

Care

Weeds: It is important to weed the young plants carefully. This should be done by hand, as their shallow roots are easily damaged by careless hoeing.

Water: Keep the soil evenly moist at all times. Brussels sprout absolutely must have enough water, especially if the weather is warm.

Mulch: This is very helpful for Brussels sprouts, as otherwise there is a lot of bare soil between the plants. It keeps the soil cooler, suppresses weeds and conserves soil moisture.

Pests: This species is prone to the same pests as other members of the *Brassicaceae* family. See **Cabbage** for more on these.

Disease: See **Cabbage** for more on these too.

Harvesting

When: The actual Brussels sprouts you eat are axillary buds and mature gradually from the bottom of the stem upwards, in the order they were formed. They do this because the apical dominance hormone produced by the growing top is only effective for a certain distance.

The sprouts generally start to form when night-time temperatures drop to 60°F. As the sprouts mature, the lower leaves may start to fade. The hardy sprouts stay in good condition even with frost (down to 20°F). In fact their flavor improves with cold weather.

How: Start picking (or rather cutting) when the sprouts are about an inch across, beginning at the bottom and working your way up to the top. Don't leave any mature sprouts on the plant, as this can affect further production.

When the plant is nearly finished, you can cut off the leafy top and eat the tender parts like cabbage.

Topping: It is possible to speed up and even out the harvest by removing the leafy growing top. This ends its apical dominance so all the sprouts start growing at once. If you want to do this, cut the top about 6 weeks before you want to harvest, just as the first sprouts are starting to form on the bottom of the stem.

Storage: Brussels sprouts may keep for several weeks when stored in a plastic bag in the fridge (don't wash them). For longer term storage they are usually frozen.

Seed saving: This is the same as for **Cabbage**.

Unusual growing ideas

Edible flower buds: If the plant has any energy left after producing all those sprouts, it may produce an edible flower bud that can be used like broccoli. If it isn't too woody, the peeled stalk is also edible.

Varieties

Brussels sprouts aren't exactly a popular crop in this country, so there aren't a lot of varieties. This is also a crop where hybrids are usually superior to open pollinated varieties (with a few exceptions). The problem with this is that many hybrids are bred for commercial farmers and tend to produce all of their sprouts at once.

Open pollinated

Long Island Improved - The old standard

Roodnerf: One of best flavored varieties. Tall.

Rubine: Sprouts are purple.

Hybrids:

Falstaff F1- Slow maturing, but tasty.

Jade Cross F1 - Compact and early maturing (85 days)

Bubbles - Tall

Kitchen use: Cut an x in the base of the stem and then steam them for 5 - 8 minutes. When cooked the stem end should barely be tender when you poke it with a knife. Whatever you do don't overcook them. Even a few minutes overcooking can make them almost inedible.

Buckwheat

Fagopyrum esculentum

Introduction: The name is derived from the visual similarity of the seeds to the larger seeds of the Beech (Boek) tree. This annual was once commonly grown as a home scale grain crop, especially in Eastern Europe. It is categorized as a pseudo-cereal as it is grown as a grain crop, yet isn't a member of the grass family. It was widely grown in the United States in the 18th and 19th centuries, but it almost disappeared along with the self-sufficient small farmers who grew it.

These days buckwheat is most familiar to gardeners as a fast maturing summer green manure crop.

Crop value: Buckwheat is unusual in that it is a very short season grain crop, able to produce in poor soil and under adverse conditions. Perhaps equally important for the home grower it is fairly easy to process into edible food. It was once an important crop for self-sufficient farmers and may be important again one day. Its biggest drawback (as with most grains) is the amount of processing required to make it edible.

Ease of growing: Few plants are as easy to grow as buckwheat. The relatively large seed germinates quickly and the plants grow vigorously and mature rapidly. If you can't grow buckwheat successfully, I suggest you stick to alfalfa sprouts (actually don't give up, just try again, it only takes a couple of months).

Climate: Buckwheat prefers cool, moist conditions (70°F is ideal), but it can't tolerate any frost. It is grown commercially in the northern states and Canada. However it is a fairly adaptable plant and quite tolerant of less than ideal conditions.

Very high temperatures may cause the flowers to die without producing seed. However it will produce more flowers to replace them and usually manages to produce enough seed to be worthwhile.

Nutritional content: The high protein grain has a better amino acid composition than most cereals and is especially high in lysine. It is also rich in complex carbohydrates and contains about 1550 calories per pound.

Buckwheat is also a rich source of rutin, a potent anti-cancer agent that also lowers "bad" cholesterol.

Soil

pH: 4.0 to 6.0
Buckwheat will grow in almost any soil, even very acidic ones, so long as it is reasonably well-drained and fairly loose. Traditionally it was grown on soils that were too poor for more valuable crops.

Planning

When: Buckwheat is a cool season crop and grows best when the weather isn't too hot. However it doesn't like cold weather and can't stand frost. Plant it any time after the soil has warmed up in spring (2 weeks after the last frost date). More commonly it is planted in mid to late summer, so it can mature its seed in cooler weather.

Buckwheat has the shortest growing season of any "grain" crop, and may mature in as little as 2 months. In ideal conditions it may flower within 5 weeks of planting. This means it can be planted over quite a long period in summer and will still have time to mature before cold weather arrives.

If your growing season is long enough, it is possible to get two crops in one summer.

Planting

Direct sowing: The easiest way to plant buckwheat is to broadcast the seeds onto the bed and then rake them into the soil. If your supply of seed is limited, you will waste less seed if you sow in rows (make the furrows ½ - 1″ deep).

Spacing: You want the plants to be spaced from 4 - 6″ apart.

Care

Watering: The seeds need moist soil for good germination, so keep them well watered. Buckwheat is quite drought tolerant, but gives higher yields if watered regularly.

Pests: Few insect pests bother buckwheat, though birds and slugs will eat the newly planted seeds and emerging seedlings. Birds may also go for the ripening grain. Deer can also be a problem for unprotected plantings.

Harvesting

When: Buckwheat will be ready to harvest 60 - 90 days after planting (the exact time depending upon the variety and climate). The seed doesn't all ripen at once, so you harvest when ¾ of it has turned dark brown. The plants can still be green when the seed is ready to be harvested. If you wait too long some of the seed will be lost (and will probably self sow).

How: Cut the seed heads with a sickle and dry them on a large tarp. Then thresh out the seeds and dry to 12% moisture for storage.

Processing: The thick seed coat (pericarp) comes off fairly easily when grinding the seed to make flour. Sift the biggest parts out of the flour before using it (you don't need to get it all though).

Seed saving: Just save some of the seed you collect.

Unusual growing ideas

Green manure: This tender annual is most familiar to gardeners as a green manure crop. It is one of the best short-term soil improving crops for the summer garden. It produces a dense fibrous root system, thrives on poor soils, adds organic matter and improves soil structure. It is also very fast growing and can be grown in a few weeks, in between other crops.

When incorporated as a green manure it is very effective at feeding and stimulating soil life. It also accumulates phosphorus and makes it more available.

Weed suppression: Buckwheat can grow up to four feet in height in only a few weeks and grows so densely it can be an effective smother crop. It actually has an allelopathic effect on many weeds and can suppress weed growth for up to 2 months. This works best when the plants are simply cut down within a week of flowering and incorporated into the soil.

A good way to establish a new garden is to plant and incorporate, two consecutive crops of buckwheat.

Buckwheat Lettuce: Some people use buckwheat as an indoor micro-green salad crop. The seeds are soaked for 3 hours and then spread out on a tray of soil, vermiculite, felt or wet paper. They are then put in a warm place and misted daily. When the seeds begin to germinate the tray is moved into full light. The greens will be ready in 1 to 3 weeks, depending upon the temperature. The plants are harvested with scissors when they are 3 - 6″ tall, leaving about an inch of stem behind. See **Microgreens** for more on this)

Caution: There is a potential problem with the frequent use of buckwheat greens. The green plant contains a toxin called fagopyrin, which can cause the skin of some individuals to become hypersensitive to sunlight. For this reason I don't recommend that you use any green parts (you may ask why I bothered to mention it then?)

Buckwheat honey: This is considered to have a very fine flavor and buckwheat is sometimes planted specifically to provide forage for bees.

Buckwheat flowers are also very attractive to hoverflies (important predatory insects that prey on aphids).

Varieties

This isn't a very important commercial crop, so there aren't very many improved varieties available (only about 6 are important commercially). They are also difficult to find, which is why I often use seed available locally, either for use as a green manure crop, or from the wholefood store. It may well be one of the following:

Giant American, Koban. Mancan, Manisoba, Manor, Spanky. Springfield

Kitchen use

Buckwheat has been an important peasant food in many parts of the world. In Japan it is used to make soba noodles, in Eastern Europe it was used to make a porridge called kasha and in North America it was used for buckwheat pancakes. You can add 20% buckwheat flour to many recipes to improve them. More recently it has been used to make gluten free beer.

Buckwheat pancakes

These are undoubtedly the best known use of buckwheat in this country.

1 cup buckwheat flour (or ½ buckwheat flour and ½ whole wheat flour)
1 tsp baking powder
2 tbsp sugar (or equivalent sweetener)
½ tsp salt
1 mashed banana
1 cup soy milk/almond milk
Oil for frying

Mix together dry ingredients, then add liquids and beat well. Fry on a lightly oiled griddle in the usual way.

Cabbage

Brassica oleracea var *capitata*

Wild Cabbage (*Brassica oleracea ssp oleracea)* is native to the coastal areas of Western Europe and is still found growing wild there. An impressive variety of cool weather garden crops have been bred from this unimpressive looking plant, including kale, collards, cabbage, broccoli, cauliflower, Brussels sprout and kohlrabi. Cabbage was probably refined into the familiar crop in Germany and is still very popular there. The word cole is an old name for cabbage (hence coleslaw).

Crop value: Cabbage was a staple food of Northern European peasants for centuries. It is an ideal crop for self-sufficiency for many reasons. It is easy to grow and store, nutritious, high yielding, hardy and can be harvested fresh during cold weather after most other crops are finished.

Cabbage was the crop to depend upon when all else failed and there are varieties for harvesting for most of the year. Perhaps because of this association with poor peasants, cabbage has never been held in very high esteem by gourmets, but it can be very good.

Ease of growing: Cabbage is pretty easy to grow if you pay attention to the minor details. Give it a good soil, water and weed regularly and plant the right variety at the right time.

Nutritional content

Cabbage is rich in vitamin C, calcium and several cancer preventing phytochemicals (anthocyanins, sulforaphane, isothiocyanates, dithiolethiones). It has been found that people who eat lots of Brassicas, have lower cancer rates than those who don't.

As a source of energy cabbage contains about 110 calories per pound, so those peasants who relied upon it as a winter food would have had to eat a lot!

About Cabbage

Seed facts
Germ temp: 45 - 85°F
Germ time: 4 - 20 days
15 days / 50°F
9 days / 59°F
6 days / 68°F
5 days / 77°F * Optimum
4 days / 86°F
Seed viability: 3 - 10 years
Germination percentage: 75+
Weeks to grow transplant: 4 - 5

About Cabbage
Hardiness: Hardy
Growing temp: 40 (60 - 65) 75°F
Plants per person: 5
Plants per sq ft: 1
Transplants:
Start: 6 wks before last frost
Plant out: 2 wks before last frost
Direct sow: 2 wks before last frost
Fall crop: Sow in late summer
Days to harvest: 70 - 200 days
50 - 150 days from transplants.

Harvest facts
Yield per plant: 1 - 2 lb
Yield per sq ft: 1 - 3 lb sq ft

Climate: Cabbage is an adaptable plant and can tolerate a variety of situations. It prefers fairly cool growing conditions (ideally 60 - 65°F) and in warm weather areas it only grows well in spring and fall (and maybe winter too). It is quite hardy (some varieties much more than others) and tolerates hard frost down to 20°F. It doesn't taste very good when grown in hot weather.

Soil

pH: (6.0 to 6.5) 7.5

Cabbages are hungry plants and must have rich soil if they are to produce well. They prefer heavy soil with lots of organic matter to retain moisture and lots of available nutrients (especially potassium and phosphorus). They don't need a lot of nitrogen however, as this can lead to sappy growth that isn't very hardy.

Cabbage doesn't like poorly drained soil. Early crops may do better in lighter soils that warm up more rapidly, or in raised beds.

Potential micronutrient deficiencies include boron and manganese.

Soil preparation: Cabbages love organic matter, so incorporate 2″ of compost or aged manure into the top 8″ of soil. This is often applied the previous fall, in which case fresh manure can also be used. They also like phosphorus.

Clubroot can be a problem in acid soil, so try to keep the pH above 7.0. Low pH may also lock up molybdenum, potentially causing a deficiency. Raising the pH with a liming agent will also add calcium which is good for cabbage.

Planning

Where: If you are growing cabbages in cold weather, they should be planted in a warm sheltered place with full sun. In warmer climates they may do better in light shade.

Crop rotation: Cabbage is prone to a host of pests and diseases, so it is important to rotate it. Don't plant it where any Brassica has been grown in the past 3 years. They often follow nitrogen fixing legumes in a rotation.

When: Cabbage doesn't do well in hot weather, as it causes excessive transpiration from the large leaves. It really needs cool weather and short days to head up satisfactorily. This means that it does best when planted early (to mature before midsummer), or late (to mature in fall). If you live in a climate with cool summers, you can harvest right through the summer. If you live in an area with mild winters, you can harvest right through the winter too.

With all of these options of when to plant, it is important to choose a variety that is appropriate for the season in which it will be grown. Many cabbage varieties are bred for growing at specific times and won't perform well if grown at the wrong time of year.

Spring: The first cabbage plants can be started 6 - 8 weeks before the last spring frost and planted out 4 - 6 weeks later. They should still be small enough that they won't be vernalized by a late cold snap, which would cause them to bolt (see **Broccoli** for more on vernalization). If you plant early and feed them well, the first plants should be mature by early summer.

Summer: In places with cool summers it can be grown almost year round, by succession sowing and using different varieties.

Fall: Start a fall crop 12 - 16 weeks before the first fall frost. This can be planted in a nursery bed, or in any vacant spot. Just be sure to give them protection from slugs and other predators. Plants grown at this time of year tend to be much better flavored than those grown in warmer weather.

Winter: In areas with mild winters cabbage can be planted in late summer as a winter crop. This will mature in late autumn and then stand right through the winter in good condition. These plants can get very big.

Cabbage can also be planted in autumn, to over-winter and mature the following spring. In milder areas it might also be planted in January for a spring crop.

Does all of this give you enough options?

Succession: Plant a succession sowing every 3 - 4 weeks. Generally you only need a few plants to mature at any one time, so you should only plant a few seeds (a dozen or so) at each sowing.

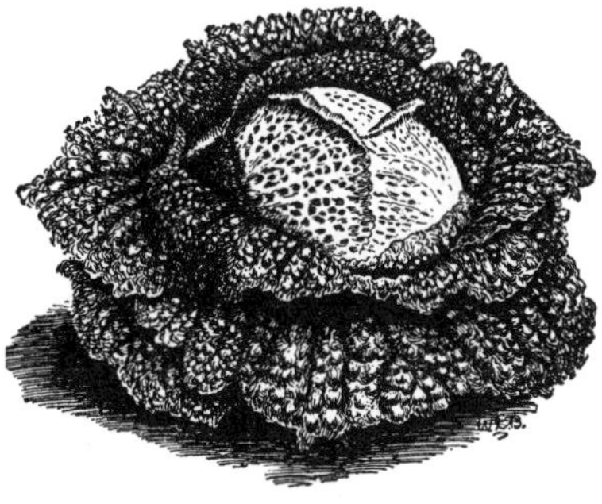

Planting

Transplants: Cabbage is hardy enough to be direct sown, but is more often grown from transplants. It actually seems to like being transplanted and is said to grow a stronger root network as a result. These can also give you an earlier start in spring.

Starting inside: The first spring cabbages are usually started indoors 6 weeks before the last frost date. Plant the seeds 1″ apart and ½″ deep and keep them warm (60 - 80°F) for fastest germination. Once they are growing, reduce the temperature to between 50 and 70°F, as they grow better in cooler conditions. When they have 2 sets of leaves they should be pricked out into a larger container, leaving 2″ between plants.

The seedlings will be ready to go in the ground 4 weeks later, when they have 4 or 5 true leaves and are about 4″ high. Be sure to plant them outside as soon as they are of sufficient size. If they sit around in containers for too long, they will get stressed and deficient and won't perform well.

You can also buy cabbage transplants of course, but they are so easy to raise yourself there is usually no reason to.

Hardening off: If transplants are to go outside while it is still cold, they must be hardened off (failure to do so can result in badly shocked plants that just don't grow well). They will then tolerate temperatures as low as 25°F. Start by putting the plants outside for 2 hours on the first day, then 4 hours on the second day. Add 2 hours every day for a week and then plant out.

If you have a cold frame you can also harden them off in there. Just open it for longer periods each day and close it at night night.

Planting out:
Planting the seedlings is pretty straightforward; just bury the stems up to their first true leaves. Press down gently around the plant to firm the soil and leave a slight depression. Water the plants the day before you transplant them, and immediately afterward to help them recover.

If cutworms, root maggots or birds are a problem in your area, you will have to take suitable preventive measures.

Cutworms: If you find whole plants laying on the ground, severed at the base, cutworms are usually responsible. Dig in the soil around the fallen plant and you will usually find a small, dark, curled up caterpillar). If you find it you can prevent it killing other plants.

Cutworms can be a real problem for young seedlings in spring. A good solution is to wrap the stems in individual cutworm collars, made of cardboard, newspaper (2 layers) or aluminum foil. These should go 2″ into the soil. You can also use a bottomless paper cup to surround the whole plant.

Starting transplants outside:
In mild weather the transplants can be started in an outdoor nursery bed. Sow the seed about 1″ apart and when they have all emerged and are growing vigorously, transplant them to stand 3″ apart. This is a much more efficient use of space than direct sowing, as the plants don't take up much bed space for the first 4 - 6 weeks of their lives.

Direct sowing: As the weather warms up, cabbage is often sown directly outdoors. The plants grow well when direct sown, though there is a danger that they may end up as dinner for some of the many hungry pests that love Brassicas.

Some people sow some turnip seed along with the cabbage, as many pests seem to prefer it and will then leave the cabbage alone. You can also plant extra cabbage seed, to compensate for some losses. The problem of predation is one reason Brassicas are often started indoors.

If you want to direct sow, plant the seeds ¼ ″ deep in cool soil and up to 1″ deep in warm soil. Space them 2″ apart, to be thinned to the desired spacing when they get big enough (you can eat the thinnings).

Spacing: This varies according to variety, soil fertility, the time of year and how large you want the plants to get. You can control the final size of the plants by the spacing - a wider spacing means larger, but fewer, plants. You can also plant closer together initially and harvest every alternate plant for use as immature greens (this goes along with planting extra to minimize the effect of pests).

Beds:
12″ spacing is for very fertile soil, summer and smaller heads.

15″ spacing is for average soil, summer and average heads.

18″ spacing is for poor soil, winter and large heads.

Rows: If you want to plant in rows, the traditional spacing is 12 - 18″ apart in the row, with 18 - 24″ between the rows (exact spacing depends upon the size of the variety).

Care

For best quality the plants must experience no check from lack of water or nutrients, or competition from weeds.

Weed: Keep down weeds around the plants. This is particularly important when the plants are young, as they can't compete very well.

Water: Cabbage needs a regular water supply to grow well, at least an inch of water per week. They are quite shallow rooted, so make sure there is plenty of moisture in the soil at all times. This is particularly important in hot weather, as dry soil can severely impact the harvest.

Consistent watering is also important. Lack of water can result in strongly flavored plants and thicker, tougher leaves. If plants are suddenly soaked after being very dry, the resulting burst in growth can cause the head to split. An extreme measure to prevent this happening (perhaps after heavy rain) is to cut some of the roots with a knife or spade. This reduces the amount of water the plant can take in.

It is best if the leaves don't get wet when watering, as several diseases can be spread in this way.

Fertilization: A liquid feed of compost tea is helpful in early spring, while the soil is cool and nitrogen is not readily available. A second feed may be given as they are heading up, to help them grow bigger.

Mulch: These widely spaced plants benefit from a mulch to keep down weeds, keep the soil cool and to conserve moisture.

Heading up: Before a cabbage begins to head up it stores nutrients in its outer leaves. These are then used during the heading up phase, when more nutrients are needed in a shorter time than the roots can easily supply.

Pests: Plants of the *Brassicaceae* family have developed a pungent and toxic oil to protect themselves from insect predators. This is very effective in most cases, however a number of insects have not only evolved some resistance to it, but are now actually attracted by it. These are serious pests of Brassicas and can make growing them much more difficult than it should be.

Aphids: These are the ever-present pests of Brassicas. Blasting them off with a strong jet (I mean strong) of water makes a big difference. It also pays to have lots of insectory plants (Ph*acelia, Asteraceae. Apiaceae*) around to feed the predators that prey on aphids.

Caterpillars: Several types of caterpillar live only on the various Brassicas and can strip a young plant to the midribs in a short time. It is important to keep an eye out for these, so you can deal with them when they first appear, rather than after they devastate your crop.

If you have only a few plants, hand picking is the best way to go. If you have a whole field then a spray of BT (*Bacillus thuringensis*) is usually recommended. Parasitic wasps can kill a lot of caterpillars if given the chance, but not if you start spraying poisons. Red cabbage is not as attractive to caterpillars as the green, though it is more attractive to aphids. Some people even go after the conspicuous white butterflies with a butterfly net.

Flea Beetles: These tiny insects are common in spring and eat small holes in the leaves of the young plants. Transplants can usually take this damage without too much problem, they will just put out new leaves, but newly germinated seedlings may be killed. If they are a big problem you could use row covers, or plant some turnip seed as a trap crop.

Cabbage Root Fly: This is probably the worst Brassica pest. It lays its eggs at the base of the plant and the newly hatched larvae work their way down to the roots and eat them. If they are numerous enough they pretty much destroy the roots and kill the plant. The first warning sign is when a plant wilts in sunny weather. If this occurs, examine the root for the small white maggots, which look like small grains of rice. If you find affected plants, remove and kill the maggots to stop them maturing and reproducing (or just to make you feel better).

The easiest way to deal with these pests is to use row covers, which prevents the fly getting near enough to the plant to lay eggs.

Another effective control is to use 6″ squares (or disks) of foam carpet backing. You cut a slit to the center of the square and put them around the stem. These work very well, because the foam can expand as the stem enlarges. These disks not only make it harder for the fly larvae to get into the root, but also provide refuges for the predatory beetles that eat the eggs and larvae. These disks have achieved 70% control, which is as good as most pesticides.

The flies prefer Chinese cabbage and will lay their eggs near it, in preference to cabbage. You could plant these near your cabbages as a trap crop.

You don't have to eliminate all of these maggots. Some damage is tolerable, so long as it doesn't seriously affect the crop.

Other pests: Cutworms, harlequin bugs, thrips, root knot nematodes, slugs and snails.

Birds: These will sometimes eat seedlings, especially in spring. If this is a problem you may have to net the plants (row covers used to prevent other pests will also work). In my garden quail are a problem for Brassicas year round, but particularly in winter. They love to eat the leaves and will tear them to shreds (sometimes they strip whole plants).

Diseases: Alternaria blight, black leg, black rot, downy mildew, fusarium wilt and wirestem.

Clubroot: (*Plasmodiophora brassicae*): This serious root disease is a big problem in some areas. It causes the roots to swell up like clubs and can kill the plant. Clubroot likes acid soil, so the closer your soil is to neutral the better. If this disease gets into your soil it can stay there for years, even without any Brassicas to infect.

Nutrient deficiency:
Boron deficiency: Brassicas generally are quite susceptible to boron deficiency, which manifests itself as hollow stems.

Harvesting

When: Harvest the first cabbage heads as soon as they are big and solid enough to be worthwhile, though you will get the biggest harvest by waiting until they are fully mature.

You can harvest the un-hearted (heartless) plants, any time they are big enough to bother with, but they will be much less productive. You could plant close together and harvest every alternate plant in this way.

If a mature head begins to crack (this may be caused by excess nitrogen, aging or irregular water supply) harvest it and use promptly. This doesn't affect edibility, but it does affect storage life.

Delaying maturation: If too many cabbages are maturing at once, you can slow their growth by cutting through some of their roots with a spade. You can also twist the head a quarter turn, to break some of the roots.

How: Harvest by cutting through the base of the stem with a knife. When you harvest early cabbage, you might want to leave a few leaves on the root (this is the fastest way to get a clean cabbage anyway). These will keep the root alive and may enable it to produce a new crop of mini cabbages (these are known as cabbage sprouts in England). If you harvest all but one of these, the remaining one might even grow into another small head

If cabbage root fly or clubroot are a big problem you might want to remove the roots after harvest and compost or burn them.

Storage: Cabbages are usually left in the garden and harvested as needed. In milder areas they will even continue to grow. In colder areas you may have to protect them with mulch.

The fleshy leaves of cabbage are intended as food storage organs, so they are one of the easiest crops to store. They can be stored in plastic bags in a refrigerator (for weeks), or in a root cellar at 32 - 40˚F and 90 - 95% humidity (for months). Don't wash them until you use them.

Seed saving: Cabbage is a biennial and takes two years to produce seed. Don't save seed from plants that flower in their first year, as you don't want to raise an annual strain that bolts quickly.

In harsh climates you may have to protect the plants over the winter. You can do this with a thick mulch of straw, cold frames, cloches or hay bales (half grown plants sometimes survive better than larger ones). You may also dig them up (leave 12″ of root attached) and store in a root cellar in damp sand.

Cabbage is usually self-incompatible and must be cross-pollinated by insects. This means there must be a number of plants flowering at the same time. Normally you should save the seed from at least 5 plants to maintain some genetic diversity.

All of the cole crops are the same species and will cross with each other. To maintain racial purity you have to ensure that only one type (and variety) flowers at once. The alternative is to isolate them, either by distance (1000 yards for different varieties, 1500 yards for different crops), or by caging them (don't forget they need insects for pollination).

The plants flower in the spring of their second year. If the head is very dense the flower stalk may have a hard time emerging. If this is the case you can cut a 2″ deep cross in the top of the head to help it get out.

A large healthy cabbage plant can produce a lot of seed and get quite top heavy. If this happens the stem may need support if it is not to break under its own weight.

The seed pods should be gathered when the older bottom pods first start to split open. Watch them carefully as they shatter easily when they are fully ripe. Cut the seedpod bearing stems and dry them in a warm place (I put small quantities in a paper grocery bag, so I don't lose any seeds). The seeds are fairly big and are easily handled and cleaned. Of course it is essential that they are thoroughly dry before storage.

Unusual growing ideas

Intercrop: The plants need a lot of space when mature, but not when young. Use this temporarily vacant space by interplanting a fast maturing crop such as lettuce.

Spring greens: This is over-wintered cabbage planted very close together (only 6″ apart). When the plants begin to touch, every other plant is harvested and eaten. The remaining plants can then either be eaten or left to head up to full size

Sprouting: If you save all of the seed from 5 plants, you will have far more seed than you actually need for planting. A good way to use the surplus is to sprout it like alfalfa. Cabbage sprouts have a nice spicy flavor and are highly nutritious.

Micro-greens: Any surplus seed can also be used to grow tasty micro-green salads materials (see **Micro-greens**).

Varieties

There are a number of different kinds of cabbage, grown for different purposes and at different times. Red, green, almost white, curly, crinkled, conical, spherical, lettuce-like, summer, autumn, winter, mammoth and tiny. The most important differences are; the time of harvest, time needed to maturity (this varies enormously), length of time they can be stored, disease resistance and their tolerance of frost. If you choose the wrong variety for your needs, it may not respond as you would like.

Early: 60 to 80 days
Copenhagen Market

Early Jersey Wakefield

Primo

Mid-season: 80 to 90 days
Brunswick

Early Flat Dutch

Late: 90 to 110 days (these are bigger, have thicker leaves and store better)

Danish Ballhead

Late Flat Dutch

Savoy: Very hardy and attractive, it is usually grown over the winter.
Melissa

Best-of-All

Red: These are the least hardy cabbages, but the most appealing visually.

Red Danish

Red Acre

Red Express

Kitchen use

A home grown cabbage, grown in cold weather and cooked really well, can be very good.

Cabbage is also great raw, in fact I actually prefer it that way.

Cole slaw

½ head cabbage (chopped)
1 green onion (chopped)
2 carrots (grated)
2 tbsp parsley leaves (chopped)
½ cup mayonnaise (or vegan alternative)
½ tsp salt
2 tsp celery seeds
½ tbsp sugar
¼ tsp black pepper
1 tbsp white vinegar

Prepare the vegetables and mix them in a bowl. In a separate bowl mix the rest of the ingredients, then pour over the vegetables to cover them evenly. Chill in the fridge for one hour (this is so simple it is hardly a recipe at all).

Couve tronchuda

Couve tronchuda
(Portuguese cabbage)

Brassica oleracea var *costata*

Couve tronchuda is a loose leaf cabbage with a hard to pronounce name. It originated in Portugal and is an easily grown and versatile plant. It is sometimes said to be a type of collards and can be grown in the same ways, but it differs in that it produces thick succulent midribs (costata means ribbed), almost like bok choy. These are more tender than those of kale or collards.

Climate: Like the collard it is more tolerant of warm weather than most Brassicas. It is also hardy enough to tolerate light frost and this can actually improve its flavor.

Crop value: This hardy, easily grown and versatile plant was a staple in peasant gardens in Portugal and is still very popular (as it is in the former Portuguese colony of Brazil). It is relatively rare in American gardens, but deserves to be more widely grown.

When: Couve tronchuda can be grown as a spring crop, but does better when grown in the fall. In milder areas it is commonly grown over the winter.

Planting: It is treated in much the same way as kale and collards, liking the same growing conditions and being affected by the same pest and diseases.

Harvest; The normal practice is to harvest individual leaves as they reach full size, as you would kale or collards. It is a fairly big plant (24″ tall x 24″ wide), so you don't need many plants.

Varieties: In Portugal there are quite a few varieties, including one that grows very tall like a tree collard. Unfortunately in this country we are usually confined to a generic "couve tronchuda" and should be thankful if we can get it. If you find any of the more unusual varieties (particularly the tree type) let me know and we can do a trade.

Kitchen use: The leaves can be eaten in two distinct ways.

The whole leaves can be used like cabbage or kale and are popular in soups, especially the traditional Portuguese dish caldo verde (green broth), where they are cut into thin strips.

The midribs can also be cut from the leaves and eaten separately.

Not quite caldo verde

1 lb couve tronchuda, sliced into very thin strips
4 tbs olive oil
8 potatoes chopped into cubes
2 medium onion, chopped
6 cloves of garlic, minced
2 bay leaves
I lb cooked white beans
½ lb vegetarian sausage (or real sausage if you are so inclined)
2 diced tomatoes
1 quart vegetable stock
salt
Pepper

Fry the onions and potato in a large pot for 5 minutes, then add the garlic and bay leaves and cook for two minutes more. Add the stock and beans, bring to a boil and simmer until the potatoes are cooked. Then add the beans, tomatoes, sausage and strips of couve tronchuda and cook for 5 minutes until the greens are tender. Add salt and pepper. Serve with bread.

Chinese Brassicas

The Chinese Brassicas tend to get overlooked by many gardeners, which is unfortunate because they are some of the most useful of all vegetables for cool climates. They are very hardy, very fast growing, very productive for the space they require, very nutritious and often very beautiful (how many times can you use the word very in one sentence?)

They are also very versatile plants as most can be used at all stages of growth. The mature leaves are good for cooked greens, younger ones are good for salads. They can also be used as micro-greens and baby greens (these are often grown under cover during the winter). If they bolt you can eat the unopened flower stalks (and edible flowers) and can ultimately gather the seed for sprouting.

Because of their hardiness they are particularly important in the winter garden.

Most Chinese Brassicas are said to be biennial, but many bolt so readily you would have to question that assumption. In the wrong circumstances they are some of the fastest bolting plants around.

They can be divided up into several distinct categories:

Chinese cabbages
Bok choy/pak choy
Tatsoi (Rosette pak choi) B. rapa var rosularis)
Choy sum (also Hon-Tsai-Tai flowering Pak Choy)
Mibuna
Komatsuna
Mizuna
Chinese Mustards(See **Mustard**)

Chinese Cabbage

Brassica rapa var pekinensis
Syn *B. pekinensis*

Introduction: The name Chinese cabbage is a fairly loose term, that has been applied to several different crops. This is the crop that produces the densely packed heading varieties, as well as some non-heading types. If you know your botanical Latin you might have noticed that this species is actually more closely related to the turnip than the cabbage.

This is a very important vegetable in China (just as cabbage was in Northern Europe) and in some poorer areas it still makes up 80% of the vegetable diet. It has been grown in the cooler parts of eastern Asia for centuries, but has only recently become popular in the West.

Ease of growing: Chinese cabbage has a reputation of being rather difficult to grow. This is because of its tendency to bolt prematurely if exposed to any kind of interruption in its growth.

Nutritional content: Chinese cabbage is rich in vitamins C and K, folate, calcium, potassium, phosphorus and is packed with beneficial antioxidants and phytonutrients. It is low in calories, with only about 60 per pound.

Soil

pH 6.0 to 7.0

This is a fairly hungry crop and prefers a rich, moist, well-drained soil with lots of nitrogen. It doesn't like very acidic or very poor soil (the latter may cause it to bolt quickly.

Soil preparation: Incorporate 2″ of compost or aged manure into the top 6″ of soil. If it is acidic add lime to raise the pH.

About Chinese Cabbage

Seed facts
Germ temp: 45 - 80˚F
Germ time: 3 - 10 days
5 days at 50˚F
3 days at 59˚F
2 days at 68˚F
1 day at 77˚F * Optimum
Germination percentage: 75+
Seed viability: 5 - 9 yrs
Weeks to grow transplants: 4 - 6

Planning facts
Hardiness: Hardy
Growing temp: 55 (60 - 65) 70˚F
Plants per person: 2
Plants per sq ft: 1
Transplants:
Start: 2 weeks before last frost
Plant out: 2 weeks after last frost
Direct sow: 4 wks before last frost
Fall crop: 8 - 10 wks before fall frost
Days to harvest: 60 - 100 days

Harvest facts
Yield per plant: 1 - 2 lb
Yield per sq ft: 1 - 3 lb sq ft

Planning

Where: In cool weather Chinese cabbage should be planted in a sunny location that is sheltered from cold winds. Don't plant it where any other Brassicas have been grown in the last three years.

When: Chinese cabbage is very prone to bolting when growing in warm weather, so is usually only grown in spring or fall.

Spring: You can try to make this plant work as a spring crop, by starting it indoors 2 weeks before the last spring frost. Plant it out 4 weeks later. It is hardy enough to be planted much earlier than this (it can survive temperatures as low as 20˚F), but the danger of vernalization and subsequent bolting is very great. It also helps to use an early maturing, bolt resistant variety.

Fall: Chinese cabbage does much better as a fall crop, because it is less likely to bolt in the shorter days. It is started in mid to late summer, 2 - 3 months before the first fall frost.

Planting

Indoors: Chinese cabbage doesn't really like transplanting (it may contribute to bolting) so plant it in cell packs or soil blocks and be very careful. If the weather gets very cold after planting out, protect the young plants with cloches, until temperatures are well above 50°F.

Outdoors: Chinese cabbages can be direct sown in mid summer, for a fall crop. Sow the seeds ½″ deep and about 3 - 4″ apart. Start thinning when the plants have 4 - 5 leaves. As plants get bigger you can harvest thin to leave the plants at their final spacing of 10 - 12″. Use the thinnings in the kitchen.

It can also be started in an outdoor nursery bed, though it doesn't like transplanting very much (it must be young to transplant successfully).

Spacing: Plant in offset rows across the bed, 10 - 12″ apart each way.

Care

Chinese cabbage will only be successful if it is able to grow without any interruption. If it doesn't get everything it needs it tends to bolt fairly quickly.

Bolting: Chinese cabbage is notorious for bolting at the slightest hint of a problem. Almost any kind of stress may cause it to bolt: the young plant being exposed to cold weather, poor soil, exposure to long days (over 14 hours), or some kind of interruption in growth (lack of water, transplanting, high temperatures). This tendency to bolt varies according to cultivar, some are much less prone to it than others.

Weeds: Keep down weeds while the plants are young, as they don't compete for nutrients very well.

Watering: This shallow rooted crop must have evenly moist soil. Never let it dry out, or it will probably react by bolting.

Blanching: The heading varieties are sometimes bound together with string (or tape or rubber bands) to blanch the inside leaves and make their flavor milder. If you do this make sure you don't trap water or slugs inside the plant.

Mulch: This is helpful to keep down weeds, conserve moisture and keep the plants cleaner.

Pests: Most of the pests and diseases that attack cabbages may also attack these plants. If anything, they are even more susceptible, for example it is more attractive to the cabbage root fly than cabbage and is sometimes planted alongside the various Brassicas as a trap crop. Pests aren't usually a big problem though. See **Cabbage** for more on the various pests.

Harvesting

When: Gather the heads as they start to firm up and feel solid to the touch. Given enough time the heads may get quite large. In warm weather they don't stay in peak condition for very long, so start using them as soon as they are big enough to be useful. In winter they stay in good condition for much longer, sometimes several weeks.

If they start to bolt, you can still eat them and should do so promptly (or you can use the resulting flower stalks instead).

They can also be used before they produce heads, even when just edible rosettes of leaves.

How: You can gather individual leaves any time, but this may reduce the final yield. A better idea is to harvest thin every other plant in a bed, leaving the rest to grow to full size.

If you leave a few leaves attached to the root when harvesting, it may put out new shoots and grow up again. This can be a good way to extend the harvest, especially in winter when it would be hard to get another crop established.

Flower stem: If a plant gets away from you completely and sends up a flower stalk, harvest it before the flower buds open and use it like broccoli. It will make more attempts to flower and these can all be eaten too. If you miss these you can always collect the seed for sprouting.

Storage: Store the heads in the refrigerator for up to 2 weeks. They may keep for several months in a root cellar at 34 - 38°F, with 90 - 95% humidity. In winter you can also store them in the ground, under a cold frame filled with straw

Seed saving: This is done in pretty much the same way as for turnip and cabbage. It is cross-pollinated by insects and will cross with any other *B. rapa* crop (which includes turnip, broccoli raab and pak choy) as well as other Chinese cabbage varieties. You should save the seed from at least 6 plants to ensure some genetic variability.

These plants will produce more seed than you need for propagation. The surplus can be used for growing cut and come again salad greens and micro-greens, or for sprouting like alfalfa.

Varieties

This is another crop where F1 hybrids are generally superior, so open pollinated varieties are disappearing from seed catalogs. Some varieties have been bred to be less day length sensitive and these do better as a spring crop.

Chinese cabbage can be roughly divided into three types, though which group some varieties belong to is open to interpretation (the Asian Brassicas can be a confusing bunch to pigeonhole).

Cylindrical heading (Michihli) type:

Michihli - Long heads to 24″ tall.

Jade Pagoda F1 - Large heads, slow bolting (65 days).

Green Rocket F1 - Early maturing (70 days).

Monument F1 - Big heads (80 days).

Barrel heading type: These heading types do best in cool conditions.

Taiwan Express F1 - Fast growing.

Rubicon F1 - Fast growing (55 days) and slow to bolt.

Nozaki Early - Fast growing (50 days).

China Express F1 - Uniform and slow bolting.

Tropic Star F1 - Heat tolerant, may bolt in cool weather. (60 days).

Wong Bok - Prefers cool weather, grown fall / winter.

Non-heading type: These can stand more heat and cold than the heading types and are less prone to bolting. Most are open pollinated, but they are not always easy to find.

Beka Santoh - Very fast growing (25 days!).

Hiroshimana - Sown year round in milder areas (45 days).

Osaka Shirona - Tolerates hot and cold (40 - 60 days.

Shantung 4S F1 - Heat tolerant.

Tyfon - A cross between a Chinese cabbage and a turnip that looks like a mustard. It grows very quickly and is often used as a green manure, as well as a food crop. I like it a lot and use it as both salad greens and as a potherb. I have found it to be less temperamental than other types.

Kitchen use

These species are very commonly used in everyday Chinese cooking, for stir-fries, soups and more. They should only be very lightly cooked, by steaming or stir-frying (they are easy to over-cook). They are also good raw in salads and sandwiches.

Bok Choy / Pak Choy

Brassica rapa var chinensis

This ancient Chinese crop has been grown for at least 2000 years and probably a lot longer. Since that time its use has spread throughout most of temperate southeast Asia and to all parts of the world where Chinese people have settled.

Though closely related to Chinese cabbage (it is the same species) it has a very different growth habit. Instead of producing a dense head of leaves, it produces leaves with characteristic broad white or green midribs. These are responsible for it sometimes being called celery cabbage. Bok choy translates as white vegetable, which is also a reference to the stem.

Bok choy is easier to grow than the heading Chinese cabbages and deserves to be more widely used in this country. It is particularly useful for cool weather growing and can be an important part of the cool season vegetable garden.

This crop is somewhat temperamental and reacts in different ways to different circumstances. It is a good idea to experiment with varieties and planting times until you find a combination that works. Try planting it at regular intervals and record how it does in your journal.

Ease of growing:

Pak choy is cultivated in much the same way as Chinese cabbage and like that plant it grows best as a fall or over-wintering crop. It isn't as difficult as that plant, but it is still prone to bolting in warm weather (even though it is supposedly a biennial). I have had plants bolt within a month of planting.

Nutritional content This crop is exceptionally rich in beta-carotene (much more than cabbage), as well as vitamin C, K and several B's, calcium and iron. It also contains valuable antioxidants, including lutein, zeaxanthin, sulforaphane and isothiocyanates which give it powerful anti-cancer properties. As an energy source it contains about 60 calories per pound.

Climate: Pak choy is generally a cool season crop, doing best at 60 to 65°F. There are some varieties that are adapted to warm weather growing however.

About Pak Choy

Seed facts
Germ temp: 45 (60 - 70) 80°F
Germ time: 3 - 10 days
5 days at 50°F
3 days at 59°F
2 days at 68°F
1 day at 77°F * Optimum
Germination percentage: 75+
Seed viability: 5 - 9 yrs
Weeks to grow transplants: 4 - 6

Planning facts
Hardiness: Very hardy
Growing temp: 55(60 - 65) 70°F
Plants per person: 10
Plants per sq ft: 2
Transplants:
Start: 2 weeks before last frost
Plant out: 2 weeks after last frost
Direct sow: 4 wks before last frost
Sow a fall crop: 6 - 8 weeks before first fall frost
Days to harvest: 30 - 60 days

Harvest facts
Yield per plant: 1 - 2 lb
Yield per sq ft: 1 - 3 lb sq ft

Soil

pH 6.0 - 7.5

This hungry crop grows rapidly and doesn't have a very vigorous root system, so needs rich, moist, well-drained soil with lots of nitrogen. In poor soil it will often bolt very quickly.

Soil preparation: Incorporate 2″ of compost or aged manure into the top 6″ of soil before planting. If the soil is poor then throw in some organic fertilizer mix too. If it is acidic add lime to raise the pH.

Planning

Where: In cool weather put it in a sunny location where it will be sheltered from cold winds. In warm weather you might try growing it in light shade. Don't plant it where any other *Brassicas* were grown in the last three years.

When: Pak choy grows best in cool weather, so the best time to plant it depends upon where you live. In places with cool summers and mild winters it can be grown almost year round (though the long days of midsummer may cause it to bolt quickly). In hot climates it can only be grown in spring and fall (and maybe winter).

Spring: This plant can be made to work as a spring crop by starting it indoors and using an early maturing and bolt resistant variety.

Sow the seed 2 - 4 weeks before the last spring frost and plant out 2 weeks after it. It is hardy enough to be planted earlier than this (it can survive temperatures as low as 20°F), but there is a danger that it will bolt as soon as the weather warms up.

Fall: Bok choy does best as a fall crop, because it is less likely to bolt in the cooler and shorter days. It is started in late summer, when the weather starts to cool down (6 - 8 weeks before the first fall frost).

Succession sowing: This is a short lived crop, so succession sowing every couple of weeks is important. In most areas you should be able to get several harvests in a season.

Planting

Indoors: Bok choy can be started indoors and transplanted. It is usually grown in cell packs or soil blocks to minimize root disturbance. If the weather turns cold again after planting out, protect the young plants with cloches, until temperatures are above 50°F.

Outdoors: Bok choy seed germinates easily and the plants grow rapidly, so it is usually direct sown. Simply sow the seeds ½″ deep and about 3 - 4″ apart. Start thinning when the plants have 4 or 5 leaves. As plants get bigger you can harvest thin, to leave the plants at their final spacing. Use the thinnings in the kitchen.

Spacing: This depends upon the variety and type of crop required. It is commonly planted in offset rows across the bed 6 - 8″ apart each way (these can be thinned later if you need a wider spacing). Plants may grow anywhere from 4 - 24″ tall, depending upon the variety and growing conditions.

Intercropping: Pak choy is so fast growing it is frequently used as an intercrop between slower growing crops. In summer it is sometimes grown in the shade underneath tall crops such as corn.

Care

Bolting: Pak choy (and most other Asian Brassicas) are prone to bolting if they don't like the conditions. Sometimes they may bolt within a few weeks of planting, which can be frustrating.

Bolting may be caused by a variety of factors, take your choice from: too hot, tool cold, too dry, long day length, low soil fertility, exposure to cold when seedlings (this may be the most important factor), extreme weather, any interruption in growth (such as careless transplanting) or simply because you look at it the wrong way.

If a plant threatens to bolt prematurely, you can simply harvest what there is, or you can let it bolt and harvest the flower shoots for use like **choy sum** (see below). You could also let it produce seed and gather it for sprouting or replanting (if it is open pollinated and not a hybrid). If it isn't big enough to be worthwhile then compost it.

This tendency to bolt varies according to cultivar, some are much more prone to it than others. It is the reason these crops are most often grown as a fall or winter crop.

Weeds: Keep down weeds while the plants are young, as they don't compete for nutrients very well.

Feeding: If your soil isn't very fertile you should give the plants a feed of compost tea or liquid kelp 2 - 3 weeks after planting and again 3 weeks later.

Watering: This is a fairly shallow rooted crop and it must have evenly moist soil. If the plant gets water stressed it will usually react by bolting. Regular watering is particularly important in summer, as you want to delay the inevitable bolting as long as possible.

Mulch: Bok choy benefits from mulch, as it helps to keep down weeds, conserves moisture and keeps the plants cleaner. Give it 2 - 3″ of organic matter such as compost or aged manure.

Pests: Most of the pests and diseases that attack cabbages may also attack these plants (slugs, snails, aphids, caterpillars, cabbage root fly, cutworms, flea beetles, cucumber beetles. See **Cabbage** for more on these.

Diseases: Clubroot, bacterial rot and damping off may all affect it.

Harvesting

When: A nice thing about bok choy is that it can be harvested at almost any stage of growth.

When the plants are mature you can pick either individual leaves or cut whole plants. When plants are a few inches high you can cut the whole rosette of 5 - 6 leaves for use as baby greens. You can also use them as even smaller micro-greens (these are often grown under cover during the winter). How tasty they are will depend upon the variety and the growing conditions.

How: You can harvest individual leaves, but they tend to be quite small so it is more common to harvest whole plants. Simply uproot every other plant in a bed, leaving the rest to grow bigger.

You can also harvest by cutting off the plants a couple of inches above soil level. With luck the remaining plant will re-grow and give you another crop. This can be especially useful in winter when it may be hard to get another crop established.

Flower stem: When the plant inevitably bolts and sends up a flower stalk you can eat it. Just harvest it before the flower buds open and use it like broccoli. Of course this is only worthwhile if the plants have reached a reasonable size. See **Choy sum** below for more on using these.

Storage: The plants can be stored for a few days in a plastic bag in the fridge. In China the leaves are often dried for use in soups.

Seed saving: This is done in pretty much the same way as for turnip. It is cross-pollinated by insects and will cross with any other *B. rapa* crop (which includes turnip and broccoli raab) as well as other Chinese cabbage varieties. You should save the seed from at least six plants to ensure some genetic variability.

Six of these plants can produce a lot of seed, which gives you plenty for growing cut and come again baby greens or micro-greens, making mustard, or for sprouting like alfalfa.

Unusual growing ideas

Multiple stages of use: A single planting can be eaten at various stages of growth. To do this it is sown quite densely (1″ apart) and then gradually harvest thinned.

The first thinning takes place after all the seeds have germinated and evens out the plants. These seedlings are the first harvest and can be used in salads or cooked.

Thin the plants again (2 - 3″ apart) when they only have a couple of leaves and no thickened midrib and are 3 - 4″ tall. These are good raw in salads or can be cooked as baby greens. They are so good at this stage, that the plants are sometimes grown purely as a cut and come again crop.

When the larger seedlings reach 5 - 6″ tall and have 5 or 6 leaves, thin them yet again by cutting the whole plants. This time to their final spacing of 4 - 8″. These larger thinnings are also good to eat.

The next harvest consists of the mature, fully grown plants.

If any plants bolt prematurely you can eat the flower stems like broccoli (before the flowers open). If the flowers have already opened, you can let them produce seed (if open pollinated, rather than F1 hybrids) and start the cycle all over again.

Baby greens: These are used when 3 - 4″ tall and only take 2 - 3 weeks to be ready for harvest.

Containers: Pak choy is a good crop for growing in containers, either for full grown plants, baby greens or microgreens.

Poly tunnels: Bok choy is one of the best crops for winter growing in poly tunnels or cold frames. They are able to tolerate wider daily temperature swings (warm days and cold nights) than most other crops. They also do well with less light (it even makes the leaves more tender) and there are fewer pests at this time.

Varieties

There are quite a few varieties available and they vary considerably in their tolerance for heat and cold and when they grow best. Success often depends upon planting the right variety for the circumstances, so it pays to experiment a little. Some varieties are intended for planting at certain times (warm weather, cold weather) and don't do well if planted at another time.

The bok choys are usually divided into three groups; white stem, green stem and baby bok choy. The babies could also go in the green or white stem categories too.

White stem

Joi choi F1 - Heat and cold tolerant, productive (50 days)

White Stem - Has a (surprisingly enough) white stem

Long White Petiole - The standard type (45 days)

Green stem

Long Green Petiole - Tolerates heat, very fast (30 days)

Taiwan bok choy - Tender, leafy and fast (35 days)

Shanghai - Heat tolerant (40 - 50 days)

Hanakan F1 - Tolerates heat, but not cold (45 days)

Tai Sai

Baby

These varieties are smaller, more tender and contain less stalk (as I imagine a baby would) so are perhaps more useful in the kitchen. They include:

Red Choi F1 - Used in salad mixes

Mei Qing choi F1 - Tolerates heat and cold (40 - 50 days)

Snowman F1 - Heat and cold tolerant (30 days)

Toy Choy F1 - Small and fast (35 days)

Kitchen use: In Asia these vegetables are usually cooked by steaming, stir frying or adding to soups, etc. Some of the milder and more tender ones can be added to salads.

In Korea bok choy is a staple for making fermented kimchee.

Other important Asian Brassicas

Tatsoi (Rosette Pak Choy)

(*Brassica rapa var. rosularis*)

This is a miniature version of bok choy and produces a rosette of thick, shiny succulent leaves. These have beautiful sculptural forms which makes them quite attractive. Unfortunately their ornamental value is limited by their short lifespan (they mature in 35 – 50 days). Tatsoi is grown in the same way as pak choy, but because it is smaller it is slightly less demanding of fertile soil. It also tends to bolt quickly in spring and does best as a fall crop.

Tatsoi is very tolerant of cold weather and can survive down to 15 or 20˚F. Some varieties are tolerant of heat and slower to bolt.

Tatsoi is used at the same stages and in the same ways as pak choy. The leaves are so small they are often cooked whole without chopping.

Choy sum (*Brassica rapa*, var. *parachinensis*)

This fast growing and vigorous vegetable is very important in southern China. It is essentially a type of bok choy that is grown specifically for its flower stalks (though the leaves and stems are eaten too). Choy means vegetable and sum means flower stem or heart. It is tolerant of low temperatures and is grown as a fall or winter crop.

The flowering stems are harvested when the buds appear, by cutting or breaking them at the point where the stem gets fibrous. After you harvest the first flower stalk, it will send up several more in succession.

The young stalks and flowers are very tender and excellent for stir-fries, though they are also usually mild enough for use in salads.

Similar and related species:

Yu Choy - Green choy sum
Used as above.

Flowering pak choi (*Brassica rapa*, var. *chinensis*)
Used as above.

Hon-Tsai-Tai (*Brassica rapa*, var. *purpurea*)
This is a purple variety of choy sum and its purple color intensifies as the temperature decreases. It is used as above too.

Komatsuna (*B. rapa* var *perviridis* (or *B. rapa* var *komatsuna*)

This Japanese plant is sometimes known as spinach mustard (or mustard spinach) because it is used like spinach, though it isn't related. Joy Larkcom, the English edible gardening expert (and my favorite garden writer) said in her fantastic book Asian Vegetables that she was tempted to give this the most underrated vegetable award

Komatsuna is an easy plant to grow and deserves to be much more widely used. It grows rapidly (it matures in as little as 35 days), is very productive and has a nice mild flavor.

This is also one of the most cold tolerant of all vegetables, growing through the winter in mild climates and often surviving under the snow in colder ones. It does very well as a winter crop in greenhouses or poly tunnels.

This plant also has some tolerance of warm weather and in some areas they can be grown year round.

Though it is often sold as simply komatsuna, there are a few distinct varieties available, including:
Summerfest

Red komatsuna

Mizuna (*Brassica rapa var japonica* or (*B. rapa var nipposinica*)

Mizuna is a very distinctive plant that forms a large rosette of divided feathery looking leaves. It is thought to have originated in China, though it is most important as a crop in Japan.

Like bok choy it can be used at any stage from seedling to flowering shoots. It is milder than bok choy however and in this country it is most often used as a salad plant (it is found in most commercial salad mixes). It is also good cooked.

Mizuna is a versatile plant, hardy enough (to 10˚F) be grown as a cold weather vegetable, but also tolerant of warm weather (to 90˚F) and more resistant to bolting than some of its cousins.

It isn't very fussy about the soil, though it should be consistently moist. It is also quite shade tolerant (especially in summer). It stays edible for a long time and doesn't get tough or highly pungent, as many Brassicas do. These virtues put mizuna on my list of indispensable, low work green vegetables and I grow it all the time.

Though mizuna is usually found as simply "mizuna", I have noticed several distinct types, some are more tender and mildly flavored than others. Some have slender stems and some have thicker white stems reminiscent of bok choy.

Mibuna (*Brassica rapa var japonica or (B. rapa nipposinica*)

The name may sound similar to mizuna and it is a close relative, but it looks quite different with its spoon shaped leaves. It is another vigorous and easy to grow plant and works well as a home garden crop.

Mibuna isn't quite as tolerant of temperature extremes as mizuna, disliking hot weather and only tolerating cold down to 20˚F. It is usually grown as a fall or winter crop.

Carrot

Daucus carota var sativus

This cool season biennial was probably first domesticated somewhere in the region of Afghanistan. It didn't get its familiar orange color until it arrived in Holland however. As you probably know the orange color is caused by carotene (a precursor of vitamin A), so the redder the root the more nutritious it is.

Crop value: Carrots are a great crop for those seeking to be more food self-sufficient. They are very nutritious, don't take up much space, are highly productive, relatively fast growing, store well and can be left in the ground for months. You may also be surprised to find that your home grown carrots generally taste better than those you can buy (or maybe you wouldn't.)

Ease of growing: Carrots are fairly easy to grow if you give them what they need. For best results you want them to grow quickly, without any interruption in growth. Good soil and prompt weeding and thinning are the keys to growing good carrots. Take care of these and you should succeed, neglect them and you may well fail.

Nutritional content: Carrots are famous for their high content of beta carotene, which the body converts into vitamin A (this is not only an important vitamin, but also a powerful antioxidant). They are also a good source of potassium and contain calcium pectate, which can lower blood cholesterol. Eating 4 raw carrots daily has been known to reduce blood cholesterol level by 10% in only 4 weeks.

As an energy source carrots contain about 190 calories per pound.

Climate: Carrot is a cool season crop, growing best at 60 - 75˚F and able to tolerate some frost. The sweetest carrots are produced when days are warm and nights are cool, as this encourages the storage of sugar in the root. They will grow well enough in warmer weather, but on warm nights (above 70˚F) the plant simply uses up the sugar in growth and doesn't store it in the root (so it won't be as sweet).

About Carrot

Seed facts
Germ temp: 45 (60 - 70) 85˚F
Germ time: 7 - 21 days
50 days / 41˚F
17 days / 50˚F
10 days / 59˚F
7 days / 68˚F
6 days / 77˚F * Optimum
6 days / 86˚F
Seed viability: 2 - 5 years
Germination percentage: 50%+

Planning facts
Hardiness: Hardy
Growing temp: 55 (60 - 70) 75˚F
Plants per person: 30
Plants per sq ft: 16
Direct sow: 2 - 4 weeks before last frost
Fall crop: Plant 8 - 12 wks before first fall frost
Days to harvest: 55 - 90 days
Height: 12″
Width: 12 - 18″

Harvest facts
Yield per plant: 2 - 6 oz
Yield per sq ft: 1 - 2 lb per sq ft

Soil

pH 6.0 (6.5) 7.0

The soil makes a big difference in how well carrot will grow (how big it gets and how sweet and tender it is). The most critical factor is porosity; a loose soil can increase the size of the roots by as much as 100%. The ideal soil is a light, humus rich, well-aerated, well-drained sandy loam, that is free of stones and fairly neutral. They don't like acid soil, heavy clay or compacted soils of any kind.

Soil preparation: Prepare the soil by loosening it to a depth of 10″ (minimum) and removing any large stones and other debris (these may cause forking). Incorporate organic matter in the form of compost or aged manure. You should also add wood ashes or greensand (for potassium), colloidal phosphate (for phosphorus) and kelp (for trace elements). Or to simplify things you could just use a complete fertilizer mix.

Carrot isn't a very heavy feeder and too much nitrogen may be a problem by stimulating top growth, at the expense of root growth.

Though aged manure is good for growing carrots, you should never use fresh manure, as it may cause them to fork and grow hairy feeder roots. If you only have fresh manure, then add it the previous fall so it can age over the winter.

If your soil is heavy, or compacted, the best solution is to double dig and incorporate lots of organic matter and then make raised beds. If this is too much work, you could grow your carrots in narrow trenches, filled with a special soil mix. If even this is too much, you could use a short stubby variety.

An easy way to ensure a good soil for carrots is to precede them with potatoes. The soil will have been heavily amended and deeply dug and any organic matter will have aged nicely. They can also follow Brassicas, or any other crop that was heavily manured.

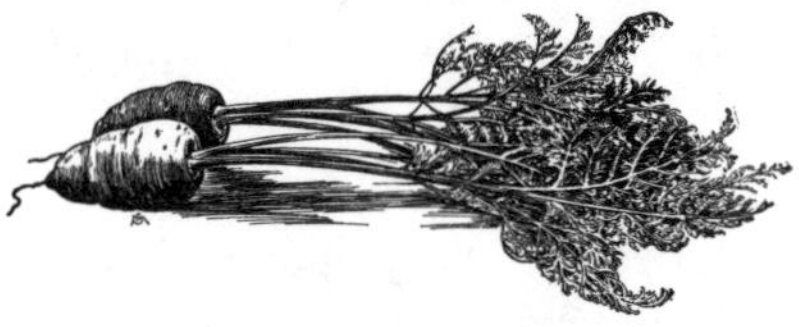

Planning

Where: Carrots need full sun for best production, though are a fairly adaptable crop and may do okay in part shade. They also like a fairly warm soil.

Crop rotation: Don't plant them where any member of the *Apiaceae* family (celery, parsnip, parsley) has grown in the last 3 years.

When: It is possible to have carrots year round if you plan carefully. They prefer fairly cool growing conditions and the conventional wisdom says they get bitter or acrid in hot weather (above 80°F). A lot depends upon the variety however.

Spring: Plant your first carrots as soon as the soil is ready to be worked in spring (it should be at least 45°F), which may be 2 - 4 weeks before the last spring frost. You can start them a few weeks earlier, if you plant them under cloches. Just be careful they don't get so big they are vernalized.

Autumn: Fall carrots should be sown from mid to late summer (a minimum of 8 - 10 weeks before the first frost) to give them plenty of time to mature before it gets too cold.

Winter: In mild climates carrots will grow right through the winter. They must be started early though, so they are almost mature by the time the first frost hits. They will then continue growing slowly all winter. If they are too small when cold weather arrives, they will simply sit in the ground until spring and then bolt.

Make one large planting for winter use, as you will be eating them for months.

Succession sowing: Carrots are in demand for the kitchen at all times, so it's a good idea to succession sow them regularly, every 4 - 6 weeks. They stay in the ground in usable condition for a while, especially in cool weather.

Spacing: The right spacing for growing carrots depends upon the fertility of the soil, the type of carrot and the size of the root you want (a wider spacing results in larger roots).

Beds:

5″ (poor soil)

3″ (good soil)

1½″ (excellent soil)

1″ (Baby carrots)

Rows: If you are planting in rows, you should sow the seeds about ½″ apart, in rows 18 - 24″ apart. These are then gradually thinned to a spacing of 3″ or so.

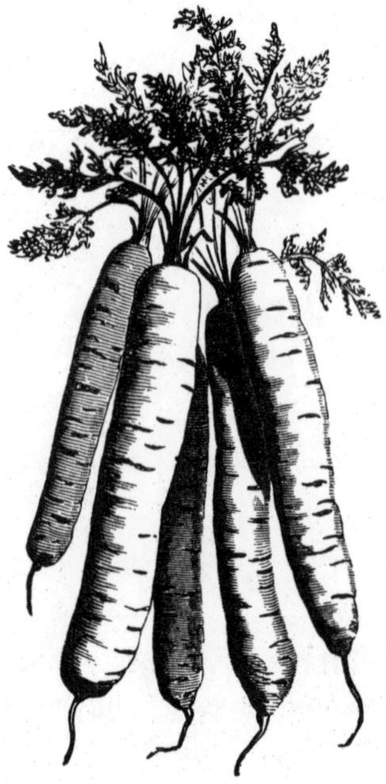

Planting

Indoors: Carrots are quite hardy and don't like transplanting, so starting indoors isn't even worth trying. If you insist on trying, then use cell packs or soil blocks to minimize root disturbance.

Outdoors: A seedbed for carrots should have a fairly fine tilth and no large stones or other debris. The seeds are pretty slow to germinate (1 - 3 weeks), which means you have to keep the soil moist for quite a long period. To make things worse, by the time the seeds germinate there is usually a healthy crop of weeds to deal with. See below for ways to handle them.

Broadcasting: You can broadcast the seeds ½″ apart and then cover them with a thin ⅛ - ¼″ layer of soil. If your topsoil has a tendency to crust, you may want to use a mix of sifted soil and compost.

The main thing to remember when broadcasting is to sow the seeds at the right density. Beginners usually plant too thickly, which wastes seed and necessitates some tedious hand thinning.

Sowing carrot seed is somewhat tricky because it is so small and light. You might try mixing it with sand, to make it easier to distribute it evenly. Pelleted seed is supposed to make it easier to get the right spacing, but I have never used it.

Rows: I favor planting short rows of carrots across the bed. It wastes less seed, they are easier to thin and it is easier to deal with weeds.

Scrape ¼ - ½″ deep furrows with a hoe and sow the seed at roughly half the desired spacing. Then close up the furrows, preferably with the same soil and compost mix used to cover the broadcast seeds.

Some people mix a little radish seed in with the carrot seed, to mark the rows and break up any soil crust.

Care of seed beds: It is important to take good care of the seed beds and young seedlings, because (as with humans) the early days can have a big impact on the ultimate harvest.

Watering: It is crucial that the seedbed be watered regularly until all of the seeds have germinated. A general rule is to allow 50% of the surface of the bed to dry out before watering it again.

Sprinkle or spray the bed lightly, if you flood it with water you may slosh the light seeds around. This will result in an uneven stand, with bare patches and very dense patches.

In hot weather you can reduce the frequency of watering (and save water) by temporarily covering the soil with burlap or cardboard. This keeps the soil cool and slows evaporation. Of course it must be removed as soon as the seedlings begin to emerge (ideally just before).

Pre-emergence weeding: Because carrot seedlings take so long to emerge, you usually have a problem with weed seedlings. There are a few ways to avoid a lot of tedious hand weeding.

A few days before you estimate the seedlings will start to emerge, you can lightly scrape a spring rake across the bed to kill any plants that have already emerged. This will give your soon-to-emerge seedlings a slight head start on the weeds. You can get a precise idea of the best time to do this by planting a sample patch of seed a few days before the main patch. As soon as the sample patch starts to germinate you should act.

Another useful pre-emergence weeding technique is flame weeding. The only problem with this is that you need a special flame-weeding torch (and fuel).

The process is simple enough, a couple of days before the seedlings emerge, you quickly (you don't want to burn the soil surface) move a flame across the bed, heating and killing all of the newly emerged weed seedlings. A significant benefit of this method is that the soil isn't disturbed, so no new weed seeds are brought to the surface, where they would germinate.

You can also sow seeds under paper tape. The seed is sown in rows in the usual way. The rows are then covered with a strip of opaque paper, such as cash register or drywall tape. This is weighted down with handfuls of soil to keep it in place. A day or so before you expect the seedlings to emerge, you remove the paper, which exposes any weed seedlings that have already germinated. These will be elongated and chlorotic from the darkness and will die when exposed to strong sunlight. This leaves a weed free strip of soil for your seedlings to emerge into. The areas between the strips are hoed in the usual way.

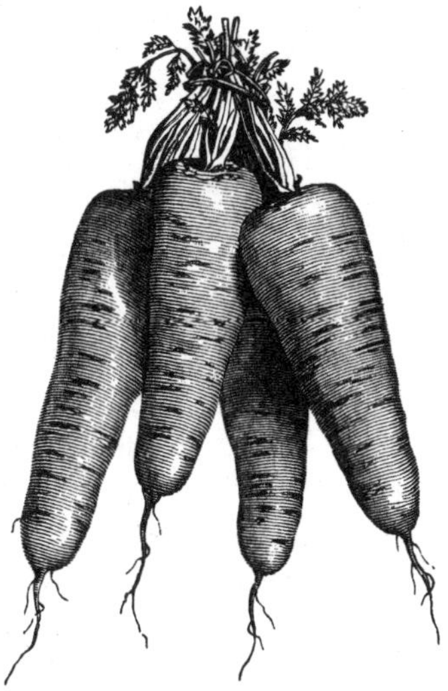

Care

Thinning: After all the seedlings have germinated and are growing well, you will have to thin them. If they are packed too closely together they simply won't produce swollen roots.

The earlier you thin (and weed) the easier it will be. The initial thinning is done when the seedlings are about 2″ tall and should leave the plants about an inch apart. If you have a large area to thin, this can be done with a wire rake (carefully!) Simply rake out excess plants.

A second thinning (and weeding) should be done 2 - 4 weeks later. This time you thin to the desired spacing by hand. Some gardeners leave this last thinning until the carrots have begun to size up and then eat them. However this may damage the remaining plants, or attract the dreaded carrot rust fly.

It is important to remove all of the uprooted plants from the area after thinning, as the smell of damaged foliage can attract the carrot rust fly. Ideally you thin on cool cloudy days, or in late evening and water afterward to reduce the smell of carrot.

Weeding: If weeds are not removed promptly they will quickly smother the sparsely leafed seedlings. Your first priority must be to weed (and thin) the newly emerged plants. Weeds will have to be removed by hand from broadcast beds. Row plantings can be hoed if widely spaced, though some hand weeding is usually needed also.

Water: Carrots need a steady and even supply of moisture for good growth. Don't let the soil dry out.

Too little water may result in excessively hairy roots (produced to search for water), or woody roots with marked rings.

Too much water can encourage excessive top growth and result in poorly flavored roots.

You might want to give the plants extra water when the roots start to size up, as this can boost yields considerably. Be careful however, as too much water after a dry spell can initiate a sudden spurt in growth, which may cause the roots to split.

Feeding: If the soil is poor you may want to give them a liquid feed of kelp or compost tea after all the plants have emerged, and then again a month later.

Mulch: If you are growing in rows a mulch is beneficial to conserve moisture and keep down weeds. It also covers the shoulders of the root, preventing them turning green and inedible from exposure to light.

In cold weather a thick mulch may also help to prevent them being heaved by frost.

Problems

Root fail to size up: You may have tried to grow carrots and ended up with lush foliage, but only small spindly roots. This happens when the plant is growing in less than ideal conditions. It produces enough food to survive, but doesn't make enough of a surplus to store in the root. This may be caused by competition from weeds or other carrots (you neglected to thin sufficiently), insufficient light or water, or from an inadequate supply of nutrients.

Splitting: This is usually caused by irregular watering, too wet, too dry, too wet.

Forking: If you have grown carrots for any length of time, you have probably harvested plants that look vaguely like a human pair of legs (sometimes with other humorously shaped appendages attached). This is known as forking (for obvious reasons) and occurs when the tip of the primary root is damaged in some way (often by contact with fresh manure, insects or stones in the soil). This forces the plant to replace it with two (or more) new growing points and so it forks.

Green shoulders: If the top of the carrot sticks out of the ground and is exposed to sunlight it will turn green and inedible. You can keep this to a minimum by pulling soil up on to the crown of the plant. You can also use mulch to cover the shoulders.

Bolting: Carrots are biennials and don't naturally flower until their second year. However they may bolt if they get vernalized. This happens when a root is sufficiently large (more than ¼″ diameter) and is exposed to temperatures below 50˚F for a period of two weeks or more. When warm days arrive it thinks winter is over and flowers.

Pests

Carrot Rust Fly (*Psila rosae*): This is the worst pest of carrots. The larvae (small maggots) tunnel into the root, causing rust colored lesions and rendering the root inedible. In some areas they make it almost impossible to grow carrots without protection. In others it isn't a problem at all.

The first line of defense against this pest is hygiene. The flies are said to be able to detect the smell of damaged foliage from more than a mile away. Keep thinning and weeding (which bruises the foliage) to a minimum and never leave the foliage lying on the ground.

If this pest is really bad in your area it's not a good idea to leave the remains of a carrot crop in the ground right through the winter. It can mean a big increase in the incidence of carrot rust fly. In such situations you should dig and compost (or eat) old carrots.

If the fly is severe some kind of barrier is probably the best way to go. Row covers are the commonest solution to this problem, but it's said that a simple plastic screen, 30 - 36″ high, around the plants will work just as well. Apparently the flies always stay close to the ground and will try to go around the screen, but they won't go over it (so long as the bed is no more than 36″ wide).

There are usually two generations of flies each year, the first in late spring and another in late summer. It is possible to avoid them both by carefully timing the planting and harvesting.

Four rows of onions, to one row of carrots, is said to disguise their smell, as is a mulch of fresh grass, or fresh sawdust.

There are now some carrot fly resistant varieties available. Apparently these work best if some non-resistant carrots are sown next to them, to act as a trap crop.

Other pests: Aphids, blister beetles, nematodes, carrot weevils, wireworms. We all know that cartoon rabbits love carrots; well gophers, groundhogs and deer do too.

Diseases: A number of diseases are occasionally a problem, including: leaf blight, downy mildew, aster yellows, rust and scab.

Nutrient deficiency: A deficiency of boron or manganese may cause the center of the carrot to turn black. You could treat both of these with a foliar feed of compost tea.

Harvesting

When: You can start pulling the roots as soon as they are large enough to be worthwhile. The larger rooted plants tend to give themselves away by having darker foliage. You can also look at the size of the orange shoulders in the ground. The main crop will be ready in anywhere from 60 days onward, depending on the variety

In the case of carrots, small isn't necessarily beautiful. Small carrots may be tender, but larger ones are sweeter, better flavored and have a deep orange color, which indicates that they are rich in carotene.

The best time to harvest carrots for maximum tenderness is when their early rapid growth starts to slow down. As the roots get much over an inch in diameter they may start to get woody (though this depends on the variety). This is why they are commonly succession sown.

Immature carrots generally have little flavor because they haven't had the chance to store much sugar. They can also be quite acrid because the aromatic terpenes (which give carrots much of their flavor) develop before the sugars. Commercial baby carrots are really just varieties with naturally small roots, planted closely together. They are still harvested when mature (unless they are the commercial fake baby carrots that are carved from larger cull carrots).

How: If you plan on harvesting a large quantity of roots, you should water them beforehand to loosen the soil and making pulling easier. In light soil you can simply pull up the roots by gently tugging on the tops. If you do this in heavy soil the tops will often break off, in which case you should loosen them with a fork before pulling. If you want to store the roots it is important to treat them gently, as any damage will encourage rot.

The usual way to harvest carrots is to start at one end of the bed and work your way down (you might also keep the bed protected with row covers).

Any carrot debris remaining after the harvest should be removed and composted. Don't leave it on the ground near the plants, as the smell of the damaged foliage may attract the carrot rust fly.

After harvest you should remove all but 1″ of the tops; they may look picturesque but they drain moisture from the roots, causing them to go flabby.

If you are going to store the roots for any length of time, you should leave them in the sun for several hours to kill the root hairs (not too long though). Select only perfect roots for storage and don't wash them. Damaged roots don't store well and should be used promptly.

Storage: Carrots usually deteriorate in one of three ways, they either dry out, sprout or rot. If you store your carrots in a cold (below 40˚F), humid place the first two won't be a problem. Rot most often occurs when the skin is damaged, which allows decay causing organisms to enter. The living carrot has the ability to heal minor wounds and prevent rot, though this declines with age. The rot factor is the reason it is so important to separate out damaged roots and not try to store them.

The best place to store carrots is in the ground. They keep better and it is a lot less work. In mild climates they will continue to grow through the winter and slowly get bigger. You just harvest them as needed. In colder climates the tops will die back when cold weather hits. When this happens cover them with 6 - 12″ of mulch (this needs to be deep to prevent the ground from freezing).

The roots actually get sweeter in cold weather as some of their starch is converted into sugar. You must dig them before growth starts again in spring, as this will make them woody and inedible. If you can't store them, then at least use them for juice, rather than wasting them

Mice can sometimes be a problem with in-ground storage (especially under mulch). If this is a problem you might try covering the bed with a wire mesh screen, before laying down the mulch.

You can also store carrots for up to 6 months in a root cellar, at 32 to 40˚F and 90% humidity (their vitamin A content actually increases in storage for several months). Put the roots in a garbage can, or a wooden box, making alternate layers of damp sand and carrots (if you don't have sand you could also use damp sawdust or peat moss) Make sure the roots don't touch each other, or they may rot. Also keep them away from apples, which emit ethylene gas and can spoil their flavor.

You can store carrots in a plastic bag in the fridge for several weeks. They can be canned or dried for longer term storage.

Unusual growing ideas

Winter Carrots: French market gardeners used to grow carrots right through the winter in the harsh climate around Paris. They did it by planting them on hotbeds of warm manure, covered with cold frames.

Giant carrots: If you want to grow a giant carrot (why?) do it in a section of 4″ drainpipe, filled with a specially prepared mix of compost, soil and sand. Water it frequently.

Containers: Carrots can do well in a container, so long as it is deep enough (twice the depth of the root), you use the right (short) variety and you keep the soil moist.

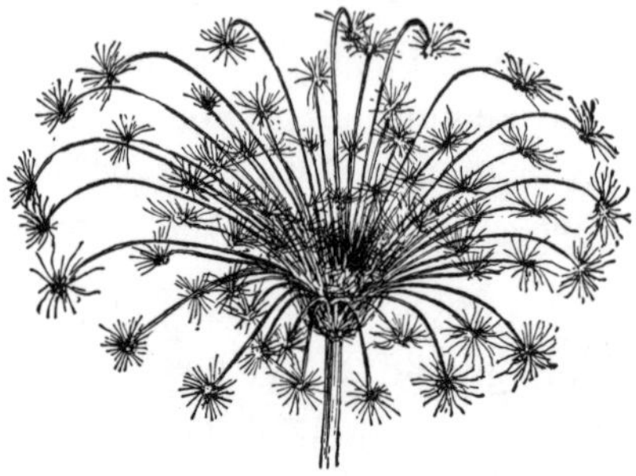

Seed saving: Carrot is a biennial, so stores food in its first year and flowers and produces seed the following year. In harsh climates you will have to protect the roots over the winter, either in the ground or indoors. Replant them in the spring and wait for them to flower.

You have to be careful which roots you use for seed production and what pollinates them. Choose your very best roots and make sure they pollinate each other. The flowers are cross-pollinated by insects and will cross with any other carrots (or the very common wild carrot or Queen Annes Lace) within a half mile. This is important, when I neglected to do it I ended up with a whole range of root colors from orange to yellow to white!

Don't gather seed from early flowering plants, uproot and get rid of them before they have a chance to pollinate the rest. You don't want to create an early bolting strain.

The best seed is produced on the primary umbel, which is the first to ripen. The second umbel is pretty good too, so take it from these two. When the seed heads are ripe, cut them and leave in a paper grocery bag to dry thoroughly.

Varieties

Size and shape are the most obvious differences between carrot varieties, with some producing 2″ spheres and others growing into huge tapered cylinders 10″ or more in length. There are other differences too, some red varieties are extremely rich in vitamin A, while others may be purple, yellow or even white. There are now quite a few hybrid carrot varieties, bred for uniformity, high carotene content, resistance to carrot rust fly, or for extra sweetness.

The variety you choose will depend upon the soil, climate and the time of year you are planting. Generally the larger types need looser and deeper soil, while the shorter ones can do well in more compact soils. Shorter ones also mature more quickly. Some varieties do much better in cold, others do better in heat, some store better in the ground.

The most important factor in growing sweet carrots is genetic; some varieties are naturally much sweeter than others. If you want to grow sweet and tasty carrots, you are much more likely to be successful if you start with a sweet and tasty variety. A high quality cultivar, can also help you to overcome some of the other problems associated with growing carrots.

Types of carrot

Nantes

These long cylindrical varieties with blunt ends are some of the best flavored and textured carrots. They are low in terpenes, high in sugar and don't develop a woody core. They are the best carrots for eating raw, but generally don't keep very well. They are easy to grow and quite fast maturing, though they do need a fertile soil.

Touchon - My favorite variety, sweet, tender, very finely flavored and doesn't get woody.

Bolero F1 - A good hybrid carrot.

Merida - A bolt resistant overwintering carrot that can be planted in fall, for harvesting the following summer.

Scarlet Nantes.- The classic Nantes variety.

Danvers

These carrots have a tapering conical shape. They are quite sweet, but have a fibrous core which makes them better for cooking than eating raw. They do well in shallow, heavy or poor soils.

Danvers Half Long - Fairly short, it does well in shallow soil.

Chantenay

These are short and conical with a broad shoulder. They can be quite sweet and tasty, but they are best used when young as they may develop a woody core with age. They are generally better cooked, rather than eaten raw.

These types aren't as fussy about soil as the Nantes and Imperator types and do better in heavy, stony and cold soil. They over-winter well in the ground and store well out of the ground.

Kuroda - Sweet, crisp and quite heat tolerant (73 days)

Red Cored Chantenay - A French classic with deep orange roots

Imperator: These long tapered carrots are bred for commercial use and are the carrots most often found in supermarkets. They store well and can be very tasty, but tend to be tougher than some other types. They do best in a deep, sandy soil and can get quite big. You need to cultivate the soil deeply when growing these types. They are not a good choice for heavy or rocky soils.

Gold Pak - Sweet and tender.

Baby: Baby carrots aren't really young carrots, they are simply varieties that don't grow very big. They may be elongated or round in shape. Their flavor is quite variable, some are good, some not so good. They don't need a very good soil, so are often used where the soil is shallow, heavy or not very fertile (they are also the best types for container growing). They don't store well.

Thumbelina - Sweet and tender.

High vitamin A: There are now quite a few of these.

Juwarot - Sweet, crisp and tasty.

A-Plus F1 - Imperator type, sweet.

Healthmaster F1 - Deep red color.

Beta III - Deep red and sweet.

Carrot Fly resistant: These are a fairly new innovation.

Flyaway F1 - Nantes Type, sweet
Resistafly F1 - Nantes type, sweet, stores well

Kitchen use

In my house no one wants to eat cooked carrots, so they are almost always eaten raw.

Chemicals called terpenes give the carrot its characteristic flavor, but they need to be balanced with sugars to make carrots that are good for eating raw. Too many terpenes and too little sugar makes for unpleasantly aromatic and acrid roots. Terpenes are broken down during cooking though, which is why cooked carrots are sweeter.

If the top of the carrot is green from exposure to light, just cut it off.

Roasted roots

A simple peasant dish

½ lb carrots
4 potatoes
1 celeriac (peeled)
1 rutabaga (peeled)
1 parsnip
1 large onion
1 turnip
½ cup olive oil
Salt
Pepper
1 tsp. paprika
¼ tsp. dill

Wash the vegetables and chop the potatoes and carrots into 1″ pieces. Chop the rest of the vegetables into smaller ½″ pieces. Put the olive oil in a roasting pan and pre-heat in a 450°F oven. Then add the chopped vegetables and seasonings and stir to coat vegetables evenly. Bake for 45 minutes, stirring occasionally to coat the pieces with oil and prevent them drying out and burning.

This is just a basic recipe and you can add lots of other stuff (garlic, green onions, tomato, mushrooms for the last 15 minutes, to cook and add flavor.

Cauliflower

Brassica oleracea botrytis group

Introduction: The cauliflower is sometimes considered to be the most refined member of the Brassica family, I don't quite know what that means, but I do know it is the most temperamental to grow. It probably originated somewhere in the Eastern Mediterranean.

Ease of growing: The cauliflower isn't a very forgiving crop and must have exactly the right growing conditions if it is to do well. It doesn't like extreme heat or cold, it doesn't like being too wet or too dry, it doesn't like poor soil and it doesn't like to sit indoors waiting to be planted out!

Cauliflower is even harder to grow organically, as it is vulnerable to the legion of pests that attack the cabbages. However if you give it exactly what it wants and time it right, then it isn't that hard to grow successfully.

Crop value: Cauliflower isn't very productive (unlike broccoli it only produces one head) or particularly nutritious, so it isn't a very important crop (unless you like it of course, which I don't particularly). They contain about 110 calories per pound.

Climate: More than almost any other common crop, cauliflower is sensitive to the weather and it will simply bolt if it doesn't like it. For this reason it is important to choose a variety that is suited to the climate and time of year.

Cauliflower needs a moist and mild climate (ideally with temperatures in the 60's) and won't tolerate drought, heat or extreme cold. Young plants will tolerate a light frost and bigger plants are moderately cold tolerant, though the head can be damaged if it freezes. Hot weather can cause plants to bolt prematurely or become unpleasantly flavored.

Nutritional content: A good source of vitamin C and potassium. It also contains the same valuable anti-cancer phytonutrients as the other Brassicas.

About Cauliflower

Seed facts
Germ temp: 45 (55 - 85) 85°F
Germ time: 4 - 10 days
20 days / 50°F
10 days / 59°F
6 days / 68°F
5 days / 77°F * Optimum
5 days / 86°F
Seed viability: 5 - 10 years
Germination percentage: 75+
Weeks to grow transplant: 5 - 6

Planning facts
Hardiness: Half hardy
Growing temp: 45 (60 - 65) 75°F
Plants per person: 5
Plants per sq ft: ½
Spring crop:
Start: 8 - 10 weeks before last frost
Plant out: 4 weeks before the last frost date
Direct sow 2 wks before last frost
Fall crop:
Start: 12 - 16 weeks before first fall frost
Plant out: 8 weeks before the first fall frost
Days to harvest: 50 - 256 days
45 - 200 days from transplant

Harvest facts
Yield per plant: 1 - 2 lb
Yield per sq ft: ½ - 1 lb sq ft

Soil

pH 6.0 (6.5-6.8) 7.4

Cauliflower must have rapid and uninterrupted growth if it is to perform well and for this it needs fertile soil. It isn't particular as to what type of soil it grows in, so long as it is fertile and moisture retentive, with lots of organic matter. It doesn't mind a fairly alkaline soil and this discourages clubroot, a serious pest of Brassicas in some areas. It doesn't like saline soil and is sensitive to a deficiency of micronutrients, especially molybdenum and boron.

Soil Preparation: Cauliflower likes nitrogen and potassium, Prepare the soil by digging deeply and incorporating 2″ of compost or aged manure. If you are organized you could add fresh manure the previous fall. It also does well if planted 2 weeks after incorporating a winter cover crop.

If the soil isn't very fertile, add colloidal phosphate (for phosphorus), wood ashes (for potassium) and kelp meal (to supply trace elements). Or put a handful of complete organic fertilizer in each planting hole.

More than most Brassicas, cauliflower doesn't like acid soils, as they can encourage clubroot and make boron less available. Add lime if necessary, preferably dolomitic lime, as this supplies useful magnesium as well as calcium.

Planning

Where: Cauliflower needs quite a lot of space for the amount it produces, so it isn't a very good crop for small gardens. It also needs at least 6 hours of sun daily. Any less than this will result in smaller heads, slower maturation and possibly leggy plants.

Crop rotation: Don't plant where another Brassica has been grown in the previous 3 years.

When: Cauliflower needs quite a long period (2 months or more) of cool weather to mature (it heads up best at 60 - 70°F). At the same time it is more sensitive to cold than most Brassicas and small plants can be injured by moderate frost.) This limits where and when it can be grown.

Cauliflower does well in the Pacific northwest as a spring-sown crop, but in most areas spring is too short. In mild winter areas it does well as a fall / winter crop, but isn't hardy enough to survive colder winters. In most places it does best as a fall crop. This is usually easier and results in larger heads.

Spring: Spring cauliflower has to be started early, so the weather will still be fairly cool when it matures. This means that there is some risk that the young plants may be damaged by frost.

Start the seed indoors 8 - 10 weeks before the last frost date and plant out 4 - 5 weeks before the last frost date (the soil should be at least 50°F and preferably higher). It needs to be planted early, because it needs a long period of cool weather to mature.

If the weather turns cold after planting, you should protect the plants with cloches or cold frames until it warms up.

Summer: In mild climates, cauliflower can be planted in spring, to mature as a summer crop.

Fall: Fall cauliflowers tends to do better than a spring crop because they are maturing in cooler weather and there are fewer pests around.

Start the seeds for a fall crop (indoors or out) 12 -16 weeks before the average first fall frost date. Plant out transplants 8 weeks before the first fall frost date.

Winter: Overwintering cauliflower is planted out in early September and matures the following spring. It is important to use a hardy variety that is appropriate for the time of year.

Succession sow: It's not a bad idea to sow cauliflower several times (each a week apart), as this increases the odds of at least some working out well.

Planting

Transplants: If you want to grow cauliflower as a spring crop this usually means starting your transplants indoors (ideally at 70°F). A fall crop may be started indoors, in an outdoor seed bed, or it may be direct sown.

Starting inside: Cauliflower doesn't really like having its root disturbed, but will tolerate it while small (if done carefully). The seeds are often sown in flats, 1″ apart and ¼″ deep. When they have two sets of leaves they are pricked out to 2″ apart.

It can also be sown in cell packs or soil blocks (plant 2 seeds to a cell and later thin to the best one) to minimize root disturbance.

The transplants are ready to go out when they are still fairly small, but have 4 - 5 true leaves. Bigger transplants are prone to bolting, especially in spring as they vernalize easily.

Hardening off: It is important the seedlings are hardened off before they go outside (failure to do so can result in shocked plants that don't grow well). Start by putting the plants outside for 2 hours on the first day, then 4 hours on the second day. Add 2 hours every day for a week and then plant out.

A simpler alternative is to put them in a cold frame, which is opened for longer periods each day and closed at night.

Setting out: Cauliflower is transplanted up to the first true leaves. Water right after planting and every day thereafter until it looks good. You might need to put on cutworm collars or cabbage root maggot disks, provide shade if it's very sunny and protect it from late frosts. It is vital that growth is uninterrupted by transplanting, as this can be enough to make it bolt.

Direct sowing: Cauliflower can also be direct sown and in some cases these have been known to mature faster than transplants. Sow the seeds ¼ - ½″ deep, with 2 - 3 seeds in each station. Thin to the best one when they are up and growing. This is most practical in climates that provide that ideal long cool growing season, or for use as a fall crop. Of course the drawback with direct sowing is that they take up space for a long time (maybe interplant it into another crop).

Outdoor nursery bed: In summer you can start transplants in an outdoor nursery bed. This is a much more efficient use of space than direct sowing, as the plants don't take up bed space for the first 4 - 6 weeks of their lives.

Sow the seed about 1″ apart and when they have all emerged and are growing vigorously, transplant them to stand 3″ apart.

Spacing: Spacing has an effect upon the final size of the head.

15″ very good soil

18″ average soil

24″ poor soil

Row spacing: Space the plants 15 - 18″ apart in the rows, with 24 - 36″ between the rows.

Care

Cauliflower needs more care than other Brassicas. You have to give it everything it needs for fast, uninterrupted growth without any checks, otherwise it may bolt prematurely.

Weeding: The plants don't compete with weeds very well, so weed regularly while they are small. Take care if using a hoe, as the shallow roots are easily damaged and this can cause bolting too.

Water: Cauliflower needs constant moisture (at least 1″ per week), so it's important to keep the soil moist at all times (lack of water can cause - you guessed it - bolting). The most critical watering time is when the head is developing, so don't let it get water stressed at this time. It is also good to get plenty of moisture retentive organic matter into the soil.

Fertilization: After the plants are established and growing well, give them a foliar feed of compost tea. Feed them again just before they start to head up (or just feed regularly every two weeks). Cauliflower is one of the crops that is most susceptible to boron deficiency (which can be caused by acid soil).

Mulch: This not only keep weeds down, it can also help to keep the soil moist and cool and helps to keep these shallow rooted plants cosy and happy.

Blanching: Many modern varieties of cauliflower are self wrapping (their leaves protect the head), but older types need to be blanched to prevent the curds turning brown from exposure to sunlight (and developing an off flavor). This is done when the head enlarges to about 2 - 3″ in diameter and starts to become visible. Even the self wrapping types will produce more desirable whiter heads if blanched.

Blanching is done on a warm dry day (so the plant is dry) by tying the top leaves together with twine (or rubber bands or clothes pins) to cover the head (do this loosely to exclude light, but allow for air circulation and so it doesn't trap water). You could also crack the leaves and tuck them over the head, or cover the head with loose leaves. You could even make a cap of aluminum foil (if you wear one too it may help to stop them bolting prematurely).

Pests: Cauliflower is attacked by the usual Brassica villains, especially root maggots (see **Cabbage**). If pests are a big problem in your area, you might want to protect the young plants with row covers. Pests are more problematic in the warm weather of spring than in the cooler weather of fall.

Disease: Cauliflower is also attacked by all of the usual Brassica diseases (see **Cabbage**).

Boron deficiency: Cauliflower is very sensitive to boron deficiency, which shows up as distorted leaf tips that often die back, Liquid kelp or compost tea can help to alleviate this.

Head problems:
Discoloration - Too much water or waiting too long to harvest.

Browning - Too much heat

Buttoning (premature and small heads) - Drought, cold, heat or any kind of stress.

Ricy (separation of curds, which looks like white rice) - May be caused by drought, cold, heat or too much nitrogen.

Leaves in curds – too much heat

Harvesting

When: Generally a planting doesn't mature very uniformly, so you need to check each plant individually.

The optimal time to harvest cauliflower is when the head has reached full size, but while it's still tight and firm. They are good later than this though and may be used until the flower clusters start to turn yellowish (rather than white) and start to separate (they are said to get ricy).

In warm weather the plants don't stay in optimal condition for very long, in which case it's better to start harvesting your first heads a little too early (this also helps to stagger the harvest season).

How: Cut off the entire head with a knife. If you aren't going to use it immediately, leave some leaves on to protect it in handling (the head bruises and discolors easily).

Storage: Cauliflower will stay in good condition for several weeks if stored in the refrigerator (make sure it doesn't contain any insects or caterpillars). The curds also freeze very well.

Seed saving: The process is much the same as for broccoli (see **Broccoli**). Cauliflower will cross with cabbage, kale and any other Brassicas. This could have interesting results, but it's probably not what you want. Take seed from six or more of the best, slow bolting plants.

Be aware that the curds of cauliflower are not flower buds like those of broccoli, but mostly only fleshy receptacles that won't develop into flowers. In fact flower development in cauliflower can be very erratic.

Unusual growing ideas

Mini-cauliflowers: This is a relatively new way to grow cauliflowers and results in miniature heads 2 - 3″ in diameter (ideal for one serving). It can be a very productive way to grow cauliflower.

Use a fast maturing summer variety for this method. Direct sow 2 seeds at each station, spacing them 6″ each way. When these are all up, thin to the strongest plant and care for them as usual. The closely spaced plants compete with each other and tend to keep each other all roughly the same size.

Varieties

In North America the choice of varieties has traditionally been quite limited, but this situation is slowly changing and some fine European and American varieties are now available. This is good because choosing the right variety can be a big factor in your success. You will probably need to experiment to find out what works best for you and at what time of the year.

Cauliflower is another crop where F1 hybrids are taking over. Some of these varieties are of very high quality and are worth trying. There are also some new varieties with spectacular orange, purple and green colored curds, but they are expensive.

Cauliflower can be divided into early, fall and winter varieties, according to their hardiness.

Early: These have a short growing season and can do well in summer (in cool areas) or fall. They are more heat tolerant too.

Snow Crown F1- 50 - 60 days

Early snowball - 65 days

Fall: These are bred for fall harvest and aren't very heat tolerant.

Fremont F1- 65 days.

Winter: These are the easiest cauliflowers to grow, because they are very hardy and tolerate cold weather. They are planted out in early fall and form large heads in late winter and early spring. The Walcheren types are among the best known.

All the Year Round - 70 days

Purple: These resemble a cross between broccoli and cauliflower. They are somewhat easier to grow than cauliflower because they don't need blanching.

Romanesco - This unusual Italian Heirloom is becoming increasingly popular. It has a very attractive spiral pattern on its pale green head. It is quite variable, with about 20% of plants not heading up and the rest doing so over a long period.

Colored types: Orange, purple, yellow or green cauliflowers are an interesting recent innovation. Unfortunately most of this color disappears in cooking and they have to be grown from very expensive seed ($3.95 for 15 seeds.)

Cheddar F1 - Orange

Panther F1 - Green

Graffiti F1 - Deep purple

Purple Head F1 - Purple (85 days)

Kitchen use: I like to use the curds raw in salads.

Celery

Apium graveolens

Introduction: This cool weather biennial is native to Europe and has been used as food at least since the time of the Romans (though this was probably leaf celery). There are three distinct types of celery commonly grown as crops. Here I am talking about the stalk celery that is familiar to all of us (in fact it is the only one most of us would even recognize. There is also root celery, usually known as celeriac, which is popular in Eastern Europe. Lastly there is leaf celery (sometimes knows as Chinese celery), which is the type most commonly used in Asia.

Ease of growing: Celery is notorious among home gardeners as being one of the hardest crops to grow well and it definitely isn't for the beginner. It is very particular about its requirements and must have all the nutrients it needs for fast, uninterrupted growth. It also needs a constant supply of moisture and a long period of cool weather. Celery is said to be even harder to grow organically and to be a true test of the organic gardeners skill.

Nutritional content: Celery mostly consists of water and fiber and has barely any nutritional value (64 calories per pound). I guess that's why it is associated with people who are trying to lose weight. It does contain some useful phytochemicals though, including apigenin, which has anti-cancer properties.

Crop value: Celery isn't a very important crop from a nutritional or productive standpoint. It does provide an interesting flavoring though.

A few people are allergic to celery and can have a severe reaction to it

Climate: Celery needs 120 days of cool (60 - 75˚F) moist weather for optimal growth. It doesn't like extreme heat or hard frost, though it can tolerate mild frost.

About Celery

Seed facts
Germ temp: 40 (60 - 70) 80˚F
Germ time: 14 - 21 days
41 days / 41˚F
16 days / 50˚F
12 days / 59˚F
7 days / 68˚F * Optimum
8 days / 77˚F
Viability: 5 yrs
Germination percentage: 55%+
Weeks to grow transplants: 8 - 12

Planning facts
Hardiness: Half hardy
Growing temp: 45 (60 - 65) 75˚F
Plants per person: 6
Plants per sq ft: 1 - 1½
Transplants:
Start 8 - 10 wks before last frost
Plant out 2 weeks after last frost
Direct sow: 2 wks before last frost
Fall crop: Start 3 - 4 months before first fall frost
Days to harvest: 85 - 200 days
75 - 120 days from transplant

Harvest facts
Yield per plant: 1 - 2 lb
Yield per sq ft: 2 - 4 lb sq ft

Soil

pH 6.0 - 7.0

Wild celery naturally grows near water and this is reflected in its preference for a rich, deep, moist (but well-drained), fairly acid soil, with lots of organic matter. It is a hungry crop, requiring a lot of nitrogen, potassium and phosphorus. The roots are fairly shallow and can tolerate wet soil better than most crops (it was originally a marsh plant).

Soil preparation: Incorporate a source of organic matter to supply nitrogen and to increase its water holding capacity (use 2″ of compost or aged manure). Add a source of phosphorus (colloidal phosphate), potassium (wood ashes or greensand) and micronutrients (kelp). If the soil is heavy, or compacted, you might also think about double digging. Add lime if the soil is very acidic.

Planning

Celery must be planned carefully, because it takes a long time to grow to maturity from seed and you often end up with a lot at one time. It is possible to sow it in succession, but this is even more complicated.

Where: Celery is an upright, compact plant and doesn't take up a lot of space (which is good, as it is in the ground for quite a long time). It prefers full sun, but will tolerate light shade for part of the day (in warm climates this may even be beneficial). However too much shade will make for tall, leggy plants that fall over easily. It needs quite a lot of attention, so should be sited where it can be watched closely and tended frequently.

When: Celery needs a long period (3 months) of cool temperatures (60 - 70˚F) for optimal quality and in warm summer areas it does best as a fall crop. It will grow in warmer temperatures, but above 75˚F growth slows down and the stalks may be more fibrous and strongly flavored.

Spring: In areas with long cool spring weather, it can be started inside 8 - 12 weeks before the last frost. It is planted out 2 weeks after the last frost.

Fall: Celery generally does better as a fall crop, planted in mid to late summer. It then gets to mature in the cool weather of fall.

Winter: In areas with mild winters, celery does well as a winter crop, planted in early fall.

Planting

Sowing: Celery seed has a reputation of being difficult to germinate, but I have never found it to be particularly problematic. I have read one piece that said fresh seed germinates best and another that said 2 or 3 year old seed is actually better because germination inhibitors have broken down. It is fairly slow to germinate (up to 3 weeks) and get going though, so you need to give it plenty of time.

Some people pre-soak the seed in hot (120˚F) water for a half hour before planting, or in compost tea overnight.

Some authorities say the seed must be scattered on the surface and left uncovered, as it needs light to germinate. Others say a light ⅛ - ¼″ covering of soil is best. I can't say I have noticed much difference either way,

Seed sitting on the surface must be kept moist at all times, as it can dry out easily which can be fatal. Germination may take as little as a week, or as long as three weeks. Some books say it is important that the temperature fluctuates below 60˚F at night during germination. Temperatures above 80˚F may inhibit germination.

Transplants

Starting inside: Celery is usually started indoors, because it is so slow growing initially. It doesn't mind transplanting when young, so is commonly started in flats, leaving 1″ between plants.

Though celery germinates best at 78˚F, the seedlings prefer a fairly cool 60˚F temperature for growth. Prick out the seedlings to 2″ apart when they have their first true leaves, as they seem to benefit from transplanting at this stage. As always, take care to keep them moist. They should take 8 - 12 weeks to reach 5″ in height and grow 5 - 6 leaves, which is the ideal transplant size.

Hardening off: If transplants are to go outside while it is still cold, the seedlings should be hardened off. They will then tolerate temperatures as low as 25˚F. Start by putting the plants outside for 2 hours on the first day, then 4 hours on the second day. Adding 2 hours every day for a week.

Vernalization: If the recently planted seedlings are exposed to extended cold temperatures (10 days below 45˚F) after a warm period they could be vernalized. They would then react to warmer weather by bolting. If cold weather unexpectedly returns after planting out, you should protect the plants with cloches.

Transplanting: When planting celery make sure you keep the root ball of each plant as intact as possible. Some people run and knife between the plants in the flat, a few days before planting to separate them.

Trench planting: An old method of growing celery was to plant in a trench. This was dug 12 - 18″ deep by 12 - 18″ wide and was half filled with compost, aged manure or other organic matter (if necessary add lime to raise the pH). This was left for a couple of weeks to settle before the transplants were planted in to it. The trench is filled in later for blanching.

Direct sowing: Celery can be direct sown if you have a suitably long and mild growing season.

Direct sowing celery is so slow it is only practical (barely) in areas with very long, cool growing seasons, such as in coastal California. There it can be planted in spring to mature in late summer or fall. Of course you still run into the usual problem with direct sowing; the small plants take up a lot of bed space that might be used more profitably for other crops (See **Outdoor nursery bed** below).

Spring celery needs to be sown as early as possible, though the soil must be at least 50°F (much lower and it will take a month to germinate). If necessary use cloches to warm the soil and protect the young seedlings during early growth. Usually the seed is sown quite thickly and the growing plants are harvest thinned several times until they reach they required spacing (the thinnings can be used in the kitchen).

Outdoor nursery bed: In summer you can start transplants in an outdoor nursery bed. This is a much more efficient use of space than direct sowing, as the plants don't take up bed space for the first 8 - 12 weeks of their lives.

Sow the seed about 1″ apart and when they have all emerged and are growing vigorously, thin them to stand 3″ apart.

Spacing: Celery is spaced fairly closely as this helps to keep down weeds and reduces the need for blanching (the soil has to be very fertile and must be kept moist for this to work).

The plants are normally arranged in offset rows across the bed. The spacing varies from 9 - 12″, depending upon the fertility of the soil. Plants have been spaced as close as 6 - get a greater quantity of smaller plants.

Care

Weed: Celery needs to be kept free of weeds at all times, but especially when the plants are small (which is quite a while in this case).

Water: Consistent watering is the single most important factor in growing good celery; the soil should never be allowed to dry out. This may mean watering daily in dry weather, though every other day is more usual.

Water is particularly critical as harvest time approaches, because this is the time of fastest growth (plants may double in size in their last month). Lack of water at this time can result in bitter, pungent, stringy plants with hollow stems and may also encourage bolting.

The best way to water celery is with a drip system or soaker hose as this keeps the leaves dry and reduces the chance of fungus disease developing.

Fertilization: Celery needs lots of nitrogen to produce succulent growth, so if your soil isn't very fertile you should feed your plants every 2 - 3 weeks with compost tea or liquid kelp. You can also put a side dressing of fertilizer mix on the soil between the plants. If plants don't get enough nutrients they may be stringy and tough.

Mulch: This is useful to conserve moisture, keep down weeds and keep the soil cooler.

Blanching: Celery was traditionally blanched (covered to deprive the stems of light) to improve its flavor and make it less fibrous. Most modern varieties don't need blanching, but a few are improved by it (it makes them milder and nuttier). When celery is planted in close blocks, it tends to self-blanch to some extent.

Blanching should only be done a couple of weeks before harvest, as too long a blanching can cause it to deteriorate or rot.

The traditional way to blanch celery is to remove the outer leaves to expose the tall stems and then surround it with a 12″ wide sheet of brown paper (newspaper isn't used as it may adversely affect the flavor). The paper is held in place by piling soil around the plant. This was one reason they were planted in trenches, as the soil could easily be pulled down to hold the paper.

A simpler way to blanch is to wrap the stem with a paper grocery bag and tie it in place (and forget about the soil).

Another method is to tie the stalks together and gradually earth them up over 3 - 4 weeks by piling soil against them (up to the base of the leaves). The disadvantage of this is that soil tends to get down between the stalks, making them gritty and hard to clean.

In cold climates celery is sometimes blanched and protected from frost at the same time, by placing a board on each side of a row and filling it with dried leaves or straw.

Problems: The month before harvest is the most critical time when growing celery. The plants are growing very rapidly at this time and need a steady supply of water and nutrients.

Pests: Celery is a relative of the carrot and is afflicted by many of the same pests. Carrot fly, celery fly, celery worms, aphids, leaf miners, slugs and snails can all be a problem at times.

Disease: Celery leaf spot, pink rot and black heart.

Harvesting

When: The first harvest you get from celery is the leaves. These can be harvested at any time for use as flavoring for salads, soups, etc.

You can harvest individual stalks of celery as soon as they are big enough to be worthwhile. This might affect the final size of the plant, but is worthwhile because it extends the harvest period.

You can start harvesting whole plants when their base is 2″ in diameter (though 3″ is better).

Spring celery should be harvested before hot weather arrives as this will cause its quality to deteriorate.

How: Harvest whole plants when the stems are 8 - 10″ tall, by cutting them down at ground level.

Storage: Celery will keep for a couple of weeks in a plastic bag in the fridge. If you want to store it for longer than this, pull it up with the root attached and re-plant it in moist sand in a root cellar. It likes to be kept at 32 - 40˚F and 90% humidity.

Seed Saving: Celery is a biennial and doesn't produce flowers until its second spring (it sometimes produces flowers prematurely in its first year, but you don't want to save seed from those plants).

The biggest problem with saving celery seed is just getting the plants to survive the winter. In mild areas they will usually do this in the ground, perhaps under a mulch to protect them from frost. In colder areas they may have to be dug up and stored in a root cellar until spring (See **Storage**).

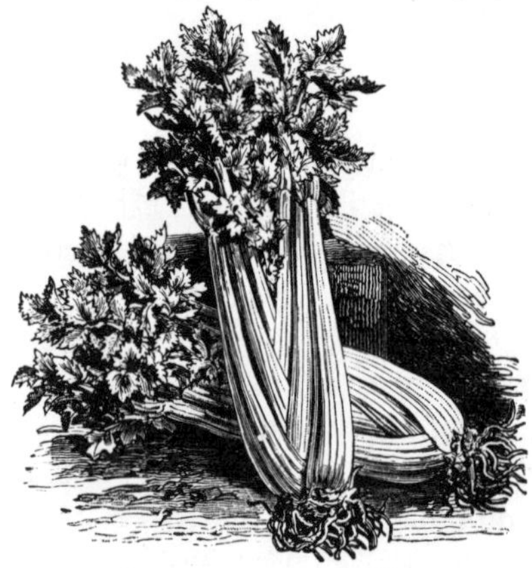

Celery flowers are cross-pollinated by insects, which makes it hard to save more than one variety at a time (unless you isolate by 1000 feet or more). One plant will produce quite a lot of seed, though you should still ideally save seed from at least 6 plants to ensure genetic variability. When most of the seed is ripe on the plant, cut the entire head and dry it in a paper bag. Be aware that some fungus diseases can be seed borne.

Celery seed is also commonly used as a flavoring for cooking.

An excess of seed could be sprouted to make delicious celery flavored sprouts or micro-greens.

Unusual growing ideas

Multi-planting: It is possible to plant celery in multi-plant blocks. Plant 6 seeds per cell and thin to the best 3 plants, when they have all emerged.

Containers: Celery can be grown in a container, though it has to be a fairly big one. The resulting plant is probably best used as a source of leaves for flavoring. Growing good stems is a lot more difficult.

Varieties:

Celery isn't a very popular garden crop, so the number of varieties available is fairly limited. There are some interesting old varieties with pink, yellow or red coloration.

Heirlooms: These have the best flavor, but generally need blanching to really bring this out.

Golden Self-Blanching - Juicy, tasty and tender (and it doesn't need blanching!)

Giant Pascal - Hardy, not fibrous.

Giant Red: Has red stalks and strong flavor.

Modern varieties: Most of these are self-blanching (and more disease resistant), which makes them easier to grow, but their flavor isn't as good.

Utah 52 - 70R Improved - A standard commercial variety.

Tango - Somewhat heat and drought tolerant.

Conquistador - Adaptable and somewhat heat and drought tolerant.

Kitchen use

Celery is most often used raw in salads, but it is also an important flavoring for soups and sauces.

In France celery is used for mirepoix, (a mix of chopped celery, carrot and onions) which is used as a base for soups, sauces and other dishes.

Celery and potato soup

3 tbsp olive oil

3 cups celery

1½ cups green onions

½ potatoes

½ tsp salt

½ cup soy milk

1 tsp salt

⅛ tsp black pepper

½ tsp thyme

Chop the celery stalks and tops finely (peel the stalks if they are stringy), then saute them with the green onions for 2 minutes. Add the potatoes, thyme, salt, pepper and 3 cups of water. Cook for 15 minutes in a covered pot until the vegetables are tender. Allow the soup to cool slightly, add the soy milk and puree it until smooth in a blender. Reheat and serve.

Leaf Celery

As the name suggests this type of celery is grown for its leaves, rather than the stems or roots. It isn't much different from wild celery and has the vigor of a wild plant.

Leaf celery is very popular in China, where it is grown as a flavoring for soups and many other dishes. I'm not going to devote much space to it here, because its cultivation is pretty much the same as for celery, though it is not so demanding (so is easier to grow).

Be conscientious about keeping the soil moist, as this not only affects growth, but also its flavor. Well-watered plants are milder and better flavored.

Varieties: There aren't many available, normally it is just leaf celery.

Parcel: The only cultivar I know of, it looks very much like curly parsley (hence the name) and I often get their volunteers confused. I believe it is a very old variety that originated in Germany. It is pretty easy to grow and self-sows regularly in my garden.

Kitchen use: The leaves are used as a flavoring herb a variety of dishes. Small amounts may be added to salads, but it is quite strongly flavored.

The small stems are used to flavor soups.

The seeds are also used as flavoring and are sometimes ground to powder and mixed with salt (to make celery salt!)

Celeriac

Apium graveolens var *rapaceum*

Introduction: Celeriac is grown for its root (more accurately this is a swollen stem base, or corm, not a root) rather than its stems, which is why it is often called celery root or turnip rooted celery. It has long been popular in Germany and Eastern Europe, where it is the most popular kind of celery. In this country it is relatively unusual however.

Ease of growing: Celeriac has pretty much the same requirements as celery and is grown in the same way. It is easier to grow though, because you don't really care about the quality of the stems, the main edible part is the root.

Nutritional content: The root is a lot more nutritious than its cousin celery. It contains carbohydrate (almost 200 calories per pound), vitamins C, K and B6, as well as phosphorus and manganese. It also contains apigenin, which has anti-cancer properties.

Climate: For optimal growth celeriac needs the same climate as celery, which means a long period of cool (60 - 75°F), moist weather. It doesn't like extreme heat or cold, though it can tolerate mild frost. In cool areas it can be grown all summer, but in hotter ones it is most often grown as a fall / winter crop.

Crop value: Celeriac is a somewhat overlooked plant and deserves to be more widely grown. It is fairly easy to grow and can be harvested for a long period over the winter.

Soil: Celeriac likes the same fertile, moisture retentive, high organic matter soil as celery.

About Celeriac

Seed facts
Germ temp: 40 (60 - 70) 80°F
Germ time: 14 - 21 days
Viability: 5 yrs
Germination percentage: 55%+
Weeks to grow transplants: 8 - 12

Planning facts
Growing temp: 45 (60 - 65) 75°F
Start: 8 - 10 wks before last frost
Plant out: 0 - 2 wks after last frost
Direct sow: 2 wks before last frost
Fall crop: Start 3 - 4 months before first fall frost
Days to harvest: 85 - 120 days from transplant

Planning

When: Celeriac needs about 100 days of cool (60 - 70°F) weather to grow to perfection. If there is a long period of cool weather in spring it can be grown at this time (this works better than celery). However it usually does best as a fall crop.

Where: A sunny spot is best, though it can also grow in light shade.

Planting

Indoors: Unlike most root crops, celeriac is often started indoors in spring, 10 weeks before the last frost date. This is simply because it is slow to get started and this saves time.

A fall crop may be started in the greenhouse or nursery bed. Sow it in midsummer, 3 - 4 months before the first fall frost. Transplant it to its permanent position 8 - 10 weeks later. See **Celery** for information on raising and hardening off seedlings.

Outdoors: Celeriac produces a better root system when direct sown For a spring crop, this is done when hard frosts are past. For a fall crop it is done in mid summer. Simply scatter the seed on the soil surface and keep moist until it germinates. Thin when all of the plants have emerged and they have a set of true leaves.

Spacing
Space the plants 10″ - 12″ - 15″ apart in the beds, depending upon the fertility of the soil. If growing in rows plant them 8″ apart, with 18 - 24″ between the rows.

Care

To produce the best roots celeriac needs to grow quickly, without a check in its growth. To do this it must get everything it needs.

Watering: Celeriac needs moist soil at all times, which usually isn't too much of a problem in the cool growing conditions it prefers.

Weeding: The small plants can't compete with weeds very well, so keep them well weeded. To avoid damaging the shallow roots (most are within a couple of inches of the surface) it is best to hand weed.

Fertilization: Celeriac is a fairly hungry crop and if the soil isn't very fertile, it is good to give the plants a feed of liquid kelp or compost tea every three weeks. If the soil is fertile this isn't necessary. Too much nitrogen can even result in excessive top growth instead of root growth.

Mulch: This is useful to conserve moisture and suppress weeds.

Pruning: Any lateral shoots that appear on the side of the root are often removed. This is done to encourage the plant to devotes all of its energy to sizing up the root, rather than growing more foliage.

Earthing up: This isn't essential but is often done to keep the expanding roots covered with soil, so they stay pale in color.

Pests: These are the same as for celery, but less problematic. Carrot fly is sometimes a problem.

Harvesting

When: You can gather the first roots when they are only 2″ in diameter, However they start to expand rapidly at this point, so the longer you wait the bigger they will get. Like many root crops they get better with lower temperatures and even light frost.

How: Dig or pull the root, brush off excess soil and cut off the tops so they don't draw moisture from the root. Don't throw these away, they can be used separately as flavoring.

Storage: The roots are best left in the ground under mulch and harvested as needed, If the ground is likely to freeze, dig them and store in a cool root cellar at 32 to 40°F. They will keep in the fridge in a plastic bag for a couple of weeks.

Seed saving: Celeriac is a biennial and doesn't produce flowers until its second spring. Saved the seed as for **celery**.

Varieties: The choice of celeriac varieties is limited, but slowly expanding. This isn't a huge problem as they are all relatively similar anyway.

Alabaster - (120 days)

Brilliant - Smooth skin and nutty flavor. Early maturing (110 days)

Monarch - A highly rated, fairly new variety (100 days)

Giant Prague - (This is the easiest variety to find (120 days).

Kitchen use

This is a plant that hardly anyone in America knows how to use. The knobby root looks a little formidable, but is easily peeled to leave a tasty white core (if the top part of the root is woody it should be discarded). They are most often used in soups or cooked in the same ways as potato, but they are also good raw in salads.

The green leafy tops and stems can be used as flavoring like leaf celery.

Mashed celeriac

2 celeriac
2 potatoes
⅛ cup olive oil
3 tbsp thyme
4 cloves garlic
Sea salt
Black pepper
¼ cup water

Cut the peeled celeriac and potato into ½″ cubes, then put in a pan with the olive oil, thyme and chopped garlic and fry for 5 minutes. Add water and simmer until soft. Mash and add seasoning and it's done. You don't even have to mash it, but then it would just be chopped celeriac.

Chard

Beta vulgaris var *cicla*

Introduction: Chard is the same species as the beet, but is grown for its edible foliage rather than the root. Though it is often called Swiss chard, it was first domesticated somewhere in the Mediterranean and was prized by the ancient Greeks and Romans for its nutritional and medicinal value.

Climate: Chard is a cool season crop, preferring to grow at 45°F - 75°F. It can grow in warmer conditions, but the leaves tend to be smaller and inferior in flavor. It can also tolerate some frost and in milder areas will continue to grow right through the winter.

Ease of growing: This is one of the easiest vegetables to grow, very productive, little bothered by pests or disease and resistant to both heat and cold. I highly recommend it as an almost foolproof potherb for the small garden.

Crop value: A useful crop because it has a long productive season (as a biennial it isn't prone to bolting in its first year) and is a nutritious green leafy vegetable.

Nutritional content: The leaves are considered to be one of the most nutritious of the common green vegetables. They contain large amounts of vitamins A and C, as well as calcium, phosphorus, potassium and iron. They also contain no less than 13 (count em) antioxidants and a host of other phytonutrients, too numerous to name.

They also contain oxalic acid, which can inhibits the absorption of calcium to some degree (see **Spinach** for more on this). They also contains about 85 calories per pound.

About Chard

Seed facts
Germ temp: 50 - 85˚F
Germ time: 5 - 21 days
42 days / 41˚F
16 days / 50˚F
9 days / 59˚F
6 days / 68˚F
5 days / 77˚F * Optimum
5 days / 86˚F
Viability: 5 years
Germination percentage: 60%+
Weeks to grow transplants: 3 - 4

Planning facts
Hardiness: Hardy
Growing temp: 45 (60 - 70) 75˚F
Plants per person: 10
Plants per sq ft: 4
Transplants:
Start: 4 wks before last frost date
Plant out: on last frost date
Direct sow on the last frost date
Fall: Plant 10 - 12 wks before first fall frost
Days to harvest: 50 - 60 days

Harvest facts
Harvest period: up to 30 weeks
Yield per plant: 10 oz (or more)
Yield per sq ft: 2 to 8 lb sq ft

Soil

pH 6.0 - 6.8

Chard has a deep, strong root system that is able to seek out the nutrients it needs, so it can grow well on fairly poor soil. However for highest yield it does best in a fertile garden soil, rich in humus, well-drained and not too acidic.

Soil preparation: Incorporate 2″ of compost or aged manure into the top 6″ of soil. Add dolomitic lime (to raise the pH and to supply magnesium) and wood ashes (to raise the pH and supply potassium).

Planning

Chard is cultivated in much the same way as beet, but it is easier to grow as it only has to produce foliage.

Where: In cool climates chard needs full sun for maximum production of foliage. It doesn't like high temperatures, so in hot climates it should be grown in part shade. It is one of the most shade tolerant of common crops.

When: Chard is quite hardy, but it germinates slowly at low temperatures, so is usually planted out around the last frost date.

Planting

As with the beet, each "seed" is actually a cluster of flowers fused together, each containing a single seed. This is why you end up with several plants, when you plant one seed. You can gently break up these clusters and get individual seeds to plant.

The seed clusters contain a water-soluble germination inhibitor, which can be leached out by soaking the seed overnight prior to planting. Don't simply soak them in a glass of water overnight however, as they may absorb water so quickly, they can be damaged. Instead they should be put on a damp paper towel, so they can absorb moisture slowly. You could take this one step further and actually pre-germinate the seeds before planting.

Transplants

Starting inside: Chard doesn't really like root disturbance, though it will tolerate it when young. For this reason it is usually grown in cell packs, plug trays or soil blocks. Germination is quite uneven, so seeds may continue to emerge for a week or more.

Planting out: Set out the transplants on the last frost date. Don't let them get too large inside, otherwise exposure to temperatures below 50°F (for two weeks), could vernalize them. They will then bolt as soon as it gets warmer. If cold weather threatens, you should protect the newly planted seedlings with cloches or row covers.

Direct sowing: This is pretty straightforward and is the preferred method of growing chard.

Broadcasting: Scatter the seeds so they are spaced about 2 - 3″ apart and cover with a ½″ of cover soil mix.

Rows: Make furrows ½ - ¾″ deep, plant the seeds 1½″ apart and re-fill with topsoil. If the soil isn't very good, you could cover with a mix of half soil and half compost.

Thinning: When all of the seeds have germinated, you can start thinning. Don't start too early though, as some may be damaged by cutworms, slugs, or other pests.

Thinning is best done in several stages, as the plants get larger. You can use the thinnings for food, or as transplants (they transplant fairly well if less than 3″ tall). The clusters don't need much thinning, as the strongest plant tends to take over.

Spacing: Chard grows fast and gets quite large so needs plenty of space. Plant it 8 - 12″ apart, depending upon the fertility of the soil and the growing methods.

Care

Chard is a robust and undemanding plant. Keep it well fed and watered and it should produce abundantly.

Water: Chard is relatively drought tolerant, though for highest quality and yields it should be well supplied with water. It is particularly important to keep the soil evenly moist in hot weather, as lack of water can encourage bolting.

Fertilization: If you are going to be harvesting intensively, you should feed the plants regularly with compost tea or liquid kelp.

Mulch: This helps to keep down weeds while the plants are young (older plants can take care of themselves). It also helps to keep the soil cool and conserve moisture.

Bolting: Chard is a biennial, but sometimes it will bolt in its first year. This is most often the result of vernalization (see **Broccoli**), but may also be caused by drought, crowding, poor soil or other stress. If a plant bolts there's not much you can do but pull it up.

Pests: Chard is little bothered by pests and disease generally. My biggest problem has been leaf miners. You can crush them in the leaf and scrape off the small white egg clusters but row covers are the best solution. Slugs and snails will eat chard if there is nothing more to their liking. In some areas nematodes can be a problem.

Disease: Cercospora lead spot is the most common disease.

Seed saving: The process is the same as for the related beet. Chard and beet will cross-pollinate so you can only save one type at a time. The seed is produced abundantly, especially if you are saving it from 5 plants to ensure some genetic diversity.

Don't count on all of you plants producing seed. Chard plants are dioecious, which means either male or female and of course only female plants will produce seed.

Harvesting

When: You can start pinching off the individual leaves as soon as they get big enough to use. I usually harvest the individual outer leaves, just as they are reaching full size (which may be 8 - 12″).

How: Chard is a great "cut and come again" crop. Keep harvesting the outer leaves as they get big enough and more will be produced. Harvest freely, but take care not to take too many from a single plant at one time. Give them a chance to recover.

You may be able to rejuvenate a tired old plant, by cutting it down to within 3 - 4″ of the ground. It should then sprout tender new growth.

Storage: Use the leaves immediately after harvest, as they are thin and don't keep for very long (only a few days in the fridge in a plastic bag). For longer term storage it can be frozen like spinach. This is useful for those times when it is producing far more than you can use immediately.

Unusual growing ideas

Spring greens: If you protect the roots over the winter, they will start growing again as the weather warms up in spring. This new growth can be harvested several times before the plants bolt. Once the plant starts to bolt the leaves aren't very good.

Ornamental: The spectacularly colored chard varieties (red, white, orange, yellow) are highly photogenic and are a favorite of upscale magazine garden photos. They can be used as foliage plants for ornamental garden beds.

Varieties

Ruby Chard:

Rhubarb Chard: These two varieties have beautiful red stems.

Bright Lights:

Rainbow Chard: These two varieties produce a combination of red, yellow, green and white stems and are beautiful enough for any ornamental garden.

Perpetual Spinach: This is an old variety with thin tender stems, that more closely resembles spinach than other chards (it is also known as spinach beet). It isn't as attractive as some of the other varieties, but is very productive and bolt resistant. It is my favorite variety (so far).

Green Lucullus: One of commonest green varieties.

Fordhook Giant: A very productive old heirloom.

Kitchen use

The leaves can be used in any recipe calling for spinach. The best way to cook them is to boil for 3 - 5 minutes, as this leaches out a lot of the oxalic acid. If the stems are tough just fold the leaf in half lengthwise and slice it off with one cut of the knife.

Supposedly the thick stems are sometimes prepared as a separate vegetable, though I imagine they would be pretty bland (those of the colored varieties may also be quite tough).

Sag Aloo

This Indian curry is normally made with spinach, but this works just as well (as does any other mild flavored green leaf).

20 oz chard leaves
1 onion chopped
5 tbsp vegetable oil
1 cup water
½ tsp black pepper
2 tbsp black mustard seed
2 cardamom seeds
2 cloves garlic chopped
20 oz potatoes in small cubes
1 small hot pepper, chopped
1 tsp ground cumin
1 tsp ground coriander
1 tsp salt

Toast the cardamom and mustard seeds in the hot oil (don't let it overheat) until they start to pop. Add the onions and garlic and fry for 2 minutes, then add the rest of the spices and cook for another 2 minutes. Then add the potatoes, hot pepper, chard, salt and water. Cook a further 30 minutes until potatoes are cooked.

You could vary this recipe by using different combinations of vegetables.

Chickpea, Garbanzo Bean

Cicer arietinum

Introduction: The common names are somewhat misleading as this plant isn't closely related to either the pea or bean. It is believed to have originated in the Middle East and has been grown there for over 7000 (it no longer even exists as a wild plant). India is by far the biggest producer of chickpeas in the world.

About Chickpea

Seed facts
Germ temp: 50 (60 - 80) 90˚F
Germ time: 5 - 14 days
Viability: 3 - 5 yrs
Germination percentage: 70%+
Weeks to grow transplants: 4

Planning facts
Hardiness: Half hardy
Temp for growth: 65 (70 - 80) 90˚F
Plants per person: 10 minimum
Plants per sq ft:
Transplants:
Start: 4 wks before last frost
Plant out: 2 wks after last frost
Direct sow: 2 weeks before last frost
Days to harvest: 90 - 100
Height: 24″
Diameter - 12″

Crop use: Chickpeas are grown for their tasty and highly nutritious protein rich seed. Like the related beans and peas they host nitrogen fixing bacteria and so enrich the soil they grow in. These features make chickpea potentially a valuable crop, but they aren't very productive, or cost effective if you compare the cost of a pound of beans against the space needed to grow them. I would consider them more of a crop for people who have lots of space and are aiming for food self-sufficiency, or who are simply adventurous in the garden (I use that term fairly loosely).

Nutritional content
Like most beans they are high in protein. They are also rich in folate, iron, manganese, phosphorus and zinc. They are very high in calories, with around 1630 per pound.

Chicpeas are also very rich in various beneficial antioxidants and phytonutients. The smaller, darker seeded, desi types are particularly rich in these.

Like other beans they are also rich in fiber, but of a particularly benefical type. This may help to lower cholesterol levels and may even reduce the risk of colon cancer

Climate: Chickpeas require a warm and fairly long growing season and don't like wet weather or cold nights. The ideal climate is dry in late summer when the pods are developing, as they are prone to rot when they get wet. Established plants can tolerate dry conditions. Unlike most beans they can also tolerate some frost and are said to be as hardy as peas.

Soil

pH 5.5 (6.4) 8.0
Chickpea will grow in most soils. It doesn't have to be highly fertile as the plant fixes its own nitrogen, but it should be well-drained.

Soil preparation: Incorporate 2″ of compost into the top 6″ of soil. They don't need a lot of nitrogen, but do like potassium and phosphorus, so you might want to give them wood ashes and colloidal phosphate.

Planning

Where: For maximum production the plants should have full sun, as any shade will reduce the harvest. In very hot areas they may benefit from a little afternoon shade. They are usually rotated with other legumes.

When: Chickpea can be planted earlier than beans because they can tolerate cooler temperatures. However the seed may rot if the soil is too cold, so plant no earlier than two weeks before the last frost date.

Planting

Inoculating: For maximum nitrogen fixation you should inoculate your seeds with a suitable chickpea inoculant (this isn't the same as a pea or bean inoculant). See **Beans** for how to do this. If you grow them fairly regularly (every 3 years or so) you won't have to inoculate again, as the bacteria can survive in the soil for that long.

Using transplants: Chickpeas require a fairly long growing season, so they are sometimes started indoors This gives them a head start and is also a good way to foil hungry birds and rodents.

Chickpeas don't really like transplanting, so use soil blocks or cell packs to avoid disturbing their roots. If germination is likely to be poor, plant 2 seeds per cell and thin to the best one when both have germinated. If you think it will be good then just put one seed in each cell.

Plant the seedlings out when they are 4 - 5″ high. If the weather is cool you will have to harden them off first.

Direct sowing: Sow the seed 1 - 2″ deep, a couple of weeks before the last frost.

Spacing:
Beds: Space the plants 4 – 6″ apart (depending on soil fertility). The plants don't mind fairly close

spacing, as they help to support each other.

Rows: Space the plants 3 - 4″ apart, in rows 18 - 24″ apart.

Care

Weed: The young plants need regular weeding until they cover the ground fully. It's best to weed by hand, as their roots are quite near the surface and are easily damaged.

Fertilizing: Chickpeas are a fairly long season crop and if your soil is poor they might benefit from a side dressing of compost in mid season (or the occasional feed of compost tea).

Water: Established plants are quite drought tolerant, but for maximum productivity you should keep the soil moist. This is particularly important in hot weather and especially when the flowers are opening and setting pods.

Chickpeas are notoriously vulnerable to rot and various fungus diseases when they get wet, especially when the pods start to develop. Try not to get the plants wet when watering (drip is best) and don't even touch wet leaves (obviously rain is bad too).

Pests: Quite a few insects enjoy chickpeas, including aphids, bean beetles, flea beetles, leafhoppers and mites. In my garden something (I suspect rodents, but it could also have been birds) actually ate the ripening seeds out of the pods.

I read somewhere that the plant can secrete malic acid onto the leaves to protect them from pests. Apparently this can irritate the skin, though I can't say I have noticed.

Disease: Potential diseases include anthracnose, blights, fusarium rot, mildew and mosaic virus.

Harvesting

When: The flowers (and subsequently pods) start to appear about 60 days after planting. The pods are quite small and contain 1 - 3 beans. They can be eaten when green like snap or shell beans and in cool, short, wet growing conditions this may be as far as you get. More often they are allowed to ripen fully and picked dry. If the weather is wet you need to get them indoors as soon as possible (for reasons I already mentioned).

How: When the pod bearing plants begin to die back and turn brown, bring them indoors to a warm, dry, well aerated place to dry fully (an old screen door works great). A fully dry chickpea is hard and will shatter if hit with a hammer.

Storage: Store the fully dry beans in a rodent proof container in a cool, dry place. They should last for several years.

Seed saving: The flowers are perfect (have male and female parts) and self-pollinating, though they are also commonly cross-pollinated by bees. Saving seed is pretty easy because that is what you are growing them for.

Varieties

You rarely see chickpea seed for sale to gardeners as it is more of a field scale crop. There are two basic types

Kabouli: These include the familiar types you see in salad bars out of a can. They tend to be bigger and rounder and often have tan skins.

Chestnut: Big seeds are good for hummus.

Black Kabouli - This is the most available of these varieties in this country. As the name suggests it has a black skin.

Desi: These are smaller and darker and are often used for flour, or split for cooking like lentils.

There are also the popping chickpeas that can be popped like popcorn, though I have never tried them.

Kitchen use

Chickpeas are used in a variety of ways, but they are best known for making hummus and falafel (see **Fava Beans** for a recipe for the latter). They can also be used like soybeans for making tofu and "milk". In India it is ground into flour (known as gram flour) which is commonly used for cooking.

The beans are soaked and cooked in the same way as other dry beans. They take 1 - 1½ hours to cook thoroughly.

Hummus

Hummus is a very variable recipe and can be changed in many ways to suit personal taste. This is a good basic recipe.

1 cup chickpeas

½ cup tahini

1 lemon

2 garlic cloves

½ teaspoon cumin

Salt

Olive oil

Parsley

Clean and rinse the chickpeas, then soak overnight in water with a tablespoon of baking soda (optional). Then boil them in fresh water until tender (1 - 2 hrs), rinse them and allow to cool. Finally puree them in with the rest of the ingredients. You can puree them by hand, but it is a lot easier with a food processor.

Chicory

Cichorium intybus

Introduction: This vigorous perennial has a history of cultivation dating back to the ancient Egyptians and has been especially popular as a salad plant in France, Belgium and Italy. It was introduced into North America as a food plant by early European settlers and is now naturalized across most of the country.

This is a rather confusing plant because it can be used in so many different ways. Apart from the cabbage (with its multitude of Brassica variations), few plants are as versatile as the underrated (in fact largely ignored) chicory. It has been grown for its leaves, hearts, flower stems, roots (for coffee) and forced shoots (known as chicons) and specific varieties have been bred for each purpose.

In recent years radicchio has become the most popular type of chicory, so I have given it a separate entry, right after this one.

Some types of chicory are sometimes known as endive, which (understandably) leads to confusion with the closely related endive (*Cichorium endivia*). The big difference is that chicory is a perennial with a strong swollen tap root that can produce large succulent shoots in spring, whereas endive is an annual. Chicory is also more cold tolerant and slower growing.

Crop value: Chicory is the source of a range of delicious salad greens and deserves to be more widely grown. This neglect is no doubt because the simple large dandelion-like leaves can be very bitter (especially in warm weather). If you first tasted a bitter leaf you might not try chicory again! To be really good, chicory has to be grown at the right time of year and picked at the right stage of growth. The best part is the blanched heart of the compact head, which is quite delicious and one of the best of all salad materials. As a bonus it is also available late in the year, when most lettuce is gone.

Nutritional content: Chicory leaves contain lots of vitamins A and C, as well as some vitamin E and folate. They are also rich in minerals, including calcium, iron, potassium and phosphorus.

Chicory is higher in calories than most leafy greens, though at about 100 calories per pound that isn't saying a lot.

About Chicory

Seed facts

Germ temp: 45 (60 - 65) 75°F
Germ time: 7 - 14 days
Germination percentage: 70+
Viability: 4 - 6 - 8 yrs
Weeks to grow transplants: 4

Planning facts

Perennial (mostly grown as annual)
Hardiness zones 3 - 11
Growing temp: 45 (60 - 65) 75°F
Plants per person: 5
Plants per sq ft: 1
Spring transplants: Start 8 - 10 weeks before last frost
Plant out 4 weeks before last frost
Direct sow: 2 - 4 wks before last frost date.
Fall crop: Direct sow 8 - 12 wks before first fall frost
Days to harvest: 90 days +

Harvest facts

Yield per plant: ½ - 1 lb
Yield per sq ft: ½ - 1 lb

Ease of growing: Chicory is a vigorous and fairly easy crop to grow, though you have to time it right so it gets suitably cool weather. This is especially critical if you want it to produce a sweet compact head of leaves.

Climate: Chicory is a cool weather plant, growing best at 60 - 70°F. It is quite hardy and can tolerate low temperatures (these result in sweeter flavor and better color). In mild winter areas it can be grown right through the winter. It will grow well enough in warm weather too, but becomes so bitter as to be pretty much inedible.

Soil

pH 5.0 - 6.8

Chicory thrives in most soil types, but for the largest roots and easier harvesting, a loose, rich, moderately well-drained, but fairly moist soil is best.

Soil preparation: Incorporate 2″ of compost or aged manure to supply organic matter. Add wood ashes for potassium and colloidal phosphate for phosphorus (or use an organic fertilizer mix).

Planning

Though chicory is a perennial, it is usually grown as an annual, as second year plants aren't usually as good as first year plants.

Where: In cool climates chicory needs full sun, but in hotter ones it may benefit from light shade during the hottest part of the day.

When: In cool climates chicory can be used as a summer crop, but in warmer ones it is only grown in spring or fall.

Spring:
Direct sowing: In areas with cool spring weather chicory can be treated like spring lettuce. Direct sow it 2 - 4 weeks before the last spring frost.

From transplants: You can grow chicory from transplants, started indoors 8 - 10 weeks before the last frost and planted out 4 weeks before the last frost.

Fall: Hot weather makes chicory leaves intensely bitter, so in warm climates it is normally grown as a fall crop. It is direct sown 8 - 12 weeks (depending upon the variety) before the first fall frost, so it can mature during a cooler part of the year. The seed is heat sensitive and doesn't germinate well above 80°F. See **Lettuce** for possible ways to overcome this.

Roots: To grow the roots for forcing or coffee, a suitable variety is planted some time in spring. It doesn't need to be started very early, as it is quite fast growing and has all season to mature.

Planting

Transplants: Chicory is often grown from transplants, which are raised like those of the related lettuce.

Direct sowing: Plant the seed ¼ - ½″ deep and 1 - 2″ apart. When all have germinated start harvest thinning, to eventually reach the desired final spacing.

Spacing:
Roots: To grow roots for forcing, space the plants 4 - 5″ apart in rows 18″ apart. This maximizes the number of roots.

Beds: Chicory may be spaced anywhere from 6″ - 9″ - 12″ - 18″ apart, depending upon the variety and soil.

Rows: Space plants 12″ apart, in rows 18 - 24″ apart.

Care

Chicory is an easy plant to grow (it commonly self-sows in my garden) and as a perennial it isn't prone to bolting in its first year.

Weeds: It is important to keep the young plants free of weeds.

Water: This deep rooted plant is very drought resistant. However a lack of water makes the plants even more bitter than usual and increases their chances of bolting. Keep the soil evenly moist at all times.

Mulch: This is useful to keep down weeds and conserve moisture. In winter it can be used to protect the plants from extreme cold.

Blanching: The plants are sometimes blanched like those of endive to make them less bitter. The easiest way to do this is to cover the plant with an inverted flowerpot (close up the drainage hole). See **Endive** (below) for more on this useful technique to make plants more palatable.

Pests and diseases: Chicory retains a lot of its wild vigor and isn't bothered by many problems. Slugs, snails and cutworms may attack it when young.

Tip burn: As the name suggests, the tips of leaves look like they have been burned. It is usually caused by excessively hot weather.

Harvesting

You can harvest individual leaves, as soon as they are of sufficient size. They are always somewhat bitter, but in hot weather they become so bitter they are uneatable.

The best part of the leaf chicory types is the blanched interior heart and to get these you must let the head form fully. You then harvest the whole head and remove all of the green outer leaves (you can eat these too, if they aren't too bitter. After this you are left with the pale, slightly yellowish and delicious heart.

Storage: Store the leafy head like lettuce, in a plastic bag in the fridge for up to a week. Store the chicons in a plastic bag in the fridge for up to 4 weeks.

Seed saving: Chicory sets seed easily if allowed to. The flowers are pollinated by insects and will cross-pollinate with endive (though apparently chicory won't pollinate endive) or wild chicory (which is a very common wild flower). To keep a variety pure you must isolate it by a ½ mile, or cage it.

It is quite hard to separate the individual seeds from the pod (you have to crush them to release the seeds), so they are often stored in the form of dried pods.

Growing chicons

Forcing the shoots: The roots are forced indoors to provide the tasty white shoots called *chicons*. This has become a major industry in Belgium and they are sometimes available in supermarkets under the name Belgian endive. They provide a fresh green vegetable in the middle of winter, when few others are available.

To grow chicons you dig the roots in late fall, after the tops have died down and they have been vernalized by cold weather. By this time they should be as big as parsnips. Cut off the dead top, leaving only an inch of stem. Also trim off the bottom of the root, so they are a uniform length of about 8″. These are then stored in a cool root cellar, or in a trench in the ground, until needed.

For forcing the roots are planted in a deep plant pot, (as many as can easily fit when spacing them 2″ apart). To start them growing they are watered and moved to a warm (50 - 60˚F) dark place.

The pale shoots take about 4 weeks to grow and are harvested when about 6″ tall. The roots will usually produce 2 crops if well cared for. In large commercial operations they are now often forced hydroponically.

Volunteer: Chicory self-sows readily and might be considered a weed if it weren't so useful. Not only is it edible and of medicinal value, but its bright blue flowers attract many beneficial insects.

Varieties

Nowhere is the chicory more highly esteemed than in Italy and a large number of types and varieties are available there. Some of these are now becoming available here too.

Dandelion types

These closely resemble the wild types, but tend to be less bitter.

Red Rib: The green leaves have red stems and are very pretty.

Catalogna: There are quite a few of these. They have long strap-like leaves like a dandelion and are sometimes known as Italian dandelion. This is one of the least developed types of chicory and is very close to being a wild plant (it has been naturalized in my garden for at least 5 years). As an almost wild plant it is commonly eaten in spring, though it becomes impossibly bitter as the weather warms up.

Catalogna puntarelle: This is a catalogna type that produces an edible flower shoot in late winter or spring. This is somewhat bitter but in Italy (especially Rome) it is highly prized as a spring treat. These are excellent in salads, but can also be cooked.

Sugar Loaf types

These are fairly similar to the raddichios and produce similar compact heads of tight leaves in cold weather. They superficially resemble a Chinese cabbage and are quite a substantial food.

The heart of these heads is naturally blanched and is succulent, bitter/sweet and delicious. These leaves are almost universally pronounced to be superior to any lettuce. They can also be used as a cooked vegetable.

The seed is planted in late spring and early summer to mature in fall and winter, when they produce their dense heads. In very cold areas it helps to protect them with a thick mulch (even though this is a pretty hardy plant anyway). They are perennial and so independent they can be naturalized.

The roots can also be dug and forced indoors like witloof.

Varieties include:

Sugar Loaf (Pain de sucre) (pan di zucchero)

Greenlof

Sugarhat

Blanc de Milan

Virtus F1

Forcing types

Witloof: This variety is grown for forcing and the resulting chicons are often called Belgian endive, even though it isn't really endive.

Totem F1

Root types

Magdeburg: This is grown for its edible roots (for coffee).

Kitchen use

Greens: The tender new spring leaves can be used in the same ways as the related dandelion, They are most often used as salad greens, but as the plant matures they become impossibly bitter. Blanching reduces this considerably and this probably led to the forcing of the roots.

Though we think of chicory as a salad plant it can also be cooked and deserves to be more widely used in this way. You can reduce its bitterness when cooking, by changing the cooking water after a minute or so.

Coffee: Chicory root has been widely used as a coffee substitute or extender and many people say it actually improves the flavor of coffee. It may also reduce its harmful effect on the liver.

To make chicory "coffee" the cleaned roots are dried thoroughly, until they are so brittle they snap easily. They are then ground to a powder and roasted in an oven until uniformly brown.

The drink is prepared by mixing a teaspoon of the roasted powder with a cup of boiling water. You can also add roasted sprouted barley, carob, cinnamon, or other goodies. It is sometimes mixed with an equal amount of coffee.

Radicchio

Cichorium intybus

Originally bred in Northeastern Italy, this type of chicory has become very fashionable in recent years. It is prized for its small dense head of colorful, sculptural, spectacular, crisp, succulent and slightly bitter leaves. However it only tastes good when grown at the right time of year (in cold weather). Plants grown when it isn't cold enough have been called rad-yuck-io.

Radicchio is cultivated in the same way as chicory. It can even be forced indoors in the same way to produce red chicons.

Varieties: From the gardeners viewpoint radicchio can be divided into two types, forcing and non-forcing. A percentage (sometimes a significant one) of both types won't produce the desired compact heads. This is one of the reasons it is often quite expensive to buy.

Forcing types: These varieties need cold weather to stimulate them to produce a compact head. Cold weather may kill the outer leaves, but the colorful head will emerge from underneath them.

Red Verona

Treviso

Non-Forcing types: Sometimes called chioggia types, these varieties produce a head even without cold weather. However you might have to stimulate them to head up by cutting off most of the top growth (leave only 2″ of leaves). The resulting new growth should then form a head

Castelfranco

Chioggia

Palla Rossa:

Giulio

Coriander / Cilantro

Coriandrum sativum

Introduction: This annual provides two quite distinct foods. The leaves (often called by their Spanish name cilantro) have a unique aromatic flavor you either love or hate (I have an old English gardening book that described the foliage as "foul smelling"). I am in a position to appreciate both sides of this argument, as I used to be one of the people who really disliked it. However over the years, through its use in Mexican foods I have grown to love it (I guess if you eat anything for long enough you eventually get to like it).

The large ripe seeds (pods) are known as coriander and have an aromatic orange-like flavor and smell. They are particularly popular in Middle Eastern and Southeast Asian foods.

I really like the immature green seeds also. They have an intriguing flavor that is somewhere between that of the leaf and the ripe seed.

Nutritional value: The leaves are actually a nutritional superfood, containing vitamins A, B1, B2, B3, B5, B6, C, E and K, as well as folate, calcium, copper, iron, magnesium, phosphorus, potassium, manganese and zinc. They also contain a variety of beneficial phytonutrients and antioxidants. We could all benefit from eating more cilantro (even those who don't enjoy it).

For what its worth cilantro also contains about 104 calories per pound (not that even the most fanatical cilantro lover would ever eat a pound of it).

Climate: Cilantro is a cool weather plant and prefers growing temperatures below 75°F. It is just about hardy enough to tolerate light frost, but anything more severe will kill it. It is also day length sensitive and bolts readily during the longer and warmer days of summer. This can be a problem if you are growing it for leaves. It often seems like it finally gets going (producing leaves) and suddenly its gone (bolted.)

Crop value: To its aficionados coriander/cilantro is an indispensable flavoring herb. To the rest of you it is a minor and rather unpleasant (foul smelling?) herb.

About Coriander

Seed facts:
Seed viability: 2 – 4 yrs
Germ time: 5 - 10 days
Germ temp: 55 (60 - 65) 75°F

Planning facts
Growing temp: 40 (50 - 60) 75°F
Spring crop: Direct sow 0 - 6 wks before last spring frost
Fall crop: Start 6 - 8 wks before first fall frost
Days to maturity: 40 - 50 leaf
70 - 90 seed
Plants per person: 3
Height 18 - 24″
Width 6″

Ease of growing: Coriander is fairly easy to grow during cool weather and in my garden it volunteers reliably every spring. It is harder to grow in summer though, as it bolts when exposed to high temperatures and long days.

This is a relatively short lived plant at the best of times and is quite prone to bolting, which can shorten its life even further. In extreme cases it will only grow 4 or 5 leaves and then flower, even if just 6″ tall.

Soil

pH 6.0 (6.5 - 6.8) 7.5

Cilantro will grow in most soil types, but does best in the average fertile, well-drained, moisture retentive garden soil. If the soil is very poor, it will bolt even more rapidly than usual.

Soil preparation: This isn't a very demanding plant, but if the soil is poor add a couple of inches of compost or aged manure.

Planning

Where: Cilantro prefers full sun when growing in its ideal cool weather. In warmer weather you will often have better luck with partial shade.

When: Cilantro doesn't like heat and bolts quickly once the weather warms up. In warmer climates it can only be grown in the cool weather of spring or early fall, but in milder areas you may be able to grow it all summer (though bolting may be a problem during the long days of mid-summer). In very mild winter areas it may continue to grow right through the winter.

It is often suggested that you plant cilantro around the last frost date, but you can plant a lot earlier than this. The seed won't be harmed by cold soil (it often self-sows) and it will germinate whenever it is ready (it knows when to do this better than you do). If you want to try and get it as early as possible you can start it inside, 6 weeks before the last frost. It can also be sown in autumn for an early spring crop.

Planting

This annual is easily grown from seed (more easily than most members of the *Apiaceae*). The familiar round "seed" is actually a capsule and contains a number of seeds.

Direct sowing: Cilantro doesn't like transplanting, so is usually direct sown. Space the seeds ¼ – ½″ deep and fairly thickly (1 - 2″ apart) to start with. You can then harvest thin every other plant as they get bigger, until they reach the desired spacing (or bolt, whichever comes first).

Starting indoors: If you want to start cilantro indoors it's best to use plug trays, cell packs or soil blocks, to minimize root disturbance. Start indoors 6 weeks before the last frost date and plant out around the last frost date. If hard frost threaten after planting, you could cover them with a frost blanket.

Fall crop: Start 6 - 8 wks before the first fall frost, or whenever the weather cools down sufficiently.

Spacing: The plants should be spaced 6 - 8″ apart in a bed. If you grow in rows you should space them 6″ apart, with 18 - 24″ between rows.

Succession sow: Cilantro is a pretty short lived plant (often only 6 - 8 weeks), but you can ensure a longer supply by making frequent succession sowings (every 2 weeks). Do this for as long as you can get usable leaves.

Care

Weeding: Cilantro isn't very vigorous when young and needs to be kept free of weeds.

Watering: It prefers moist soil and needs watering regularly in dry weather. Dry soil may contribute to bolting.

Pests and disease: Cilantro is fairly pest and disease free. In fact it actually attracts beneficial insects such as predatory wasps.

Bolting: Cilantro is notorious for its penchant for bolting. This is most often caused by high temperatures combined with long days, but it can also be caused by poor soil, root disturbance due to careless transplanting.

Saving seed: If left alone this insect pollinated plant will eventually produce seed and will often self-sow. There aren't many varieties, so you probably don't have to worry too much about cross-pollination.

Harvesting

The leaves can be gathered as soon as the plants are big enough. If you plant thickly you can harvest thin to extend the harvest. Do this by removing every other plant and using them in the kitchen.

The small white flowers are a nice addition to salads.

Gather the seed heads when the seeds start to turn brown. Put them in a paper bag in a warm place to dry fully and then separate out the large seeds from the chaff.

Storage: You can keep the leaves in a plastic bag in the fridge for a few days. They don't keep their flavor very well when dried. The best way to store them and retain their fresh taste is to freeze them. You can freeze the leaves whole in a plastic bag, or you can put the chopped leaves in ice cube trays and cover them with water. Once they are frozen you can transfer them to a plastic bag.

The dry seeds will be good for several years.

Unusual growing ideas

Containers: Cilantro does pretty well in containers and can even be grown indoors in this way.

Microgreens: If you must have fresh cilantro in the heat of summer salsa season, you could try growing it as microgreens. You can do this outside in a shady bed (maybe use misters to keep it cool) or inside.

Varieties

For a long time if you wanted to grow this plant there was just one type of generic coriander/cilantro seed (sometimes labelled as Chinese parsley). This has changed in recent years and now quite a few varieties are available, mostly bred with the aim of slowing down bolting (these can help a lot).

Slow bolt aka Santo - As you might guess this variety was bred to be slow to bolt.

Long standing - This variety was bred to be long standing (aka slow to bolt!)

Calypso - This one was bred to be even slower to bolt than Slow Bolt (by 3 weeks!)

Kitchen use

A very international plant, the seeds and leaves are important in Mexican, Vietnamese, Thai, Indian and other cuisines. I read somewhere that the roots are edible too, though I'm not sure I believe it.

Of course this is an essential ingredient for salsa (see **Tomato** for a good recipe for this).

Warm weather cilantro alternatives

The frustrating thing about cilantro is that it doesn't grow well in hot weather, when you have all those tomatoes, peppers, garlic and onions crying out to be made into salsa. Fortunately there are a number of other similar tasting plants that actually thrive in hot weather (they don't taste exactly the same, but they are close enough for most purposes). If you crave cilantro during the summer, you will probably be interested in trying these heat loving alternatives. Once I found these I became less concerned about cilantro bolting.

Culantro

(*Eryngium foetidum*)
I would say this small tender plant has the closest resemblance to cilantro of the three. It is usually grown from seed and takes up to 21 days to germinate. It is a fairly slow growing plant and takes about 75 days to start producing a worthwhile amount. It is normally started indoors early and planted out after the weather has warmed up.

I have never had a lot of success with culantro in my garden, it just grows too slowly to be of much use. I'm assuming this is because the nights here are too cool. I haven't really pursued it though, because the other two grow so easily.

Papalo

(*Porophyllum ruderale*)
This species is commonly used in its native Mexico as a warm weather substitute for cilantro. In restaurants there it is often found in a vase on tables, to be added to food to diners taste. It is now in demand for gourmet restaurants in this country.

Papalo isn't related to cilantro (it's a member of the daisy family) but it tastes quite similar. It is a vigorous, almost weedy, plant and may eventually grow to 4 feet in height, but is best harvested when about 12″ tall. It likes well-drained soil and full sun.

I have found the biggest drawback of using papalo is finding seed to plant; it simply isn't available in many places. When I finally found some it never germinated. Then I got some at a seed exchange and it germinated very easily. I now consider it a garden essential.

Vietnamese Coriander

(*Polygonum odoratum)*
This sub-tropical plant needs moist soil and can even be grown in water gardens. The first time I grew it I never realized this and only gave it water sparingly. It survived but didn't really thrive until I increased the amount of water they received. In ideal conditions it can be very vigorous and can grow like a weed.

This tender perennial isn't considered very hardy, but it usually survives the winter in my garden and has been there for at least five years now. It has even survived a cold snap where we had frost every night for two weeks. If you want to grow it in marginal situations you have to look for warm microclimates to put tender it.

My plants haven't produced seed (to my knowledge), but are easily propagated by division or cuttings.

Vietnamese coriander has become a fixture in my garden because it is a do nothing plant. It just grows and I just harvest. The flavor is slightly different from cilantro, but close enough for most purposes.

Corn

Zea mays

Introduction: This warm weather annual differs from all other common garden vegetables in being the only a member of the grass family (*Poaceae*). It is thought to have originated somewhere in Central America, though it is no longer found anywhere as a wild plant (it may be descended from the closely related Teosinte, which is still found in the wild in Mexico). Native Americans have cultivated corn for over 5000 years and in many places it was not only a staple food, but also an integral part of their culture.

Corn was introduced into Europe in the sixteenth century and spread from there to all suitable climates around the world. There are several different types of corn (see **Varieties**), but they are all grown in much the same way, only their uses differ.

Nutritional content: Sweet corn is rich in carbohydrate, as well as soluble fiber, folate, niacin, thiamin and phosphorus. It also contains useful phytochemicals. Yellow varieties also contain vitamin A.

Field corn is rich in protein, carbohydrates, potassium, calcium and the amino acids leucine and methionine (the latter is lacking in beans, which is why they go together so well).

Niacin: When corn was introduced to the rest of the world in the sixteenth and seventeenth centuries a little snippet of important information was left behind in its homeland. The niacin in corn is not very available and requires special processing before humans are able to make use of it.

As corn became a staple food in many poor areas a problem developed, as some people started to show symptoms of niacin deficiency. This results in an unpleasant deficiency disease called pellagra.

In its native land corn is soaked in an alkaline solution of water and calcium hydroxide (slaked lime) or wood ashes. This process is known as nixtamalization and has several important effects. The most important is that it makes the niacin in the corn more available. It also softens the cellulose in the seed, making it easier to grind and making it possible to make it into dough for making tortillas.

Crop value: Sweet corn is one of the ultimate treats of the summer garden (it makes my mouth water thinking about it), but it isn't really a good crop for small gardens. You need quite few plants to ensure good pollination and they aren't very productive for the space they require.

From a nutritional and self sufficiency viewpoint field corn is much more important than sweet corn. It is one of the easiest and most productive of all cereal crops to grow and process and it can be used in a variety of ways for making cornbread, tortillas, polenta and more.

Anyone seeking food self sufficiency in a warm climate will probably end up growing a lot of corn (emulating many peasants around the world).

If you want to use corn as a staple food it needs to be processed to make its niacin available. Fortunately this is pretty easy to do (see **Nixtamalization** below).

Ease of growing: Corn is a fairly easy and reliable crop to grow if you give it moist, fertile soil and warm weather.

Climate: Corn is a subtropical plant and uses C4 photosynthesis, which enables it to grow more efficiently in high heat and light levels. For best growth it needs warm weather and as much sunlight as it can get. If it doesn't get full sun all day it will grow more slowly and won't be as productive.

Soil

pH 5.5 (6.0 - 6.8)

Corn grows well in a variety of soils, but it is a hungry plant and needs a lot of nutrients for maximum production. The ideal soil is rich, moisture retentive and well-drained. Field corn isn't quite as demanding as sweet corn, but the better the soil the better the crop.

Soil preparation: This vigorous and fast growing crop needs generous amounts of nitrogen, phosphorus and potassium, as well as all of the other plant nutrients.

Incorporate 2″ of compost or aged manure into the top 8″ of soil, along with colloidal phosphate (for phosphorus) and wood ashes (for potassium). Add kelp to supply the necessary trace elements. Alternatively you could use an organic fertilizer mix to supply these nutrients,

Corn is sometimes planted into a bed 2 weeks after a nitrogen fixing winter cover crop (such as fava beans) is incorporated.

Legend has it that Native Americans put a fish in each hill of corn, to supply the necessary nutrients. This isn't true though, when soil fertility started to decline they would just move their gardens to new soil (one of the advantages of not "owning" land).

Planning

Where: Sweet corn can be grown in an intensive bed, but it should be in a large block for best pollination. It is a tall growing plant, so must be planted where it won't shade other plants. If you are growing SH2 or SY types they need to be isolated from other types, either by time (10 days) or distance (at least 25 ft).

Field corn should probably be grown in its own separate patch, as you will need to plant quite a large area if you want to produce a significant quantity of food. You might want to try growing it in a polyculture with squash and beans (see **Three Sisters** for more on this).

Crop rotation: Don't plant corn in the same soil for at least 3 years. In a rotation it commonly follows a nitrogen-fixing legume.

When: Don't plant corn until at least 2 weeks after the last frost date, when the soil has warmed up to a minimum of 60°F (75°F for the more temperamental supersweet varieties). Native Americans traditionally waited until the plum trees bloomed, or the oak leaves were emerging before planting. In cold soil, the seed takes a long time to germinate and there is a much greater chance of loss to rot or some hungry creature.

Day length: Though it isn't as critical as with some crops, corn is day length sensitive to a varying degree (some varieties more than others). If it is planted too late in the year it will often flower while the plants are quite small and there won't be much of a harvest.

About Corn

Seed facts

Germ temp: 50 (60 - 75) - 95°F
Germ time: 3 - 10 days
22 days / 50°F
12 days / 59°F
7 days / 68°F
4 days / 77°F * Optimum
4 days / 86°F
3 days / 95°F
Seed viability:
Sweet Corn 1 - 3 yrs
Field Corn 3 - 5 yrs
Germination percentage: 75%+
Weeks to grow transplant: 3 - 4

Planning facts

Hardiness: Tender
Growing temp: 50 (60 - 75) 95°F
Plants per person: 15
Plants per sq ft: 1 plant needs 1 - 2 sq ft
Transplants:
Start: 2 wks before last frost
Plant out: 2 wks after last frost
Direct sow: 2 wks after last frost
Days to harvest: 60 - 150 days

Harvest facts

Harvest period: 2 - 3 weeks
Yield per plant: 2 - 4 ears
Yield per sq ft: 1 - 3 ears

Succession sowing: In the home garden you don't want a lot of corn ripening at once (unless you are going to freeze it). You can stagger the harvest, by succession sowing a block every 2 - 3 weeks. You could also plant several varieties with different maturation times.

Planting

Transplants

Starting inside: Corn can be started indoors, but this is only worthwhile for very early corn, where the growing season is exceptionally short (or cool), or to avoid predators such as birds and mice.

Use cell packs, soil blocks or plug trays as corn doesn't really like disturbance. Sow 2 seeds in each cell or block and thin to the best one when they have all emerged. If germination is very good, you might just plant one seed per cell. The seedlings grow rapidly and will get root-bound if left in their containers for too long. Ideally they should be out of their pots and in the ground within 3 - 4 weeks.

Direct sowing: Corn is usually direct sown, because it grows fast, doesn't like transplanting and it is less work. In spring when the soil is cool, it should be planted only 1″ deep. Later in the year, when the soil is warm, it may be planted as deep as 4″. The less vigorous seed of hybrid varieties is usually planted only ¾ - 1″ deep (this should be consistent as they are sensitive to this). Plant twice as many seeds as you need and thin to the desired spacing when they are several inches high.

To get the plants off to a good start, you can soak the seeds overnight prior to planting (sweet corn is more temperamental than field corn and needs more moisture to germinate). For an even faster start you could pre-germinate them, but be careful not to break the brittle roots

In some areas mice or birds can be a major problem in spring, in which case you can use rows covers (these also keep the seedlings warmer).

Hill planting: Native Americans used to plant their corn in hills. These were quite literally small flattened mounds about 18″ in diameter. They planted 6 - 8 seeds in each hill, at a depth of 2 - 4″ and spaced evenly in a circle about 9″ in diameter. The hills were spaced about 4 feet apart in the rows and there was about 4 feet between the rows.

Row planting: Corn is usually planted in rows, but to ensure good pollination (which means full ears) it is important that the rows be in blocks. These should consist of at least four rows each.

Spacing:
Rows: Put the plants 6 - 8″ apart in the rows, with 24 - 36″ between the rows.

Beds: Plant in offsets rows across the bed. The distance apart depends upon the soil:
18″ (poor soil)
15″ (average soil)
12″ (excellent soil)

Poor emergence
This may be caused by several factors; cold or wet soil, poor seed, birds, mice, rotting of seed, soil compaction or crusting, insects, disease or too deep planting. Sweet corn is more vulnerable than other types because it contains less food in the form of starch (the sh2 and se types are particularly temperamental).

Care

Weeding: It is important to weed the plants carefully while they are young. After they reach 12″ in height they can deal with almost any weed. The young plants can be hoed quite closely, as they don't have shallow roots.

Water: Sweet corn is a thirsty plant and needs a constant supply of water for best growth. This is especially crucial during tasselling and subsequent ear maturation. A soaker hose or drip system is the best way to irrigate. Be careful when overhead watering as it can interfere with fertilization during the pollen shedding stage.

Generally field corn needs significantly less water than sweet corn, especially those varieties bred for growing in dry climates.

.**Fertilization**: It is a good idea to give the young plants a boost of nitrogen (such as compost tea or liquid kelp) when the seedlings are about 12″ tall and growing rapidly. Give them another boost when the silks appear.

Pollination: Corn is wind-pollinated and getting good pollination is a critical aspect of corn growing. If you don't get good pollination, the ears may be only half filled and you won't have a good crop. Overhead irrigation and wet weather can impede pollination

The male tassel on top of the plant gives off pollen for a couple of days before the female flowers (the silks) become receptive. When the silks are receptive, you can improve pollination by gently shaking the plants, so pollen comes cascading down from the tassels. This should be done on a still day of course.
In some cases the type of pollen a plant receives will determines its taste characteristics. This means you should ideally only have one kind of corn flowering at one time (unless you are prepared to hand pollinate).

Genetic purity is most important with the super sweet hybrids and they should probably be isolated from all other types of corn. It is not so important for field corn, unless you are saving the seed for planting (in which case you may want to hand pollinate).

It is helpful to note when half of your sweet corn plants are showing silks, because they will be ready to harvest from 18 - 22 days later. The exact time depends upon temperature and growing conditions.

Suckers: Corn plants often produce suckers, smaller stems, which if left alone may eventually flower and produce small ears. Some people believe theses drain energy from the plant and remove them as they appear. This isn't really necessary though.

Pests: Many pests attack corn at various stages of growth. These include cutworms, corn rootworms, wireworms, aphids, flea beetles, corn earworm, corn borers, Japanese beetles, sap beetles, raccoons, squirrels and birds.

Corn Earworm: This is perhaps the most common corn pest. It burrows down into the ear, eating the seeds and making quite a mess. It isn't usually a problem on early corn, but can affect almost every ear of a late planting.

The good news is that corn earworm damage is mostly cosmetic and is usually confined to the tip of the ear. All you have to do is chop this off and the person eating the corn won't even be aware there was a problem (if only all garden pests were so easy to deal with). Supposedly some varieties have tighter husks than others and so are less affected (i.e. Country Gentleman).

Diseases: Potential disease problems include: bacterial wilt, maize dwarf mosaic, corn leaf blights, root rot and rust.

Corn Smut (*Ustilago maydis*): Corn smut is a fungus disease that infects corn plants, producing swollen growths on the ears. In the United States it is considered a pest and is destroyed whenever it occurs. In Mexico it is known as huitlacoche and is considered a delicacy that is actually worth more than corn. It has an earthy, sweet mushroom-like flavor and is said to be very good (I have never been lucky enough to get any to try).

Attempts have been made to popularize corn smut as a food in the United States by re-naming it Mexican truffle. Perhaps one day it will become a useful crop here too. I have no doubt high end restaurants would eat it up if you could grow it for them.

For culinary use this fungus should be gathered while it is still moist and immature, about 2 - 3 weeks after the initial infection. The mature fungus eventually releases a cloud of brown spores. If you are lucky enough to have corn smut, you could try collecting some of the spores. The Aztecs used to deliberately infect their plants with them and you could try doing the same.

Nutrient deficiency:
Nitrogen deficiency is common in corn, especially if the soil is cold or unusually wet or dry. Young plants will be spindly and their leaves will be pale and slightly yellow (rather than deep green). Treat it by feeding your plants compost tea or other high nitrogen liquid fertilizer.

Harvesting

Sweet corn:
When: More than almost any other crop, it is important to gather sweet corn at the right time. The ears mature from 17 - 23 days after pollination (depending upon the weather) and there are many indicators of maturity.

How to tell when sweet corn is ripe

The silks wither and turn dark brown.

The ear feels fat.

The end becomes rounded rather than pointed.

The ear tilts away from the stem.

To check if an ear is ripe, pull open the top of the husk and squeeze a kernel. If it is fat and spurts milky juice, it is ready. If it is dimpled and spurts watery juice it's not yet ripe (just close up the husk). Be aware that some super sweet varieties may have clear juice and still be ripe.

If the kernel is fat and tough, the ear is probably over-mature and will be starchy and not very good.

Wait for raccoons to show an interest.

Sweet corn ripens quickly in warm weather, so watch it carefully and harvest when it is ready (it is only really good for a few days). If you can't use it immediately, freeze it, or give it away. If not harvested at the right time it will be wasted.

How: Snap the ripe ear from the plant by pulling it downwards, being careful not to break the plant, or damage its neighbors.

Field Corn: Harvesting field corn is much easier than sweet corn; simply leave the ears until the entire plant turns brown and dry. Then remove the husks and dry the whole ears.

Watch for birds when the corn is ripe as they will sometimes strip seed from the whole ears. If they start to do this harvest immediately.

Storage:
Sweet corn: Most types of sweet corn are best when used immediately and deteriorate quickly after picking. The super sweets can be stored for a few days in the fridge (the low temperature slows down the conversion of sugar to starch.

Field corn: The dry ears can be stored whole (they are quite decorative), but the seed takes up less space if you remove it from the ears. Make sure the seed is completely dry before storing it, otherwise it will go moldy.

Seed saving: Saving corn seed is a little more complicated than most other crops, because you have to worry about inbreeding (corn strains are very inbred). If you want to maintain a pure variety indefinitely you need to save seed from at least 50 plants (some say the absolute minimum is 100 with 200 being ideal) to maintain sufficient genetic variability.

If you are growing field corn this isn't a big deal, you can just collect a few seeds from each mature ear and use the rest for food. It is a problem with sweet corn though, because you have to let the ears mature and dry fully to get the best seed. This essentially means you have to let one whole ear of sweet corn mature on each plant and only eat any others. Of course saving all of the seed from 200 ears is a huge amount of seed.

All of this makes keeping sweet corn seed pure and vigorous a special project, rather than an incidental activity. This is made even more difficult by the fact that sweet corn is quite short lived, so you can't just do it once every few years. Saving sweet corn seed probably makes most sense as a community project, to be undertaken cooperatively by many gardeners (or by small commercial growers).

If you just want to save a little money on seed, you can forget about all I have just said. Just save the seed from a few ears and plant it the following year. The next year you could buy a packet of new seed and mix it with your own seed to deepen the gene pool. This isn't ideal from a genetic standpoint, but what have you got to lose?

The other problem with corn is that it is wind pollinated and can cross very easily. To keep a strain pure you must either hand pollinate, grow only one variety at a time, or separate it from other tasselling plants by at least 250 yards (1000 yards is better). You should also collect your seed from the center of the stand, where there is less chance of stray pollen coming in.

Native Americans saved their own field corn seed for thousands of years, but they didn't worry about the purity of a strain. In fact they encouraged diversity in their seeds, by collecting seed from a variety of plants, rather than simply the 'best', as we tend to do.

Hand pollination: This isn't difficult, but takes some time, especially if you are pollinating 100 plants. The first step is to put a bag over the female flowers before the silks emerge, to prevent them being pollinated by any stray pollen. This must be taped shut, to prevent any pollen entering. The next morning, after the dew has dried, you go out and gently shake pollen from the newly opened tassels into a paper bag. Then simply transfer a little pollen onto the silks of each plant with a brush. You then replace the bags and leave them on until the silks go brown. Mark the ears carefully so they don't get eaten accidentally (which would be a pain after all that extra effort).

Unusual growing methods

Early corn: If your growing season is short, or you just want to get very early corn, start your seedlings indoors a couple of weeks before the last frost date. It also helps to warm the soil under black plastic for a couple of weeks before planting out. Plant the seedlings on the last frost date and cover with row covers, or cloches, to keep them warm until the weather warms up.

Baby corn: These are the tiny immature cobs seen in Chinese restaurants. Any kind of sweet corn can be used, but there are special varieties (Baby Asian, Chires Baby Corn) that produce multiple ears per stem (Chires is said to produce up to 40 ears per plant).

Baby Corn is grown in exactly the same way as sweet corn, though you can plant it closer together (as close as 8″ in fertile soil). The ears are harvested a couple of days after the silks show. As you might imagine this isn't a very productive crop.

Dry garden: Field corn can be dry farmed using only the water that's held in the ground. The plants must be spaced further apart for this to work. If you want to experiment with this then try and find a variety that was developed in a dry climate.

Three sisters

Native Americans called corn, beans and squash, the three sisters and devised a very efficient method of growing them together. This works just as well today as it ever did and you may want to experiment with it. The corn stalks give the beans support, the squash creates a living mulch over the bare soil between the corn hills and the beans supply nitrogen. Even the foods they provide complement each other.

The corn is planted as described above, with 5 - 6 seeds in each hill. These are left to grow until they are about 10″ tall and are then hilled up with soil to a height of about 6″ (this makes them more stable). After hilling, 10 - 12 pole beans are planted in a circle around the growing corn, a few inches away from them. These sprout within 7 - 10 days. A week after they have germinated, 5 squash seeds are planted around them, about a foot further out.

Once everything is growing there is little left to do, except ensure that they aren't overtaken by weeds and have enough water. You may want to help the individual pole beans find corn stalks to climb up. The squash will eventually cover and shade the ground, though you might feel the need to direct growing shoots to bare areas, so they fill in more evenly.

Varieties

If you grow a lot of corn, you can save money by buying your corn seed in bulk from a farm supply store, rather in packets from the garden center. Of course you can also save your own open-pollinated field corn seed for use in future years.

Field corn

If you mention corn to a gardener, she will almost certainly think of sweet corn, as most of the corn grown by American gardeners is of this type. Yet in the history of corn as a food crop, field corn is actually far more important.

Field corn varieties can be divided into several groups, according to the type of starch they produce. There is also considerable difference in color, with blue, white, red and yellow varieties.

Dent Corn: *Z mays var indentata*
The kernels of dent corn have a depression in the middle (hence the name) and their starch is a mixture of hard and soft. Almost 80% of commercial field corn is of this type. Depending upon when they are picked, the kernels can be used for cornmeal, hominy, roasting corn or sweet corn.

Gourdseed corn is a type of dent corn that is prized for making high quality cornmeal.

Flint Corn: *Z. mays var indurata*
Flint corn grows better in cooler climates than most other types.The starch in the semi-translucent seeds is very hard, which is how it gets its name. It is used for cornmeal, though it is so hard it can be difficult to grind.

Soft Corn: *Z. mays var amylacea*
The seeds contain mostly soft starch hence the name. This type of corn is easily ground to meal and is commonly used for bread, tortillas and corn chips.

Popcorn: *Z. mays var everata*
Popcorn kernels have a very hard outer layer and a soft inner layer, a combination which makes them pop readily. They can also be used for cornmeal. Popcorn is a great crop for children to plant, as they get an extra special reward at the end of it.

Strawberry Popcorn - This is the easiest variety to find.

Japanese hulless - I have had good luck with this one.

Sweet Corn

Z. mays var saccharata
Sweet corn differs from field corn in that it is harvested while immature and most of its food is in the form of sugar rather than starch. This is why it is so sweet and why the seeds shrink when dried. It also makes the seeds somewhat temperamental in their germination capacity and accounts for their short storage life.

The sweetness genes in sweet corn are recessive so there must be a copy of the gene in both the flower and the pollen. If sweet corn is pollinated by field corn it will be starchy instead of sweet.

Corn is one of the few crops in which hybridization has made a big difference. Hybrids are superior to non-hybrids in that they mature more uniformly and are often sweeter. Unfortunately you can't save the seed of a hybrid, as they don't come true to type (of course you may not care as it isn't the easiest plant to save seed from anyway). There are several types of sweet corn

Normal sugary (su) - Hybrids
The (su) gene is found in all older sweet corn varieties (open pollinated and hybrids) and its sugar starts to convert to starch soon after picking. These varieties aren't as sweet as other types, but often make up for it with good corn flavor. These types do better in less than ideal conditions, such as cool soil.

Silver Queen F1 - Late season (90 days), sweet and tender. It was the standard corn for a while.

Honey & Cream F1 - Vigorous plants, sweet bicolor corn, a classic.

Normal sugary (su) - Open **pollinated**
Some traditionalists maintain that sweetness isn't everything and that open pollinated varieties simply have a better corn flavor. If you grow them, you have to be more on top of things, as they don't maintain their sweetness for very long. When harvesting you get to perform the boil water before harvesting ritual.

Country Gentleman - A shoe peg corn (kernels not in rows), a classic for roasting.

Golden Bantam - A favorite for 100 years.

Painted Mountain - Multi-colored and genetically diverse. Can also be ground to flour.

Super sweet corn

These were bred for commercial growers, as they remain sweet for much longer than conventional varieties. They can be divided into 3 types, supersweet (sh2), sugary enhanced (se) and synergistic (sy).

Super Sweet (sh2): These contain the sh2 gene which not only makes them very sweet, but also means that their sugar converts to starch very slowly. It is important that they be fully mature before use, as they don't develop much corn flavor until this time. They are known for being quite crisp in texture (some people call them tough).

These types don't contain a lot of starch, which makes them somewhat temperamental to germinate in less than optimal conditions. They shouldn't even be planted until the soil is at least 65˚F and preferably 70˚F. They also need to be isolated from other varieties while tasselling, otherwise the resulting kernels will be tough and starchy.

Honey 'n Pearl F1 - One of best bi-colored sh2's

Xtra-Tender F1- White super sweet.

Sugary Enhanced (se) (se+)

These contain a gene that enhances the normal sugary gene (su) and makes the kernels sweeter and more tender (some people think it is mushy). In addition the sugar is only slowly converted to starch after picking. These varieties don't require isolation from other varieties.

Sugar Pearl F1 - An early white corn.

How-Sweet-It-Is F1- One of the sweetest corns around.

Kandy Korn F1 - Stays sweet for 2 weeks.

Sugar Buns F1 - An early (70 - 80 days yellow corn.

Synergistic (sy)

These varieties contain (su) (se) and (sh2) genes, which makes them both tender and very sweet. They also need to be isolated from other varieties when tasselling. They tend to be more vigorous than the sh2 types.

Montauk F1 - A big bicolor (80 days).

Kitchen use

Traditional sweet corn begins to lose its sweetness as soon as it is harvested, because the sugar is gradually converted into starch. The sooner you cook it, the less sweetness will be lost. Corn epicures say you should have the water boiling before even picking your corn (and preferably out in the field on a camp stove. Sadly this obsessive ritual is dying out because the newer hybrids stay sweet much longer.

You can also cook corn in its husk on a barbecue or campfire.

Other uses: Corn has traditionally been used for bread, tortillas, mush, beer, whiskey and animal feed. It is now a major industrial crop, with thousands of uses from cornstarch to ethanol based motor fuel. It is also the source of the notorious high fructose corn syrup which finds its way into a huge number of processed foods.

Sweet corn chowder

2 carrots
1 stalk celery
1 onion
1 sweet pepper
2 cups corn kernels
2 cups vegetable broth or water
1 cup potatoes
1 cup soy milk
1 tbsp flour
1 tbsp olive oil
Salt and pepper

Saute the carrot, celery onion and pepper in the oil for a few minutes then add the water and potatoes and simmer 10 minutes. Add the corn and cook for another 10 minutes. Then mix the soy milk and flour and salt and pepper and add to mix. Simmer for another 10 minutes.

Nixtamalization

This is the process of treating field corn to make it more nutritious and versatile. It is a fairly simple process, but somewhat time consuming. The end product is known as corn masa meal.

Put 4 tbs pickling lime (calcium hydroxide) in 4 quarts of water and bring to a boil (wood ashes can also be used, though I'm not sure of the quantity). Then add 3 cups of washed dry corn and simmer until the skin of the corn kernels start to peel off (how long this takes will vary from 1 - 3 hours). Then take the pan off the heat, cover and leave overnight.

Next day you rinse the corn several times to remove all of the lime. The corn can then be ground to a coarse meal for immediate use or dried for later use. If you want a finer meal you have to remove the skins of the kernels too.

Cornsalad

Valerianella locusta
Syn *V. olitoria*

Introduction: Cornsalad is a small, weedy, slow growing plant, that produces a low rosette of edible leaves. It gets its English name because it was a common edible weed of cereal fields (corn was once a general word for all cereal grains). It was also once commonly called lambs lettuce (supposedly because sheep like to forage on the wild plants).

It has recently become popular as a gourmet green under its French pseudonym mache. Presumably because if you want to promote any food it doesn't hurt to associate it with France.

Cornsalad is small and slow growing, so you need a lot of plants if your family expects to get regular salads from it. This could be the reason why some people use it as a cover crop!

Nutrional value: Cornsalad is a good source of vitamins A, B6 and C, as well as iron, potassium and manganese.

Climate: Cornsalad is one of the hardiest of all salad plants (down to 10˚F) and can thrive when few other plants can even survive. It doesn't grow well in warm weather and won't even germinate above 70˚F.

Crop value: Cornsalad is significant because it grows and produces food in winter, when edible plants are scarce. For this reason it has been an important spring salad green in Western Europe for many generations. If well established in fall, it can produce right through the winter, even in colder areas.

Ease of growing: Cornsalad is a tough plant and doesn't need much care. It is easy to grow in cool weather, but has a tendency to bolt when it gets too warm. It volunteers in my garden in winter and early spring.

About Cornsalad

Germ temp: 40 (55 - 65) 70˚F
Germ time: 10 - 14 days
Viability: 5 - 10 yrs
Growing temp: 40 - 70˚F
Sow out
Spring: 6 wks before last frost.
Fall: 6 - 8 wks before first frost
Days to harvest:
50 - 60 days (summer)
60 - 90 days (winter)
Height 8 - 10″
Width: 5 - 8″

Soil

pH: 5.5-7.5

Cornsalad will grow almost anywhere, but does best in a sandy well-drained soil that is rich in nitrogen. If the soil is poor it will grow very slowly and may bolt at the first opportunity.

Soil preparation: If the soil is not very fertile incorporate 2″ of compost into the top 8″ of soil.

Planning

Where: In cool weather cornsalad should be put in a warm sheltered spot, where it will get full sun. In warmer weather it can be planted in part shade.

Spring: I haven't had a lot of success with spring planting cornsalad in my garden, it seems like it just gets going and then it bolts.

A spring crop should be planted early to give it a long period of cool weather, as it will bolt when warmer weather arrives. Apparently in cool climates it can be succession sown right through the summer, for a continuous harvest.

Fall: Because of its predilection for bolting, cornsalad does much better as a fall and winter crop. The cool weather and short days help to minimize this tendency.

Cornsalad can tolerate hard frost and in many areas it will keep growing right through the winter. It actually grows better in cold weather as it gets bigger and better flavored.

Plant when the weather starts to cool down in fall, 6 - 8 weeks before the first fall frost. It can also be planted in late fall for a spring crop (the seed will sit in the soil and germinate when it is ready in late winter).

Planting

Outside: Cornsalad is usually direct sown like spinach, either by broadcasting, or by sowing in rows. In my experience the seed doesn't have a very good germination rate, so sow fairly thickly. Plant the seed ¼ - ½″ deep and 1″ apart in rows 10 - 24″ apart. Keep the soil moist until it germinates.

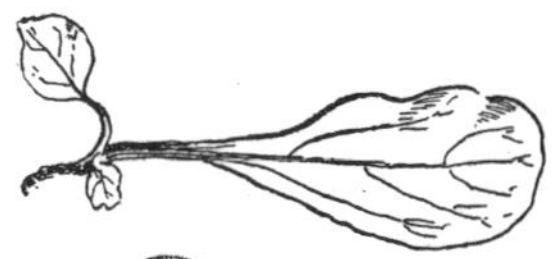

Spacing: Harvest thin the rows by taking out every other plant, until they are at the desired spacing of 4 - 6″ apart (eat the thinnings). If using transplants space them 4 - 6″ apart in offset rows. You can leave them closer than this, but the plants won't get as big.

Care

Weeds: This is a low and fairly slow growing plant (especially when young) and needs to be kept free of weeds. Of course most weeds are growing slowly in cool weather too.

Watering: Cornsalad needs a constant supply of moisture, but this is rarely a problem in cool weather.

Pests and disease: Few pests are active in the cool weather that cornsalad prefers. Slugs, snails and birds are the ones you are most likely to encounter.

Harvesting

Start harvesting the leaves as soon as they are big enough to be worthwhile. They won't produce for very long once the weather warms up in spring, so make the most of them.

If your seed was sown fairly thickly, you can harvest whole plants by taking every alternate one. You can also cut off the entire plants, just leaving a couple of inches behind to regenerate. You can also pick individual leaves, though they are quite small. You can harvest from the plants right up until they produce flowers.

Some people blanch the plants for a few days prior to harvest, by covering with plant pots.

Storage: The leaves are quite perishable, but can be kept for a few days in a plastic bag in the fridge. Don't wash until you use them (I mean the plants not you).

Seed saving: Cornsalad will produce an abundance of seed without any help from you and will commonly self-sow. It is cross-pollinated by insects, but there are few varieties available (and fewer being grown) so keeping it pure isn't usually a problem. Watch the plants carefully as the seed ripens, so you can gather it before it all falls.

Save seed from the last plants to bolt, rather than the first ones. You don't want to develop a fast bolting strain.

Unusual growing ideas

Volunteers: Allow some plants to self-sow and they will produce new plants in autumn. Cornsalad has been growing by itself in my garden for years now.

Summer shade: In cooler climates it may be possible to grow cornsalad in summer, by interplanting it in the shade of tall growing crops like corn or sunflower.

Winter crop: Cornsalad is a good winter crop for growing in cold frames or tunnel cloches. The additional warmth will greatly increase growth.

Cover crop: If you have enough seed, cornsalad can be grown as an edible winter cover crop, alone or with a nitrogen fixer such as fava beans.

Varieties

When I first tried cornsalad, the packet of seed just said "Cornsalad", but in recent years a few more refined varieties are appearing (whether these are that much different is open to question). They may even be divided into two distinct types.

Large seeded types: These produce bigger plants, up to 8″ across. They can grow in higher temperatures than the small seeded types.

Gros Graine (Big Seeded) - Larger leaves on a bigger plant

Baval - Faster growing, larger plant

Small seeded types; These produce smaller plants up to 5″ across. They tend to be the best flavored.

Verte De Cambrai - One of the best for flavor.

D'Etampes - A French heirloom.

Kitchen use: Cornsalad is most popular in France and Italy (which suggests it should be good). The flavor is mild and nutty and it is commonly used like lettuce as a mildly flavored base for salads. It can also be cooked as a potherb like spinach. The older leaves can get somewhat bitter in warm weather, but not inedibly so.

Wash the leaves carefully before use, as these low growing plants often get splashed with soil.

Golden or Italian Cornsalad

(*Valerianella eriocarpa*)

This is a different species than the above, with larger, lighter colored leaves. It is used in the same ways though (if you can find any seed to plant).

This Mediterranean native is not as hardy as the above, but is more heat tolerant (especially if given some shade during the hottest part of the day). It is also less prone to bolting.

Cowpea

Vigna unguiculata ssp unguiculata

Introduction: Cowpea is an unfortunate name for this legume and certainly doesn't inspire gourmet fantasies (black eyed pea is a slight improvement, but still not great). This unfortunate name probably came about because of its use as feed for livestock. Southern pea is probably the best name for them (though it isn't a pea).

Cowpea originated in Africa where it has been cultivated for at least 6000 years and is still a very important crop there. It is not a pea, it is another type of bean, though from a different family than the bush and pole beans.

Cowpea is very much a tropical species and is more tolerant of heat, drought and poor soils than most legumes. It was once widely grown in the southeastern states, having been introduced along with African slaves, but has declined in importance as a commercial crop (often replaced by soybean). Black eyed peas and crowders are still more widely grown in gardens in that area than anywhere else though.

Cowpea is a versatile crop and can be used in many different ways. The young leaves can be eaten like spinach, the immature pods like green beans, the immature seed like shell beans and the fully ripe seed as dry beans.

Nutritional content

Dry seed: These are rich in protein (23%), though like most beans they are deficient in some amino acids (which is why beans are commonly eaten with grains such as corn. They are also a good source of carbohydrate, potassium and fiber. They contain approximately 1520 calories per pound.

Shell beans: These are rich in protein as well as vitamins A and C.

About Cowpea

Seed facts
Germ temp: 60 (65 - 80) 90˚F
Germ time: 5 - 10 days
Seed viability: 4 - 6 yrs
Germination percentage: 70%
Weeks to grow transplants: 3 - 5

Planning facts
Hardiness: Tender
Temp for growth: 60 (70 - 85) 95˚F
Plants per person:
Plants per sq ft:
Transplants
Start: On the last frost date
Plant out: 4 wks after last frost
Direct sow: 4 wks after last frost
Harvest: 80 days (shell peas)
120 days (dry peas)
Height: Bush 18 - 36″
Vining 36 - 144″
Diameter: 12 - 30″

Harvest facts
Harvest period: 6 - 8 weeks
Yield: ½ - 1 oz / sq ft
Yield per plant: 1 - 3 oz

Ease of growing: Cowpea is grown in much the same ways as the soybean and likes the same warm days and nights and moist fertile soil. If it gets these things it is pretty easy to grow.

Climate: Cowpea is a tropical plant and grows best when given four months of warm humid conditions, but it is also quite tolerant of drought. They thrive in the same climate as corn, which means they like heat and can't take any frost.

Soil

pH 5.5 (6.5) 7.0

Cowpea can be grown in a wide range of soils and is valued for its ability to grow well on poor soil. However it will be most productive on a light, moderately fertile, well-drained, slightly acid one, It doesn't like wet soil.

Soil preparation: This is a deep rooted plant and if your soil is compacted you should think about deep cultivation (or even double digging).

Cowpea likes organic matter so incorporate a couple of inches of compost into the top 6 - 8″ of soil. It doesn't need a lot of nitrogen, as this can result in lush growth, delayed maturation and lower yield. It likes moderate amounts of phosphorus and potassium, so add these if the soil is lacking in them.

Planning

Where: For best growth the cowpea needs a warm site with full sun.

When: Don't plant cowpea until all frost danger is past and the soil is at least 65˚F (and ideally 80˚F). In colder soil the seed may rot before it germinates. If you want to get an early crop, you will have to warm the soil beforehand, with cloches or plastic mulch (or start them inside). Raised beds also help because they warm up faster.

Planting

Using transplants: If you have a short growing season it is possible to start cowpeas indoors as you would beans. Start around the last frost date and sow out a month later. This is a lot more work than direct sowing though.

Direct sowing: Sow the inoculated seeds as you would other beans. They should be planted 1″

deep in cool soil and 1 ½″ deep in warmer soil.

If planting in rows simply make suitably spaced furrows, put the seed in at the correct spacing and refill the furrows. If planting in beds, place the seeds on top of the prepared seedbed at the correct spacing. Then simply push them down into the soil with your finger and close up the hole.

Inoculation: Like most legumes cowpea plants fix nitrogen, but only if the appropriate rhizobium bacteria are present in the soil. If you haven't grown them in the past 3 - 5 years you should probably inoculate them. See **Bush and Pole Beans** for more on this.

Spacing: This depends upon the size of the variety. Space the seeds of bush types 2 - 4″ apart in the row with 20 - 30″ between the rows. The vining types need more space, so plant them 3 - 6″ apart in the row.

Support: The vining types can be supported in the same ways as other beans (See **Bush and Pole Beans)**. The bush types tend to mutually support each other.

Care

In the right climate cowpeas are a fairly easy and undemanding crop

Weed: Weed the plants carefully while they are young. Older plants can compete against weeds fairly well.

Fertilizing: This isn't essential, but a regular feed (every 3 weeks) of compost tea or liquid kelp can increase productivity.

Water: Cowpea is famed for being one of the most drought tolerant crops, but it will be most productive if irrigated regularly, with at least 1″ of water per week. If water is in short supply you can economise by only watering during flowering and pod development. Try not to get the leaves wet as it can encourage disease.

Pests: Root knot, nematodes, cowpea curculio, aphids, green stink bugs, cornstalk borers, spider mites, deer, rabbits, birds.

Disease: The usual bean suspects: damping off, root rot, southern blight, mosaic virus, bacterial wilt, fusarium wilt. These are most often a problem in warm humid conditions.

Pollination: Cowpea is mostly day neutral and self-pollinating.

Harvesting

Leaves: The tender young leaves are edible and can be used raw or cooked. Of course you don't want to take too many of these or you may affect the production of pods.

Green beans: The pods are best gathered just as they are reaching full size, but before the beans start to swell. They should still snap in half easily (if they don't they are probably too old and will be tough and stringy).

Gather the pods carefully so you don't damage the plants. Hold on to the vine and pull down on the pod, so there is no danger of tearing the plant, or pulling it out of the ground.

Shell beans: These are sometimes called southern peas and are harvested as soon as they reach full size in the pod, but before they toughen up (which should be 4 - 8 days after the pods reach full size). Pods vary from 3 - 10″ in length and contain anywhere from 6 - 18 seeds.

Dry beans: These are gathered after the pods have shrivelled and dried on the vines (you can sometimes hear the seeds rattle inside the pod). You can gather small quantities of pods individually, but for larger harvests pick the whole plants and lay them on a tarp to dry. Carefully thresh out the seeds to free them from the pods and then dry thoroughly.

Storage: The green pods can be stored in plastic bags in the fridge for up to 2 weeks, but are best used fresh. For longer storage they can be dried, pickled or frozen. Shell beans can also be frozen.

Fully dry peas can be stored in a rodent proof container in a cool place, and will stay edible for several years.

Seed saving: Cowpeas are generally self-pollinating so you don't have to worry too much about cross-pollination. They are treated like other beans and allowed to dry fully on the vine. The peas are then removed and dried further before storing.

Unusual growing ideas

Green manure: This plant is a useful warm weather green manure crop to add nitrogen to the soil. To achieve this the plants must be incorporated into the soil soon after flowering. If it is allowed to produce seed, it puts most of the nitrogen it has fixed into these.

Cowpeas are sometimes used to rehabilitate very poor or damaged soils, as they are able to grow in poorer soils than most legumes.

Interplanting: In its African homeland subsistence farmers commonly interplant cowpea with corn, millet or sorghum. It has also been interplanted experimentally with leaf amaranth.

Dry gardening: In many parts of the world cowpeas are important for their ability to produce well without irrigation, even in hot dry areas. If you want to try this, space them further apart, so they have a greater volume of soil to take moisture from.

Companion: Cowpeas were once commonly planted with corn, to provide feed for animals (either greens for forage or seed for chickens).

Varieties

These are divided into several groups according to the appearance of the seed or pod. They may be further sub-divided into bush, semi-vining or vining (not so common) varieties.

Black eyed peas – These have a dark colored eye (not always black) and the pods are not crowded.

California Blackeye Pea - There are a number of these, each with a different number (#5, #45, etc).

Pinkeye Purple Hull - Semi-vining plants, purple pods (85 days).

Queen Anne Blackeye Pea - Heavy producer (70 days).

Crowder peas – Have tightly packed seeds that are either speckled or one color.

Black Crowder - Long pods, black seeds (70 days).

Calico Crowder - Old heirloom, Long vines (70 days).

Colossus - Big seeds (60 days).

Cream cowpeas – These aren't crowded and have cream colored seed.

White Whipoorwhill - Prolific (75 days)

Zipper Cream - Bush type, white seed (60 days).

Kitchen use

The immature pods can be cooked in the same ways as snap beans.

The shell peas are removed from the pods and cooked for 20 minutes in just enough water to cover them.

The dry peas are cooked in the same way as dry beans. They are usually pre-soaked for 4 - 8 hours, then rinsed and boiled in fresh water until tender. The cooked peas/beans can be used in any bean recipe.

Yardlong bean

(*Vigna unguiculata ssp sesquipedalis*)

This is an Asian subspecies of the cowpea and is grown in the same way. It is a pole bean and has to be grown on a tall support.

The pods may actually get up to a yard in length in some cases, but are at their best when up to a foot long and 3/8″ in diameter (which takes 65 - 80 days from planting). They can also be used for shell or dry beans and the leaves are edible too.

You might assume that the pods should be boiled like snap beans, but they are actually much better when stir fried or steamed.

Chinese Red Noodle - Long red beans on tall vines (80 days).

Green Yard Long Bean - Long green pods with black seeds.

Cucumber

Cucumis sativus

Introduction: This tropical species is thought to have come from India or thereabouts and has a very long history of cultivation there. It reached Europe early enough to have been widely grown by the time of the Romans.

Nowadays cucumbers are one of the most popular home garden vegetables. This isn't surprising as they are tasty, productive and have an extended harvest season (though they do take up quite a bit of space).

Nutritional content: Cucumbers are a good source of water (96%). They also contain some vitamin C, potassium and antioxidants. As a source of energy they contain 68 calories per pound (not exactly rocket fuel).

Climate: Cucumber is a tropical plant and needs warm (70 - 80°F) sunny days, mild nights and plenty of water for best growth. They can't stand any frost at all.

Ease of growing: Like the related squash the cucumber is a pretty easy plant to grow, so long as it gets good soil and warm weather (and pests and diseases don't get too bad).

Crop value: Cucumber rates close to the bottom on the self-sufficiency scale. It takes quite a bit of room to grow and is very low in nutritional value (you could starve to death growing and eating cucumbers).

Soil

pH 6.0 (6.8 - 7.0) 7.5

Cucumbers grow rapidly once established and to sustain their high level of growth they need a rich soil. It should be loose, moisture retentive and well-drained, with lots of organic matter. Raised beds are good because they help the soil warm up quickly and provide good drainage.

Soil preparation: Incorporate 2″ of compost or aged manure into the top 6″ of soil. Add lime if the soil is acidic, as they don't like a low pH. They don't like salt either, so watch what kind of manure you use.

In cool areas with plenty of rain, cucumbers are often grown in raised hills, ridges or beds, as this helps the soil to warm up faster. This doesn't work so well in hot dry areas though, as they tend to dry out more quickly and so need more irrigation.

Planning

Where: For maximum production cucumbers need full sun (at least 8 hours daily). They can grow well enough with light shade, but will be less productive.

Don't plant cucumbers where any of the Cucurbits (cucumber, melon or squash) have grown within the last three years.

When: Cucumbers are native to the tropics and absolutely must have warm soil (60°F minimum - 70°F better) for good germination and growth. Consequently they are among the last crops to be planted out in spring. Most varieties fruit better in short days, so tend to be more productive later in the summer.

Cucurbits in general (squash, melons, cucumbers) are all easy to start from seed, though they don't like transplanting.

About Cucumbers

Seed facts

Germ temp: 60 (65 - 75) 105°F
Germination time: 3 - 10 days
13 days / 59°F
6 days / 68°F
4 days / 77°F
3 days / 86°F * Optimum
3 days / 95°F
Germination percentage: 80%+
Viability: 2 - 5 years
Weeks to grow transplants: 3 - 4

Planning facts

Hardiness: Tender
Growing temp: 60 (70 - 80) 90°F
Plants per person: 1
Plants per sq ft: ¾

Transplants:

Start: On last frost date
Plant out: 3 - 4 wks after last frost
Direct sow: 2 - 4 wks after last frost.

Harvest facts

Days to harvest: 70 - 100 days
Harvest period: 8 - 12 weeks
Yield per plant: 4 lb (10 - 20 fruit)
Yield per sq ft: 3 lb sq ft

If your growing season is long you can start them outside 2 - 4 weeks after the last frost date (or whenever the soil reaches 60°F).

If the growing season is short then start the seeds inside on the last frost date (they grow fast) and plant out 3 - 4 weeks later. Don't start them too early, as you can't put them out until the soil is warm and if they sit inside too long, they may get root bound.

Don't be in too much of a hurry, as plants set out at the right time will usually outgrow those planted too early. If necessary you can speed up soil warming in spring by using black plastic mulch or cloches.

Support: The bush cucumbers are quite compact, but the vining types take up a considerable amount of space if left to sprawl across the ground. Fortunately they are good climbers and will be perfectly happy growing vertically. Trellised plants may take up only one tenth of the bed space of unsupported ones.

Trellising can also increase yields by as much as 100%, because fewer fruits are lost to rot, disease or slugs and there is more light for photosynthesis. Fruits are also straighter and cleaner.

If building a trellis seems like a good idea, but too much work, you may be able to plant them along a wire fence. You can also use cages of 6″ mesh steel reinforcing wire, 3 ft in diameter and 6 ft high. These can work well, though the plants may eventually outgrow them. These cages can even be covered with plastic to protect the young plants from late frost. You can also open these out to create a wire tunnel, which can also be covered in plastic in cold weather.

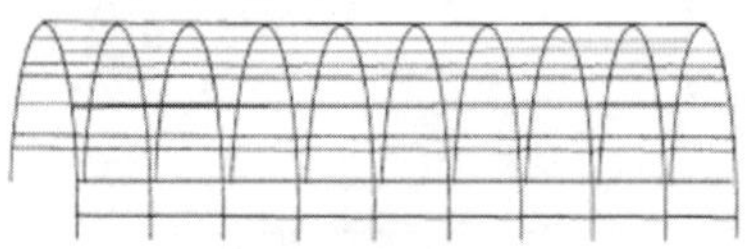

Many kinds of supports have been used for cucumbers, including fencing wire, nylon netting and bamboo canes. Be creative, but make sure it is strong enough to support the weight of a fruiting crop (and wind and rain), you don't want it to collapse.

If you are going to create a support your cucumbers, you should set it up before planting. This will minimize disturbance to the young plants.

No support: Supporting the vines up in the air isn't always a good idea. In hot, dry areas it is better to leave the plants close to the ground, where they can create their own little humid microclimate and so lose water less rapidly.

Planting

Transplants

Starting inside: Early cucumbers are usually started indoors, because the soil outside may not be warm enough for good germination (even though the air may be warm enough for their growth). They dislike transplanting, so are usually started in individual 3 or 4″ containers, 2 seeds to a pot (later thinned to the best one). Don't use smaller containers, as the seedlings grow so quickly you will soon have to re-pot them.

Planting out: Dig a hole and half fill it with a couple of handfuls of compost, then plant out the seedlings up to their first true leaves. Water immediately after planting. If the weather turns cold after planting you should cover them with cloches or row covers.

Direct sowing: Once the soil has warmed up it is simpler to sow cucumbers directly in the soil 2 - 3″ deep. In good conditions they grow very quickly and will often catch up with transplants, even though they were started several weeks later.

In dry conditions you might want to soak the seed overnight before planting to hasten germination. You can even pre-germinate them (this is fairly straightforward because they are so big).

Planting methods

Beds: When growing in intensive beds, the compact bush varieties work best. Plant them in two alternate rows down the bed. You may want to interplant a fast growing crop at the same time, to take advantage of the temporarily vacant space.

You can use vine cucumbers in a bed too, but you will have to give them support so they can grow vertically.

Hills: Vine cucumbers were traditionally planted in hills. You can do this by digging a large hole 12″ in diameter and 12″ deep (you can line this with gopher wire if necessary). Half fill this hole with compost and then return the soil to the hole. The result is a slightly raised mound that warms up quickly and provides good drainage. Several seeds (5 to 6) are then sown on top of the mound. When these have several leaves they are thinned to the best 2 or 3 plants.

The disadvantage of raised hills is that they dry out quickly, so don't work so well in dry climates. In such circumstances you can flatten the "hill" until it is flat. In extreme cases you might even make it into a slight depression (an anti-hill).

Ridges: In the cool climate of Britain outdoor cucumbers are often sown on raised ridges of soil, as these warm up better. To make a ridge you dig a trench and fill it with compost or aged manure and then replace the soil to form a ridge. You then plant your cucumbers in a row along it.

Spacing: There are quite a lot of options for spacing, depending upon the type of cucumber you grow and how you grow them:

Intensive bed spacing varies from 18 - 24″ apart, depending upon the soil and the variety. If growing in two parallel rows you might have 24″ between the plants and rows.

Trellised vine cucumbers can be grown 12″ apart in the row, with 24 - 36″ between the rows.

Cucumber hills are planted 36″ apart, with 2 or 3 plants in each hill.

Plants in rows should be 24 - 30″ apart, with 48 - 72″ between the rows.

Succession sow: Make another sowing 4 - 6 weeks after the first one (and if your growing season is long maybe another a month or so after that). You then have vigorous young plants to take over as the older ones start to decline in productivity.

Care

Cucumbers are pretty vigorous plants and don't usually require a lot of attention.

Watering: Cucumbers are mainly composed of water and for best growth you should keep the soil evenly moist, but not wet, at all times. This is particularly important when they start producing fruit. Give them a minimum of 1″ water per week. Ideally this should be lukewarm (70°F), so it doesn't shock the plants or cool the soil significantly.

The best way to water cucumbers is with a drip system or soaker hose. This keeps the leaves dry and so reduces the chance of disease problems. If you must use a sprinkler do it in the morning, or early evening, so the leaves have a chance to dry quickly. You don't want them to stay wet all night.

Mulch: This is beneficial to conserve moisture and keep weeds under control (as an added benefit it also keeps the fruit clean). The soil must be warm before you put this on though, as mulch insulates the soil and prevents it from warming up.

A living mulch of annual clover can work well with cucumbers.

Fertilization: When the seedlings have recovered from transplanting, give them a liquid feed of liquid kelp or compost tea, to give them a boost. If your soil isn't very fertile, then continue to feed them every 2 - 3 weeks (or at least after the first flowers appear).

Pruning: In some circumstances you might want to pinch out the growing tip of the young plant to encourage branching. Some people pinch them back twice, so they produce four growing tips.

Pollination: Cucumbers are monoecious (they produce male and female flowers on the same plant) and the first few flowers to appear are usually males. These don't bear fruit of course.

Female flowers are easily recognized by the tiny "cucumber" at the back of the petals. These appear soon after the first males and will to bear fruit if pollinated successfully. If the weather is cool this may not happen, in which case they will simply shrivel and drop off. Apparently cold weather encourages the production of male flowers, while warm weather encourages female flowers.

If your plants aren't setting fruit you could try hand-pollinating some of the female flowers (seed savers do it all the time). This isn't usually necessary though, just be patient and they should start to produce eventually.

Pests and diseases: I have found cucumbers to be fairly free of pests, though they do have a few serious ones.

Cucumber beetles: This is the biggest problem when growing cucumbers (no surprise really, with a name like that). This pest doesn't just eat the plants (which is bad enough), but can also spread bacterial wilt disease. Row covers will work until the plants get too big, Another approach is to plant blue hubbard squash nearby, as these will attract the beetles away from the cucumber (in theory at least).

Other pests: Squash bugs, aphids, pickle worms, squash vine borers.

Diseases: Powdery and downy mildew are the commonest diseases of cucumbers. Keep the leaves of plants dry and make sure there is good air circulation. Other diseases include alternaria blight, angular leaf spot, anthracnose, mosaic virus and bacterial wilt. Some varieties are resistant to some of these diseases.

Bitterness: Bitterness in cucumbers is caused by chemicals known as cucurbitacins and is partly genetic, though high temperature and lack of water can make things worse.

The easiest way to avoid bitter cucumbers is to plant a non-bitter variety that is low in cucurbitacins. An added benefit of these is that they may be less attractive to cucumber beetles. You should also make sure the plants have plenty of water, especially in hot weather.

Harvesting

When: The fruit will be ready for harvest 15 - 18 days after pollination (which is roughly 2 months after planting). The first fruits are usually quite small, simply because the plants themselves aren't very big.

Once the plants start producing, you should check them every 2 - 3 days and harvest any fruits that are ready. The plants regulate the number of fruits they have growing, so if they are already holding a lot, they won't produce many new ones.

For maximum yield you should harvest the fruits just before they reach full size. You can gather them when smaller than this, but you won't get as much food. They grow very quickly, doubling in size in 24 hours, so don't leave the fruits too long, or they will start to develop hard seeds and the skin will toughen. Definitely don't allow any fruits to mature on the vine, as this can stop the plant producing altogether. Pick the fruits regularly, even if you just throw them at a wall.

If you want small fruits for pickling, you can harvest ordinary cucumbers while they are still small, but the specially bred pickling varieties will be much more productive.

How: It's better to cut the fruit from the vine, rather than pulling it off. The stem is quite tough and it's easy to break part of the vine accidentally. Ideally you should leave a short section of stem on each fruit, to prevent moisture loss. Brush any small spines off of the fruit with your hands.

Storage: Cucumbers are at their best when eaten immediately after picking. They are very perishable, but will keep for a week or so if stored in a cool place (40 - 50°F). Don't keep them in the fridge. For longer term storage they are often pickled. I don't advise trying to dry them as they are 96% water!

Seed saving: Cucumbers are cross-pollinated by bees, so must either be isolated by 1000 yards or hand pollinated. Hand pollination is fairly straightforward because the flowers are so large. It is done in the same way as for Squash (see **Squash**). Take seed from 5 of the best and most typical plants to avoid inbreeding depression.

If you are saving seed, the fruit must be allowed to mature properly. It will turn yellow and start to wither when fully ripe. Separate the seeds from the pulp and ferment them for a couple of days in the same way as you would for tomato.

Finally separate the cleaned seeds from the fermented mush and dry them thoroughly. Ideally they should have a moisture content of around 6% for storage. Be aware that a number of diseases can be seed borne.

Unusual growing ideas:

Ornamentals: The vining types are vigorous climbers and can be used to cover a wire fence or trellis and turn it into a temporary and quite ornamental screen. They are such good climbers they can even be trained over an arbor to provide summer shade.

Containers: The bush varieties do quite well in containers, so long as you keep them well watered.

Varieties:

A lot of breeding work has gone into the cucumber and the result is a lot of variation. The shape of the fruit varies considerably, from foot long green ones to tennis ball sized white or yellow ones. Some varieties are resistant to specific diseases. There are also gynoecious varieties that produce all female flowers and are self-fertilizing (parthenocarpic) for growing in the greenhouse.

Bush cucumbers are favored in small gardens because of their compact habit, though they aren't generally as productive as the vine types.

Vining cucumbers are often preferred in warm moist climates as they get better air circulation, so are less vulnerable to disease. They may suffer more from sunburn however.

When choosing a cucumber remember that bitterness is partly genetic. If you have had a problem with this in the past then be sure to choose a non- bitter type, such as one of these listed below.

Pickling: These produce large numbers of small, light green fruits, ideal for pickling (what else?)

Parisian Pickling: This famous heirloom is not only outstanding for pickles, but is also good for fresh eating if it gets bigger.

Slicing: These produce the large dark green cucumbers you see in markets. They tend to be productive and disease resistant.

Diva F1: Sometimes said to be the best flavored cucumber. It produces all-female flowers that don't require a pollinator.

Persian cucumber - Early and productive, the thin skinned fruits are never bitter.

Boothby's Blonde - The light colored fruit are non-bitter. This is sometimes said to be the best cucumber.

Sweet Slice, Carmen, Country Fair are all non-bitter.

Long:

Telegraph Improved - Old English heirloom, long, sweet fruits.

Yamato - Produces an abundance of long fruit (to 20″). Can also be pickled.

Japanese climbing - The long, non-bitter fruits are produced abundantly. Often said to be one of the best cucumbers.

Satsuki Madori - Vigorous, productive and produces delicious non-bitter fruit. Sometimes said to be the best cucumber.

Round:

Crystal Apple - This Australian heirloom is round, sweet and white.

Lemon Cucumber - Very similar to the above, but light yellow.

Kitchen use

Cucumbers are almost always eaten raw of course.

Pickles

3 lb cucumbers (3 - 4″)
8 cups water
¼ cup cider vinegar
⅓ cup salt
8 garlic cloves (peeled)
2 small fresh hot peppers
2 tbsp whole mustard seeds
2 tsp celery seeds
1 tsp turmeric
1 tsp freshly ground black pepper
6 to 8 seed heads dill

Thoroughly mix the vinegar, spices, garlic cloves, dill heads and salt (it should all dissolve) with the water and pour over the cucumbers into a large ceramic bowl. Put a plate over the bowl to push the cucumbers under the surface. Cover with a cloth and leave for 48 hours. Finally put the pickles into jars with a clove of garlic and cover with brine (remove the dill). They will keep in the fridge for about 3 months.

Edible Flowers

Edible flowers have become quite fashionable of late and for good reason. A handful of flowers will transform a mundane salad into an edible work of art that makes you feel like Martha Stewart. Flowers don't only add color however; many also add unique and delicious flavors.

You probably already grow edible flowers in your garden, you just don't realize it and think of them as simply ornamentals. My belief is that if you have them, you should make use of them. I am not going to give any cultivation directions here, I just want to make you are aware of what is out there. Things you might already have, or might choose to grow in the future.

Caution: The golden rule with eating anything is "know what you eat". Never put anything in your mouth that you don't know to be edible. Not all flowers are edible (edibility has no connection with beauty) and a few are quite poisonous. Some plants have edible flowers, while the rest is poisonous, so don't take anything for granted.

Even when a plant is considered to be edible, there is still the possibility that it could cause an adverse reaction in some people (some members of the Daisy family are known for this). When you taste a plant for the first time, it's a good idea to eat only a small amount and see if there is any problem, before consuming more. It's probably a good idea to always eat flowers in moderation (which is what most people do anyway).

You should also be aware that flowers in other peoples gardens (or anywhere else) may have been sprayed with toxic chemicals.

Taste: Just because a flower is considered to be edible doesn't mean it tastes good, or that you will like it. The only way to know that is to taste it yourself.

Which part of a flower you eat will depend upon what it is. Sometimes you eat the whole thing and sometimes only a part of it. In some cases only the petals are good, in which case you will have to remove the sepals (green leafy bits underneath the petals), stamens and pistils (these are the reproductive parts and often taste different from the petals). The stamens commonly contain pollen which can occasionally cause allergies). Sometimes even the white base of the petals isn't good and should be removed. You need to experiment to find out what you like and what you don't (this really is a matter of taste).

Identification: Before you can safely eat any flower you know is edible, you need to be sure that you have got the right plant. Common names can sometimes be confusing, as the same name may be applied to more than one plant (this is why we have unique Latin names for every species).

Gathering: I make it a habit to pick a few flowers whenever I am out gathering salad materials. Gather them when they have just opened fully, ideally while it is still cool, but the flowers are dry. Usually you don't need many, so you can be picky and choose only perfect ones.

Cleaning: If the flowers have just opened and haven't touched anything you don't really need to clean them (they are clean), just check them carefully to make sure they don't contain hidden insects or other surprises. Nothing spoils the dinner party like a guest crunching on an earwig (you can be sure Martha Stewart doesn't have insects in her flowers). If the flowers aren't clean, you can dip them gently in water, shake and dry on a paper towel. They must be dried carefully and rapidly otherwise they will deteriorate.

Using: Flowers can be used in many different ways. The most obvious is to add them to salads, but they can also be used as a edible garnish to add beauty, color and flavor for any dish. You can also add them to ice cubes for drinks, or candy them for decorating desserts.

The best edible flowers

A lot of edible flowers are mostly for show; they add color and make a dish look spectacular, but don't add much flavor. It you are happy with edible flowers that look great and don't care if they add flavor, then there are a lots to choose from. If you want something that also adds a unique flavor then you are much more restricted. Here are the ones I have found to be the most useful.

Anise Hyssop (*Agastache foeniculum*): The flowers are small, but add a lovely blue color and anise flavor.

Arugala (*Eruca vesicaria*): The white flowers taste like arugala.

Basil (*Ocimum basilicum*): The small white flowers taste like basil.

Batchelors Buttons (*Centaurea cyanus*): Beautiful bright blue color.

Brassicas: All Brassica flowers are edible and have a pleasantly pungent mustard flavor.

Bee Balm (*Monarda didyma*): Beautiful and aromatic

Borage (*Borago officinalis*): Use only the blue (or white) petals, remove the hairy calyx and stamens

Calendula (*Calendula officinalis*): A reliable standby if nothing else is available, Calendula flowers can be found almost year round in my garden. The ray flowers (petals) don't have much flavor, but are worth adding for their vivid orange or yellow color (they are sometimes called poor mans saffron).

Chives (*Allium schoenoprasum)*: The purple, onion flavored florets are very good.

Cilantro (*Coriandrum sativum*): The white flowers are tasty, but small. Even better are the green seeds, which are a delightful combination of cilantro and coriander.

Day Lily (*Hemerocallis* species): These are commonly eaten in Asia. Their flavor varies a lot so taste them to find the best kinds (some are not pleasant).

Dill (*Anethum graveolens*): Nice dill flavor.

Garland Chrysanthemum (*Chrysanthemum coronarium*): Also known as shungiku, the petals are aromatic and pungent.

Garlic (*Allium sativum*): If your garlic produces flowers, they can be eaten for their pungent garlic flavor.

Ox Eye Daisy (*Chrysanthemum leucanthemum*): The white ray flowers ("petals") are good.

Fennel (*Foeniculum vulgare*):: The yellow flowers, buds and immature seeds all have a delicious (and quite strong) anise flavor.

Garlic Chives (*Allium tuberosum*): The pretty purple flowers have a nice garlic flavor.

Lavender (*Lavandula angustifolia* is best): The aromatic flowers are used to flavor a variety of foods (lavender cookies are good).

Leeks (*Allium porrum*): The florets have a nice onion flavor.

Lovage (*Levisticum officinale*): The flowers have that delicious lovage flavor

Marigold (*Tagetes tenuifolia*): Only a few varieties are good (Lemon Gem and others) so taste first.

Nasturtium (*Tropaeolum majus*): One of the best edible flowers. Big and colorful with a delightful aromatic/pungent/sweet flavor all their own.

Pea (*Pisum sativum*): This is the common garden pea (not Sweet Pea - *Lathyrus odoratus*, which is poisonous). They have a nice (you guessed it) pea flavor.

Pineapple Guava (*Feijoa sellowiana*): The thick succulent petals are sweet and very good.

Pinks and carnations (*Dianthus caryophyllus* - Clove Pink is best): Flavor varies a lot so try any you find. Remove the white base of the petal and eat the colored part.

Radish (*Raphanus sativus*): The flowers and green seed pods have a pungent mustard flavor.

Roses (*Rosa* species): Not to everyone's taste, but the scented petals are used to flavor a variety of various dishes and drinks.

Salvia (*Salvia* species): Pineapple sage, common sage and clary sage are all good, but some others can be mildly toxic.

Squash (*Cucurbita* species): The stuffed blossoms are a delicacy. The petals are eaten, but the rest is usually removed.

Sweet Cicely (*Myrrhis odorata*) Sweet anise flavored flowers can be used raw or as flavoring.

Violas (*Viola* species): The strongly scented Sweet Violet (*V. odorata*) is the best. Other types add color but not much flavor.

Other edible flowers

This is pretty much just a long list, as to go into more detail would take up more room than is really justified. This list is potentially almost endless because anything that isn't actually poisonous could probably be eaten in the small amounts. These are all considered edible flowers, though their quality varies lot. Many add color and beauty, but not much flavor. You could experiment with any of these species:

Alkanet (*Anchusa azurea*): Petals only.

Alliums: Almost any wild or cultivated species can be used.

Alyssum (*Lobularia maritima)*: Small white flowers are pungent.

Angelica (*Angelica archangelica*)

Apple (*Malus* spp): Can eat a few petals but not too many, as they have a chemical that turns into cyanide when eaten.

Balloon flower (*Platycodon grandiflorum)*: Blue flowers are quite good.

Bean (*Phaseolus vulgaris*): Flowers have a green bean flavor.

Black Locust (*Robinia pseudoacacia*): Eat the flowers only, all other parts are toxic.

Burnet (*Sanguisorba minor*): Cucumber flavor.

Carrot (*Daucus carota*): Nice carrot flavor

Catnip (*Nepeta cataria*): Strong mint flavor

Chamomile (*Chamaemelum nobilis)*

Chervil (*Anthriscus cerefolium*)

Chicory (*Cichorium intybus*)

Citrus: Taste first, some are not very pleasant.

Clover (*Trifolium* species): Sweet

English Daisy (*Bellis perennis*)

Dandelion (*Taraxacum officinale)*: Use individual petals

Cottage Pink (*Dianthus plumarius*): Can be very good.

Elder (*Sambucus* species): Flowers only (other parts toxic). They have a distinctive aromatic flavor.

Evening Primrose (*Oenothera biennis*): Yellow flowers are quite good.

Forget-Me-Not (*Myosotis sylvatica*): Use flowers in moderation, contains toxins

Freesia: Aromatic

Fuchsia: Eat only the petals, discard the rest.

Gardenia (*Gardenia jasminoides*): Used raw, pickled, for tea.

Ginger (*Zingiber officinale*) Fragrant flowers have a ginger flavor.

Gladiolus: Taste first, some are good and some are not pleasant.

Hawthorn (*Crataegus* species)

Hollyhock (*Alcea rosea*): Flowers add more color than flavor

Honeysuckle: (*Lonicera japonica*)

Horseradish (*Armoracia rusticana*)

Hibiscus (Hibiscus rosa-sinensis)

Hyssop *Hyssopus officinalis*

Impatiens (Impatiens walleriana)

Jasmine (*Jasmine officinale*): Traditionally used in tea.

Kudzu (*Pueraria montana*): Aromatic and sweet

Lemon Verbena (*Aloysia triphylla*): The flowers are small but aromatic

Lilac (Syringa vulgaris)

Linden (*Tilia* spp.)

Mallow (*Malva sylvestris*)

Manzanita (*Arctostaphylos* species): Some species are good.

Marjoram (*Origanum majorana*)

Marsh Mallow(*Althaea officinalis*)

Mexican Tarragon (*Tagetes lucida*): Flowers taste like tarragon.

Mimosa (*Albizia julibrissin*)

Mints (*Mentha* spp)

Moringa (*Moringa oleifera*)

Mullein (*Verbascum thapsus*)

Okra (*Abelmoschus esculentus*): Flowers used like hibiscus.

Oregano (*Origanum vulgare*)

Oregon Grape (*Mahonia aquifolium*): Yellow flowers are slightly acidic.

Parsley (*Petroselintum crispum*)

Passionflower (*Passiflora* species)

Pelargonium: Taste first, some scented varieties are good, others are not.

Peach (*Prunus persica*): Can eat a few petals but not too many, as they have a chemical that turns into cyanide when eaten.

Pear (*Pyrus communis*): Can eat a few petals but not too many, as they have a chemical that turns into cyanide when eaten.

Phlox (*Phlox paniculata*): Flowers spicy

Plum (*Prunus* species): Can eat a few petals but not too many, as they have a chemical that turns into cyanide when eaten.

Poppy (*Papaver rhoeas*) Red petals add color.

Primulas (*Primula vulgaris*)

Redbud (*Cercis canadensis*)

Rose of Sharon (*Hibiscus syriacus*)

Roselle (*Hibiscus sabdariffa*)

Rosemary (*Rosmarinus officinalis*)

Safflower (*Carthamus tinctorius*): Dried flowers used like saffron

Savory (*Satureja Montana*)

Scarlet Runner Bean (*Phaseolus coccineus*)

Society Garlic (*Tulbaghia violacea*): The pretty violet flowers are edible and taste like onion.

Spiderwort (*Tradescantia virginiana*)

Stock (*Mathiola incana*)

Strawberry (*Fragaria* species): These are edible, but every time you take one you potentially lose a strawberry.

Sunflower (*Helianthus annuus*): (petals)

Sweet Rocket (*Hesperis matronalis*): Add color more than flavor.

Sweet Woodruff (*Galium odoratum*)

Thyme (*Thymus* spp.)

Tiger Lily (*Lilium lancifolium*)

Tuberose (*Polianthes tuberosa*): Was cooked and eaten by the Aztecs.

Tuberous Begonias (*Begonia x tuberhybrida*): These can be good, but should be eaten in moderation.

Tulip (*Tulipa* species): Flowers are sweet and crisp, other parts can be toxic

Red Valerian (*Centranthus ruber*)

Water Hyacinth (*Eichornia crassipes*)

Water Lily (*Nymphaea odorata*): Edible but almost too pretty to use.

Wisteria (*Wisteria sinensis*): Flowers only, other parts are toxic.

Yucca (*Yucca* species): Tasty, sweet and crunchy

Eggplant

Solanum melongena

Introduction: This subtropical species was first cultivated by the great civilizations of China and India almost 6000 years ago. It gradually moved west to the Mediterranean with early traders and has been grown in the warmer countries of Europe since at least the 16th century. It is a tender perennial, but is treated as an annual in temperate countries. It is one of the prettiest vegetables and doesn't look out of place in the ornamental garden.

Nutritional value: The fruit are a useful source of vitamins A, C and some B's, including folate, as well as calcium, magnesium, potassium and phosphorous. They are a very good source of various antioxidants and phytonutrients. They contain about 110 calories per pound.

Ease of growing: Eggplant can be quite slow to get going initially, but once it is established in the right growing conditions it isn't too difficult to grow.

Crop value: Eggplant is a fairly nutritious plant, but it isn't eaten in quantity It isn't particularly productive or easy to grow either, so isn't a very important crop from a food self-sufficiency standpoint.

Climate: The eggplant is of subtropical origin and needs a long (3 - 5 months), hot (70 - 90°F) growing season for best growth. It won't grow well if it isn't warm during the day and doesn't like cold nights (below 70°F is cold for eggplant). However there are some varieties that do okay in cooler climates.

In cool climates it is sometimes grown in a greenhouse or tunnel cloche.

Did I mention that eggplant doesn't like extreme heat either?

About Eggplant

Seed facts
Germ temp: 60 (75 - 90) 95°F
Germ time: 14 - 21 days
13 days / 68°F
8 days / 77°F
5 days / 86°F * Optimum
Viability: 6 - 10 yrs
Germination percentage: 60%+
Weeks to grow transplants: 6 - 8

Planning facts
Hardiness: Tender
Growing temp: 65 (70 - 85) 90°F
Plants per person: 2
Plants per sq ft: ½
Start: 6 - 8 wks before last frost
Plant out: 4 wks after last frost
Plant size: 24 - 72″ tall
18 - 24″ wide

Harvest facts
Days to harvest:
From seed: 100 - 150 days
From transplant: 55 - 85 days
Yield per plant: 4 lb (5 - 20 fruit)
Yield per sq ft: ½ - 1½ lb sq ft

Soil

pH 5.5 - 6.8

Eggplant likes the same kind of soil as peppers, fertile, well-drained, deep and loose. They need a fair amount of nitrogen and moderate amounts of phosphorus and potassium (a fair amount is slightly more than a moderate amount).

Soil preparation: Incorporate 2″ of compost or aged manure into the top 6″ of soil. Raised beds are good as they help the soil to warm up faster.

Plastic mulch: When growing eggplant in cooler areas, some people use plastic mulch to keep the soil warmer.

Planning

Where: Eggplant needs a warm, sunny spot, sheltered from cold winds.

Eggplant is quite slow growing, so you may want to plant a fast growing intercrop (lettuce is good) in between the transplants. This may even be beneficial as it acts as a living mulch.

When: The seed must be started indoors quite early (10 - 12 weeks before setting out), so the plants have enough time to size up before transplanting time.

I must emphasize again that eggplants must have warm conditions if they are going to make much progress (80 - 90°F is ideal).

Planting

Transplants

Eggplant is usually grown indoors and transplanted, because it needs warm conditions for germination. If you waited until the soil outdoors was warm enough (at least 60°F) before sowing seed, you could waste a lot of time.

Starting inside: Eggplants don't like root disturbance, so are best started in cell packs or soil blocks. Plant 2 - 3 seeds per cell and when they all emerge, thin to the best one. Be careful when transplanting, as any damage will show up as poor growth and delayed fruiting.

Eggplant is one of the most temperamental of all the common crop seeds. It germinates best at higher temperatures than most crops (ideally 75 - 85°F) and even at the optimal temperature of 85°F, you should only expect about 60% of seeds to actually germinate. Soaking them overnight may speed up germination.

If your greenhouse (or other growing setup) isn't warm enough you could try using heating cables, or simply start them indoors somewhere really warm. Just be sure to put them out in bright light as soon as they start to germinate.

For most rapid growth you should feed the seedlings twice a week with a dilute liquid kelp (use double the recommended quantity of water).

When your seedlings have 2 sets of true leaves you should prick them out into individual 4″ pots.

Hardening off: By the time it is warm enough in spring to plant your eggplants outside, it will be pretty hot in the greenhouse. To avoid any kind of transplant shock, you should harden off the plants to get them accustomed to the cooler conditions outside. Do this slowly over a week, by reducing the amount of water they get and by leaving them outside for longer periods each day.

Hardening off isn't necessary in warm summer weather, but it doesn't hurt to keep them outside in the shade for a few days before planting out.

Buying plants: Because eggplants are so slow to start, many people prefer to buy their plants. The only drawback to this is that you have a lot less weird and wonderful varieties to choose from. When buying plants look for stocky ones that aren't rootbound, don't have any flowers or fruit and look deep green and healthy (with no signs of disease, pests or deficiency).

Planting out: Eggplants can't tolerate cold weather, so they are among the last plants to go outside in spring (usually a couple of weeks after tomato). The soil temperature should be at least 60°F and the air temperature at least 70°F. It is possible to set them out earlier, if you warm the soil with black plastic or cloches (and then protect them with cloches).

You don't usually need many eggplants, so you can take special care when planting them. Make a fairly big hole, throw in a couple of handfuls of compost and a handful of organic fertilizer mix and then plant the seedlings up to their first true leaves. Water straight after planting of course.

Direct sowing: If you have a very long growing season you could start the seed outdoors. The best way to do this is to plant them in a nursery bed (a small area specifically designated for growing seedlings) and later transplant them to their final position.

Spacing:
Beds: Put transplants 18 - 24″ apart in the intensive beds.

Rows: Space them 18 - 24″ apart in the rows, with 24 - 36″ between the rows.

Care

Weeds: Eggplants are quite shallow rooted, so don't use a hoe around them. Weed carefully by hand instead.

Water: The plants are fairly drought tolerant, but if they are to produce an abundance of tasty fruit they need plenty of water. Keep the soil evenly moist by watering deeply once or twice a week (never allow them to wilt). Don't over-water them though, they do not like wet soil. They don't like wet leaves either, so drip irrigation works best.

Fertilization: Once the seedlings have started growing well, give them a dose of compost tea or liquid kelp (they especially need nitrogen and potassium). Repeat this every 3 - 4 weeks for maximum production.

Mulch: In warm weather mulch is helpful to conserve soil moisture and keep down weeds (in very hot conditions it also helps to keep the soil cool). This shouldn't be applied until the soil is warm though.

Pruning: Pinch out the growing tip when the plant is about a foot high, to make it branch and get bushier. If you want large size fruit, don't let a plant produce more than a half dozen. Prevent this by pinching out new flowers and any lateral side shoots. You might also do this if you live in an area that is marginal for growing eggplant, so at least a few get to ripen.

Support: Eggplants are usually fairly sturdy, but the fruiting plants can get top heavy and fall over. If this starts to happen you can carefully add some bamboo cane supports (or try and coax them into a tomato cage).

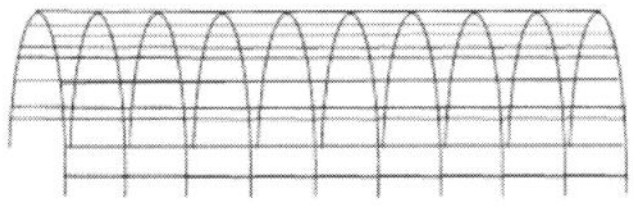

An arch of concrete reinforcing wire makes a great support. While the plants are small it can be covered in plastic to keep them warm. As they get bigger they can grow through it and sprawl on top.

Protection: If a frost threatens (in spring or fall) you should protect the plants with a frost blanket, or anything else you have available.

Problems: To produce well, eggplant needs warmth, good soil and abundant moisture. They are somewhat temperamental though and sometimes you give them these things and still they don't do well. Planting out too early is a common cause of failure; if a young plant gets severely chilled it can be permanently retarded.

If it is too cold (especially at night) or too dry, the plant may drop its flowers instead of setting fruit.

Pests: Eggplant is a member of the *Solanaceae and* is susceptible to the same pests as tomato and potato.

Flea beetles: These pepper the leaves with tiny holes and are a common problem. Fortunately they are not usually serious and can be ignored.

Cutworms: If these are a common problem in your area, protect your transplants with cutworm collars.

Disease: Eggplant is affected by most of the same diseases as the tomato and potato. Avoid getting the leaves wet and give the plants good air circulation.

Harvesting

When: Traditionally the fruits are harvested just as they reach full size, while their skin is still shiny. If the skin has turned dull, the seeds are ripening (they turn brown) and it is too old.

Small: In Asia they often pick the fruit while it is the size of an egg, or only slightly larger. These young fruit are tastier and have a better texture than older ones. Picking smaller fruit also increases the harvest, as a plant can produce many more of them. It also lengthens the harvest, as they will produce over a longer period of time.

How: Cut the fruit from the plant with a knife or secateurs, without pulling on the plant too much. Leave an inch of stem attached to the fruit.

Storage: Eggplant should be treated like a tomato, which means picked when ripe and used immediately (it doesn't mean eat them raw). Keep them at a cool room temperature (not in the fridge) and they should be good for a week or so. For longer term storage they fruits can be cut up and frozen.

Seed saving: The plants are generally self-pollinated, but some cross pollination by insects also occurs. To keep a variety pure only one variety should be grown at one time, or it should be isolated by at least 50 feet. To ensure genetic variability, you should save the seed from at least 6 plants.

To get ripe seed, you need to let a fruit ripen completely. Separate the seed from the fruit by grating the seed bearing flesh and then mashing it in water. The seed is then dried for storage. Eggplant seed is quite long lived if stored properly and may last for up to ten years.

Unusual growing ideas

Ornamental: With its mauve flowers and shiny fruits, eggplant is one of the most attractive vegetables and can easily blend into the ornamental garden.

Containers: If you live in a less than ideal climate you might try growing eggplant in a container. You can put it outside when it is warm and bring it indoors if it gets too cold. It also helps that the soil in a pot will get warmer than it would in the ground. It should be a fairly big pot (at least 12″ deep) though and you must take care to keep the soil moist.

Tunnels: In cooler climates eggplant may be grown in plastic tunnels to give it additional heat. Open these up whenever it is warm enough, so bees can pollinate the flowers.

Varieties

If you don't have the ideal climate for eggplants you should choose an early maturing variety. Most of the eggplant varieties that are available are of two main types.

American / European: These are the eggplants you see in stores, fairly big and somewhat pear shaped with shiny purple skin. There are also some less common white fruited varieties that are the reason this plant is known as eggplant.

Black Beauty - An old favorite.
Casper - A beautiful and tasty white variety.

Asian: The small Asian eggplants are considered to be tastier than the larger western varieties. They can also be more productive, as the fruits are picked when smaller (so more will form.) They are often more attractive too.

This is another crop where F1 hybrids are taking over the seed catalogs. However there are still many fantastically multi-colored (orange, white, green, yellow, purple) open pollinated heirloom varieties from Asia. These are becoming much more widely available and can be quite spectacular. In fact they are some of the prettiest vegetables you will ever see. I make no claim to be an eggplant expert, but these varieties are highly rated:

Ichiban - Long purple fruit, does well in cooler areas.

Little Fingers - Small purple fruit, not much bigger than your fingers.

Millionaire - Purple fruit, very early (54 days from transplanting).

Orient express F1- Does well in cooler areas. Fast maturing (60 days from transplanting).

Rosa Bianca - Italian heirloom, medium size, purple fruit (80 days from transplanting).

Rosita - Pink / purple fruit (80 days from transplanting)

Thai Green - Long narrow green fruit, vigorous (80 days from transplanting)

Fairytale F1 - One of best tasting varieties, white / purple fruit.

Kitchen use

Probably more than any other common vegetable, cooking and recipe is all important with eggplant. A badly cooked eggplant is almost inedible, while a well-cooked one is absolutely delicious.

Eggplants have a natural affinity with barbecues and are a good meat substitute.

Garlic, basil and marjoram all go well with eggplant.

Eggplant with Garlic

3 or 4 oriental eggplants chopped into 1″ cubes
2 cloves garlic
4 green onions chopped
1 tsp chopped fresh ginger
1 tsp chili sauce
1 tsp wine vinegar
1 tsp sugar
½ tsp ground black pepper
1 tbsp cornstarch
4 tbsp water
4 tbsp soy sauce
1 tbsp sesame oil

Mix the sugar, soy sauce, chili sauce and pepper in a bowl. In another bowl mix cornstarch and water. Saute the garlic, 2 green onions and ginger in a little oil for several minutes. Add the eggplant and soy sauce mix and simmer 15 minutes. Finally add the cornstarch and rest of the onions and cook for a few minutes more.

Endive

Cichorium endivia

Introduction: Endive (or escarole) is a close relative of chicory, which is sometimes (rather confusingly) called endive, However it differs in that it is a biennial (though grown as an annual) rather than a perennial and is less cold tolerant

Endive is often overlooked because people don't know how to grow it properly. This can be a problem because if it is grown at the wrong time of year it can be very bitter. When grown properly it is an excellent salad plant for cooler climates and is particularly prized in France and Italy.

There are several different types of endive, the most popular are the frisee types with their finely cut feathery foliage. These find their way into many (if not most) commercial salad mixes.

Nutritional content: The leaves are rich in vitamins A C, E and folate, as well as the minerals calcium, iron, potassium and phosphorus. The contain about 80 calories per pound.

Climate: Endive is a cool weather plant and doesn't do well with heat (though it can tolerate more than lettuce). In warmer areas it can be grown either in spring (okay) or fall (better).

Crop value: Endive isn't a particularly nutritious or productive crop, but it does produce some of the best tasting salad materials.

Ease of growing: As with the related chicory, endive is a vigorous and fairly easy crop to grow.

However for best flavor you have to time it right so it gets suitably cool weather. This is especially critical if you are growing the cornet types that produce a sweet compact head of leaves (the best kinds).

About Endive

Seed facts
Germ temp: 45 (60 - 65) 75°F
Germination time: 5 - 14 days
Germination percentage:
Viability: 5 - 10 yrs
Weeks to grow transplants: 4

Planning facts
Hardiness: Hardy
Growing temp: 45 (60 - 65) 75°F
Plants per person: 5
Plants per sq ft: 1

Transplants:
Start: 8 weeks before last frost
Plant out: 4 wks before last frost
Direct sow: 2 - 6 weeks before last frost date
Fall crop: Sow 12 weeks before first fall frost

Harvest facts
Days to harvest: 100 - 140 days
Yield per plant: 6 - 12 oz
Yield per sq ft: 6 - 12 oz

Soil

pH 5.0 (5.5 - 6.8) 7.0

Endive prefers a rich soil with lots of moisture retentive humus. It should be well-drained (as with most cold weather crops), otherwise the roots may rot over the winter. It grows well in quite acid soil.

Soil preparation: Incorporate 2″ of compost or aged manure into the top 6″ of soil.

Planning

Endive is grown in much the same way as the related lettuce.

Where: Full sun is important for this cool weather plant.

When: The plant is similar to lettuce in many ways, including its tendency to turn very bitter or bolt in hot weather (it is also day length sensitive too).

Spring: In cool climates endive can be grown as a spring crop. It can be direct sown 2 - 4 weeks before the last frost, or even earlier if protected by cloches.

It can also be started indoors, 8 - 10 weeks before the last frost and planted out 4 weeks before the last frost. You need the plants to grow rapidly and mature before the weather gets too warm, otherwise you are wasting your time.

Fall: Endive is most successful as a fall crop, as it has less tendency to bolt in the cool short days. It also tastes less bitter when grown in cool weather and may even be improved by light frost. Start the seeds about 12 weeks before the first fall frost. As with lettuce, warm soil can hinder germination (see **Lettuce** for ways around this).

Over-Winter: Endive is quite hardy and in mild winter areas it can be grown right through the winter. It can also be started in fall and over-wintered in the ground, to provide an early spring crop.

Planting

Transplants: Transplants are grown in the same way as lettuce, started 8 - 10 weeks before the last frost date and planted out 4 weeks before. They should be about 3″ tall when planted out.

Direct sowing: Endive can be direct sown using any of the techniques I have described for lettuce. The seeds are usually planted ¼ - ½″ deep. I plant quite thickly initially and slowly harvest thin to the desired spacing, starting when they have all emerged and are 1″ tall.

Spacing: Give the plants enough space, crowding can cause them to bolt.

Bed: Put the plants in offset rows across the bed. Space them 6″ - 9″ - 12″ apart, depending upon the soil and variety.

Row: Row spacing should be anywhere from 6 - 12″ in the rows with 12 - 18″ between the rows.

Care

It is important that spring sown plants grow rapidly (so they have time to mature before it gets too warm), so they need to be pampered.

Water: The soil must be kept evenly moist, otherwise their flavor may be inferior and the plants may bolt.

Fertilization: For good growth the plants must have all the nutrients they need. If the soil is poor give them a liquid feed of compost tea or liquid kelp every 3 weeks.

Blanching: The leaves are commonly blanched to reduce their bitterness and make them sweeter. There are several ways to do this.

Tie the outer leaves together for 10 days before the harvest (or for up to 3 weeks in winter). Do this when the plants are dry, because if any water gets trapped inside the heart it may cause it to rot. Also don't tie slugs up inside the heart.

A simpler way to blanch them is to cover with an inverted flowerpot (close up the drainage hole). They have even been blanched by simply laying a board of wood on top of them. The inner leaves often get somewhat blanched naturally, just by being covered by the outer ones.

There is a downside to blanching. It not only reduces their bitterness, it also reduces their nutritional value. Of course you probably wouldn't eat them otherwise, because they would be too bitter (which invalidates this argument).

Pests: These are much the same as with lettuce. Slugs can be a nuisance with young plants, or when blanching. Premature bolting is generally more of a problem than pests.

Harvesting

Harvest like lettuce, taking the whole heads, individual leaves, or most of the heart (the part remaining will often re-sprout). Eat any thinnings in salads.

Storage: You can store the heads in a plastic bag in the fridge for up to 10 days.

Seed saving: The procedure for saving seed is the same as for chicory. It is somewhat easier to save endive seed however, as it can't be pollinated by chicory (or by the ubiquitous wild chicory). Don't save seed from any plants that bolt prematurely, as you don't want to produce a strain of quick bolting plants.

Unusual growing ideas

Salad mix: The frisee endives are one of the most popular plants for growing in salad mixes. See **Salad Mix / Mesclun** for more on this.

Varieties

The endives can be roughly divided into four types.

Escaroles: These varieties have large broad lettuce-like leaves, usually entire and undivided. They are the hardiest of the endives and are usually grown as a fall or winter salad crop. Some people prefer their flavor.

Full Heart Batavian - Large, succulent leaves, big head. All America winner in 1934.

Broadleaf Batavian - Large lettuce-like leaves. An old heirloom.

Curly leaved: These varieties have divided leaves and are commonly known as endives. They are more tolerant of warm weather than the escaroles, so are more often grown in spring and fall.

Frisees: These varieties have finely divided, almost fuzzy leaves that are visually very appealing and find their way into many salad mixes. They are more tolerant of warm weather, so are commonly grown in spring as well as fall (and not so tolerant of cold weather).

Rhodos - Frilly leaves used in salad mix (42 days)

Salad King - Italian Heirloom (95 days)

Tres Fin Maraichere - French heirloom, great in salad mix (55 days)

Escaroles En Cornet: These are so rarely grown that they don't even have an English name, yet many people (mostly French and Italians) consider them the best of all the endives (if not the best of all salad plants). These are prized for the large, succulent sweet and delicious heart. They are sometimes confused with the fairly similar sugarloaf chicory, but they are actually endive.

Cornet D'Anjou

Cornet de Bordeaux

These two are difficult to find in this country. I found the second one in a packet of Italian salad mix.

Kitchen use

Endive was originally used as a potherb (braising is good), but is now more generally eaten raw in salads.

Garlic

Allium sativum

Introduction: Garlic originated in the Caucasus region of central Asia and is thought to be one of the first cultivated plants (it no longer even occurs as a wild plant). It has been prized as a culinary flavoring for over 7000 yrs, having been cultivated by almost every ancient civilization, from the Chinese, Indians and Egyptians onwards. China is now the worlds biggest producer, growing something like 70% of the total world crop.

Ease of growing: Garlic is a fairly easy crop to grow and I find it one of the most satisfying. Harvesting the garlic crop is one of the highlights of my gardening year.

Garlic is very productive and it is easy to grow enough for a whole year. It is also fairly easy to store and some varieties can keep for up to 10 months.

Crop value: Garlic isn't hugely important from a nutritional standpoint because it is only eaten in small quantities, but it is extremely important from a culinary viewpoint. It is second only to the onion in importance as a kitchen flavoring. No serious cook could conceive of not having garlic on hand.

Nutritional content: Garlic contains so many valuable phytochemicals (including allicin, ajoene and allyl sulfide) that it is an important medicine / food. It has anticarcinogenic, antioxidant, antifungal, anticlotting, antiseptic and antibiotic properties (and probably a few more too).

Garlic has so many benefical qualities that there has been a lot of hype in recent years about its value as a medicine / food (I refuse to use the word nutriceutical) and countless commercial preparations are available. However a lot of its benecifical chemicals are quite delicate so eating them as a food is much more effective than swallowing them in a manufactured product.

You can maximize the beneficial qualities of your garlic by letting it sit for a while after chopping

Garlic contains about 670 calories per pound. I'm not quite sure why I'm telling you this, as I can't imagine anyone has ever eaten a pound of garlic at one time!

About Garlic

Planning facts
Hardiness: hardy
Growing temp: 45 (55 - 75) 85°F
Plant:
Fall: 8 - 10 wks before first frost
Spring: 4 - 6 wks before last frost
Days to harvest: 90 - 220 days
Plants per sq ft: 4
Plants per person: 10 - 15
Height 12 - 24″
Width 6 - 12″

Harvest facts
Harvest period: 2 - 3 weeks
Yield per sq ft: ¾ - 2 lb
Yield per plant: 2 - 4 oz

Climate: Garlic originated in central Asia with its cold winters, cool springs and warm dry summers. It needs warm days (cool nights are fine) for best growth. Too much heat (above 95°F) can hasten maturation, which isn't good as it means the plant has less time to store food and so results in smaller bulbs. Rain while the bulbs are maturing isn't good either.

Garlic is very hardy and can tolerate temperatures down to 0°F or lower. If the soil doesn't freeze, its roots will continue to grow right through the winter. The tops will also grow whenever the temperature is above 40°F, in fact they grow best in fairly cool conditions.

Hardneck varieties are hardier than the softnecks and so a better choice for colder areas. The softnecks are more suited to mild winter areas. Most commercial garlic is the softneck type, grown in central California with its mild winters, mild springs and warm, dry summers.

Soil

pH 5.5 (6-6.5) 7.0

Garlic will grow well enough on poor soil, but the bulbs won't get very big. For big beautiful bulbs it needs a light, rich, deep, moist, well-drained loam with lots of organic matter. Drainage is important for this over-wintering crop, as the roots may rot if they stay wet and cold for too long.

Soil preparation: Garlic sends down roots 2 feet or more, so the ideal soil is deep, loose and friable. It doesn't like compacted soil, so if the soil is at all heavy or compacted, then double digging and incorporating organic matter will help. Raised beds are also beneficial as they help to ensure deep soil and good winter drainage (which is important).

Incorporate 2″ of compost or aged manure into the top 6″ of soil, along with a source of potassium (wood ashes) and phosphorus (colloidal phosphate). Garlic has a particular liking for sulphur.

Garlic does well following a recently incorporated summer green manure crop, as it benefits from the newly released nutrients. You might even plant a crop of buckwheat specifically to fertilize a following garlic crop. Wait two weeks for the crop to decompose before planting the garlic.

Don't overdo the fertilization for garlic, as it can make the bulbs less flavorful.

Planning

Where: Garlic needs full sun, the more the better. It doesn't tolerate weeds very well, so try to choose a spot that doesn't have a lot of them.

Crop rotation: Don't plant garlic in soil where any Allium (garlic, onion, shallot, leek) has grown within the last 3 years.

When: The most important factor in growing good garlic is planting it at the right time.

Fall: In places where garlic will survive the winter it does better and gets larger when planted in fall. This gives it plenty of time to put on vegetative growth and store food before the long days of the following summer trigger bulbing.

In mild climates, set out your cloves from August onwards (at least 2 months before the first frost date). You want the plants to be well established before the onset of cold weather.

You can also plant garlic in fall in colder areas (until November). They won't make any top growth, but their roots will grow and give you an early start in spring. The bed should be mulched with 4 - 6″ straw to protect the cloves from frost and prevent heaving. When the coldest part of the winter is over (early spring) you should remove the mulch to allow the soil to warm up.

Spring: In areas with very cold winters, fall planted garlic may not survive outside and in such places it must be planted in spring, 4 - 6 weeks before the last frost. It can go in the ground as early as early as February if you protect it with cloches.

Don't wait too long in spring to plant your garlic, or you may run into a problem with lack of chill. The dormant cloves and / or young plants must be exposed to a period of cold weather (6 - 8 weeks below 50°F) before bulbing can occur. If they don't get this the cloves will simply get bigger, rather than dividing into the familiar bulbs. These are known as "rounds" and can be eaten (though they aren't very big) or left in the ground for another year.

Spring planting works okay, but isn't usually as productive as fall planting.

Planting

How: Garlic is propagated vegetatively from individual cloves. Gently break open the bulb, without bruising the cloves inside (you don't want them to lose their protective skin). Do this just before planting, as separating the cloves may initiate root growth.

Some people say larger cloves make larger bulbs. Others say it doesn't matter much what size the clove you plant (within reason), the final bulbs will be about the same size. I say if you bought bulbs to plant, then plant them. Do you care if some of the resulting bulbs are slightly smaller than others? If you have plenty of planting material, you might use very small ones for growing garlic greens.

Plant the cloves 2 - 3″ deep (1″ in mild areas), making sure they are upright. This means planting them pointed side up and flat side down (planting upside down does not help). If the soil is very loose you can just push the clove down into the soil, but if it is hard the ensuing pressure may damage the base of the clove. In such circumstances you should loosen the soil before planting.

Sometimes the newly planted cloves will be dug up by cats using the freshly planted bed as a litter box. The best way to prevent this is to lay a piece of wire fencing on the bed for a few weeks. The sprouts can emerge through this easily, but it prevents digging.

Spacing:

Beds: Space the plants 4 - 6″ apart, in short offset rows across the bed. Use the closer spacing in very fertile soil and the wider spacing in poor soil. If you want to be able to hoe between the rows, make the rows slightly wider (8″) apart.

Rows: Space the plants 4 - 6″ in the row, with 15 - 24″ between the rows.

Bulbing: As with the related onions, bulbing is determined by day length. Bulb formation is triggered by long days and once the right day length comes along, the plant will form a bulb, no matter what size the plant. Once bulbing starts, leaf growth comes to a halt. Bulbing is also affected by temperature, soil fertility, plant size and vigor, but to a lesser extent.

The bulb consists of specialized storage leaves. Bulbing occurs when the plant stops producing new leaves and starts to store food in the leaves it has. This causes their bases to expand, which creates the bulb. When the bulb is mature, all of the food has gone from the rest of the leaves, so they wither, fall over and die.

For large bulbs you want maximum leaf growth before day length triggers bulb formation. In ideal conditions the plants may get two feet tall. Poor leaf growth means small bulbs, with small cloves that are so tedious to peel they often don't get used (don't throw them away though, see **Green Garlic** below).

Care

Weeds: Garlic only has a few strap-like leaves and can't compete with weeds very well, so it's important to keep it well weeded at all times. This is all the more important as the plants are in the ground for a long time (parts of two growing seasons). The roots are shallow, so hand weeding is preferable to hoeing.

Water: This is another critical factor in growing good garlic. The plants need to have a steady and constant supply of moisture when putting on leaf growth and bulbing up. Do not allow the soil to dry out at this time. At the same time you don't want the soil to be too wet, as this can encourage fungus disease, so don't over-water.

About 2 - 3 weeks before the plants are ready to harvest, you should stop watering, to allow them to dry out. This hastens maturation and starts the curing process.

Mulch: I like to lay down a 2 - 3″ straw mulch after planting, to conserve moisture, keep the soil cool and suppress weeds.

In cold climates a thick mulch is used to protect the cloves over the winter. This should be removed in early spring to allow the soil to warm up. When the soil is warm you apply a thinner mulch to suppress weeds and conserve moisture.

Fertilization: Garlic isn't a very hungry plant, but it needs a steady supply of nutrients for best growth. Young plants need an adequate supply of nitrogen, so you may want to feed them in spring while the soil is cool and not much nitrogen is readily available.

If your soil isn't very fertile it is a good idea to give them a regular foliar feed of compost tea or liquid kelp. Start this when the plants are 3″ tall and repeat every 2 - 3 weeks during the growing season (stop about a month before bulbing starts). If you don't want to do this, you can simply feed them once in spring when they start growing vigorously. They need micronutrients as much as NPK.

The yellowing of some leaf tips is quite normal in garlic; it doesn't necessarily indicate any kind of nutrient deficiency.

Bolting: Hardneck garlic usually send up a scape (flower stalk) in late spring, just before it starts to bulb up. Many people consider this to be undesirable and remove it to prevent it using energy that could be used for enlarging the bulbs. However some growers say it is best to leave it on as the bulb stores better (even if it is very slightly smaller).

One good reason to remove the scape is that it is edible (don't throw it away). In Asia these are highly prized as food and special varieties are grown to produce them. See **Scapes** below for more on this.

Softneck garlic doesn't produce scape routinely, though they may do so if stressed. If these start to bolt you should remove the scape promptly.

Pests and diseases: Garlic is generally free of most pests and diseases, though it is more afflicted in cool wet climates. It is occasionally attacked by onion maggots (a relative of the dreaded cabbage root fly/maggot) and thrips. Of course gophers will eat it too (plant by plant, right down the row, if given the opportunity).

Harvesting

Garlic is propagated vegetatively, so all of the cloves of a variety are genetically identical. The ultimate size of a bulb is determined by timing, growing conditions and to a lesser extent by variety (some naturally get larger than others).

The size and number of cloves in a bulb is determined by the variety. Sometimes a bulb may have a small number of large cloves and sometimes it may have a large number of small cloves.

When: Garlic is harvested when half of the lower leaves have turned yellow (there should still be 5 or 6 green leaves). At this time you should be able to clearly see the swollen bulb when you move the mulch aside. Pull up a few random bulbs and inspect them carefully before harvesting all of it.

If garlic is left in the ground too long all of the leaves turn brown and the over-mature bulbs may start to split open. This may not look very nice, but doesn't affect its edibility. These might not store as well though (they may dry out faster), so should be used first.

How: If your soil is very loose often you can simply uproot the plants by pulling on the tops. If the soil is very firm, you will have to loosen it with a fork first. Garlic bruises easily, so handle it carefully at all times and never throw it around.

Don't leave the bulbs on the ground in the sun for too long, as they may get cooked. They then turn a translucent yellow and are ruined.

Curing: Newly harvested garlic should be cured at around 70°F before storage. This not only lengthens its storage life but also improves its flavor (newly harvested garlic may be somewhat bitter).

If the weather is dry, you can cure the bulbs by leaving them in a shady place for a week or two. If it's wet, you will have to cure them Inside (the greenhouse is a good place, as it's dry and warm). Once they are dry the leaves don't smell of garlic very much.

The dry bulbs are prepared for storage or sale by cutting off the shriveled tops (leave about 2″) and trimming the stringy roots (to ½″). They are also cleaned by removing any discolored outer wrapper layers. If you have several varieties that look similar you might cut the stems of each variety to different lengths, to help identify them.

If you want to make garlic braids, save the bulbs with the best tops (don't cut them off of course).

Storage: The bulbs must be thoroughly dry before storing them in a cool dry place, with 50 - 60% humidity and good air circulation. If the bulbs are to be used fairly quickly, they can be stored at 50 - 60°F. For longer-term storage (and for the bulbs that will be re-planted in fall) they should ideally be kept at 35 - 40°F.

Store the bulbs in wooden boxes, mesh bags, or the traditional garlic braids. It is tempting to hang these attractive braids in the kitchen, but it is usually too warm and dry there. When stored above 70°F some of the bulbs may dry out before you get around to using them.

In the kitchen its best to keep garlic in a terracotta garlic keeper or a doubled brown paper bag.This ensures it has the high humidity necessary to prevent it drying out.

Different types of garlic have different storage properties. The softneck types store better than the hardnecks.

Seed saving: Garlic doesn't produce viable seed, so it is propagated vegetatively from the same cloves you use for cooking. Simply save some of the bulbs for re-planting at the appropriate time. These must be stored carefully though, otherwise they may dry out, or sprout prematurely. You can't leave the bulb in the ground of course, because it will eventually start to grow again and form a crowded cluster of plants.

If you use the same strain for long enough, it will eventually adapt to your climate.

Unusual growing ideas

Containers: Garlic is a fairly compact plant and can do well when grown in a container. Just make sure it is big enough - at least 12" deep and that you use a good potting mix. The most difficult thing about growing garlic in a pot is that cloves are planted in fall, so will need attention for quite a while. The most important thing is to not let the soil dry out too much.

Bulbils: You can grow garlic from the bulbils that are sometimes produced on the flower umbel (head), but you won't get mature bulbs for two years. Some types produce these more readily than others (notably the Asiatics and turbans)

Green Garlic: In China a lot of garlic is planted for use in the green stage. Any surplus, or unusually small cloves (such as the aforementioned ones that are too small to peel) can be planted like green onions in a couple of square feet of bed. Single leaves can be cut off from the bulbs as needed (they will produce more). The whole young plants are also eaten. If you overlook a bulb and it sprouts in the garden, you can use the multiple stems in the kitchen.

Scapes: In China and Japan when a bulb bolts it is considered to be an opportunity, rather than a loss. The scape (flower stalk) is highly prized and constitutes an extra (and early) crop from the maturing bulbs. They are cut off as they emerge and the bulb continues to mature. In Asia they even have special varieties that reliably bolt, but still produce good sized bulbs.

Varieties

There are over 400 varieties of garlic, which may come as a surprise if you are only used to seeing the big white bulbs in the supermarket. Apparently a lot of garlic varieties came from the Soviet Union after 1989, which is why there are now many more varieties than were previously available. You can buy many strains by mail order, while a few may be available in local retail outlets. You should only need to buy a variety of garlic once, as it's easy to save bulbs for next year.

You can grow garlic from cloves purchased in a supermarket, but it will probably be a softneck that is adapted to the California (or Chinese) climate. You will do better with locally grown bulbs from a farmers market, as they should be of a variety that does well in your area. When buying bulbs intended for food use, you should be aware that some diseases can be spread vegetatively in the cloves.

The kind of garlic you choose to grow is usually dictated by your climate or taste preferences. You should also think about their storage properties. You don't want all of your garlic to be a variety that doesn't store very well.

There are two main types of garlic, but they are divided into several groups.

Hard neck types

(*Ophioscordon* ssp)
These get their name from the distinctly woody flower stalk which goes through the center of the bulb. They don't usually get as big as the softnecks and have fewer wrapper leaves and fewer (but bigger) cloves. The latter is a good thing if you are growing in poor soil, because even small bulbs will produce a few good sized cloves.

Hardnecks are better suited to colder northern areas than the softnecks (in fact in very warm areas they may be hard to grow). They are divided into 3 main groups.

Rocambole

These varieties usually have thinner wrapper leaves, purple streaks and aren't very white. They usually produce 8 - 10 cloves, arranged radially around a woody scape. They are some of the best flavored and most pungent garlics, but many don't store for very long (about 6 months). The scape does a double loop as it emerges. They like cool winter and spring weather for best growth. They are hardier than the porcelain types.

Carpathian, German Red, Killarney Red, Spanish Roja.

Porcelain

These beautiful garlics have thick papery white or purple wrappers, usually containing a small number (4 - 6) of large cloves (which means you need to save more bulbs for replanting). They have a rich strong flavor (often hot) and store well (8 months or more). They do best in the north, but can be grown in most places. They are considered the best varieties for medicinal purposes.

Georgian Crystal, Georgian Fire, Music, Northern White, Romanian Red.

Purple stripe

These types have thick white wrappers with distinctive bright purple stripes (color intensity varies with growing conditions). The scape usually makes ¾ loop. They have very good, often complex, flavor (they are a favorite for baked garlic) and aren't very pungent. They produce a small number (5 - 6) of large cloves and store for about 6 months. They are hardier than the porcelain types

The purple stripes may be subdivided into three separate groups.

Standard Purple Stripe
Belarus, Chesnok Red, Persian star

Marbled Purple Stripe
Bogatyr, Gourmet Red, Siberian

Glazed Purple Stripe
Brown Tempest, Purple Glazer

Weak bolting hardneck types / softnecks

These types were once thought to be softnecks, but now they are considered to be a separate group. This group contains some of the most interesting and unusual types.

Asiatic

These sometimes send up scapes in spring and sometimes not. This does an inverted U as it emerges. As the name suggests they were developed in Asia. They usually contain from 9 - 12 cloves. The flower umbel may produce a few medium sized bulbils that can be eaten or used for propagation.

Asian Rose, Asian Tempest, Korean red, Sonoran

Turban

These are called turban garlic because the large flower umbel somewhat resembles a turban (these produce a lot of small bulbils that can be used for propagation too). These often have good color and strong flavor, especially when raw. They are earlier, produce less cloves (only 6 or so) in a bulb and don't store as well as other softneck types. They do well in dry climates.

China Dawn, Chinese Purple, Shandong, Tzan, Xian, Chinese Pink (early).

Creole

These are sometimes considered to be a separate group and sometimes included with the softnecks. They are the least common type of garlic and are still rare in most areas. They originated in Spain and southern France and are some of the best types to grow in warm climates (zone 7 - 10). They are quite tough and tolerate adverse growing conditions better than most types. They usually have very good flavor and are some of the best for eating raw. They also store well. Their biggest drawback is that they still quite hard to find

Ajo Rojo, Burgundy, Creole Red, Cuban Purple, Pescadero Red, Spanish Morado

Soft neck types

(*Sativum* ssp)
These don't have the hard scape of the hardnecks, hence they are known as softnecks. They are the type of garlic commonly sold in supermarkets. They grow well in mild climates, which is why most American garlic is produced in central California. They often do well when planted in spring.

Softnecks store better than the hardnecks and have more cloves (12 - 20), with larger ones on the outside and smaller ones in an inner cluster. This means the bulbs need to get to a good size to produce reasonably sized cloves.

Artichoke

This is the type of garlic most often seen in supermarkets. These varieties are less temperamental than other types and so easier to grow (probably the easiest) and can get quite big. They have a soft central stalk and a large number of cloves (12 - 20), They store quite well. Their flavor varies a lot, some are mild and some are quite pungent.

California Early, California Late, Early red Italian, Inchelium Red, Italian Late, Polish White

Silverskin

These are the best keeping varieties (10 months or more) and have soft pliable tops, which make them the best for braiding. They are easy to grow, fairly late and have a stronger flavor than the artichoke types. The wrappers are white, though the cloves may be colored. They don't get as big as the artichoke types, but have more cloves. This can be a problem if the bulb isn't very big, as many of the cloves will be small.

Mexican Red, Mild French, Nootka Rose, Silverskin.

Kitchen use

Garlic doesn't develop its characteristic flavor until the cell walls are ruptured. This releases as enzyme called alliinase which converts the alliin in the cells into the yummy diallyl thiosulphinate we all love.

The flavor of garlic varies according to how it is prepared. Many cooks insist that it should be chopped for best flavor. They say you should never crush it in a garlic press.

Green Garlic: In China they don't just eat garlic cloves. They eat the whole plant; young leaves, young plants, flower stalks. These can be used in the same ways as green onions.

Garlic soup

You have to try this, it's a variation of the soup that earned me a marriage proposal. Not in any way pungent or harsh, it is rich and delicious. I believe it originated in Provence.

2 bulbs (not cloves) garlic peeled and chopped
4 tbsp olive oil
8 cups water
3 potatoes cut into small cubes
3 celery stalks (chop finely)
3 carrots sliced finely
1 tsp chopped parsley
1 tsp dried basil
1 bay leaf
Salt and pepper

Saute the garlic in the oil for a couple of minutes and then add everything else. Simmer for about 45 minutes until the full flavor develops. It should be eaten immediately as its flavor starts to deteriorate if left for any length of time. Unlike many soups it does not taste better the next day.

Hamburg Parsley

Petroselintum crispum var *tuberosum*

Introduction: Hamburg parsley, also known as parsley root or turnip rooted parsley, is a relatively little known and under used crop plant, that originated somewhere in Central Europe (Germany is my guess!) It is a dual purpose plant, in that it produces a sweet parsnip-like root and parsley-like foliage.

Nutritional content: The green parts contain vitamins A, C, K, folate, iron and potassium, as well as various antioxidants. The root is rich in carbohydrates and vitamin C. They are fairly low in energy, containing only about 160 calories per pound.

Climate: This plant prefers fairly cool temperatures in the 60's and low 70's°F. It doesn't like hot weather and in warmer climates it is best grown as a fall crop. It is quite hardy (it can tolerate moderate frost) and often stays green well into the winter.

Ease of growing: Hamburg parsley takes a while to get started, but it is an undemanding and fairly easy crop to grow.

Crop value: This is a dual purpose crop, but you could argue that it isn't that good at either thing. Parsnip produces bigger roots in a shorter time, while leaf parsley tastes better.

Soil

pH 6.0 - 7.0

This plant does well in most soils, so long as they are moisture retentive and fairly loose.

Soil preparation: Incorporate 2″ of compost or well-rotted manure into the top 12″ of soil and remove any rocks, twigs or other debris. It doesn't like a lot of nitrogen, so don't use fresh manure. It does like phosphorus, so add colloidal phosphate.

About Hamburg Parsley

Seed facts

Germ temp: 40 (50 - 85) 90°F
Germination time: 14 – 28 days
29 days / 50°F
17 days / 59°F
14 days /68°F
13 days /77°F * Optimum
12 days / 86°F
Seed viability: 1 - 5 yrs
Germination percentage: 60%+
Weeks to grow transplant: 8 - 12

Planning facts

Hardiness: Hardy
Growing temp: 45 (60 - 65) 75°F
Plants per person: 10
Transplants:
Start: 6 weeks before last frost
Plant out: on last frost date
Direct sow: 6 weeks before last frost
Fall crop: Sow 3 months before first frost

Harvest facts

Days to harvest: 90 - 150 days
Yield per plant: 4 - 8 oz
Yield per sq ft: 2 - 4 lb

Planning

When:

Spring: Hamburg parsley is a pretty hardy plant and can be direct sown 6 weeks before the last frost date. However the seed takes a long time to germinate in cool soil. For reasonably prompt germination it needs fairly warm soil (around 70°F), so you might want to wait until around the frost-free date. To save time it can be started indoors about 6 weeks before the frost-free date and planted out on the frost-free date. In cool climates there is no rush to get it started, because it can grow all summer.

Fall: In warm climates Hamburg parsley does best when grown as a fall and winter crop. Start this in mid-summer.

Where: This plant can tolerate more shade than most crops and still do quite well (in hot weather they will even benefit from it). However for best production it should be given full sun.

Planting

Germination problems: Parsley is notorious for being slow to germinate, especially in cool soil. Apparently the reason for this is that it has to go 7 (or 3 or 9) times to the devil and back before it will germinate (which obviously takes some time). I don't know how you could speed that journey up, but you can soak the seed overnight prior to planting, to leach out germination inhibitors. You might also warm up the soil with plastic mulch or cloches for a couple of weeks before planting.

Parsley seed is fairly short lived, so seed left over from a couple of years ago may not germinate. It's a good idea to use fresh seed annually, or even better to save your own and plant that.

Another approach is to sow the seed in fall and leave it over the winter to germinate in early spring. This simplifies things in that you don't have to worry about germination or when to plant. It will just appear when the time is right. You can simplify this even further by allowing plants to flower and set seed and plant themselves!

Outdoors: Sow the seed almost on the surface (⅛ - ¼″ deep), either broadcast or in rows. Radish is often sown with it to mark its location, as it can take weeks to appear. It is a good idea to sow 3 or 4 times as much seed as you need because germination can be erratic. When all have germinated thin as necessary.

Indoors: Like most root crops Hamburg parsley is usually direct sown, rather than being transplanted. According to folklore transplanting parsley is actually bad luck. If you are prepared to take this risk (loss of property, injury, sickness) then start them in soil blocks or plug trays to minimize root disturbance (it doesn't like transplanting).

Spacing: Hamburg parsley is sometimes spaced quite closely (3 - 4″), to get a large quantity of small roots for eating while they are still young and tender). Alternatively you can plant further apart (up to 6″) and allow the roots to reach full size.

Care

Water: Though the plants are actually quite drought tolerant, it is important to keep them well watered for best growth and flavor.

Mulch: Use mulch on established plants to conserve moisture and keep down weeds.

Weeds: Young plants don't compete with weeds very well, so must be weeded carefully and regularly. This should be done by hand, as hoes can easily damage the shoulders of the root. Older plants are better able to compete against weeds, as they produce an abundance of foliage.

Mulch: This is helpful to keep down weeds, conserve soil moisture and keep the soil cool.

Pests: Hamburg parsley may be attacked by the same pests and diseases as carrot and parsnip, but it is less often troubled.

Harvesting

When: The roots can be used as soon as they are large enough to be worthwhile, but taste best when 6 - 8″ long.

The leaves can be used like parsley as soon as they are of sufficient size. Just don't take too much from any single plant, as the top growth is needed to provide food for the roots. Generally the foliage isn't as good as that from a leaf variety though.

How: If the soil is loose, you can pull the roots up by the tops. If the soil is heavy you will have to loosen them with a fork before pulling. After harvesting you should remove the tops, to stop them draining moisture from the root.

Storage: The roots are best left in the ground under mulch until you need them, as they actually improve with frost. If this isn't possible, store them like carrots in moist sand or sawdust, in a root cellar at 32 - 40°F with 90%+ humidity.

Seed saving: Saving seed is quite simple, just leave the plants alone to flower and set seed. It is cross-pollinated by insects, so don't save seed from different varieties at the same time (it will also cross with leaf parsley).

Unusual growing ideas

Naturalizing: You don't have to do anything to get this biennial to naturalize, just allow it to seed itself. The following spring plants will germinate everywhere the seed falls. These will flower the following year and set seed of their own.

Ornament: Parsley foliage is attractive enough to not look out of place in the ornamental garden.

Varieties: For a long time it was hard to find any varieties in this country, all you ever saw was just plain old Hamburg parsley. However in recent years superior cultivars have been appearing, mostly imported from Europe.

Arat is a fast maturing (75 day) variety.
Berliner
Eagle

Kitchen use

This plant is widely used in Eastern European cooking, where the roots are used like parsnips. They are good roasted, or used in soup.

The leaves can be used in sauces, salads and as the all-purpose garnish. They may not be as good as those of a leaf variety, but they are certainly worth using for something.

Parsley

Petroselintum crispum

Parsley originated in the Mediterranean region and was popular with the ancient Greeks and Romans It is cultivated as described above for Hamburg parsley. It is actually easier to grow though, as it doesn't need to produce a large swollen root.

Once parsley is established it will pretty much grow itself and if you allow it to produce seed it will usually self-sow. I rarely even plant it anymore, as I have enough self sown plants.

You probably won't need a lot of plants, 3 or 4 should be plenty (unless you are a real parsley addict)

There are now quite a few varieties available, though I haven't paid much attention to them (as I said mine usually self sows). The flat leaf parsleys are said to have the best flavor, but the curly varieties are more popular, because they are prettier.

Horseradish

Armoracia rusticana

Introduction: Horseradish is native to Eastern Europe, but it has been widely cultivated in temperate areas around the world and is now naturalized in most of them. This is typical of this persistent plant, where it is planted it stays.

Nutritional content: You wouldn't think of horseradish as a major source of nutrients, simply because it is too pungent to eat in quantity. However it is full of potent phytochemicals (glucosinolates) with anti-cancer properties. It is also rich in vitamin C.

All of the brassicas contain the beneficial glucosinolates, but horseradish contains up to 10 times more of them. This means that even the small amounts you are likely to eat can go a long way to improving your health.

Ease of growing: Few plants are as easy to grow as horseradish. It is essentially a wild plant and will commonly grow without any input from you. Just plant it in a vacant spot and leave it alone.

Soil

Ph: 5.5 to 7

Horseradish will grow in almost any well-drained soil, but it will be most productive in a rich, moist one that contains lots of organic matter.

Planning

Where: Horseradish does best in a fairly cool climate and likes full sun. It will also grow in shade too, though not quite as well.

This is a persistent perennial so it isn't a good idea to put it in the middle of an annual bed. It isn't an invasive plant, in that it doesn't spread aggressively, but once it gets established it can be difficult to remove. This is because any fragment of root left in the ground can grow into a new plant. Save yourself some trouble and plant it in a remote place, where it can be left to its own devices.

You can also plant horseradish in a container, partly buried in the ground (it needs to be deep). This makes harvesting easy, as you simply dig up the container and dump it out on to the ground.

When: Traditionally horseradish is planted 2 - 4 weeks before the last frost date, though if the ground isn't frozen it can be planted any time from winter to early spring. In mild areas it can be planted in fall too.

If you can't plant your root when you get it home, store it in the fridge in a plastic bag.

Planting

Vegetative: Horseradish is not grown from seed, but is propagated vegetatively from pieces of root. Usually when a plant is harvested, the smaller rootlets are trimmed off from the large roots. These are saved for replanting, while the larger roots are eaten. Very small rootlets take two years to produce usable roots. Larger roots will be ready to harvest in only one year.

Horseradish is a tough plant and doesn't need meticulous care in planting (it grows as a perennial and persistent weed in many places). It is common to dig a fairly large hole and refill it with half compost and half soil. Plant the root with the crown just below the soil surface.

Spacing: Space the plants 12 - 18″ apart. You don't usually need many of them (unless you are some kind of horseradish fanatic).

Care

Mulch: This is helpful to keep down weeds, hold in moisture and provide nutrients.

Feeding: The root will get bigger if it gets plenty of nutrients. If the soil is poor you may want to give it a foliar feed occasionally.

Water: Horseradish is somewhat drought tolerant and can handle neglect, but such plants won't get very big. For big beautiful roots it needs a regular supply of water.

Pests: The only problem I have had (admittedly a significant one) was with gophers eating the roots.

Harvesting

The roots can be dug at any time of year, but are at their best after they go dormant, from late fall until early spring (when they start growing again). In loose soil, the roots of older plants may grow to be three feet in length, but smaller roots are generally of better quality for food.

How: The brittle roots need to be dug carefully, as they break easily. Any fragment remaining in the ground will grow into a new plant, which can be good or bad, depending upon where it is.

Storage: In mild winter areas the roots can be gathered as needed through the winter. In cold areas, where the ground freezes, you may want to dig them in late fall and store them over the winter in damp sand.

Seed saving: Horseradish has been propagated vegetatively for so long that it doesn't produce seed. Of course it doesn't need to, it saves itself.

Unusual growing ideas

Wild garden: Horseradish doesn't need the pampered soil and growing conditions to be found in the intensive beds. It will be happy in almost any vacant spot in the garden (you will be happier too).

Containers: Horseradish does quite well in a container, so long as it is deep enough and it gets watered regularly.

Varieties: Maliner Kren is the commonest variety (in fact usually the only one available). I originally bought my horseradish root from a vegetable market (it is cheaper and readily available), so don't even know what variety it is.

Kitchen use

An intact horseradish root has no pungency at all, the acrid oil that gives it its characteristic flavor only appears when the root is damaged. Damage (such as grating) ruptures the cell walls, allowing an enzyme to react with a glycoside to form mustard oil (allyl isothiocyanate). The relatively bland root then quickly develops enough pungency to take your breath away.

Like most plants that produce mustard oil, horseradish irritates the kidneys and mucous membranes and so is toxic to some degree. However it is hard to eat enough to have any deleterious effect beyond a sore tongue.

Horseradish is an acquired taste. A bite of the raw root may be the hottest thing you have ever eaten (if you have led a sheltered life) and this extreme pungency limits its use as food. It is far from insignificant however, as it is used to make the famous horseradish sauce, as well as salad dressings.

Try making "horseradish bread" instead of garlic bread.

If you dislike the pungency of the raw root, try cooking it. This prevents the acrid mustard oil from forming and leaves you with a relatively bland root vegetable. The root is also a good addition to soup.

Leaves: The first tender spring leaves can be added to salads, or cooked with other greens as a potherb. These are so good that the roots have actually been forced indoors like chicory (*Cichorium*) to provide winter greens.

Horseradish Sauce

2 oz grated horseradish
1 oz sugar
Pinch of sea salt
2 oz breadcrumbs
¼ cup plain yogurt
½ cup mayonnaise
1 tbsp lemon juice

Mix together all the ingredients and then add enough wine vinegar to make a paste. Chill in the fridge before enjoying all of those antioxidant phytochemicals.

Kale, Scotch

Brassica oleracea var *acephala*

Introduction: This cool season biennial is the most primitive of the cabbage family crops and isn't far removed from the wild *Brassica oleracea*. It is not very common on dinner tables in this country, which is unfortunate as it is one of the most nutritious vegetables. It hasn't always been so neglected though; it was once one of the most widely used green vegetables in Northern Europe

Many Americans think of kale as an attractive curly garnish (it is often used in restaurants as a cheap substitute for parsley), which isn't intended to be eaten. This is a shame because well-grown kale, harvested in cold weather, is very good. At the same time I should add that poorly grown kale, harvested in warm summer weather, can be tough and almost inedible.

Nutritional content: Kale is a highly nutritious plant, being rich in vitamins A, C and K, chlorophyll and many important phytochemicals (including isothiocyanates, sulfuraphane, lutein and zeaxanthin). It is said to contain even more antioxidants than other Brassicas (which are all a good source of them). They contain almost 200 calories per pound, which is quite a lot for a leafy green vegetable.

Climate: Kale is a cool season plant and really comes into its own in the depth of winter, when other crops die off. It can survive temperatures as low as 0°F and will continue to produce food when most other crops are just frozen sticks. It can even be gathered from under the snow when frozen solid (though of course it won't be growing then).

Kale doesn't just tolerate cold temperatures and frost, the flavor of the leaves is actually improved by it (they become sweeter and more tender).

Kale grows quite well in warm weather, but at temperatures much above 75°F, the flavor deteriorates and it can become tough.

Ease of growing: Kale isn't far removed from a wild plant and shows it by being pretty easy to grow. It is even easier in cold weather, when it leaves most of its potential pests and diseases behind.

Crop value: Kale was a staple winter food for many Northern European peasants (Scottish vegetable gardens were commonly known as kale-yards). It is very nutritious and was especially important as it produced during late winter and early spring, when it was one of the few fresh foods available (one cultivar was actually known as Hungry Gap for this reason). It can still be very valuable for this.

Another benefit of kale is that it can be harvested repeatedly, often sending out new leaves for 6 months or more.

Soil

pH 6.0 - 7.5

Kale is more tolerant of poor soil than other Brassicas, but the most palatable leaves are produced by rapid uninterrupted growth. For this the soil must be rich, well-drained and moisture retentive with lots of organic matter. Of course with a winter crop, drainage is usually more of a concern than water retention. If the soil is too wet in winter the roots may rot.

About Kale

Seed facts

Germ temp: 40 (45 - 95) 95°F
Germination time: 4 - 9 days
15 days / 50°F
9 days / 59°F
6 days / 68°F
5 days / 77°F * Optimum
4 days / 86°F
Seed viability: 4 - 6 yrs
Germination percentage: 75+
Weeks to grow transplants 5 - 6

Planning facts

Hardiness: Very hardy
Growing temp: 40 (60 - 65) 75°F
Plants per person: 10
Plants per sq ft: to 1
Height: 18 - 36″
Spread: 18 - 36″

Transplants:

Start: 6 wks before last frost
Plant out: 2 wks before last frost
Direct sow:
Spring: 4 – 6 wks before last frost
Fall: 2 wks before first frost

Harvest facts

Days to harvest:
50 - 70 days from transplant
80 - 100 days from seed
Harvest period: 16 - 26 weeks
Yield per plant: 1 - 2 lb

Soil preparation: Kale likes organic matter, so amend the soil by digging in 2″ of compost or aged manure. It also likes a neutral pH, so add lime to raise the pH if necessary. Its nutritional requirements are similar to those of cabbage, in that it needs a significant amount of phosphorus and potassium, but not a lot of nitrogen. If your soil isn't very fertile you may also want to add some fertilizer mix.

Planning

Where: Winter kale will be growing in the coldest part of the year, so should be planted in the warmest, sunniest, most sheltered part of the garden.

Kale is one of the most shade tolerant garden vegetables, though it won't be quite as productive as when in full sun. In warmer weather it is usually happier in light shade. If this is from a deciduous tree, it will mostly disappear in winter, which is ideal.

Crop rotation: Kale should not be planted where another Brassica has grown in the past 3 years.

When

Spring: Kale can be planted in spring for harvesting in early summer. It is started indoors 6 weeks before the last frost date and planted out 2 weeks before the last frost date. If you plant too early the plants can be vernalized and may bolt soon after planting out.

Kale will actually grow right through the summer, but doesn't taste very good in warm weather. It really needs cool weather to make it tender and sweet.

Fall: As I already mentioned kale is most useful as a fall crop, planted in mid-summer, at least 2 - 3 months before the first fall frost date. The plants need to be fairly big by the time of the first frost, so they are vigorous enough to keep growing. In mild climates it will continue to grow all winter without disruption and can be harvested continually for months (it will also be in peak condition in the cool weather).

It is a good idea to plant your autumn kale as an intercrop

between an existing summer crop. It will gradually take over the space as the weather gets cooler and the summer crop fades.

Late kale can succeed a mid-season crop such as potatoes or beans.

Winter: Your fall kale crop will gradually become your winter kale crop, especially in milder areas. If you want to use kale as a staple winter crop you should probably grow quite a lot of it. It grows slowly in winter, so you want to have quite a few plants to harvest from (so you don't stress any one plant too much).

Planting

Direct sowing: The easiest way to grow kale is to sow it directly into the garden. The seed germinates easily and grows quickly, even in fairly cool soil. Plant the seeds ¼ - ½″ deep and 2″ apart. Start harvest thinning when all the seedlings have emerged and are of sufficient size.

Transplants

Starting inside: Kale is often started indoors to get an earlier crop in spring. It will germinate and grow much faster in warmer conditions, enabling you to plant out a thriving seedling, rather than a seed. Transplants may also be used where insects or other pests are a problem.

Kale doesn't mind transplanting so can be started in flats, as well as cell packs and soil blocks. Plant the seed 1″ apart in a flat and when the seedlings are big enough prick out into another flat, leaving 2″ between the plants. The plants are ready to go outside when they have 3 - 5 true leaves, a stem diameter of about ⅛″ and are 3 - 5″ tall.

Hardening off: If transplants are to go outside while it is still cold, they should be hardened off first. They will then tolerate temperatures as low as 25°F. You do this by putting the plants outside for 2 hours on the first day, then 4 hours on the second day. Add 2 hours every day for a week and then plant out.

A simpler alternative is to put them in a cold frame, which is opened for longer periods each day and closed at night.

Planting out: Transplant the seedlings slightly deeper than they grew in the flats, up to the depth of their first true leaves. Water well after planting (of course).

Protection: Early growth is often slow in cool weather. You might want to use cloches to keep the plants warmer and so speed this up.

Bolting: In spring a potential problem with using transplants may occur if you are too successful and grow big healthy transplants. If these are then exposed to cold weather they may be vernalized, which will cause them to bolt. To avoid this your transplants should have stems no thicker than ⅛″.

Starting transplants outside: In terms of bed space, a kale seed takes up as much space as an 8 week old transplant, so direct sowing isn't very space efficient. You can use bed space more efficiently by sowing your fall kale in an outdoor nursery bed (this only works in warm weather of course). Leave them there until they are of transplant size and then plant them out at their full spacing in early fall.

Spacing: Kale plants can get quite big, so give them plenty of room:

Beds:
12″ apart in excellent soil
15″ apart in good soil
18″ apart in poor soil

Rows: If you want to plant in rows, space them 18 - 24″ apart, with 12″ between the plants.

Care

Weeds: Kale is pretty independent once established, so you only really need worry about weeds while it is young.

Watering: Kale has large leaves and can lose a lot of water in warm weather (another reason not to grow it then). It is actually moderately drought tolerant, but for the best quality (texture and flavor) you must keep it well supplied with water.

Fertilization: If the soil isn't very fertile, feed the plants with compost tea or liquid kelp. Start feeding them as soon as they have recovered from transplanting and every month thereafter. This is especially important if you are going to be harvesting for weeks on end.

Mulching: Use a mulch in summer to keep down weeds, keep the soil cool and conserve soil moisture. In winter a mulch can help to protect the roots by moderating soil temperature and preventing frost heaving.

Pests and diseases: Kale is less vulnerable to pests than other Brassicas (even to clubroot), but it still has its share, especially in warm weather. See **Cabbage** for more on these pests and how to deal with them.

Birds In my garden quail have a particular affection for Brassicas such as kale and they may strip whole leaves from the plants. In my last garden they got so bad in winter that I had to net the 4 ft tall plants.

Harvesting

When: Kale produces an abundance of foliage right through the growing season, but it is at its best during cold weather. This is because cold weather stimulates the conversion of starches in the leaves into sugars (a similar thing happens in Jerusalem artichokes and parsnips). A few nights of freezing temperatures are enough to make this happen. The cold also makes the leaves more tender.

You can gather kale leaves for as long as they are produced, sometimes right through the winter. In extreme cold you might cover them with mulch for extra protection. Even the frozen leaves can be eaten and are actually very good.

The new shoots, produced when the plant first starts growing again in spring, are also good.

When kale bolts in spring, the flower buds can (and should) be gathered and used like broccoli. They are a nutritious and tasty treat, that is not to be missed. If they are infested with aphids, blast them off with a jet of water.

How: For a longer and bigger harvest it is best to gather single leaves as they get large enough. Don't take them from the growing point and only take 1 or 2 leaves from a plant at one time.

You may be able to stimulate an old plant to put out tender new growth, by stripping off all of its leaves.

Seed saving: Plants over-wintered in the ground will flower the following spring. Kale will cross-pollinate with any other Brassica crop (broccoli, Brussels sprout, cabbage, collards), so only one variety can be flowering at one time. Save the seed in the same way as you would **cabbage**.

The plants will produce an abundance of seed. In fact they sometimes get so top heavy with seed they need staking to stop them falling over.

If you save kale seed you will end up with a lot, especially as you should save the seed from at least 5 plants to maintain some genetic variability. This is far more than you will ever need for planting. You can sprout most of it like alfalfa, or use it to grow **micro-greens**.

Unusual growing ideas

Winter indoors: In very cold areas kale can be grown in winter in an unheated greenhouse or cold frame. It has even been grown indoors as a winter houseplant.

Ornamental use: Some kales have very attractive foliage and can be used in the flower garden. The specially bred ornamental kales are edible too and can be quite good.

Container growing: Kale does well in containers, so long as it has enough room, good soil and plenty of water.

Growing as a perennial: You can get some of the hardier kale varieties to survive for several years, by not allowing them to flower and set seed. You can propagate them by taking green stem cuttings in summer.

Cover crop: Kale is sometimes planted as a green manure or winter cover crop. In areas with mild winters it will produce a lot of foliage over the winter and has the additional benefit that it is edible. In spring you can eat the tender new flower shoots, before incorporating the rest of the plants into the soil.

The drawback to using kale as a cover crop, is that it is a member of the Brassica family and so prone to all of the same pests and diseases.

Varieties

There are several different types of kale:

Curly kale: This is the commonest and most familiar type.

Dwarf blue curled - Frilly blue leaves (55 days).

Redbor F1 - Frilly purple leaves (50 days).

Plain kale: These have smooth flat leaves and include the hardiest and most trouble free varieties. They are getting to be hard to find though.

Miscellaneous kale

Lacinato - This Italian variety is known in Italy as Cavolo Nero or black cabbage. It is more tender and delicately flavored than most types.

Thousand headed kale: This very hardy variety produces more than one growing point, hence its name. It can be persuaded to grow as a perennial in some areas.

Ornamental Kale: This multi-colored and quite spectacular plant is commonly used to add fall color to gardens. Though not considered as tender or tasty as other types, it can sometimes be surprisingly good (it depends on the variety and growing conditions).

Kitchen use

In cool weather the tender young leaves are good enough to eat raw. Older leaves can be steamed, stir-fried, used in soups or dried for chips. They are quite substantial and don't shrink down nearly as much as some other greens, so you don't need to gather as much.

If the main leaf stem is tough, it is easily removed by folding the leaf in half and slicing it off.

Ribollita

This Tuscan soup has a lot of ingredients because it is made to use up leftovers.

½ cup olive oil
2 onion
6 leeks
3 celery stalks
3 zucchini
5 garlic cloves
4 carrots
½ savoy cabbage
1 bunch cavolo nero (black kale aka laciniato kale)
1 bunch spinach (or other greens)
5 potatoes
1 cup green beans
2 ½ cups cannelloni beans
6 cups vegetable stock
5 sage leaves
4 tbsp tomato paste

Cover the beans with 2″ of water and soak overnight. Next day add the Sage and simmer until cooked. Sauté the onion and Leek in oil until cooked, then add the chopped Garlic and sauté another minute or two. Then add the rest of vegetables (chopped), the stock and the beans (with their cooking water) and cook in a covered pot for 30 minutes. Stir occasionally. Add salt and pepper.

Traditionally this was eaten as soup on the day it was cooked. The following day the leftover soup was put in a casserole dish, covered with a layer of garlic bread (or bread with a layer of onion on top) and baked in the oven. If any was still left on the third day it was re-heated with a little olive oil.

Collards

Brassica oleracea var *acephala*

Introduction: Collards are the same sub-species as Scotch kale, but differ in being more tolerant of hot weather (it is often a bigger plant too, with broader, fleshier leaves). Their heat tolerance has made them an important crop in warmer parts of the world, notably in Africa, Brazil and around the Mediterranean. In North America they are most widely grown in the southeastern States, where they are grown year round (but not usually harvested much during the summer months).

Nutritional content: Collard greens are similar to other Brassicas in their nutritional content, or even slightly superior.

How to grow: Collards are cultivated and used in pretty much the same ways as kale, so I won't repeat all of that information here.

Collards are such a long season crop, they are usually direct sown 2 - 3″ apart in mid spring. Wait until the cold weather has passed, so there is no chance of this biennial being vernalized (which could cause it to bolt).

As the planting fills in, it is gradually harvest thinned, first to 6″, then to 12″ and then to a final spacing of 15 - 18″. If conditions are right it will continue to grow right through the summer, fall and into winter. The fully grown plants are very tolerant of cold weather, smaller ones less so.

Harvest: Though collards tolerate hot weather, the leaves taste better in cool weather and it is as a winter crop that it really comes into its own. If you only gather a couple of leaves from a plant each time, it will continue to grow strongly. Take them from the bottom of the plants and leave the growing heart alone.

Unusual growing ideas:
Wild garden: This is quite an independent plant and can do well in the wild or forest garden.

Varieties: These are some of the most commonly available cultivars.

Georgia - Tender blue/green leaves (65 days)

Vates - Dark Green leaves (70 - 80 days)

Champion - High yielding, slow to bolt (70 days).

Green Glaze - Sometimes called greasy collards, it is an old heirloom (1820) with bright green leaves. (80 days).

Top Bunch F1 - A fast growing hybrid, similar to Georgia (50 days).

Kitchen use: Collard greens are a classic southern dish and are traditionally eaten on new years day with black eyed peas. They are commonly prepared by tearing the leaves into shreds (discarding the thick stems) and boiling in salt water with ham hocks for anywhere from 45 minutes to 2 hours.

I'm all for tradition, but I can't help thinking that 45 minutes cooking is a little too long. I prefer to use the more tender greens, cut off any tough stems and cook the leaves by steaming them for 5 minutes or so.

If the leaves are tough you can remove the thick fibrous midribs and just use the more tender leaf blades (fold the leaf in half and slice off the stem with one movement).

I have read that if you put summer harvested collard leaves in the fridge for a few days, their flavor will improve (I haven't tried it though).

Kale / Collard chips

These are a genuinely nutritious snack that tastes so good they encouraged me to grow Scotch kale again. They can also be made with collards, They are pretty simple to make, you just sprinkle the leaves with sea salt and dry them.

The simplest (and most nutritious) way to dry the leaves is in a dehydrator at 110°F until dry (usually overnight). Put the dried leaves / chips in a bowl and sprinkle with olive oil and nutritional yeast.

If you don't have a dehydrator you can do it in an oven by using the lowest temperature and turning it off occasionally.

Kale, Siberian / Russian

Brassica napus var *pabularia*

As you might guess from the name, this plant originated in Northeastern Europe and neighboring Asia. It is an entirely different species from Scotch kale, but is often grouped together with it. This is understandable as they are both called kale, are both Brassicas and are grown and used in the same ways. However they differ in that most Siberian kales aren't as hardy, they have thinner leaves and they taste better in warm weather.

I think Siberian kale is a better food plant than Scotch Kale. It is milder in flavor and so tender in texture that it is sometimes used raw in salads. It is a fantastic home garden crop plant, very hardy, nutritious, tasty and easy to grow. I can't praise it enough.

In Britain this species is known as rape kale, which is a good name because it is actually a type of rape (*B. napus*) and more closely related to rutabaga than to Scotch kale.

Nutritional content: This plant is rich in all of the nutrients you would expect to find in the Brassicas. These include vitamins A, C and K, chlorophyll, manganese, copper and several important antioxidants. The red colored types are particularly valuable because the red color comes from beneficial carotenoids.

Crop value: This plant is a staple winter green vegetable in my garden. I have planted it in late spring (if you plant it too early it will bolt almost immediately) and it has fed us through the summer, fall, winter (in our mild winters it doesn't even slow down) and into early spring. It then bolts and produces an abundance of nutritious and tasty flower buds that can be used like broccoli (if they are infested with aphids, blast them off with a jet of water). Eventually the flowers open and go on to produce a lot of seed (often several ounces per plant). This can be used for sprouting, micro-greens and to grow future crops.

This species is good to eat at any time, though it is at its best in cool weather, when the leaves become sweeter in flavor. It is also most useful at that time, when fewer other leafy crops are available.

Growing Siberian kale:
This species is grown in the same way as Scotch kale and prefers similar conditions. It will be most productive in fertile soil, but tolerates poorer soil than most Brassicas. It does need fairly moist soil though and growth will slow if it gets too dry.

Seed saving: This species won't easily cross-pollinate with any *B. oleracea* species, though it will cross with rutabaga. When collecting seed take it from a minimum of 10 of the best plants (remove any poor specimens to prevent them pollinating the plants you want).

Varieties: This is such a wonderful crop plant it's becoming increasingly popular with vegetable gardeners and quite a lot of new (and old heirloom) varieties are now becoming available. Some of the most interesting include:

Siberian Kale – Tender enough to be good raw as well as cooked.

Dwarf Siberian Kale - A smaller variation of the above.

White Russian – A hardy type that also tolerates wetter soil than most.

Wild Kale – A very variable type.

Red Russian: 60 days. This old Russian heirloom is also known as Ragged Jack (because of its ragged frilled leaves). It grows well in heat and cold, though is not as hardy as some cultivars. It is one of the best flavored varieties, with succulent and tender leaves.

Western Front – One of hardiest varieties and if you pamper it a bit, it can even be convinced it is a short lived perennial.

Kitchen use:
These kales tend to be more tender than the Scotch types and don't need cooking for as long. In fact many are good raw too.

Colcannon

This simple Irish peasant dish was traditionally eaten at Halloween.

1 lb kale (strip out any tough midribs and chop finely)
1 lb mashed potatoes
1 finely chopped onion or 2 small leeks or 4 chopped scallions
5 fl oz milk
Butter
Salt
Black pepper

Cook the kale until tender. At the same time simmer the onions in the milk for 5 minutes. Mix the finely chopped kale with the mashed potatoes and then add the milk. Reheat it for a few minutes then put in a dish. Sprinkle with salt and pepper and then make a well in the center for the butter.

Perennial kale / collards

These are some of the most useful and practical perennial vegetables for temperate gardens.

Purple tree collards
This plant has become very popular around the San Francisco bay area and in other mild winter areas. It grows and produces year round in the maritime climate and can actually live for up to 20 years. It won't do so well in colder areas, or where there are a lot of pests and diseases (cabbage root maggots and clubroot come to mind).

This plant is grown in pretty much the same way as Scotch kale, so I won't say much about cultivation here. The most significant difference is that it is propagated vegetatively from cuttings, rather than from seed,

In most places this isn't an easy plant to find, you rarely (more like never) see it in garden centers, though it does show up at various garden fairs and related events. Probably your best chance is to get some cuttings from a local gardener.

This plant is easily propagated by stem cuttings taken from non-woody parts (each should have 5 - 6 leaf nodes). Take these by cutting the top off the plant (the remainder will send out side shoots), or by cutting off and rooting the side shoots. Remove all but the top leaves and put the cutting in a pot filled with rooting medium (peat moss, perlite, vermiculite). Cover with a plastic bag and wait until they root, which can take anywhere from 3 weeks to 3 months.

If this plant will grow in your area you should try it. It is easy to build up a stock of these plants and have kale greens available almost year round with little or no work.

When growing this plant you have to make sure you always have some vigorously growing young plants, so you can keep on taking cuttings. Old woody parts don't root well.

These plants are semi-sterile and don't often produce seed. Though this year one of mine decided to produce some - I can't wait to see what it produces.

When growing in ideal conditions these plants can get so big they fall over, so they often need staking. The stake should be sturdy and tall, as they can get to 10 ft in height.

Walking Stick Cabbage

This type is much easier to find than the above, as it is usually propagated from seed. It can also be propagated vegetatively from stem cuttings however and this is the way to go when you find a particularly good plant.

This independent plant has grown wild in my garden for years, despite total neglect.

Walking stick cabbage gets its common name because the woody stems have been used for making walking sticks. This variety was originally bred in the British Channel Islands for cattle feed and grows up to 10 feet tall. Humans can also eat the leaves, though they tend to be somewhat tougher than the above.

You can make this plant more palatable by cutting out the midribs of the leaves (simply fold the leaf in half and slice it off with a knife).

Kohlrabi

Brassica oleracea var *gongylodes*

Introduction: This somewhat bizarre looking vegetable is relatively rare in American gardens and kitchens; in fact many people wouldn't even recognise it.

The edible part of the kohlrabi is not a root, though people usually assume it is. It is actually the swollen above-ground portion of the stem, and is very much like a fat juicy broccoli stem. It is sometimes said to be a cross between a cabbage and a turnip, but that is just because it seems like one. More likely it was developed from a thick stemmed forage cabbage.

Kohlrabi (the name is German and translates as cabbage turnip) was developed in Italy or Germany around 500 years ago. It is still most popular there, so hasn't really spread very much, though it is now popular in parts of Asia too.

Climate: Like all Brassicas this is a cool season plant, preferring to grow in temperatures of 60 - 70°F. In cool climates it can be grown all summer, but in warmer ones it must be grown in spring and fall (it grows best in the latter). It is quite hardy and can stand moderate frost.

Ease of growing: Kohlrabi is a very useful crop, tasty, fast growing, compact, nutritious and slightly more tolerant of warm weather than most Brassicas. Much that has been said about cabbage also applies to kohlrabi.

Crop value: Some people (those who are most familiar with it) consider kohlrabi to be the best tasting of all the Brassicas and prize it very highly (they also recommend it as a good plant for children to grow). Individual plants don't produce much food, so you need to have quite a few of them to make it worthwhile. Fortunately it doesn't require a lot of space and matures pretty quickly (60 days).

Nutritional content: This is much the same as cabbage, which means high vitamins A and C, folate, potassium, calcium and lots of antioxidants. It contains about 120 calories per pound.

Soil

pH 6.0 - 7.0

To grow to perfection, kohlrabi needs a light, rich, moisture retentive soil, with lots of organic matter.

Soil preparation: Incorporate 2″ of compost or aged manure into the top 6″ of soil (you could add fresh manure the previous fall), along with a fertilizer mix. It is a light feeding crop and doesn't need a lot of nitrogen, but it does like potassium (add greensand or wood ashes). It also likes calcium and a fairly neutral pH, so lime if necessary.

Planning

Where: Kohlrabi grows best in full sun, though it will tolerate light shade.

Crop rotation: Kohlrabi should not be planted where any other Brassica has grown in the previous 3 years, as this can lead to disease or pest problems.

When: Like most Brassicas, kohlrabi grows best in the cool (40 - 70°F) weather of spring and fall.

About Kohlrabi

Seed facts
Germ temp: 40 (45 - 95) 100°F
Germ time: 3 - 10 days
15 days / 50°F
9 days / 59°F
6 days / 68°F
5 days / 77°F * Optimum
4 days / 86°F
Seed viability: 4 yrs
Germination percentage: 75%+
Weeks to grow transplant: 5 - 6

Planning facts
Hardiness: Half hardy
Growing temp: 40 (60 - 65) 75°F
Plants per person: 10
Plants per sq ft: 4

Transplants:
Start indoors: 6 - 8 wks before last frost
Plant out 2 - 4 wks before last frost
Direct sow: 4 - 6 wks before last frost
Fall sow: 6 - 8 weeks before first fall frost

Harvest facts
Days to harvest: 55 - 90 days
30 - 40 days from transplanting
Yield per sq ft: 1½
Yield per plant: 6 oz

Spring: Sow the first spring crop 4 - 6 weeks before the last frost date (it will grow at 40°F). The fast maturing types work best in spring.

Fall: Kohlrabi generally does better as a fall crop, sown 6 - 8 weeks before the first fall frost date. Autumn kohlrabi can be allowed to get larger than 2 - 3″, because cold weather seems to keep them tender for longer (it also increases their sweetness). Any type can be used at this time of year.

Succession sowing: In spring you can make several succession sowings, 2 - 3 weeks apart (very early sowings may be vernalized and bolt). In cool climates you can continue to succession sow all summer.

Planting
Like most Brassicas it can be either transplanted or direct sown, both work well.

Transplants
Starting inside: Kohlrabi is such a fast growing crop, that starting indoors is probably only worthwhile if your growing season is very short, or if space is limited. Sow the seeds 3 - 4 weeks before planting out. It doesn't really like transplanting so it's best to use cell packs, soil blocks or plug trays.

Planting out: Transplant the seedlings outside 2 - 4 weeks before the last frost date. Plant them to the depth of their first true leaves.

Direct sowing: Kohlrabi is usually direct sown, Sow the seed ¼″ deep in rows or broadcast it and cover with a thin layer of cover soil. Sow quite thickly initially and thin when they are around 4″ high (eat the thinnings).

Spacing: Make sure the plants aren't crowded, or they won't size up properly.

Beds: Plant kohlrabi in offset rows across the bed, 4″ - 6″ - 8″ apart (the exact distance depends upon the fertility of the soil).

Rows: When growing in rows plant 1″ apart initially and slowly thin to 4 - 6″ apart. Space the rows 12 - 18″ apart.

Care
Kohlrabi must grow fast for best quality, so give the plants all the water and nutrients they need.

Thinning: It is important to thin (and weed) the plants properly, so they have enough room. If they are crowded they won't bulb up properly.

Weeds: Control weeds by hand weeding, as hoeing can easily damage the shallow roots and swollen stems. A mulch will help to suppress weeds.

Water: Keep the soil evenly moist, or the bulbous stems may turn woody. Fortunately this isn't often an issue with this cool weather crop. The plants have their greatest need for water when the bulbs are forming, so make sure you keep the soil moist at this time.

Mulch: This is helpful to keep the soil moist and to suppress weeds (the leaves are fairly sparse and don't create a lot of shade).

Fertilization: If the soil isn't very fertile, you should give the plants a feed of liquid kelp or compost tea every 2 - 3 weeks.

Pests: The same pests that attack cabbage also go for kohlrabi, but they aren't usually as bad (See **Cabbage**). In spring you may have to protect the seedlings from birds.

Harvesting

When: Start harvesting the bulbous stems when they are 1½ - 2″ in diameter, as they are most tender at this stage. You can eat the larger 3″ diameter roots, but in warm weather they often develop a woody core and their flavor deteriorates. In late fall and winter even the larger bulbs can be good.

How: Cut the stem an inch below the bulb, or simply uproot the entire plant if they aren't growing too closely together (don't disturb neighboring plants). For storage you should cut off the leaves and roots.

Storage: Kohlrabi stores very well and will keep for several weeks in the fridge in a plastic bag. It may last for several months in a root cellar at 32 - 40°F and 90%+ humidity. It also freezes well.

Seed saving: This is the same as for cabbage. In very cold climates you may have to lift the plants in fall (keep their roots intact) and store them in moist sand in a root cellar over the winter. Replant them in early spring, somewhere they won't be in the way

Unusual growing ideas

Intercrop: This compact and fast growing plant can be very useful for intercropping between slower growing plants.

Varieties

Up until recently there weren't many varieties available in this country, but now new ones are appearing all the time, including a lot of hybrids from Europe.

Green Vienna (better flavored)

Purple Vienna (hardier)

Early White Vienna (what's this with Vienna?)

Gigante (Superschmeltz): Can get very big without getting woody and tolerates low temperatures.

Eder F1: Fast growing (only 38 days).

Winner: Exceptional flavor.

Kossack: Stores well.

Kitchen use

The bulbous stem is good cooked, but is also mild enough to be eaten raw (sliced or grated) in salads. The thick skin is usually peeled off, though if the root is small and tender it may be eaten. The young leaves can be used like kale.

Leek

Allium porrum

Introduction: This non-bulbing relative of the onion is native to Eurasia and was first cultivated somewhere in the Eastern Mediterranean. It has been a food of the common people since the ancient Egyptians and still is in many parts of Europe. This is in stark contrast to the United States, where leeks are often considered a luxury food, with prices to match its elevated status. When you start growing your own leeks you soon come to understand why they are so important in French cooking.

Ease of growing: The leek is a satisfying crop to grow and much more straightforward than the onion. It is a biennial so you don't usually have to worry about premature bolting and it doesn't produce a bulb so you don't need to think about day length and its effect on bulbing. It is also very hardy and winter leeks can simply be left in the ground until needed for the kitchen.

Crop value: The leek is not only one of the hardiest of common crops, but also one of the most useful and it was once very important for Northern European peasants. It would supply food right through the winter and still be good in early spring, when little else is available. Its sweet and delicate onion flavor was widely used to flavor more bland staple foods. Of course it is equally useful today and should be considered one of the garden staples.

Climate: Leeks prefer cool (50 - 70°F), moist growing conditions, but also do well in warmer climates if well supplied with water. Many types are very cold tolerant (down to 20°F) and are often one of the last plants standing in a frozen garden.

Leeks will grow quite happily in warm weather (above 75°F, but won't taste as good as in cooler temperatures.

About Leek

Seed facts
Germ temp: 40 (60 - 75) 95°F
Germination time: 14 - 21 days
30 days / 41°F
13 days / 50°F
7 days / 59°F
5 days / 68°F * Optimum
4 days / 77°F
4 days / 86°F
Germination percentage: 75%+
Viability: 1 - 5 years
Wks to grow transplants: 10 - 12

Planning facts
Hardiness: Hardy
Growing temp: 45 (55 - 75) 85°F
Plants per person: 30 - 50
Plants per sq ft: 9

Transplants:
Start: 10 - 12 wks before last frost date
Plant out: On last frost date
Direct sow 4 wks before last frost date
Sow fall crop 12 - 16 weeks before first frost

Harvest facts
Days to harvest: 110 - 200 days
75 - 100 days from transplants
Yield per plant: 8 oz per plant
Yield per sq ft: 2 - 9 lb sq ft

Nutritional content: Leeks are a good source of vitamins A, C, K and several B's, as well as potassium, iron and some beneficial phytonutrients. They are also relatively high in calories, with around 270 per pound.

Soil

pH 6.0 - 7.0

Leeks need a deep, rich, fairly neutral soil. They don't mind heavy soil, but it should be well-drained, because the plants will often remain in the ground through much of the winter and are susceptible to rot in wet soil.

Soil preparation: Leeks need rich soil to grow well. A common practice is to plant leeks in soil that was heavily amended and cultivated for a previous crop, such as potatoes. If it is low in organic matter, or particularly heavy, incorporate 3 - 4″ of compost or aged manure into the top 12″ of soil.

Leeks do very well in deeply cultivated intensive beds. If your soil is compacted, you might want to consider double digging because (remember) leeks like loose loam. They also like potassium and phosphorus, so add colloidal phosphate and greensand or wood ashes (or an organic fertilizer mix).

If your soil is poor, you might grow them in trenches, enriched with aged manure or compost. This is how they get those prize nine pound leeks.

Leeks can be planted fairly early in the spring, so gardeners often prepare the growing bed the previous fall.

Planning

Where: Leeks need full sun, especially if growing in winter. For best growth they should also be sheltered from cold winter winds. Leeks take quite a long time to grow and will be in the ground for most of the growing season, so put them where they won't be in the way. Fortunately they don't take up much space and are good for intercropping, as their foliage is relatively sparse for much of their early growth.

When:

Spring: Leeks are very hardy and prefer a long cool (not much above 70°F) growing season, so they are one of the first spring vegetables to be started indoors.

Leek seedlings grow quite slowly, so they are usually started indoors, about three months before they are planted out (sometimes as early as December or January). The earlier you start them, the larger they will get. Unlike many crops they don't get over-mature quickly, they just get bigger. The seedlings are transplanted outdoors on the last frost date (after being hardened off.)

Leeks can also be direct sown, about a month before the expected last frost, or as soon as the soil can be worked. The protection of cloches or poly tunnels will speed up growth.

Some people start leeks both indoors and outdoors. The transplants are for eating over the summer, while the direct sown ones are for using the following winter.

Fall: In areas with mild winters, leeks are best grown as an over-wintering crop. They are started in early summer (indoors or out) and can be harvested as needed through the winter. Any plants that are left by spring will put on a burst of growth and then bolt.

Planting

Transplants:

Starting inside: Leeks transplant easily so are usually started in flats. They don't have much foliage so can be planted quite close together and you can get a lot of plants in one flat. The seeds germinate and grow slowly, so start them early, water regularly, feed occasionally and be patient. They should be ready to plant out in 8 - 12 weeks when they are about 8″ tall and about ⅛″ in diameter. Some people advise trimming the tops and roots, to make planting easier (they can get quite long and easily fold up in the planting hole).

Hardening off: If spring transplants are to go outside while it is still cold, they should be hardened off first. You do this by putting the plants outside for 2 hours on the first day, then 4 hours on the second day. Add 2 hours every day for a week and then plant out.

A simpler alternative is to put them in a cold frame, which is opened for longer periods each day and closed at night.

Planting out: There is no point transplanting the seedlings outside before the soil has warmed up, they will grow faster inside. Wait until a month after the last frost date.

In my opinion the only way to plant leek seedlings is with a dibber. In fact a desire to plant a lot of leeks is a sufficient reason to get a dibber (or make one out of a broken spade, shovel handle or piece of stick). Mark out the required 4 - 6″ hole depth (depending on size of plants) on the side of the dibber, so you know how deep to go.

To plant you simply punch a series of holes in the soil and drop a plant into each hole. When you have planted a good sized section you water them all with a trickle of water. There is no need to fill the hole, enough soil will wash down into the bottom to cover the roots. It couldn't be easier or quicker.

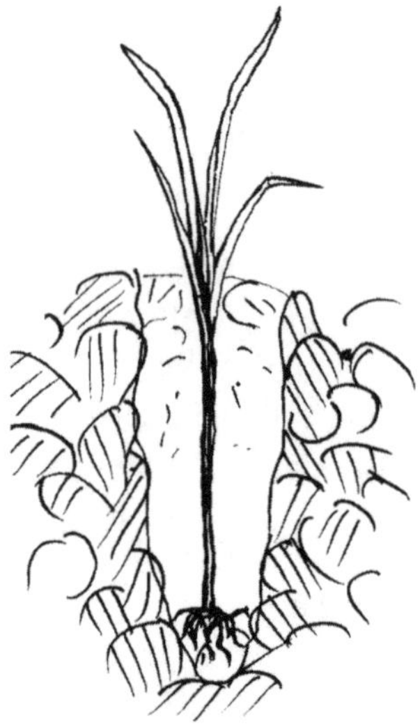

You can also transplant the seedlings into a 6 - 8″ deep trench, Plant with a dibber as described above and when the plants are growing well gradually fill the trench with soil. This blanches the stems and provides a greater length of the desirable white stem.

Leeks can also be planted in a row on level ground. They are then hilled up as they grow, to blanch the lower stems.

Starting outside: Fall leeks are often started outdoors in a nursery bed and then later transplanted to a permanent site. This is much more space efficient than direct sowing and the seedlings are more easily protected from pests.

Direct sowing: Summer leeks can be direct sown in early spring at a depth of ¼ - ½″. Space the seed ½″ apart and gradually harvest thin to the desired spacing.

There are a couple of problems with direct sowing into the beds. One is that it wastes bed space because they are so slow growing. Another is that you have to find another way to blanch the stems. To do this you either have to sow the seed into a trench as described above, or you earth them up with soil (see **Blanching** below for more on this).

Spacing:
Beds: Leeks are usually planted in offset rows across the bed. The spacing ranges from 3 - 6″ depending upon the fertility of the soil (to get the highest yield of large plants space them 6″ apart). You might want to use a wider spacing, so you can get a hoe between them for weeding.

Rows: When you plant in rows it is easier to earth them up. Space the plants 2 - 6″ apart in the row, with 12 - 24″ between the rows. If you use the closer spacing align the plants so the leaves point perpendicular to the row (leek leaves always emerge opposite each other).

Care

Leeks need looking after carefully, because they grow slowly and don't have a lot of foliage (a newly planted leek bed actually looks pretty pathetic). They should always have an abundance of available nutrients and water for best growth.

Weeds: The lack of foliage makes young leeks vulnerable to competition from weeds. It is especially important to keep them well weeded when they are young and spindly, as they don't shade the soil very well (or compete with weeds). They are quite shallow rooted, so be careful when weeding with a hoe (it's safer to hand weed).

Water: Leeks grow best in moist soil, so make sure they have a constant supply of water. Water them deeply once or twice a week. Don't over water though, as this can encourage disease problems.

Fertilization: Leeks are often in the soil when it's cold and nutrients aren't readily available. It helps to give them a feed of compost tea or liquid kelp, as soon as they are well established.

If the soil isn't very fertile you should feed them every 4 weeks until late summer and then stop (later feeding can make them more susceptible to cold damage).

Mulch: Mulch is very beneficial for leeks. Their lack of foliage means that the soil is prone to drying out in sunny weather and a mulch shades the soil and helps it to retain moisture. It also helps to keep down weeds and is a source of nutrients for the soil.

In areas where winter temperatures drop well below freezing you should protect the plants with a deep mulch. It not only protects the plants from cold, but also stabilizes the soil temperature. This prevents frost heaving, which can damage the roots. It's best to apply this in fall while the soil is still warm.

Blanching: Leeks are often blanched (deprived of light) to get a longer area of white stem, as this is considered superior to the green part.

Blanching is usually done with soil, either by earthing up the stems, or filling up the trench they are growing in. Some gardeners wrap corrugated cardboard collars around the plants before blanching, to prevent soil getting lodged between the leaves (no one likes gritty leeks). You can also blanch the stems with a deep mulch, which has the advantage of not being gritty.

Pests: Theoretically leeks are susceptible to the same problems that afflict the related onions, but generally they are quite pest free. They are occasionally bothered by onion maggots or thrips (see **Onions**).

Diseases: Leeks may be affected by the same diseases as onions, including botrytis, purple blotch, white rot and downy mildew. Most of the time they tend to be remarkably healthy though.

Harvesting

When: Leeks can be harvested as soon as there is enough to be worth eating. If you plant more thickly to start with, you can harvest thin to the desired spacing, without eating into your leek harvest.

The main harvest comes when the stems are ¾ - 1″ in diameter, though their flavor and texture generally stays good even when they get bigger than this. Leeks only really deteriorate when they start to bolt, as they develop a woody inedible core. If you really want to use bolting leeks remove this before cooking.

How: In loose soil you can sometimes harvest leeks by simply pulling them out of the ground. If the tops break off before they come free, you will have to loosen them with a garden fork first.

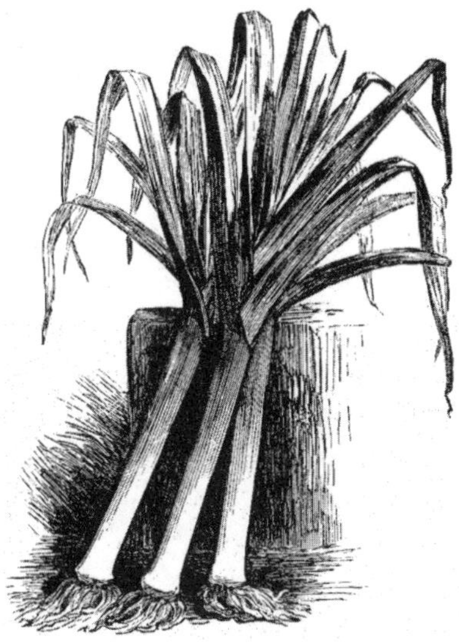

If you are harvesting leeks before they reach full size, you should harvest alternate plants, as this gives the remaining plants more room to grow. Just be sure you don't disturb their roots. Alternatively you could take the largest plants first, leaving the others to size up.

Storage: Leeks are so hardy they are usually stored in the ground and harvested as needed (cover with mulch in cold climates). The outer skin may turn somewhat slimy in very cold weather, but the interior will be fine.

You can store leeks for several weeks in a plastic bag in the fridge. In very cold climates you can store them in a root cellar at 32 - 40°F. Trim off the excess tops and roots and plant them in a box of damp sand.

Seed saving: It's easy to save leek seed, simply leave the best plants in the ground instead of eating them. Save the seed from at least 12 plants to ensure enough genetic variation. Leeks are biennial and will produce their spectacular flowers in spring (and ripe seed in early summer).

Leeks are cross-pollinated by insects, so you don't want any other varieties flowering within a mile. In most cases this isn't likely as few people allow their leeks to flower, If it is possible then you could cage the plants.

You may want to dig the seed-leeks from their bed while they are dormant and move them to a more convenient location. This frees up the bed they were growing in for another crop.

Unusual growing ideas

Multi-planting: You can plant leeks in clusters, rather than as single plants, simply plant 4 or 6 seeds together. This is usually done in soil blocks, but could also work in flats or cell packs. These clusters must be spaced further apart than single plants to give their roots more room and prevent crowding.

Ornamental: Leek flowers look a lot like ornamental Alliums and aren't out of place in the ornamental garden.

Vegetative propagation: After leeks flower they produce offsets at the base of the stem, which will grow into new plants. These are known as leek pearls and can be used for propagation or eaten.

Competitive gardening: In parts of Britain the cultivation of the biggest and most perfect leek is a very competitive activity. It results in monster leeks weighing 9 lb or more. I find it amazing how humans can turn even the most unlikely activity into a competition!

Perennial: Leeks can be treated like perennials, as they propagate themselves vegetatively by means of offsets. They can also self-sow. There is also a perennial leek (the Babbington leek), which produces bulblets on the flower head instead of flowers. These can be used for propagation too.

Varieties

These differ in their hardiness, time to harvest, color and size of stem. In North America the choice of leek varieties has been quite limited until recently. Fortunately many European varieties are now becoming more widely available. Leeks can be divided into two kinds (can't everything), according to their hardiness: the summer leeks and the winter leeks.

Summer Leeks: These fast growing leeks aren't as hardy as the winter types and don't store as well. They are grown in summer for immediate consumption.

Gros Long d″Ete
Runner F1
Megaton F1
King
Richard
Varna

Winter Leeks: These leeks grow quite slowly, but are very hardy and can remain in the ground over the winter. They often have a bluish tinge to their leaves and are considered the best flavored types.

Alaska
American Flag
Bandit
Bleu Solaise
Carenton
Giant Musselburgh
Lyon
St.Victor
Tadorna
Scotland

Kitchen use:

Leeks are considered one of the finest flavored members of the onion family and are especially highly esteemed in France. They are a main ingredient of the famous leek and potato soup (made from two peasant staples).

In France the dark green parts are often used separately to make soup stock.

Leek and potato soup

4 leeks
1 onion
1 lb potatoes
½ tsp sea
4 cloves garlic
4 cups vegetable stock
2 tablespoon olive oil
2 tsp rosemary

Chop the leeks and onion and sauté until they become translucent. Add the chopped garlic and cook another minute. Add the potatoes (chopped into ½″ cubes) and the vegetable stock and simmer for 20 minutes in a covered pan. Allow the soup to cool so you can put it in a blender along with the rosemary and salt and blend until smooth. Re-heat before serving.

Elephant Garlic

Allium scorodoprasum

An elephant garlic bulb look like a giant garlic and is even divided into a number of cloves, but it is actually more closely related to the leek than it is to garlic. Its flavor is garlic-like, but a lot milder.

Elephant garlic is a hardy and easy to grow plant (just treat it like big garlic). Plant the large cloves 3 - 4″ deep and 8 - 10″ apart, in rows 18 - 24″ apart.

If any flower stems start to emerge, remove them so the plant devotes all of its energy to bulb production. Unlike garlic the flowers will produce seed if left to their own devices.

Elephant garlic is not a substitute for garlic and if you use it like that you will be disappointed. It isn't a very important flavoring because the flavor is very mild. You can use it in any of the ways you might use a sweet onion. It is best used raw, to add a mild garlic flavor to salads and sandwiches. It is good on pizza and can also be sauteed, but be careful not to overcook it, as this will make it bitter.

Lettuce

Lactuca sativa

Introduction: Lettuce is probably descended from *Lactuca serriola* and originated somewhere around the Mediterranean or Near East. Some types have been grown since the time of the ancient Egyptians.

Lettuce is almost synonymous with salad. It is easily the most popular salad ingredient, as countless restaurant salads consisting of a bowl of lettuce with a couple of cherry tomatoes will testify. The lettuce available in supermarkets rarely measures up to those you can grow yourself.

Ease of growing: Lettuce is easy to grow if you give it the right conditions, which means fairly cool and moist weather. The challenge comes in getting it to grow when you want it, as it doesn't like hot weather. The other problem is that once it is mature it doesn't stay in prime condition for very long before it turns bitter and bolts.

Nutritional content: This varies a lot depending upon the type. Head lettuce is the least nutritious (though not negligible and leaf and romaine types are the most nutritious. They contain protein, calcium, vitamins A, C and K, as well as several B vitamins. They are also a good source of copper, magnesium, manganese, phosphorus, potassium and various antioxidants. They are pretty low in calories, with about 60 per pound.

Soil

pH 6.0 (6.8) 7.5

Lettuce needs to grow fast for best quality, which requires a good soil. It should be fertile, moisture retentive, well-drained and rich in organic matter. The pH isn't particularly important. Light soils that warm up quickly are good for early lettuce.

About Lettuce

Seed facts
Germination temp: 35 - 80°F
Germination time: 2 - 15 days
49 days / 35°F (may rot)
15 days / 40°F
7 days / 50°F
3 days / 60°F * Optimum
2 days / 77°F
3 days / 86°F (only 12% germination)
Seed viability: 2 - 5 yrs
Germination percentage: 80%+
Time to grow transplant: 5 - 6 wks

Planning facts
Hardiness: Half hardy
Growing temp: 45 (60 - 65) 75°F
Plants per person: 4 per sowing
Plants per sq ft: 4

Transplants:
Start: 6 - 8 wks before last frost
Plant out: 2 - 4 wks before last frost
Direct sow spring:
Leaf: 4 - 6 wks before last frost
Head: 2 - 4 wks before
Fall crop: 6 - 8 wks before first fall frost
Succession sow: every 2 - 3 wks

Harvest facts
Days to harvest: 50 - 100 days
Yield per plant: 6 - 12 oz
Yield per sq ft: 1 lb

Soil preparation: Lettuce has a weak root system and isn't a very efficient feeder, so the soil needs to be quite fertile.

Its first requirement is for nitrogen (add compost or aged manure), but it also needs moderate amounts of potassium (add wood ashes or greensand) and phosphorus (add colloidal phosphate). It also likes calcium, so you might also want to give it some dolomitic limestone. To simplify things you might just add an organic fertilizer mix at the recommended rate.

Prepare the soil by adding 2″ of compost or aged manure (unlike most plants it is also happy with fresh manure), along with any other amendments. This needn't be dug in very deeply as lettuce is quite shallow rooted (the weak roots only penetrate about 4 - 8″). For very early crops you might want to prepare the soil the previous fall.

Planning

Where: In cool climates lettuce needs full sun, but in hotter ones it will benefit from light shade during the hottest part of the day.

When: Lettuce germinates quite well in cool (40°F) soil and will continue to do so until the temperature gets up to 75°F (after this it gets erratic). With careful planning and a little ingenuity it is possible to have lettuce for 6 - 9 months of the year (though much depends on the climate).

Spring: The first spring sowing should be of leaf lettuce, as this is the hardiest kind. It can be direct sown 6 wks before the last frost, or started indoors 8 weeks before the last frost and planted out 4 weeks later. Properly hardened seedlings can take frost down to 20°F. For the earliest crops you may want to warm the soil with cloches and use transplants.

Head lettuce is less hardy than the leaf types, so is usually started indoors 6 weeks before the last frost date. Seedlings can be planted out 2 weeks before the last frost date.

Summer: Lettuce doesn't like hot weather. At temperatures above 75°F only 50% of the seed may germinate and the plants may turn bitter and bolt quickly.

To have lettuce through the warmest part of the growing season you have to be creative. Use a heat tolerant variety, water every day and plant it in the shade of larger plants. If a spell of cooler weather is forecast, you can take advantage of it to sow some lettuce. See **Unusual Growing ideas** for more on this.

Autumn: Sow fall lettuce 4 - 8 weeks before the first fall frost date (or whenever summer temperatures start to moderate). Pests are very active at this time, so you may want to start them inside or in a protected place.

Winter: Some hardy varieties of lettuce can tolerate temperatures as low as 25°F and can be grown as a winter crop in milder areas. Start the plants (inside or out) about 4 - 6 weeks before you expect the first frost. Though they are quite hardy, they still do better when given protection from hard frost. The additional warmth of a cold frame or cloche can greatly boost growth.

In very cold areas you can grow lettuce in the greenhouse or cold frame. If you do this, make sure they stay cool (35 - 45°F), as low light levels and short days, combined with higher temperatures, can encourage bolting.

Succession sowing: Most lettuce is only harvested once and then it is gone, so you need a constant supply of new plants. To get this you need to sow a small quantity of seeds every 10 - 21 days (depending on time of year). There is only a short time between lettuce maturing and lettuce bolting (especially in warm weather), so you don't want to have many mature plants at one time.

To spread out the harvest you can plant different varieties with different maturation dates. You can also start harvesting the plants while they are immature.

Planting

Transplants

Starting inside: Lettuce is often grown from transplants, as this gives the fastest harvest, saves on bed space and avoids various garden hazards. Seedlings are easily raised and don't mind root disturbance, so you can use flats, cell packs, plug trays or soil blocks.

When using flats space your seed 1″ apart. When the seedlings are about 2″ tall and start to touch each other, prick out into another flat, leaving 2″ between the plants.

Cell packs, plug trays and soil blocks should be big enough that the plants don't need transplanting to large containers. Sow 2 or 3 seeds in each cell and remove the weaker seedlings when the best one is 2″ tall.

It is said that some kinds of lettuce need light for germination. This is easy to arrange, just don't cover the seed with soil. Of course you must then take extra care to ensure it doesn't dry out.

Planting out: Lettuce transplants easily in cool weather. In hot dry weather you must take precautions to ensure that the young plants are kept moist.

Direct sowing: This is simple enough in cool weather, as the seeds germinate easily and the plants grow rapidly. You may run into problems when the soil gets warm, as the seed doesn't germinate very well above 75°F. In this situation you can pre-germinate the seed in the fridge as described below.

Planting in rows: Lettuce is commonly sown in rows, with 1″ between the plants and 5″ between the rows. Plant at a depth of ⅛″ in cool soil and up to ¾″ deep in warm soil.

Planting in beds: Lettuce can also be broadcast, spacing the seeds 1 - 2″ apart.

Thinning: When the plants are 2 - 4″ high, they can be thinned to the required spacing. The thinnings can either be eaten or replanted elsewhere at the final spacing. Transplanting will slow them down a little and can help to extend the harvest. Careful sowing of seed can help to reduce the need for thinning.

Raising transplants outside: Lettuce germinates readily in cool soil, so you can easily start your transplants outdoors in a nursery bed. This is commonly done in mild climates and saves on greenhouse or bed space. Just transplant the largest seedlings as space becomes available in the intensive beds.

Hot weather germination: In warm soil (75°F or above) lettuce seed will germinate poorly, if at all. You can get around this by pre-germinating the seed in the fridge on a paper towel. You don't have to keep it in the fridge until it has germinated, just 5 days will be enough to break its dormancy. It will then germinate in warm soil.

Spacing: This varies depending upon the type of lettuce and the variety grown. Don't crowd the plants as they won't produce large heads and won't grow rapidly, which is important if you are to grow the best tasting lettuce.

Head Lettuce: Plant this in offset rows: 15″ - 12″ - 10″ apart, depending upon the variety and soil fertility.

Leaf Lettuce: Plant this in offset rows: 12″ - 8″ - 6″ apart, depending upon the variety and soil fertility.

Care

Lettuce needs to grow quickly for best quality. This can only occur if you give the plants everything they need.

Weeds: The young plants are vulnerable to weeds, so keep well weeded. Their roots are shallow so be careful with the hoe.

Water: Lettuce is largely composed of water and it responds to irrigation by giving a larger and better tasting harvest. If you think the plants might need water they probably do.

Good watering practices can help offset the negative effects of summer heat, so it is important to keep the soil constantly moist. In hot weather this may mean watering every other day. At the same time don't over water and try to keep soil from splashing on to the leaves.

Fertilization: If your soil is not as rich as it could be, give the plants a feed of compost tea or liquid kelp about a month before harvest. This is especially important with the crisphead varieties.

Mulch: This helps to conserve soil moisture, keeps down weeds and helps to keep the plants clean. If you apply it early, it can also help to keep the soil cooler in hot weather. On the negative side, it may also harbor lettuce loving slugs.

Pests: Lettuce can fall victim to quite a few pests, but they are not usually too serious. These include tarnished plant bugs, thrips, aphids, leaf miners, flea beetles: These small creatures may be controlled by using row covers.

Slugs and snails: These molluscs love the tender young leaves and are the commonest problem you will face when growing lettuce.

Cutworms: These can be a real problem for young seedlings in spring. Some gardeners use individual cutworm collars of cardboard, newspaper (2 layers) or aluminum foil). If you find plants laying on the ground, dig in the soil around them and you can usually locate the small dark caterpillar that is responsible. If you find it you can prevent it doing further damage.

Mammals: Deer, rabbits and groundhogs can quickly devastate even a mature lettuce patch. A fence may be necessary if you have these problems.

Disease: Lettuce may be afflicted by various blights, spots, rots, rusts, mosaics, mildews and yellows, but none are particularly significant when growing on a garden scale.

Other problems

Bolting: A mature lettuce will flower (bolt) when the day length gets up to 14 or 16 hours (the exact day length depends upon the variety), even if the weather is cool. Warm weather (above 75 - 80°F) frequently accompanies the long days of midsummer and may hasten bolting, but it isn't the primary cause. Likewise crowding can contribute to bolting.

Bolting will also occur when a plant reaches full size and has all the resources it needs to flower. When the plant has enough large leaves they signal the plant that it is ready to flower. The onset of bolting may be retarded somewhat by the frequent picking of single leaves, but it won't stop it.

When a plant starts to bolt, it turns bitter, the head elongates and the new leaves begin to take on an elongated shape. The plants can be quite beautiful at this stage and if left alone the flower stalk will appear and ultimately produce an abundance of seed. I often allow them to produce seed, as I use a lot for growing **cut and come again salad** and **Micro-greens**.

Bitterness: This is a characteristic sign of imminent bolting, but it may also be caused by water stress or unusually warm weather.

Tip burn: Burnt looking leaf tips may indicate a shortage of calcium, or night temperatures over 65°F.

Harvesting

When: Lettuce is most nutritious if used fresh and doesn't keep well, so it's best to harvest it right before a meal. When grown for sale they should be harvested in the cool of early morning.

You can start harvesting leaf lettuce only a few weeks after planting, as soon as there are enough leaves to be useful. Head lettuce is harvested when the heads are firm, or at least have formed. There is no reason to wait for them to reach full maturity, as they will bolt soon afterwards. It is always better to harvest too early than too late.

How: I commonly gather individual leaves as I need them for salads. This works out well, so long as you leave enough on the plant for it to recover. Picking individual leaves may even slow down bolting.

Traditionally the whole lettuce is cut off at the base. If you leave a few leaves on the stem, rather than cutting at actual ground level, the head will be cleaner. The stem remaining in the ground may then continue to grow and sprout new leaves. It may even grow some little lettuces.

Storage: Leaf lettuce has thin leaves and won't keep for much more than a week in a plastic bag in the fridge.

Crisphead lettuce has stiff, fleshy leaves and keeps very well, in fact that is why it is so popular with commercial growers. It will keep for several weeks in a plastic bag in a refrigerator.

The other types are somewhere in between. Don't wash any lettuce until you are going to use it.

Seed saving: It is fairly easy to save lettuce seed and if you save it from your best plants, you can develop better strains than you can buy (and have higher quality seed). The plants are mostly self-pollinated, though there may be some cross-pollination from insects. It is recommended that varieties be separated by 25 ft to keep them pure, which is simple enough. It will also cross-pollinate with wild lettuce (several *Lactuca* species) so remove any you see within 200 ft of your flowering plants.

I often save lettuce seed with no thought for purity, as I want it in volume for growing cut and come again lettuce. I don't really care if the variety is somewhat mixed up (in fact I probably wouldn't even notice if it was).

I often gather seed from plants that have bolted, but you shouldn't gather it from the first plants to bolt. Early flowering is not a trait you want to perpetuate.

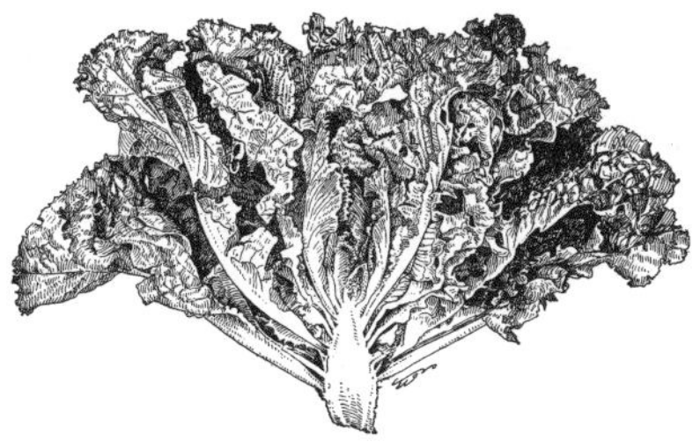

Head lettuce can present a problem when it comes to seed saving. The head may be so dense that the flower stalk may not be able to get out. If this is the case, you may have to cut an X in the top of the head, to enable the flower stem to emerge (as you would with a cabbage). If the flower stem is very big you may have to stake it to prevent it from falling over when it gets loaded with seed.

The yellow flowers are followed, 2 to 3 weeks later, by fuzzy dandelion-like seed heads. Gather the seed as it ripens by holding a paper bag over the head and shaking (I really dislike the smell the plants leave on your hands when doing this).

The seed ripens sequentially, so you must collect it every few days to get all the ripe seed. Keep on collecting until you have all the seed you need, or until it is blown away by the wind.

Alternatively you can cut the entire head when about 50% of the seed has ripened and dry it in a paper grocery bag. Clean the seed and remove the fuzz, then dry and store it in a cool place.

Newly harvested seed usually won't germinate for a couple of months.

Lettuce mosaic virus can be seed borne so watch out for it if you save your own seed, or swap seed with others.

Unusual growing ideas

Intercrop: Lettuce is a compact and fast growing plant, perfect for intercropping between a slower maturing crop. It will be out of the ground before the other crop needs the space. This works well with slow growing crops such as parsnip peppers or tomato. If you have a ready supply of transplants, you can fit a few lettuces into any small vacant space that appears.

Cut and come again:

If lettuce plants are packed very closely together, the plants don't produce a head at all, they just produce an abundance of single leaves, the perfect size for using in salads. This gives you a completely different way to grow lettuce, either alone or in a salad mix.

The seed is broadcast directly on to the bed, so there is a seed roughly every ½″. You may want to cover the seeds with a very light covering of soil, to stop it drying out.

Start harvesting when the leaves are 2 - 3″ tall, leaving at least an inch of stem on the plant when cutting, so that it can regenerate. I like to make a small sowing every 3 weeks to maintain a steady supply of leaves.

When grown in this way lettuce needs only about half the space it would for growing heads. I like this method so much, I stopped growing individual lettuce for a while.

See **Salad Mix** for more on growing salad greens at close spacing.

Multi-planting: Leaf lettuce can also be multi-planted. Sow 2 or 3 seeds in each block or plug tray and allow them all to grow to maturity. Plant the clusters out 12″ apart.

Containers: Lettuce does quite well in containers, so long as they contain a fertile soil mix and you keep them watered. Because containers are so portable you can move the plants to cooler locations in warm weather.

Hot weather growing: The best way to grow summer lettuce is as a cut and come again crop. Use a heat tolerant variety and grow it in the shade (use shade netting or interplant under taller plants). Apply cold water daily to keep the soil moist and cool. Cut the leaves frequently to make the most of the harvest and to slow down bolting. Of course you should also use a heat tolerant variety (see below for a few of these).

Volunteers: If you allow lettuce to flower it will often self-sow. You can aid this process by scattering some of the abundantly produced seed in suitable places. In spring you can often simply transplant these seedlings to where you want them. If they are of different varieties, they can give quite an extended harvest period.

Varieties

Four types of lettuce are commonly grown, looseleaf, crisphead, butterhead and semi-heads (romaines). There is a lot of variation within these types, with many cultivars bred for specific purposes. Some are especially good for a specific season, some are for growing under glass and some have even been bred for container growing.

There are now a huge number of lettuce varieties available, so I'm just going to mention a few from each type.

Looseleaf
Lactuca sativa
This is the easiest to grow, the most tolerant of heat or cold, the fastest to mature and the most nutritious. It comes in various colors and sizes and usually matures in 40 - 50 days.

Oakleaf
Black Seeded Simpson
Deer Tongue
Salad Bowl
Red Sails
Bronze arrow
Flame
Sunset

Butterhead / Bibbs
Lactuca sativa var *capitata*
These have soft, loosely packed heads and very good flavor. They are fairly easy to grow and tolerate some heat. These mature in anywhere from 65 - 80 days.

Buttercrunch
Tom Thumb
Merveille de Quatre Saisons

Romaine (Cos)
Lactuca sativa var *longifolia*
These produce heads of tender green leaves with crisp midribs. They are better flavored and more heat tolerant than most other lettuce. They mature at around 70 - 85 days.

Little Gem
Paris Green Cos
Valmaine
Winter Density

Crisphead / Iceberg
Lactuca.sativa var *capitata.*
These have dense heads of crisp leaves and need a long period of cool weather for best growth. Head lettuce is the most difficult to grow, the slowest, the most demanding and the least nutritious. It is very popular however, because of its crisp and crunchy texture. It is prized by industrial agriculture for its ability to survive handling, shipping and sitting on supermarket shelves. These take the longest time to mature, anywhere from 80 - 95 days.

Crispino
Great Lakes
Iceberg
Webbs Wonderful

Heat tolerant lettuce
There are quite a few of these when you start looking.

Black Seeded Simpson
Deer Tongue
Green Star
Jericho
Lollo Rossa,
Oakleaf
Merveille de Quatre Saisons
Red Sails
Webbs Wonderful

Cold tolerant lettuce
Lettuce is quite a hardy crop all around, but some varieties are more hardy than others.

Arctic King
Brown Dutch Winter
Merveille de Quatre Saisons
Red Oakleaf
Rouge d'Hiver
Valdor
Valmaine
Winter Density

Kitchen use:
We tend to use lettuce raw in salads and sandwiches, but it has other uses as well. It has been used as a potherb, stir fried, added to soups and used as wrapping for other foods.

Celtuce
Stem Lettuce
Lactuca sativa var angustata

Introduction: This is a type of lettuce that isn't grown for its leaves (which are edible, if not always very good), but for its succulent edible flower stem. This is supposed to resemble celery, hence the name celtuce (cel - tuce celery - lettuce), though it doesn't really.

Celtuce originated in China and has been a popular crop there for a long time, but was only introduced into America by Burpee in the 1940's. This explains why the name sounds like something an ad agency came up with (it probably is).

Celtuce has pretty much the same growing requirements as lettuce and is grown in the same way, so I will only mention the differences here.

Ease of growing: Though rarely grown in American gardens, celtuce is fairly easy to grow. It makes a virtue of the problem that is the bane of many lettuce growers; that of bolting.

Nutritional content: The leaves are richer in vitamin C than lettuce.

When to plant: In mild summer areas celtuce can be grown all summer, but in warmer ones it is most often grown as a spring or fall crop.

In spring you can start the seed indoors 6 weeks before the last frost date. Plant the seedlings outside 2 weeks before the last frost date. You should be able to make several succession sowings (every 2 weeks) before the weather gets too warm.

A fall crop is started 2 - 3 months before the first fall frost (you can succession sow several times after this). It is hardy enough that in mild winter areas it can be grown as a winter crop.

Spacing: The plants can get quite big so space them 12″ apart in beds, or 12″ apart in rows with 18″ between the rows.

Feeding: Give the plants compost tea or liquid kelp at about 30 days and again at 60 days. You want the plants to grow as large as possible before they bolt, so you will get larger stems and more edible material.

Harvest: You can gather the very young leaves for salads, but older ones tend to be bitter. Don't take leaves from plants you are growing for their stalks. They should be allowed to put all of their energy into producing large and juicy stems.

The stems are harvested when about 1″ diameter and about 12″ tall. After harvesting you can strip off the leaves and use them like lettuce (they are usually cooked in China).

Use the stems as soon as possible as they don't store very well. Harvest for greens in 60 days, or stems in 90 days.

Kitchen use: The stem is a bit like a broccoli stem, in that it has a fibrous skin which should be peeled off. This is more important than it is with broccoli, as the skin contains a bitter sap. After peeling it should be washed to remove any sap.

The heart of the stalk is good raw, sliced or shredded in salads. They can also be steamed or used in stir-fries and soups.

Luffa

Luffa species

Introduction: These vines are widely cultivated in the tropics for food and for their sponges. They are related to the squashes and their cultivation is quite similar.

About Luffa

Germ temp: 60 (70 - 95) 105°F
Germination time: 14 - 21 days
Seed viability: 2 - 5 years
Days to harvest: 70 - 100 days
Growing temp: 60 - 75°F
Start inside: 2 wks before last frost
Sow out 2 - 4 wks after last frost

Ease of growing: I have found it similar to the squash, though the seed is somewhat more reluctant to germinate.

Soil

Incorporate 2″ of compost or aged manure into the top 6″ of soil. Luffa doesn't need a lot of nitrogen, (it may encourage excessive leaf growth), but it does like phosphorus (give it colloidal phosphate) and potassium (wood ashes).

Climate: For best growth these tropical plants needs a long, warm growing season, with plenty of sun.

Planting

Starting inside: In northern climates the luffa is treated in much the same way as the squash. It is started in the greenhouse 4 - 6 weeks before it can be planted out. The seeds have a hard seed coat that must be softened before they can germinate. You should probably soak the seed overnight prior to planting. They don't like having their roots disturbed, so should be started in cell packs or soil blocks.

Planting out: Plant them outside when they have at least 3 true leaves and all danger of frost has passed. Plant them up to their first true leaves.

Direct sowing: Luffas are slow to germinate and so can only be started outside in areas with long growing seasons. It is sown like cucumber.

Spacing: Sow the plants in hills 36″ apart. Trellised plants can be grown 12″ apart in two rows 36″ apart.

Care

Watering: They need even moisture for best fruit production, so water regularly.

Support: These vigorous sprawling vines produce better fruit when grown on a trellis. They also suffer less from pests and diseases.

Pests: They may be attacked by the same pests that bother squash.

Harvesting

Food: The flowers should appear about 6 weeks after transplanting. If you are using the immature fruit for food, you should gather them while they are under 6″ in length. As with squash, regular harvesting will keep them producing well.

Sponges: The fruits are left to mature fully and turn pale green or yellow. If you want to get big sponges, don't allow too many to mature on one plant.

Processing sponges: Allow the ripe fruit to dry for a couple of weeks, then cut off the ends and shake out the dry seeds. Dry them thoroughly and keep them for next year. To remove the skin soak the fruit overnight (or boil for a few minutes). The softened skin will then peel off. To get the familiar clean pale luffa (loofah), soak it for a half hour in a dilute solution of bleach (it doesn't take much bleach).

Seed saving: This is easy, just save the seed when you process the mature fruit. Like other cucurbits they are insect-pollinated, but there is little danger of cross-pollination, as few varieties exist (and few people grow them anyway).

Unusual growing ideas

Ornamental: This vine is quite ornamental and can be grown on a trellis as a deciduous screen.

Varieties

Chinese Okra - *L. acutangula*: This species has 10 prominent ridges on the fruit. It is the best species for food, but not as good for sponges.

Sponge Gourd - *L. cylindrica*: (Syn. *L. aegyptiaca)*
This species has smooth skin. It is the best for sponges, but not as good for food.

Kitchen use

The immature fruit can be used like summer squash, or eaten raw in salads.

Apparently the leaves are also edible and can be used as a salad or potherb. I haven't tried them though.

Melon

Cucumis melo

Introduction: The melon has been called "The noblest production of the garden". It is a member of the Cucurbit family and is grown in much the same way as the related cucumbers. It isn't quite as vigorous when young however.

This succulent tropical fruit probably originated in Asia and has been eaten for over 4000 years. It was first grown in Britain in the sixteenth century using hotbeds made from manure.

Ease of growing: Melons are fairly easy to grow in a warm hospitable climate, not so easy in cooler areas.

Nutritional content: The fruits contain vitamin C, beta-carotene, potassium, pectin and several beneficial phytochemicals, including lycopene and zeaxanthin. Their energy content is about 160 calories per pound.

Climate: Melons do best in a hot (for best flavor), dry (to reduce disease) climate. If it's too cool they will grow slowly and the fruit won't taste very good. They can't stand any frost.

Soil

pH 6.0 to 7. 0

The ideal soil for melons is loose, moist, fertile, well-drained and fairly neutral. In cool climates a light soil is good as it warms up faster (raised beds are good too).

Soil preparation: Incorporate 2″ of compost or aged manure (they love old manure) into the top 6″ of soil. If you don't have a lot of compost, then simply put a shovel full in each planting hole.

About Melon

Seed facts
Germ temp: 65 (70 - 95) 100°F
Germination time: 3 - 10 days
8 days / 68°F
4 days / 77°F
3 days / 86°F * Optimum
Germination percentage: 80+
Viability: 2 - 4 yrs
Weeks to grow transplants: 3 - 4

Planning facts
Hardiness: Tender
Growing temp: 65 - 75°F
Plants per person: 2
Plants per sq ft: plant needs 2 - 4 sq ft

Transplants:
Start: on the last frost date
Plant out: 4 wks after last frost
Direct sow: 4 wks after last frost
Succession sow: about 4 - 6 weeks after first sowing

Harvest facts
Days to harvest: 70 - 150 days
Harvest period: 12 weeks
Yield per plant: 2 lb (2 - 4 fruit)
Yield per sq ft: ½ - 1½ lb sq ft

Melons don't need a lot of nitrogen, as this encourages leaf growth at the expense of fruit. They do like phosphorus (bonemeal or colloidal phosphate) and potassium (wood ashes), as well as boron and magnesium. You can add all of these at the same time by using an organic fertilizer mix. They dislike acid soil, so lime if necessary using dolomitic lime (which also adds magnesium).

Planning

Where: Melons must have hot weather (ideally 90°F) if they are to make the sugar needed to produce sweet fruits. In cooler areas you need to give them as much sun and heat as possible (a south or west facing slope is good). They should also be sheltered from cool winds.

I must emphasize that if melons don't get enough heat they won't taste very good (even if you do grow them successfully.) In a cool climate it's a waste of time trying to grow them outside, grow them in greenhouses, or under cloches or cold frames.

Crop rotation: It isn't a good idea to plant Cucurbits (melons, squash, cucumbers) in the same soil more frequently than every 4 years.

When: Melons need warm weather to germinate and grow, so don't plant them until all danger of frost is past and the soil temperature is at least 60°F. If you want to grow melons in areas with short growing seasons, start them indoors and warm the soil with black plastic, or cloches, before planting.

Succession sowing: If you want to have a continuous harvest of melons, you should make several sowings, perhaps 3 - 4 weeks apart. You can also plant several varieties, with different maturation times.

Planting

You might want to pre-soak the seeds overnight before planting, especially if you are sowing directly outside.

Transplants

Starting inside: If your growing season is short, you will want to start your melons indoors. Like most Cucurbits they dislike root disturbance, so should be started in cell packs, soil blocks or individual pots. Plant 2 seeds to a block and thin to the best one after both have emerged. The seedlings will be ready to plant out in 3 - 5 weeks, when they have at least 3 or 4 true leaves.

Don't start your melons too early, as you don't want them to get root-bound. If it is too cold to put them out when they are ready, you will have to move them into larger pots.

Planting out: Plant out the seedlings up to their first true leaves and water immediately. When they have recovered from transplanting give them a liquid feed to get them growing again. In cool areas you might want to put them under cloches or row covers until the weather warms up. You might also warm the soil in this way before planting.

Direct sowing: If your growing season is long and hot enough, it is better to direct sow your melons. They will germinate and grow rapidly in warm (75°F) soil.

Sow the seeds 1″ deep, with 4″ between the plants. When they have all germinated, thin the row to leave a plant every 18″. You may be able to transplant some of the thinnings if you do it very carefully.

Hills: Melons are often planted in hills, slightly elevated above the surrounding soil. This helps the soil to warm up faster and provides better drainage (melons rot easily in wet soil.

To make a hill remove 2 shovelfuls of soil, dump in 2 shovelfuls of compost or aged manure and then replace the soil. Mix it all together and shape it into a low mound. Plant the seeds on edge, ½ - 1″ deep, sowing 5 - 6 seeds on each mound. When these are growing well, pinch out the inferior seedlings, to leave the best 3 plants to grow on.

Spacing:

Hills: Space the hills 3 - 5 ft apart, with 3 plants to a hill.

Rows: Space the plants 18- 24″ apart, in rows 72″ apart (or 24 - 36″ apart in rows 60″ apart).

Beds: Intensive gardeners plant melons 15″ - 18″ - 24″ apart, depending upon the soil and variety. They are usually planted in rows, to facilitate supporting them. If they grow upwards they take up a lot less space.

Care

Watering: Melons are quite shallow rooted, so need fairly constant water. This is most critical when the fruits are sizing up and they should get all the water they can use at this time. In hot weather this can be up to 2 gallons a day for each plant (1″ a week). Ideally this should be lukewarm so it doesn't cool the soil. When the fruits have reached full size you should ease up on watering, otherwise they may split.

The best way to water melons is with a drip system, as they don't like having wet leaves (this encourages fungus disease). If you must use overhead watering then do it in the morning or early evening, so the leaves can dry out quickly.

No-watering: There is an alternative way to water melons, which is to not give them any water at all. You will get fewer and smaller fruits, but they will be sweeter. For this to work you have to space the plants further apart, so they have more volume of soil to extract water from. The exact spacing will depend upon your soil and its moisture holding capacity.

Weeds: It is important that the plants be kept free of weeds, especially when young. Be careful when hoeing as they have shallow roots.

Mulch: This is useful to suppress weeds, conserve moisture, reduce the incidence of disease from splashed soil and to keep the fruit cleaner. Don't apply it until the soil has warmed up however

Fertilization: When the flowers start to set fruit, you might give the plants a feed of compost tea or liquid kelp. Feed them again as the fruit begins to size up.

Be careful when fertilizing melons, as too much nitrogen may encourage a young plant to produce excessive foliage at the expense of fruiting. Too much nitrogen during fruiting may also result in inferior (and later maturing) fruit.

A low-tech way to feed melons is to bury a 1 gallon plant pot alongside the plant and half fill it with vermicompost or manure. Fill it with water every day and let the water slowly seep out (and leach nutrients with it).

Protection: In cool climates you can use cloches to keep the plants warmer. They must have heat if they are to produce sweet fruit.

Pruning: The seedlings should be pinched back twice, so they produce four growing tips. These are then allowed to grow and flower.

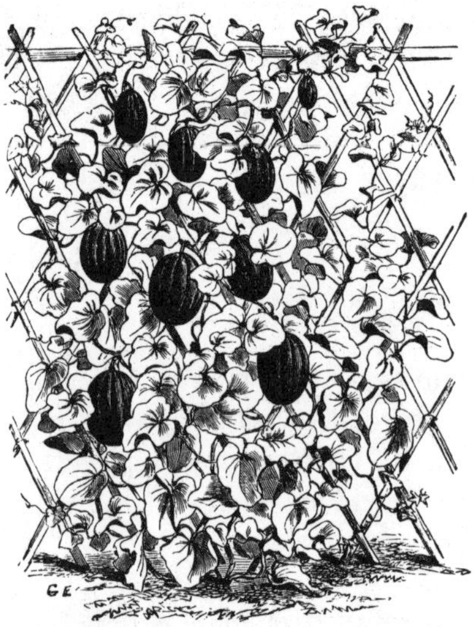

Support: The plants can be trained up trellises to save space, just as you would with cucumber. This should be fairly sturdy to support their considerable weight. The fruits are heavier than cucumbers and usually need individual supports (slings made from old panty-hose work well.)

Fruiting: The first flowers to appear are usually male and don't produce fruit. Female flowers follow soon (7 - 10 days) afterwards and these will bear fruit if they are pollinated (honeybees are important pollinators).

Growers often allow one fruit to develop on each branch and then pinch off any others that form. The more fruit you allow to develop, the smaller they will all be.

Pollination: If you want to make sure your plants are pollinated, you can do it by hand. This isn't normally necessary however, as insects will usually do the job. Hand pollination is most often done in greenhouses or cloches, where insects may not be able to get to them easily.

Care of fruit: As the melon swells it can get quite heavy. If it is growing on a trellis it should be supported in a sling. If it is growing on the ground you can insert a tin can, plant pot, tile or stone underneath it, to keep it off of the soil.

Pests: Melons are related to cucumbers and suffer from many of the same afflictions. They are particularly vulnerable when small, so should be watched carefully at this time. Melon aphids, melon worms, pickleworms, squash bugs, squash vine borers, mites, whiteflies and cucumber beetles (which spread fusarium wilt) may all cause problems. Rabbits, raccoons and birds will eat the ripe fruit.

Diseases: Like most cucurbits they are prone to a variety of diseases when growing in humid conditions. These include mosaic virus, downy mildew, powdery mildew, alternaria leaf blight, anthracnose, fusarium wilt and bacterial wilt. It is important to keep the leaves dry where possible.

Harvesting

When: The first fruits will be ready to harvest in mid to late summer, about 35 - 45 days after pollination. The key to great melons is to pick them at the peak of ripeness, so don't pick a melon before its time (it won't be as good as it could have been). If you leave it too long it will start to deteriorate, so it's important to get this right.

There are several ways to tell when a melon is ripe, though not all of these indicators may be present at the same time. You will learn to get it right by experience.

> **When a melon is ripe**
>
> It develops a very strong aroma.
>
> The blossom end (the one opposite the stem) gets soft.
>
> Muskmelons and canteloupes develop cracks around the stem.
>
> Gently roll the fruit in your hand, if it separates (slips) easily from the vine it is ready.
>
> The tendril closest to the fruit usually shrivels up.
>
> The spot where the melon was resting on the ground will turn from white to yellow

How: It is best to cut the fruit from the vine, leaving a couple of inches of stem attached. Handle the fruit carefully once it is harvested, as it will bruise easily.

Storage: For best flavor melons should be eaten as soon as possible after harvest, preferably while still warm from the sun. Otherwise they should be treated like tomatoes and kept at room temperature. They can be stored in a fridge for a couple of weeks, but their flavor will slowly deteriorate.

Seed Saving: Melons are cross-pollinated by insects so you can grow only one variety at one time. If you want to grow more than one the best idea is to hand pollinate, though you could also cage them (isolating by a ½ mile requires a very large garden).

Hand pollinating melons isn't difficult, though the flowers are smaller than other Cucurbits. The flowers are most receptive to pollination before any fruit start growing. Once there are fruit maturing on the plant they become less inclined to pollinate successfully.

You need to prepare to pollinate the flowers the night before, by finding some male and female flowers (the female has a tiny "melon" behind the flower) that are about to open the following day. Tape them shut with a little piece of masking tape (don't tape it too well or it will be hard to remove without damaging the flower). This prevents them from opening and being pollinated before you get to them.

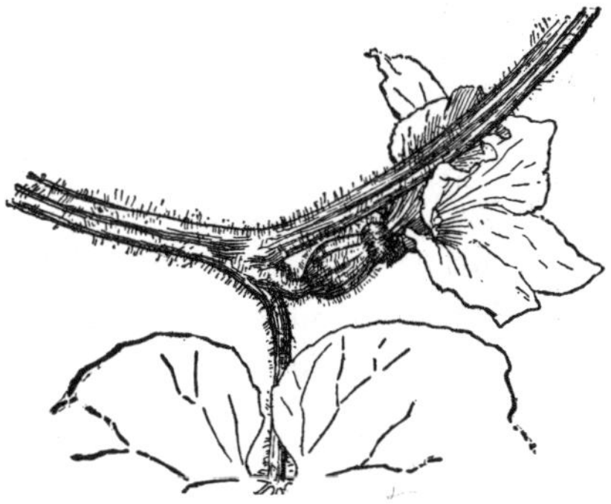

The next day pick a male flower and remove its tape and petals. Then carefully open a female flower (from a different plant), being very careful to not damage the petals. Insert the male flower into a female flower and brush the pollen from the anthers on to stigma. Finally tape the female flower closed again. The petals will soon fall off and if pollination was successful the tiny fruit will begin to grow.

It is often tempting to try planting seed from a particularly delicious melon you have eaten. Unfortunately many commercial melons are F1 hybrids and their seed won't produce a melon like its parent. If you know the melon wasn't a hybrid then go for it (it does seems a shame not to be able to use some of those seeds).

Varieties

When choosing a melon it is important to choose one that will grow well in your area. Melons are divided into several categories.

Summer melons

European Canteloupe Melons

(*C. melo* var *cantalupensis*)

These usually have hard, ribbed (not netted), pale green skin and are not the familiar fruits we call canteloupes. These are not widely grown in North America.

Charentais

Boule d'Or

American Canteloupe Melons, Muskmelons

(*C. melo* var *reticulatus*)

These are the fruits Americans call canteloupes and have the familiar netted skin. They need hot weather to ripen properly and don't ripen well off the vine, so wait until they are fully ripe before picking.

Persian

Haogen

Galia

Jenny Lind

Blenheim Orange

Winter melons

These are sometimes called winter melons because they take longer to ripen and often the weather has started to cool (they are somewhat hardier than other types).

Casaba, Crenshaw, Honeydew and Persian melons

(*C. melo* var *inodorus*)

As the Latin specific name suggests they don't have a strong scent. Their skin is smooth (not netted) and tougher so they can be stored for a longer time. Crenshaw is a cross of casaba and Persian melons.

Earlidew F1
Honeyloupe

Japanese Melons

The Japanese have taken melons to a whole other level. The Yubari King greenhouse melon is often given as a gift and is highly prized. When I say highly prized I really mean prized highly - a pair were recently sold in auction for over $15,000. More proof (if we needed it) that some people just have too much money.

Japanese melons tend to be very sweet and fairly small.
Emerald Jewel,
Emerald sweet
Sakatas Sweet

Kitchen use

As with beer Americans usually consume melons cold, as it makes them more refreshing. However (also as with beer) low temperatures also reduce their flavor. For the best taste experience melons should be eaten at room temperature (or even better warmed by the sun).

Salad greens: Yes you can get salad greens from melons, just sprout the seeds like those of sunflower.

The cleaned seeds can also be toasted in a skillet until golden brown, then shelled and eaten.

Micro-greens

Introduction: Micro-greens are the seedlings of a variety of salad plants, gathered after they have formed their first true leaves. They bridge the gap between sprouted seeds from the kitchen and salad mix from the garden. Apparently they are no longer quite the hip and trendy thing they were a few years back (if you care), but they are still the same versatile and nutritious fresh food they always were. They are easily grown at home and give you a way to grow nutritious salad materials year round.

There is a precedent for micro-greens. In Britain inexpensive trays of "mustard and cress" grown on fiber pads have long been available in markets, to be clipped as needed for salads and sandwiches. In North America people have been growing trays of buckwheat "lettuce" and sunflower "lettuce" for years. These are both used in the same way, and cut when they produce their first true leaves (or even before). The idea of micro-greens takes this a step further and introduces a wide variety of new plants to provide a unique taste treat rather than extra nutrition (though they have that too).

Growing micro-greens gives you a practical way to make use of some of the excess seed that inevitably accumulates when you start saving your own seed (in fact it is a good reason to start saving seed).

Crop use: Growing microgreens is a practical way to grow flavoring and salad materials year round, and can be very useful if you live in a very cold or very warm climate.

Ease of growing: Growing micro-greens is closer to sprouting than it is to vegetable gardening. They are grown for such a short time and in such a controlled environment that there is little chance of things going wrong (though inevitably mishaps can happen occasionally).

Nutritional content: The nutritious young plants are rich in vitamins A, B's, C, E and K as well as calcium, iron, magnesium, phosphorus and potassium. They also contain various antioxidants and beneficial phytochemicals.

Days to harvest: This can be anywhere from 3 - 21 days, depending upon the crop and growing conditions.

When: One of the nice things about micro-greens is that they can be grown inside or outside. This means you can have cheap fresh salad materials at any time of the year, no matter how cold or hot it gets outside.

In winter you can grow them in the house or greenhouse. In spring and fall you can grow them in the greenhouse or cold frame. In summer you can grow them in a shady part of the garden, or back in the house (for growing cool weather crops).

Containers: Almost any type of container can be used to grow microgreens. The kind you choose will depend on what you want. If you want to grow as much as possible as quickly as possible you might use the same wooden flats used for starting transplants, or large plastic trays. If you want something cute to put on your kitchen window you might use decorative ceramic or terracotta pots (if they don't have drainage holes, you can put some gravel in the bottom for drainage). If you live in an apartment you might use the plastic containers that fruit or salad mix comes in (just put some drainage holes in the bottom).

Soil mix: The mix is more important for anchoring the plants and supplying water than it is as a source of nutrients, because they are in the ground for such a short time. It is best not to use garden soil to fill the containers, as it contains weed seeds and living soil organisms.

You can buy a potting soil mix, but it is relatively expensive and you can easily make it yourself (a simple mix would be 1/3 sand, 1/3 peat moss and 1/3 compost). You don't need to completely fill the container either, you only need to put an inch or two in the bottom.

Seeds: Use only untreated seed as you don't want anything with fungicide on it. You will need quite a lot of seeds to grow microgreens and this can get expensive if you are using individual seed packets (though you can use those left over from planting the garden). You can save money by searching out bulk seed or seed sold for sprouting.

The best place to get seeds for microgreens is your own garden, by saving them yourself. Seed saving is a perfect complement to growing microgreens because it gives you a way to use up a lot of those surplus seeds that often just sit around until they die.

You can use a mix of seed for microgreens, but you may have a problem if they germinate and grow at different rates. An extreme example would be if you mixed heat loving basil with fast growing cold tolerant bok choy. You would have a crop of bok choy before the basil has even germinated! If you plant more than one kind of seed in a container it is important that they grow at roughly the same rate, so you can harvest at the same time.

It is usually simpler to plant each type of seed in a separate container, as each one can then grow at its own rate. You then just cut what you want and mix it together.

Planting: The seeds are scattered on the moist growing medium, keeping them very close together (¼″ apart maximum). Don't cover them with soil as it will make for soil covered microgreens. Keep the containers in a warm place (70°F is optimal for most salad crops). The container should be misted as necessary to keep the growing plants well supplied with moisture.

Succession sowing: Micro-greens are a very short term crop and the frequency of succession sowing will depend upon how much you plant and how much you use. After a couple of sowings you will work this out for yourself.

Warmth: Micro-greens don't need much attention, so long as it is warm enough for germination and growth. The ideal temperature is around 70°F in the day (and slightly lower at night), though it varies with each crop. Many grow faster if it is warmer than this.

You can achieve a warm temperature in a cold house by putting them near a heat source, or using a seed tray heating pad. Of course in cooler temperatures it makes sense to concentrate on cold tolerant crops such as Brassicas and lettuce.

If the temperature gets too hot for the germination of lettuce you can pre-germinate it in the fridge. See **Lettuce** for how to do this.

Watering: The soil in the containers needs to be kept moist at all times, so the seeds don't dry out (which they can do easily when they are sitting exposed on the surface). A spray bottle works well for watering as it gently mists the plants without splashing the seeds around too much.

Professional growers often water from below by immersing the containers in a tray of water for a minute or so to thoroughly moisten the soil. This keeps the tops drier, cleaner and less prone to rot. They may also put lids on their containers to keep the plants moist.

Light: The seeds don't need light until they have germinated, so you can start them anywhere. Once they have germinated they need plenty of light for good growth. The best source is the sun, so a greenhouse is probably the best place to grow them (unless its warm enough to have them outside). A sunny windowsill is also good (and more convenient) but usually limited in size. I don't really like electric lights, but they are a necessary evil if you have no better light source.

Of course the seedlings don't last for very long anyway, so it doesn't matter if they don't get full sunlight all of the time Even if they are somewhat light deprived you can still eat them.

Harvesting

When: The best time to harvest is about 5 minutes before sitting down to eat. Commercial growers harvest in the early morning when the plants are cool.

The plants are usually cut within 2 - 3 weeks of planting, when they have their first true leaves. However you can let them get somewhat bigger if you want. This will make the harvest bigger, though the leaves may be less tender and mild (though I'm sure your teeth can still handle them).

How: Before harvesting you should gently brush off any seed husks that remain attached to the leaves.

The best way to harvest is to cut them with scissors just above the soil level, so you don't disturb the remaining plants (try not to get them dirty as you want to minimize washing). If necessary rinse them carefully and use straight away. Unfortunately, unlike mesclun, they won't regrow after cutting, they are a one time deal.

Kitchen use: These plants can be used as a salad in their own right, but are so precious (expensive) they are usually combined with seed sprouts, edible flowers and other salad materials from the garden. In posh restaurants they are commonly used as a garnish for soups, sandwiches and salads.

Outdoor growing: In warm weather the best place to put your microgreen containers is outside in the shade.

In theory it could be possible to grow microgreens in the ground in a growing bed, but they are so small and close to the ground that it would be hard to keep them clean enough for use (misting instead of sprinkling would help a lot.) You could also try building wooden frames for growing them slightly off the ground.

Varieties; The best seeds for growing microgreens are those that grow rapidly and taste good, which includes:

Beet and chard: Prized for their color more than their flavor.

Brassica family: There are a lot of these and they tend to be fast growing and pungent in flavor. All of them are good, but arugala, bok choy, garden cress, mizuna, mustards, radish and turnip are perhaps the fastest (you can be eating them in a week).

Lettuce: The staple of micro-greens and mesclun mixes, they are tasty and sometimes spectacularly beautiful too.

Basil: Slower than the others (and needs more heat), but has a wonderful flavor.

Celery: This is fairly slow, but adds a great flavor.

Fennel: Delicious anise flavor.

Sunflower: Fast and tasty (needs warmth for fast growth).

Other useful plants

These are also worth experimenting with as micro-greens:

Amaranth
Chervil
Chia
Chicory
Cilantro
Clover
Cornsalad
Dill
Escarole
Fenugreek (one of my favorites)
Flax
Onion
Plantain
Purslane
Quinoa
Radicchio
Sorrel
Spinach
Water Pepper

Millet, Proso

Panicum miliaceum

Millet is a somewhat confusing crop because it is actually the name for a group of several different species of small-seeded cereal grains, rather than just one. Here I am going to only talk about the species that is best adapted for growing human food in temperate climates, the proso millet. This is the kind you buy in the store for human consumption.

Proso millet was one of the first grains to be domesticated and has been grown for 10,000 years or more (it predates wheat). It grows in a variety of soil types and has a very short growing season (only 60 - 75 days. It is also the hardiest of the millets and was a staple food in Europe until it was displaced by wheat.

It is sometimes called broom corn because the heads of the plants were (and still are in some countries) used to make brooms.

I don't claim to be an expert on millet, but I have done my best to put together a coherent article because of its ease of growing and nutritional value. I did this because I wanted to include some foods that could help you stay alive.

Nutritional content: Millet is higher in protein (15%) than corn and is also rich in vitamins C. E and several B's (especially niacin, B6, pantothenic acid and folate). It also contains calcium, iron, potassium, magnesium, phosphorus, and zinc. It is one of only a few alkaline grains and is packed with energy (1700 calories per pound).

Crop use: Proso millet is a valuable grain crop for the homesteader as it has such a short growing season. It is also one of the best crops for low water situations, as it needs less water than any other common cereal.

About Millet

Germ time: 2 - 21 days
Germ temp 45 (50 - 90) 100°F
Growing temp: 68 (70 – 75) 85°F
Days to maturity: 60 - 90
Seed viability: 2 - 4 years
Yield: 1 lb / 10 sq ft
Grows 1 - 4' high

Ease of growing: Proso is an undemanding crop to grow. The hardest part is finding a way to hull the seeds so you can eat them.

Climate: Millet prefers warm growing conditions, though it will grow in cooler ones too (it can't tolerate any frost though). It doesn't need a very long growing season.

Millet uses water very efficiently (it uses C4 photosynthesis) and is commonly grown in dry areas.

Soil

pH 5.5 (6.5) 7.0

Millet is famous for its ability to grow on poor soil but it is more productive when growing on a fertile one. It likes the same kind of soil as corn, especially well-drained loam. It doesn't like wet soil.

Soil preparation: This is pretty much the same as for corn, a couple of inches of compost and a source of potassium and phosphorus (maybe wood ashes and bonemeal), Alternatively you could just add some fertilizer mix, as it likes nitrogen too.

Planning

Where: Any sunny place will do, so long as it is well-drained.

When: Proso likes warm weather and dislikes frost. It is a very short season crop, so doesn't have to be planted early, it can go in any time in early summer that gives the most suitable weather (and avoids drought). Ideally the soil should be at least 65°F for planting. Of course it has to be planted early enough so that it matures before the first fall frost.

Planting

Raising transplants: Only a workaholic would try growing millet from transplants. If you want to try it, use the same procedure as for wheat.

Direct sowing: When the soil is warm enough make 1″ deep furrows and sow the seed 2″ apart, in rows 12″ apart.

Spacing:
Bed: Space the plants 6 - 8″ apart each way.

Rows; Space the plants 2″ apart in the row, with 12″ between the rows.

Care

Water: Proso produces food with less water than any other common grain, because it uses it very efficiently and has a short growing season. If you plant it in spring when the soil is moist it shouldn't need much watering at all.

Later in the season you usually water to get the plants well established and then give it an occasional watering. It will simply stop growing if it gets too dry and start again when it gets moisture.

If water is abundant then irrigate regularly for best production.

Fertilize: Proso millet uses quite a lot of nitrogen, so you might want to give it a foliar feed of compost tea occasionally.

Mulch: This can be helpful to keep down weeds and minimize water use.

Weeds: The young plants will need weeding, as they don't compete against weeds very well. Older ones are quite vigorous and can smother most weeds.

Pests: Generally millet isn't seriously bothered by pests, though it may be attacked by mites, grasshoppers, armyworms, rodents and birds. The latter love it, which is hardly surprising when you consider it is commonly used as bird feed.

Disease: Smut can occasionally be a problem.

Harvesting

When: Millet is harvested when the whole plant has turned golden brown and half of the seeds are ripe (the rest may be soft, but should be brown). Don't wait too long otherwise the seeds will start to fall and the birds will start to feast.

How: Cut the whole seed heads and dry in the sun for several days (this makes threshing easier).

Threshing: The ⅛″ seeds are freed from the plant by beating the heads with sticks until the grains come loose. The seed should then be dried further (ideally to 13% moisture for long term storage.

Hulling: This is the hard part and requires some machinery (though you can convert a corona hand mill to do it, Go to this website for instructions on this:

http://www.savingourseeds.org/pdf/grain_dehuller.pdf

Storage: The grain stores very well and was once kept as an emergency food source. Keep the dry seed in a vermin proof container in a cool dark place.

Seed saving: Just save some of the seed you have collected (take it from the best plants).

Varieties

Finding seed: Proso millet isn't widely grown, so you aren't going to find seed in the average seed rack in a garden center. When I first tried it I had to get my seed by mail order. Very few varieties are available to the gardener.

Kitchen use

The small grains of millet can be used is a variety of ways, boiled, steamed or ground to flour. It doesn't contain gluten so must be mixed with wheat for a raised bread.

If getting the husks off is too difficult, you can use the seed for sprouting. This also has the added benefit of making them more nutritious.

Millet has (like almost everything else) been fermented to make beer.

Mustards

Brassica juncea

Introduction: This species is believed to be a hybrid of *B. rapa* and *B. nigra.* It has been most highly refined in China, where it is a very important cool season vegetable.

This is the green leaf mustard, not the condiment mustard, which is made from the ground seeds of *B. nigra* and *B. alba.* However this species can be used for making mustard too.

Ease of growing: If given the right conditions mustards are one of the most easily grown and fast maturing crops you can grow. They produce heavily in a small area and require little effort to grow.

Crop value: I have to admit that I overlooked the mustards for a long time. I guess I was put off for a long time because they can get very pungent in hot weather. Only relatively recently have I come to appreciate their many virtues (speed of growth, nutritional value and (often) mild flavor.

The mustards definitely deserve to be more widely cultivated in the west, especially in small gardens where space is limited. We in the west have a lot to learn from China about growing food in small spaces.

The one place you commonly find mustard leaves is in commercially grown salad mixes.

Nutritional content: These are some of the most nutritious leafy greens, rich in vitamins A and C, as well as calcium, iron and potassium. Like other Brassicas they also contain a variety of cancer preventing phytochemicals.

Mustard seeds are very rich in the glucosinolate phytonutrients (these are powerful antioxidants), as well as selenium, magnesium and omega 3 fatty acids. All of these are responsible for making the condiment mustard (see recipe below) a surprisingly nutritious food and medicine. When you eat mustard for its flavor you can be smugly satisfied that you are also eating a very beneficial food supplement (though even this can't turn a hot dog into a health food).

About Mustards

Seed facts
Germination temp: 45 - 95°F
Germination time: 2 - 7 day
Viability: 3 - 8 yrs
Germination percentage: 75%+
Seed viability: 4 years
Weeks to grow transplant: 3 - 4

Planning facts
Hardiness: Hardy
Growing temp: 45 (55 - 65) 75°F
Plants per person: 5
Plants per sq ft: 4

Transplants
Start: 6 wks before last frost
Plant out 2 wks before last frost
Direct sow: 2 wks before last frost
Fall crop: Sow 6 - 8 wks before first frost
Succession sow: Every 4 weeks

Harvest facts
Days to harvest:
20 - 40 days (summer)
60 days (winter)
Harvest period: 8 - 10 weeks
Yield per plant: 1 lb
Yield per sq ft: 2 - 4 lb

Soil

pH 5.5 - 6.8

Mustards aren't particularly fussy about soils, but will be most productive on rich moisture retentive ones.

Soil preparation: If the soil is poor, dig in 2″ of compost or aged manure, as well as wood ashes or greensand (for potassium), colloidal phosphate (for phosphorus) and kelp (for trace elements). You could also simply use a fertilizer mix to supply all of these.

Planning

Where: The ideal spot for mustards depends on the weather. If it's cool they should be planted on an open sunny site. If it's warm they will benefit from some shade during the hottest part of the day.

Mustards are in and out of the ground quickly, so are commonly grown as an intercrop between slower growing plants.

Crop rotation: They should not be planted where another Brassica has grown in the past 3 years.

When: These fast growing plants will grow well in both warm and cool weather, but taste better when it's cool.

Mustards can be planted at any time as a cut and come again crop. Just plant a small section of bed every two weeks (space the plants ½″ apart), keep cool and well watered and see how it goes.

Spring: Mustards can be started indoors 6 weeks before the last frost and planted out 2 - 3 weeks later. Start direct sowing about 2 weeks before the last frost date, so they have time to mature before it gets hot. They are somewhat prone to bolting when planted at this time however and generally do better as a fall crop.

Summer: In cool climates, it is possible to succession sow the mustards all summer.

Fall: Mustards generally work best as a fall crop and (like many Brassicas) cold weather actually improves their flavor. Direct sow a fall crop at least 8 weeks before the first fall frost is expected.

Winter: Mustard thrives in cool weather and can even take quite a bit of frost (some varieties will take temperatures as low as 18°F). In milder areas it makes a great winter crop. It will also work in colder areas if it is grown under cloches or in poly tunnels.

Planting

Mustards can be direct sown or transplanted.

Transplants

Starting inside: Mustard doesn't mind transplanting, so is easily started indoors in flats or soil blocks. However you gain little time by doing this because it germinates well at low temperatures and grows quickly outside. I suppose it may be worthwhile in early spring to get a head start, or if you want to save bed space or avoid pests.

Direct sowing: Mustard is usually direct sown, by broadcasting and then covering with ¼ - ½″ of soil (or a mix of half soil and half compost). It doesn't mind being crowded so plant thickly and slowly thin to the proper spacing (eat the thinnings).

It can also be sown in rows, just make shallow ½″ deep furrows and space the seeds ½″ apart.

Spacing:
Beds: Space the plants 6 - 12″ apart each way. Exact spacing depends upon the variety.

Rows: Space the plants 1 - 4″ apart, in rows 12 - 24″ apart.

Care

For best quality you want your mustard plants to grow as fast as possible, which means giving them everything they need.

Water: If the soil is too dry the plants will develop a bitter and pungent flavor. If you want tasty, mild flavored mustard greens you must keep it moist at all times

Fertilization: If the soil is less than ideal, you may want to feed your plants with a foliar fertilizer such as compost tea. Do this after thinning them to their final spacing and again as necessary.

Mulch: This is primarily of value to keep down weed growth and keep the soil moist. It can also help to keep the soil cool, which can delay bolting.

Pests: Mustards suffer from the same pests as the other Brassicas, but especially flea beetles and cabbage root fly (see **Cabbage** for more on these).

Slugs and snails can be a serious problem early spring when there is not much else for them to eat. They can wipe out a new planting almost overnight. The best approach is to go out with a flashlight after dark and hand pick them.

Harvest: Harvest mustards by cutting the whole plants, leaving several inches of stem behind. The remaining stem will then resprout and grow another crop (you can sometimes cut them several times).

Alternatively you can harvest single leaves, as soon as they get large enough (about 3″ high).

If the plants bolt before you get a chance to harvest them, all is not lost. If it is big enough, the immature flower stalk can be eaten like broccoli raab. The flowers and green seedpods can be added to salads. Of course you can also collect the seed for various purposes.

Seed saving: It's easy to save seed from these annuals. Just treat them like kale and gather the seed at the appropriate time. Be careful not to let it self-seed too much, as it can become a weed if it gets established (though perhaps not an unwelcome one).

Mustard can produce far more seed than you need for propagation. You can use the surplus for growing cut and come again salad greens and micro-greens, or for sprouting like alfalfa (they make excellent, slightly spicy sprouts). They can even be used for making the super-nutritious condiment mustard (see below).

Unusual growing ideas

Cut and come again salad greens: Pungent mustard leaves are a basic ingredient of salad mixes. The red types are particularly prized, as they add color as well as flavor. (See **Salad mix**).

Micro-greens: This is just a smaller version of the above. You plant the seeds ¼″ apart and harvest them when the first true leaves appear, which of often within a few days. **See Micro-greens**

Winter crop: Some mustard varieties are very hardy (especially the oriental types) and make excellent winter crops for mild climates. They can also be used in colder climates if protected by cloches, or grown in a cold frame or greenhouse. If it gets very cold they may stop growing, but they won't be damaged and will resume growing when the temperature rises sufficiently.

Ornamentals: Some mustards have unusual foliage and are quite ornamental. These may be planted in ornamental borders to fill any unsightly gaps. Start the seedlings inside, or in a nursery bed and transplant them as vacant spaces appear.

Green manures: These fast growing plants are often grown as green manures, as they produce a large amount of biomass in a short time. An advantage is that you can also eat them. A disadvantage is that they are members of the Brassica family and so subject to all of their afflictions.

Varieties

There is a lot of variation in this crop.

Western mustards

These are some of the most commonly used varieties.

Southern Giant - Large, hardy plant, very productive (55 days)

Florida Broadleaf - Large mild tasting leaves (45 days)

Savannah F1 - Early and slow bolting (35 days)

Tendergreen - This is commonly thought of as a mustard, but is actually a kind of turnip (see **Turnip**).

Eastern mustards (Gai Choy)

The mustards are much more important vegetables in Asia than they are in the west. They can be divided into a number of different types.

Broad leaved Mustard
(*Brassica juncea var rugosa*)
Osaka Purple
Red Giant
Ruby Streaks
These are all good for salad mixes as they add color as well as flavor.

Leaf mustard
(*Brassica juncea var foliosa*)
San-Ho Giant - Very large plant for fall growing.

Curled Mustard
(*Brassica juncea var crispifolia*)
Green Wave: This curly mustard is very hardy, fast growing and resistant to pests.

Green-in-the-Snow, Snow Cabbage, Shi-Li-Hon (*Brassica juncea var multiceps*). This very hardy (down to 20°F) type is grown in cold weather (as the name suggests). It doesn't work well in warm weather.

Kitchen use

The tender leaves can be used raw in salads, cooked as a potherb, or in soups and stir-fries. If they are very pungent try cooking with blander greens, or change the cooking water half way through.

Prepared Mustard

1 tbsp coriander seeds
6 tbsp mustard seeds
1 tbsp black peppercorns
¼ cup chopped onion
½ tsp dried thyme
2 cup water
2 tsp honey
¼ cup red wine vinegar
½ tsp ground turmeric

Toast the coriander seeds in a skillet, then crush them with the mustard seeds, and peppercorns. Mix with the thyme, onion, turmeric and leave for three hours. Add water and vinegar and honey and simmer 10 minutes, being careful it doesn't burn. It will get thick.

New Zealand Spinach

Tetragonia tetragonioides

Introduction: This species is native to coastal areas of New Zealand and Australia, where it grows on sand dunes and beaches. As the name suggests it can be used like spinach, but is rarely found for sale in markets so you may not have heard of it. It finds its way into the home vegetable garden as a warm weather substitute for spinach.

Nutritional content: Like many greens it is high in vitamins A, B1, B2 and C. Like spinach it also contains oxalic acid.

Climate: New Zealand spinach is best known for being much more tolerant of hot and dry weather than spinach. It is actually a perennial, but it can't stand frost, so must be grown as an annual in all but the mildest areas (zone 10 or 11). It grows best at fairly moderate temperatures.

Ease of growing: I haven't had a huge amount of success with this plant, mostly because I like amaranth so much that I really haven't given it a fair chance. The last time I tried it the plants grew well, until quail shredded them all.

This is fairly easy plant to grow once it has germinated (this is quite slow) and once it gets going it grows rapidly. It is rarely bothered by pests and tolerates high temperatures.

About New Zealand Spinach

Germ temp: 50 (60 - 70) 90°F
Germination time: 14 - 21 days
Germination percentage: 40%+
Viability: 3 - 5 yrs
Weeks to grow transplants 3 - 5
Sow outdoors: 2 wks after last frost
Start indoors: 2 wks before last frost
Plant out: 2 wks after last frost

Planning facts

Hardiness: Tender
Growing temp: 60 (65 - 75) 95°F
Days to harvest: 60 - 90 days
Plants per person: 2
Plants per sq ft: 1

Transplant facts

Start: 4 wks before last frost
Plant out: 2 wks after last frost
Direct sow: 2 wks after last frost
Height: 12″
Width: 24 - 36″

Harvest facts

Days to harvest: 60 - 75 days
Harvest period: 12 - 20 weeks
Yield per sq ft: 1 - 2 lb
Yield per plant: 1 - 2 lb

Soil

pH 6.0 - 7.0

New Zealand Spinach grows best in the typical ideal garden soil, moisture retentive, well-drained and fertile. It is quite tolerant of saline and alkaline soils and grows wild along the coast of California (which is pretty close to its native habitat). It is quite drought tolerant, but prefers to grow in moist soil (on the coast near here you usually see it growing wild in damp spots).

Soil preparation: Incorporate 2″ of compost into the soil, as well as some fertilizer mix. If the soil is poor it may bolt quickly.

Planning

Where: In cool climates this plant needs full sun, but in warm weather it does better with light shade during the hottest part of the day. It is a low growing, sprawling plant and is independent enough to do well in wilder parts of the garden.

When: This is a warm weather crop and can't stand any frost. There is no point in starting it until all danger of frost has passed and the soil has warmed up to at least 60°F (usually at least 2 weeks after the last frost date). If you want to start it earlier you can warm the soil with cloches or plastic mulch (or start it inside).

Planting

The seeds are a little temperamental in their germination and may take 3 weeks to emerge. They are often soaked overnight prior to planting, to soften the skin.

Each "seed" is actually a capsule and contains several seeds. When all have germinated you should thin to the best one (or you could transplant the extra seedlings).

Transplants: If the growing season is short it should be started indoors about 4 weeks before the last frost date. Plant the seedlings out 2 weeks after the last frost.

Direct sowing: In hot climates it is easier sow the seed directly in the garden. Plant them ¼″ deep.

Spacing: Space the plants 12 - 18″ apart in the beds, or 12″ apart in rows 24 - 36″ apart.

Care

Watering: This succulent plant is quite drought tolerant, but you should always keep the soil moist. If it gets dry the quality of the leaves deteriorates and growth slows down drastically.

Mulch: This is useful while the plants are young, to suppress weeds and keep the soil moist and cool. As the plants mature they sprawl over the ground and form their own living mulch.

Pests: New Zealand spinach is considered pretty pest free and when I have grown this crop in other areas I had no trouble at all. However at my present garden quail have taken a liking to it and will strip off all of the succulent parts if given the opportunity. To prevent this I have to net them.

Harvesting

When: Don't start harvesting until the plant is about a foot tall and has enough vigor to tolerate cutting.

How: If you only harvest the growing tips the plant will regenerate quickly and can be harvested for months (this is the preferred method). You can also cut it down almost to the ground and (hopefully) it will sprout up again.

The plants is best used fresh, but can be kept in the fridge in a plastic bag for a few days. If you suddenly have a glut you can cook and freeze it like spinach.

Seed saving: This couldn't be simpler, just leave it alone and it will produce seed (you don't need to know any more). If you allow it to produce seed, it will often self-sow too.

Unusual growing ideas

Cuttings: In mild climates, where this succulent plant can be grown as a perennial, it is commonly propagated vegetatively from cuttings. These root very easily.

Wild garden: This plant is so independent it can be grown as a semi-wild plant. Use it in a sunny part of a forest garden (it doesn't really like shade), or any vacant spot. If it likes the conditions it will self-sow.

Ornamental use: The dark green triangular leaves make this quite an attractive plant and it can be used as a border or backdrop for ornamentals. It might also be used as a temporary groundcover.

Container growing: It does quite well as a container plant, though you need to keep it well watered for best flavor.

Varieties

I haven't seen any, but apparently there is one called Maori. Usually it is just plain old generic New Zealand spinach.

Kitchen use

I don't think the fleshy leaves are very good raw, though some people like them. They make a pretty good spinach substitute when cooked though. Use them in any recipe calling for cooked spinach.

Some people say you should blanch the leaves for 3 minutes and then cook them in fresh water to reduce their oxalic acid content.

Oat

Avena sativa

Introduction: This is one of the most useful grain crops for small scale growing. It contains very high quality protein, is fairly easy to grow and does well in cool climates.

Nutritional content: Oats are rich in high quality protein, dietary fiber, thiamin, folate, zinc, selenium, copper, iron, manganese, magnesium and various antioxidants.

Crop value: Oats are highly nutritious and grow in poorer soil and cooler conditions than most other grains. They aren't very productive for the amount of space they require though, so are only worth considering as a home garden crop if you have a lot of space.

Ease of growing: Oat is a fairly easy plant to grow, the difficulty comes (as with many grains) in converting it into food you can use. The naked seeded types are much easier in this regard, as they don't need processing to remove their tough seed coats.

Soil: Oats like a moist fertile soil. They don't need too much nitrogen as it can cause them to lodge (fall over). It does need to be fairly well drained though.

Planning

When: This very hardy plant doesn't mind the cold. It will just take advantage of the warmth whenever it comes.

Spring: Oats can be planted in spring (as early as possible) to be harvested in early summer.

Fall: It can also be planted in fall as an over-wintering crop, to be harvested in spring. If the climate is right, this usually works out better.

Spacing: People think of grasses as being spaced closely together, like a lawn, but most grains should actually be planted quite far apart. Space the plants 5″ apart in the beds, to allow for the fact that they send up several tillers (stems).

Planting:

Transplants: Start the seed indoors in flats, about 8 - 10 weeks before the last frost. When the plants are about 2″ high they are transplanted outside. They are quite hardy.

Direct sowing: If you have lots of seed it can be broadcast and then raked in to the soil (uncovered seed will get eaten by birds). If you don't have a lot of seed it should be sown in drills (shallow furrows.)

Care

Weeding: The wide spacing means that the young plants can't compete against weeds very well, so they should be kept well weeded.

Watering: Oats grow best with a steady supply of water, so don't allow the soil to dry out.

Pests: Few pests bother oats when it is growing on a small scale.

Harvesting

Harvest the plants before the seed is perfectly ripe and the stems have turned completely yellow. Bind the plants into bundles and store them in a dry place until they are completely ripe. When the seed is fully ripe it is somewhat crunchy. Thresh the seed from the plants by walking upon it on a hard floor. If you used a hull-less variety that is all you need to do.

Oats are quite high in fat and don't store as well as most other grains

Organic matter: The straw remaining after threshing is a good source of bedding for chickens (they will find and eat any remaining seeds). It is also a good source of carbonaceous material for the compost pile.

Seed saving: Just reserve some of the seed you have grown to eat.

Varieties

Hull-less oats (of the species *A. nuda*) have hulls that aren't well attached to the grain and so come off easily. The only drawback is that they are somewhat less productive.

Kitchen use

Oats are a very versatile food and can be used in a variety of ways. They can be ground to flour for baking, rolled and made into oatmeal, used for granola and much more.

Oat straw doesn't sound like a very exciting tea material, but oat straw tea is actually quite pleasant. It is not only drunk for pleasure though, it is a good source of calcium and magnesium (it is said to be beneficial for the bones and joints.) It is also a diuretic and is sometimes even used for anxiety.

Oca

Oxalis tuberosa

Introduction: In its native Andes the oca is second only to the potato in importance as a staple root vegetable. This is largely because it can be productive under more adverse growing conditions.

Unlike its compatriot the potato, oca has never been very well known outside its native range. This is somewhat surprising when you consider of its many virtues. I think it's time is coming though and that it is going to become much more popular as a garden crop in the near future. For some reason it is already quite widely grown in New Zealand and it is known as New Zealand yam in some places.

Oca is propagated vegetatively from tubers like the potato. These are absolutely beautiful, coming in different colors (red, yellow, pink, white, purple) and having a shiny, jewel-like quality.

Ease of growing: Oca is a rugged and independent plant; it tolerates poor soil and harsh climates, is fairly easy to grow and can be very productive. The only drawbacks are that it is day length sensitive and needs a fairly long growing season (see **Climate** below).

Climate: Oca is native to subtropical mountains and grows best with a long, relatively cool growing season (they don't like extreme heat).

Oca is day length sensitive, needing short days (less than 12 hours) to produce tubers, which means that it doesn't really start producing tubers until after the fall equinox. For this reason it does best in mild areas where fall frosts come late. It is well suited to my California garden, where it grows as a low maintenance perennial.

About Oca

Perennial
Hardiness zones: 7 - 11 (in colder areas tubers must be taken inside for the winter)
Growing temp: 55 (65 - 75) 95°F
Plant out: On last frost date
Days to harvest: 170 - 240
Yield per plant: 2 - 3 lb
Plant size:
Height: 12 - 18″
Width: 18 - 24″

If your garden gets early frost in September or October oca is unlikely to do well without protection (you can cover them to protect from light frost). Dedicated growers have grown them in poly tunnels, but of course this increases the amount of work required.

Crop value: Oca isn't anywhere near as productive as the potato, but is a pretty good substitute for it in the kitchen. As it is day length sensitive it will only produce tubers in fall, which means you can only get one crop a year. Newer varieties are less day length sensitive and lower in oxalic acid, which can only add to its appeal.

Nutritional content: The tubers are fairly nutritious, being high in carbohydrate, calcium, iron, phosphorus and vitamin A.

Oca also contains oxalic acid, which is considered bad because it can combine with calcium and prevent it getting absorbed by the body. However this is no more of a problem in oca than it is in spinach (which is not much of one).

Soil

pH 5.3 - 7.8

Oca is known for its ability to grow and produce well in poor soils (so long as they are well-drained). However it will be most productive in a fertile, sandy soil.

Soil preparation: For maximum productivity incorporate 2″ of compost into the top 8″ of soil. Also put a handful of an organic fertilizer mix in each planting hole.

Planning

When: Oca is really a fall crop, so there is no rush to get it into the ground in spring (unless your growing season is very short of course). Start planting around the last frost date. A hard frost will kill anything above ground (don't worry it will regrow), so wait until the last frost date (or later) before planting. If your growing season is short you can start them inside in 4″ pots and plant them outside a couple of weeks after the last frost date.

Where: Oca is commonly planted as an annual crop like the potato. If you live in a mild climate you can also give it a permanent home in the semi-wild or forest garden. It needs full sun.

Planting

This is an easy crop to get started as it is grown from tubers. Plant these 2″ deep and 24″ apart. If you intend to earth them up, this will be easier if you plant them in rows.

Starting indoors: If your growing season is short you can start the tubers in 4″ pots to save some time.

You might also start indoors if you have just bought some expensive tubers and don't have many (to ensure there are no mishaps).

Spacing: Space the plants 12 - 24″ apart (or even wider in some cases). The bigger the spacing the larger the plant will get (they can reach 24″ in height and 24″ in width). They start out fairly upright and compact, but eventually sprawl into a heap, with stems rooting where they touch the ground. Wider spacing tends to produce bigger plants which means more big tubers, which is good.

The plants don't need a lot of space for the first few months, so you might want to interplant something between them.

Care

Watering: Oca doesn't need a lot of water, but for best production the soil should be kept evenly moist. The plants produce a lot of foliage through the summer and the bigger they get the more tubers they will produce.

Oca will be more productive if you give it extra water when the tubers start to form (not too much though).

Weeding: Keep the young plants well weeded. Established plants can compete with weeds quite well.

Earthing up: If the plants are earthed up after 3 months, they will produce more tubers (this isn't absolutely necessary though).

Mulch: This is helpful to conserve moisture and suppress weeds, especially if you are growing your tubers in a wilder part of the garden. You can't easily mulch and hill up though, so must do one or the other.

Fertilizing: The plants will benefit from feeding in late summer when tuber start to form. You could either side dress with a fertilizer mix or feed with compost tea or liquid kelp.

Pests: I haven't noticed any insect pests or diseases (which is a nice change from the potato). However rodents will eat the stored tubers if given the chance.

Frost protection: The tubers start to develop quickly after the fall equinox and the longer they can keep growing after this time, the bigger the harvest. Protect them from early frost with anything you have (ideally fleece frost blankets, but cardboard or plastic sheet will also work). Keep protecting them for as long as you can, ideally until mid November or December.

Harvesting

When: The tubers don't start to develop until the day length drops below 12 hours, which may be anywhere from 4 - 6 months after planting.

After the tops have died down (or been killed) you wait a couple of weeks for the tubers to mature and then start to harvest. As a mountain crop it has evolved to deal with frost and the tubers continue to grow for a while after the tops are dead. If it gets seriously cold before this time and the soil threatens to freeze, then you will have to harvest the tubers, otherwise they may be damaged.

In mild climates you can simply leave the tubers in the ground and harvest as needed. Any you don't harvest will start to grow again the following year.

How: The tubers are found fairly close to the plant and are quite shallow, so are easily dug with a fork. Most are also pretty brightly colored and so easy to spot.

Storage: The best place to store the tubers is in the ground. In colder climates you should cover them with mulch to prevent the ground freezing. If it isn't practical to leave them in the ground, they can be stored like carrots, in a root cellar in damp sand or sawdust (or simply in slatted wooden boxes). They will keep in a plastic bag in the fridge for several weeks.

Unlike potatoes the tubers don't need to be kept in the dark, in fact if they are exposed to sunlight it reduces the amount of oxalic acid they contain and makes them less sour.

In their native Andes they are often dried for storage.

Seed saving: Oca produces perfect (have both male and female parts) 5 petalled yellow flowers. You don't need to worry about them though, as oca is usually propagated vegetatively.

You need to save some tubers for replanting, so don't eat them all. I usually eat the larger tubers and save the small ones for replanting.

Unusual growing ideas

Ornamental: The plants have attractive clover-like foliage and are pretty enough to be grown as an ornamental border. Though of course this border won't look so pretty when you dig it up.

Containers: Oca will grow well enough in containers filled with fertile soil mix, but they will need to be fairly big if you are going to get many tubers for your efforts.

They can also be grown in grow bags as described in **Potatoes**.

To save bed space some people grow then in containers for a while and plant them out when they start to get big.

Perennial: In a mild climate oca will grow quite happily as a perennial, you just have to leave it alone.

Varieties

Finding any oca tubers to plant isn't easy, finding named cultivars is even harder. The tubers come in a range of colors, but mostly pink, red, purple and yellow (or a mix thereof). Some newer varieties may be lower in oxalic acid.

Kitchen use

The root can be used in the same ways as the potato, though they don't need peeling and are easy to clean. They can be boiled, baked, roasted, fried and used in soups. Unlike the potato it is also quite good raw, being crisp and slightly tart. In Mexico they are eaten with salt, lemon and chile pepper. They can also be pickled.

In its native Andes they sometimes leave the tubers in sunlight to improve their flavor. Apparently this reduces the amount of oxalic acid they contain and increases their glucose content.

The growing tops are also edible and can be added to salads. However they should be used in moderation as they contain oxalic acid.

Okra

Abelmoschus esculentus
Syn *Hibiscus esculentus*

Introduction: This relative of cotton is often said to be native to Africa because of its popularity and the diversity of types grown there. However it may also have originated in southern Asia as it is widely used there too. It isn't found as a wild plant anywhere.

Nutritional content: Okra contains vitamin A, folate, calcium, phosphorus, potassium and around 140 calories per pound. The seeds are rich in protein and edible oil.

Ease of growing: Okra is a fairly easy plant to grow if it has a warm climate. If it is too cool it will only grow slowly and won't be very productive.

Climate: Okra is a true tropical plant and likes long warm days and warm nights. This is why it is most popular in the southeastern states. In my garden the days are warm enough, but the nights are too cool for it to be really happy.

Soil

pH 6.0 to 8.0

Okra is a vigorous and fairly greedy plant, so the soil should be rich in all nutrients. It should also be well-drained and have a fairly neutral pH (it doesn't like acid soil).

Soil preparation: Add organic matter in the form of 2″ of compost or aged manure. You might also add wood ashes to supply potassium and colloidal phosphate for phosphorus.

About Okra

Seed facts
Germ temp: 60 (70 - 95) 105°F
Germination time: 5 - 10 days
27 days / 59°F
17 days / 68°F
13 days / 77°F
7 days / 86°F * Optimum
6 days / 95°F
Seed viability: 4 - 5 yrs
Germination percentage: 50%+
Weeks to grow transplant: 5 - 7

Planning facts
Hardiness: Tender
Growing temp: 65 (70 - 85) 95°F
Plants per person: 3
Plants per sq ft: 1

Transplants:
Start: 2 - 3 weeks before last frost
Plant out: 4 weeks after last frost
Direct sow: 4 weeks after last frost
Days to harvest: 100 - 130 days
Height: 3 - 10 ft
Width: 12 - 36″

Harvest facts
Harvest period: 6 - 10 weeks
Yield per plant: 8 oz
Yield per sq ft: 8 oz

Planning

Where: Okra can get quite tall, so make sure it doesn't shade other crops. Most varieties only get to 4 or 5 feet, though some can reach 10 feet or more. The flowers and leaves are quite attractive, so it doesn't look out of place in the ornamental garden.

Because okra is planted so late, it can often go into the space previously occupied by an early crop, such as peas or fava beans.

When: This tropical plant thrives in heat and can't stand any cold whatsoever. It shouldn't be planted until all frost danger is past and the soil has warmed up to at least 60°F. If the growing season is short, you might use cloches or black plastic to warm the soil.

Planting

Sowing: Okra is easily raised from seed and grows quickly in good conditions. Some people soak the seed overnight before planting to speed germination in dry soil.

Transplants

Starting inside: If your growing season is short you should start okra inside to save time. It doesn't like root disturbance, so plant it in cell packs or soil blocks. Start the seed 2 - 3 weeks before the last frost date and plant out about a month later.

Direct sowing: In areas with a long growing seasons, okra is often direct sown. The soil should be warm before you plant (60°F minimum), as the seed will simply rot if planted in cold soil. Plant the seeds ½″ deep in heavy (or cool) soil, or 1″ deep in light (or warm) soil. Space the seeds 4 - 6″ apart, to be thinned to the desired spacing later.

Spacing:

Beds: Space the plants 12 - 18″ apart, depending upon the size of the variety.

Rows: Plan on spacing the plants 12 - 18″ apart (depending on the size of the variety), in rows 2 - 6 ft apart. Two rows work well in an average garden bed.

Care

Water: Okra must be kept well watered at all times if it to produce well. This is especially important in very hot weather.

Weeds: The young plants should be kept free of weeds. Older ones can look after themselves, especially if mulched.

Fertilization: Okra is a fairly hungry plant. If the soil isn't very rich, give it a liquid feed of compost tea, or liquid kelp every 2 - 3 weeks. It especially likes nitrogen.

Mulch: Once the soil is warm apply 3″ of mulch to keep the soil moist and keep down weeds.

Pruning: If the plants get too big, you can cut them down a bit. They will usually respond with vigorous new growth and start producing again.

Pests: In a warm climate okra may be attacked by aphids, leafminers, nematodes, stinkbugs and some caterpillars. Pests are less problematic when it is growing in cooler areas.

Diseases: Diseases include southern blight, fusarium wilt and various molds and fungi.

Harvesting

When: The flowers should appear about 60 days after planting, but cold weather, or lack of moisture, may cause them to drop off without being pollinated. The pods are ready about 5 days after the flowers are successfully pollinated. They are at their best while they are soft and small (2 - 3″ long) and snap easily. As they get bigger than this, they can start to get tough and are not so good.

Caution: Okra plants are covered in tiny spines and may cause skin irritation in some people.

How: The plants grow fast in warm weather and can produce a lot of pods. Pick the new pods conscientiously every day or two, as the more you pick, the more you get. If any pods mature on the plant, they may cause it to stop producing. Use them as soon as possible after harvest, as their flavor deteriorates quickly.

Seed: If the pods get over mature, you can always shell out the soft green seeds and use them like peas.

The dry seeds are rich in high quality protein and it has been suggested that they could be more valuable for their seeds than for the pods,

Storage: Fresh okra pods should be used within a day or two, as they deteriorate quickly. The simplest way to store them for any length of time is to freeze them.

The pods can also be dried for storage, though their flavor will be quite different from that of fresh plants (but still quite good).

Seed saving: Okra will self-pollinate if no other plants are growing nearby. However the flowers are very attractive to bees and if any other okra is growing nearby they will probably be cross-pollinated. For this reason you should only grow one variety at a time, or you must isolate the plants. The best way to do this is by bagging, which means covering the flower with a small muslin bag (you could also make bags from old pantyhose) to prevent any pollinating insects getting to it.

The whole process from flower to fully ripe seed takes about 5 weeks and may cause the plants to stop producing new pods. Some people forget about further food production about 6 weeks before the first fall frost date and allow their plants to start producing ripe seed.

To ensure genetic variability you should save the seed from at least 5 of your best plants.

The dry pods can be even more irritating than the green pods, so wear gloves and long sleeves when harvesting. Separate the seeds from the pods carefully and dry thoroughly before storage.

Unusual growing ideas:

Ornamental: Okra is attractive enough for the ornamental garden, and works well as an edible ornamental.

Varieties

Some of the old varieties were as much as 12 feet in height, but modern varieties tend to be much more compact. There are quite a few varieties out there, but most of them are quite hard to find (Southern Exposure Seed exchange is a good place to look).

Clemson Spineless - The commonest variety.

Cowhorn Okra - Has long pods with great flavor.

Hill Country Heirloom Red - An attractive variety with red pods.

Louisiana Green Velvet - A vigorous plant with smooth pods.

Perkins Mammoth - Can get very big. Not easy to find.

Red Burgundy - Has red pods.

Star of David - Unusual flavor.

Kitchen use

Okra is related to the mallows and has the same mucilaginous (slimy) quality that some people object to. You can minimize their sliminess by cooking them in a way that doesn't involve water

Okra is most popular in the southeastern states, where a traditional dish is fried okra.

Fried Okra

1 lb okra pods
1 egg
1 cup cornmeal
2 tbsp water
2 dashes hot sauce
Oil

Wash and trim the okra and cut into ½″ slices. Beat the egg and water in bowl, then add the okra, hot sauce and cornmeal. Roll around to coat all pieces and then sauté in a pan slowly so the okra dries out in cooking. If you want to make it more authentic it was traditionally deep fried.

Onion

Allium cepa

Introduction: The onion is one of the essential kitchen ingredients, that no cook can do without. It probably originated somewhere in central Asia, but has been cultivated by every major civilization from the Egyptians, Greeks and Romans onward. Its use as a flavoring has spread around the world and it is prized by people everywhere.

Apparently the word onion comes from the Latin unio meaning one, because it only produces one bulb, unlike the related garlic, shallot and potato onion.

Onions are biennial and spend their first year growing a nutrient filled bulb. In their second year they flower and set seed (and then die). When growing onions you have to be careful not to vernalize them, as this will cause them to flower in their first year (see **Bolting** below).

Ease of growing: The most important thing to remember about growing this biennial is that it is day length sensitive. It is programmed to produce bulbs when the appropriate day length arrives, no matter how big or small it is.

It is your job as a gardener to get the plants as big as possible before the onset of bulbing. To do this you must use a variety that is appropriate for the day length of your location. You should also plant them as early as possible, so they can put on the maximum amount of vegetative growth before they start to produce a bulb.

If you do everything at the right times, you will find onions are a pretty easy crop to grow.

About Onion

Seed facts

Germ temp: 50 (60 - 65) 85°F
Germ time: 7 - 28 days
136 days / 32°F
30 days / 41°F
13 days / 50°F
7 days / 59°F
5 days / 68°F * Optimum
4 days / 77°F
4 days / 86°F
13 days / 95°F
Seed viability: 1 - 4 years
Germination percentage: 70%+
Weeks to grow transplant: 10 - 12

Planning facts

Hardiness: Hardy
Growing temp: 55 (65 - 75) 80°F
Plants per person: 25
Plants per sq ft: 16

Transplants:

Start: 10 - 16 weeks before last frost
Plant out: 2 - 4 wks before last frost
Direct sow: 4 - 6 wks before last frost
Fall crop: Plant 6 - 12 before first fall frost

Harvest facts

Days to harvest:
Seed: 160 - 180 days
Sets/plants 90 - 120
Yield per plant: 4 oz
Yield per sq ft: 1 - 4 lb

Crop value: Though the onion isn't the most nutritious crop, it is so indispensable in the kitchen that it is one of the most important crops you can grow.

Nutritional content: Actually the nutritional value of onions shouldn't be underestimated, as they are eaten in quantity. The bulbs are a good source of vitamin C, potassium and calcium. They also contain a variety of beneficial phytochemicals, including diallyl sulfide, kaempferol and quercitin. They contain about 200 calories per pound.

The leaves are rich in vitamin A.

Climate: Onions grow best if it is cool (55 - 75°F) for all of their vegetative growth, but warm (70 - 80°F) and dry when they are bulbing up and ripening. They are very day length sensitive, so it is important to plant at the right time and choose the right variety for your latitude.

Soil

pH: 6.0 (6.8) 7. 5

Onions are not very efficient feeders because their roots are weak and shallow (they may only venture about 6″ from the plant). Consequently they need a loose, rich, moisture retentive soil with lots of organic matter. They don't like compacted, heavy, dry, acid, weedy, salty, or poorly drained soils. They are very sensitive to wet soils and their roots may rot if it is too wet (especially over the winter).

Onions don't require a lot of nutrients, but they aren't very efficient feeders, so they need to have plenty available. For example they only need about 150 pounds of nitrogen per acre, but you may have to add 300 pounds for them to get even that much.

Soil preparation: Prepare the soil by incorporating 2″ of compost, or aged manure, into the top 10″ of soil, which is where most of their feeder roots are to be found. For an early spring planting you could do this in fall, using fresh manure if necessary. Cultivate the soil deeply, remove stones and debris and make a nice seed bed. This encourages their weak roots to penetrate more deeply.

Onions don't need a lot of nitrogen, but they do like potassium (wood ashes or greensand) and phosphorus (colloidal phosphate), so add some to the soil if necessary. They also need plenty of micronutrients, so seaweed can be a big help.

If the pH is low then add lime, as they don't like acid soil.

Raised beds work very well for onions, as you can give them the perfect deep, well-drained soil.

A traditional method of growing onions is to dig a trench 6 - 8″ deep and 6 - 8″ wide and put a layer of fertilizer mix in the bottom. Mix compost (or aged manure) with the soil and put it back in the trench. You then plant into this.

You might also add a layer of phosphorus fertilizer 3″ down, to further improve their growth.

Planning

Bulbing: The onion bulb is a food storage organ comprised of layers of specialized leaves. Bulbing occurs when the plant stops producing new leaves and starts to store food in the base of the leaves. This causes them to swell and form the bulb. When the bulb is mature, all of the food has gone from the leaves to the bulb, so they wither, fall over and die.

Each of these leaves forms a layer of the onion bulb, so the more of these there are the bigger the bulb will get. A fully mature onion will ideally have 12 - 13 leaves when it starts to bulb up.

Day length: The main trigger of bulbing is day length; the plants will start to produce bulbs when they receive a certain number of hours of daylight (or more accurately hours of darkness). Different varieties require different day lengths, which is why we classify them as either short, intermediate or long day length.

Onion day length

Short day: Under 13 hours

Intermediate day: 13 - 14 hours

Long day: 14 hours or more

Very long day: 16 or more hours

A few varieties are day neutral

Generally short and intermediate day varieties are grown below 36 degrees latitude, while long day types are grown above this line (which is roughly from San Francisco to Washington DC.

If a long day variety is planted where the days are too short, it will grow well enough as a green onion, but will never produce a bulb. It can be used for green onions though.

If you plant a short day variety where the days get too long, it will bulb prematurely when it gets the day length it needs, so the bulbs won't get very big.

Temperature; This also affects bulbing: cool weather may slow it down slightly, while warm weather may hasten it.

Where: Onions prefer a warm, sunny site, protected from strong winds. It is important that the soil is well-drained, especially if they are to be in the ground over the winter.

Onions are vulnerable to weeds, so a very weedy site isn't good.

Crop rotation: Don't plant onions where any other Alliums have grown in the past 3 years.

When: It is important that bulb onions are fully grown when the appropriate day length arrives, so they will bulb up fully. You have several options as to what and when to plant, but remember the more time the plants have to grow, the bigger they will get and the bigger the bulbs they will produce. If the winter is cooperative this usually means planting in fall or early winter, If this isn't possible then you will plant in early spring.

If you don't plant onions early, they won't have time to produce large plants before bulbing starts and you will end up with small bulbs. Of course they may also grow slowly for some other reason (poor soil, root damage, pests) and they will only produce small bulbs too.

Spring: Spring planted onions must be started early if they are to grow large enough before long summer days trigger bulbing. This means putting sets or seedlings into the ground (or starting them inside) as early as January or February. They will put on vegetative growth steadily through spring and early summer and bulb up when the days get to be the right length. They need warm weather to ripen and cure the bulbs.

You can speed up early spring growth by growing them under tunnels or cloches.

Fall: One way to give the plants more time for vegetative growth is to start them in autumn (if the climate is suitable). Some varieties are specifically intended for over-wintering and these will work best.

Timing a fall planting is somewhat tricky because if the plants grow too big over the winter they will bolt when spring arrives (this is why sets and transplants don't usually work out well). On the other hand if you plant too late they may not survive the winter.

Fall crops are best grown from seed, planted 6 - 12 weeks before the first fall frost. The exact date will depend upon your growing conditions and you may have to experiment a bit to get it right.

Planting

You have three choices of planting method when growing onions; you can use seed, transplants or sets. All of these are fully hardy and can be planted as soon as the soil is workable in spring. When you first try growing onions it isn't a bad idea to try two different planting methods at the same time, to see which works best for you.

Seed

Growing your own onions from seed gives you the greatest choice of varieties. The problem is that they are quite slow, growing only half as fast as lettuce.

Onion seed is one of the shortest lived of all common vegetables, so it is important that it is fresh. Fresh seed germinates quickly (7 - 10 days) and grows more vigorously. It is most common to use the seed to grow transplants, but you could also direct sow it, or use it to grow your own sets

Direct sowing: This is slower than transplanting of course, but easier and can work well in some situations (especially if you have a long growing season).

This is considered the best way to plant onions in fall for a spring crop, as they are less likely to bolt than transplants or sets. Time your fall planting so the seedlings are well established before frost arrives. In cold areas, protect them with mulch over the winter.

Onions are very hardy and can be direct sown as soon as the ground can be worked in early spring. This may be 6 weeks before the last frost (the soil should ideally be 50°F).

You can either broadcast the seed, or sow in drills ¼ - ½″ deep. Keep the soil moist and free of crusting until all of the seed has germinated. It is usual to sow quite thickly and gradually thin it out to the desired spacing (you can eat the larger thinnings). Thinning is very important if you want to grow large bulbs, so don't neglect it.

Onion sets

These are small onion bulbs (⅜ - ¾″ in diameter) grown in crowded conditions, so as to induce premature bulbing. They are the easiest way to grow onions, as you don't have to worry about germination and are actually starting with a small bulb.

The problem with using sets is that there are very few varieties available. In fact often packages of sets often don't even say what type they are, other than yellow, red or white onions! Hopefully the sets sold in your area will at least be appropriate for your day length.

Buying sets: Every spring sets are available in every garden center, so they are probably the commonest way to grow onions. It is good to get and plant them as soon as they become available, if left too long they will eventually start to sprout in the bag.

Growing sets: This is easier than you might imagine and has the advantage in that you can grow whatever variety you want. Simply scatter the seed on a prepared bed in spring, ¼″ apart and cover with ¼ - ½″ of sifted soil / compost mix. Don't feed the plants and go lightly on the watering. Because they are growing so close together they will crowd and stunt each other, which is what you want When the tops turn brown, dig and dry the small bulbs for at least 10 days. Store them in the fridge or root cellar (below 40°F). Sets with a diameter of less than 1″ are the best, as they are less likely to bolt.

Planting sets: This is pretty straightforward, simply place them on the ground, with the right (pointed) side up, at the desired spacing (adjust if necessary). If the soil is very loose you can just push the sets down into the soil to the proper depth (they should be just barely visible) with your finger and close up the hole. If the soil is dense pushing on the bulb may damage it, in which case you should either loosen it with a fork beforehand, or poke a small hole for each bulb.

Some gardeners sort out their sets and use the small ones (dime size or smaller) for bulb onions and larger ones for scallions. This may seem counter intuitive, but the larger ones are more inclined to bolt.

You may have to protect the newly planted bed from birds (they sometimes pull the sets out of the ground) or cats (who use it as a litter box). To foil cats just cover the bed with a piece of wire mesh fencing until they are established.

Transplants

Using transplants gives you the largest onion bulbs and is generally considered the best way to grow onions.

Buying: Many people buy their transplants (either by mail order or from the garden center) in bundles of 50 - 80 plants. These work well, but are a little expensive, especially when you consider how easy it is to raise your own. They also have quite a big interruption in growth while they are in transit to your garden.

If you can't plant your bundles of transplants when you get them, keep them in a cool moist place for up to 2 weeks.

Growing transplants: Start the seeds about 8 - 12 weeks before planting out time. Remember the longer the plants grow before bulbing, the bigger the bulb can get. Onions don't mind transplanting (it may even encourage good root growth), so are usually planted in flats (or plant pots), ¼″ apart and ½″ deep (cover with a sifted soil / compost mix). You can grow a lot of plants in a small area.

The seeds will germinate much quicker if you put them in a warm place (75 - 80°F). Once they have germinated they should be moved to a cool place (60 - 70°F), as this gives you stockier, hardier plants.

If the stems are smaller than ¼″ diameter when you plant them out, you shouldn't have to worry about vernalization (see **Bolting** below). However you want them to be close to this size, so the bulbs will get bigger. If you don't plant them out until the weather has warmed up, you won't have to worry about this too much anyway.

Planting transplants: The seedlings can be transplanted out 2 weeks before the last frost date, but I prefer to wait a bit longer, to avoid the possibility of vernalization. Use only the largest, healthiest seedlings and plant them 1″ deep. Some people cut off part of the top and root before transplanting, claiming it encourages new root growth and vigorous recovery.

The transplants may take a week or so to recover from transplanting before they put on much growth. Keep the soil moist and feed them every 3 weeks or so to maximize growth.

Spacing: Onions don't like competition so spacing has a direct effect on the final size of the bulbs. A wider spacing results in larger bulbs, but of course you get less of them. For maximum production of food you should plant fairly closely. The individual bulbs may be fairly small, but you will get a lot more of them (often small bulbs are more convenient than large ones anyway). Close spacing can also result in faster maturation.

Of course the fertility of the soil also affects spacing. In rich soil you can put the plants closer together.

I like to plant onions in offset rows at a fairly wide spacing across the bed, so it's easier to weed them with a hoe. Some gardeners initially plant at half the final spacing and remove each alternate plant for use as green onions (if growing from seed you can afford to be extravagant).

Bed spacing:
Large bulbs: 4 - 5″ apart

Medium bulbs: 3 - 4″ apart

Pickling bulbs: 2 - 3″ apart

Green onions: 1 - 2″ apart

Row spacing: Put the plants 3 - 5″ apart, in rows 12″ - 15″ - 24″ apart (exact spacing depends upon variety and soil).

Care

You want onions to grow as fast as possible, so by the time the day length is right for bulbing, they will be have stored enough food to produce large bulbs. This means spacing them properly and giving them all the nutrients and water they need.

Weeds: Onions don't produce much foliage and don't get very big, so they can't shade out, or outgrow weeds as they mature. This means that competition from weeds can be a major problem, especially for direct sown crops. It is critical that they are weeded methodically, especially during their first two months in the ground.

You need to be careful when weeding, as their shallow roots are easily damaged by careless hoeing. As the plants get bigger, a mulch is helpful to keep weeds down.

Water: Though onions are quite drought tolerant, a lack of water makes the bulb smaller and more pungent. It can also make the plant liable to bulb prematurely, which also means smaller bulbs. For best flavor and largest bulbs, you should keep the soil moist at all times, so there is no interruption in growth.

Give your onions water in the form of frequent shallow watering (there's no point watering these shallow rooted plants very deeply). It is best to water in the morning, so the tops dry out quickly, as this reduces the potential for diseases such as downy mildew. Don't over-water though as too much water may result in bulbs that don't store well.

Stop watering the bulbs when they stop enlarging, as they need to be dry for curing. If the soil isn't dry enough the bulbs may start to put out new roots.

Thinning: It is important that the plants have enough room to grow without competition, so thin if necessary. Use the thinnings as green onions.

Frost protection: Use row covers to protect seed beds from hard frost, as this could damage them.

Fertilization: If your soil isn't very fertile and the plants aren't thriving, give them a feed of compost tea or liquid seaweed every 2 - 3 weeks. Alternatively you could side dress with a fertilizer mix every 4 weeks. Stop feeding when the bulb ceases to grow rapidly.

Mulch: The sparse foliage doesn't shade the soil very much, so a mulch is helpful to conserve soil moisture in dry weather. It will also help to keep down weeds. Mulch also insulates the soil, so don't apply it until the soil has warmed up.

Special problems

Bolting: Sometimes onions will bolt instead of bulbing, or bolt while bulbing. This usually happens because the plants were vernalized.

For a plant to be vernalized it must be at least ¼″ in diameter (smaller plants aren't usually affected) and must be exposed to temperatures below 50°F for two weeks. When warmer weather returns the plant thinks it has gone through a winter and so sets about following its destiny, which is to produce seed. This sometimes happens when there is a very late cold spell in spring.

This phenomenon means you must be careful when planting onions in fall or early spring. If they get too big (over ¼″ diameter) they may bolt when spring arrives.

If a plant bolts remove the whole flower stalk promptly. Don't just pinch off the flower, otherwise the plant will continue to waste energy on the remaining stem (which will swell up).

Bolting doesn't affect edibility, you can just remove the woody stem core when chopping the bulb. However it does mean the plant is wasting energy, so the bulb won't get as big as it could have. Bolted onions don't store as well, so should be used first.

Pests: Onions are relatively pest free, except for a couple of (not insignificant) insects.

Onion maggots: This small fly is found in the northern (above 40° latitude) United States and Canada. The larvae burrow into onion bulbs and seedlings, stunting or killing them, or causing them to rot in storage I have had no experience with them, but row covers are an effective solution

Onion thrips: These creatures suck juices from the plants. They survive the winter in weeds so keep the garden clean. Spanish onions are resistant.

Disease: Though the Alliums in general are rarely affected by pests, there are quite a few potential disease problems. Onion leaf blight and purple blotch are the most serious, especially in wet or humid weather (provide good air circulation).

Other diseases include fusarium rot, downy mildew, rust, smut, pink root, onion smudge and neck rot (I can't help thinking that the people who named these diseases didn't display much creativity).

Nutrient deficiency

Tip burn: A deficiency of potassium or manganese may cause the tips of older leaves to die back. Liquid kelp will supply both of these (as will compost of course).

Harvesting

When

Bulbs: For immediate eating you can start harvesting bulbs as soon as they are big enough to be worth using. However if you want to store the bulbs for any length of time, they must be fully mature.

When bulbing is complete the tops turn yellow and die back, as they have no more energy in them. Stop watering at this time, to allow the bulbs to dry out and cure.

Some gardeners knock over any remaining green leaves at this point, to hasten their drying. Don't do this prematurely though, wait until at least a half of the tops have fallen by themselves and take care not to bruise the bulb. Leave the bulbs for another week to die back fully.

How: Lift the bulbs with a fork and leave them in a dry place with good air circulation for a few days to dry.

Onion bulbs are fairly delicate, so handle them carefully at all times and don't throw them around. This is particularly important if you want to store them. Damaged or bruised bulbs will rot easily.

If it isn't too hot and sunny you can leave them outside, but if the sun is hot, you should move them into the shade, as they can be cooked by very strong sunlight.

If there is danger of rain or dew you should move them under cover, as you don't want them to get wet while they are drying!

Indoor drying is often done on screens or slatted shelves in a warm, dry, well ventilated place. You can also dry them on sheets of newspaper. After the tops have dried out completely, it is common to cut them off, leaving just 1″ on the bulb, but some people say they store better if the tops are left on. Obviously if you want to braid your onions you need the tops intact. Finally put the bulbs in a warm, dry place for 2 - 3 weeks, to cure fully.

Greens: You can harvest individual leaves from your bulbing onions at any time. Just don't take too many or it will affect bulb formation. Actually it is a better idea to leave the bulb onions alone and plant extra plants for scallions (use the largest sets, or the weakest looking plants). Even better is to plant some perennial welsh onions or Egyptian onions to supply green onions.

Storage: How long your onions will store depends upon what variety they are. The sweeter ones don't store well and must be used relatively quickly. The more pungent ones may keep for many months.

Before storing the bulbs, you should examine them carefully. The papery outer skin should be in good condition, there should be no bruising and the neck should be dry and papery. If the neck is still thick it didn't mature properly and won't store very well. Any bulbs that are less than perfect should be used first.

Store the bulbs in boxes or mesh bags (old panty hose works well). You can also make onion braids. Ideally keep them in a cool dry place at 32 - 50°F with 60% humidity.

Excessive moisture will encourage sprouting, so the fridge isn't a good place for them.

Large onions can be sliced and dried, small ones can be pickled.

Onion braids look great hanging in the kitchen, but it is too warm and dry to store them there for any length of time (they will dry out). You could make small braids and bring them into the kitchen as you need them.

If your onions start to rot in storage, it is usually either because they weren't cured properly or because of fungal infection.

Seed saving: Onions are cross-pollinated by insects, but this isn't usually a big problem as there are no close wild relatives and most people don't let their onions flower. They will cross with shallots, potato onions and welsh onions (even though the latter is a different species).

Onions are biennial and will flower in the spring of their second year. In mild climates you can leave the bulbs in the ground over the winter, but in cold climates you may have to store them inside and re-plant in spring.

Use the best onions you have for seed. Larger bulbs produce larger flowers (they sometimes get to 4 feet in height) and more (and perhaps healthier) seed.

Make sure the flower heads are thoroughly dry before collecting seed. When they are fully dry remove the seed from the head and dry it some more before storing. Onion seed doesn't remain viable for very long, 2 - 3 years is probably typical.

Unusual growing ideas

Interplanting: Onions are commonly interplanted with carrots, but do well with many crops.

Containers: Green onions are well suited to growing in containers and don't require much work. Bulb onions can be grown too, though they need a deeper container and you probably won't get a very big harvest.

Green onions: These are varieties of bulbing onion, sown in fall and harvested as scallions or green onions in spring (which is why they are sometimes known as spring onions). They can be planted very closely together, with as many as 30 plants per square foot.

Green onions can also be multi-planted, with up to 10 seeds in one soil block, or plug tray (in this way you can grow a bunch of green onions.

There are varieties specifically bred for this purpose (White Lisbon is one), or you can use any surplus onion sets.

Green onions may be hilled up with soil to increase the length of white stem.

If you grow a long day onion in a short day area, or vice versa, you may end up with green onions by accident.

Varieties

More than with most crops, the selection of the right onion variety for your location and purpose is extremely important. You must choose a variety that is suited to your day length.

I already mentioned how onion varieties are commonly classified according to the amount of daylight they require to produce bulbs. European varieties tend to be long day, because they come from more northerly latitudes. For some reason seed packets often don't contain day length information, which seems rather negligent.

Short day onions

These are grown in the south, up to 36° latitude and bulb when the day length is under 13 hours. If you plant them further north they tend to bulb prematurely.

In very mild climates it is common to plant them in fall to grow over the winter and bulb in spring.

Pungent - California early red, Ebenezer, Red Creole, White Creole

Sweet - Texas Early Grano, Texas super sweet, White Bermuda, Yellow Granex,

Intermediate day onions

These are grown from 34° - 38° N and bulb when the day length is 13 - 14 hours. Generally they don't store well.

Pungent - Stockton Red, Super Star, Australian Brown, Southport Yellow globe, Italian red, White Portugal.

Sweet - Candy, Red Candy Apple, Walla Walla,

Long day onions

These are grown in the north, above 36° N and bulb when the day length is more than 14 hours. They are often hard and pungent and generally store well.

Pungent - Ailsa Craig, Copra, Early yellow globe, Red Zeppelin, New York Early, Yellow globe danvers, Sweet Spanish, Cipollini.

Sweet - Walla Walla

Other types of bulb onions

Storage onions

These tend to have pungent flesh and thick skins.

Copra, F1, Ebenezer, Yellow Globe, Yellow Of Parma

Sweet onions

These have such a mild flavor they are often eaten raw. Their skins tend to be rather thin and they contain a lot of water, which means they don't keep very well. They are mostly short day types (but not all).

Yellow Granex F1, Walla Walla

Cipollini onions

These flat Italian onions have a fairly mild, sweet flavor and store for up to 5 months. If you grow them well they can get quite big. They are long day onions, though may do okay in intermediate areas too. They are often planted in fall to mature in spring.

Borettana
Red Cipollini

Japanese onions

These are simply Japanese varieties that have been bred for growing in mild climates. They are planted in late summer or fall and harvested the following summer, slightly before other bulb onions.

Senshyu Semi-Globe
Imai Early Yellow
Shonan

Kitchen use

Onions resemble garlic in that their pungent flavor only develops fully when cell walls are ruptured. If you bake a whole onion this will inactivate the enzymes and the flavor won't be anywhere near as strong.

Onion Bhaji

1 large onion
1 small hot pepper (de-seeded and chopped, the hotness is up to you)
4 oz chickpea flour (grow your own)
1 oz cilantro
¼ tsp chili powder
½ tsp turmeric
½ tsp baking powder
½ tsp ground cumin
Salt
Water
Vegetable oil

Mix all the dry ingredients together in a bowl, then add enough water to make a batter (this should have the consistency of whipping cream). Let it sit for 15 minutes. Cut the onion into ¼″ thick slices and coat them with the batter. Then fry in 350°F oil (it needs to be hot) first on one side until crisp and then turn over (you can also deep fry, but this takes more oil).

Drain well on kitchen paper and serve hot with mango chutney.

Onion, Welsh

Allium fistulosum

Introduction: This perennial onion has nothing to do with the country of Wales, it's name is thought to come from the German *welsche* meaning foreign. Though a relatively minor crop in Western countries, it is the most important type of onion in Asia and has been grown in China for thousands of years. It is also known as **Japanese Bunching Onion** because of this.

Welsh onion doesn't produce a swollen bulb, but tillers and sends up several stems.

Crop value: This is a very reliable and hardy crop plant and deserves a more prominent place in the vegetable garden. It has much the same cultural requirements as the bulb onion, but you don't have to worry about bulbing.

Ease of growing: Welsh onion is easy to grow and low maintenance. As a perennial it will come back every year and just be there, waiting for you to use it.

Climate: Welsh onions grow best at a cool 50 - 70°F. You don't need to worry about day length with these types, because they don't produce a bulb.

Soil
pH 6.5 to 7.5
As with other onions it has a shallow and not very vigorous root system, so needs to grow in rich, moist soil for best performance.

Planning

Where: The plants can tolerate some shade, so long as they get at least 4 hours of sunlight per day.

It is a good idea to plant quite a lot of this, so you can harvest occasionally from each individual without causing too much damage. With 12 - 16 plants per sq ft they don't take up much space.

The perennial clumping types can be planted in the ornamental, wild or forest garden.

When: This perennial plant can be harvested in spring and early summer, thus filling the gap between stored winter bulbs and the first summer crop.

Japanese bunching onions are usually grown as annuals. They are planted in autumn to mature early the following summer. In very harsh climates they can also be started indoors in very early spring (8 - 12 weeks before last frost), to mature in early summer. They can also be grown over the winter in a cold frame.

Planting

Welsh onions can be direct sown, but are more often started indoors (or in a nursery bed) and transplanted to their final position. Once you have a good stand, you can divide the clumps to multiply them.

Starting seedlings: In Asia these plants are not usually direct sown, but are started indoors or in a nursery bed. They transplant quite easily and in China they are sometimes transplanted several times, just to slow down their maturation.

Sow the seed ¼″ deep in flats, cell packs or soil blocks (you can multi-plant them, sowing several seeds per station). They germinate best at 60 to 65°F.

Direct sowing: This is pretty easy, just sow the seed where you want it.

Spacing: Space the seedlings 2 - 4″ apart.

Care

This is pretty much the same as for onion.

Mulch: In colder areas protect them over the winter with a thick mulch.

Division: Divide overcrowded colonies every couple of years, or when you want to start new colonies.

Pests: They are subject to the same problems as other onions, but to a lesser extent. When grown as a perennial there is a greater chance of pests building up in the soil, so be watchful.

Harvesting

Bunching onions can be eaten at several stages of growth. The very young plants can be thinned and eaten like chives. The green leaves can be eaten anytime, as can the thickened white bases (these are sometimes blanched to make them longer).

In loose soil you can harvest by simply pulling on the tops. If you do this in heavy soil, they will just break off. In this situation you must loosen the soil with a trowel before harvesting.

Seed saving: Just allow the plants to flower and set seed. Cross-pollination probably won't be a problem. Of course as they are a perennial you don't need to save seed at all.

Welsh onion is so closely related to the onion that it can cross-pollinate and many varieties are actually crosses of the two species (these are often sterile however.)

Unusual growing ideas:

Interplanting: Japanese bunching onions don't take up much space, so they are a good crop for interplanting between other crops.

Varieties:

Evergreen Bunching Onion - Tender, mild, a standard variety (70 days)

Franz - An old heirloom

Deep Purple - Base of onion is purple (60 days)

White spear - Heat resistant

Japanese bunching onions

The Asian varieties are generally more vigorous and refined than the European types, which isn't really surprising as they are much more important there.

There are attractive red and purple cultivars, varieties for cold winter growing and varieties for hot weather.

The Asian types don't form clumps as well as the Europeans, in fact they are usually grown as annuals. I value this crop as a perennial so I prefer the clumping types.

Japanese types:

Evergreen White Nebuka - A splitting (clump forming) type with slender white stems (60 days).

He-Shi-Ko - A standard (60 - 80 days).

Ishikura Improved - Stalks may get 20″ long x 1″ diameter (40 - 50 days).

Red Beard - A splitting type with red bases (40 - 50 days).

Onion, Egyptian

Allium cepa var *viviparum* (*proliferum* group)

This uncommon type of onion grows like a green onion, but then puts out a cluster of small bulbils instead of flowers. These in turn produce their own green onions and even more bulbils. Eventually the stem bends over and the bulbils touch the ground and take root. These then send up clusters of green shoots of their own. The plant is sometimes called the walking onion because this trait gives them the ability to move from their original location.

Egyptian onion is grown in the same ways as the other onions and likes the same conditions.

Ease of growing: I like the Egyptian onion because it is so easy to grow it is almost weed-like. Once established you can forget all about it, except for harvesting.

Climate: It will grow as a perennial in zones 5 - 9. In colder areas you could bring the bulbs indoors for the winter.

Planting: The plant is propagated vegetatively by means of the bulbs or bulbils, planted an inch deep and six inches apart. It grows in most soil types, so long as it gets full sun. I often plant entire bulb clusters in vacant spots around the garden. They grow into a whole new bunch of green onions.

Harvest: Don't over-harvest the leaves, or you may damage the plants, The way to avoid this is to have a large patch (or several small patches), so you can pick from each plant in turn and give the others time to recover.

Weeds: Like other onions they are vulnerable to weeds, so should be kept weeded (this is important because they are in the ground all of the time).

Mulch: This helps to suppress weeds, conserve moisture and keeps the soil cooler.

Harvest: The leaves, small bulbs and bulbils can be used at any time they are available.

Seed saving: This plant doesn't produce flowers or seed. It is propagated vegetatively from the bulbils that form instead.

Varieties:

Catawissa: This is said to be an unusually vigorous type.

Kitchen use: The whole plant is edible, basal bulbs, green stems and small bulbils (peel and eat raw or cooked). Of course if you eat the main bulb you kill that particular plant.

Orach

Atriplex hortensis

Introduction: Orach (pronounced or-ack) is native to Northern Europe and is notable for being one of the first plants ever cultivated in Europe (it was an old potherb even to the ancient Greeks and Romans). Also known as mountain spinach, it is a relative of amaranth and is used as a vegetable in the same ways.

Ease of growing: This plant is little changed from a wild plant and grows like one (which is another way of saying that it is usually easy to grow.

Crop value: Orach is a spinach substitute that requires very little work to grow. If you allow it to produce seed it will often volunteer and you won't even need to plant it.

Climate: Orach is a cool climate plant and does best as a spring or fall crop. It is somewhat heat tolerant though and doesn't bolt as easily as spinach. It can also tolerate some frost.

Nutritional value: Orach is a good source of vitamins A and C, as well as calcium, iron, phosphorus, magnesium and various phytonutrients. As far as I can determine it doesn't contain oxalic acid (don't quote me on this though, I could be wrong).

Soil:

pH 6.5 - 7.5

Orach does well on most soils, even quite alkaline ones. However for best results it should be grown in fertile, well-drained soil with lots of organic matter. It is very tolerant of saline soil.

About Orach

Germ temp: 50 - 65°F
Seed longevity: 3 - 5 yrs
Germ time: 5 - 10 days.
Sow out: 2 - 3 wks before last frost
Days to harvest: 40 - 50
Plant size:
Height: 4 - 6 ft
Width: 18 - 24″

Planning

When: This annual generally grows best as a spring or fall crop, though in milder areas it can be grown in winter too.

Where: In cool climates orach does best in full sun, but in hotter ones it prefers light shade. It is a good plant for growing in a wild or forest garden, as it is also very independent.

Orach can cast quite a bit of shade itself (it can grow to 6 feet or more) so don't plant it where it might shade sun loving neighbors.

Planting

Start your first plants in spring, 2 - 4 weeks before the average last frost date. Sow the seed directly into the garden ½ - 1″ deep and 2″ apart. When they are a couple of inches high they should be thinned to the required spacing. You can eat the thinnings, or transplant them to another spot (they transplant quite easily).

Succession sowing: In cool climates you can sow every 3 weeks or so, from March until August.

Spacing:
Beds: Space the plants 6 - 12″ apart.

Rows: Space the plants 6 - 12″ apart in the row, with 12 - 18″ between the rows.

Care

This is a pretty independent plant and doesn't need much attention.

Weeding: The young plants need weeding, but older ones can take care of themselves.

Water: Orach is quite drought tolerant, but needs moist soil if it is to produce an abundance of foliage.

Feed: An occasional liquid feed may help it to produce more plentiful and succulent growth.

Mulch: This helps to keep down weeds and conserve soil moisture.

Pruning: Pinch off the flowers as they appear unless you want to save seed. Regular picking encourages new growth and lengthens the harvest season.

Pests: They are relatively pest free, though aphids can be a problem (wash them off with a jet of water).

Harvesting

Start gathering the leaves and growing tips about six weeks after planting. Gathering the growing tips causes them to get bushier. Older leaves aren't as good as younger ones (they are best left on the plant), so you always want to encourage new growth.

Storage: Normally you simply harvest the leaves as you need them, but they will keep for a few days in a plastic bag in the fridge. For longer term storage you can freeze them like spinach.

Seed saving: Just allow them to flower and set seed. Your biggest concern is collecting it before it falls. Apparently the seed can live for up to 7 years, but I haven't had much luck with seed that wasn't fresh.

Orach will commonly self-seed if given the opportunity; I haven't grown it for several years and I still occasionally get volunteers appearing.

Unusual growing ideas

Ornamental use: This is quite an attractive plant and comes in red, purple, yellow or various shades of green. It is often used in edible landscaping.

Varieties

Purple – Quite ornamental, both in the garden and on the plate.

Red– Quite ornamental, both in the garden and on the plate.

Yellow – Some consider this the best tasting type.

Green – It comes in several shades of green.

Kitchen use

The leaves are usually cooked as a potherb and in soup (this was traditional in parts of Eastern Europe). The young leaves can also be eaten raw in salads.

Parsnip

Pastinaca sativa ssp *sativa*

Introduction: The parsnip has been an important crop since the time of the Romans. It was actually a staple root vegetable in Europe for centuries, until it was eventually displaced by the potato. It is still much more popular there than it is in North America and is a common sight in their vegetable gardens.

Crop value: The parsnip is a valuable crop for several reasons. It tastes good, is nutritious, is easy to store (simply leave it in the ground) and easy to grow. The main drawback is that it is slow growing and in the ground for quite a long time.

Ease of growing: Parsnip is an easy plant to grow, as once established it is capable of looking after itself. When I first started gardening and carrot used to give me problems, I never had any difficulty with parsnip.

Climate: The parsnip is a cool season crop, growing best at 60 - 65˚F. It grows well enough in warmer weather, but warm nights (above 65˚F) cause the plant to use the sugar it produces for further growth, rather than storing it in the root. Such roots won't be very sweet.

Parsnips are very hardy and can tolerate a considerable amount of frost, which actually improves their flavor by making them sweeter.

Nutritional content: The root contains carbohydrates, vitamin C, folate, calcium, manganese, potassium and lots of fiber. It is quite a good source of energy with 340 calories per pound.

About Parsnip

Seed facts
Germ temp: 35 (50 - 70) 85°F
Germination time: 10 - 21 days
172 days / 32°F
57 days / 41°F
27 days / 50°F
19 days / 59°F
14 days / 68°F * Optimum
15 days / 77°F
32 days / 86°F
Viability: 1 yr
Germination percentage: 60%+

Planning facts
Hardiness: Hardy
Growing temp: 40 (60 - 65) 75°F
Plants per person: 25
Plants per sq ft: 9
Direct sow
Spring: 2 wks before last frost
Fall: Sow mid summer
Days to harvest: 120 - 200 days

Harvest facts
Yield per plant: 2 - 16 oz
Yield per sq ft: 1 - 4 lb sq ft

Soil

pH 6.0 - 7.0

The ideal soil for parsnips is a fairly neutral, loose, well-drained, moderately rich loam. It should be deep because the roots may go down 2 feet and also fairly free of stones. They won't be very productive in poor soil.

Soil preparation: Incorporate 2 - 4″ of compost or aged manure into the top 12″ of soil. Don't use fresh manure, as too much nitrogen encourages foliage growth at the expense of the roots (it may also make the roots fork). Like most root crops they need lots of potassium (add greensand) and phosphorus (add colloidal phosphate or wood ashes), but relatively little nitrogen. Add lime if the soil is acidic.

If the soil is compacted, double digging is recommended, as it ensures the soil is loose and free of large stones. If it is really bad, you might consider growing the shorter varieties and planting in trenches filled with a special sifted topsoil / compost mix.

Parsnips are a good crop to plant after potatoes. They like the deeply dug soil and the previous heavy fertilization.

Planning

Where: Parsnips do better than most common crops in light shade, though they are more productive in full sun. They are in the ground for a long time, so should be located where they won't interfere with late garden operations, such as fall bed preparation.

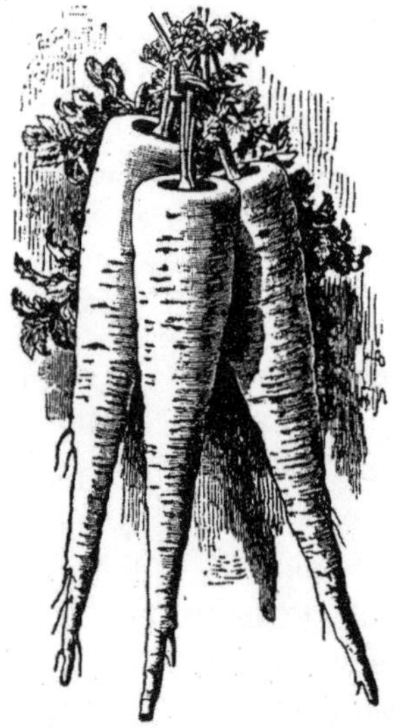

When: Parsnip planting should be timed so the plants mature in the cool weather of autumn. It is quite a long season crop (it can easily take four months to reach maturity) and when you plant it is largely determined by the length of your growing season.

Spring: In areas with a short growing season you plant it in spring for a fall harvest. You can sow the seed as early as 2 weeks before the last spring frost date, but unless there is a rush to get them in the ground, you may as well wait a few weeks until the soil has warmed up. If you look at the germination times you will see that it takes the seed almost 2 months to germinate at 40°F, but only a month at 50°F.

Fall: In areas with a longer growing season they are usually planted in midsummer, so as to mature around the time of the first fall frost. They can then sit in the ground until needed. Start thinking about planting them 4 months before the first fall frost.

Planting

Direct sowing: Parsnip seed is considered to be temperamental and you often read warnings against using seed that is more than one year old. I haven't had much difficulty in getting 2 year old seed to germinate, but for best results it is best to use fresh seed where possible. You should also plant lots of it (you may as well use the whole packet as it doesn't keep well anyway). It is better to sow slightly too thickly (and have to thin) than it is to risk not having enough plants.

The seed is quite slow to germinate, taking 2 weeks even at the optimal 68°F. It may not germinate very well if the soil is warm, which could be a problem if you are planting in midsummer. See **Lettuce** for more on persuading seed to germinate in cool weather.

The most critical aspect of sowing is depth, as the seedlings aren't very vigorous and must not be sown too deeply (¼″ is enough). Some people plant a few radishes along with the parsnips under the theory that the fast germinating radishes break up the soil surface, making it easier for the parsnips to emerge (they also mark the rows).

Broadcast sowing: Scatter the seed so there is an inch separating each one. Be careful of high winds blowing the light seeds as they are designed to be scattered by the wind. Also make sure you sow enough seed, because after you plant it might take a whole month before you realize your stand is too sparse. Cover the seed with a thin ¼ - ½″ layer of soil (or a mix of sifted topsoil and compost).

Row sowing: Sow the seed ½ - 1″ apart in shallow furrows Then re-fill the furrows with a thin layer of sand, or a mix of sifted topsoil and compost (ideally you want to plant them ¼″ deep.) You can also sow it in wide rows.

Water gently after sowing. Too much water, applied too quickly, may wash these light seeds around. This results in bare patches and very dense patches, which isn't good.

Spacing: The distance between plants largely determines how big they can get.

Beds: If you want very large roots space them 4 - 5″ apart in the beds. For average sized roots space them 3″ apart.

Rows: Space the plants 2 - 4″ apart in the row, with 18 - 24″ between the rows.

Thinning: If the plants are to grow quickly, without competition from neighboring plants, they must be properly thinned. As with carrots, this is one of the most crucial aspects of raising good parsnips.

When all of the seedlings are up and about 3″ tall, thin them to the desired spacing, taking out the weakest plants where possible. Don't wait too long to do this, as their roots and tops will soon get tangled.

Care

Weeds: The young plants don't compete with weeds very well, so must be weeded carefully. This should be done by hand, as hoes can easily damage the shoulders of the root. Older plants are able to compete against weeds pretty well, as they produce a dense canopy of foliage.

Watering: Parsnips need constant moisture (especially when the roots are sizing up), so don't let the soil get too dry. Give them at least 1″ of water per week.

Fertilization: If the soil isn't very fertile, give your plants a regular feed of compost tea or liquid seaweed every month.

Mulch: If growing in rows it is helpful to lay down mulch between the rows. It keeps the soil moist, suppresses weeds and covers the shoulders of the roots.

Pests: Parsnip can be affected by most of the pests that attack the related carrot, but it tends to be a pretty problem free crop and isn't usually badly affected.

Leaf Miners: The only pest I have encountered has been leafminers, but as we don't eat the leaves their damage is usually fairly inconsequential. If they get bad, you might want to use row covers.

Canker: This disease is commonest in poorly drained, acid soils and causes the root to rot. Most modern varieties have some resistance to it.

Harvesting

When: Parsnips generally take around 120 - 150 days to reach maturity. They can be dug any time they are large enough, but they are at their best from late autumn onwards, after the tops have died down and they have been exposed to several weeks of frost and cold weather. Low temperatures cause the starch in the root to be converted into sugar, which makes them sweeter.

Generally the roots are gathered after the foliage has died down and it's getting cold. As with carrots the young roots are the most tender, but they are not as sweet or tasty as older ones. You can continue to eat parsnips all winter until you run out, or until they start to grow again the following spring (which they do quite early).

How: If the soil is very loose, you can simply pull the roots up by the tops. If the soil is heavy they will just break off if you try this. You then have to loosen them with a fork before pulling. After harvesting you should remove the tops, to stop them draining moisture from the root.

Don't harvest any more roots than you can use in the next meal, as they store better in the ground. If you still have roots in the ground in late winter, you should dig them all, as they will turn woody and unpalatable once they start growing again.

Storage: Parsnips are one of the best crops for winter use. They are so hardy they can be stored in the ground all winter and dug as required. A thick mulch of straw can be used to prevent the ground from freezing so they are easier to dig (it may also protect the roots). In extremely cold areas they may be covered with 4 - 6″ inches of soil and then a layer of mulch put on top of this.

If mice are a problem you may have to lay down wire mesh before you apply the mulch.

The roots can be stored for several weeks in a plastic bag in the fridge.

For long term storage, treat them like carrots and store them in a root cellar, in damp sand or peat moss. Large quantities can also be stored in a clamp (see **Potato**). Smaller quantities may be sliced and frozen.

Seed saving: It's easier to save parsnip seed than most other biennials, because they are so hardy there is no problem getting them through the winter. You don't have to store the roots inside, or even protect them outside (though you might want to move them to a more convenient place).

Parsnips flower in the spring of their second year. They are cross-pollinated by insects, so you should grow only one variety at a time (or you could isolate them). They will also cross with wild parsnip, which is the naturalized wild form of this plant (it is common in some areas). Save seed from at least a half dozen plants to maintain some genetic diversity.

Gather the ripe seeds from the umbels in summer (don't wait too long or they may start to disperse) and dry thoroughly. They will need at least a month of after-ripening before they will germinate.

Unusual growing ideas

Intercrop: Parsnip is so slow to get started that it is common practice to plant a fast growing intercrop, such as lettuce or spinach, in between the newly sown rows. These will be harvested before the roots need the room.

Greens: The tender new leafy growth of second year plants is sometimes eaten in salads. Surplus roots are sometimes forced indoors to supply early spring greens.

Varieties

Some parsnip varieties can produce large, spindle shaped roots up to 18″ in length, with a diameter of 3″ at the top. These larger roots need a very deep and loose soil to perform well.

Most modern varieties are resistant to parsnip canker. The commonest varieties include:

All American
Cobham Improved
Improved Hollow Crown
Harris model

Kitchen use

Parsnips are best known for their use in winter stews and soups, but can be used in lots of other ways too. Try roasted parsnips, French-fried parsnips, stir-fried parsnips, steamed parsnips or baked parsnips.

Baking is particularly good as some of their starch will be converted into sugar and they become very sweet.

When sugar was expensive parsnips were sometimes used to sweeten cakes and to make desserts (and they still can). In Britain they have been used to make a surprisingly good wine.

Pea

Pisum sativum

Introduction: This crop originated somewhere in central Asia about 8000 years ago and is now cultivated all around the world. In their dry state peas are a highly nutritious, protein rich food and were once a staple food of Northern European peasants. However for modern gardeners peas are more popular in their green stage and increasingly as edible pods.

Peas are members of the *Fabaceae* and share the most important characteristic of many members of that family. They have a symbiotic relationship with nitrogen fixing bacteria that live in nodules on their roots. This makes them important for organic growers, because they can add nitrogen to the soil, rather than taking it out.

It is important to understand that the pea plants themselves don't fix nitrogen, they simply play host to nitrogen fixing bacteria. If this bacteria isn't present in the soil then the growing plants will take nitrogen from the soil, just like any other plant. See **Inoculation** below for more on this.

If you are growing dry peas any nitrogen that is fixed may be converted into protein rich peas, rather than entering the soil.

Crop value: Dry peas are one of the best cool weather sources of high protein food for the home garden. Home grown green shell peas are one of the taste highlights of the spring garden. The plants can be very productive, especially when growing edible pods varieties. The growing leafy shoots and flowers are also edible.

Peas are all the more valuable for their ability to enrich the soil with nitrogen.

As a cool weather spring crop they can be out of the ground by June, leaving plenty of time for a warm weather crop to succeed them.

About Peas

Seed facts

Germ temp: 40 (60 - 75) 85
Germination time: 6 - 17 days
36 days / 41°F
14 days / 50°F
9 days / 59°F
8 days / 68°F
6 days / 77°F * Optimum
6 days / 86°F
Germination percentage: 80%+
Viability: 3 years
Weeks to grow transplant: 4

Planning facts

Hardiness: Hardy
Growing temp: 55 (60 - 65) 70°F
Plants per person: 50
Plants per sq ft: 8

Planting facts:

Start: 8 wks before last frost
Plant out: 4 wks before last frost
Direct sow: 4 - 6 wks before last frost
Fall crop: 8 - 12 wks before first frost
Succession sow: every 2 - 4 wks

Harvest facts

Days to harvest: 55 - 120 days
Harvest period: 4 - 6 weeks
Yield per plant: 2 oz
Yield per sq ft: 1 lb

Nutritional content: Green peas contain vitamins C and B6, along with folate, iron and several anticancer phytochemicals. They contain around 350 calories per pound.

Dry peas are high in protein and contain over 1500 calories per pound.

Ease of growing: I have always found pea to be one of the easiest and most foolproof crops (so long as they are protected from birds). The only time they didn't do well for me was when I planted late and it got hot early. Even then they did okay, but the harvest period was very short.

Climate: Peas are very much cool weather plants, growing best at a temperature of 60 - 70°F. The flowers don't usually set pods above 80°F, so high temperatures severely affect production.

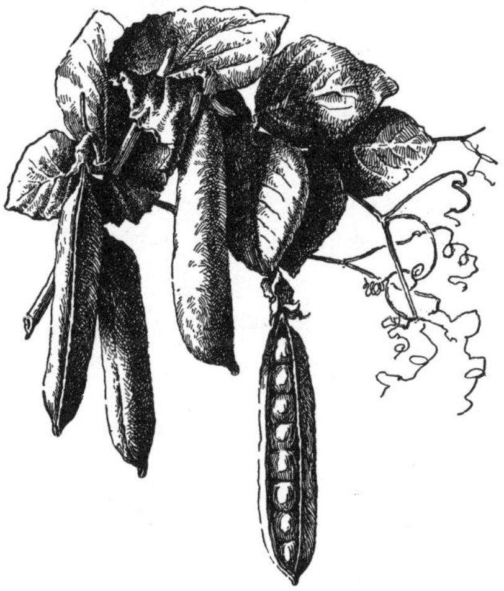

Soil

pH 5.5 (6.0 - 6.5) 7.5

The best soil for peas is a loose well-drained loam. If the soil is compacted then double digging is beneficial. If it is poorly drained, use raised beds, especially for early plantings, as they don't like wet soil. In very poor soils it may pay to plant your peas in trenches, filled with a mixture of soil and compost.

Peas don't need a soil that is high in nitrogen, as they can obtain their own. In fact if nitrogen is too easily available they won't bother to fix any. They do need phosphorus (colloidal phosphate) and potassium (wood ashes), as well as calcium and magnesium (use dolomitic limestone). You can also supply all of these with an organic fertilizer mix.

Soil preparation: Dig in 2″ of compost or aged manure (it can be fresh if applied in fall), as well as colloidal phosphate and greensand.

Peas are one of the first crops to be planted in spring, so many gardeners prepare the soil the previous autumn and cover it with mulch. This must be removed several weeks before planting, to allow the soil to warm up.

Planning

Where: Peas need full sun and lots of room for good growth. The climbing habit of the pole varieties can be an advantage, as it keeps them up off the ground and so saves garden space. However it also makes the plants vulnerable to high winds, so they should be planted in a sheltered spot.

When: Peas are cool weather plants, hardy down to 20° (28°F when flowering). They prefer mild growing temperatures (60 - 75°F) and don't usually set pods above 80°F. In areas with hot summers they are grown as a spring or fall crop. Unlike most cool weather crops they usually do better when planted in spring.

Spring: It is important to plant your crop early enough, so that it has sufficient time to mature before hot weather sets in. Normally the first peas are planted 4 - 6 weeks before the last frost date. The exact date depends upon the soil temperature, it should be at least 40°F and preferably 60°F. If it is too cold they may rot before they germinate (or be eaten by rodents or birds). Some gardeners plant their first peas even earlier than this, but run the risk of their being killed or injured by frost. When this works out you get very early peas, so it is often worth the risk.

You can make earlier crops less risky by warming the soil with black plastic or cloches two weeks before planting. You can leave the cloches on after planting to protect and warm the young plants (which speeds up growth).

Summer: In cool climates you can grow peas right through the summer (they aren't affected by day length). This won't work in warmer climates though, as they don't like heat.

Fall: Plant a fall crop 8 - 12 weeks before the first fall frost, so it matures in cool weather.

The seed may be sown in autumn for an early spring crop, though there is some risk that the seed may rot over the winter.

Succession sowing: In cool climates you can succession sow every 3 weeks, until the weather warms up. This doesn't work so well in warmer climates as later sowings often catch up with the earlier ones. In such cases a better solution is to plant several varieties with different maturation times.

Support

Just as with beans there are both bush and pole varieties of peas. Unlike beans however, even the bush types may do better with some support and repay the extra work with a larger harvest.

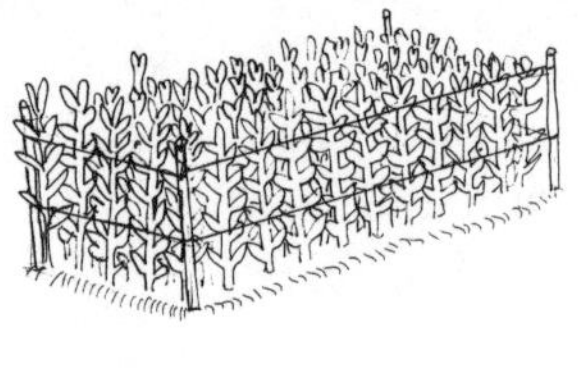

Climbing peas that don't have anything to climb will be very unhappy as they struggle along the ground and will rarely produce well,

Install any support structure before you plant the seeds. Once they have germinated it takes considerable finesse to install it without damaging the young plants.

Whatever type of support you use should be tall enough that your plants don't outgrow it and flop about. If they threaten to get too tall you can pinch out the growing tops (these are edible and very good). It should also be strong enough to bear the weight. The tangled full size vines and their load of peas can weigh quite a lot, especially when they get wet. A strong wind can cause additional stress.

Peas climb by means of slender tendrils and need a thin structure to grab on to; they can't grow up thick poles. This means they need a different kind of support from beans. A pea tendril will take about an hour to curl around a slender twig.

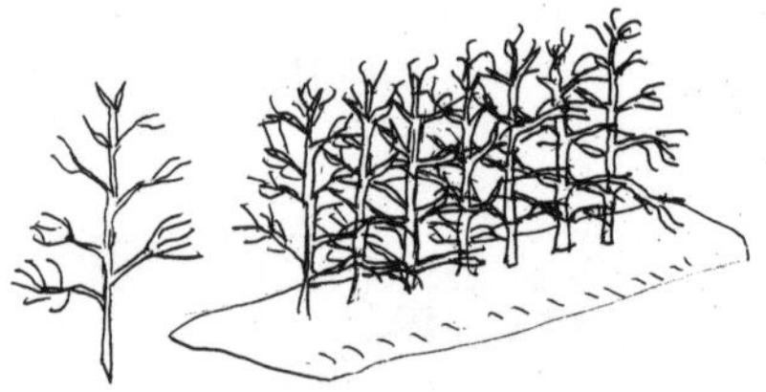

In England peas were traditionally supported with tall branches of hazel shrubs (though any brushwood will work). These were trimmed to a flat 2 dimensional plane so they could be placed close together in a row You just stick the butt ends firmly into the ground.

You can buy plastic netting that is specifically intended for use as plant trellis, but I find old wire fencing is more durable and easier to work with. It can be fastened to a trellis or shaped into a self-supporting cage.

If you are creative, you can rig up something from poles and string or netting. You might then use it a second time for a following crop of cucumbers or melons.

Ordinary tomato cages (which aren't needed so early in the season) can work to support bush peas, but aren't tall enough for the vining types. If you make your own 6 ft tall tomato cages out of hog wire these will work for the vines. These also look quite ornamental when covered in foliage.

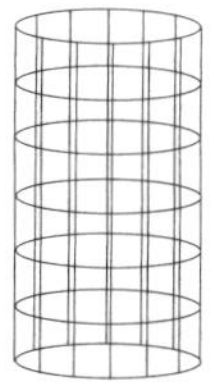

If you intend to grow a lot of pole types, probably the easiest field scale support consists of 8 of 10 ft metal T posts, with a ¼″ nylon rope along the top with horticultural netting (or wire fence netting) wired to it.

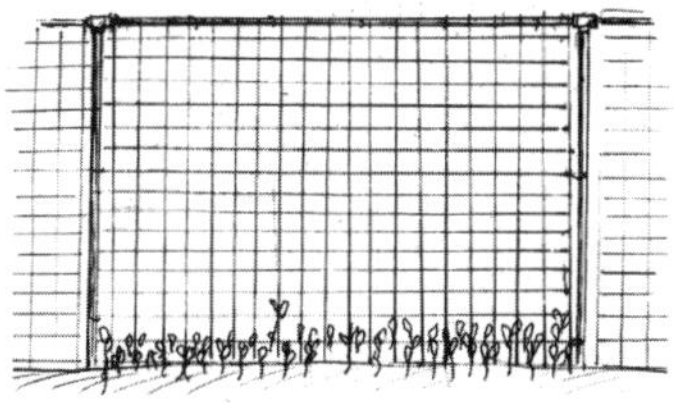

Planting

Inoculation: The nitrogen-fixing bacteria that live in nodules in pea roots can survive in the soil for 3 - 5 years. If you haven't grown peas within that time, you should inoculate your seeds with a commercial inoculant. This can make a big difference to the amount of nitrogen that is fixed. This in turn may increase the yield of pods by as much as 75%. See **Beans** for more on seed inoculation.

Protection: In my experience spring peas are irresistibly attractive to birds and if you don't protect a planting it will be severely damaged. This means covering the bed with bird netting until the plants are growing well. Don't put the netting too close to the plants, otherwise they will quickly get entangled, making it hard to remove.

Transplants

Starting inside: Peas are traditionally direct sown because they are hardy and dislike transplanting. However starting them indoors does have its advantages. It allows you to get a very early start on the season, which can help you to get an early harvest. Perhaps more importantly it is easier to protect the germinating seeds indoors, so you lose less to rodents and birds.

Peas don't like transplanting, so to minimize root disturbance they must be started in individual containers such as cell packs, or soil blocks. Start them about 3 - 4 weeks before planting out and don't forget to inoculate them.

Don't keep them indoors any longer than necessary, or they will suffer.

Hardening off: If you are putting your plants out early into a cold garden it is important to harden them off properly. You do this by putting the plants outside for 2 hours on the first day, then 4 hours on the second day. Add 2 hours every day for a week. A simpler alternative is to put them in a cold frame, which is opened for longer periods each day and closed at night.

Planting out: This is pretty straightforward, just be careful not to disturb their roots while doing it.

Direct sowing:

Pea seeds will germinate over a wide temperature range, but do so much faster in warm soil. At 40°F they may take over a month to germinate (if they don't rot, or get eaten in the meantime). At 70°F they may take only a week.

If the soil is dry you can speed up germination by pre-soaking the seeds for 4 hours before sowing. The best way to do this is to put them between moist paper towels. Soaking them in a bowl of water can cause them to absorb water too rapidly and may actually injure them.

You can also pre-germinate the seeds to improve emergence in cold soils. Sprout the seeds on paper towels in a warm place and plant them out as soon as the roots start to appear (don't wait too long).

Don't forget to erect your supporting structure before you plant your seed, so you don't disturb the young plants later.

Peas are commonly planted in rows, as this simplifies the task of supporting them. The traditional way to do this is to make furrows, as deep (usually 1″) and as far apart as required. Put the seed in the furrow at the required spacing and re-fill it with soil. Peas seed is quite vigorous and is not usually bothered by crusting. It's a good idea to sow a few extra seeds at the end of a row, so you have extra plants to fill in any gaps.

Bush peas can be planted at equidistant spacing right across the bed. Just lay out the seeds on the surface at the required spacing. When you are happy with this, push the seeds down to the proper depth with your finger.

When the soil is cold in early spring, plant your peas 1″ deep (it will be too cold down at 3″). Later plantings in warmer soil can go 2 - 3″ deep (where it is cooler and more evenly moist).

If the soil isn't moist you need to water straight after planting.

Spacing: This depends upon whether you are using bush or pole varieties.

Bush varieties: These short varieties don't need much support, so are commonly planted in offset rows across the beds 4 - 6″ apart each way.

You can also plant them in rows down the bed. Put the seeds 2 - 3″ apart in the rows, with 24″ in between the rows.

Pole varieties: Pole varieties are usually grown in rows because it is easier to support them. They are best planted in double offset rows, with 2 - 3″ between the plants and 6″ between the rows. You can get two of these double rows in a 5-foot wide bed (space them 24 - 30″ apart).

Care

Weeds: Weed the young plants carefully (preferably by hand), to avoid damaging their shallow roots. Older plants are usually vigorous enough to overwhelm most weeds.

Mulch: This is helpful to keep down weeds, keep the soil cool and conserve soil moisture.

Water: Peas need constantly moist soil, but water is particularly important when they start to produce pods. If you allow the plants to get dry during this time the harvest will decrease dramatically.

In cool spring weather peas usually get enough water from rainfall so that you don't have to irrigate. Watering at this time may encourage mildew and can actually reduce yields.

If the soil is dry by the time the flowers appear, you should give them extra water. This improves the set of pods and hastens their maturation.

Feed: Generally peas don't need additional feeding, though if the soil is very poor the young plants might benefit from a feed of compost tea or liquid kelp.

Pests: Quite a few pests may attack peas, including aphids, tarnished plant bugs, cutworms, mites, leafminers, leafhoppers, cucumber beetles, pea weevils and various caterpillars

Diseases: These include fusarium wilt, mosaic virus, blight, downy mildew, powdery mildew and pea enation virus.

Mice and birds: These can be major pests and have been known to systematically eat whole plantings (birds break off the new sprouts, mice eat the seed in the ground). If mice are a problem there are repellent seed coatings available (kerosene was once commonly used). Netting can keep the plants safe from birds, but it's a real pain to deal with.

Slugs and snails: These are mostly a pest of unsupported plants. They don't really like peas very much, but will eat them if there's nothing better available.

Deer, rabbit, groundhog: All of these animals enjoy the young plants and must be kept out with fences or dogs.

Harvesting

Peas mature quickly after pollination, so you have to check on the plants regularly (every day or so). This is particularly important as the weather warms up and they develop rapidly.

You must pick the pods when they size up, even if you don't want to eat them, otherwise production will decline. In cool weather, a well managed planting may yield for as long as 6 weeks, though if the weather turns hot it may be as short as 2 weeks.

I find a lot of peas get eaten in the garden, no matter what type they are.

Shell peas: Fresh green shell peas seem to have disappeared from the diet of most Americans as too much trouble. This is unfortunate as fresh peas in their prime are one of the great treats of the spring garden.

When: Picking peas at the right time is almost as important as it is with sweet corn. Too early and they are very small, too late and they are starchy and not very good. To determine the best time just taste them at different stages and decide which is best.

The peas will be ready to eat 3 - 4 weeks after blooming. They should be just about full size in the pod (each pod contains 4 - 10 peas) and should be very sweet (taste them). When they over-mature the pod turns leathery and the peas become starchy.

How: The pods start to ripen at the base of the plant first. Remove them from the plants carefully, so you don't damage the vines. This is usually a two handed job, you hold the plant with one hand and pull down on the pod with the other.

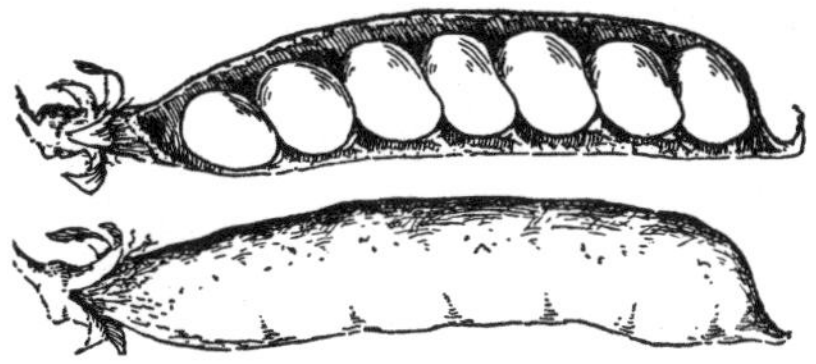

Snap peas: These should be picked as soon as the peas reach full size and the pod is nice and fat and round. Taste them to see if they are ready, they should be sweet, crisp and succulent.

If the pods have a string down each side, the best technique is to snap off the pod by bending it to one side. This breaks the pod but not the strings, so if you then pull on the pod, it will peel off the strings and leave them attached to the plant.

Snow peas: These should be picked after the pods have reached full size, but before the peas inside start to swell. Don't make the common mistake of harvesting smaller pods in the belief they will be better. They may be tender but they won't be very sweet.

Dry peas: To get dry peas simply allow the pods to ripen and dry fully on the vines. You can gather small quantities of pods individually, but for larger harvests pick the whole plants and lay them on a tarp to dry. Carefully thresh out the seeds to free them from the pods and dry them thoroughly.

A dry pea should shatter when crushed. If you can make a mark with your fingernail it isn't dry enough. An easy way to see if they are dry enough is to put a few in a closed jar for a few days. If condensation forms on the inside of the jar, they are still too moist.

Storage: The sugar in shell and snap peas begins to turn to starch soon after harvesting, so they don't store well. For this reason they should be used promptly for best flavor. If you have to store them, put them in the fridge in a plastic bag for up to 2 weeks. The best way to store them for any length of time is to freeze them.

You can store properly dry peas in any cool dry place.

After harvest: Cut the plants down to ground level, leaving the nodulated roots in the ground to rot. You can compost the tops, or just dig them into the soil.

Seed saving: Peas are one of the easiest crops to save seed from. They are self-pollinating, though a small amount of insect pollination may also occur. Ideally you will have only one variety flowering at a time. You can also isolate flowering varieties by at least 150 feet.

In dry weather all you have to do is leave the pods to mature and dry on the vine. In wet weather you may have to cut the vines and dry them under cover. When the pods are crisp and brown remove the seeds. These should be dried further and stored in a cool dry place.

Unusual growing ideas

Green Manure: Bush peas are a very good cool weather green manure crop for soil enrichment. This will also give you more edible leafy tips than you could ever eat.

Pea greens: Peas can also be grown specifically for their leafy green tips, which are very good.

You can start harvesting the first growing tips when the plants are about 12″ tall. This will cause them to branch out and get bushier. Keep on harvesting the new tips as they are produced. They are best used immediately after picking.

Varieties

The cheapest place to buy pea seed is at an agricultural supply store, where you can buy them in bulk by the pound.

Bush peas start to bear earlier than the pole types, but the latter give a more abundant and longer harvest. Many gardeners plant both types to get the best of both worlds.

Peas can be separated into several quite distinct group, depending upon their purpose.

Garden Peas: These seeds are wrinkled when dry because they contain more sugar and less starch (like sweet corn). They are intended for use as green fresh shell peas, but can also be used as somewhat inferior dried peas. There are early, mid-season and late varieties.

Bush types: These are bred to grow without staking and to produce a lot of pods in a short Time, which are useful traits for commercial growers. They also tend to be earlier. Most new pea varieties are bush types.

Green Arrow - Fine flavor (68 days).

Laxtons Progress - Old British heirloom (63 days)

Little marvel - Small productive plants (65 days).

Pole types: These are better suited to home growing as they produce over a longer period. They do need supporting however.

Alderman - Very tall, fine flavor (78 days).

Champion of England - To 10 ft tall and very productive (60 - 75 days).

Petit pois: As the name suggests these originated in France and are the 'gourmet pea'. They are green shell peas, harvested when still very small and sweet. As you might expect from a French food they are superior in flavor and texture to other types.

Sweet Provence - High quality (65 days).

Waverex - Very sweet, bush type (65 days).

Sugar peas: These originated in China and are the original edible podded peas.

Oregon Giant - Large pods, mildew resistant bush (70 days).

Oregon Sugar Pod II - Productive and adaptable bush type (68 days).

Snap Peas: A more recently developed edible-podded pea, this one originated in America. The pod is thicker and more succulent than that of the snow pea. These are probably now the most popular home garden pea varieties, because there is no work in shelling and very little waste.

Super Sugar Snap - The best known variety. A mildew resistant vine (60 days).

Amish Snap - I once read an article in Organic Gardening magazine about how the original Sugar Snap pea was painstakingly developed. They could have just started with this old heirloom, as it is almost identical (60 - 70 days).

Magnolia Blossom Snap - Purple flowers and extra tendrils, tall vine.

Soup or Field Peas: These varieties are hardier than the garden peas and are starchy, rather than sweet. They are grown as protein rich dry peas for use in soups.

Alaska - Can be eaten as shell peas too (56 days).

Blue Pod - Dutch heirloom vine (85 days)

Early peas:

Sugar bon

Burpeana early

Maestro - Bush

Little marvel

Sugar daddy

Mid season peas:

Cascadia - Bush

Mammoth melting sugar

Oregon Giant

Oregon sugar pod II

Lincoln

Super snappy

Late peas:

Green arrow - Bush

Wando - Bush

Alderman - Pole

Snowflake

Kitchen use

Green shell peas, snow peas and snap peas are all excellent raw, steamed or stir-fried.

Tender pea greens (the leafy tips of the plants) can be eaten raw in salads, or sauteed in olive oil with onion.

The flowers can be added to salads
.

Pea recipe

My family prefer snap peas raw, rather than cooked. This simple recipe is good though.

1 lb snap peas
3 tbsp olive oil
1 clove garlic minced
⅛ cup soy sauce
¼ tsp sesame oil
1 tbsp tahini

Remove ends of pea pods and spread them on a baking tray pan. Mix garlic into oil and pour over the pods. Broil in oven for 5 minutes until cooked. Mix the soy sauce, sesame oil and tahini to make a sauce to pour over the cooked pods.

Peanut

Arachis hypogaea

Introduction: Apparently also known as goobers, though I have never heard anyone actually call them that (except in magazines attempting to be folksy). The peanut is native to South America and has been cultivated for over 5000 years. It is an important crop in India, China, West Africa and the United States.

The seeds of the peanut are produced underground in the familiar leathery seedpods and are not really nuts at all.

Ease of growing: Peanut isn't a difficult crop to grow if you have a suitably warm growing season. If you don't, you might be able to get it to grow with a little pampering and persuasion, but you probably won't get a very big harvest.

> **About Peanut**
>
> **Transplants**:
> Start 4 weeks before last frost
> Germination temp: 70 - 95°F
> Plant out: 2 weeks after last frost
> Direct sow: 2 weeks after the last frost date.
> Growing temp: 60 (85) 95°F
> Minimum night temp 60°F
> Days to harvest:
> 90 - 100 days green
> 110 - 140 days dry
> Yield per plant: ¼ - 1 ½ oz

Crop value: Peanuts are potentially an important crop for those seeking greater self-sufficiency because they are high in protein and fat (two nutrients lacking in many vegetables). Of course they are only of value if you have the right climate for reliably growing them in quantity.

You will need quite a bit of space to make growing peanuts worthwhile. Their productivity per square foot is about the same as dry beans.

Nutritional content: We all know peanuts are very rich in protein and fat (48g per 100g). They are also a good source of niacin, thiamin, pantothenic acid, folate, magnesium, phosphorus and zinc.

Their high fat and protein content makes peanuts a great source of energy. They contain around 2500 calories per pound!

Climate: The peanut is a tropical plant and likes hot sunny weather (it grows best at 80 - 95°F). It doesn't like cold weather and even night temperatures should be a minimum of 60°F (and preferably much higher).

Soil

pH 5.5 - 6.5

Peanuts prefer a light well-drained soil. It doesn't need to be very rich in nitrogen as the plant plays host to nitrogen fixing bacteria, but it should contain plenty of calcium.

They don't like heavy or compacted soils (the flowers and pods can't penetrate them easily).

Planning

When: This South American plant likes a long hot growing season and does best in warmer areas. However it can be grown in cooler northern areas if you have the right microclimate.

Don't plant peanuts until the soil has warmed up to at least 60°F (you can use black plastic or cloches to speed this up).

Where: Peanut is very much a warm weather crop and must be planted in a warm and sunny spot.

Inoculation: If you haven't grown this crop before, it will fix more nitrogen if inoculated with a suitable strain of nitrogen-fixing bacteria. See **Beans** for how to inoculate.

Planting:

Transplants: In cool climates, or where the growing season is short, peanuts are often started inside in cell packs or soil blocks. Like most legumes they don't like root disturbance.

Direct sowing: In warm climates peanuts are usually direct sown (the soil should be at least 65°F). Plant 1″ deep in cool soil, or 3″ deep in warm soil.

Spacing:

Beds: Space the plants 9 - 12″ apart, in offset rows across the bed.

Rows: Put plants 6″ apart in rows 20″ apart.

Care

Weeding: The young plants should be kept well weeded. This should ideally be done by hand to avoid damaging the shallow roots.

Hilling: When the plants are 12″ tall they should be hilled like potatoes, to help bury the flowers and increase yields.

Mulch: This is useful to keep down weeds and conserve moisture.

Watering: Water is most critical from the time the flowers appear until harvest. Water regularly during this period to keep the soil moist. Try not to get the leaves wet when watering, as it can contribute to disease problems.

Pests: Peanut can be attacked by a host of pests, especially in warmer climates. These include armyworms, corn earworms, corn rootworms, corn borers, cutworms, leafhoppers, mites, stink bugs, thrips, whitefly, wireworms and a variety of caterpillars. The good news is that peanuts are renowned for their ability to tolerate damage and still produce well.

When growing in cooler climates you may see no problems at all.

Disease: There are a number of potentially serious diseases (black rot, leaf spot, tomato spotted wilt virus, white mold and more).

Pod formation: The plants start to flower about 40 days after they emerge. They produce showy infertile flowers and inconspicuous fertile flowers. Once the latter are fertilized they send out a stalk (called a peg) that grows down into the soil and produces a pod. These take a further 60 - 70 days to mature.

Harvesting

When: You can harvest the pods after the leaves start to die back in September or October. Don't dig them too early, as the pods may not be fully filled (or may even be empty).

The actual stage of harvest is a matter of personal preference, some people like them somewhat green, others prefer them to be fully ripe.

How: Harvest by lifting the whole plants and shaking off the loose soil. Hang them in a warm dry location for 2 months to allow the pods to dry thoroughly. It is essential that they be out of the reach of rodents, otherwise there won't be a single seed left (mice love peanuts).

Seed saving: The plants are mostly self pollinating, so this is just the same as harvesting the seeds for eating. Make sure they are properly dry before storing, or they will go moldy. Save the seed from at least five plants to ensure sufficient genetic variation.

Unusual growing ideas
Peanuts can be grown in pots, or as an ornamental.

Varieties

Peanuts can be divided into several types.

Virginia - (2 - 3 seeds per pod) These are the highest yielding and most versatile types and have the largest peanuts. They produce fairly small, creeping plants, about 24″ tall with a spread of 30″. They take 130 - 150 days to mature.

Valencia - (3 - 6 seeds per pod). Some people consider these the best flavored types. Their seeds have bright-red skin and mature in 95 - 100 days. They grow to be large, upright plants, often 50″ high and 30″ wide. The pods are generally found close to the plant.

Spanish (2 - 3 seeds per pod). Spanish peanuts are small, with reddish-brown skin and mature in about 120 days. They are very rich in oil and are commonly used for oil and peanut butter, as well as for snacks.

Runner type (2 seeds per pod). These grow as a low bush and mature in 130 - 150 days. They are usually roasted.

Kitchen use: Prepare the nuts by roasting them for 20 minutes at 300°F. They can also be cooked by boiling in salt water for anywhere from 1½ - 3 hours (the length of time depends upon how soft you like them).

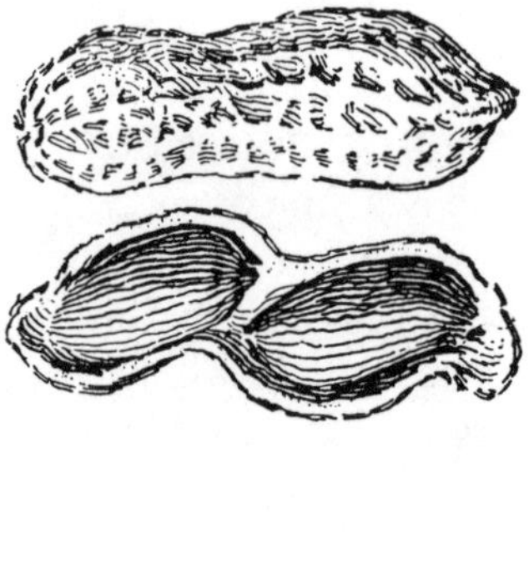

Peppers, Hot / Sweet

Capsicum annuum

Introduction: Peppers are native to Central and South America and have been an important crop in that area for over 5000 years. There are two distinct kinds of peppers, with quite different uses: the hot peppers and the sweet peppers. Their flavor and uses differ considerably, but they are grown in pretty much the same way.

Sweet peppers are tasty and quite productive for the area they take up, but they are nowhere near as important to cooking as the hot peppers. These are highly prized for their fiery flavor and after the colonization of the New World they became an important spice all around the world. They are especially prized in parts of Asia and in China, India and Thailand they are now as important as any native spices.

Ease of growing: I have always found peppers to be pretty straightforward, so long as they have enough heat. They can be slow to get started if it isn't warm enough.

Crop value: Sweet peppers are one of the most popular garden crops, though they aren't particularly nutritious, aren't particularly productive and aren't a very important crop from a self-sufficiency standpoint.

I consider hot peppers to be very important in the kitchen, because they can spice up a huge variety of bland foods and make them into something special.

About Peppers

Seed facts
Germ temp: 60 (85) 95°F
Germ time:
Hot peppers: 14 - 28 days
Sweet peppers: 7 - 14 days
25 days / 59°F
13 days / 68°F
8 days / 77°F
8 days / 86°F * Optimum
9 days / 95°F
Viability: 2 - 4 yrs
Germination percentage: 55%+
Weeks to grow transplant: 8 - 12

Planning facts
Hardiness: Tender
Growing temp: 75 - 85°F day
55 - 65°F night
Plants per person: 4 Sweet
2 Hot
Plants per sq ft: 1 (or less)

Transplants:
Start: 4 - 8 weeks before last frost
Plant out: 2 - 4 wks after last frost
Succession sow: After 6 - 8 wks

Harvest facts
Days to harvest:
120 - 150 days from seed
50 - 75 days from transplanting
Harvest period: 12 weeks
Yield per plant: 1 - 2 lb
Yield per sq ft: ¼ - 1 lb sq ft

Climate: Peppers originated in the tropical highlands of Central and South America and grow best with warm days, cool nights and high humidity. They don't really like extreme heat and if the soil gets above 85°F in summer it can slow growth. Air temperatures above 90°F can cause flowers to drop instead of producing fruit.

Nutritional content: Peppers contain vitamin C and A (beta carotene) as well as some important detoxifying antioxidant phytochemicals, including, lutein, zeaxanthin and capsaicin. They contain about 125 calories per pound.

Capsaicin (the chemical that puts the hot in peppers) is most concentrated in the placenta, but as the fruit matures it seems to spread to the seeds and fruit itself. Humans can detect this fiery chemical in concentrations as low as 1 part per million. Sweet peppers don't contain any capsaicin (if they did they would be hot peppers). They do contain other beneficial phytonutrients though.

Soil

pH 5.5 - 7.0

Peppers like a deep, loose soil that is fairly rich in all of the plant nutrients (especially magnesium) and organic matter. They don't mind acid soil, but don't like salty ones.

Soil preparation: Peppers aren't very hungry plants and don't need a lot of nutrients. Dig 2″ of compost or aged manure deeply into the top 10″ of soil, along with colloidal phosphate (for phosphorus), greensand or wood ashes (for potassium) and kelp (for trace elements). You may also want to add some kind of calcium, either lime or gypsum, depending upon soil pH. This should provide all of the nutrients they need. Alternatively you could simplify things by just using an organic fertilizer mix.

If your soil isn't well-drained then use raised beds, as peppers don't like having wet roots.

Planning

Where: Peppers need a warm, sunny, sheltered spot. In very hot climates (where temperatures regularly get up into the 90's, they will benefit from light shade during the hottest part of the day.

Crop rotation: All members of the Solanum family (eggplant, potato, tomato) are subject to the same pests and diseases. Don't plant peppers where any related plant has grown in the last 3 years.

When: Peppers grow best with warm (70 - 80°F) days, cool (55 - 65°F) nights and high humidity. Don't plant them out until the average daytime temperature is at least 65°F and the average night temperature goes no lower than 55°F. The soil should be at least 60°F.

Peppers won't grow well if it's cold and may be permanently damaged by temperatures below 55°F.
In cool weather sweet peppers won't get as big or sweet, while hot peppers won't get as hot. In such situations you might think about growing them under cloches or in a greenhouse. You should also use an early maturing variety.

Peppers need to be started early, because they are slow to get going. Start them indoors 4 - 8 weeks before the last frost date. They are generally one of the last crops to be planted out in late spring, a couple of weeks after tomatoes (4 weeks after the last frost). If the temperature threatens to go below 55°F after you plant them, then cover with mulch, frost blankets or cloches.

Succession sowing: In areas with a long growing season you might want to make a second sowing 6 - 8 weeks after the first one.

Planting

Transplants

Starting inside: Peppers are started in pretty much the same way as tomatoes, but they are a bit more temperamental. This is because they need warmer temperatures for germination and growth than almost any common crop. The soil should be a minimum of 60°F and preferably 80°F. You can see from the germination numbers in the table that temperature has a dramatic effect on germination time. At 60°F they take almost a month to germinate, while at 80°F they take only a week or so. You need to take this into account when deciding when to start the seed.

To get your peppers going as quickly as possible start them somewhere really warm. If you can't put the whole container inside, you could pre-germinate the seeds (see **Pre-germination**). Wherever you put them make sure they have good ventilation to avoid diseases such as damping off.

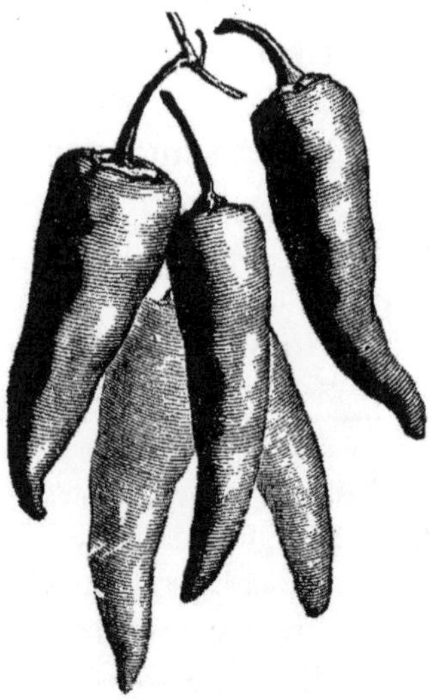

Seed starting mix: Some hot pepper aficionados recommend soilless mixes and say you should avoid both soil and peat when growing pepper transplants.

Seed treatment: Soaking the seed overnight is said to remove germination inhibitors and so may speed germination.

It is sometimes recommended that before planting you soak the seeds in a 10% bleach solution (or hydrogen peroxide solution) for 10 minutes, to kill any disease spores (the seed should then be rinsed carefully). It is said that this treatment may also speed germination by several days.

Pre-germination: To speed up growth and save time you can pre-germinate the seeds. Place them on a strong (tear resistant) paper towel, roll this up and put it in a plastic bag. Place this in a warm place (85°F is best) and start checking it after 3 days. As soon as the seed starts to germinate, plant it out, even if you have to pick out individual seeds. If they don't germinate within 3 weeks, you should probably get new seed.

Planting: Plant the seeds 1″ apart and up to ¼″ deep in the flat (they don't mind transplanting) or in cell packs or soil blocks (put 3 seeds in each, to be later thinned to the best one).

It is a good idea to water the seedlings with tepid water, to avoid cooling the soil. It is also important not to over water; so allow the soil surface to start to dry out before watering again.

Pricking out: When the seedlings are about 2″ tall, prick them out into individual 4″ pots (it's a good idea to add extra phosphorus to the potting mix). You can bury them somewhat deeper each time you transplant, as they will form roots on their stems. When the transplants are 4 - 6″ tall they are ready to go outside.

Hardening off: If you are planting peppers in cool spring conditions, they must be hardened off carefully before they go outside (failure to do so can have serious consequences).

Do this slowly over a week, by reducing the amount of water they get and by leaving them outside for longer periods each day. Start by putting them outside for 2 hours at midday and give them 2 additional hours every day, until they are out all day (or simply put them in a cold frame and leave it open during the day). This helps them to slowly get accustomed to the somewhat less than ideal conditions to be found outside.

In warm summer weather there is no need to harden them off. However you may want to keep them outside in the shade for a day or two, so they can get used to the drier conditions.

Planting out: The soil must be warm (at least 65°F) before these tender plants are set out. If necessary you could use black plastic mulch to hasten warming. If the air temperature is still cool at this time, you could protect the plants with cloches to speed their growth.

The actual planting is simple enough, just make a large hole, add a handful of organic fertilizer mix and plant them out so they are a couple of inches deeper than they were growing in their pots. If cutworms are a problem, you can make protective collars of newspaper or aluminum foil.

Direct sowing: It is possible to direct sow peppers, but it isn't very practical unless you have a long growing season. Plant the seed ½″ deep when the soil has warmed up sufficiently (a minimum of 60°F - and ideally 80°F).

Spacing:
Space sweet peppers 12″ - 15″ - 18″ apart, according to the fertility of the soil and the size of the variety. Some particularly large varieties may need even more.

Hot peppers can get bigger than sweet peppers and so may need anywhere from 12 - 24″ between the plants (again it depends upon the variety).

Care

If your peppers are growing in ideal conditions they can be quite problem free.

Water: Peppers are somewhat drought tolerant (especially hot peppers), but lack of water can affect fruiting so they need to be kept moist for best production. This is most critical from the time the flowers appear until the fruit reach full size. This is particularly important for sweet peppers; if they don't get enough water, the fruits will often get blossom end rot, or develop a slightly bitter flavor.

Don't give the plants water too frequently however, they don't like wet roots and waterlogged soil. Also don't leave water on the leaves overnight as this encourages disease. Drip irrigation works well with peppers.

Fertilization: If your soil is poor you could feed the plants with compost tea or liquid kelp, after they have recovered from transplanting. Feed them again as they start to flower to help in setting fruit. They need phosphorus and potassium, but not too much nitrogen (which may result in big vigorous plants, but few fruits). You should be able to tell if they need fertilizing by the amount of growth they are making.

Mulch: This is recommended to conserve moisture and to keep down weeds around these shallow rooted crops. Don't apply it until the soil is warm though; ideally wait until they are flowering. In very hot weather mulch is sometimes recommended to keep the soil comfortably cool.

In cooler areas black plastic mulch is sometimes used to give the plants extra warmth. People have also been known to put flat rocks around the plants, with the idea that these will absorb heat during the daytime and radiate it back to the plants at night.

Pruning: You may want to pinch out the growing tip when the plant is about 6 inches tall, to make it branch and become bushier.

If your plants start to produce flowers while they are still small, it's a good idea to pinch them off. At this stage you want your plants devoting all their energy to growth, rather than to producing fruit.

Pollination: Peppers don't flower until they have produced about ten nodes on the stem. It is common for the first flowers to drop off without setting fruit, usually because night-time temperatures are too cool (below 50°F). Don't worry too much about this, as soon as it gets warmer they should start to set fruit.

Lack of pollinating insects can also cause flowers to not set fruit. If this is a problem you can hand pollinate with a small paintbrush

If the fruits drop off after they have started to swell it could be temperatures above 90°F, an excess of nitrogen or a deficiency of boron.

Support: Peppers are more sturdy and upright than tomatoes, but heavily laden plants will often benefit from staking, especially in windy sites.

Pests: Peppers have more than their fair share of potential pests (as do other members of the *Solanaceae*), but often they are fairly pest free. Possible problems include aphids, hornworms, leafhoppers, mites, nematodes, pepper weevils, leaf miners, flea beetles and Colorado potato beetles.

Disease: Peppers can be affected by a number of diseases (anthracnose, bacterial spot, southern blight, early blight, verticillium wilt).

To minimize disease problems you should keep the foliage dry, make sure they have good air circulation and practice good sanitation. If you start to have problems then try using disease resistant varieties.

Tobacco mosaic virus: This often-fatal virus disease can be transmitted via cigarette smokers, so keep them out of the garden. Some varieties are resistant.

Boron deficiency: The fruits of boron deficient plants are often small and bitter. A deficiency usually shows up in light alkaline soils (high pH reduces its availability), as plants normally get enough boron from compost or other organic matter. Kelp and granite dust are also good sources.

If you are really sure your soil is deficient in boron, you might try dissolving a teaspoon of borax in 10 gallons of water and spraying it over 100 square feet of bed. Be careful though, larger amounts may result in boron toxicity, which is worse than a deficiency.

Magnesium deficiency: This is common and causes leaves to turn yellow and drop off. Dolomitic limestone is the long term remedy, but is slow to take effect. A faster solution is a foliar spray, made from one teaspoon of Epsom salts (magnesium sulfate) in a pint of water. This should be enough to cover 100 sq ft.

Sunscald: This manifests itself as papery bleached tan patches on the fruit. The damaged parts may then be open to fungal infections, which cause them to rot. Sunscald isn't a disease, but is literally caused by too much direct sun. This can happen to almost any plant, though it is most common on widely spaced and sparsely foliaged ones (as you might imagine).

Avoid sunscald in the future by spacing the plants closer together, to give the ripening fruit more shade. Staking the plants can also help as it prevents them falling over and exposing the fruit to sunlight.

Blossom End Rot: See **Tomato**.

Harvesting

When: Sweet Peppers take 4 - 5 weeks to reach full size from pollination and another 4 - 5 weeks to ripen fully.

The fruits can be harvested anytime after they reach full size. To get the highest yields you can harvest them as soon as they reach full size and are still green. When fruit starts to ripen it invariably slows the plant down.

It's useful that peppers can be eaten while green, but unless you are very impatient, or frost threatens, I don't recommend it. Their flavor and nutritive value improves markedly as they ripen (in most countries they are never eaten green). If you want more fruit it makes more sense to simply grow more plants to make up for the lower yield of ripe fruit.

Remove all small fruit about a month before you expect the first fall frost. These wouldn't have time to ripen anyway and removing them allows the plant to channel all of its energy into ripening the remaining larger ones. Once they reach full size the green fruit will ripen indoors like tomatoes. You can also eat fruits that haven't reached full size, but they aren't usually very good.

How: Harvest peppers by cutting the fruit from the plant, leaving a short stem on the fruit. You can break them off, but the stem is quite tough and there is a risk of damaging the plant.

Storage: Sweet peppers can be stored in a plastic bag in the fridge for several weeks. For longer term storage the fruits can be chopped and frozen, though they will only be good for cooking once frozen.

Most hot peppers are easily dried for storage, either to the leathery stage, or so they are brittle enough to grind to powder. However some of the fleshier types (like the Jalapeno) hold too much moisture to dry easily, so are traditionally smoked (a smoke dried jalapeno is known as a chipotle). They can also be pickled. I find that freezing works well for all hot peppers and is very simple.

Seed saving: Though peppers are mostly self-pollinated they do cross-pollinate to some extent. To ensure purity you should have only one variety flowering at a time, or you can isolate them by 400 feet, or cover with row covers. Hot peppers are more prone to cross-pollination as their styles protrude more from the flower than those of sweet peppers.

It's easy to save pepper seed; just let the fruits ripen fully and collect the seed when you prepare them for eating. Take seed from the first and biggest fruit to appear on the best plants, as these will produce the best seeds. Ideally you will take seed from a minimum of 5 plants to ensure genetic variation.

Dry your pepper seed thoroughly and store it in a cool dry place. Ideally as close to freezing as possible, but not below.

Take the seed out of a hot pepper pod before drying it; don't dry the whole pod and then remove the seed. You may want to use rubber gloves when handling the seed of hot peppers as the juice can by quite irritating to the skin.

Unusual growing ideas

Houseplants: Hot peppers are often grown in pots and can make interesting houseplants. You can pot them up in fall and bring them indoors for the winter. Plant them back outside the following spring. They are a tender perennial and may last for several years if treated like this.

Ornamental use: Peppers are quite attractive plants and with their colorful (green, red, yellow, orange, purple) fruits don't look out of place in the ornamental garden. Some of the hot pepper varieties are quite spectacular.

Containers: Peppers can grow quite well in containers (use a 2 gallon pot for each plant). These have the advantage that you can move them around to take advantage of a warm microclimate. They can also be treated as a perennial and brought inside in cold weather. They have even been used as house plants!

Increasing light: Aluminum foil mulch has apparently increased yields by 30%, by increasing light levels on the plant. However I'm not sure that would be good enough reason to have sheets of shiny metal in my garden.

Cuttings: Soft cuttings of peppers can be rooted (in water or vermiculite) and this is one way to get plants for overwintering. The length of time they take to root varies a lot though.

Unusual uses

Insecticide: Hot pepper fruits have been used as an insecticide and repellent for many pests.

Fungicide: Capsaicin is a natural fungicide, in fact its purpose may be to prevent the slow germinating seeds from rotting before they germinate.

Bleeding: Powdered hot peppers are an excellent wound treatment and sprinkled on a cut they stop bleeding within minutes. People often think I'm joking when I suggest putting such a fiery substance on injured areas, but it really does work and doesn't sting that much (no more than iodine).

Varieties

Peppers tend to be very regional and a variety that does well in one area may not do well in another. It is important to choose varieties that will grow well in your area.

When reading catalogs remember that days to maturity usually means the time from the transplant being set out, to the green fruits reaching full size (but not turning red). Don't ask me why its not from seed to ripe fruit, I don't know.

Sweet Peppers: If you are adverse to intentionally inflicting pain on yourself, you may be more interested in these. There are now a lot of hybrid varieties available, but they don't offer huge advantages (and seed saving is so easy with the open pollinated types).

Bell peppers

California Wonder - Introduced in 1930 and still very popular (70 days from transplant).

Gypsy F1 - A standard hybrid red pepper for hot or cool areas (60 days from transplant).

Purple Beauty - Heirloom with dark purple fruit (75 days from transplant).

Sweet Chocolate - Sweet chocolate brown fruit (65 - 85 days from transplant).

Specialty peppers (not bell shaped)

Corno Di toro - Italian heirloom with bulls horn shaped fruit (80 days from transplant).

Cubanelle - Small fruit prized for frying (75 days from transplant).

Jimmy Nardello - Sweet Italian pepper for frying (75 days from transplant).

Lipstick - Very sweet small fruit are produced abundantly (70 days from transplant).

Red Ruffled - Small, pleated, sweet fruit (85 days from transplant).

Hot Peppers: Like many people who love food, I find hot peppers more interesting than sweet peppers (See Scovile scale for varieties).

In 1912 Wilbur Scoville devised a rating system for determining the hotness of hot peppers. This isn't an exact science, as the amount of heat varies according to growing conditions and the hotter the climate the hotter the pepper (there can be a considerable difference within a variety). It is useful for comparing the relative difference between varieties however.

Kitchen use

Sweet peppers - These are most often used raw, but can also be bakes, grilled and roasted. They have a unique flavor that goes well with basil, garlic, tomatoes, olive oil, onion and rice.

Hot peppers - These are more important than sweet peppers from a culinary standpoint. They can be fried, roasted, dried and baked to spice up a multitude of dishes. It's unfortunate that their use often results in blisteringly hot foods, because this overshadows their wonderfully flavors.

Capsaicin is very irritating to delicate skin and mucus membranes. This is especially noticeable when frying them, and when it comes to shedding tears some varieties can put onions to shame. Some people are much more susceptible to their effects than others. If you've experienced this you won't be surprised to hear that capsaicin has been used as a bear and dog repellent and as a riot control agent.

Easy hot sauce / dog repellent

This is quick and easy way to use up an abundance of peppers. You can even give it as a gift.

20 hot peppers (the type will depend upon how hot you want it. jalapenos are good)
1 tsp vegetable oil
4 cloves garlic (finely chopped),
1 medium onion (finely chopped)
1 cup white wine vinegar
2 cups water
¾ tsp salt

Sauté the peppers, garlic, onion and salt in a glass or enamel pan for 4 minutes, then add the water and simmer for 20 minutes (stir so it doesn't stick). Then allow to cool and puree in a food processor until completely smooth. Add the vinegar to the puree and it is done. It is best to put in canning jars and keep in the fridge, where it should last 6 months. Some cooks think a little sugar improves the flavor.

The Scoville scale

Sweet (0)
Banana (100 - 500)
Anaheim (100 - 1000) mild

Ancho, Poblano (1000 - 1500) This fairly mild pepper is known as ancho when dried and poblano when eaten green.
Jalapeno (2500 - 5000) This is one of the most popular peppers, It can get pretty hot, but also has a nice aromatic flavor.
Serrano (5 - 15,000) good flavor and dries well.

Here we reach my limit. Call me a wimp but I don't really enjoy peppers much hotter than this.

Cayenne (30 - 60,000) Dries well.
Tabasco (30 - 50,000 (very hot)
Chiletepine (50 - 100,000)
Thai Dragon (150,000) Very hot

Habanero / Scotch Bonnet (200,000) - The hottest common peppers. Here we enter the realm of the truly macho/masochistic. They are sometimes said to be a different species *C. chinense,* but aren't. When you get to this point I don't know whether to admire the eaters dedication to the cause, or laugh at their juvenile machismo. Someone just gave me some habanero seeds, but I'm not quite sure what to do with them!

Naga Jolokia, aka **Bhut Jolokia** or **Ghost pepper** (855,000) - A single seed of this almost mythical Indian variety is said to cause intense burning for 30 minutes (yum.)

Potato

Solanum tuberosum

Introduction: Potatoes originated in the mountains of Central and South America and have been cultivated for over 6000 years. A huge number of varieties are still grown in that region.

The potato wasn't initially a success when brought to Europe around 1580, probably because they were short day varieties and didn't start to produce until late in the year (and because they were related to many poisonous plants). However better varieties were developed eventually and when people realized its many benefits its use spread throughout Europe.

The potato was introduced into North America in 1621, but didn't become a significant food crop for almost a century until Irish settlers arrived in 1719 (in some places it is still called Irish potato to this day).

Potatoes are the fourth biggest crop in the world overall and by far the most important vegetable crop (over 320 million tonnes in 2010). This is mostly for local consumption as they are quite perishable and aren't traded internationally like other major commodity crops.

In recent years there has been a huge increase in potato production in many third world countries. This isn't surprising as they may yield from 10,000 to 30,000 pounds per acre and provide more usable protein per acre than any other crop (up to forty times more than cows).

Apparently only about 20% of gardeners regularly grow potatoes, I'm not really sure why this is, maybe people think they need a lot of space, are cheap to buy and don't taste much better than shop bought.

I grow quite a lot of potatoes and find that they are actually one of the most space efficient crops you can grow, considering the amount of nutrition they provide. A 10 square foot planting can yield 20 pounds of tubers. Organic potatoes are never cheap where I live; they generally range from $1 to $2 per pound and at those prices growing potatoes becomes a pretty good deal.

Home grown potatoes also taste better than those you buy and are one of the great treats of the summer garden. Also over 80% of conventional potatoes contain some pesticide reside, so its good to eat organic ones.

Crop value: Potatoes are the single most useful garden crop from a self-sufficiency standpoint, because of the combination of their exceptional nutritional value, their productivity, ease of growing and ability to store well. They are unique as the only garden crop you could live on (at least for a while). At one time Irish peasants really did live on a diet of potatoes and milk and their population increased rapidly (until the potato famine).

I enjoy growing potatoes and find them to be one of the most rewarding crops of all. They emerge quickly, don't need much attention and harvesting is so much fun that even my children used to help.

Potatoes are also a beneficial crop for the garden, as their growth and harvest loosens the soil, improves its tilth and suppresses weeds. This feature makes them useful as pioneer plants for starting a garden, or for reclaiming rough land (see **Unusual growing methods**).

If you have a small garden I would say that they are only cost effective if you have a fairly fertile soil and treat them well. If you are getting less than a pound of potatoes per square foot, it may not be worth it.

If you are ambitious and intend to grow a lot of potatoes it is important that you have somewhere to store them all. They are fairly perishable and won't keep well if you don't give them the right conditions. The last thing you need is a ton of rotting potatoes.

Ease of growing: Potatoes are easy to grow if they have the right conditions. The only time I have had major problems was in Washington state when they were afflicted with late blight, due to wet weather.

Nutritional content: The potato is a substantial and nutritious food. Most people know it is a major source of carbohydrates, but are less aware that it is an important source of protein too. It also contains a lot of vitamin C, several B vitamins and the minerals copper, iron and potassium. These all make an important contribution to the diet because it is eaten in quantity (this isn't horseradish) Apparently blue / purple potatoes also contain valuable anthocyanin phytonutrients.

Potatoes are a major source of energy, with about 350 calories per pound.

Climate: Potatoes are native to tropical mountains and prefer mild temperatures, ideally in the range of 60 - 70°F. They grow best in fairly dry climates and can be affected by a variety of diseases when growing in wet conditions. In mild winter areas, with few frosts, they are sometimes grown in late fall or early spring.

Potato plants don't like frost or cold weather and don't do well if it is too hot. Soil temperatures above 70°F inhibit tuber formation and this stops altogether if it gets much above 80°F).

Having said all that, potatoes are actually quite adaptable and can do well in a surprising range of situations.

About Potatoes

Planning facts
Perennial
Hardiness: Half hardy
Soil temp for planting:
45 (55 - 65) 70°F
Growing temp: 60 - 70°F day
45 - 50°F night
Plants per person: 15 - 20
Plants per sq ft: 1
Plant: 2 - 4 wks before last frost date
Days to harvest: 90 - 140 days

Harvest facts
Yield per plant: 1 - 2 lb
per sq ft: 1 - 2 lb
per 10 ft row: 6 - 17 lb

Soil

pH 4.8 (5.5 ideal) 6.5

Potatoes will grow and produce well in most soil types, even those that are too acidic for most crops. For best results they prefer light, deep, well-drained sandy soils. They like a more acid soil than most vegetables, as it increases yield and decreases the incidence of scab (a disease that mostly occurs when the pH is above 6.0.)

Potatoes don't like heavy clay or rocky soil because the tubers can't easily expand as they grow, Nor do they like wet soil, which can cause all kinds of problems with disease and rotting. You can solve both of these problems fairly easily by creating raised beds of loose, well-drained soil.

Soil preparation: Potatoes aren't a fussy crop, but they respond well to soil improvement. They like loose soil, so if yours is heavy or compacted, deep cultivation such as double digging is beneficial.

Deep digging also enables you to add the all important organic matter in the form of 3″ of compost, leaf mold or aged manure (some people avoid manure saying it encourages scab, but I haven't found any problem with composted manure). All types of soil will be improved by the addition of organic matter.

If organic matter is in short supply then simply put some in the planting trench or in each planting hole. A fertilizer mix is also a good idea (or alfalfa or seaweed meal).

Never lime the soil when planting potatoes. If the soil is too alkaline then add sulphur, pine needles or another acidifying agent to lower the pH.

Potatoes are so adaptable and tolerant that they are often used as the first crop when establishing a new garden.

If your soil is really bad (or you don't have any at all) you can grow potatoes in raised beds, pots or grow bags.

Fertilization: Potatoes are fast growing plants and respond well to high fertility.

An old practice is to provide nutrients to potatoes in the form of fresh plant material. Wilted comfrey leaves or seaweed were laid in the trench along with the tubers (up to a pound per tuber), to feed the plants as they decompose. You can also plant the tubers directly into a newly incorporated green manure or cover crop.

Nitrogen: Potatoes aren't big nitrogen users and too much can result in abundant top growth, but fewer (and inferior) tubers. A potato rotation is often scheduled to follow a heavy nitrogen user like corn.

Potatoes do need some nitrogen however, especially in the first few weeks, when they are putting on a lot of leaf growth. They use 75% of all the nitrogen they need in the first 4 weeks of growth. Too little nitrogen may result in the premature production of small tubers, so use your judgment.

Potatoes aren't very good at getting nitrogen, so it should be in an easily available form (compost, seed meal, comfrey).

Phosphorus: Potatoes should have a good supply of phosphorus, though they aren't heavy users. Use colloidal phosphate and compost.

Potassium: This is the most important primary nutrient for potatoes, increasing yield, improving quality and hastening maturation. Potatoes need a steady supply of potassium throughout their lives, but especially when their tubers are forming. Adding 5 pounds of wood ashes per 100 square feet of bed can increase yields by as much as 30%. If using wood ashes would raise the pH too much, you could use greensand, though this isn't as easily assimilated.

Calcium: Potatoes also like calcium, though most sources run the risk of raising the ph, which isn't good. Gypsum doesn't do this though and can be applied at 5 lb/100 sq ft.

Planning

Potatoes are usually propagated vegetatively from tubers, or pieces of tubers. These are known as seed potatoes, though they aren't actually seeds at all.

Crop rotation: Potatoes are susceptible to the host of diseases that affect members of the *Solanum* family. Don't plant them where tomato, pepper or eggplant have been grown within the last 3 years. If scab is a problem avoid planting after beets too.

Where: Potatoes need full sun if they are going to be really productive, so make sure they have a prime garden spot.

If you plan to grow potatoes as a staple food you will have to devote a significant portion of your growing space to them. At the same time you also have to rotate them for at least 3 years, so they usually form a separate rotation group of their own.

When: Potatoes grow best in mild temperatures (below 70°F) and don't tolerate heat well (especially when forming tubers). The soil temperature should ideally be between 55 - 70°F. In areas with hot summers they are usually grown as a spring or fall crop. In mild climates they can be grown all summer.

The chitted tubers can go in the ground as early as 6 weeks before the last frost (though 2 - 4 weeks is more common). The young plants will tolerate a light frost, especially if covered with straw. Even if they are damaged they should recover quickly.

Potatoes are tropical plants and evolved to grow with short day length, so they grow best in spring and fall. Long summer days may actually delay tuber formation somewhat. In warmer areas you may be able to plant them as early as February (if you can find seed potatoes to plant).

Succession sowing: You may want to grow several crops in succession to maintain a constant supply of new potatoes. You can also plant early, maincrop and late varieties at the same time.

Early crop: The minimum soil temperature for planting potatoes is 45°F, though 50 - 55°F is better.

The first crops can be started as early as 6 weeks before the last frost date, though you must take care to protect them from any frost. This is pretty easy when they are barely poking out of the ground; just cover them with soil, mulch, row covers, cloches, tarps or old blankets (some varieties can even take mild frost).

Main crop: This is usually planted around the last frost date (2 weeks before to 2 weeks after). Don't leave it too long as long days can slow down maturation.

Late crop: In many areas you can get two crops of potatoes a year. Time the second crop to mature around the time of the first fall frost (the shorter days actually hasten tuber formation).

It can be a problem to find seed potatoes for this second planting, as they generally disappear from stores after the spring planting season. You might have to buy them in spring and store until required. You can also store some of your spring harvest in the fridge (temperatures below 50°F will help to overcome their dormancy period). Chitting them isn't really necessary when planting into warm soil.

Where I live finding seed potatoes isn't that easy even in spring, unless you want to buy a pound of them in a little mesh bag for $5.00 (which has a significant impact on the economics of growing them.) Apparently a lot of stores are reluctant to carry them in bulk because they are so perishable. It is good to buy yours early, when you first see them for sale. They may as well sit in your house as in the store.

Before planting

Certified disease free tubers: You can grow perfectly good potatoes using old potatoes from the market (supposedly they are often sprayed to prevent them sprouting, but they do sprout eventually). The problem is that these may be infected with virus diseases, which will then become established in your garden. Once a virus is established in your garden it is there to stay and can infect every subsequent crop (and maybe even tomatoes, peppers and eggplants as well).

Because of the potential for disease problems most authorities recommend planting only certified disease free tubers. Its hard to get optimal yields from poor quality seed potatoes, no matter how good your soil and cultural practices. I used to think this was just a way to get you to buy much more expensive seed potatoes, but since I have had a problem from replanting infected tubers I know better. It can waste a lot more in time and effort than you save in money.

Selecting seed potatoes:

A tuber is not a root. It is a swollen stem adapted to be a food storage organ and has a small scar on one end where it was attached to the plant by the stolon. The other end of the tuber (the rose end) has a cluster of dormant buds known as eyes, which have the ability to grow into new plants. There are also eyes in other parts of the tuber and you can cut one tuber into several pieces. You just have to make sure that each piece has an eye that can grow (even a potato peeling can grow if it has an eye). However the rose end contains the most vigorous shoots.

There is much debate over the ideal size of a seed potato (this is the kind of thing that makes gardening so exciting), but it is smaller than many people think. Most books recommend 2 - 4″ (3 - 4 oz) tubers, saying smaller ones produce smaller plants and hence smaller tubers and lower yields. They say that larger tubers produce bigger plants and hence larger tubers. However it is now thought that whole tubers of 1 - 3 oz are ideal.

Agricultural researchers in England obtained their highest yields by planting very small (⅓ oz) tubers very close together (only 9″ apart). They found that larger tubers (spaced further apart) sent up several shoots that essentially became separate plants and eventually competed with each other. Using smaller tubers can also reduce seed potato costs significantly.

Of course many gardeners get the same results by cutting larger tubers into several pieces, each with 2 or 3 eyes. However cut pieces are more prone to rot unless they are left for a few days, so their cut surfaces can dry out and toughen. They can also be dusted with sulphur powder and left for 24 hours in indirect light. These measures usually work out okay, but take time. It would be simpler to just use smaller tubers (called single drops by farmers) in the first place.

If you do cut the tubers it is best done after chitting, as it results in some moisture loss (and of course you can cut the tubers according to the sprouts they have made). Some experts frown on cutting seed potatoes for early crops which will grow in cool soil because of the greater potential for infection and rotting.

When you buy seed potatoes they shouldn't have started to sprout very much, as the brittle and delicate shoots are easily damaged once they start to elongate.

When you get your seed potatoes home, put them in a cool, humid place until you are ready to chit or plant them. To prevent premature sprouting store seed potatoes at 40 - 50°F. If they already have sprouts take care not to break them off (the first sprouts to appear are the strongest and best).

Sets: If you buy seed potatoes by mail order they may very well be in the form of sets. These consist of a single eye from a tuber with a small plug of potato attached. Sets are not a very satisfactory way to grow potatoes. Even if you are fortunate enough to get sets in good shape, they won't perform as well as whole tubers with their large reservoir of food to draw from. They may also be coated with fungicide for interstate shipment.

Chitting:

It is to your advantage to plant tubers that already have healthy shoots, because it gets them off to a faster start and so reduces the chance of rot. This is most important for early planting, as the tubers may sprout slowly in cool spring soil. Later plantings don't need chitting as they will sprout rapidly in the warm soil.

About 2 - 3 weeks before you wish to plant the tubers, you should start chitting (sprouting) them. Do this by setting them out, rose end up, in indirect light (not direct sunlight, but still fairly bright- never dark) at a temperature of 55 - 65°F (warmer temperatures may cause them to shrivel).

The aim is to get 2 - 4 sprouts each 1 - 2″ long on each tuber. If you can't plant them out as soon as they get to this stage, you should then return them to cooler conditions. If they sprout very slowly you can speed this up by giving them warmer conditions for a while.

Don't worry if the tubers turn green, the solanine produced may help to prevent them rotting.

You should rub off any excess sprouts (above the 2 - 4 required), as soon as they start to sprout, so the tuber doesn't put too much energy into them. Leaving too many sprouts can mean smaller potatoes. Of course if you are going to cut a tuber into pieces you need some sprouts on each piece, so don't rub them off until after you cut them up.

Some gardeners allow the shoots to grow to 6 - 8″ in length, claiming this increases yields by up to a third and reduces the time to harvest. However the long sprouts are easily damaged and must be handled very carefully.

It is actually possible to remove the sprouts from the tuber and plant them separately (or leave one or two on the tuber and plant the others separately). This might be worth trying if you only have a couple of unusual tubers. It is also possible to eat part of the tuber and plant the peel, so long as it has some eyes on it. Of course these techniques you give you lower yields and they will take longer to mature.

Planting

Planting depth

New tubers only form above the old one, so the deeper the tuber is set into the ground, the higher the potential yield. This is one reason potatoes were traditionally hilled up.

The actual planting depth varies according to soil and season. In England (where spring weather is cool) they tend to plant their potatoes quite shallowly (2 - 3″) and hill them up later. They do this because the tubers can easily rot if planted too deep in cool soil.

In warm soil you can plant the tubers much deeper. They might be 4″ deep in a heavy soil and up to 8″ deep in a light soil.

Rows or beds: If your soil consists of very fertile and loose raised beds and you don't plan on earthing them up, you can grow potatoes on equidistant spacing. If you plan on hilling them up you should grow them in rows.

Spacing: Potatoes are grown at a wide variety of spacings, depending upon the soil, water availability, and other factors.

Spacing is the biggest factor in determining the final tuber size. The closer the spacing, the more competition and the smaller the tubers (however you get more of them). Researchers have found the optimal spacing for highest yield per square foot (of fairly small tubers) is two plants per square foot, which averages out to be about 9″ apart. This could be worth trying, unless you really want large tubers.

Closer spacings are used for early potatoes, or when you have ideal growing conditions, don't mind smaller tubers, or when space is limited. They don't work if the soil isn't very fertile, as potatoes don't like having to compete with each other.

Wider spacings are used for maincrop potatoes, when the soil isn't very fertile, when water is limited, when you want large tubers, or if you have lots of room and don't need high yields per square foot. You might be able to grow a fast growing intercrop (such as spinach or mustard) in between the widely spaced plants to help increase productivity.

Bed spacing: The traditional spacing ranges from 9″ - 12″ - 15″ depending upon variety, tuber size and soil fertility. You may want to start with 12″ and see how that works.

Row spacing: Traditionally they are planted 8″ – 12″ – 15″ in the rows, with 18″ - 24″ – 36″ between the rows. Start with 12 x 24″ and see how that works.

Dry gardening: If you want to grow potatoes without irrigation you might try 18″ between plants and 48 - 60″ between rows.

Planting methods

Rows/ trenches: The traditional way to plant potatoes is in trenches and this is probably still the best way if you want to grow them in bulk as a staple food. One advantage of planting in rows is that it is easy to hill them up later. A potential disadvantage in wet weather is the soil in the trench may stay wet for longer.

Begin by digging a trench one spade deep and one spade wide (put the soil you remove evenly on both sides for later earthing up). Put all of the amendments that potatoes love (compost, wilted comfrey leaves, seaweed, wood ashes, alfalfa pellets, greensand, fertilizer mix) into the bottom of the trench.

The tubers are then placed in the trench at the desired spacing and about 4″ of soil is pulled back into the trench to cover them. When the plants reach 6″ in height you can fill the trench up with soil.

Beds: If you don't want to use trenches you can simply dig holes in the wide beds, at the desired spacing (use a bulb planter to speed this up). You then simply place your tubers in the holes and cover with 3 - 4″ of a mix of compost and soil. If the soil is cold don't water the bed until the plants have emerged, to reduce potential rotting problems.

Growth pattern

The growth of a potato plant can be divided into four distinct stages.

Vegetative stage

For the first 30 - 70 days a potato plant produces main shoots and lots of foliage. The larger the plant at the end of this stage, the larger the eventual yield can be. Watch out for pests such as Colorado potato beetle during this stage. Vegetative growth goes along best during the long days of early summer.

Tuber formation

After 70 - 90 days of vegetative growth the main shoots stop growing and side branching occurs. At this time tubers start to form on stolons coming from the feeder roots. A soil temperature of 60 - 70°F is said to be optimal for tuber formation and it slows down as the temperature goes above this, until it stops altogether at above 80°F (hilling can help to keep the soil cooler).

Tuber formation usually coincides with the onset of flowering and is a good indicator that tuber formation has begun. It is not physiologically related however and in some situations flowers may not appear at all.

Tuber enlargement

As the plants come into full bloom the tubers enlarge rapidly and the plant has its greatest need for potassium. This is also the most critical time for water and for maximum growth they need a steady supply. You can start digging new potatoes at this stage and mine often get no further than this. Fungus diseases sometimes attack plants at this time.

Maturation

When the plants reach maturity the tops wither and die back and the skins on the tubers thicken (this is important for storage). When 75% of the foliage is dead, water them for the last time, wait 10 - 14 days and they are ready to dig.

Care

Hilling: If you planted the tubers at a shallow depth you should hill them (also known as earthing up) as this can greatly improve the crop. Hilling increases the depth of soil for tuber formation and ensures they aren't exposed to the sun (which would turn them green). It is also a good way to eliminate weeds and can help to keep the soil cool in hot weather. It also prevents the plants sprawling and gives the tubers nice loose soil to grow in.

Hill up the plants when they are 6 - 8″ tall, by burying the bottom half of the plant. You should repeat this 2 - 3 weeks later and perhaps a third time several weeks after that (adding a couple of inches more soil each time, until the hill is 6″ tall). Don't over-do the hilling though or you can reduce their ability to produce food by burying food producing foliage.

Hilling up is easy if you planted in widely spaced rows, but not possible if you planted in beds (use mulch instead).

Mulch: Potatoes are commonly mulched with compost, shredded leaves, hay or seaweed (potatoes have a special affinity for seaweed). This conserves moisture and helps to keep the soil cool, which is important in warmer areas.

Of course you can't use mulch if you plan on hilling up the plants, but a thick mulch can actually be used instead of hilling (see **Unusual growing methods**).

It is best to avoid mulch if you have problems with slugs.

Weeding: Potatoes are vigorous plants and can compete against weeds pretty well. However you should weed while the plants are small. Do this carefully so you don't damage the shallow roots. When you earth up the plants you will eliminate all of the weeds in the bed.

Feeding: The young plants need nitrogen for fast uninterrupted growth. Give them a foliar feed of compost tea, comfrey tea or liquid kelp, 3 - 4 weeks after the shoots emerge from the soil and are 4 - 6″ tall (or side dress with fertilizer mix). This could also help to remedy any minor nutrient deficiency.

For maximum yields (or in poor soil) they should receive a foliar feed every 2 weeks until they start to flower.

Water: It is important to keep the soil evenly moist (but not wet) for best growth, as lack of water results in poor yields of small tubers. It is also important to water uniformly, making sure it penetrates through the dense foliage and down to the full root depth of 18″ (or at least the top 12″ where the greatest proportion of roots are found).

Potatoes should get at least an inch of water per week, though the exact quantity will depend upon the weather. Continue watering regularly until the tubers are almost ready for harvest and then stop.

If water is in short supply, just give them 4 gallons per square yard at the crucial time when the tubers start to form (when the flowers appear). In humid climates many gardeners stop watering when tuber formation starts, so they don't grow too fast. Excess water may cause hollow heart, where the interior grows so rapidly it cracks (this is most often seen in the bigger potatoes).

Try not to get the foliage wet when watering as potatoes are very vulnerable to fungus diseases. Drip irrigation is best for this reason. Otherwise water in the morning or early evening, so foliage can dry out quickly (you don't want it to stay wet all night).

Pests

The potato has more than its fair share of disease and insect pests. Fortunately these aren't found everywhere; in some favored areas potatoes have few problems and are very easy to grow. The severity of potato pests also varies from year to year, with different growing conditions. In some years they do little harm, in other years they can be devastating. Warm humid conditions are the worst for potatoes.

The best thing you can do for your plants is keep them well fed, so they can (hopefully) deal with pests and diseases as they arise.

Colorado potato beetle: Both adults and larvae feed on potato leaves and they can be a big problem if they get out of hand. On a small scale you can simply hand pick off any beetles you find and scrape off the tiny orange egg masses from under the leaves (and any newly hatched larvae). The larvae are eaten by many predators, though the adults are fairly poisonous.

Other pests: Aphids, blister beetles, flea beetles, nematodes, leafhoppers, tuberworms and wireworms.

Diseases

The potatoes is prone to more than its fair share of diseases, a few of which are listed below.

Viruses: Virus infection may show itself as pale, distorted or mottled leaves and stunted plants, but often there are no obvious symptoms except reduced yield (this can progressively decrease each time they are planted). You may avoid these by using certified seed and not saving your own tubers for planting.

Removing viruses: It is possible to get a virus-free plant from an infected tuber. You plant the tuber in a container of sterile potting mix and keep it in a warm place to grow. When the shoot reaches 6 - 8″ high you cut it off 2 - 3″ above the soil line (it should never touch the soil or the rest of the tuber). The shoot can then be rooted in another container of sterile potting mix. It will then hopefully be virus-free, just hope that your garden is also, when you plant it out.

Verticillium wilt: This fungus shows itself by the tops dying off prematurely (it's also known as early dying fungus). You may still get a small crop of potatoes from affected plants, but they won't store well. This disease may last for 7 years in the soil and to eliminate it you can't plant potatoes in the same spot for at least 4 years. Other members of the Solanum family are also affected, so they can't be grown either (except for a few resistant varieties).

Scab (*Streptomyces scabies*)
This very common disease is caused by a fungus in the soil. It is undetectable above ground and the damage is mainly cosmetic, so it is not very serious unless you are growing for market (it reduces their marketability).

Alkaline soil (above 6.0 pH) and lack of moisture are the main causes of scab. It persists in the ground for several years and can also infect other root crops such as carrot, beet and turnip. The best ways to prevent scab is to rotate annually and to keep the pH of the soil somewhat acid (below 5.6 pH), so don't lime it. Abundant water may reduce damage from scab.

If your garden has conditions that encourage scab, you may want to use a resistant cultivar.

Late blight (*Phytopthora infestans*): This is the disease that caused the famine that depopulated Ireland, by killing one and a half million people and causing another million to emigrate. It is called late blight because it likes warmer weather and usually occurs after tomatoes (which are also susceptible) have flowered. It doesn't much bother early crops, so planting early is a good preventative.

This fungus first manifests itself as spots on the lower leaves in cool, wet weather, but then the leaves die and brown patches appear on the tubers. The only thing you can do is dig the tubers 2 weeks after the tops die down and use them. This disease affects yield, but doesn't affect storability (of course you wouldn't use infected potatoes for seed. Many modern varieties have some resistance to late blight.

Early Blight (*Alternaria solanii*)
This fungus disease occurs earlier in the season and isn't as big a problem as late blight. It appears as irregular shaped dark brown concentric spots on the shaded lower leaves. These slowly enlarge and merge until badly infected leaves eventually die (those at the bottom of the plant first and then progressing upward). If you recognize it early enough you may be able to treat with Bordeaux mixture.

You can minimize its effects by keeping plants well fed and watered, by removing crop debris, keeping leaves dry, preventing soil from splashing onto leaves and removing infected plants.

Blackleg (*Pectobacterium carotovorum*): This bacterial disease most often occurs in cool/warm wet weather when the plants are growing well (or even flowering). It shows itself as black slimy decay around the base of the stem (hence Blackleg). Leaves turn yellow and then brown and eventually die. The tuber rots from the stem end and becomes a slimy, smelly mass.

Though infection most often results from infected seed potatoes, the bacteria may also enter the plant through wounds in the tuber (such as from scab or insect damage).

To avoid this disease use certified disease-free seed potatoes. Use whole tubers (rather than cutting them up) and rotate them annually. Also remove any volunteers from the ground.

Bacterial ring rot (*Clavibacter michiganense* ssp *sepedonicus*)
The first symptom of this bacterial disease is yellowing and browning of leaves and wilting of some stems (though usually not all). In mild cases there may not be any obvious symptoms until you cut a tuber in half and see the characteristic ring of discoloration (in mild cases) or rot (in severe cases). Though it doesn't kill the plants it is significant because it makes the tubers unsalable (and in severe cases unusable).

This disease can only live in living plants (it can't survive in the soil) and infection is usually the result of planting diseased tubers (it can be spread to healthy tubers by the process of cutting them into smaller pieces with an infected knife). If you save your own seed potatoes it is important that you don't plant any that contain this disease (the best safeguard is to plant only certified seed potatoes). You should also remove any volunteers from the garden, as well as any plants that show signs of wilting, before they can spread infection to other plants.

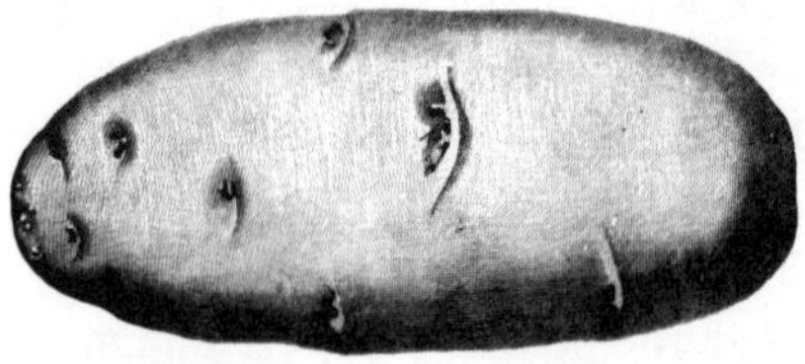

Harvesting

When: You can start harvesting new potatoes 70 - 90 days after planting (after the plants have been flowering for a while). Just root around beneath the living plants until you find some sizeable tubers. New potatoes taste great, but taking them reduces the final yield, so only take a couple from each plant (if you really like them, then grow some plants specially for this). The skins of new potatoes are very thin and they are high in sugar, so they don't store well.

The main potato harvest begins when the leaves start to lose their green color and die back (late in the season they may be killed by frost before this happens). If you want to store the tubers you should leave them in the ground for 2 weeks after the tops turn yellow and die down. This allows the skins to toughen up. If the skin rubs off easily with a finger they are not ready to store. Once the tubers are mature you should dig them, otherwise they may eventually start to sprout again.

It is a lot easier and less messy to harvest potatoes when the soil is fairly dry.

How: Digging the tubers is a very rewarding activity. It feels like digging for buried treasure (which it kind of is), but is a lot more fruitful. Dig the tubers with a spade or spading fork, starting at least a foot away from the plants to minimize accidental spearing. Tubers will always be found above the seed potato (which is usually still recognizable), but may be some distance to one side.

Some people like to dig a hole alongside the first plant and then pull the plant over into it. The second plant then goes into the hole left by the first one (this method ensures thorough soil cultivation).

Always handle the tubers gently to minimize damage. Even the slightest skin abrasion can cause a tuber to rot in storage and this can spread to nearby tubers.

When you have finished digging, let them dry out and sort the tubers into three piles: badly damaged (speared or chopped) ones for immediate eating, grazed ones for use in the near future and perfect ones for storage. You will also sort out any partially green potatoes that have been exposed to light and are inedible.

Green tubers: Any tubers that are not fully covered with soil or mulch will turn green from exposure to light. These are mildly toxic and the common advice is that they shouldn't be eaten (though you can often cut off the green parts). However recent studies show that most of this is concentrated in the skin, rather than the flesh. This suggests that they could be peeled and eaten in an emergency – though a better idea might be to save them for planting.

Storage

Careful storage is very important with potatoes. If they are not given ideal conditions they will soon become inedible, due to rotting, turning green or sprouting. Even under the best conditions they will gradually deteriorate over time (your job is to lengthen this period).

Unlike most other root vegetables potatoes can't be left in the ground until needed (a few weeks is okay). If the soil is fairly warm and moist they will sprout as soon as their dormancy period of 2 - 3 months is over. If it is cold and wet they may rot, or develop diseases such as scab. If the soil freezes they will probably rot.

Temperature is the most critical storage factor. If conditions are too warm (above 50°F) they will sprout as soon as their natural dormancy period is over in 2 or 3 months (of course this won't matter if you only have a 2 months supply of tubers to store). If it is too cold (below 40°F) their starch may turn to sugar and give them an off flavor (apparently you can convert this back into starch by storing them above 65°F for a couple of weeks). The fridge isn't a good place for potatoes as it is too cold.

Prepare the tubers by air-drying in a dark place for several days (don't wash) and then store them at 60°F for two weeks to cure. They should then be stored at 40 - 50°F with high humidity (90%). Keep them in wooden boxes, or sacks, with good air circulation (never in plastic bags) and check periodically for rot. Keep them in the dark of course, or they will turn green.

Properly stored potatoes can last for at least 5 - 6 months, though you should keep checking them for signs of rot or deterioration. Potatoes that are sprouting can still be eaten, just rub off the sprouts.

Other storage options for potatoes are somewhat limited, as they can't easily be frozen, dried or canned.

Clamp: Large quantities of potatoes can be stored over the winter in a clamp. This works best in light, well-drained soil and should be in a sheltered position.

Start by digging out the soil in the area of the clamp to a depth of 10″ and then lay down a 3 - 6″ layer of straw or dry leaves (you might first lay down a layer of gopher wire to foil rodents).

A piece of perforated pipe is arranged in the center and the roots are placed around it to form a cone or prism shaped pile (a vent can also be constructed from straw).

The pile is then covered with a 6″ (more in very cold climates) layer of straw, or leaves.

Finally the straw is covered with a 6″ layer of soil, which is packed down with a spade. Some of this soil comes from the original excavation; the rest is obtained by digging a drainage trench around the clamp. Keep the vent open on top of the clamp, unless it gets very cold, in which case it should be closed up with straw.

Seed saving: When we talk about seed saving with potatoes we are usually talking about seed potatoes, rather than actual seed. Saving your own seed potatoes can save you a bit of money if you grow a lot, as well as the trouble of having to find them to plant. It also helps you to another level of food self-sufficiency, as you don't have to depend upon anyone else. It is also appealing if you want to grow unusual varieties that are hard to find.

Unfortunately there is a problem with saving your own tubers and it is frowned upon for the same reason as using supermarket tubers: it can lead to problems with disease. Plant an infected tuber and every tuber the plants produces will be infected at least as badly and perhaps worse. The disease may also spread to healthy plants via insects or infected tools.

The advisability of saving your own seed potatoes largely depends upon where you live and how much disease you have encountered. It worked well when I lived up in Washington, but down here in warmer California I have encountered serious problems with disease, notably bacterial ring rot. After one totally unproductive attempt I went back to buying certified seed potatoes.

If you want to save your own seed potatoes, just choose the best tubers, check them for disease symptoms and store them very carefully instead of eating them.

Potato seed: You may want to experiment with true potato seed as well (see below). The fruits are produced readily in many cases, so all you have to do it allow them to ripen (this takes about 2 months from flowering). Squeeze out the seeds into a bowl and wash them. The good seeds sink and bad ones float.

If you grow seed from a vegetatively propagated variety they won't come true to type, but will produce entirely new varieties. If you like any of these you can propagate them vegetatively and name the new variety after yourself.

There are some true potato seed varieties that come true to type, but they are not easy to find.

Companion plants: Some gardeners interplant marigolds or beans with potatoes as a way to repel Colorado beetles. Researchers have found that the presence of these plants in a stand of potatoes does seem to confuse the insects (and most importantly there are fewer beetles to be found).

Of course any time you plant anything among the potatoes, it is going to be disturbed and uprooted while harvesting. This means that any edible interplanted crop must be harvested before the potatoes are ready. It will also take up space, water and nutrients that the potatoes could have used.

Unusual growing ideas

True potato seed: When I first started gardening many years ago there was much fanfare around the introduction of true potato seed, as the wave of the future. As a young and inexperienced gardener at the time, I thought it was a silly idea that wouldn't catch on. I reasoned that one of the advantages of growing potatoes is that you don't have to start with tiny seeds. I was right that it didn't catch on, but wrong in thinking it was a silly idea. Growing from true potato seed actually has some significant advantages.

Advantages of true potato seed

The seed will be much less likely to be carrying any kind of disease

You can start the seed at any time you need potatoes (often seed potatoes are only readily available in spring).

They are a lot cheaper. A packet of seed (that might produce 100 plants) would only cost the same as a pound or two of seed potatoes.

True potato seed can also be stored for several years, whereas seed potatoes are very perishable.

You can save your own seed quite easily.

Potatoes are no harder to grow from seed than the related tomato and are treated in pretty much much the same way. The catch is that you have to find a variety that comes true to type.

I think true potato seed will become important in the future, as it allows you to save them from year to year without having to worry about disease.

New potatoes: If you have lots of seed potatoes you could grow some plants specifically to produce delicious new potatoes. These can be planted as close as 6″ apart, as they will be harvested as soon the new potatoes form.

Mulch planting: Potatoes will grow quite happily in a layer of mulch instead of soil. This also makes it easy to take a few new potatoes from the living plants; you simply pull the mulch aside. The only real problem with growing in mulch is getting the large quantity of mulch material needed.

You can just put the seed potatoes on the ground and lay a 3″ layer of mulch (compost, straw, chopped leaves, aged manure) on top of them. Add more mulch as the plants get taller, until it is 8 - 12″ deep. This is necessary to keep light from turning the tubers green and because tubers only form above the seed potato.

Another method starts the previous fall, when you pile chopped tree leaves where you want the potato patch to be (do it as you clean them up). The following spring you plant sprouted tubers 6″ deep in the leaves. Hill up the plants with more mulch as the pile settles and the plants grow.

You can also combine mulching with trench planting. Lay the tubers at the bottom of a 12″ deep trench and cover with 3″ of chopped leaves. As the plants grow keep filling up the trench with more leaves.

Land clearing: Potatoes are the best vegetable crop for starting a new garden on uncultivated ground. Simply dig trenches and plant as described above. The amending, digging, hilling and harvesting will loosen and improve the soil and make it more suitable for other crops.

You can also use mulch to start a new garden on grass or weed infested land. Simply put the tubers on the ground and cover with a thick 3″ layer of mulch. As the plants grow you add more mulch. The combination of a thick mulch, deep shade and the considerable soil disturbance will eliminate existing plants and leave you with a nice clear bed of loose soil.

Container growing: Potatoes are well suited to growing in containers and if you do it right they can be surprisingly productive. This is the way to go if you only have a small space (or just a patio or balcony)

Container growing isn't just a novelty, or for patio gardeners. It can also give you a useful way to multiply one special tuber. It could also be used to grow your own seed potatoes, as it gives you a much greater control over the spread of disease. It is also a good way to get very early or very late potatoes.

Yellow Finn and Red Pontiac both work well for this. Early varieties don't work so well, as you want types that continue to produce more tubers, rather than setting them all at once.

How: You can grow a single potato to be enormously productive in the following way. Obtain a large garbage can, put drainage holes in the bottom and fill it with a foot of good soil mix (try equal parts compost, good garden soil and sand).

Plant one large seed potato in the soil. As the plant grows, slowly fill the can with more fine compost, always covering only a third of the plant. With a little luck the end result will be one very large plant, completely filling the whole can with tubers. When the plant dies back, empty out the can and collect the tubers.

The most important thing when growing in containers is to water carefully, too much, or too little, water will cause problems.

A refinement of this is to use tires (or slatted wooden bins). Start with one tire filled with soil and as the plant grows add more tires and soil. The advantage of this method is that the plant gets maximum light at all times and is never growing in the bottom of a can.

Another variation on this is to use a bottomless wooden box, or even a wire cage 18 x 18″ in size (these can even be stood on driveways).

You can also use a standard 15 gallon plastic plant pot or a large fiber pot.

Grow bags: Many European urban gardeners have discovered the joys of growing potatoes in plastic bags. They often buy bags of prepared mix, but its easy to make your own. This is very similar to container growing.

Start with a large tough garbage bag, put some holes in the bottom for drainage and half fill it with a mix of equal parts sandy soil and compost. They need to get good sun, so fold down the edges of the bag. You then plant two chitted potatoes in the bag and add water. As the plants grow you fill the bag with more of the soil / compost mix. Be careful to keep them well watered (not too little or too much).

Dry gardening: In most areas a spring potato crop can be produced without irrigation, as there is usually a lot of moisture in the soil from the winter. You simply space the plants further apart than normal (18 - 24″). Your yields may be slightly smaller, but the tubers will contain less water and so be more nutritious and better flavored. They may also store better as their skins tend to be tougher. This can give you an easy, low cost way to grow an important food crop.

You need to keep moisture robbing weeds under control when doing this. A mulch is good if you have enough of it.

Autumn planting: In mild areas any tubers overlooked during the harvest will survive the winter underground and volunteer the following year. This shows that it is possible to plant potatoes in autumn for a spring harvest. You might use some of the small tubers harvested earlier in the year. Plant them in October or November for harvest in spring.

Fall planting is something of a gamble depending upon the amount of frost and rain you get. It didn't work for me because the plants became horribly infected with powdery scab (a disease I had never even seen before).

Varieties

Though only a half dozen varieties are widely cultivated commercially, there are an enormous number of potato cultivars, with different shapes, sizes and colors (white, yellow, red, blue) and other attributes (waxy, starchy or all purpose). Some do better on heavy soils, some are more resistant to cold or disease, some contain more vitamin C, protein or antioxidants and some taste better.

Generally the heavy yielding commercial varieties tend to contain more water, but farmers like them because they get paid just as much for water as for potato. Older, lower yielding types are often more nutritious.

Russets: These have characteristic brown russeted skin and are best for baking because they are high in starch.

Butte - Classic russet, very high in vitamin C

Russet Nugget - Good flavor. Late,

Yellow:

Yukon Gold - One of most popular potatoes, yellow flesh. Early.

Yellow Finn - One of best flavored potatoes, yellow flesh. Mid

Red:

All Red - Red skin, pink flesh. Mid

Red Cloud - White flesh, Heat tolerant. Mid.

Red Norland - White flesh, early.

Sangre - One of best tasting red potatoes. Mid

White:

Kennebec - High yielding, tolerant of adverse conditions. Mid

White Rose - High yielding, does well with irrigation. Early

Blue:

I once grew some amazingly productive blue potatoes, but I never did find out what variety they were. Unfortunately my family wouldn't eat them, claiming they tasted weird. I don't believe they did, but I have to admit that eating blue mashed potato was strangely disconcerting.

Caribe - Red/purple skin, white flesh.

Purple Viking - This has purple skin and white flesh. Mid

Fingerlings:

French Fingerling - Small pink tubers with excellent flavor. Mid

Purple Peruvian - Deep purple flesh, late.

Russian Banana - One of the most popular fingerlings, easy to grow. Late.

Early potatoes: These fast maturing (less than 90 days) varieties are usually eaten immediately. They are good for areas where spring is short and summer is hot. They are also good for new potatoes.

Early Rose
Mountain Rose
Purple Viking
Red Norland
Red Pontiac
White Rose

Midseason potatoes: These mature in around 100 days.

Colorado Rose
Desiree
French Fingerling
Maris Piper
Red Lasoda
Rose Finn Apple
Yukon Gold
Yellow Finn

Maincrop potatoes: The late maturing varieties are commonly stored for winter use. They produce large crops of tubers that store well.

Bintje
Butte
German Butterball
Russian Banana
Katahdin
Kennebec

Kitchen use

Of course potatoes are famous for the infinite number of ways in which they can be used: boiled, baked, fried, chipped, casseroled, stewed, roasted, mashed, scalloped, twice baked and more.

Starchy or floury potatoes are prized for baking and frying. Waxy potatoes are firmer and hold their shape, so are used for boiling whole and for potato salad. All purpose types can be used for all purposes.

Potato latkes

8 potatoes

2 eggs

1 onion

1 tsp salt

½ cup flour oil

Grate the washed potatoes (don't peel) into a bowl. Beat the egg into another bowl, then mix in the grated onion, along with the flour and salt. Squeeze the excess moisture from the potatoes and add them to the egg mix.

Heat some oil in a skillet until it sizzles and drop in large tablespoonfuls of the mix. Flatten the mix and allow it to cook until golden brown. Then flip it over and cook the other side. Serve with apple sauce.

Quinoa

Chenopodium quinoa

Introduction: Quinoa (pronounced keen-wa,) has been cultivated in its native Andes mountains for 6000 years and was a staple food of the Incas. They looked upon it as more than simply a food crop, it was also considered a sacred grain (the name means mother grain). It was believed to give a person special endurance (and even heightened psychic abilities) above that to be expected from its nutritive qualities. As with amaranth, the Spaniards suppressed its growth as symbolic of pre-conquest culture, so its use declined.

Quinoa is sometimes referred to as a pseudocereal (along with amaranth and buckwheat), as it is grown as a grain crop, but isn't a member of the grass family. In recent years it has become hip and trendy and as a result (like food, nightclubs, clothes, property and everything else) the price has risen considerably. In consequence it now costs up to 3 times what it did a few years ago. Ironically this means that peasants in its homeland can no longer afford to eat it!

Ease of growing: Quinoa is an undemanding plant that is closely related to a common garden weed. It is fairly easy to grow and can do well in conditions that don't suit most other crops. It does need a suitably cool growing environment though, and you need to use a suitably adapted variety (some old varieties prefer to grow at high altitude).

Though quinoa is a fairly new crop in North America, it has big potential as a garden crop for the future when greater self-sufficiency may be a goal.

Crop value: Quinoa is that rare commodity a starchy, high protein grain that can easily be raised and processed on a small scale (it is the best temperate climate substitute for rice). If the growing situation is right, quinoa can be an outstanding crop for food self-sufficiency. It is productive, nutritious, easy to grow and requires relatively little processing.

Nutritional content: Quinoa is one of the most well balanced and nutritious of all grains. It contains from 7 - 22% almost complete protein (said to be similar to that of dried milk), with a better balance of amino acids than almost any vegetable food. It even includes lysine which is missing from most vegetable proteins. It also contains vitamin E, several B's, calcium, iron magnesium, manganese, potassium and zinc.

The seed is a major source of energy, with almost 1700 calories per pound.

The leaves are rich in vitamins A and C, as well as calcium and iron (and some less desirable oxalic acid).

Climate: Though quinoa originated in tropical latitudes, it doesn't have the needs of a tropical plant. It is actually a mountain plant and grows best in fairly cool climates. It doesn't like very hot weather and doesn't set seed very well at temperatures above 90°F. It has the potential to be an important crop for Canada and the northern U.S.A.

Quinoa prefers cooler temperatures than amaranth (another Incan staple) and so was the main grain crop at higher altitudes. It is well adapted to the high levels of UV light and daily temperature extremes found in high mountains.

The growing plants can tolerate light frost (to 30°F), and when seed is ripe and the plants are dying back they can survive temperatures as low as 20°F. As a (high altitude) tropical plant it needs short days to start flowering, though modern cultivars don't show this somewhat awkward trait very strongly.

About Quinoa

Seed facts
Germ temp: 45 (50 - 55) 65°F
Germination time: 3 - 7 days
Viability: 5 - 7 yrs
Germination percentage: 70%+

Planning facts
Hardiness: Tender
Growing temp: 50 (60 - 70) 90°F
Plants per sq ft: 1
Direct sow: 2 weeks after last frost
Days to harvest:
90 - 120 days - seed
40 - 60 days - greens
Height: 4 - 6 ft

Harvest facts
Yield per sq ft: 1 - 2 oz
Yield per plant: 1 - 2 oz

Soil

pH: 5.0 (6.0 - 7.0) 8.5

Quinoa will grow well in any soil so long as it is well-drained, but it will be most productive in a light fertile loam. It is extremely adaptable and in South America it is often grown on very poor, marginal soils that are wet, dry or very alkaline (8.5) or acidic (5.0).

Soil preparation: This fast growing plant likes nitrogen, so give it 2″ of compost or aged manure and an organic fertilizer mix. It also likes phosphorus.

Planning

When: Quinoa needs up to 4 months from planting to harvest, so is usually planted in spring, starting 2 weeks after the last frost date (the soil must be at least 45°F). The latest date for planting is determined by counting back 4 months from your first fall frost. Don't wait too long to plant, or it won't have time to mature before cold weather arrives.

Where: Quinoa needs full sun for highest productivity. It doesn't grow well in shade

Planting

Direct sowing: Quinoa is usually direct sown, because you need a lot of plants and it germinates well in cool soil (it germinates best at 45 - 55°F). In fact if the soil is much above 65°F it often doesn't germinate satisfactorily (I wondered why it didn't germinate in my greenhouse!) Plant the seed ¼ – ½″ deep, either by lightly broadcasting or in rows.

The seed germinates quickly, so you can soon see if any areas have poor germination. If this is the case then sow more seed to fill in.

A problem with broadcasting quinoa is that the seedlings look exactly like those of the weed lambs quarter. This makes it hard to know what to take out and what to leave in. The best solution to this is to plant in rows, so you can just remove everything that isn't in the predetermined line.

Thinning: Quinoa is usually planted more closely than the final spacing (perhaps 3″ apart), to ensure a good stand. You can then thin at your leisure to achieve the desired spacing. As a bonus you can eat the plants you remove as greens (they are good).

Spacing: The plants are spaced from 8 - 18″ apart, depending upon the variety and the size of plant required. Some varieties can get quite tall (5 - 8 ft). If you want to plant in rows, put the plants 6 - 12″ apart, in rows 18 - 24″ apart.

Some experiments suggest that the closer spacings (3 - 4″ in row with 24″ between rows) can produce higher yields, earlier and more uniform maturation and plants with single unbranched heads. Of course these traits are well suited to mechanical harvesting.

Care

Watering: Quinoa has a strong root system and is naturally quite drought tolerant, so it doesn't need a lot of water (it can produce a good crop with as little as 10″).

Generally there is enough water in the soil for early growth and as it gets bigger you only need to irrigate if it gets very dry (which is usually later in the season). More water results in bigger plants, but this doesn't necessarily translate into higher yields (it may also cause greater seedling mortality).

Weeds: The plants grow fairly slowly when young and will need weeding regularly (planting early can reduce weed problems). Once they reach about a foot in height, they are able to take care of themselves.

Mulch: This helps to conserve soil moisture, keeps the soil cool and keeps down weeds. However older plants don't really need it as they shade the soil and suppress weeds themselves.

Pests: Quinoa is bothered by the same pests as its relatives chard and spinach. Armyworms, caterpillars, flea beetles and aphids sometimes attack the plants, but generally these vigorous plants will just keep on growing and aren't greatly affected.

When I planted quinoa in Western Washington it was plagued by leaf miners (which also attack lambs quarters) and apparently this is common in some of the eastern states.

Happily birds don't usually go for the seeds because they are protected by their coat of bitter saponins (though persistent rain may wash away some of this defense).

Disease: When grown on a field scale, quinoa is sometimes affected by the same viruses and other diseases that affect chard and spinach.

Rain: Heavy rain when the seed is mature can sometimes cause it to sprout. In this situation it should be harvested and dried as quickly as possible.

Harvesting

When: Quinoa is usually harvested when the leaves start to die back. In some areas this may be after the first frosts (this doesn't harm the ripe seed heads).

You can tell when the seed is ready because it will pop out when you rub the tops. If you can just about dent a seed with a fingernail it is fully ripe.

How: In dry weather you can gather the seed by bending the heads over a bucket and gently rubbing the loose ripe seed into it. The seed doesn't all ripen at the same time though, so you may have to harvest the primary heads first and come back a couple of weeks later for the rest.

You can also cut the entire seed heads and leave them in a dry place (on a screen with good air circulation) to dry out fully. You then have to loosen the seed from the heads by any threshing means possible. This is fairly easy, as it isn't tightly held.

The separated grain can then be cleaned by screening and winnowing. Finally it should then be dried even more (it must be fully dry for storage).

Leaves: The seed is not the only part of the plant that is edible. The young leaves can be used as a potherb like the related giant lambs quarters and spinach. It is not a good idea to take leaves from grain producing plants, but you can use any plants that have to be thinned out (and unwanted volunteers).

Storage: The dry seed can be stored in a rodent proof container in a cool, dark, dry place.

Seed saving: If you are growing quinoa for seed, then saving seed for planting isn't very difficult. Just set aside some of the seed you have collected. It is generally self-pollinated, but some degree of cross-pollination may occur.

If you want to be sure to keep a variety pure, you should probably just grow one variety. If you don't particularly care about purity, just grow whatever kinds you can find and save seed from your best plants. Do this for a while and you can create your own locally adapted variety (I think this is the best approach).

Quinoa seed is fairly small and you don't need a lot for planting. A pound of seed is enough to plant an acre of land.

Unusual growing ideas

Ornamental: Quinoa is quite attractive and some varieties have found their way into the purely ornamental garden. Their value for this is somewhat limited because you need a lot of them if you want to grow much grain.

Varieties

The main thing that has been holding quinoa back in this country has been a lack of suitably adapted varieties (many weren't well adapted to North American conditions). This is changing and there are now quite a few available and more are being developed (though they may not be easy to find). The grains may be yellow, red orange, purple or black.

Some growers seem interested in its ornamental qualities and are selecting for bright colored flower heads.

Brilliant Rainbow - Multi-colored

Cherry vanilla - Pink and cream

Red Head - Bright red seed heads.

Faro - One of the first varieties to be successful at low altitude.

Cahuil - Another of the first varieties to be successful at low altitude.

Temuco - Orange seed heads. Works well in wetter climates.

Kitchen use

Leaching: The seeds have a bitter coating of saponins which must be removed before they can be eaten. Don't do this until you want to use the grain though, as it keeps better if unwashed. There are several ways to leach the grain.

The simplest way is to soak the seed in water for several hours, change the water and soak for several more hours (agitating the water can speed this up). You then rinse them until the water is no longer foamy.

You can also put them in a blender at low speed and keep changing the water until it is no longer foamy.

It's been suggested that you could put the seeds in a muslin bag and run them through the cold cycle of a washing machine. Saponins are a kind of detergent and will foam up if agitated in water, so maybe you could wash some clothes at the same time!

The seed you buy is white because the saponins that give it a yellow color have been washed out.

Using: The leached seeds need no further preparation, they are ready to cook. This is usually done by simmering one cup of grain in 2 cups of water for 15 minutes until it is soft. It can also be added to soups and stews.

The seed can also be ground to flour and mixed with wheat flour for baking. The Incas also made beer from it.

The young leaves can be eaten as a salad or green vegetable.

Related species

The *Chenopodium* genus has more than its share of good potherbs, they include:

Good King Henry

Chenopodium bonus henricus

This species differs from the rest of the *Chenopodium* potherbs in that it is a perennial. Though not a very common crop, it is been sporadically cultivated for centuries in its native Europe for its tasty spring shoots. These can be one of the first greens to be harvested in spring.

Ease of growing: Good King Henry is a pretty hardy plant and about as low maintenance as you can get.The hardest part about growing it is finding plants or seed to get it established.

Where: This Northern European plant doesn't like hot weather and in warm climates it does best in part shade. It is not a very productive plant (considering it takes up space year round) and is better suited to semi-wild cultivation, rather than the intensive garden. It is well suited to the forest or wild garden, because of its shade tolerance.

Soil: Good King Henry likes nitrogen and does best on rich, moist soil.

Planting: Though this plant is perennial, most people start it from seed initially. This can be planted directly in the garden in early spring (it is very hardy). It can also be started in the greenhouse and transplanted out after the last frost date.

Once you have some established plants, you can propagate it vegetatively. Just divide the biggest and best plants while they are dormant.

Good King Henry is naturalized as a wild plant in parts of the east. If you can find it, you can collect the seeds, or transplant some plants to your garden.

Care: This plant grows vigorously once established and spreads to form colonies. This makes it an ideal low-maintenance food crop.

Watering: For best production keep the soil fairly moist at all times. This plant doesn't like to be dry.

Harvest: The leaves are at their best when they first appear in spring, though new growth can be eaten at any time it is available. The emerging flower stalk can be eaten like asparagus.

Seed saving: Good King Henry will produce seed with no help from you, just leave it alone. There is no need to worry about varieties as there aren't any (that I know of).

Unusual growing ideas:
Wild Garden: This is the ideal semi-cultivated crop. It can be planted in a suitable location and pretty much left to its own devices except for harvesting. Plant lots of individual plants and harvest a little from each, when you need it.

Kitchen use: The fleshy leaves are used in much the same way as spinach (they even contain oxalic acid).

Strawberry Spinach

Chenopodium capitatum

If you approach this plant with the word strawberry in your head you will be sadly disappointed (though strawberry flavored spinach would be a bit odd anyway.) There is no relationship, connection or similarity between this plant and the strawberry. If you think of the word spinach you will be a lot closer to the mark.

This plant gets its name because the red fruit are said to resemble a strawberry (though to my mnd it looks more like a raspberry). It is also known as beetberry, which makes more sense because it is related to the beet and does produce what looks like a berry.

Beetberry can be used like the related spinach, as a potherb or raw in salads. It is a good addition to salads as the berries add color, as well as a rather bland green taste. Native Americans used the berries to dye skin, clothes and basket material.

Beetberry self-seeds in my garden. I planted it several years ago and it still reappears occasionally. I don't consider this a very important plant, but since we are talking about useful *Chenopodium* species, I thought I should mention it

Huazontle

Chenopodium nuttaliae

This species was an important vegetable crop for the Aztecs (it is sometimes called Aztec spinach). It is grown from seed in much the same way as quinoa and may actually have the same ancestors.

Huazontle has the same kind of vigor that you find in its weedy relatives and is very easy to grow. If you give it the opportunity it will even self sow.

The young plants can be used as a potherb like spinach, but the tender flowering tips are the real star. These are gathered up until the flowers open and are boiled or steamed for 5 - 10 minutes. They shrink quite a lot in cooking so gather plenty. These flowering tips have a lovely firm texture and delightful flavor. They are one of the best green vegetable I have ever tasted; they are really good (I was not surprised to read recently that they are starting to become trendy among foodies).

In Mexico the flowering tops are boiled for 5 minutes, squeezed into bunches, dipped in eggs and fried.

Giant Lambs Quarters

Chenopodium giganteum

The leaves of this species can be used like spinach, while the flowering tops can be used like huazontle. I highly recommend it as a low work vegetable that self-sows readily and does well in both warm and fairly cool weather.

I don't grow this plant in the same way as most other vegetables (or even think of it in the same way). It bridges the gap between weed and crop plant and essentially interplants itself around the garden. If you let is produce seed once it will appear all over the place for the next several years. Some people would consider this a bad thing and call it a weed, but I appreciate it and call it delicious.

I do have a fairly liberal attitude to weeds, in that I don't think a completely weed free bed is always a good thing. Instead I look upon them as a potential additional crop and having weeds that are as eminently edible as this one certainly helps.

I collect the abundantly produced seed each year and scatter some of it in areas where I want it to grow. This doesn't even have to be the the vegetable garden, any disturbed soil will do.

I now have so many self-sowing *Chenopodiums* in my garden I don't know which is which. I just eat them all.

The only type I have ever seen is named **Magenta Spreen**, which has magenta patches on its leaves.

Radish

Raphanus sativus radiculata group

Introduction: The main virtue of radish is that it is quick; some varieties may mature in as little as 3 - 4 weeks. Actually I would say that its only virtue is that it is quick, as I am not a big fan of radishes. They are not very nutritious and are way down near the bottom of my list of useful garden crops.

I actually value radish more for its tasty, spicy seed sprouts than as a root vegetable. The young leaves, flowers and green seedpods are all good in salads.

Climate: Radish is a cool weather crop, growing best at a cool 60°F and with moist conditions. Hot weather causes them to develop a very pungent flavor, similar to the related horseradish.

Ease of growing: The Latin species name means "easily reared", because this is one of the simplest vegetables to grow. It is often one of the first vegetables a new gardener tries and is commonly recommended for children (though I can't imagine many children enjoy eating it very much).

Nutritional content: The root is fairly rich in vitamins C and B6, as well as folate, potassium, magnesium, copper, and calcium. It is pretty low in energy, with only about 75 calories per pound.

About Radish

Seed facts
Germ temp: 45 (70 - 80) 95°F
Germination time: 3 - 10 days
29 days / 41°F
11 days / 50°F
6 days / 59°F
4 days / 68°F
4 days / 77°F * Optimum
3 days / 86°F
Seed viability: 5 years
Germination percentage: 75+

Planning facts
Hardiness: Hardy
Growing temp: 45 (60 - 65) 75°F
Plants per person: 20
Plants per sq ft: 16
Direct sow:
Spring: 2 – 4 wks before last frost
Fall: 8 - 10 wks before first frost
Succession sow: 10 - 14 days

Harvest facts
Days to harvest: 20 - 40 days
Yield per plant: 1 oz
Yield per sq ft: 1 - 5 lb sq ft

Soil

pH 5.5 - 6.8

Radish roots don't go very deep so the ideal soil is loose and well-drained, such as a sandy loam. They don't like heavy soil. It should also be slightly acidic.

Soil preparation: Most soils will benefit from 2″ of organic matter (compost or aged manure), which should be incorporated into the top 6″ of soil to loosen it (this is particularly important in heavy clay soil). It's also a good idea to remove any rocks or debris you come across.

In very poor soil you can dig a special trench and fill it with a mix made from compost, sand and soil.

Like most root crops radishes don't need a lot of nitrogen (don't give them fresh manure), but they do like potassium and phosphorus.

Planning:

Where: In cool weather radishes are grown in full sun. In hot weather they may benefit from light shade during the hottest part of the day.

Because the roots are in the ground for such a short period, they are rarely planted in their own bed space. They are usually interplanted between slower growing crops, such as Brassicas.

When: Radishes grow best with moist soil, cool weather and short days (ideally less than 12 hours long). In most areas these conditions are most easily found in spring and fall (the latter is best).

You can grow radishes in summer too, but temperatures much above 70°F cause them to be very pungent. At this time of year you have to use the right varieties and give them light shade and plenty of water.

Spring: A rule of thumb would be to start planting radishes 2 - 4 weeks before the last frost date. You can plant earlier than this, but if the soil temperature isn't at least 45°F germination will be slow (at 40°F they may take a month to germinate). You could get them going earlier by warming the soil with black plastic or cloches.

You can plant radishes every 2 weeks until hot weather arrives. Take a break until the hottest days of summer are over and then start your fall planting.

Fall: Radishes often grow better in fall than they do in often spring, as they get to mature in the cool days of autumn.

Winter: In mild climates radishes can often be grown into early winter.

Succession sowing: Radish roots are only in optimum condition for a short time, so it's best to only plant a few seeds at one time. Succession sow every 10 - 14 days (the shorter time is for warmer weather).

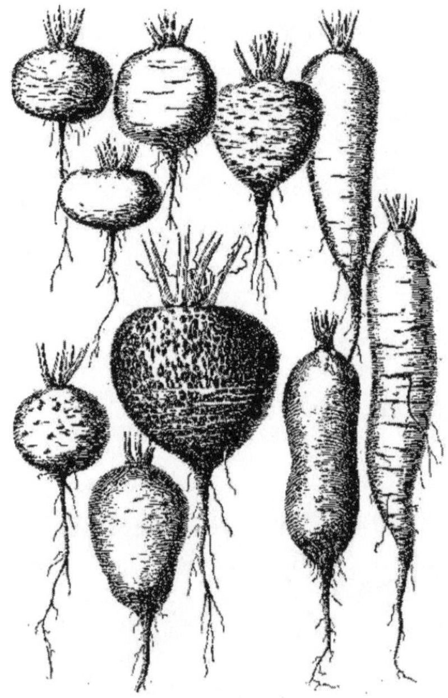

Planting

Direct sowing: There is no reason to start radishes indoors, because they germinate easily in cool soil and the plants grow rapidly. Like most roots they don't transplant well.

The seed is sown directly into the garden ½ - 1½″ deep and 1″ apart. A deeper planting may give you slightly larger roots, especially if you give them a slightly wider spacing (1½″). Bigger seed may also result in larger roots.

Thinning: When the plants have 2 - 3 leaves you should thin to the desired spacing.

Spacing: Space the plants 1″ - 2″ - 4″ apart, depending on the fertility of the soil.

Care

They need to grow rapidly for best quality, which means giving them everything they need.

Thinning: Proper thinning is essential if you are going to grow good radishes. If the plants are crowded they won't produce useful roots. You can eat the thinnings in salads.

Weeds: These small plants don't compete with weeds very well, so should be hand weeded regularly. Don't use a hoe too near the plants as their shoulders are easily damaged.

Watering: Radishes must have a steady supply of water, so keep the soil evenly moist at all times (in dry weather this often requires watering every other day.)

Too little water can result in woodiness and excessive pungency (often such roots are also pithy and have marked growth rings). Too much water may encourage top growth at the expense of the roots. Irregular watering can cause them to crack.

Mulch: This keeps the soil cool, which is important in warm weather. It also retains moisture and keeps down weeds. Generally they aren't in the ground for long enough for this to be worthwhile though.

Pests and diseases: Radishes are susceptible to the usual host of Brassica pests. Flea beetles will commonly eat small holes in the leaves, but this isn't usually a major problem. You can protect your plants against many pests by using floating row cover.

Cabbage root maggot: This is the big pest of the radish and is most problematical in spring and late summer. See **Cabbage** for ways to deal with it.

Radishes are sometimes planted as a trap crop, to lure the little worms away from more valuable Brassicas.

Common problems: Though radishes are one of the easiest crops to grow, beginners often have problems.

No root: If a radish doesn't produce a swollen root, it is usually because the growing conditions weren't good enough. It simply wasn't producing enough food to have a surplus to store in the root and make it swell. This most often occurs because they weren't thinned properly, resulting in competition from neighboring radishes (or weeds). It may also be the result of low light levels, too high growing temperature or insufficient water or nutrients.

Excessive pungency: High temperatures (above 70°F) or dry soil may cause the root to be excessively hot. This may also occur when the roots get past their prime.

Woodiness: Insufficient water, or high temperatures (above 70°F) can also cause the roots to be woody or pithy.

Bolting: Radish is an annual and will bolt when it has built up enough food reserves to produce seed. Crowding, poor soil, lack of water and other types of stress may hasten bolting, as may the long days of summer (another reason they are easier to grow in fall).

Harvesting

When: The rapid growth of radishes can be a problem in that the roots are only at their peak for a short time and soon get over-mature. It is important to harvest as soon as they are ready. They will actually age more slowly in the fridge than they will in the ground.

Check to see if a root is ready for harvest with a little careful digging. They are generally best when still small (under 1″ diameter), as they often get woody or pithy as they enlarge.

If a root gets past its prime, you can just let it flower and go to seed. You can then eat the flowers and unripe seed pods, or you can gather the seed for planting or sprouting.

How: Uproot the plants by hand and cut off the tops to prevent them taking moisture from the root.

Storage: The roots will keep for several weeks in a plastic bag in the fridge.

Seed Saving: Radishes are insect pollinated and will cross with any other variety, or with wild radishes (the latter is so common around here that it would be hard to isolate them by the required ½ mile). However if you have a clump flowering together they are going to be mostly pollinated by each other. If you really want to do it right they should probably be isolated by caging,

I mostly use the seed I collect for sprouting, rather than growing more roots, so I'm not that motivated to keep them pure. I just allow the pods to ripen and gather the seed.

Unusual growing ideas

Pod Radishes: These are grown for their enlarged seedpods rather than their roots. These are fleshy and pungent and are a nice addition to salads. I actually rate them more highly than the roots.

Containers: Radishes can be grown in 6″ deep pots. They will need frequent watering if they are to produce edible roots.

Indoors: Radishes have been grown indoors in a container in winter, You would have to be a radish addict to bother with them though.

Trap crop: These easily grown plants are commonly planted as trap crops to lure Brassica pests away from more valuable plants. If you simply sow a few more seeds than you need, your regular radish crop could perform this function too.

Sprouting: Any excess seed from your radishes can be sprouted to provide one of the best salad sprouts. See **Sprouting seeds**.

Varieties

Round:

Champion - Bright red (25 days).

Crimson Giant - Red bulbs get bigger without turning pithy (30 days).

Cherry Belle - A favorite, as it resists turning pithy. (22 days)

Easter Egg - A mix of colors (30 days).

French Breakfast – More tolerant of heat than most.

Helios – Yellow roots are fairly sweet and mild (30 days).

Ping Pong F1 - Roots are white and mild (30 days).

Long/cylindrical:

White Icicle - Grows fast to 5″ long 30 - 35 days).

D'Avignon - Red with a white base (21 days).

Shunkyo Semi-long - Roots pungent and sweet (32 days).

Kitchen use

The roots are generally used raw in salads and sandwiches. They can also be cooked in soups or pickled. In Germany slices of radish are traditionally eaten with salt in beer halls (there is even a variety names after this practice - **Munchen bier.)**

The tender young leaves can also be eaten, either raw in salads or cooked as a potherb.

The immature seedpods are good in salads and can also be pickled.

Rat-tail radish

(*Raphanus sativus* **var** *caudatus*)

This is grown for its long edible seed pods (which do somewhat resemble a rats tail) and doesn't produce an edible root. These can be planted a couple of weeks before the last frost. It is much more tolerant of hot weather.

Radish, Winter

Raphanus sativus var *niger (longipinnatus)*

Introduction: Winter radishes are most often associated with Japan, where a quarter of all vegetables grown are radishes. However they were actually popular in Europe before the familiar small radishes were introduced. Like the turnip they were an important winter food for peasants.

The roots get much larger than ordinary radishes and sometimes reach 3″ diameter and 18″ long. They are called winter radishes because (like winter squash) they were stored for winter use. They are treated a lot like turnips.

Most of what was said about growing radishes also applies to winter radishes, so I will only mention the differences here.

Soil

The soil needs to be more fertile than for radishes and should be rich, loose and friable (ideally a rich, sandy loam). The roots go a lot deeper too, so you need to loosen the soil to a greater depth (ideally 12″).

Planting

When: If you plant winter radish in warm summer weather they will merely produce leaves and bolt, without producing a large swollen root. The plants appreciate the warm weather, but need cool nights to produce large roots.

The plants need a minimum of 65 days to produce roots, so plant them in late summer, about 60 - 90 days before the first autumn frost is expected.

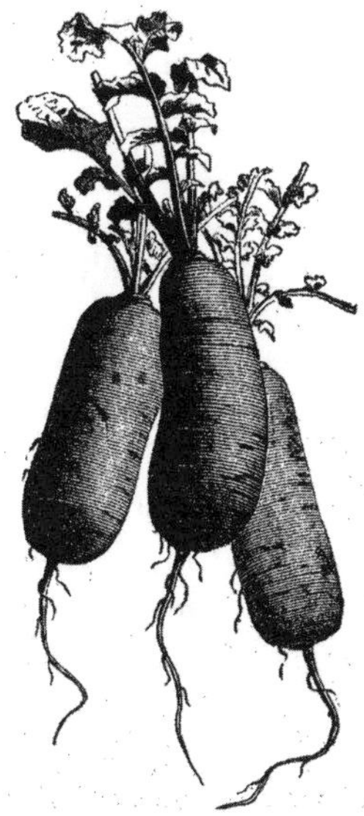

Spacing: Space the plants 6 - 18″ apart, depending on soil and variety.

Sowing: Sow the seed ¾ - 1″ deep and 2″ apart.

Watering: The plants need consistently moist soil for good growth. Abundant water after a dry spell may cause the roots to swell rapidly and split.

Seed saving: This is done in the same way as for the turnip.

Unusual growing ideas
Compact soil: Daikon radishes have a very strong and deep penetrating root and are sometimes planted to loosen compacted soil, as an easy alternative to digging.

Harvest: The flavor of the root can be improved by frost, so don't harvest too early.

Some radishes are grown for their edible leafy tops, which are eaten like turnip greens.

Storage: When possible the roots are left in the ground until needed (a thick mulch will protect them from cold weather). If this is not possible they can be stored in moist sawdust, or sand, in a root cellar at 32 - 40°F. The harvested roots will keep in a plastic bag in the refrigerator for several weeks.

Varieties: Some varieties have very beautiful roots.

Open pollinated:
Giant Luo Bo: Large oval roots are sweeter than many. 80 - 100 days

Myashige: The medium spiked roots are often pickled. 60 days

Tokinashi: Is quite pungent. 60 days.

Shogoin: This turnip shaped radish is usually cooked. 70 days

Sakurajima: This variety can get very big. 80 days

Wayakama White: Long white roots. 70 days

Hybrids:
April Cross F1: A giant spiked root, slow to bolt. 60 days

Minowase summer cross F1: Another giant spiked root, heat tolerant and does better in warm weather. 60 days

Leaf radishes: In Asia some varieties of radish are grown for their edible leafy tops, rather than their roots. These include:
Four season F1
Hattorikun F1
Pearl leaf F1
Saisai Purple

Kitchen use: The roots are peeled and eaten raw, cooked like turnips, pickled (very popular in Japan), stir-fried and dried. The grated root is often used in sauces in Japan.

The immature seedpods are good in salads or pickled. The ripe seed is sprouted like alfalfa.

Rhubarb

Rheum rhabarbarum

Introduction: Rhubarb was first grown in gardens for medicinal purposes, but later began to be eaten as a food. It eventually became popular in the cooler areas of northern Europe as a substitute for fruit in desserts (it can be harvested early in the year, before any real fruit is available). Presumably this only happened after cheap sugar became available to sweeten it, as it is very sour.

Rhubarb is quite an acquired taste and some people can't see any virtues in it at all. However others, usually people who have grown up with it, come to love it (and even crave it in spring).

Ease of growing: If your climate is right this perennial is one of the easiest things you can put in your garden. Just put it in the ground and it will grow and produce.

Nutritional content: Rhubarb contains vitamins C and K, as well as magnesium, calcium, potassium and manganese. It is also rich in fiber. It contains about 100 calories per pound.

Rhubarb also contains oxalic acid, which can prevent the absorption of calcium. This is a relatively minor effect however and nothing for anyone with a reasonable intake of calcium to worry about.

Climate: Rhubarb is native to Siberia and so very hardy (to -20°F). It prefers cool moist summers (no higher than 75°F) and cold winters (below 40°F) with some freezing. When growing in cool climates rhubarb needs a sunny site, where it won't get too much frost (which could delay early harvests). In hotter ones it benefits from some shade during the hottest part of the day.

Rhubarb can deal with a long period of hot dry weather by going dormant, though of course this doesn't do anything for its productivity.

About Rhubarb

Perennial
Hardiness zones: 2 - 9
Viability: Plant may live for 20 years
Growing temp: 50 (55-75) 80°F
Plants per person: 2
Plants per sq ft: 1 plant needs 4 sq ft
Yield per plant: 1 - 6 lb
Yield per sq ft: ¼ - 1 ½ lb
Height: 36″
Width: 48″

Soil

pH 5.0 to 6.8

Rhubarb is a heavy feeder and prefers a deep, rich, moisture retentive soil with lots of organic matter. It needs to be well-drained, otherwise the roots may rot over the winter (raised beds help in this).

Soil preparation: Rhubarb is a perennial and will be in the ground for a long time, so you should incorporate lots of organic matter into the soil before planting. You might even double dig to get some of that organic matter down deep. You could also add some organic fertilizer mix to supply additional nutrients.

Planning

Where: Rhubarb is in the ground for a long time, so choose a site where it won't be disturbed. It should be well away from shrubs or trees, whose roots might take nutrients away from it. If the soil is not well-drained, you should grow it on a raised bed. Don't use a raised bed in a warm dry climate though, as it will dry out too quickly.

I grow rhubarb in a far from ideal climate of hot dry summers and mild wet winters, and it still does surprisingly well. In this climate it does best with light shade, as the large leaves can lose a lot of water on a hot day. It also benefits from a cooler microclimate.

When: Rhubarb can be planted any time the roots are dormant, from late autumn to spring. Of course pot grown plants can be planted at any time.

Planting

Rhubarb is grown from crowns, which are pieces of root with growing buds attached. The usual method of planting is to dig a large hole (three times the size of the plant) and heavily amend it with compost or aged manure and some fertilizer mix. The crowns are then planted so the bud is a couple of inches below the surface.

Growing from seed: Rhubarb isn't often grown from seed, but this is easy to do. It germinates readily and the seedlings grow rapidly (in the tropics it has actually been grown as an annual!)

There are several potential problems with growing rhubarb from seed. One is that the plants take several years to reach useful size. Another is that it doesn't come true to seed, so the seedlings will be quite variable, with some being inferior to their parents. Usually you select the best seedlings and propagate them vegetatively, while discarding the inferior ones (sow a lot of seed so you have plenty to choose from). You could even argue that the genetic variability is good.

Sow the seed 1″ apart in a flat in a greenhouse, or in a cold frame (plant extra so you can choose the best plants for growing on). The seedlings grow quite quickly and will need to be pricked out when they have 3 - 5 leaves. When they are large enough, plant them outdoors in a nursery bed, taking care to water regularly during their first year. Plant out the best plants in their permanent positions the following spring.

Spacing: Rhubarb can get quite big and likes to have plenty of room so don't crowd it. Overcrowded plants are more likely to have disease problems.

Beds: Plant the crowns 24 - 36″ apart in each direction.

Rows: Space the plants 24 - 36″ apart, in rows 36 - 48″ apart.

Care

Rhubarb is a tough and independent plant and can survive with relatively little care, however it will be more productive if you give it a little TLC.

Weeds: Remove all perennial weeds from the bed before planting (this is one of the benefits of double digging). A mulch will take care of any annual weeds.

Watering: Rhubarb is a cool weather plant with large leaves and requires quite a lot of moisture. In dry climates it will need regular watering to keep it productive. If it doesn't get enough water in hot weather the large leaves will wilt during the day and may even die back. If this occurs too often the plants may simply go dormant.

Fertilizing: Rhubarb is a heavy feeder, however an annual application of aged manure or compost (as mulch) should supply all the necessary nutrients.

Mulch: Apply a 2 - 3″ layer of compost or aged manure annually. This keeps down weeds, conserves moisture and feeds the soil (which then feeds the plants).

Winter protection: In very cold climates a thick mulch of leaves or straw can be useful to protect the plants over the winter.

Deadheading: Any flower stalks that appear should be removed promptly to stop the plant devoting energy to seed production. Remove the whole flower stalk, not just the flowering top (otherwise it will keep trying to flower). Never let it produce seed as this would waste even more energy.

Thinning: Rhubarb is a long lived plant when growing in ideal conditions, but after a few years it can start to get crowded (the stalks will be smaller in size and may be affected by pests or disease). To avoid this the plants should be thinned every 3 - 5 years, by dividing them and removing excess crowns (you can replant, give away or sell these).

Divide each root to leave at least one (and preferably 2 - 4) bud on each piece. Replant these so the top of the bud is covered with 2″ of soil.

Forcing outdoors: In northern Europe it was once a common practice to force rhubarb. This would give an early crop, up to 6 weeks before the unprotected plants. This was done by covering the crown (it stayed in the ground) with a bottomless bucket (the lid was left on). Leaves, manure or soil was piled around the bucket to insulate it.

The resulting shoots were pale pink and extra succulent from being deprived of light. After the harvest, the bucket was removed, a layer of mulch was applied and the plants were left to continue growing as normal.

You can hasten spring growth by covering the plants with clear plastic.

Pests: Obviously any time you have a problem with a perennial plant it is more serious than with an annual. Rhubarb is relatively pest free, but you may occasionally have problems with Japanese beetles, or leafhoppers.

My biggest problem has been with gophers. These rodents will completely destroy a plant, which is a problem in a plant that takes several years to grow. If you live in gopher country you should plant rhubarb in wire baskets.

Diseases: Potential disease problems include anthracnose, crown rot, foot rot, leaf spot and verticillium wilt.

Harvesting

When: Don't harvest any stalks in the first year after planting and only a few in the following year. This gives the plant time to grow as big as possible, so it produces large, succulent stems. In the third year you can start harvesting regularly. You harvest the stems after they have reached full size and the leaves have opened fully.

How: Harvest by twisting the stalk, so it separates from the root. You then remove the leaf otherwise it will draw moisture out of the stalk and it will quickly go floppy. You have two options in harvesting:

You can either harvest all of the stems on a plant at the same time (and then leave it for a long period to recover.

Alternatively you can take 3 - 4 stems from each plant (never taking more than half of the stems from a plant at one time). In this way you can harvest fairly regularly.

Some people harvest intensively for about two months in spring and then leave the plants alone so they can build up reserves of food. This makes sense, as real fruit becomes available later anyway.

Storage: The stalks will keep for a week or so in a plastic bag in the fridge. They can be kept fresh by keeping them upright in a jar of water.

For longer term storage it can be chopped and frozen.

Seed saving: Rhubarb produces seed readily if you allow it to; in fact the usual problem is stopping it. It doesn't often self-sow, but doesn't need to because it is a long lived perennial. The wind pollinated flowers are hermaphrodite (have both male and female parts).

Unusual growing ideas

Ornamental: Rhubarb has a strong bold shape and can be useful as an ornamental (though picking the stalks won't help its appearance).

Wild garden: Rhubarb is a good plant for the wild or forest garden because it tolerates light shade (though in cooler climates it will do best in sunny clearings). It is a very independent plant and often survives in abandoned gardens for years.

Containers: Rhubarb can do well in containers, though you have to give it a large one and plenty of water and nutrients.

Protection: You can speed up the growth of rhubarb in spring by covering the bed with a cloche.

Varieties

There aren't many.
Glaskins Perpetual - English heirloom, easily grown from seed.
Crimson Red - Prized for its fine flavor.
Victoria - Another classic variety.

Kitchen use

Rhubarb is something of an acquired taste and you either like it or you don't. It can be very sour and needs a lot of sugar to make it palatable. It is often combined with strawberries to make pie.

Rhubarb crisp

1 cup whole wheat flour
1 cup oats
1 cup sugar
½ cup butter
4 cups chopped rhubarb
2 tbsp cornstarch
1 cup water

Combine the flour, oats, ½ a cup of sugar and melted butter in a bowl and mix well. In another bowl mix another cup sugar with the cornstarch, add a cup of water and stir until smooth. Pour this mix over the chopped rhubarb and then cover with the flour and oat mix. Bake for 40 minutes at 350°F, until the top is golden brown and the rhubarb is tender. Eat warm, with whipped cream or ice cream.

Rutabaga

Brassica napus

Introduction: One of the classic fall root vegetables, rutabaga originated in a garden somewhere in Eastern Europe as a hybrid between turnip (*B. rapa*) and cabbage (*B. oleracea* var *capitata*).

Rutabaga is often confused with the similar looking turnip, but it is bigger, hardier (because it contains less water) sweeter, longer keeping and slower maturing. It came to Britain via Sweden, which is why they know it as swede (a contraction of Swedish turnip). The name rutabaga is Swedish and apparently means root-bag.

I hated this food while growing up in England and long held a lingering animosity to it. My mum knew better than to give it to me, but I was traumatized by school lunches and memories of puddles of overcooked translucent yellow slime) However a few years ago I grew it for my wife and was very surprised. Like many crops, it was very different when harvested fresh from the organic garden and was actually really good. I hold this as proof that you can heal those childhood scars.

Nutritional value: The rutabaga is a good source of vitamins A and C as well as calcium and potassium, but it is chiefly valued as a source of carbohydrates.

Ease of growing: Rutabaga is well known for being an undemanding plant. If you give it moist, fertile soil and plant it at the right time (in suitably cool fall weather) it should perform for you.

About Rutabaga

Seed facts
Germ temp: 40 (60 - 85) 95°F
Germination time: 3 - 10 days
Seed viability: 2 - 5 yrs
Germination percentage: 75+

Planning facts
Hardiness: Hardy
Growing temp: 40 (60 - 65) 75°F
Plants per person: 5
Plants per sq ft: 1½
Direct sowing:
Spring: 4 - 6 wks before last frost.
Fall: 3 to 4 months before first frost
Height: 12″
Width: 9″

Harvest facts
Days to harvest: 80 - 120 days
Yield per plant: 1 - 2 lb
Yield per sq ft: 2 - 4 lb

Climate: This is a cool weather crop (no surprise there, as it was developed in Sweden) and is traditionally grown as a fall / winter crop. It prefers cool days (60 - 65°F) and cool nights (50 - 60°F). The latter are needed to encourage the storage of carbohydrates which results in sweeter roots. It can tolerate cold down to around 20°F.

Crop value: This nutritious and easily grown root has long been an important winter food crop for humans and animals in cold northern climates. Before the introduction of the potato it was a staple crop for European peasants and is still potentially important for those seeking greater food self-sufficiency. A major virtue is that it can be left in the ground to provide food for an extended period over the winter.

Soil

pH 6.0 (6.5-7.0) 7.5

Rutabaga is less fussy about the soil than most Brassicas, but the ideal soil is fairly heavy, not too high in nitrogen and contains lots of potassium. It should also be fairly neutral (acidic soil encourages clubroot) and well-drained. The plants are very sensitive to boron deficiency.

Soil preparation: If the soil isn't very fertile, incorporate 2″ of compost or aged manure into the top 8″ of soil (this provides essential boron and holds moisture). Add wood ashes to supply potassium and lime to raise the pH if necessary.

Deep cultivation to loosen the soil to a depth of 12″ doesn't hurt when growing rutabagas. This also allows you to remove any stones or other debris.

Planning

Where: Like most cool weather crops rutabaga needs full sun for best growth and productivity.

When:

Spring: This hardy plant will work as a spring crop if early summer brings mild days (60 - 70°F) and cool (50 - 60°F) nights. If the weather is consistently above 80°F it is too warm. It will germinate in cold (40°F) soil, so can be planted as early as 4 - 6 weeks before the last frost.

In many cases spring sown plants aren't very satisfactory, as the warmer temperatures cause them to develop lots of leaves and small, pungent roots that don't taste very good. If this happens you can always eat the leaves, though they aren't as good as those of turnip.

Fall: Most areas of the country get too warm in early summer for rutabaga to be successful as a spring crop. In such cases (and all other cases too) it does much better in its traditional role as a fall crop. Plant 3 - 4 months before the first fall frost.

Crop rotation: Rutabaga should not be planted where another Brassica has been grown in the previous 3 years.

Planting

It has been found that large seeds germinate faster and grow better than smaller ones, so some people sift them to remove the smallest seed.

Direct sowing: Like most root crops rutabaga doesn't like transplanting, so it is pretty much always direct sown. Sow the seeds ¼ - ½″ deep and 2″ apart initially. Thin out the excess plants in two stages to reach the final spacing.

Spacing:

Beds: Space the plants 6 - 9″ apart in the bed. The exact spacing depends upon the fertility of the soil.

Rows: Space them 6 - 9″ in the rows, with 18 - 24″ between the rows.

Care: This robust plant doesn't usually require a lot of attention.

Water: Rutabaga needs constantly moist soil for best quality roots. If it's too dry the flavor won't be as good and the roots may split.

Mulch: This benefits the plants by keeping the soil cool, supplying nutrients, conserving moisture and suppressing weeds. In very cold weather a thick mulch is useful to keep the ground from freezing.

Weeds: Weed the young plants regularly as they are vulnerable to weed competition. Be careful about using a hoe as it can damage the shoulders of the roots.

Pests: The same pests that attack cabbage (aphids, flea beetles, slugs, snails) may bother rutabaga, but they are usually less troublesome. Root maggots may attack early plantings. If any pest becomes problematic you can use row covers to protect your plants.

Disease: It is prone to the same ailments as cabbage: clubroot, wirestem, mildew, boron deficiency.

Harvesting:

When: The roots are usually harvested when 3 - 6″ in diameter (bigger roots may get tough). They are improved by frost, but not by being frozen, so should be protected from extreme cold with a thick mulch. Harvest spring roots as soon as they reach useful size and before the weather warms up.

How: Dig the roots with a fork.

Storage: One of the advantages of rutabagas is they are so hardy they can be left in the garden until needed. If it gets so cold they could freeze solid, you can dig them all and store in a root cellar at 32 to 40°F.

Greens: If any plants remain in the ground in early spring, you can use their new foliage as spring greens (first year growth is generally tough and not as good as that of turnip.) The flower buds can be used like **Broccoli Raab.**

Seed saving: Rutabaga is a biennial, growing one season and producing seed in the following year. It is hardy enough to over-winter in the ground, before flowering in spring. Usually all you have to do is leave a few plants unharvested. If you stored them inside, you will have to replant the best ones in a convenient spot.

Rutabaga will cross-pollinate with Siberian kale, so only one crop should be flowering at one time. If necessary stake the tall plants (the tops can get quite heavy with seed) and leave them alone. Save seed from at least 5 plants to maintain some genetic diversity.

These plants produce a lot of seed, far more than you will ever need for planting. You can sprout some of the surplus seed like alfalfa to produce nutritious salad greens. You could also use it to grow micro-greens.

Unusual growing ideas

Forcing: Any surplus roots can be used as a source of winter greens. They are potted up and forced inside like those of **chicory**.

Varieties

Rutabaga isn't very popular in North America, a fact reflected in the relatively small number of varieties that are available here. There are lot of different types in Europe, but they can be hard to get hold of.

American Purple Top - Big purple shouldered roots (90 days).

Collet rouge - The name translates as red neck because the skin on top is red, while the bottom is yellow.

Collet Vert - This one has a green neck and yellow bottom.

Joan - Sometimes said to be best flavored variety (90 - 100 days).

Laurentian - An improved Purple Top (100 days).

Kitchen use

The roots are similar to those of the turnip, though they are generally considered to be superior. They are a traditional ingredient in winter soups and can be used in most of the same ways as potatoes (the two are sometimes eaten together.) Some people like it raw in salads or even sandwiches.

Mashed rutabaga

1 lb rutabaga
3 tbsp butter

The root is peeled and cut into pieces, put in boiling water and simmered for 15 minutes. When suitably soft it is mashed to a puree with the butter. It is then put back in a pan and re-heated to dry off some of the excess moisture. You could leave out the butter if you want less fat, but then this wouldn't really be much of a recipe.

Salad Mix / Mesclun

Introduction: The original salad mix was probably the French mesclun which originated in Provence and was a mix of lettuce, endive, arugala and chervil. In recent years the idea of salad mix has expanded to include a wide variety of different salad plants and commercial salad mixes are now very popular.

The clever part of growing salad mixes is the concept of sowing the plants so close together that they produce single leaves instead of hearted plants. The individual leaves are then cut as they reach suitable size. I have had such success with this method that I now grow most of my salad crops in this way.

Nutritional content: Salad greens are packed with vitamins (especially A and C), minerals and beneficial phytonutrients. We could all benefit from eating at least one salad every day.

Ease of growing: Few things are as easy to grow as salad, mix: it is about as close to foolproof gardening as you can get. It is certainly much simpler than growing a bunch of different plants. It is also fast, in some cases you can start harvesting within a couple of weeks.

Climate: The majority of common salad plants prefer cool, humid weather. If you choose the seeds yourself (rather than planting a pre-packaged mix) you can tailor your choice of plants and varieties to suit the climate. It is possible to create a mix that will do well in warmer situations too.

Crop use: I rate salad mix as an essential garden crop because of its high nutritional value, ease of growing and productivity. As far as I am concerned, no garden should be without its salad beds. This is a very productive way to use garden space and should be one of your highest priorities.

Soil

pH 6.0 to 7.0

The soil is called upon to produce a lot of foliage in a short time, so it should be fertile, fairly neutral, moisture retentive and well-drained.

Soil preparation: Raised beds are the best way to grow salad mixes, as they provide the ideal rich well-drained soil. They are also convenient in that you can simply plant a few square feet of bed every week or two, to keep a continuous supply coming.

Be generous in your fertilization program, starting by incorporating a 2″ layer of compost into the top 6″ of soil. You should also add seaweed, wood ashes and colloidal phosphate (or an organic fertilizer mix).

Planning

Which plants to use: You can buy packets of "salad mix" seed, but if you choose your own individual varieties you have more choices. You can decide the proportion of bland, sour, bitter, and different textures and colors and you can adapt it according to the growing season. You might create a warm weather mix and a cool weather mix, so you can keep the salad coming all through the growing season. You might also create a longer lasting mix by avoiding plants that bolt quickly. See **Varieties** for more on the choice of plants.

How much: Plant at least 2 sq ft of mixed salad greens per person at each planting. Of course exactly how much to plant depends upon how much salad you eat.

When: The season makes a big difference as to what you can grow in a salad mix. You have to adapt your growing methods (and the species of plants) to the weather.

Spring and fall: Most traditional salad plants do best in cool weather, so these are the easiest and the most productive growing times. Many of these plants are very hardy and can germinate at temperatures as low as 40°F, so you can start them pretty early. You can use cloches or poly tunnels to warm the soil and speed germination and growth.

Summer: If you want to grow salad mix in summer heat, you have to be a bit more resourceful, but it is certainly possible. Bolting (the bane of summer salad growing) is less of a problem because the plants won't be around long enough to get the chance.

In warm weather the biggest problem is that cool weather crops, such as lettuce, don't germinate very well (if at all) at higher soil temperatures. You can get around this by pre-germinating them in the fridge as described in **Lettuce**. You can also search out more heat tolerant species and varieties.

Winter: In Europe cold tolerant varieties of salad greens were commonly grown under glass (cloches, cold frames, poly tunnels) in winter and this can work well, as most of them prefer cool weather.

They will take longer to mature at this time of year, so make bigger sowings (or do it inside in containers). Your protected winter salad beds will be the perfect vacation resort for slugs and snails to spend the winter, so watch out for them too.

You can also move indoors entirely and grow them in the greenhouse (or under lights) in flats or large trays. See **Microgreens** for more on indoor salad growing.

Succession sowing: Make a planting of salad mix every 1 - 3 weeks (depending upon how much you eat and how fast they grow – which in turn depends upon the weather and the soil). The default option is to simply sow a patch every 10 days or so. If you end up with more salad than you need it will encourage you to eat more, which is not a bad thing.

Where

You don't need a lot of space to grow salad mix, because you get a lot of plants in a small area. In cool weather the plants will grow best with full sun, but can do okay with some shade (there is nothing to lose by trying). If you want to grow them in hot weather they will usually do better with some shade during the hottest part of the day.

Planting

Direct sowing: Salad mixes are almost always direct sown because you are dealing with so many plants, so closely spaced together, that transplanting would be impractical. There are two common ways of planting.

One way is to simply scatter (broadcast) the seed on the surface of the bed, so there is a seed every ½ - 1″. Spread this out carefully so the mix is evenly distributed and cover it with a light sifting of soil (or a mix of soil and sifted compost). When doing this it is important to scatter the seed evenly, you don't want bare patches and congested patches. If you are new to this you could practice scattering the seed on to a sheet or a large piece of cardboard.

The other method is to make shallow furrows ¼″ deep and 3″ apart. Plant into these at ½ - 1″ spacing and then scrape the disturbed soil back into them.

You can sow different kinds of seed into the same area of bed. However it is important that the strongest growers don't overwhelm the weaker ones, so make sure they have sufficient space (it helps to mix the seed up thoroughly before planting). You can also harvest judiciously to prevent this happening.

You can also plant each variety separately in its own short rows or block. This is better than mixing in many ways, because it allows you to compensate for different growth rates (some plants grow faster than others and will need planting more often). It also allows you to grow and harvest as much of each variety as you want.

Water immediately after planting to thoroughly wet the soil and give the seeds a good start.

After watering you might want to cover the bed with cardboard, row covers or shade cloth (this is better as you can water right through it). This will slow evaporation from the bed and so reduce the frequency of watering. It is important to remove this as soon as the seeds start to germinate though, otherwise they will elongate and become chlorotic in their search for light.

In many places you will have to protect the bed from birds, cats and other creatures. The usual way to do this is with bird netting draped over plastic hoops. I prefer to support the net with tunnels made from hog wire fencing.

Spacing: Careful spacing is important because you don't want the plants to be too crowded. If you are broadcasting you want your seeds to be ½ - 1″ apart (no wider and no closer). If you plant in rows you want ½ - 1″ spacing in the rows, with 3″ between the rows.

Care

The best salad material comes from plants that grow rapidly, so you need to make sure they have everything they need for good growth.

Thinning: Once all of the seeds have germinated you can start harvest / thinning, to give each plant enough room.

Weeding: The bed will need weeding when young, to ensure that weeds don't take over before the salad plants get established.

Watering: There are a lot of plants taking water from a small volume of soil, so the beds must be kept evenly moist at all times. This is especially critical in summer. Of course you don't want the soil to get waterlogged either, so be aware of what is happening.

Feeding: You may be able to speed up regrowth by watering the plants after harvest with a dilute liquid kelp. I prefer not to use my old compost tea standby on them, because they will be eaten fairly soon afterwards.

Pests and disease: Slugs and snails love salad mix and will eat the seedlings as they emerge. They can be hand picked at night, or you could surround the bed with some kind of barrier (such as a copper strip).

If insect pests become a problem you can grow your salad mix under row covers.

Birds also appreciate the tender succulent seedlings and they can be a problem in both cold and hot conditions. If so you may have to net the whole bed.

Bolting: If any plants bolt you should remove them immediately. They won't produce anything edible (the flower stems are too small to be of any use) and are just taking up space. Remove them and you leave more room for neighboring plants.

Harvesting

When: You can start harvesting individual leaves when they are 2 - 3″ tall, which takes about 3 - 4 weeks. This can continue for as long as the bed is producing a worthwhile amount, which depends upon the crop, variety and climate. Some plants can be harvested for a month, some for only a week or two. Generally you should expect to get at least 2 cuttings from a bed.

Salad mix is very perishable and for maximum nutrition and flavor it is best to harvest just before you are going to eat it. However it is often more convenient to harvest every few days and keep it in a plastic bag in the fridge until needed.

Commercial growers harvest early in the morning when the plants are at their coolest (heat is the enemy of salad mix).

How: I will describe three ways you can harvest the plants. You can use just one of these methods, but you get more flexibility by using a combination of all three.

You can cut whole small plants (or clumps of plants) with shears, leaving the bottom inch of stem behind to regenerate. This enables the plants to continue growing, so you can get a second (and sometimes even a third) harvest. This is often known as 'cut and come again', because the same plants are harvested more than once.

You can also pick the largest leaves from individual plants, to give you a longer harvest period.

Another alternative is to harvest entire plants and thereby thin overcrowded areas (do this strategically so you thin the most crowded areas first). By doing so you can slowly thin out most of the bed over time. The plants that remain can be allowed to get bigger.

You need to wash the salad before eating and to check for insects and unwanted weeds.

Storage: Salad mix doesn't store well so it's best to cut only as much as you need for the next meal. It will keep for a week in the refrigerator in a plastic bag, but it will slowly deteriorate.

Unusual growing ideas

Hot weather salads: Many plants that bolt quickly in hot weather might still be grown as a salad mix because you are harvesting the plants when they are little more than seedlings and they won't have time to bolt.

There are also things you can do to cool down the summer salad bed. Start by putting it where it will be coolest, which usually means in light shade (under a trellis, or to the north side of trees, fences or your house), or make a sunshade of shade cloth or wooden lath. Water daily to keep the entire area cool and moist and to prevent the plants from developing very strong flavors. Misters work great to cool the plants and provide water. You should also look for varieties and species that don't mind some heat.

Containers: Salad mix can be grown in containers, but I have dealt with that separately (see **Micro-greens**).

Ornamental use: A bed of salad mix is quite attractive (if temporary) and can be used for its ornamental effect. You can make patterns of different shapes, colors and textures.

Foraging; To bulk up the salad and make it more interesting, you can go around the garden gathering various edible leaves and flowers. These can be gathered without significant harm to any plants and leave the garden looking untouched. Throw in a few sprouts and edible flowers (see those separate sections) and you have a salad that not only taste great, but looks spectacular and is highly nutritious.

Seed Saving: Eventually any remaining plants will start to bolt. I sometimes allow a few of the most interesting types to grow up and set seed, as this supplies the seed that will be needed for growing next years salad mix.

Varieties

The ideal plants for a salad mix taste good (not too bitter or pungent), are tender and succulent, look good, germinate and grow quickly and don't bolt easily.
The choice of suitable plants will vary according to the growing conditions. Finding salad plants that tolerate hot or cold weather is more challenging than finding ones that grow well in mild temperatures.

When choosing plants, you will want a variety of flavors.

Bland: This is for the bulk of the salad. Lettuce is almost always the first choice, as there are so many kinds and they work so well. The best types of lettuce for this are the romaines, though leaf lettuce also works well. Usually you will have more than one variety in a mix.

Other bland green include amaranth, komatsuna, miners lettuce, spinach, chard and beet greens. Cornsalad is good too, but will probably need to be planted separately because it is fairly slow growing.

Pungent: Mustards are the most commonly used, because they so fast and easy to grow. Arugala is also popular, if you like its distinctive pungent flavor. Kale, green onion, garden cress, peppergrass, radish, land cress, Chinese cabbage and other Asian greens (mizuna, tatsoi and various mustards) are all possible options.

Bitter: Dandelion, chicory, fenugreek, radicchio (adds color too) endives (the curly frisee types are almost an essential because they add unique texture).

Sour: Sorrel

Succulent: Purslane is a great hot weather crop. Miners Lettuce does well in cool moist conditions.

Aromatic: Basil, green onion, chervil, cilantro, shiso and shungiku.

Wild plants and weeds: If you are creative (and know what you are doing) you can add a number of garden weeds to your mix, to bulk it up and add nutrition (and flavor).

Other plants: Of course you can add anything else that is edible in your garden. See **Edible flowers** in particular.

Cold tolerant: Cornsalad, Brassicas, chicory, Asian greens and some lettuce.

Heat tolerant: Mizuna, basil, amaranth, lambs quarter, purslane, chard, kale, collards, garden sorrel, New Zealand spinach and some lettuce.

Kitchen use

Combine your salad mix with some edible flowers and wild greens for the ultimate salad.

Tahini Salad dressing

4 tbsp tahini
Juice of a lemon
1 tsp mustard
1 or 2 garlic cloves (crushed)
2 tbsp tamari
½ tsp pepper
2 tbsp water

Mix everything together thoroughly and its ready.

Salsify

Tragopogon porrifolius

Introduction: This old European crop with the thin pale edible roots is also known as oyster plant because these are supposed to resemble oysters in flavor. It is a biennial and is grown in much the same way as the completely unrelated carrot.

Climate: Salsify is native to Southern Europe, but grows and tastes best at a relatively cool 75°F. Temperatures above 85°F can result in fibrous roots.

Ease of cultivation: This is a fairly easy plant to grow, as it is not that far removed from a wild plant.

Nutritional content: The root contains carbohydrates, B vitamins, calcium and potassium.

Soil

pH 6.5 - 7.5

Salsify will grow in most types of soil, but the roots will get bigger in a deep, loose and fertile one, that is not too rich in nitrogen. Very rocky soil, or fresh manure, may cause the roots to fork.

Soil preparation: Incorporate 2″ of compost or aged manure, along with wood ashes and phosphate rock. Lime if the soil is acid.

Planning

When: Plants that are harvested in warm weather aren't very good to eat, so you should time your planting so they mature as the weather starts to cool down (the flavor is also improved by frost).

In areas with a short growing season salsify may be started in spring 2 - 4 weeks before the last frost. The soil should be at least 40°F before planting.)

About Salsify

Germination temp: 40 - 85°F
Germination time: 12 - 21 days
Seed viability: 1 - 3 years
Hardiness: Very hardy
Growing temp: 45 (55 - 75) 85°F
Direct sowing
Spring: 2 - 4 wks before last frost
Fall: 12 - 16 wks before first frost
Days to harvest: 120 - 180 days
Yield: 1 - 5 lb sq ft

In areas with a long growing season they are usually planted to mature in fall, which means sowing 3 - 4 months before the first fall frost. In very mild climates the plants will continue to grow all winter, and can be harvested over a long period.

Where: Salsify grows best in full sun, but in hot climates it will benefit from light shade during the hottest part of the day. The roots are inferior when growing in warm weather.

Planting

Direct sowing: Like most root crops salsify doesn't like transplanting, so is almost always direct sown. Use fresh seed and don't sow it too thickly, 1″ apart and ½″ deep is about right.

The seed germinates fairly slowly, especially in cool soil, so don't panic if they don't appear immediately. When the seedlings have all germinated and are a couple of inches high, thin to their proper spacing.

Spacing:

Beds: 3 - 5″ apart in offset rows.

Rows: 3 - 4″ apart in the row, with 12″ between the rows.

Care

Water: It is important to keep the young plants well watered. Once they are well established they are more independent, but should still be kept evenly moist for best growth and quality. Lack of water results in fibrous roots.

Weeds: Salsify is fairly slow to get going and has sparse grass-like foliage, so you need to keep the plants well weeded.

Fertilize: The plants are in the ground for a long time, so give them a side dressing of fertilizer mix after a couple of months.

Mulch: Straw mulch is useful to conserve moisture and suppress weeds. In winter a thicker mulch may be necessary to prevent the ground from freezing.

Pests and disease: Carrot rust fly will also attack salsify (see **Carrot** for more on this). Other than that it seems to have few serious problems.

Harvesting

When: You can start to harvest the roots as soon as they are big enough to be worthwhile, but their flavor is improved by exposure to frost and cold weather.

How: Use a fork to loosen the soil, so you can pull the slender roots without breaking them. Breaking a root not only means less to eat, but it won't keep for very long

Storage: The roots don't keep well once harvested, so it is better to leave them in the ground where possible. In areas with mild winters this is easy, but where the ground freezes you may need to use a mulch to protect them.

The roots can be stored in a plastic bag in the fridge for a week or so (remove the tops of course), but they are thinner than carrots and don't keep as well.

In very cold climates the roots are usually dug (cut off the tops) and stored in moist sand in a root cellar, at 32 - 40°F. They should keep for several months when treated like this.

Seed saving: The seed isn't very long lived, so it is a good idea to save some regularly. This is pretty simple, just leave the plants alone and they will flower in their second year. They are insect pollinated, but there are so few varieties this isn't usually an issue. However they can also cross with wild salsify (which is a common weed in many areas.)

Collect the fluffy dandelion-like seeds before they blow away.

Unusual growing ideas

Ornamental: The flowers are quite attractive, though they don't appear until the second year.

Tops: The tops and immature flower stems can be eaten when the plants begin to grow again in their second year. Use them in salads or cook like asparagus

Varieties

Mammoth Sandwich Island - This is the only one you are likely to see.

Kitchen use

Use the roots raw or cooked, in the same ways as parsnip or carrot. The tough skin has to be removed, but this isn't too difficult. Just wash them and peel with a potato peeler. You can also peel them after they have been cooked. They have an affinity for cream.

The flowers and new spring greens can be added to salads (it is sometimes grown specifically for the latter).

Scorzonera

(Scorzonera hispanica)

This uncommon crop plant is also known as Black Salsify because of its black root. It is grown in much the same way as salsify, except that it is a perennial and is sometimes allowed to grow for 2 years to reach a larger size.

The root is eaten in the same way as salsify. The flowers and new spring greens can be added to salads.

Spanish Salsify

(Scolymus hispanicus)

This species is even rarer than the above rarity. It is cultivated and used as above.

It may be rare as a food crop, but in California this plant is known as Common Golden Thistle and is considered a noxious weed!

Sesame

Sesamum indicum

Introduction: The nutritious oily seeds of sesame have been an important crop for at least 5000 years. It is generally thought to have originated in Africa and was introduced into North America with African slaves. It isn't a very important crop in the US, either for farmers or gardeners.

Though sesame is rarely grown as a garden crop I have included it here because it is exceptionally nutritious and is a good source of oil (which isn't commonly found in most garden crops).

The seed is the source of one of the best edible oils and could potentially be an important crop for gardeners aiming for any kind of food self sufficiency.

Sesame is generally a long season crop, though some varieties mature in as little as 90 days.

Crop use: Sesame is outstanding as a source of oily, protein rich seeds. It is also one of the most practical crops for making your own vegetable oil (though probably not very cost effective at the moment).

Ease of growing: If you have a suitably long and hot growing season it should be fairly straightforward to grow. It is more difficult to grow in cooler areas though.

Nutritional content: The seeds are rich in protein and fat (they contain up to 50% oil by weight), as well as calcium, copper, iron and manganese. They are also an exceptional source of vitamin B1 and various beneficial antioxidants. The seeds just squeak past peanuts and sunflower seeds for the title of highest energy food in this book. A pound of seed comes packed with a total of 2578 calories.

The seed also contains some less welcome things too, including phytic acid and oxalic acid, both of which can make nutrients less available to the body.

About Sesame

Seed facts
Germ temp: 60 (70 - 80) 95˚F
Germ time: 5 - 14 days
Viability: 4 - 5 yrs
Weeks to grow transplants: 8

Planning facts
Hardiness: Tender
Temp for growth: 65 (70 - 85) 95˚F

Transplants:
Start: 4 wks before last frost
Plant out: 4 wks after last frost
Direct sow: 4 wks after last frost
Height: 2 - 8 ft
Diameter - 18″

Harvest facts
Days to harvest: 90 - 150
Yield: ¼ -2 oz / sq ft

Climate: As a native to the tropics sesame is very heat and drought tolerant. It needs a long hot growing season to thrive and does well in the same conditions as cotton and lima bean.

Soil

pH 5.5 (6.4) 7.0

Sesame can do well in most soils, even those that aren't very fertile. It will be more productive when growing in a moisture retentive and fertile soil though. It should also be well-drained, as sesame doesn't like wet roots. It doesn't like saline soil either.

Soil preparation: Add 2″ of compost to the soil along with some organic fertilizer mix. Don't give it too much nitrogen, as this can encourage leaf growth instead of seed production.

Sesame is a strong rooting plant and can improve the soil it grows in.

Planning

Where: Sesame is a warm weather crop and should be placed in the warmest and sunniest part of your garden. It won't thrive if it isn't warm enough. It should also be sheltered, as it is a fairly tall plant and can be blown over by strong winds.

When: Sesame shouldn't be planted outside until all frost danger is past and the soil is at least 65˚F (or preferably 70˚F), which may be 4 weeks after the last frost date. In areas with a short growing season this may be too late for this long season plant to mature, in which case it may have to be started indoors. It is a short day plant and flowers as the days shorten in late summer.

Planting

Sesame can be quite tricky to get established as it needs warm, moist soil and the fairly weak seedlings can have a hard time emerging if the soil is at all crusted. This could be an argument for starting it indoors if you only want a small number of plants.

Using transplants: Start seed indoors 8 weeks before you wish to plant out.

Direct sowing: Sow the small seed about ¼ – ½″ deep. They should germinate within a week or so.

Spacing: 6– 10″ is probably a good spacing, though commercial plantings are often closer.

Care

Weed: Sesame grows slowly when young and is vulnerable to weeds. Keep it well weeded at this stage.

Water: Young plants need moist soil to get established, but older plants are quite drought tolerant (they have a very wide spreading root system). However in dry climates regular irrigation will make the plants much more productive.

Don't give them too much water though, the plants can be harmed by this (it can also adversely affect the flavor of the seed).

Pests: Sesame isn't very attractive to most leaf eating insects, though it is occasionally bothered by aphids and thrips.

Diseases: Sesame may be affected by fusarium wilt, and various root rots, leaf spots and blights. Damping off is sometimes a problem during germination. Keep the leaves dry when possible and grow in well drained soil.

Harvesting

When: Sesame is indeterminate with individual seed pods ripening consecutively up the stem. These are 1 – 1 ½″ long, contain 8 rows of seeds (50 - 100 seeds in all) and turn brown when fully ripe. You have to be careful when harvesting as they shatter easily when ripe and a lot of seed can be lost.

How: The whole plant can be harvested when the first of the lower pods are fully ripe and start to open. They are sometimes tied together in a shock (also known as a stook) and left to dry in the garden.

Cut the whole seed heads and dry them on a sheet. Then thresh them to free the seed and dry thoroughly before storage. Drying the seed properly can be difficult, but it is important if it is to store well.

Storage: The dry seed (6% moisture max) stores well and can keep for several years.

Ornamentals: Sesame has attractive white bell shaped flowers, but they open slowly over a period of several weeks, so the plants aren't very showy.

Varieties

Finding suitable sesame seed varieties isn't easy because it is so rarely grown as a home garden crop.

Commercial growers generally use fast maturing unbranched types, with non-shattering seed pods.

Kitchen use

In America the oily seeds are most often found on baked goods, especially white hamburger buns (which is a sacrilege for such a wonderful food). They are also commonly available in the form of tahini, while sesame oil is one of the best cooking oils.

The seeds have strong, rich flavor that enhances many foods. It is often toasted to improve its flavor. This is easily done in a dry skillet and only takes a couple of minutes.

Apparently the seed has also been sprouted, though I have never tried it.

The leaves are also edible but not particularly good.

Tahini

I love this stuff and it makes the seeds more digestible. It is pretty easy to make.

Though most commercial tahini is made from hulled seed, you can use unhulled seed too (which is helpful if you are using home grown seeds. It will be slightly more bitter than the commercial stuff and probably also more nutritious.

Start by soaking your seed overnight in warm salt water to leach out the phytic acid. Then drain, rinse and put it in a dehydrator at 115°F for 4 - 6 hours until dry (you can also toast them lightly in an 300°F oven for 20 minutes, stirring occasionally). Then pulse / chop them to a paste in a food processor. If this seems too dry then add a little sesame oil to make it thinner and easier to grind.

Shallot

Allium cepa aggregatum group

Introduction: Some gourmets consider the shallot to be the most refined of all the Allium family and it certainly is milder and more delicately flavored than onion or garlic. It is the commonest kind of multiplier onion, a group that also includes potato onions and Egyptian onions. Each plant produces a cluster of up to 10 or so bulbs, each up to 2″ in diameter and connected at their bases.

Ease of growing: The shallot has similar growing requirements as the onion, though it is easier to grow, as you don't have to worry so much about day length. You can grow it as an annual, or you can leave it in the ground year round.

Crop value: Shallot is a very dependable crop for the home gardener and I highly recommend it. It is easy to grow, tasty, doesn't require much space, is quite productive and doesn't take a lot of work to grow. The bulbs also store better than onions.

Climate: Shallots prefer the same climate as the onion, which isn't surprising as they are simply another type of onion. They like cool weather (50 - 70°F) for growth and slightly warmer 70 - 80°F (and dry) weather for bulbing and ripening.

Like onions they are day length sensitive, with long days triggering bulbing. I didn't realize this for a long time though, because I always plant in fall, so they have plenty of time to grow before day length triggers bulbing.

Day length isn't such a big issue because they are perennial and in the ground for a long time. As long as each shoot has at least 4 or 5 leaves you can rest easy and happily watch them bulb up when they are ready.

Nutritional content: Like the onion they are rich in vitamin C, potassium, calcium and a variety of beneficial phytochemicals.

About Shallot

Perennial
Hardiness zones: 3 - 10
Soil temp: 50 (60 - 65) 75°F
Seed viability: 1 - 4 years
Yield: 1 - 4 lb sq ft
(1 lb sets gives 5 - 7 lb bulbs)
Yield per plant: 2 - 8 oz
Days to harvest: 90 - 120 days
Growing temp: 50 (60 - 70) 75°F
Plants per person 5 - 10

Soil

pH 6.0 (6.5) 7.0

Shallots prefer the same kind of soil as onion, well-drained, rich, loose and moisture retentive. However they will do fine in a less than ideal soil. It does need to be well-drained though, as they may rot over the winter if it is too wet. If your soil isn't very well-drained, you should grow them in raised beds, or on ridges of soil.

Soil preparation: Incorporate 2″ of compost or aged manure into the top 6″ of soil, to supply nutrients and aid in moisture retention. This is particularly important if your soil is light and doesn't hold water well.

You may want to add colloidal phosphate to supply phosphorus and wood ashes or greensand for potassium. You could also use a standard fertilizer mix, though they don't need a lot of nitrogen.

If the soil is very acidic add lime to raise the pH.

Planning

Where: Shallots don't take up much space, so it's fairly easy to find a place for them. If you are growing them as an annual, put them in a raised bed. If you are growing them as a perennial, put them in any vacant spot where they won't be in the way. You can even plant them singly around the garden. Just remember that they need full sun.

When: Depending upon where you live, shallots can be either planted in fall or spring. You might even plant at both times, as extra insurance. Spring planted bulbs are also less likely to bolt.

Spring: The bulbs are quite hardy and can be planted 4 - 6 weeks before the last frost date (they actually prefer to grow in cool soil). Starting early is important to give them as long a growing season as possible before they bulb. They grow well in the long days of spring and early summer, and should be ready to harvest in mid to late summer.

Fall: In mild climates they are usually started in fall at the same time as garlic. If winter isn't too harsh this is generally the best way to go and results in bigger bulbs. A deep mulch can help them to survive severe cold (though watch for mice getting in there and eating the bulbs). Fall planted bulbs are more likely to bolt than spring planted ones, which may be an issue with some types.

Planting

Vegetative: When shallots are grown from bulbs they are planted directly in the garden. Plant them so the pointed tip of the bulb just shows above ground level and the flat end is down. If they somehow work their way out of ground (birds often have something to do with this), just put them back in.

Seed: Seed grown shallots are usually grown in the same way as onion, which means starting them indoors as transplants. See **Onions** for how to do this.

Once you have raised your first crop of bulbs from seed, you can start propagating them vegetatively.

Spacing:
Beds: 4″- 6″ - 8″ apart
Rows: 4 - 6″ apart in rows 9″ apart

Care

Weed: As with the related onions, shallots have quite sparse foliage and are vulnerable to weed competition. They should be weeded regularly, preferably by hand, as the bulbs are easily damaged (be very careful if using a hoe near the plants). A mulch can be a big help in keeping weeds down.

Water: Shallots are somewhat drought tolerant, but need evenly moist soil for best production. Don't let the soil dry out too much as it can reduce the final yield.

Fertilization: If your soil is poor give the plants a foliar feed of compost tea when the shoots are about 6″ high. Feed them again about a month later.

Mulch: A couple of inches of straw mulch may be applied when the shoots have appeared. This helps to keep down weeds and reduces the rate at which the soil dries out in hot weather.

Unearthing: Shallots like to grow half out of the soil. If the bulbs get partially buried, scrape away the soil to expose them almost down to the roots.

Pests: Shallots are bothered by the same pests as onions (thrips, onion maggot, slugs and snails, gophers, leafhoppers), but are usually relatively pest free.

Disease: The plants can be afflicted by all of the same diseases as onions, as well as damping off, downy mildew, rust and more. One of the commonest problems is bulb rot caused by cold, wet soil. Generally they are quite trouble free though.

Bolting: Some types of shallots may occasionally try to flower. If this happens cut off the entire flower stalk promptly, as it takes energy from the bulbs (the vegetative types can't produce viable seed anyway).

Harvesting

When: The bulbs are ready to harvest when the tops have died down, usually in July or August.

You can harvest the green tops at any time for use like scallions.

How: Pull the whole bulb clusters (you can almost just pick them up off the ground) and leave in a warm, dry, shady place for a few days to dry.

Storage: Shallots keep very well (some varieties better than others). They generally last longer than onions, and were once saved until the store of bulb onions had gone.

They keep best in a cool dry place, at 32 - 50°F and 60% humidity. Don't keep them in the fridge for very long, as it is too humid (too much moisture can encourage sprouting or mold).

Don't break up the bulbs until you are going to use them, as it may start them sprouting.

Seed saving: There are actually two types of shallots, those that are propagated from seed and those that aren't. The latter don't produce fertile flowers and so can't produce seed. With these you simply save some of the bulbs for replanting.

If your plants produce viable seed you can save it in the same way as for onion. The flowers are cross-pollinated by insects, but this isn't usually a problem as there are no close wild relatives and most people don't let their onions flower. Seed production just happens, all you have to do is not stop it. Collect the seed from the dry head and dry it thoroughly before storing. The seed doesn't remain viable for very long, often only a couple of years, so don't try and keep it too long.

Unusual growing ideas

Greens: You can grow shallots as a source of scallions. The best way to do this is to have a permanent colony of the plants (or small patches in different parts of the garden).

Interplant: You could plant a low growing / fast maturing intercrop in between the rows of shallots, to make the space more productive.

Containers: Shallots do quite well in containers, so long as they are deep enough.

Indoor greens: Shallots can be grown indoors in winter to supply green onions.

Varieties

Though many garden centers simply sell "shallots", there is actually a considerable difference between the different types. These differ in color, flavor, keeping qualities, the day length they require for bulbing and how you grow them.

You could try growing shallots that are sold for food, just be aware that there is some danger that the bulbs may contain virus disease. You will have the best chance of success with bulbs that were locally grown and are organic. Chemically grown bulbs are commonly treated to retard sprouting (and may rot before they sprout).

Types of shallot

The information on shallots is often contradictory and confusing. It can be difficult to know what is a shallot and what is not a shallot.

True shallots

These are only propagated vegetatively and can't be grown from seed.

French Red - This is the most commonly available type (or group of types). It has pink flesh and does better than the gray type in southern areas.

French Gray (Griselle) - The French consider this the one true shallot, with the one true shallot flavor. If you want to grow it you will probably have to go on-line and hunt it down. It doesn't keep as well as the other types (only 4 - 6 months). Also it often doesn't do well in more southerly areas.

I'm not sure whether the following are true shallots (the French would probably say not), but they are usually propagated from bulbs.

Picasso - This Dutch type has red brown skin and pink flesh.

Yellow moon - A Dutch variety with yellow skin.

Seed grown shallots

Vegetative propagation is fine for the gardener, but commercial growers prefer to grow from a small quantity of easily stored seed, rather than a large volume of perishable bulbs. Consequently there is a whole range of commercial varieties (usually hybrids) for growing from seed. The big shallots you see in supermarkets are this type.

Shallot connoisseurs consider these to be just a small perennial onion, rather than a shallot. Whatever they are they are still a useful crop that is well worth growing. They include:
Picador
Saffron
Conservor

Kitchen use

Shallots are an essential ingredient in French cuisine and they specify certain types for certain recipes.

Shallots work great if you only need a small quantity of onion.

The greens are very good too.

Potato Onion

Allium cepa aggregatum group

Introduction: The potato onion is a type of multiplier onion (like shallot) that is thought to have originated in Scandinavia. It has the same growth habits as the shallot and is cultivated in exactly the same ways. The major difference is that it produces much larger bulbs (up to 3″ in diameter), so is actually more useful. It doesn't have any connection to the potato except that it is usually propagated vegetatively (which is a pretty slender connection).

Growing potato onions is ideally suited to home growing, as it is so simple as to be almost foolproof. You simply plant a bulb and harvest a clump of bulbs!

This was a popular crop plant in America when people grew their own food and many families handed it down, mother to daughter for generations (the very definition of an heirloom crop). Use of this plant declined drastically when people stopped growing much of their own food, to the point where it is now almost forgotten. It is even difficult to find bulbs to plant.

Crop value: If the value of a plant is indicated by the number of pages written about it, then I should write a lot more about this one. However most of what I have written about growing onion and shallot is also relevant here, which means this entry is fairly short. Nevertheless this is an outstanding perennial food crop (probably the best overlooked one) and really should be grown by everyone.

Ease of growing: In many ways this is the easiest of all the onions to grow. It has the advantage of vegetative propagation as in the shallot, but produces bigger bulbs.

Like other onions the potato onion is day length sensitive, so should be planted in fall or early spring. This gives it plenty of time to grow before the appropriate day length triggers bulbing.

How they grow: The bulb send up several shoots and grows into a cluster of green plants. Eventually the old bulb shrinks away and each shoot in the cluster forms a new bulb on the soil surface. Generally each plant will produce 3 - 5 bulbs, but sometimes there is as many as 12.

As a rule of thumb you can expect to harvest at least five times what you plant, which should give you some idea how much you need to plant (and save) to supply yourself with onions for the year.

I have read that if you plant a large bulb it will make a cluster of many small ones, whereas if you plant a small bulb it will make one large one. I can't verify this though, because I haven't paid that close attention (I only have a short attention span). If it is true then it means you should plant a number of big and small bulbs every year. The small ones will then grow into big ones for eating, while the big ones will grow into small ones for replanting.

Soil: Same as for onion and shallot.

Fertilization: Same as for onion and shallot. It doesn't need a lot of nitrogen.

When to plant:
Fall: In milder climates the bulbs are often planted in fall, along with garlic and shallot. As the plants then have longer to grow they should give you a bigger harvest (though this doesn't always happen). Another advantage is that if you plant in fall, you don't have to store them over the winter.

In cold climates fall planted bulbs might not survive a particularly cold winter, so there is some risk. Fall planting also encourages bolting, whereas spring planting doesn't. This is good if you want to save seed, bad if you don't.

Spring: In colder climates spring planting makes the most sense, especially if you don't want them to bolt (which takes energy from the bulbs). You can plant as soon as the ground can be worked in spring, which may be a month before the last frost (or even earlier in some cases).

Spring planted bulbs usually mature a little later than those planted in fall. If you have enough bulbs you could plant at both times, to spread out the harvest and provide a little extra insurance against loss.

Spacing:
Beds: Space the plants 6 - 8″ apart in wide beds.

Rows: Space the plants 3 - 4″ apart in the rows, with 18 - 24″ between the rows.

Planting: Plant as you would a shallot, so the bulb is just covered with soil (some people plant deeper in fall for better protection from the cold).

Growing from seed: The potato onion can be started from seed quite easily. The difficult part is finding seed to plant (if you can't find any contact me, I usually have some). The disadvantage of vegetative propagation is that over the years bulbs can get infected with virus diseases, which can result in small (though perfectly usable) bulbs. When plants are grown from seed they can produce big, beautiful virus free bulbs, 3 - 4″ in diameter, in their first year.

Plants grown from seed will also show a lot more genetic variation because they aren't all clones of the same plant. There may be differences in color, size, shape and bulbing habit. You can simply choose bulbs of those you like best for replanting the following year and propagate them vegetatively.

Care: These are surprisingly tough plants. I have had small plants appear to die in hot dry conditions, only to reappear and produce bulbs the following summer.

Watering: Water the plants regularly while they are growing rapidly. Stop watering when the bulb forms and the leaves start to turn yellow, so the neck can dry out.

Mulching: In cold climates overwintering bulbs will benefit from the protection of a thick mulch. This should be removed after all hard frosts are past, so the soil can warm up.

Problems: The only major difficulty I have found with potato onion is finding seeds or bulbs to plant. It is a lot easier to grow than it is to find. This is unfortunate because if more people could try it, then it would be much more popular. This would make it more available, so even more people could try it. Fortunately it is gradually becoming easier to find.

Insurance: The problem with growing perennial vegetables such as this is if something goes wrong you can lose everything. One year all of my stored potato onion bulbs were eaten by wood rats, fortunately I had overlooked a few bulbs in the ground. These produced seed and I was able to start over again. Avoid this by encouraging friends and neighbors to grow it too. This provides invaluable insurance against loss.

Another form of insurance is to plant some of your bulbs in fall and some in spring. Then if your fall bulbs meet an unanticipated fate, you haven't lost everything.

Seed saving: Many people say it is hard to get potato onions to flower and produce seed, but I haven't found this to be a problem. In fact my fall planted bulbs produce seed so readily I have had to start spring planting too.

If a bulb produces seed it will use all of its energy for that and will shrivel and become pretty much inedible.

Harvest:

When: This is a fairly short season crop and a spring planting can be harvested in late summer, when the leaves start to die back.

How: The mature bulbs sit on the ground and can often be simply picked up. If the soil is hard you may have to loosen it with a fork first.

Curing: After harvest you need to keep the bulbs in a dry place to cure (just as you would other onions).

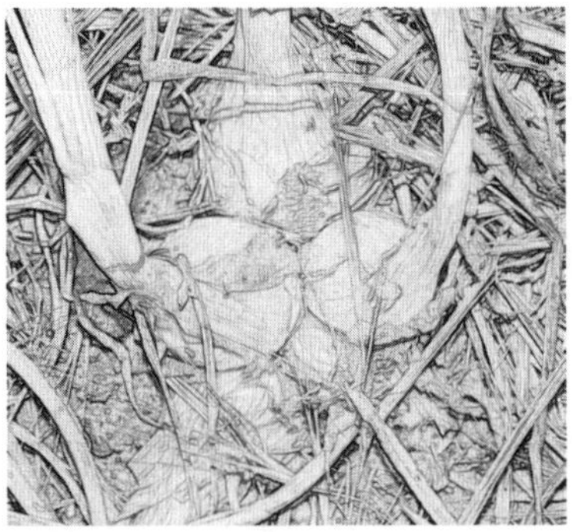

Storage: Store your best bulbs in a cool, dark, rodent-proof place (this is especially important for any bulbs you will use for replanting). Potato onions store exceptionally well and will often stay good for up to 12 months.

Of course you need to set aside a portion of your crop for replanting the following year.

Varieties: A few do exist, but you are usually lucky to find any potato onions at all. Even if you find somewhere to get the bulbs, you may have another problem in that they are only usually available at the end of the growing season (around October) and often sell out quickly. When you find somewhere that sells them order early.

If you grow them from seed you will find quite a bit of variation in each plant and can create your own varieties.

Kitchen use: You can use the bulbs and green leaves as you would those of onions. The bulbs will be different sizes so you can choose the size you need for whatever dish you are cooking.

The potato onion is nice when fried with potatoes (which is another very slender connection between the two).

Shungiku

Chrysanthemum coronarium

Introduction: Shungiku is actually a species of Chrysanthemum (it is sometimes called Garland Chrysanthemum), though not a very showy one. It is native to the Mediterranean, where it is known as crown daisy, but it is only commonly used for food in Asia (how it got there must be an interesting story, but I don't know it). It has a nice aromatic, almost floral flavor that goes great in salads. You don't need a lot of plants as it is quite strongly flavored.

Climate: In its native Mediterranean shungiku is a late winter / spring flower. It grows best at a mild temperature of 60 - 70°F. Hotter temperatures usually cause it to bolt fairly quickly. It will tolerate light frost.

Nutritional value: Like most leafy greens it is high in vitamins, including A, B1, B2, B6, C, K and folate. It is also rich in minerals including calcium, phosphorus and potassium, as well as various beneficial antioxidants.

Ease of growing: Shungiku isn't a very demanding plant and is pretty easy to grow. The only problems I have had is with its unseemly haste to flower when the weather warms up.

Soil

pH: 5.2 - 7.5

This weed-like annual does well in most soil types, but (as usual) it gets bigger and more succulent in rich, well-drained, moisture retentive soil.

About shungiku

Germ temp: 60 - 70°F
Days to germinate: 7 - 21
Days to harvest: 30 - 50
Direct sow
Spring: 2 wks before last frost
Fall: 8 - 10 wks before first frost

Planning

When: Shungiku prefers cool weather and in most of the U.S. it must be grown as a spring or fall crop. In cooler areas it can be grown all summer too. In areas with mild winters it is commonly planted in fall as a winter salad green. In less mild areas it can be grown under cold frames or in tunnels.

Where: Shungiku will be most productive in full sun, but in warmer climates it will benefit from light shade during the hottest part of the day.

Planting

Transplants: Shungiku isn't usually started indoors because it is quite hardy and germinates well in cool soil, but it is easy enough to do. It doesn't mind transplanting so you can use flats or cell packs.

Direct sowing: Plant the seed ¼ - ½″ deep and 1 - 2″ apart, to be thinned to the desired spacing later.

Spacing:
Beds: When growing in beds space the plants 4 - 6″ apart.

Rows: If you want to grow in rows space the plants 3 - 6″ apart, in rows 12 - 20″ apart.

Succession sowing: The plants aren't very long lived, so you may want to plant every 3 - 4 weeks to ensure a continuous supply.

Care

Watering: Keep the soil evenly moist for best growth.

Weeds: Shungiku doesn't compete with weeds very well, so keep it well weeded.

Feeding: Plants may benefit from an occasional foliar feed to keep them growing rapidly.

Frost protection: Shungiku tolerates light frost, but will need protection from harder ones.

Pests and disease: I can't remember ever having a problem with it. In fact the plants attract beneficial insects to the garden.

Harvesting

You can harvest thin whole plants until you get to the final spacing and then start picking leaves individually (take single leaves from a number of plants and they won't even notice). Gathering regularly may delay flowering. Pinch out any flower shoots as they appear (they are edible too, so don't just throw them away).

You can also harvest by cutting off the entire top of the plant, leaving a couple of inches of stem to regenerate. It should re-grow a couple of times before it will need replacing.

Seed saving: Shungiku produces seed readily if allowed to flower (somewhat too readily actually). You probably don't have to worry about keeping a variety pure because there are so few of them. Just cut the ripe seed heads and dry them in a paper bag.

Unusual growing ideas

Ornamental: This species is occasionally grown in the ornamental garden for its small, daisy-like yellow flowers.

Varieties

Shungiku is sometimes sold under the name chop suey greens, garland chrysanthemum and tong ho (its Chinese name). There aren't many varieties and usually you see the fern leafed type, which closely resembles the wild plant. However there is also a broad leafed type too, which is said to be somewhat more refined and better flavored.

Kitchen use: This species adds an interesting flavor to salads and I like it a lot. Apparently it has also been cooked as a potherb or braised, but I haven't tried this.

The edible flower petals (not the whole flower) can be added to salads.

Sorrel, French

Rumex scutatus

Introduction: This species isn't very well known in this country, but it is grown all around the world where suitable conditions exist (it is most popular in Northwestern Europe). I am including it here because it is easy to grow and thrives in fairly inhospitable conditions. I am not going to say a lot about it however.

Climate: This cool weather plant prefers mild temperatures (50 - 70°F) and plenty of moisture. It is quite a tough plant though and will tolerate hotter and drier conditions too.

Ease of growing: French sorrel is essentially a no-work plant. It is a perennial and once established it will spread vegetatively to form a dense clump. It will also self-sow and quite literally grow itself.

Nutrional content: This species is very rich in vitamins A, B9 and C, as well as iron, magnesium, and calcium and some powerful antioxidants. It also contains mildly toxic oxalic acid (which is actually responsible for its lemon-like flavor), so should be used in moderation (don't try to live on it for long periods). See **Spinach** for a bit more on oxalic acid.

Soil

pH: 5.5 (6.0 - 6.5) 6.8

Sorrel will grow in most soil types, so long as they aren't too alkaline, It will be most productive in a rich, moisture retentive, well-drained one.

Planning

When: Sorrel is a perennial so you don't need to get it started particularly early. In fact it is probably best to wait until the soil has warmed up in spring. You can also sow it in fall to germinate in spring.

Where: This is a perennial, so it's best not to put it plant in the annual beds. Give it space somewhere it can grow without disturbance. It grows best in a mix of sun and shade, which makes it a great plant for a forest garden situation,

Planting

This plant is easily grown from seed, either started inside or direct sown. Once you have plants growing vigorously, you probably won't need to plant it again. If it doesn't self-sow enough for you, then you can get more plants by dividing the clumps. This is actually beneficial as it rejuvenates the plants.

Spacing: This perennial spreads vegetatively to form large clumps. Plant it with a spacing of 12 - 15″ apart, though this will gradually get smaller as they grow and fill in.

Care

Watering: Sorrel is quite drought tolerant and does fine in my garden, where it is lucky to get watered once a week. However for maximum productivity and best flavor it should have a moist soil.

Feeding: To keep the plants growing well, mulch it with compost every spring. You might also give it a little fertilizer mix.

Control: In the right conditions this plant can become something of a nuisance, as it slowly spreads vegetatively and self sows enthusiastically. If you don't want it springing up everywhere remove the flower stalks as they appear (this will also make the plant devote more energy to vegetative growth).

Pests: Sorrel is generally quite pest free, though sometimes leaf miners will be a problem. Deal with them by discarding infested leaves, or simply cut off the inhabited parts and use the rest.

Harvesting

Pick the leaves as they reach full size (they will still be tender). The newly emerged spring leaves have a milder flavor, but you get less of them. The flavor deteriorates after flowering, so remove the flower stalks. Regular harvesting encourages further growth.

The thin leaves wilt quickly after harvest, so gather just before you want to use them.

Seed saving: Sorrel can produce a lot of seed if given the chance. Usually the problem is stopping it.

Unusual growing ideas

Wild garden: Sorrel is too permanent and too vigorous to be put in the intensive beds (and doesn't need such rich soil anyway). Just plant it in the semi-wild garden and let it fend for itself. It is an ideal forest garden crop and could almost be used as a groundcover.

Varieties

There aren't many of these, usually it is just 'French Sorrel".

De Belleville: This is the only variety I have seen.

Kitchen use

The sour leaves are most often used to give salads a little extra flavor (they can even replace lemon juice or vinegar). They are a little too strong to make a whole salad out of though.

The leaves can also be used as a potherb and this reduces their sour flavor considerably, though they shrink a lot in cooking. Many recipes for sorrel also call for cream or milk because it combines with the oxalic acid and neutralizes the acidic taste.

In France sorrel is traditionally cooked with eggs and used to make soup or sauce for fish.

Related species:

Sorrel – *Rumex acetosa*

Patience Dock - *Rumex patienta*

Both these species are grown and used like the above.

Sorrel soup

This is a traditional peasant recipe throughout much of Northern Europe. It is known as schav in Slavic countries.

4 tbsp olive oil
½ cup green onions (or onion)
4-6 cups sorrel leaves
6 potatoes
Salt
3 tbsp flour
1 quart vegetable stock
1 egg
½ cup cream (or milk)
1 bay leaf

Heat the stock to simmer and add the potatoes, bay leaf and salt. While this is happening sauté the chopped green onions and sorrel in the olive oil for 5 – 10 minutes. Then add them to the stock and simmer until the potatoes are tender (15 minutes). When they are cooked reduce it all to a puree in a blender.

The next step is to beat the egg with the half cup of cream and a ¼ cup of soup (you don't want the egg to cook before it is mixed). Then add the egg/cream mix to the soup and cook on a low heat for 5 minutes (don't let it boil). Keep whisking all the time until it gets thick.

Spinach

Spinacia oleracea

Introduction: Spinach originated in Asia and reached Europe during the Middle Ages. It is one of the most popular leaf vegetables because it is quick and highly productive. The harvest can start within a month of planting and it can be out of the ground within 2 months.

Climate: This is very much a cool weather crop, growing best at a mild 60 - 65°F during the day and even lower at night (down to 40 - 45°F). It is quite hardy and can tolerate temperatures as low as 20°F.

Spinach doesn't like hot weather and will be unhappy (and probably bolt) when it gets above 75°F.

Nutritional content: Spinach is rich in iron, but this is very water soluble and easily leached out by boiling. It is also a source of vitamins A (beta carotene), C and K, folate, luteine and various useful phytochemicals. It contains about 100 calories per pound.

Spinach also contains mildly toxic oxalic acid, which can make calcium somewhat less available in the body. Fortunately this is not a significant problem to anyone with a reasonable intake of calcium. You will still get more calcium from eating spinach than you will lose from ingesting the oxalic acid.

Oxalic acid may also contribute to the formation of kidney stones, so anyone prone to them should probably avoid spinach.

Ease of growing: As with many other crops, spinach is easy to grow if you give it the right conditions, which in this case means cool

About Spinach

Seed facts
Germ temp: 35 (55 - 65) 75°F
Germination time: 5 - 22 days
62 days / 32°F
22 days / 41°F
12 days / 50°F * Optimum
7 days / 59°F
6 days / 68°F
5 days / 77°F
Seed viability: 2 - 4 years
Germination percentage: 60%
Weeks to grow transplants: 3 - 4

Planning facts
Hardiness: Hardy
Growing temp: 60 - 65°F day
40 - 45°F night
Plants per person: 10 per planting
Plants per sq ft: 9

Transplants:
Spring crop:
Start: 8 wks before last frost
Plant out: 4 wks before last frost
Direct sow:
Spring: 6 wks before last frost
Fall: 6 - 8 wks before first frost
Succession sow: Every 2 wks

Harvest facts
Days to harvest: 40 - 60
Yield per plant: 6 - 8 oz
Yield per sq ft: ½ - 2 lb sq ft

weather and short days. It is usually grown as a spring and fall crop, with the latter being easiest. Forget about trying to grow spinach in warm weather, no sooner does it reach any size than it bolts (in fact it sometimes bolts before it reaches any size at all!)

Soil

pH 6.0 (6.5) 7.0

Spinach is a fast growing and fairly hungry plant and does best in a soil that is rich in humus, moisture retentive and contains lots of nitrogen and potassium. A light and well-drained soil is best as it will warm up quickly in spring. It should also be fairly neutral as spinach doesn't like acid soil. It is quite tolerant of saline soil.

Soil preparation: For best growth spinach needs a steady supply of available nutrients. It likes organic matter, so incorporate 2″ of compost or aged manure into the top 10″ of soil (where most feeder roots are found), along with a fertilizer mix. It loves manure and can even thrive in soil containing fresh manure (though ideally this should be incorporated the previous autumn).

Spinach doesn't like acid soil, so lime if necessary. Not too much lime though, as it doesn't like very alkaline soil either!

Planning

Where: Spinach really doesn't like heat and in warmer areas it will do better on a site that has light shade during the hottest part of the day. When growing in cool weather it should be in full sun. Raised beds are good because they warm up quickly in spring and tend to be well-drained.

Rotate spinach (and the related beet, chard and quinoa) so it doesn't grow in the same place for at least 3 years. The plants should have good air circulation to minimize disease problems.

When: More than any other common crop, spinach doesn't like warm weather, in fact it actually germinates best at only 50°F. If you look at **Seed facts** you will notice that it germinates more rapidly at higher temperatures, but less seed will germinate. At 70°F only about half of the seeds may germinate.

You have several options of when to grow spinach:

Spring: You must sow spinach early if you are to get a useful crop before heat and lengthening days cause it to bolt. Start the first spinach plants indoors about 8 weeks before the last frost date and plant it out about 4 weeks later. Direct sow your first outdoor crop 6 weeks before the last frost date.

Don't stop with one planting, you should be able to make 2 - 3 succession sowings 2 weeks apart, and maybe more, depending upon how quickly the weather warms up.

Summer: If you live in a climate with cool summers you may be able to grow spinach right through the summer. Just succession sow every 2 - 3 weeks.

If you don't have cool summers then forget about spinach, there are plenty more fish in the sea. See **Warm weather alternatives to spinach** below.

Autumn: Spinach does best as a fall crop, as it is much less prone to bolting in the shorter, cooler days and the leaves grow larger and more succulent. Sow the seeds when the soil starts to cool down, which may be a couple of months before the first autumn frost date.

The biggest problem when planting fall spinach comes when the soil is too warm. It must be cool enough for good germination (ideally below 60°F), otherwise germination may be poor. To improve your chances you might try cooling the soil by frequent watering, and using shade cloth. Another option is to pre-germinate the seed in the fridge. Put the seeds on a moist paper towel, put it in a plastic bag and store in the fridge for a week. They should then germinate quite well.

Winter: In areas with mild winters, some varieties of spinach can be grown as a winter crop, starting 4 - 8 weeks before the first fall frost. They are hardy down to 25°F and don't bolt in the cool, short days.

The key to success as a winter crop is for the plants to get big enough before cool weather hits. They will then continue to grow throughout the winter. If they are not big enough, they will just sit there looking sorry for themselves.

Spinach won't take hard frost unprotected, so in harsher climates it is often grown under the cover of cloches, cold frames or poly tunnels.

Planting

Direct sowing: This is easier than using transplants and generally more satisfactory. Sow the seed ½″ deep (¼″ in cold soil) and 1 - 2″ apart (either broadcast or in wide rows).

Spinach sown directly into cold spring soil is slow to germinate, so some gardeners pre-germinate it before planting. Alternatively you could warm the soil with plastic mulch or cloches. Some gardeners mark the location of the slow germinating seeds by sowing a few radishes along with the spinach.

Thinning: When all of the plants have emerged, thin them to 2 - 4″ apart. When they are 4″ high thin them again to a final spacing of 4 - 8″ (eat any thinnings that are big enough to be worthwhile). Spinach doesn't like being overcrowded and will often react by bolting.

Transplants

Starting inside: Spinach doesn't like transplanting (it can cause bolting), so this is only done under special circumstances. You might do it when you want to get an early start to the season, or in late summer, to give it cooler conditions than it would get outside.

To minimize root disturbance you should use cell packs or soil blocks. You can also multi-plant it by putting several seeds in each cell.

The plants germinate and grow best in cool conditions, so don't let them get too warm, otherwise they may not perform well when transplanted outdoors.

Spacing: A single spinach plant doesn't produce a lot, so you need quite a few plants to keep yourself supplied with spinach.

Beds: Spinach works well when grown in a wide bed, though it should be spaced carefully to avoid overcrowding. The exact spacing will vary according to the soil and the variety grown, but generally the following is good:

8″ (poor soil)

6″ (average soil)

4″ (good soil)

Rows: Space the plants 2 - 5″ apart, in rows 12 - 24″ apart. If growing rows on a wide bed you could plant 3 or 4 rows 10″ apart.

Care

Spinach must grow quickly to produce the highest quality food. This means giving it optimal conditions; as much water and nutrients as it requires and no competition from weeds or crowded neighbors (all these factors can contribute to bolting).

Water: Keep the soil evenly moist (not wet) otherwise the plants may bolt. Fortunately this isn't usually a problem in the cool weather preferred by spinach.

Spinach is vulnerable to fungus disease so it is good to keep the leaves dry when watering. Use drip irrigation, or water early enough so leaves can dry out quickly and not stay wet all night.

Fertilization: Spinach needs a good supply of nitrogen for best growth, but it grows in cold soil when not much nitrogen is readily available. If your soil isn't very fertile you should give the plants a feed of compost tea, or liquid seaweed, every 2 weeks. You really want to keep those plants growing rapidly.

Pests: Pests aren't usually a huge problem in the cool weather that spinach prefers. Slugs and snails, flea beetles and caterpillars will all eat the leaves, but the commonest are leaf miners. These tunnel into the leaves and make them useless. Remove any affected leaves (or squash the tiny grubs) and rub off the egg clusters. If they are very bad you will have to use row covers.

Aphids and leafhoppers can sometimes be a problem because they transmit virus diseases.

Many animal pests will go for spinach, particularly rabbits and deer.

Disease: Downy mildew is the commonest disease problem, though anthracnose, curly top and mosaic virus can all afflict spinach. Keep the leaves dry and provide good air circulation to minimize problems.

Bolting: Spinach will bolt when the day length is from 12 ½ - 15 hours (the exact number depends upon the variety, some are more sensitive than others). As with lettuce, warm weather (above 75°F) may hasten bolting, but doesn't really cause it. Poor soil, overcrowding, vernalization may also cause the plants to bolt.

Cool weather (below 65°F) may retard bolting, as can frequent harvesting of leaves.

Nutrient deficiency: Spinach is somewhat vulnerable to a boron deficiency, which shows itself as small yellowish leaves and dark colored roots.

Harvesting

When: You can gather whole plants (harvest thin to begin with), or you can pick individual leaves (carefully) as soon as they are of sufficient quantity and size (3 - 4″). Don't take too many leaves from any one plant and don't let them get larger than 6″. You can also cut the whole plants, leaving a couple of inches to regenerate so you can harvest again at a later date,

Once the plants start producing you should harvest regularly and enthusiastically, Spinach doesn't usually stay in peak condition for very long, so take advantage of it.

The flavor of fall spinach is improved by cool weather and even light frost. It can also be harvested for a lot longer and is less inclined to bolt.

When spinach gets ready to flower the top leaves become noticeably triangular and the stem elongates. When you see this starting to happen you should harvest as much as you can.

How: Pinching out the leaves encourages new growth, so keep it cropped even if you don't need it (freeze it). If the leaves get too big and tough, try cutting the whole top off of the plant, leaving about 3″ to re-sprout.

Storage: Use the leaves as soon as possible after harvest, as they will only last for a few days in a plastic bag in the fridge. If you can't use them immediately then freeze for later use.

Seed saving: Spinach plants are dioecious (there are separate male and female plants) so all plants don't produce seed. The first plants to flower are males, which are taller but have smaller leaves. You don't need a lot of males, but some are necessary for fertilization (1 male for every 2 females).

Spinach is wind pollinated so it is hard to keep it pure (it must be isolated from other varieties by at least a mile). This essentially means only having one variety flowering at a time (of course you can't do anything about other plants in the neighborhood). Because of this it is best to grow the plants in a cage covered in row cover fabric - it needs to be able to exclude very fine pollen)

Saving the seed is fairly straightforward, just allow a patch of plants to bolt (remove any plants that bolt earlier than the rest, or are unusual in any way) and let the seed ripen and dry on the plant. Then put the seed heads in a paper bag and allow them to dry completely indoors.

One female plant can produce a lot of seed, so you don't need many plants. Only save seed from your best plants of course. Ideally you would save seed from at least 20 plants to maintain genetic variability.

Unusual growing ideas

Intercrop: When grown in ideal conditions, spinach is very fast growing and makes a useful crop for interplanting between slower maturing crops.

Salad mix: This fast growing plant makes an excellent salad mix crop. Sow the seeds ½ - 1″ apart. Individual leaves are gathered as they reach a useful size (anywhere from 2 - 5″). These are carefully pinched off (or snipped), leaving enough behind to enable the plant to regenerate. Spinach works very well when grown in this way, as bolting isn't as much of a problem. See **Salad Mix** for more on this.

Indoor Crop: Spinach is very cold tolerant and makes a good winter crop for the cool greenhouse or growing frame. If you are lucky it may grow all winter without bolting.

Varieties

Many modern spinach varieties are lower in oxalic acid, as well as being more bolt resistant. You will have to experiment to find the best types for your area. Spinach is sometimes divided into smooth and wrinkled leaf (savoyed) types.

Smooth leaf: The leaves are lighter in color and fairly flat, which makes them easy to clean. This is the most popular type on the west coast. It is commonly used for salads and as baby greens.

Monstreaux De Viroflay - An old French heirloom with big leaves, does well in winter (50 days).

Red cardinal f1 - Red veined - bolts quickly - for baby leaves (30 days).

Giant Noble - Slow to bolt (45 days)

Oriental Giant F1 - Vigorous plant with big leaves (35 days)

Monnopa - Low oxalic acid (45 - 55 days)

Wrinkled leaf (savoyed): These have darker, wrinkled (obviously) leaves that are harder to clean than the smooth types. They do better in colder weather and tend to be slightly slower to bolt.

Bloomsdale Long Standing - A classic old variety (40 - 60 days).

Giant Winter - A very cold hardy type (45 days).

Merlo Nero - Italian heirloom (48 days)

Hybrids:

Emu F1 - The most bolt resistant type (42 days).

Regiment F1 - Productive, bolt and mildew resistant (40 days)

Tyee F1 - Bolt and mildew resistant (40 days)

Correnta F1 - Heat tolerant and bolt resistant for a longer harvest (45 days).

Kitchen use

Spinach must be washed carefully to get all of the soil off the leaves. This is especially important with the wrinkled leaf varieties.

The nutrients in spinach are easily leached out by boiling water, so they should only be cooked for a short time. The best way to leach out the maximum amount of oxalic acid, while losing the minimum nutrients is to boil for one minute in a large volume of boiling water in an uncovered pot.

I like to use spinach raw in salads. The smooth leaved varieties are considered superior for this, as they are easier to clean.

Spanakopita

2 lb spinach
¼ cup parsley
1 oz dill leaves
1 cup crumbled feta cheese
½ cup ricotta cheese
4 tbsp olive oil
1 large onion, chopped
1 bunch green onions
4 cloves garlic, minced
2 eggs, beaten
10 sheets phyllo dough
¼ cup olive oil

Sauté the onions, green onions and garlic in olive oil until translucent. Add spinach and chopped parsley, cook until wilted and then leave to cool.

Mix the beaten eggs, dill, feta and ricotta cheese and then stir in the onion and spinach mix. Oil and layer 5 sheets of phyllo dough into a 9″ square pan, then spread in the spinach cheese mix. Fold edges over mix and then oil and layer the other 5 sheets of phyllo dough on top. Fold edges down into pan to seal. Bake in preheated 350°F oven for 30 minutes until golden brown.

Warm weather alternatives to Spinach

When the days get to be too long and too hot for spinach, you have to look at some of the other options. At least one of the following will work for you in such situations:

Chard - Has the advantage in being a biennial and so doesn't bolt in its first year. It also has an advantage in that it will grow in both hot and cold conditions (though it doesn't really like heat and its quality suffers somewhat). (I like the variety called Perpetual Spinach) See **Chard** for more on this.

Amaranth - This is my favorite for hot weather growing. Few crops are easier to grow or taste better. See **Amaranth** for more on this.

Giant Lambs Quarter - This is as good as amaranth and just as easy to grow. See **Giant Lambs Quarters** for more on this.

Orach - This isn't as bolt resistant as some of the other plants mentioned here, but does well in both warm and cool conditions. See **Orach** for more on this.

New Zealand Spinach - Many people like this, but I haven't used it to the full, because I already like the above crops so much. See **New Zealand Spinach** for more on this.

Malabar Spinach - This highly productive vine is the plant to go to if your summer means really hot and humid weather. My garden is too cool for it, so I have never really experienced what it is capable of.

Sprouting Seeds

When I rewrote this book I considered deleting this section because sprouting isn't really gardening, but I kept it because it is such an easy way to grow food. It allows people who live in colder climates (or on stored food) to keep on growing a little bit of garden indoors through the winter. It gives you a quick and easy way to produce highly nutritious salad materials, even to the point of sprouting an entire meal.

Sprouting is an extension of the garden in that it gives you a way to grow food using the abundance of seed your garden plants will produce if given the opportunity. In some cases these sprouts can be more useful than the original crop and you might grow a crop specifically to produce seed for sprouting (I've just planted some alfalfa for this).

Nutritional content: Sprouted seeds are some of the most nutrient packed foods we have. They are full of vitamins, minerals, chlorophyll, antioxidants, enzymes, phytochemicals and probably things we don't even know about yet. Everyone really would benefit from eating more sprouts

Ease of growing: Sprouting isn't really gardening because it is just too easy. There are very few ways you can really go wrong (and you don't lose much if you do).

Containers: There are all kinds of commercially available sprouting trays, but they tend to be quite expensive, presumably because they don't sell in very large quantities. I spent $30.00 on a few cents worth of flimsy plastic trays because I wanted to experiment with them. They work well enough, but not really any better than a large jar (I like one gallon pickle or mayonnaise jars), with a piece of cheesecloth screen (some people use old panty-hose), stretched over the mouth and held in place with a rubber band. You could also make your own sprouter trays out of wooden frames and some fine screen material.

Some seeds (basil, chia) are too mucilaginous (slimy) to sprout well and these can be grown on moist paper towels (or vermiculite or peat moss). This is getting into the realm of micro-greens though, so I'm not going to say any more about them here. See **Micro-greens**.

Choosing seed: It is always best to use fresh seed, as it should have the highest germination rate.

You can mix seeds together to create a sprout mix (so long as they have relatively similar germination times). In winter you can use this as the basic salad and just add other stuff to spice it up.

Where: You can sprout pretty much anywhere, so long as it is sufficiently warm (70 - 80°F is ideal). In cooler conditions they will take longer to grow and some types may even rot before they are big enough to be useful.

When: You can sprout anytime, so long as it is warm enough. Most sprouts take anywhere from 2 - 10 days to grow, which is faster than any other food plants.

Light or dark: You don't need full sun to grow sprouts, in fact some grow bigger and better if kept in the dark for most of the time. They are germinated in the dark and left there for a few days to elongate. They are then given light for their last few days so they can develop some nutritious chlorophyll.

How

Cleaning: Check your seed before sprouting and remove any obviously damaged (moldy, damaged, shriveled or broken) seeds and any other debris. This stuff can start to rot if it is kept wet for a week.

Soaking: This provides the seed with the moisture it needs to begin germinating. The length of soaking depends upon the seed. Small ones may be soaked for only 20 minutes, while large beans may get 8 - 12 hours (usually overnight)

Rinsing: This is necessary to provide the sprouts with fresh water and to wash off the old water. Twice a day is usually enough, but more doesn't hurt, especially in warm weather.

After rinsing it is important to ensure the sprouts are well-drained; if they stay wet perpetually they may rot.

Harvest: You can start eating sprouts as soon as they are big enough to be worthwhile. In warm conditions they may be ready in only 2 - 3 days, but if it is cool they may take 4 - 6 days. Some of the slower germinating types may take as long as 2 weeks.

Final rinse: After you give the sprouts a final rinse, you should drain them well and leave them for 8 hours for all excess water to drain away. This is very important as wet seed may start to rot after a few days.

Storage: Store the sprouts in a plastic bag (or plastic container with lid) in the fridge and they should stay good for a couple of weeks. They are alive so they can last for a while.

Problems

Temperature: If the temperature is too low the seed will sprout very slowly, which can potentially lead to rotting if it takes too long.

Water: Seeds dislike highly chlorinated water and in extreme cases it can kill them (this makes you wonder what it does to us!). If you suspect this is a problem you could switch to boiled water (maybe water that has been left in the kettle after making a cup of tea – cool of course). You could also leave the water overnight in an open container, which allows a lot of the chlorine to dissipate.

Rotting: If the seed is old a significant proportion may not germinate. This is a problem not only because it means less sprouts, but because dead seed may start to rot if it sits around too long. Sometimes the seed hulls (and any ungerminated seeds) will collect together at the bottom of the screen and start to rot, which then spreads to the sprouts. If this starts to happen you should separate the growing seed from the dead seeds and other debris.

Kitchen use: Sprouts are commonly grown in the kitchen as well as prepared for eating there.

Varieties

The easiest sprouts to grow are alfalfa, clover, mung beans and sunflowers which is why they are the most commonly available in markets. There is no reason to stop there however, there are many more possibilities than you might imagine. In fact you can try the seed of pretty much any edible plant. The main criteria is that it produces a lot of seed easily and germinates fairly quickly.

The best sprouts

Alfalfa: The standard sprout.

Broccoli: These are very high in antioxidants

Clover: Another standard sprout, these are like large alfalfa sprouts.

Fenugreek: Have a great flavor (though slightly bitter) and are one of my favorites

Lentil: Easy to grow and substantial. Any variety will work, though their flavor varies.

Mung bean: Mung beans taste best if kept in low light most of the time, as it keeps them white and succulent.

They are great for cooking or eating raw.

Pea: Delicious pea flavored sprouts in 2 - 4 days.

Radish; Produces a pungently flavored sprout that spices up a salad.

Sunflower: Can be sprouted, but more often they are grown on a paper towel or soilless medium.

Other seeds for sprouting

Herbs

Dill: This takes up to 14 days to produce delicious dill flavored sprouts

Fennel: This takes up to 14 days to produce delicious fennel flavored sprouts

Garlic chives: Tastes like garlic, but is slow to sprout, taking up to 14 days (which is another way of saying what I just said above).

Vegetables

Arugala: 3 - 6 days. Is great if you like its strong flavor.

Cabbage: Takes 3 - 7 days to produce tasty sprouts. Red types are prettier than the green.

Kale: 3 - 6 days. Red Russian kale sprouts are beautiful and tasty. Scotch kale works well too.

Leek: Takes 10 - 15 days to produce a delicious onion flavored shoot.

Oriental mustards (Bok choy, tatsoi): A pungent sprout in 3 - 6 days.

Onion: Takes 10 - 15 days to produce a delicious miniature onion.

Turnip: A very tasty, mild flavored sprout in 3 - 6 days.

Winter radish: Produce a pungent sprout in 3 - 6 days.

Pulses

Most beans contain digestive inhibitors (a few also contain other toxins) so their sprouts should be cooked rather than eaten raw (sprouted beans cook a lot faster than dry ones). They should be soaked overnight before sprouting and kept in indirect light (or in the dark).

Adzuki bean: Take 2 - 7 days, depending upon how big you like them. They can be eaten raw or cooked.

Beans (Pinto bean, black turtle beans, etc). These take 2 – 6 days. They are cooked like dry beans after sprouting. They take a lot less time to cook when sprouted and are more nutritious.

Soy bean: Somewhat more temperamental than other beans, they take 2 – 6 days.

Black Eyed Pea: Treat like dry beans.

Chickpea: Take 2 - 5 days, depending upon how you like them. They are more digestible raw than most beans.

Peanut: Best when they just start to sprout, which takes 2 – 5 days.

Miscellaneous

Amaranth: The tiny sprouts are produced in 2 - 5 days

Buckwheat: This grows fast and can be used in as little as 2 days. It needs thorough rinsing before use. This isn't the same as buckwheat lettuce.

Hemp: These nutritious sprouts are ready to eat in 3 - 6 days, or until the police arrive to arrest you, in which case you should eat them immediately (unless you live in Colorado or Washington of course).

Quinoa: The sprout doesn't get very big and is ready in as little as 1 day (or as long as 3). Should be washed to remove saponins before sprouting.

Sesame: Are ready in 1 - 3 days. Older sprouts can get bitter.

Grains

These are only sprouted for 2 - 3 days, until they have small white shoots showing (any longer and they get fibrous and start turning into grass). They have a sweet flavor when sprouted and are often used for baking. Of course sprouted (malted) barley is the essential ingredient for making many kinds of beer.

Barley

Corn

Millet

Oats

Rice

Rye

Triticale

Wheat

Edible weeds

The seed of almost any edible leaf plant can be used, if you can get it in sufficient quantity and it germinates rapidly. Be aware that some very fresh seed may have a dormancy period and won't germinate well until this is up. These should be looked upon as experimental.

Dock

Lambs Quarters

Plantain

Purslane

Sorrel

Squash, Summer

Cucurbita pepo var melopepo

Introduction: The squashes originated in the Americas and have been cultivated for over 5000 years. The summer squash are a group of varieties that are eaten while the fruit is immature and soft skinned. They are called summer squash to differentiate them from the longer lasting winter varieties.

Summer squash are one of the most popular crops for home gardeners. Just a couple of plants can produce more fruit than the average family can eat and they have a reputation for being so productive that it's hard to keep up with them. They are actually something of a gardeners joke and countless magazine articles about them open with some ostensibly humorous variation on the theme that everyone eventually has so many they have to resort to desperate measures to get rid of them.

Ease of growing: In warm weather summer squash are productive, fast growing and very easy to grow. They are not so easy if the weather is cold, or if they are attacked by hordes of squash vine borers, squash bugs and cucumber beetles. These pests can make life difficult for the unsuspecting squash grower.

You always see summer squash seedlings for sale at garden centers, but there is little point in buying them. The plants will be happier if grown from seed and it will cost a lot less.

Nutritional content: Summer squash aren't particularly nutritious, they contain vitamin A, folate,

About Summer Squash

Seed facts
Germ temp: 60 (65 - 85) 100°F
Germination time: 3 - 10 days
16 days / 59°F
6 days / 68°F
4 days / 77°F
3 days / 86°F * Optimum
Germination percentage: 75+
Viability: 3 to 6 years
Weeks to grow transplants: 3 - 4

Planning facts
Hardiness: Tender
Growing temp: 60 (65 – 75) 90°F
Plants per person: 1
Plants per sq ft: ⅓

Transplants:
Start: 2 wks before last frost
Plant out: 3 wks after last frost
Direct sow: 2 wks after last frost
Succession sow: Every 4 - 6 weeks

Harvest facts
Days to harvest: 50 - 120
Harvest period: 12 weeks
Yield per plant: 15 - 20 fruits
Yield per sq ft: ½ - 2 lb

potassium and a small amount of manganese. They don't provide many calories either, only about 75 per pound (any time a food grows very quickly it will be low in calories).

Crop value: Summer squash can be very productive, but they take up quite a bit of space and aren't very nutritious. All of this means they rate fairly low on the self reliance scale.

Climate: Squash originated in the tropics and need warm weather. They can't tolerate any frost.

Soil

pH 6.0 - 7.0

Summer Squash is a hungry and fast growing crop that produces a lot of biomass. To do this it needs a fertile soil with lots of organic matter, so that it retains moisture, but drains well. It doesn't do well on acid or saline soils.

Soil preparation: Squash have a very vigorous root system, which may go down 6 feet in its search for nutrients. Add 2″ of compost, or aged manure, to the top 8″ of soil, to supply nutrients and to increase its ability to hold moisture.

If the soil is poor you can plant into individually amended holes (you won't need many).

The traditional method of sowing squash in hills probably originated to help the soil warm up faster and to provide good drainage. Prepare a hill by digging a hole 12″ deep by 18″ wide and half filling it with compost. Return all of the soil to the hole to form a small mound or hill. Generally these should have a slight depression in the top to aid in water absorption otherwise they can be hard to water.

You might try growing squash on the site of an old compost pile.

Planning

Where: Squash are large plants that take up a lot of room, but make up for it by being very productive. You may only get one row (or two offset rows) of plants in a wide bed. I like to put them at the edge of the garden, where they act as a buffer zone with the rest of the garden. This is definitely the place for the vining types, as they can be allowed to wander off into vacant space.

All of the squash must have full sun for good growth.

Rotation: Don't plant squash where any other member of the *Cucurbitaceae* (cucumber, melon, pumpkin, winter Squash) has grown within the last 3 years.

When: Summer squash are quite frost tender, so can't be planted until all danger of frost has passed and the soil has warmed up (at least 3 weeks after the last frost). If the weather is very variable at this time, cover them with cloches to keep them warm.

Don't sow squash seed before the soil has warmed up to at least 60°F and preferably 75°F). If it's too cold they may simply rot in the ground before they germinate. You can use black plastic to warm the soil if necessary.

Succession sowing: You may want to make at least one succession sowing 4 - 6 weeks after the first one, so you can replace declining plants. If your growing season is long enough you might even do a third sowing 4 - 6 weeks later.

Planting

Direct sowing: Plant 2 seeds at each location and when both have germinated thin to the best one They germinate and grow fast in warm soil and soon produce vigorous young plants.

If the soil is only marginally warm enough, you could pre-sprout the seed (take care not to damage it). Such extra effort is rarely worth it however; it's better to be patient. You can warm the soil with black plastic to get them off to a faster start and protect them under cloches until the weather gets warmer.

Transplants

Starting inside: Summer squash grows quickly when direct sown into warm soil, so this is the preferred method of growing them. Starting indoors is usually only worthwhile if the growing season is short and spring growing weather is less than ideal. By doing this you may be able to save a few weeks. You may also find that a direct sown crop planted a month later, actually catches them up (and that you wasted your time).

Squash dislike transplanting, so should be started in individual containers. Plant two seeds in each pot and after they have both emerged, you remove the inferior one (pinch it off to avoid disturbing the other one).

I like to use 4″ pots as they allow some time before the fast growing seedlings must be planted out (you don't need many of them). If containers are smaller than this you may have to pot them up before planting out, which is an additional chore.

Planting out: Plant your squash out as soon as they have 3 leaves, as they will quickly outgrow their pots and get root-bound (if it's too cold outside then plant into a bigger pot).

To plant them make a large hole, add a shovel of compost and a handful of fertilizer mix and plant as deep as their first true leaves.

Hills: They can also be planted in hills as described under **Winter Squash.**

Protection: If cold weather threatens to return after you have planted, you can cover them with cloches. In many areas it's a good idea to protect the young plants with row covers, to keep pests from attacking the young plants.

Spacing: Squash grow into big plants that need a lot of space.

Beds: In intensive beds they are spaced 18″ - 24″ - 36″ apart, depending upon how large the particular variety gets.

Rows: You could plant your squash in a row down the center of the bed, spaced 18 - 24″ apart, and fill in the rest of the space with a fast growing crop. You could also use 2 offset rows, to fill the bed more completely. Normally you don't usually need very many plants, unless you are growing for sale.

Hills: The hills (which are clusters of plants) are usually spaced 36 - 48″ apart in the row, with 48 - 72″ between the rows.

Care

Weed: Once squash get going they grow so rapidly that weeds generally aren't a big problem. They should be weeded while small however. It's always a good idea to keep weeds to a minimum in the beds, if only to prevent them setting seed.

Watering: The plants should have evenly moist soil all the time. The leaves wilt readily in the hot afternoon sun to slow down water loss. Normally they will recover quickly in the evening as the temperature drops. If they don't they either need water or (bad news) you have a disease or pest problem.

The best way to water squash is with soaker hose, as wet foliage can lead to fungus diseases.

A low tech way to water and feed the plants is to bury a one gallon pot alongside the plant and half fill it with compost. Then fill it with water a few times a week.

Fertilization: If your soil is poor give the plants a liquid feed of compost tea every 2 - 4 weeks.

Mulch: This is helpful with these widely spaced plants, to keep down weeds and conserve moisture. You can also use a living mulch of annual clover or hairy vetch.

Pollination: The first few squash flowers to appear will be males and won't produce any fruit. These will soon be followed by female flowers, which have what look like a tiny fruit behind them. If these are fertilized, the fruit will swell within 4 - 5 days. If the temperature is very cool (below 50°F) the females may not be pollinated and the tiny 'fruit' will drop off. It is easy enough to hand pollinate (see **Seed Saving** below), but this is rarely necessary.

Pests: Depending upon where you live, squash aren't much bothered by pests, or they may be so badly affected that they may be impossible to grow.

Squash vine borer: Many pests simply do some damage (often not serious), but this one will usually kill the plant unless drastic measures are taken. If you aren't very observant, by the time the damage is apparent the plant is wilting and close to death.

If a plant starts to wilt, the commonest course of action is to cut the plant open and pry out the worm like caterpillars (I don't like killing things but it's hard not to feel satisfaction when removing these). The borers give away their location by the sawdust-like frass that comes out of little holes in the stem. After digging out 8 or 10 borers the plant may be pretty well shredded, but you might save it if you bury the stems in soil, so they can send out new roots. Another course of action is to inject B.T into the stem.

It would be much better if you could prevent the borers from entering the plant in the first place. One idea is to lay a sheet of aluminum foil 'mulch' under the plant, apparently it is supposed to fool the parent moth so she doesn't find the stems. You might also wrap the stem with aluminum foil. I moved away from the area (and left this pest behind) before I had a chance to try this.

Squash Bugs; These small brown bugs can be a big problem if they get out of hand. Hand pick adults and nymphs and remove egg clusters.

Cucumber beetles; These attack the plants at all stages and are a problem not only because they eat the plants, but also because they spread bacterial wilt disease.

If you manage to avoid the vine borers and the squash bugs, you may be faced with a variety of other pests, including aphids, mites and pickleworms.

Diseases: Potential problems include angular leaf spot, alternaria blight, bacterial wilt, downy mildew, mosaic and powdery mildew.

You can avoid many of these problems by keeping the foliage dry and providing good air circulation. Also succession plant, so you can simply remove old plants before they succumb to disease.

Blossom end rot isn't a disease, but is caused by an irregular water supply. See **Tomato** for more on this.

Harvesting

When: Harvest the fruit when they are 4 - 8″ long, which should be about 4 - 6 days after pollination. Generally it's better to harvest them when still fairly small (4″ is good), though often they are still good when twice this size. If you pick them while they are small it's easier to consume all that are produced, so less are wasted.

Whatever the size you like it is very important to pick the fruit regularly and not let any mature on the vine. Those jumbo fruits take a lot of energy and can stop the plant producing altogether.

Gather the edible flowers on the day they open, ideally in early morning while they are still cool. Put them straight in the fridge and use them the same evening. Usually you use the males for food, leaving a few to pollinate the females.

How: Cut the fruits from the plant with a sharp knife to minimize damage to the vine. Leave a small section of stem on the fruit to prevent moisture loss and so improve storage life.

Storage: The fruits are best used fairly promptly. They will keep in good condition in the refrigerator for 2 weeks, but by that time you will have many more new ones. I don't know of a good way to preserve them.

Seed saving

Squash are cross-pollinated by insects. They will not only cross with other varieties of summer squash, but possibly also with some kinds of winter squash too. This means you have to have only one type flowering at one time. If you have more than this you can try hand pollinating them. As with most Cucurbits you should save the seed from at least 5 plants to ensure enough genetic variability (which is a lot of seeds). Fortunately they are quite long lived (and you can always eat some of the seeds too.)

Hand pollination isn't as difficult or complicated as you might imagine. Go out in the evening and find some male and female flowers that are about to open the following day and tape them shut with ¾″ masking tape. It doesn't matter if they are on the same plant.

The next day you open a male flower and remove its petals. You then carefully open the female flower without damaging the petals, brush the pollen-laden anthers from the male on to the pistil lobes of the female and then tape it closed again (to prevent further pollination). This procedure should work 50 - 75% of the time. It works even better if 2 males flowers are used to pollinate each female.

You will soon know if the above procedure has worked because a successfully pollinated flower will swell rapidly. If it wasn't successful the flower will soon wither and fall off. Mark the hand pollinated fruit prominently so it isn't accidentally harvested and leave it to mature fully on the vine. This will slow down further fruit production, or may even stop it altogether.

When the fruit is fully ripe it will get woody like a winter squash. It takes time for the fruit to ripen fully, so allow plenty of time before frost - at least 60 days). You then clean the ripe seed, dry it thoroughly and store in a cool dry place.

Unusual growing ideas

Volunteers: You will often find healthy young squash seedlings popping up in your garden (especially around compost piles). Unfortunately you don't know what they were pollinated by (though you may have an idea if you only grew one kind) and may end up with some strange and inedible fruit.

In mild climates some people sow squash seed in the fall, in the belief that only the most vigorous and hardy seeds will survive until the spring.

Containers: The bush varieties do quite well in containers, so long as they are large enough and you keep them well watered.

Varieties

Most summer squash have a bush habit, though a few are vines. There is considerable variation in the kinds of fruit they produce, in both shape and color (green, yellow, white).

There are now a lot of hybrid varieties, especially disease resistant ones. I don't think they offer a huge advantage though, certainly not enough to give up being able to save the seed (squash are already pretty vigorous anyway).

The main groups are:

Zucchini – These produce the familiar long, green fruit you see in stores (though some are yellow - mostly F1 hybrids).

Black Beauty

Cocozelle

Black Zucchini

Raven

Gold Rush F1

Crookneck / Straighneck – Yellow and bulbous with a crooked or straight narrow neck.

Summer Crookneck

Cougar F1

Zephyr F1

Round – These resemble a small green melon.

Ronde De Nice

Eight Ball F1

Pattypan – A round and flat with scalloped edges. Some people consider them among the best flavored types, though I'm not sure there is much difference.

Bennings Green Tint

Peter Pan F1

Scallopini F1

Sunburst F1

Vining types - These aren't very common, as most gardeners now grow the more compact bush types. The only one of these I have grown wasn't really a vine in the same way as a winter squash, it was more like a bush type that just kept getting longer and longer (to 10 ft or more).

Costata Romanesco

Long Green Trailing

Tender and True

Tatume

Trombocino – This is actually a variety of *C. moschata*, that grows as a vine and is more pest resistant than other types.

Kitchen use

Squash are quite versatile in the kitchen. My favorite ways of cooking squash include frying in tempura and making vegetarian "burgers" from them. Tender young ones can also be eaten raw in salads.

Squash flowers may be fried in batter, stuffed and baked, added to soups and eaten in quesadillas.

Vegetarian burgers

1 cup grated squash
1 cup oats
1 cup grated onion
Salt and pepper
Oil for frying
Herbs for flavoring

This is the basic recipe. Just mix all the ingredients together and shape into patties for frying. You can flavor them with a variety of herbs and spices (basil, coriander, jalapeno, etc) according to your tastes and what you have available.

Squash, Winter and Pumpkins

Cucurbita species

Introduction: The winter squash and pumpkins belong to various species, including *C. pepo, C. mixta, C. moschata* and *C. maxima.* They are grown in pretty much the same ways as the summer squash (some types are actually the same species), so if I don't mention something here it is because I already covered it there.

Winter squash get their name because they were the squash you ate during the winter (even though you grew them in summer).

Nutritional content: The fruits are rich in complex carbohydrates (180 calories / lb), beneficial fiber, vitamins A, several B's (including folate) and C. They also contain copper, iron, magnesium, potassium and zinc. Some are also a good source of antioxidants and other phytonutrients. They contain about 150 calories per pound.

The seeds are rich in protein and beneficial oils and contain about 2500 calories per pound. This could mean the seeds inside the pumpkin contain more energy than all the rest of it.

Ease of growing: Winter squash are easy to grow if the weather is warm and they aren't attacked by squash vine borers or hordes of squash bugs, all of which can make life difficult.

Once established these vigorous and fast growing plants can compete with any weeds, so long as their roots are in good soil and they are well fed and watered.

Crop value: Winter squash can be a valuable plant for those aiming for greater food independence. They produce two useful foods, the flesh of the fruit and highly nutritious edible seeds. They are easy plants to grow, quite productive (for the amount of work they require) and easy to store.

Winter squash do require quite a lot of space, but they are willing to share it with other plants. Native Americans traditionally grew squash with corn and beans in a polyculture they called the three sisters. This is a good space saving idea, as they produce almost as well as when growing alone. See **Three Sisters** in **Corn** for more on this.

Planning

Where: Winter squash grow to be large sprawling vines, so don't plant them in the middle of the intensive garden. The best place for them is out on the edge of the garden where they can run off into unused space without causing trouble. If you don't have this option they will take up a lot less space if grown vertically on trellises or cages. Of course they will then require extra work to grow (and may create shade).

If you plan on growing a lot of winter squash you will also need somewhere to store them.

About Winter Squash

Seed facts

Germ temp: 65 (80 - 95) 100°F
Germination time: 3 - 10 days
16 days / 59°F
6 days / 68°F
4 days / 77°F
3 days / 86°F * Optimum
Germination percentage: 75+
Seed viability: 3 - 6 years
Weeks to grow transplant: 3 - 4

Planning facts

Hardiness: Tender
Growing temp: 50 (65 - 75) 90°F
Plants per person: 3
Plants per sq ft: ⅓

Transplants:

Start: 2 wks before last frost date
Plant out: 3 wks after last frost
Direct sow: 2 - 4 wks after last frost

Harvest facts

Days to harvest: 90 - 120
Yield per plant: 3 lb (5 fruits)
Yield per sq ft: 1 lb sq ft

Planting

Transplants

Starting inside: Winter squash are often started indoors to get a few extra weeks of growing time (which can be important in cool climates). The naked seeded varieties of pumpkin rot easily unless given ideal conditions and so are usually started indoors. See **Summer Squash** for more on this.

Direct sowing: You only need to plant winter squash once in a year, so do it properly.

Hills: The traditional method of growing squash is in hills, which are small mounds. Prepare the hill by digging a hole 24″ wide by

12″ deep and half filling it with compost (line it with a gopher basket if necessary). Then return the soil to the hole to create a low mound with a depression on top. Plant 4 - 6 seeds (½ - 2″ deep depending on how warm the soil is) in each hill and thin to the best 2 or 3 when they have all germinated.

In hot dry situations hills don't work so well, as they tend to dry out quickly. In this situation you may find it best to flatten the hills out, or make them into slight depressions (use the same process though). Then any irrigation water will moves toward the plants, rather than draining away from them.

Spacing: Winter squash hills are usually spaced 4 - 6 feet apart. The exact distance depending on the variety and the fertility of the soil.

If the plants are to be grown up supports they can be planted closer together, perhaps as close as 30″ apart.

Care

Weed: Once the plants get going they are vigorous enough to look after themselves. You need to keep the young plants weeded though.

Water: Winter squash are fairly drought tolerant, but do better if the soil is kept evenly moist, especially in dry weather.

The big leaves of these plants wilt very easily in hot weather, but recover equally easily when the temperature drops. If they don't it means they need water (or you have a problem with pests or disease).

Fertilization: If your soil isn't very fertile you may want to feed the plants every 3 weeks with compost tea or liquid kelp.

Pruning: About a month before frost is due, pinch back the growing tips. This ensures the plants put all of their energy into ripening the fruit they already have and won't start any more.

To get larger fruit you simply limit the number of fruit they produce. Do this by pinching off unwanted female flowers and small fruit.

Frost protection: These tender plants will be killed by freezing temperatures. If an early frost threatens give them protection by covering with frost blankets or mulch.

Pests: They are bothered by the same pests as summer squash, but slightly less so. Squash vine borers seem to prefer C. pepo species to the others.

Harvesting

When: Winter squash must be fully ripe for optimal flavor and keeping qualities. It takes 2 - 3 months from pollination to full ripeness (up to 4 months for pumpkins).

The fruits are normally gathered after the skin turns dull and the dry stem snaps easily. For good storage properties the skin must be too tough to dent with a fingernail. If they are not fully mature they won't store well. The fruits must also be picked before frost does any damage.

How: Cut the ripe fruit from the vine, leaving about 6″ of stem attached.

Storage: Cure for 2 weeks in a warm place (80 - 90°F) and then store at around 50 - 60°F and 60 - 70% humidity. They may last 6 months or more in storage, which is why they were once so important for self-sufficient farmers.

Seed saving: This is the same as for summer squash. It takes time for the fruit to ripen properly so allow plenty of time for them to mature before frost.

Unusual growing ideas

Three Sisters: Winter squash are the third sister (the others are corn and beans) in this Native American polyculture. See **Corn** for more on this.

Volunteers: Squash occasionally volunteer and produce healthy young seedlings. Unfortunately you probably don't know if they crossed with anything and may end up with a pretty strange fruit (of course you can try eating it anyway).

Screen: You can train the vigorous climbing varieties along a wire fence to make a deciduous screen.

Giant fruit: To grow giant show pumpkins plant several seeds in a hill made from almost pure compost and thin to the best plant. Feed weekly with manure tea or liquid kelp and allow only one fruit to develop on each plant. You could allow three to grow if you just want big ones for your own use.

Signature: You can scratch your name on a squash or pumpkin and it will get bigger as the fruit matures.

Soil cleanup: These plants are very efficient at absorbing polycyclic aromatic hydrocarbons (such as benzene) from the soil. If you grow the plants and then remove them, you can remove these contaminants from the soil.

Varieties

Most winter squash are of the sprawling vining type, though there are some bush varieties that require less space.

The fruits vary greatly in their eating qualities; some are excellent and some are rather bland.

Winter squash (and pumpkins) belong to several different species:

Cucurbita maxima
Banana Squash
Hubbard Squash
Turban Squash
Small Pumpkins
These large vines have very big rounded leaves and soft hairy stems. They can be distinguished from *C. moschata* because the leaves are rougher in texture and their margins are more ragged. Also the stem on the fruit is swollen.

Buttercup, Marina di Chioggia, Queensland Blue, Blue Hubbard, Red Kuri.

Cucurbita moschata
Butternut Squash
Crookneck Squash
Another large spreading plant, the leaves are softer than the above and more entire. The flowers have large sepals. The stem of the fruit is 5 sided and distinctly flared.

Butternut, Chirimen, Musquee de Provence, Ponca

Cucurbita mixta **Cushaw Squash**
This species resembles *C. moschata* (some people say it is the same) but the leaf tips are more rounded and the 5 sided fruit stem doesn't flare out as much.

Green Striped Cushaw, Tennessee Sweet Potato

Cucurbita pepo
Summer Squash
Golden Acorn
Spaghetti Squash
Table Queen Squash
Pie Pumpkins
This species includes the summer squash varieties as well as several interesting winter types. It is easily distinguished by its prickly stems (all the others have smooth stems), prickly lobed leaves and the hard angular stem on the fruit. They are more vulnerable to squash vine borers than other types.

Delicata, Royal Acorn, Table Queen, Spaghetti Squash (used like spaghetti), **Lady Godiva** (naked seeded)

Immature acorn squash can be picked and used like summer squash.

Kitchen use

The mature fruits were once an important winter food in some areas.

Butternut Squash are commonly used to make commercial "pumpkin pie" filling.

Squash flowers can be dipped in batter and fried.

The seeds are all edible and may be roasted at 160°F for 20 minutes. The naked seeded types are most useful as they don't need shelling.

Strawberry

Fragaria x *ananassas*

Introduction: I didn't include the strawberry in the first version of this book because it is a fruit (though I did include melons). However I have included it this time because it is grown in the same ways as the vegetables and really fits into the vegetable garden very well.

Crop value: The strawberry is the small fruit that no garden should be without. It is delicious, easy to grow, produces a lot of fruit in a small area (each plant can produce a quart of berries) and takes little effort to grow. It is also perennial so only needs be planted once (though it is sometimes grown in more intensive ways, or even as an annual).

The enjoyment of fresh strawberries was once limited to early summer, but since the introduction of day neutrals and everbearers, they are now available for a much longer period (often through most of the summer).

Ease of growing: The strawberry is surprisingly easy to grow, especially if you use vigorous newly propagated, virus free plants.

With several types of strawberry available, which one you choose will depend upon the climate and how you want to grow them.

If your growing conditions are suitable the easiest way to grow them is as a low maintenance, long term perennial.

Nutritional content:
Strawberries are rich in sugars, vitamin C, potassium and a variety

of beneficial antioxidants (including ellagic acid). They are all the more important because they are eaten in quantity (and are easy to eat in quantity). They contain about 150 calories per pound.

About Strawberry

Planning facts
Perennial
Hardiness zones: 3 - 10
Growing temp 65 - 75°F
Plant height: 6 - 9″
Plant diameter: 8 - 18″
Plants per person: 5
Plants per sq ft: 1 - 5

Harvest facts
Harvest period: 6 weeks
Yield per plant: 1 lb
Yield per sq ft: ½ - 2 lb

Climate: Strawberries prefer a mild climate and grow best from 50 - 80°F. Warm days (70 - 80°F) day and cool nights (60 - 65°F) produce the best flavored berries. They don't like very hot weather and won't set fruit very readily when it gets much above 80°F.

Strawberries need a period of cold weather (between 34 - 55°F) in winter, to allow them to go dormant. Without this rest they won't produce many flower buds and fruit production will suffer. This can be a problem in milder areas as they are quite hardy and will often continue to grow right through the winter. In such cases they are often treated as annuals and grown from pre-chilled plants.

The plants are quite hardy, but the flowers are easily damaged by late frost. Rain is bad when the plants are fruiting as it can lead to various diseases

Strawberries are grown over a wide geographical area so it is important to choose a variety that is suitable for where you live. Some are day length sensitive and fruit best when there are less than 14 hours of daylight.

Soil

pH 5.5 (6.0) 7.0
Strawberries can grow in most soils, but prefer a fairly acidic, well-drained, light loam that is rich in organic matter. They don't like wet soil, so if it is poorly drained you should grow them on a raised bed. They don't like dry soil either, so make sure the soil has lots of organic matter to retain moisture.

Soil preparation: Before planting you should dig the soil thoroughly, to loosen it and remove perennial weeds.

Add 3 - 4″ of compost or aged manure to the top 10″ of soil before planting, along with some fertilizer mix. As it is a perennial you won't be able to incorporate anything else into the soil for a while.

Be careful not to over-fertilize with nitrogen, as it can result in excessive leaf growth at the expense of flowering and fruiting. It may also make plants more vulnerable to winter frost injury.

For spring planting it is good to grow a green manure/cover crop over the winter and incorporate it into the soil a couple of weeks before planting. Of course you will have to do this quite early in spring, so you can get the plants in the ground and growing.

Strawberry life cycle

Strawberries differ from most of the plants in this book in that they are perennial and propagate themselves vegetatively. A mature plant sends out a stolon (runner) about 6″ long and then produces a vigorous new plant. Another stolon may arise from this plant and then another stolon, to produce a whole series of plants. A single mother plant can produce up to 10 plantlets in this way.

A plant start out as a runner in its first year, produces an abundance of berries in its second and third years and then starts to decline. Each individual plant can live for up to 5 or 6 years, but they are usually removed after 3 years, to make way for new plants.

In late summer and fall the plant makes buds that will produce the following years flowers. These go dormant in winter and flower the following spring.

Planning

Strawberries can be grown in a variety of ways. They have been grown as annuals, for two years (they reach peak bearing in this year), three years, five years or as a permanent bed.

Where: Full sun (6 hours or more). It's a good idea to give your plants their own permanent bed out at the edge of the garden where they can grow undisturbed for several years. A strawberry bed isn't particularly attractive, but can work as a groundcover.

Avoid planting strawberries in wet areas and frost pockets, especially for early spring crops. Beds recently converted from grassland are not good as they may contain pests that like to feed upon strawberry roots. There should be good air circulation to reduce disease problems.

Ideally you shouldn't plant strawberries where any Solanum crops (eggplant, peppers potatoes and tomatoes) have grown within three years, as they are all vulnerable to verticillium wilt.

You can plant strawberries in semi-shade, such as around fruit trees. They won't be as productive as plants in full sun, but if they are filling otherwise unused space then they are a bonus anyway. You could use some of the surplus runners in this way.

When:
When you plant depends upon your climate and the type of strawberry you are growing.

Spring: Day neutral and everbearing strawberries can produce a large crop in their first year, so they should be planted as soon as the soil is dry enough in spring (you want the maximum early growth, so they will fruit later). With Junebearers early planting isn't so critical as they have a whole year to get going.

Fall: In mild winter areas strawberries are often planted in fall and may continue to grow slowly right through the winter. Very hard frosts can damage young plants, so cover with mulch if this threatens.

Transplants: Strawberries are most often grown from commercially available transplants. These should be certified disease-free because strawberries are susceptible to virus diseases.

You can often get plants for free from gardening friends, but this brings with it the risk of disease. You have to weigh up whether this risk outweighs the expense of buying plants (it often does, but a lot depends upon where you live) Inspect your free plants carefully, you want large, vigorous, productive plants with plump, light colored roots and dark green leaves (and of course no sign of disease).

Before planting: Newly purchased bundles of plants can be kept in the fridge for a week or so, just be sure to keep them moist. Wrap them in a moist (not wet) paper towel and store in a plastic bag. It's not a bad idea to soak the roots in water for a while before planting.

Planting

This is best done on a cloudy day, or at least late in the afternoon. Take your time with planting and do it right, your plants will appreciate it.

The best way to plant is to make a hole large enough to accommodate the fully spread roots (the size of this will vary from plant to plant). Many people make a cone shaped mound of soil at the bottom of the planting hole and spread the roots out evenly over this. Don't fold the roots over to make them fit, or plant with the roots all matted together.

It is important to put the plant in the ground at the right depth, with all of the roots covered and the fleshy crown on the surface of the soil. If the crown is too high the plant may dry out. If it's too low it may rot.

Water thoroughly after planting.

Spacing

A typical row spacing is 15 -24″ apart in the row, with 36- 48″ between the rows. However the exact spacing depends on what kind of berries you are growing and how you are growing them.

Spacing June bearers

June bearers produce lots of runners and are often grown in "matted rows" whereby the plants are spaced 18 - 24″ apart with 48″ between the rows. They are allowed to produce runners and form a densely matted row (you want about 5 plants for every square foot). After harvest the plants may be cut down (they are often actually mown) to within 2 ½″ of the ground.

Spacing Everbearers

These are most often grown on a mound system which consists of narrow raised beds about 8″ high and 24″ wide. The plants are grown in two offset rows with 12″ between the plants. Runners are usually removed as they appear to encourage the mother plants to produce more crowns and berries. This system usually produces the largest and highest quality fruit, but requires more work.

A variation on the mound system is the hedgerow system which allows for some runners to create new plants around the mother plants.

Spacing day neutral strawberries

These can fruit abundantly for a long period in summer, but are more temperamental than the other types and don't produce many runners. They are usually grown on the mound system, in the same way as the everbearers,

Care

Strawberries can be grown fairly casually as a low work crop, but they will be more productive if you look after them.

Watering: For maximum production the plants require

a steady supply of moisture, especially in hot weather (which is why good soil is important. Lack of water can seriously reduce yields especially when fruit is growing). It can also impact flower bud formation for the following year.

Give the plants at least 1″ of water a week during vegetative growth and maybe even more during fruiting (this depends upon the weather of course). Drip works well and helps to minimize disease.

Water is also very important during late summer, as the flower buds are developing at this time, This will determine the amount of fruit produced next year.

You can damage strawberries by giving them too much water, as wet soil can cause the roots to rot. Don't just water routinely, you have to be observant and look at local conditions.

Weeding: Strawberries are vulnerable to weeds because they aren't very tall and don't cover the ground completely. Keep the bed well weeded and you will get higher yields (this is particularly important when they are getting established). Usually this means hand weeding as hoeing isn't practical once the plants start to spread.

Removing flowers: When growing June bearers you traditionally pinch out any flower buds that appear during the first year to prevent any fruit being produced. This allows them to devote all of their energy to vegetative growth and results in bigger plants and bigger harvests in future years. However if the plants get big enough you can let them produce some fruit in the first year. With ever-bearing and day neutral varieties you pick off flowers for the first 4 - 6 weeks of flowering to allow the plants to get bigger. After this time you let them flower and produce fruit.

Renewal: Common practice is to allow a plant to produce for two years (its most productive years) and then replace it with a vigorous new runner after its third year.

Runners: Everbearers and day neutrals often have their runners removed during their first year, so they keep on producing the maximum amount of fruit (rather than wasting some of their energy producing new plants). In the second year some runners may be allowed to root (these will replace the mother plants the following year).

You can direct the runners to vacant areas where you want them to root (there is no need to detach them from the mother plant). The first daughter plants are usually the best. Runners that form early in the year on Junebearers will produce berries the following season.

Runners are useful for producing new plants, but you don't want them to produce so many they get overcrowded. Once the bed has the desired density (5 plants per sq ft) you should pinch out extra runners (or root and remove). These late runners often won't have time to produce fruit buds anyway.

Fertilization: Strawberries are very productive plants and should be fertilized regularly. In particular they should get plenty of phosphorus and potassium as this aids in fruit production.

Top dress with a fertilizer mix annually after fruiting in late summer. This will help the plants produce fruit buds for the following year.

Though fertilization is important you don't want to over-fertilize, as this can result in excessive leafy growth, which is vulnerable to frost. It also means the plants produce less fruit.

Frost control: Plants should be protected from late frosts as these can damage the flowers and their buds. You can protect them from light frosts with row covers or mulch. Commercial plantings are often protected by overhead sprinklers.

Summer mulch: Mulch is beneficial during the growing season because it suppresses weeds, conserves moisture, keeps the soil cool and keeps berries from contact with the soil. Straw is the commonest mulch though pine needles also work well (and provide desirable acidity).

Plastic mulch (black or green) is now widely used by commercial strawberry growers, as it suppresses weeds and holds in moisture. The plants need to grow and cover the plastic before it gets very warm, otherwise the soil may get too hot.

Winter mulch: In cold winter areas the plants are often covered with several inches of loose mulch (straw or pine needles) to protect the buds over the winter. This is applied after the plants have gone dormant and temperatures start to drop below 20°F. Remove it in early spring so the soil can warm up (not too early though).

Pests: Slugs, snails, tarnished plant bug, mites, strawberry weevils and spittlebugs can all be a problem.

Birds: In many areas these are one of the biggest problems as they peck the fully ripe fruit. If they become a serious problem you will probably have to net the plants.

Diseases: Strawberries are quite vulnerable to disease when they get overcrowded, are growing in wet soil, or if the fruit and foliage gets wet.

Common diseases include powdery mildew. verticillium and botrytis (fruit rot), leaf spot and red stele.

Viruses: As a long lived perennial, strawberries are prone to virus diseases which can reduce vigor without being obvious. This is why it is best to start with certified disease free plants, rather than using free runners from existing plants.

Various kinds of rot. There are several of these fungus diseases, including gray mold, tan rot, hard rot, leather rot, black seed rot and stem end rot. Help avoid these diseases by using mulch to keep the fruit from contact with the soil. Also provide good air circulation, don't let the plants remain wet for long periods and don't allow any fruit to decay on the plant.

Harvesting

When: Strawberries ripen about 4 - 5 weeks after the flowers open.

The most important thing to remember about harvesting strawberries is that they don't continue to ripen after picking. They must be allowed to ripen fully on the plant, which means they should be fully colored for at least two days. The foolproof way to decide when they are ripe is to eat one - if it tastes great it is ready. If it never tastes great you are growing the wrong variety.

Harvest the fruit every 2 days for best quality and least losses (or even every day during peak season).

You should wait until the berries are dry before harvesting, as wet berries are prone to rot.

How: The fruits bruise easily so be gentle. Pick the whole berry with the calyx and a short ½″ stem attached, by pinching them with your fingernails. Don't leave the harvested berries in the sun for any length of time, it is important to keep them cool.

It is also important to remove any diseased, pecked, damaged or over-ripe berries from the plants as you move along the rows harvesting. This will help to minimize problems with pests and disease.

After harvest care:

This is a big step towards getting a good harvest the following year.

Fertilize after harvest to supply the plants with necessary nutrients.

June bearing varieties are sometimes mowed to a height of 2 ½ - remove top growth. This is high enough not to damage the crowns.

Thin out the runners so the plants don't get overcrowded. You can cut out as many as half of the plants and they will soon fill in again.

Keep watering and weeding to maintain general plant health.

Mulch the plants after they go dormant.

Storage: The berries can be stored in the fridge for several days in a shallow covered pan (don't wash them). For longer term storage they can be frozen (if you have a use for strawberry flavored mush), or made into preserves. They are best used immediately though.

Seed saving: Strawberries are rarely grown from seed, but this is pretty easy to collect. The easiest way is to put the fruit in a blender with water for a few seconds. The heavy seed will settle to the bottom, where it can be collected and cleaned.
You can dig up rooted runners while dormant during the winter and plant them elsewhere. You can also root them directly into a plant pot.

Unusual growing methods

Annual growing: In warmer areas, where they don't get enough winter chill, strawberries are commonly grown as an annual. These are planted in fall, grow right through the winter, are harvested the following spring and summer and are then replaced.

Growing from seed: Almost all garden strawberries are propagated vegetatively, but there are a few varieties that can be grown from seed. This is pretty easy as the seedlings are quite vigorous. Seed may take 2 - 8 weeks to germinate at 65 - 75°F.

Containers: Strawberries are often grown in containers or even hanging baskets.

Semi-wild growing
If your climate is well suited to growing strawberries you may want to try growing them as wild plants. Simply plant them in suitable spots and let them run wild.

Varieties

Strawberry varieties tend to be quite variable and what does well in one area may not work at all in another. When choosing a variety it is important to find one that will perform well in your garden. They are available in three distinct types.

Junebearers – These are the original strawberries and bear one very large crop over 2 – 4 weeks in early summer. After this they send out an abundance of runners, which grow into new plants. These are the most widely adapted and dependable strawberries and are ideally suited to growing berries for preserves or freezing. There are early, mid-season and late varieties so you can extend the harvest quite a lot by planting several varieties.

Early: Chandler, Earliglow, Annapolis, Delmarvel

Mid-season: Redchief, Honeoye, Guardian, Surecrop

Late: Allstar, Jewel, Sparkle

Day neutrals - These bear fruit in several flushes through the summer, which spreads out the harvest considerably. They are fairly temperamental and require favorable conditions (not too hot or too dry), but can work very well. They don't produce many runners because they concentrate on fruiting instead.

Seascape, Selva, Tribute and Tristar

Everbearers - These bear two or three times during the summer and don't produce many runners, because they concentrate on fruiting instead. They do best in long day areas, where they can produce fruit for months.

Fort Laramie, Ozark Beauty, Quinault

Alpine Strawberry

Fragaria vesca

Though this species is one of the ancestors of the garden strawberry, it is quite a bit different. The plants (and fruit) are much smaller and they rarely produce runners.

This species is justly famous for its delicious fruit, which make up in flavor and aroma what they lack in size.

The young plants can't compete against weeds very well, but older plants are quite vigorous. In good growing conditions they can be very productive and will bear fruit for many months. In my garden I have harvested fruit in almost every month of the year (though admittedly not many from December to February).

As with other strawberries the fruit needs to be fully ripe to develop good flavor. Birds are less attracted to the yellow or white fruited types as they don't ever look ripe (some people prefer their taste too).

Alpine strawberry is easily grown from seed, though it is quite slow to germinate. The plants will produce fruit in their first year, especially if you start them early. You could also divide the plants, but this is only really worthwhile if you get a unique plant you really like (otherwise seed is so easy).

This plant will be most productive in a fertile, well-drained, but moisture retentive soil. It will grow well in full sun or light shade.

Sunflower

Helianthus annuus

Introduction: The sunflower is native to North America and was long grown by Native Americans, but first became an important commercial crop in Russia. This occurred after breeders produced a variety with unusually large, oil rich, seeds. Their use quickly spread throughout eastern Europe until they were the most important oil seed crop grown there. It is now an important crop in its native land as well, though even today many varieties are of Russian origin.

Many people think of sunflowers as an ornamental, rather than an edible crop, but the seeds are highly nutritious.

Crop use: The sunflower is valuable as a source of high protein seeds, but it could also be important as a garden scale source of oil (fats can be hard to grow in the garden). It is also very pretty (spectacular even) and provides food for beneficial insects.

Ease of growing: This is a pretty easy crop to grow if it has fertile soil, plenty of water and warm weather. It is rarely bothered by pests up until the seed starts to ripen (then birds and squirrels can be a problem).

Climate: Sunflowers like warm, humid growing conditions, similar to those for corn.

Nutritional content: Sunflower seeds contain about 20% protein, 20% carbohydrate, 40% fat (which is very rich in essential fatty acids), several B vitamins A, calcium, iron potassium and zinc.

With all of that fat and protein it should come as no surprise that the seeds contain over 2500 calories per pound.

About Sunflowers

Germination temp: 70 - 85°F
Germination time: 7 - 14 days
Seed viability: 3 - 5 years
Hardiness: Tender
Growing temp: 50 (60 - 75) 95°F
Yield: 3 lb / 100 sq ft.
Days to harvest: 90

Soil

pH: 6.0 to 7.0
Sunflowers are very hungry plants and for good growth they need rich moist soil with an abundance of nutrients. They like phosphorus and potassium, but not too much nitrogen as this may encourage leaf growth rather than flowering.

Soil preparation: Sunflowers are hungry crops, so enrich the soil generously before planting. Incorporate 3″ of compost or aged manure, along with wood ashes, colloidal phosphate and kelp powder (or an organic fertilizer mix).

Planning

When: You can start planting sunflowers 2 weeks after the last frost date, when the soil has warmed up to at least 50°F.

Rotation: Sunflowers have a reputation for exhausting the soil if continually planted and harvested on the same piece of land. Always leave at least 3 years between crops.

Planting

Indoors: Sunflower are often started indoors for an early and protected start. The seedlings grow rapidly, so are best started in 4″ pots (to give them plenty of room). Plant 2 - 4 seeds in each pot and when all have germinated you can thin to the best one (or two).

Outdoors: Sunflower seeds germinate and grow so rapidly they are usually direct sown. Plant them ¼″ deep.

Spacing: Space the plants 12 - 24″ apart, depending upon the variety.

Care

Weeds: The young seedlings can't compete with weeds very well, so weed them carefully. Once they get going they will soon outgrow any weeds.

Water: Sunflowers are thirsty plants and for maximum production they need a constant supply of water.

Mulch: In hot climates a mulch is useful to conserve soil moisture and keep down weeds.

Pests and disease: Birds love sunflower seeds and can be a major pest in some areas. Squirrels and raccoons may also develop a taste for them and become a problem.

Harvesting

When: When the seeds are ripe the whole head will start to droop and the seeds will be fat and plump. Open a few seeds and see (and taste) if they are fully ripe. Watch carefully or birds will get the seed before you do.

How: The easiest way to harvest the seeds is to cut off the whole heads. Dry them in the sun and then rub the heads against a screen (or against each other) to free the seeds.

Storage: The seeds must be dried carefully if you want to store them for any length of time, otherwise they will mold. Store the dry seeds in a cool, rodent-free place.

Unusual growing ideas

Sunflower Lettuce: Sunflower seeds can be grown indoors as a seedling salad crop. Soak the seeds for 3 hours and then spread them out, one seed deep, on trays of soil, peat moss or wet kitchen paper. Keep them in a warm place and mist daily. When the seeds begin to germinate move them into full light. The greens will be ready in 1 - 3 weeks (depending upon the temperature). Cut the plants with scissors when they are 3 - 6″ tall, leaving about an inch of stem behind. See **Microgreens** for more on this.

Smother crop: Their luxuriant and rapid growth makes sunflowers useful as a smother crop. A dense stand of the tall plants will crowd out and eradicate persistent weeds.

Canary plant: Sunflowers are very sensitive to low soil moisture and can be used as indicator plants for the whole garden. Watch your sunflowers and when they wilt it means soil moisture is low and it is time to water the garden.

Temporary screen: These tall growing flowers can be used to make a quick (and pretty) temporary screen. If you feel ambitious you could try growing a sunflower maze.

Fertilizer: Sunflowers use four carbon photosynthesis which makes them more efficient when growing under high heat and light intensities. This means they can grow very quickly and produce an abundance of organic matter.

They are sometimes grown as a green manure crop, which is incorporated just before the flower buds appear (which is when the plants start to turn woody). They can also be grown to produce organic matter for the compost pile. If you want to try this its cheaper to use bulk raw seeds from a whole food store.

Apparently even their hunger for nutrients has been put to use. The plants have been used to remove an excess of nitrates from the soil.

Seed saving: Sunflowers are cross-pollinated by insects, so you can only save the seed from one variety at a time (they may also cross with any wild sunflowers).

Saving the seed is pretty easy, except for the fact that birds and squirrels may take every full kernel if you don't protect them.

Varieties

There are lots or ornamental sunflower varieties, but most don't have large enough seeds to be very useful for food. The best edible seeded varieties include:

Skyscraper - As you might imagine it is tall, with huge seed heads (75 days)

Mammoth Russian - The classic heirloom sunflower (80 days).

Snack Seed - Big fat seeds.

Kitchen use

The raw or roasted kernels can be used like nuts: eaten out of hand, in baked goods, granola and trail mix. Native Americans often ground the whole seed to meal for baking bread and thickening soups.

Edible oil: Modern varieties of seed may contain up to 60% oil. This can be extracted by pressing the crushed seeds using a hand press such as the Piteba. You can also do as Native Americans used to do, boil the kernels in water and skim off the edible oil that floats to the surface.

Sprouts: The raw whole seed can be sprouted for salad greens (see **Sprouting seeds**). Don't let the sprouts get too big or they may develop an acrid taste.

Eating sunflower seeds

If you are to grow sunflowers for their edible seeds, you really need to learn how to eat them. Start by putting a seed vertically between your molars (chewing teeth) so the seed holds in the indentations. Crack the seed gently, then use your tongue to separate the smooth seed from the rough shell. Finally you spit out the shell.

This is harder to do than it is to describe and it takes quite a bit of practice to get it down smoothly. Eventually you can have a store of seeds in one cheek, crack them on the other side of your mouth and spit out the shells in a continuous stream.

Sweet Potato

Ipomoea batatas

Introduction: The sweet potato is native to the Americas and was introduced into Europe very early in the history of European colonization (about 1500). Many of the earliest references to the potato probably actually mean this species. Predictably it didn't do very well in chilly Northern Europe, but was taken from there to India, China and other tropical countries where it became an important food crop.

Sweet potato should not to be confused with the yam, which is a member of the *Dioscoreaceae* family. It is actually a relative of the morning glory, which is apparent if you see their flowers.

Crop use: In the right climate the sweet potato is one of the most nutritious and productive vegetables you can grow. In places that are too hot to grow potatoes it often takes their place as the staple vegetable crop. It can be an important crop for those aiming for food self-sufficiency in warm climates.

Ease of growing: In a suitably warm climate the sweet potato is pretty easy to grow, though it is vulnerable to quite a few pests and diseases.

Climate: Sweet potato is actually a perennial in tropical climates, but in temperate regions it can't survive the cold winters and so must be grown as an annual.

It does best in a hot, humid climate with a long growing season (ideally 4 - 5 months of warm or hot weather) and moderate, evenly distributed rainfall. For best quality it needs warm nights (a minimum of

60°F and ideally over 70°F) as well as warm days. In the United States it is most widely grown in the southeastern states.

The sweet potato can also be grown in less than ideal conditions, but you have to work at it and give it some protection in cool weather. I've done it a couple of times in my garden, but the nights are too cool for it to be very productive.

About Sweet potato

Planning facts
Perennial
Hardiness: Tender
Growing temp: 65 (70 - 85) 95°F
Plants per person: 5
Plants per sq ft: 1
Weeks to grow transplants: 8 - 12
Plant out: 4 weeks after last frost
Days to harvest: 130 - 170

Harvest facts
Yield per plant: 4 oz - 3 lb
Yield per sq ft: 1 - 3 lb

Nutritional content: Sweet potato is an important food crop from a nutritional standpoint. It is a good source of vitamin C and B6, while those with orange flesh are rich in vitamin A (beta carotene). It is also a good source of calcium, potassium and pectin, as well as some beneficial phytochemicals including lutein and zeaxanthin.

Site: Sweet potato is a fast growing and vigorous vine and most types requires quite a lot of space, though there are a few more compact bush varieties. All need as much sun as they can get.

The plants are quite vulnerable to pests and diseases, so should be rotated regularly. Don't grow them in the same place again for at least 3 years.

Soil

pH 4.5 (5.5 - 6.5)7.0

Sweet potato can be grown on soil that is too poor for most crops, though (as is usually the case) better soil will give you a larger crop. The ideal soil for sweet potatoes is a rich, deep, well-drained, sandy but moisture retentive loam. It should be fairly acidic, as disease problems are more common in neutral soils. Clay soil can produce slender roots, while poorly drained soils can result in root disease.

Soil preparation: Incorporate 2 - 4″ of compost or aged manure into the top 6 - 10″ of soil. No matter what type of soil you have, adding organic matter will be beneficial when growing sweet potatoes. It lightens a heavy clay soil and improves its texture. It helps a sandy soil to retain moisture (and improves its texture too). Double digging is a good idea if the soil is heavy.

Like most root crops sweet potatoes need phosphorus (colloidal phosphate is good) and potassium (add greensand or wood ashes). They don't need a lot of nitrogen, as it encourages the growth of foliage rather than roots (and can result in inferior quality roots).

Ridges: When growing sweet potatoes in cooler areas, the soil is often shaped into ridges, as these warm up (and drain) faster than flat soil. This doesn't always work in hotter areas, or with very sandy soil though, as they tend to dry out too quickly.

Lighter soil can be shaped into ridges 6 - 8″ high and 12″ wide, with 30″ between the ridges. On heavy soil they may be 12 - 15″ wide and 36 - 48″ apart. Raised beds also work well.

Planning

Where: These creeping tropical vines need plenty of sunlight and a lot of growing space. In cooler climates they must be planted in the warmest and most sheltered spot you have. They should also be planted where they can sprawl without interfering with other crops.

When: Sweet potatoes are tropical plants and don't tolerate cold very well, so there is no point in trying to get them in the ground early. Don't plant them out until at least 3 - 4 weeks after the last frost date and the soil is at least 60°F (65°F or higher is better). If you need to gain some extra time you can warm up the soil with black plastic for a couple of weeks before planting. The roots need to be harvested before the soil temperature drops down to 55°F in fall.

Buying plants: In many areas of the country slips aren't readily available and you may have to buy them by mail order.

Planting

Sweet potatoes are propagated vegetatively by means of shoots taken from the tubers, known as slips. Whole tubers aren't usually planted because they send out too many shoots which would eventually compete with each other.

Though sweet potatoes are usually fairly easy to grow, I have encountered a problem in obtaining planting material. In traditional sweet potato growing areas (the southeast) they can be purchased from nurseries and in most other areas they can be bought by mail order (these don't always arrive in the best shape, but usually do fine).

My problem in California is that you can't buy them locally and you can't easily buy them by mail order from another state because of quarantine restrictions (though there are some exceptions). I have got around this problem by raising my own slips from tubers I buy at the store. There is some danger of introducing virus diseases when using shop tubers though and it is better to use certified disease free slips where possible.

Starting your own slips: It is pretty easy to grow your own slips if you have some unsprayed tubers. The best source of tubers are those you have grown yourself, so it is a good idea to save a few of the best ones (they should be fairly thick, at least 1 ½″ in diameter).

You can also use organic tubers from the supermarket or health food store. Avoid conventional tubers as they are commonly sprayed with a sprout inhibitor, in which case they won't sprout.

Indoors: Start sprouting the tubers 2 - 3 months before you want to plant them out. The usual way to do this is to half bury them in a bed of damp sand or peat moss (some people cover them with plastic to retain moisture). They should be kept at a temperature of 70 - 90˚F (the warmer it is the faster they will sprout). In 4 - 8 weeks they should produce a number of vigorous shoots with healthy roots on them. You should be able to get 10 - 12 slips per tuber.

Commercial operations sprout the tubers with bottom heat and you might want to try this. In the old days this was done in hot beds filled with fresh manure, covered with a few inches of sand or soil. Now it is done with electric soil heating cables.

You can also suspend a tuber half in water with toothpicks (like an avocado pit). Just make sure the top (flat end) is upright. I haven't had any luck with this method, as the tuber rotted before it sprouted. Also they don't tend to have as good a root system.

When the slips are large enough they are carefully detached from the tuber. You can remove individual slips as they get big enough and leave the tuber to produce more.

If you detach the slip with all of its root attached it will recover faster, but you will transfer any disease from the tuber. If you cut it an inch away from the tuber it will take longer to recover, but you may leave any disease behind. You can put these in 4″ pots until they grow roots and then plant out.

If it's still too cold outside, you might have to transplant them into bigger (1 gallon) pots, or a deep flat.

Outdoors: If it is warm enough you can start slips outdoors (or under cloches or cold frames) following the procedure described above.

Planting out: I prefer to plant the slips in individual holes. Make a large hole, add a couple of handfuls of compost, along with some wood ashes. Then bury most of the slip, leaving just the tip sticking out and make a slight well to hold water. If the weather is still cool, cover with cloches to keep them warm and happy. If the weather is hot make sure you give them plenty of water until they are settled in.

In some areas you may have to use cutworm collars to protect the newly planted slips.

Spacing: Sweet potatoes are commonly planted in rows, as it is a lot easier to hill them up. Space the plants 12 - 18″ apart, in rows 36 - 48″ apart. Bush types can be spaced somewhat closer.

Care

These plants are quite independent and don't really need much care once they are established.

Water: Established plants are quite tolerant of drought, but the soil should be kept evenly moist (at least 1″ per week) for maximum production. If water is in short supply then just water while they are young.

Irregular watering (too wet, too dry, too wet) can cause the tubers to crack).

Too much water isn't a good idea, as it encourages foliage growth rather than root growth.

Weeds: Sweet potatoes are vigorous plants and weeds aren't a big problem once they get established, but you will need to weed while they are young. If they have to struggle against a lot of weeds during early growth it can reduce the harvest by as much as 20%.

The plants should be weeded 2 - 3 weeks after they go in the ground (and again 3 - 4 weeks later). If you are using a hoe, don't go too deep as it's easy to damage the shallow roots. You will also remove weeds later on when you hill the plants. A layer of mulch will help to keep weeds under control (but makes it hard to hill them).

Fertilization: It isn't necessary to feed the plants, unless the soil is very poor, in which case give them a feed of compost tea when the tubers are developing. Don't over-feed, as this can encourage lush foliage growth at the expense of tuber production.

Mulch: In cool climates a black plastic mulch is often used to give the plants extra heat. The slips are planted through slits in the plastic.

In hot climates an organic mulch may be used to keep down weeds and conserve soil moisture. Don't apply this until the soil has warmed up nicely though.

Hilling: As soon as the plants are making good healthy growth they should be hilled up as this can increase the final yield. Of course this is impractical if you are using black plastic mulch, or if they are not planted in rows.

Frost: Sweet potatoes are very tender and any frost will kill the tops.

If a late spring frost threatens, you should cover your plants with frost blankets or a few inches of loose mulch (and maybe a cloche or bucket for extra insurance). This is usually easy because the plants are pretty small at this point.

If an early fall frost threatens, it pays to protect them with straw mulch, cloches or even sheets. This is extra work but you may be rewarded with several more weeks of growing weather. The plants grow rapidly towards the end, so there can be a big benefit in leaving them in the ground as long as possible. When a hard frost threatens, dig the tubers immediately. Don't wait too long as any damage to the tubers will affect their storability.

Pests: A lot of pests may potentially attack sweet potatoes, but generally they are so vigorous this isn't a problem (just make sure they get all of the nutrients they need).

One of the few advantages of growing them in the cooler north is that there are less pests to deal with.

Pests include: cucumber beetles, cutworms, flea beetles, Japanese beetles, nematodes, sweet potato leaf beetles, sweet potato weevils, tortoise beetles, wireworms and more.

Diseases: Sweet potatoes are vulnerable to several diseases, including black rot, fusarium wilt, internal cork, pox, scurf, soft rot, stem rot and various fungal, bacterial and viral pestilences.

Use resistant varieties, certified disease free slips, good sanitation, rotation and careful storage to minimize disease problems (some diseases develop during storage). Most diseases are less problematic in the north and in acidic soils.

Sweet potatoes are vulnerable to several diseases in storage, so it is important to harvest carefully (without damaging the skins) and cure properly.

Harvesting

When: You can start harvesting and eating the tubers as soon as they reach a useful size. However if you want to store them you must wait for them to mature fully (the lower leaves will start to turn yellow and die back

Sweet potatoes continue to grow and get bigger until cold weather kills the tops, so it is a common practice to wait until frost threatens and then harvest. If a forecast warns of severe frost you must harvest before it hits, as it can damage any tubers lying near to the surface). Also harvest before the soil drops to 50°F as this can result in internal damage. Don't worry if a lot of the tubers are small, they will still taste good.

How: The tubers tend to grow vertically and cluster directly underneath the plant (they don't generally spread out a lot). You will have to dig deep to get them whole, without breaking them.

Always handle the tubers gently as they are easily damaged and even a small wound can lead to decay (some gardeners even line the harvesting container with soft cloth).

Let the newly harvested tubers air dry for a couple of hours and then brush off excess soil. Don't leave them exposed to the sun for more than an hour though, as this can damage them (some people wait until it is cloudy before harvesting).

The next step is to sort the roots into three piles. The first one for seriously damaged tubers, which should be eaten immediately (though they won't taste as good if not cured) The second pile is for slightly damaged tubers, which should be eaten fairly promptly. The final pile is for undamaged tubers which can be stored.

Curing: The flavor of the tubers becomes sweeter after curing, as this encourages the formation of an enzyme which converts some of their starch into sugar. It also heals minor injuries.

Remove any excess soil clinging to the roots before curing, but don't wash them. Cure the tubers by keeping them at 80 - 90˚F (with 85 - 90% humidity) for 10 days. If the temperature is only 70˚F then leave them for 2 - 3 weeks.

Storage: Store the tubers in paper lined boxes in a dark, humid, well ventilated place at 50 - 60˚F (they may rot if it's colder than 50˚F). This is not only the best temperature range for storage, but also encourages the conversion of starch to sugar, so they taste better.

Sweet potatoes don't like being stored at very low temperatures and can be damaged if kept in the fridge for a long period.

Even under the best conditions sweet potatoes don't store for very long, If treated well they should keep in good condition for several months (but not much longer). They often decay in storage though, so it's good to check them frequently for rot or deterioration.

Seed saving:
Sweet potatoes rarely flower outside the tropics and even more rarely set seed, so it isn't used for propagation.

Save some of the best tubers for propagating slips. These should be stored as described above, but even more carefully, as they need to keep longer.

Unusual growing ideas

Cuttings: If you have a long, warm growing season you can propagate sweet potatoes by taking green cuttings from growing plants and rooting them in water.

Indoor plants: Sweet potato vines have been used as indoor plants, though I can't imagine they produce very much when grown in this way.

Container growing: The bush varieties have been successfully grown in containers. They are also well suited to grow bags, just be sure to use a fertile mix (see **Potato** for more on this).

Animal food: In the south a significant proportion of the sweet potato crop is used to feed livestock.

Growing in cooler areas:
Though sweet potatoes do best where summers are long and warm, it is possible to grow them in colder areas, if you are prepared to do some extra work. You need to use a fast maturing variety, warm the soil with plastic mulch and maybe even use cloches to keep the plants warmer.

Interplanting: Sweet potatoes work well with corn, just give it a couple of weeks head start.

Overwintering: Take some of the smaller tubers from your harvest and pot them up for the winter. Keep these in the greenhouse or windowsill and the following spring you can separate out the new shoots that emerge and plant them in individual pots. When the right time approaches in spring just plant them out.

Other uses: Sweet potatoes can be used as a temporary groundcover (or a permanent one in tropical areas). They can also be used as a soil improving crop to loosen clay soil.

Varieties

Sweet potatoes may be divided into the dry fleshed types and the moist fleshed types (these become sweeter and softer when cooked). The skin color ranges from brown, copper, pink to purple.

In marginal northern areas the choice of variety is important, as you will need to grow a short season variety such as Georgia Jet. There are also special varieties for feeding livestock that produce abundantly but aren't so sweet.

Moist flesh types: The most popular and widely used sweet potatoes are of this type.

Beauregard

Centennial - 90 days

Covington

Georgia Jet - 85 to 90 days

Jewel

O-Henry

Puerto Rico - A compact bush type

Dry flesh types: These are mealier and not quite so popular.

Japanese

Jersey Orange

Kitchen use

The roots should be baked at 350 - 375˚F to maximize their sweetness.

Tomatillo

Physalis ixocarpa

Introduction: The tomatillo has been grown in Central America for around 3000 years, but it is often as much a weed of cultivated fields as it is a crop. In this country it is commonly found in parts of the country with large Latino populations, but is becoming increasingly popular in other areas too.

Tomatillo means small tomato, and was presumably given because it is a relative, though it is quite a bit different. It does have fairly similar cultivation requirements, though it is somewhat more independent.

This species is sometimes called the husk tomato because of the papery lantern (actually a calyx) that surrounds the fruit.

Nutritional content: The fruit contains vitamins C and K as well as copper, iron, magnesium, manganese, phosphorus, potassium. It is also rich in niacin and folate.

The fruits contain about 150 calories per pound, which is quite a bit more than the tomato.

Crop use: The tomatillo is a pretty easy plant to grow and can be quite productive for the amount of work it requires (which isn't much). It isn't very important from a nutritional standpoint, but does have some culinary interest.

Ease of growing: In suitably warm climates tomatillo is very easy to grow; in fact it often volunteers and grows itself like a wild plant.

Climate: The tomatillo is a sub-tropical plant and does best in a warm, humid climate (it will happily tolerate temperatures in the 90″s °F). However I have also read reports of it growing and producing well in cool, wet England, so it is obviously more adaptable than we usually give it credit for.

About Tomatillo

Seed facts

Germ temp: 60 (65 - 70) 75°F
Germination time: 5 - 14 days
Days to germinate: 5 - 14
Germination %: 75
Seed viability: 4 - 7 yrs
Weeks to grow transplants: 4 - 8

Planning facts

Hardiness: Tender
Growing temp:
Day: 65 (70 - 85°F) 90
Night: 55 to 65°F
Plants per person: 2

Transplants:
Start: 6 - 8 wks before last frost
Plant out: 2 - 4 wks after last frost
Direct sow: 2 wks after last frost
Days to harvest: 60 - 80 from transplant
Yield: 1 - 8 lb per plant
Yield per sq ft: 4 oz – 1 lb

Soil

pH 6.0 - 7.0

Tomatillos aren't as hungry as tomatoes, but will be most productive in a well-drained, moisture retentive loam, with lots of organic matter. However they will grow in almost any well-drained soil.

They don't need a lot of nitrogen and too much can result in lots of vegetative growth and few fruits.

Soil preparation: If your soil is less than perfect the plants will benefit from the addition of 2″ of compost or aged manure. You might also put a handful of fertilizer mix in each planting hole.

Planning

Where: These plants need the same conditions as the tomato: as much sun as possible, good air circulation and a warm sheltered site.

When: Tomatillo is usually started indoors like tomato 4 - 8 weeks before the last frost date (the length of time they take to grow will depend upon how warm they are). However if you have a long growing season, or a fast maturing variety, it is possible to direct sow them.

Planting

Planting indoors: Plant the seed in a flat 1″ apart and ¼ - ½″ deep (they like to be covered.) Prick them out into another flat when their first true leaves appear, spacing them 2″ apart. You can also grow them in cell packs or soil blocks.

Harden off: Before transplanting outside you must harden the seedlings off, so they become accustomed to somewhat less than ideal conditions (see **Tomato** for how to do this).

Transplanting outside: Bury most of the stem when transplanting and roots will form all along its length. If the plants are very leggy you should pinch out the lower leaves before planting.

If the weather is cool at transplanting time, you can warm up the soil with cloches or black plastic.

Sowing outdoors: The seed should be planted ¼ - ½″ deep, after the soil has warmed up. Pre-germinating the seed inside may help to speed things up.

Direct sowing these widely spaced plants isn't a very efficient way to use precious bed space. It is much better to start the seeds in a nursery bed and only plant them out when they are good sized transplants.

Spacing: Tomatillo plants can get quite big, so space them 24 - 36″ apart each way.

Support: These tend to be quite sprawling plants and some people grow them in tomato cages to keep them under control. If you have space its easier to let them run wild at the edge of the garden.

Care

Generally tomatillos are independent, almost weed-like plants and don't need a lot of attention.

Water: Tomatillos are quite drought tolerant, but will be much more productive if watered regularly.

Fertilization: If your soil isn't very fertile, give them a feed of compost tea or liquid kelp when the flowers first appear.

Mulch: This is helpful to conserve moisture and keep down weeds.

Control: The tomatillo is a sprawling vigorous plant and in the right climate it can really spread. When a stem touches the ground it will commonly root, so you can easily end up with a jungle of tomatillo. Avoid having it root where you don't want it to by moving the growing shoots promptly.

Frost: You can extend you harvest season by protecting the plants from early fall frosts. Cover them with fleece frost blankets/row covers, or whatever you have available (cardboard, bed sheets, a layer of straw).

Pests: Tomatillos have a lot of potential enemies in the form of hornworms, fleas beetles, cucumber beetles, Colorado potato beetle, aphids, nematodes, stink bugs and more. However I have found them to be relatively untroubled.

Disease: Tomatillos are attacked by the same diseases as tomatoes, but aren't usually as susceptible. These include early and late blights, anthracnose, mosaic virus, southern bacterial, verticillium and fusarium wilts and of course damping off (which can infect almost anything). Powdery mildew is a common problem where air circulation is poor (as always).

Harvesting

The fruits are ready to harvest one to two months after flowering (depending upon the variety). When the fruit is ripe the husk will turn yellow (or purple or brown) and will be completely filled by the fruit (often to the point where it splits open).

Tomatillos will ripen off the plant, so you can pick the fruit while it is still green (so long as it fills the husk). Some people say slightly unripe fruit is actually better for salsa.

You will often find ripe fruit in their papery husk, sitting on the ground. These are still edible and will stay good to eat for quite a while.

Storage: The fruit can be kept for a couple of weeks at room temperature, sitting in their husks. They can also be made into salsa and canned. You can freeze the puree as you would that from tomatoes.

Seed saving: Just remove the seeds from the ripe fruit before you eat them and process as for tomato. The fruit is more variable however, so save seed from the best flavored plants.

I have always believed tomatillos to be self-pollinating like tomatoes, however when I looked online I found many sites claiming that they are self-incompatible and needing cross pollination (the internet nearly always provides contradictory information, so this wasn't a big help). As it makes sense to have at least two plants anyway, this isn't a big issue. The flowers are very attractive to bees and I have never had any problem with fruit set.

Unusual growing ideas

Volunteers: If any fruits fall to the ground and rot, you will most likely get volunteers the following year and forever after (it does this much more successfully than the tomato). These will be just as good as their parents so can be allowed to mature and bear fruit. If they like your garden you may never have to worry about planting them again (which could be a good or bad thing depending upon how much you like them.)

Dry gardening: Tomatillo is independent enough to grow without any irrigation, even in quite dry climates. They may not get as big as irrigated plants, but they will be big enough.

Dry gardening requires that the plants be spaced further apart, to give each one more root room. See **Tomato** for more on this.

Containers: Tomatillo does well in a container, so long as you give it good soil, plenty of water and a deep pot (it can grow to be a big plant, so a 5 gallon pot isn't too big).

Varieties

There are only a few varieties commonly available, but more keep appearing.

Purple De Milpa: This is considered to be one of the best flavored. It is almost a wild plant and often volunteers.

Cisneros - Produces the biggest fruit of any common variety,

Purple - Large purple fruit for purple salsa verde (or should I say salsa morado!)

Toma Verde - Yellow green fruit.

Kitchen use

The tomatillo is important in Mexican cooking, for its use in the classic salsa verde, as well as other dishes (it's good roasted). It is not usually eaten out of hand.

Salsa Verde

12 tomatillos
1 medium onion
½ cup clime juice
5 cloves of garlic
¼ teaspoon sugar (optional)
1 to 2 finely chopped jalapeno peppers
1 tsp salt

Chop all the ingredients and mix thoroughly in a bowl. That's all there is to it. It is better is left overnight before eating.

Related species

Ground Cherry

Physalis peruviana

Also known as cape gooseberry, this species is a close relative of the tomatillo and is cultivated in the same way. The fruit looks like a small tomatillo, but it has a pleasant sweet/sour flavor and is good enough to be eaten raw.

Like the tomatillo the ground cherry enjoys hot weather, but it is significantly hardier and in milder areas (zone 8 and higher) it can be grown as a tender perennial. It will often survive for several years and be more productive after its first year. In areas with colder winters it must be grown as an annual though.

This species is naturalized in some areas of the country and in a few it is actually considered an invasive species. If it likes your garden it will often volunteer from fallen fruit. Once you have an established plant you it can be multiplied by taking (and rooting) soft cuttings.

Harvest: Like the tomatillo, the fruit comes wrapped in its own husk and may be picked before it is ripe. They sometimes fall from the plant before they are ripe and lay on the ground, which is presumably where the common name comes from. Unlike the tomatillo the fruit doesn't completely fill the husk.

Kitchen use: The ripe fruit is soft, yellow and sweeter than the tomatillo, so is more commonly eaten as a dessert. They can be eaten raw, or cooked in preserves and sauces. They can also be frozen whole to preserve them.

Varieties:
Goldenberry
Giant
Yellow husk

Strawberry Ground Cherry

Physalis pruinosa

This annual is used like the above. Some people say it has better flavor.

Aunt Mollys Ground Cherry - This Polish variety is the most commonly available type. It produces small sweet fruit.

Goldie - Has bigger fruit.

Golden Ground Cherry

P. pubescens

Another annual that is used like the above.

Cossack Pineapple - An Eastern European variety.

Tomato

Lycopersicon esculentum

Introduction: Tomato is native to South and Central America and was introduced into Europe in the sixteenth century. It took a long time for it to be accepted there as a safe and wholesome food. It first became popular in Italy, and is still closely associated with Italian food. Tomato is actually a tender perennial, but must be grown as an annual in temperate climates.

The tomato is the most popular garden vegetable crop in America and more square footage of garden magazine space has been devoted to it than any other vegetable. It is popular because it is easy to grow, very productive (it is one of highest yielding vegetable crops) and because home grown fruit is generally far superior to commercial fruit. Few food crops have suffered as much as the tomato in the search for agribusiness perfection.

With the exception of the ripe fruits, all parts of the tomato are somewhat poisonous (not to mention unpleasant tasting).

Nutritional content: Tomatoes contain vitamin C and A (beta carotene) and a whole range of valuable phytochemicals (lycopene, lutein, zeaxanthin and more). They are not a good source of energy, with only about 80 calories a pound!

Climate: The tomato prefers warm weather and doesn't like it when night temperatures drop below 50°F, They don't like very hot weather either and may fail to set fruit above 95°F.

About Tomatoes

Seed facts

Germ temp: 60 (75 - 85) 90°F
Germination time: 5 - 14 days
43 days / 50°F
14 days / 59°F
8 days / 68°F
6 days / 77°F * Optimum
6 days / 86°F
Seed viability: 3 - 7 years
Germination percentage: 75%+
Weeks to grow transplant: 4 - 10

Planning facts

Hardiness: Tender
Growing temp: 50 (70 - 75) 95°F
50 - 55°F at night
Plants per person: 3 - 5
Plants per sq ft: ½

Transplants:

Start: 2 - 6 wks before last frost
Plant out: 2 wks after last frost
Succession sow: 6 wks later

Harvest facts

Days to harvest: 80 - 120
50 - 85 days from transplanting
Harvest period:
Determinate: 4 - 6 weeks.
Indeterminate: 6 - 12 weeks
Yield per plant: 2 - 6 lb
Yield per sq ft: 1 - 3 lb sq ft

Ease of growing: In a suitably warm climate the tomato is pretty easy to grow, which is part of the reason it is the most popular home garden crop of all. They are so easy to grow they even show up in office buildings and volunteer in cracks in sidewalks.

Crop use: The tomato isn't the most nutritious crop, but it is very much a kitchen essential, as it is used in a huge number of dishes.

Soil

pH 5.5 (6.0 - 6.8) 7.5

Tomatoes aren't particularly fussy about soil, but generally the better the soil the larger the fruit. The perfect soil for tomatoes is a deep loam with lots of moisture retentive organic matter. It should also be well-drained as they are prone to root rot in wet soils. Early crops do better in light sandy soil because it warms up faster. They prefer a fairly neutral soil, but aren't very sensitive to pH.

Tomatoes are fairly heavy feeders, using quite a lot of nitrogen (180 lb /acre), a moderate amount of phosphorus (21 lb / acre) and a lot of potassium (280 lb / acre). They have deep roots that may go down 5 feet, but most of their feeder roots are in the top 2 feet.

Soil Preparation: Tomatoes are fairly hungry plants, so incorporate 2″ of compost into the soil generally and then put any additional amendments directly into the planting hole.

Nitrogen: This is most important during the initial vegetative growth stage, though some is also needed for fruit set.

Some gardeners make the mistake of giving the plants too much nitrogen. This isn't good as it can result in plants with too much lush foliage and not enough fruit.

Phosphorus: This is probably the most important nutrient for tomatoes, so put a handful of colloidal phosphate in the planting hole. This will supply phosphorus for early growth and good fruit set (a lack of it can delay maturation).

I read somewhere that Alan Chadwick used to put a layer of

phosphorus in the top 4″ of soil and another down 18″ deep to account for this (but I never could pay that much attention to the details).

Potassium: This is also important while the plants are young. Put a handful of greensand or wood ashes in the planting hole,

Calcium: Tomatoes need quite a bit of calcium and a lack (when combined with irregular watering) can result in the common affliction known as blossom end rot.

The commonest source of calcium is ground limestone (such as dolomitic lime) and if your soil pH is low this is the best source. If you don't want to alter your soil pH very much then you could use gypsum, eggshells or even calcium antacid tablets. You can put these directly in the planting hole, so it is immediately available to the plants roots.

Other nutrients: Tomatoes need trace elements right through their growth cycle. If you have added lots of well-rotted compost, aged manure, or seaweed to the soil before planting, this will supply all of the micronutrients they need. If you haven't then you may want to feed regularly with liquid kelp.

Planning

Where: To grow the very best tomatoes you need a warm sheltered site and 10 or more hours of sun daily (they can be grown with as little as 6 hours daily, but they won't be as productive).

It is best to avoid wet sites and those with poor air circulation, as disease can be more problematic there. If the climate is cool, put them against a south facing wall or on a south facing slope. You could also grow them under cloches, or in the greenhouse.

When:
Tomatoes are very tender and have little tolerance for frost. They are usually started indoors anywhere from 4 - 10 weeks before the last frost date. The seedlings can be planted out a couple of weeks after the last frost date.

Generally determinate varieties need 4 - 8 weeks to be ready for transplanting outside. The rather slower indeterminate varieties may take 6 - 10 weeks to attain a suitable size. If you have a very long growing season you can direct sow them outside.

The reason for the big variation in start date is because the rate of seedling growth is very much determined by temperature. If your greenhouse is a cool 60°F the seedlings may take 10 weeks before they are ready to go outside. If it is a cosy 85°F they may be ready to go in as little as 4 weeks. In very warm conditions they will grow like weeds.

It is good to get the starting date right, because you don't want to have plants sitting around inside in pots for too long (if they start to flower it is definitely too long).

Succession: Though tomatoes will produce fruit for quite a while, they do have a peak bearing season and eventually get less productive (even indeterminate types). You might want to start a succession sowing 4 - 6 weeks after the first (or direct sow some plants when planting the first batch out). If your growing season is long you might even plant a third one a month or so after that.

You can also stretch out the season by planting several varieties with different maturation times.

Cuttings for succession: A quick way to get plants for a second sowing is to use cuttings. Pinch out some of the suckers from your favorite plants and root them in water. These cuttings will give you new plants faster than you could grow them from seed.

Crop rotation: Don't plant tomatoes where any other member of the *Solanaceae* (eggplant, pepper, potato) has grown within the last 3 years.

Planting

Buying transplants: This is the easiest way to get tomatoes, though you don't get as much choice as to varieties. You may also buy problems in the form of disease, weeds or insect pests, so check them carefully before you buy.

The best transplants are about 8″ tall and stocky (never leggy). Don't buy plants with flowers, or tiny fruit, in the belief this will save you time. Premature flowering is actually a sign of stress.

The larger the plant, the greater the setback from transplanting, which is why smaller plants usually do better in the long term.

Transplants

Starting indoors: The seeds should be planted ¼ - ½″ deep in flats, soil blocks or cell packs and put in a warm place to germinate. They germinate best at a temperature of around 75 - 85°F during the daytime and 10°F lower at night.

A common mistake is to plant far more seeds than you need; don't grow 50 plants if you only have room for 10. If you sow 3 seeds for every plant you require, that should be plenty. When you only plant a small number of seeds, you can also give them plenty of room - an inch apart is good.

When their first true leaves appear, the seedlings should be transplanted to individual 4″ pots. Plant them deeper than they were growing, as they will produce roots all along the buried stem. Temperature can also be slightly lower (65 - 75°F in the day and 55 - 65°F at night).

You must now give the seedling everything it's little green heart desires: water, humidity, warmth, all the nutrients it needs and plenty of light.

It is not good to have your tomato plants sitting around in the greenhouse for too long. Once the roots have filled the soil in the pot, you must either plant them out or move them to bigger pots. Don't let them linger inside, as the roots will start to circle around and it will get root-bound. They may even start to flower, which (as I just explained) is not good.

Hardening off: If you are planting tomatoes out in cool spring conditions, they should be hardened off carefully. Do this slowly over a week, by reducing the amount of water they get and by leaving them outside for longer periods each day. On the first day put them outside for two hours during the warmest part of the day. Next day give them four hours, then six and so on. This helps them to slowly get accustomed to the somewhat less than ideal conditions to be found outside. You can also put them in a cold frame, which you open during the day and close at night.

In warm summer weather there is no need to harden them off. However you may want to keep them outside in the shade for a day or two, so they can get used to the different growing conditions.

Planting out: It is important that the soil be sufficiently warm (60°F minimum) for planting tomatoes outside. If it is too cold they will simply sit there without growing and may even be permanently retarded. For very early plantings you might warm up the soil with plastic (clear or black) and use cloches to protect the young plants.

The best time to transplant tomatoes (or anything else) is on a cool cloudy day, if rain threatens even better. If you don't get cool cloudy days, then transplant them in the early evening, not in the heat of the day.

You can give tomatoes a lot of attention while planting, because you don't usually plant very many. Dig a fairly large planting hole and amend it with a couple of handfuls of compost. The hole should be deep enough so you can bury most of the seedling (pinch off the lower leaves), leaving just the top few leaves sticking out of the ground. When you do this additional roots will grow all along the buried stem.

If the soil is still fairly cool when you plant, you can lay the plants almost sideways in shallow trenches, rather than deep holes. The plants will benefit from the warmer soil at this depth and will still produce roots all along the buried stem. This is also a good way to plant very large or leggy plants.

Water well after planting and keep the plants moist until they are well established. It is a good idea to put the supporting stakes, or cages, in the ground at this time, to avoid disturbing the plants later.

If you have a cutworm problem, wrap collars of aluminum foil or paper around the stem near ground level. A ring of wood ashes might also help.

Direct sowing: Sowing seed directly outdoors is only a practical proposition in areas with a very long growing season.

The seed should be planted ¼ - ½″ deep, after the soil has warmed up. If you are in a hurry you can pre-germinate the seed inside to speed things up.

Of course the problem with direct sowing is that the plants take up bed space from the moment they are planted, but don't give any return for months. It is much more

Determinate or indeterminate

Determinate plants only grow to a certain height and then flower and produce fruit. They produce one flower cluster on each side branch and then stop growing. They are then finished. These varieties are hardier, shorter (good for under cloches), earlier and produce a lot of fruit in a short time (usually 4 - 6 weeks).

Indeterminate plants never stop growing (at least theoretically). The side branches keep growing and can eventually turn into another stem, producing many clusters of flowers. They take longer to start bearing, but keep producing for much longer. They produce more poundage of fruit per square foot than the determinates.

efficient to raise transplants in an outdoor nursery bed (this is a specially protected outdoor bed that is used specifically for raisng transplants).

Spacing: The ideal spacing for tomatoes varies a lot, because of the difference in the size of the varieties and in the fertility of the soil.

Beds: Intensive bed spacing puts plants at 18″ - 24″ - 30″ apart.

Rows: They may be spaced anywhere from 18 - 36″ apart, in rows that are 36 - 60″ apart.

You could also experiment with closer spacings. This reduces the yield per plant, but may actually increase the yield per area, as you grow more plants. Sunlight isn't needed for ripening the fruit, so the foliage can be quite dense.

Care

For highest productivity tomatoes need lots of sun, enough room and a steady supply of available water and nutrients. If you give them all they need, they will respond by flowering earlier and fruiting more profusely.

Watering: Tomatoes are quite drought tolerant and don't really need a lot of water. More water means more and larger (but less tasty) fruit, while less water means fewer (but better flavored) fruit.

You don't need to water these deep rooted plants very often, but you should water regularly (unless you intend to try dry gardening). This is especially important when the fruits are sizing up. At this time you might water deeply twice a week.

Don't wait until they show signs of water stress as this can lead to problems with blossom end rot. Uneven watering may also cause fruit to split.

Don't get tomato foliage wet, as it can invite the spread of fungus disease. Drip irrigation is the best way to water, as it keeps the soil evenly moist but the plants stay dry. If you must use overhead watering then do it early enough in the evening, so that the foliage can dry out quickly and doesn't stay wet all night.

Fertilization: High nitrogen fertilizer is a help when the plants are growing rapidly, but once the flowers appear they need phosphorus more than nitrogen.

If your soil is poor you may give your plants a foliar feed of compost tea or liquid kelp every week until they start to flower. Then feed every 2 - 3 weeks.

Instead of using liquid feed you could top dress with a fertilizer mix, or use compost as mulch.

Mulch: Mulch is useful to keep down weeds, conserve moisture and keep the fruit clean. It can also reduce disease problems by keeping soil off of the foliage. In very hot areas mulch is also useful to keep the soil cool.

Don't put down an organic mulch until the soil is warm (when plants start to flower), as it insulates the soil and can prevent it from warming up quickly.

In cooler areas tomatoes are sometimes planted through black plastic mulch, which suppresses weeds, holds in moisture and keeps the soil significantly warmer. Some experiments using red plastic have shown significantly earlier and higher yields.

It is also possible to grow tomatoes with a living mulch such as clover (See **Unusual growing ideas**)

Support

No support: It isn't absolutely essential to support your plants, they can just sprawl on the ground. Determinate varieties work best when grown in this way, as they tend to be smaller. Indeterminate varieties can get quite large and do better if given some kind of support.

Allowing plants to sprawl along the ground can work okay in hot dry climates. In more humid ones it is just inviting problems with disease because of the much reduced air circulation and proximity to moist soil. Pests are also a bigger problem as there isn't much distance between the fruit and the soil with its multitude of hiding places.

I have to say I haven't had much luck with letting plants sprawl on the ground and don't recommend it. There are situations where this will work, but my garden isn't one of them (I lost a large proportion of the fruit to pests and disease).

Support: Raising the plants off of the ground has distinct advantages. It keeps the plant away from the soil with its pests and diseases. There is also better air circulation so leaves dry out more rapidly and are less vulnerable to disease. When plants grow vertically, rather than horizontally, they take up less space, so you can grow more of them in a given area. All of these things result in a significantly larger harvest that offsets the additional work involved.

I tend to go for the easiest kind of support, because I always try to get the most results for the least effort. In my opinion this is the wire cage. Commercial tomato cages are widely available, but often tend to be too small. I find it's cheaper and better to make my own, using 6″ square concrete reinforcing wire mesh. You can make cylinders 18″ in diameter and any height you want (3, 4, 5 or 6 feet tall).

In windy areas it is a good idea to fasten the taller cages to short stakes (or to each other), so they don't get blown over. In cool spring weather you can wrap the bottom of the cage with clear plastic to keep the plant warmer.

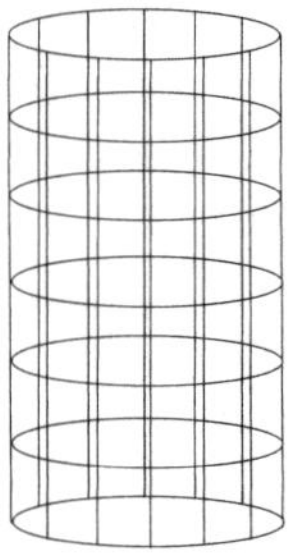

You can also open up these cylinders and spread them across the bed to form a wire tunnel (like a cloche frame). The plants will grow up through the mesh and sprawl on the top. In spring you can cover it with plastic to turn it into a cloche for early growing.

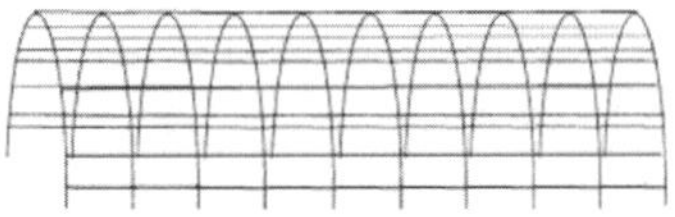

The simplest and cheapest supports are bamboo or wooden stakes. Their length is determined by the eventual height of the plants, plus the 12″ or so that goes down into the ground. They may need to be 4 feet tall for some varieties, 6 feet tall for others. It's a good idea to put these in the ground while planting, to minimize future root disturbance. The plant can be tied to the stake with strips of cloth or wire ties.

If your plants start to outgrow their supports you can always add a couple of taller stakes (carefully so as not to damage too many roots).

Pruning:
Some people prune their indeterminate tomatoes (they are mostly control freaks without enough to do). It basically consists of pinching out all the suckers (these appear in the axils of leaves) you don't want to grow into stems. Determinate plants should never be pruned, as it will reduce their already limited yields.

Pruning is most often done in cool climates to reduce the number of fruit produced and give them a better chance of ripening. It can also improve fruit quality by increasing the amount of light entering the plant and increasing aeration (though light isn't needed for ripening). It may hasten maturation by as much as two weeks and allows for closer spacing of plants.

The drawback to pruning is that it reduces the area for photosynthesis, so means less fruit per plant (yields may be half that of unpruned plants).

I don't bother with pruning, it just seems like extra work I don't need to do. The most efficient way to grow tomatoes is to use indeterminate varieties, unpruned, in cages.

Double stem: More fruit can be obtained if you allow one sucker to develop into a second stem (this is really training rather than pruning). You pinch out all of the suckers, except the one below the first flower cluster. This will quickly grow into a second stem. It can be supported by planting two flexible stakes together and spreading them apart at the top with a small stick. One stem is trained up each stake.

A third stem could produce even more fruit, but this gets even more complicated.

Frost protection: Tomatoes can't stand any frost, which can be a problem because you may encounter it at either end of the growing season

Spring frost protection: This is rarely needed because you don't plant tomatoes until the soil is warm. If a rare late frost threatens, it is not difficult to cover the low plants with row covers, mulch, plant pots or whatever is at hand.

Fall frost protection: This is important, as an early frost will usually kill unprotected tomato plants. If you can help your plants make it through this first frost there may not be another one for several weeks, during which time you can get a lot more ripe fruit. You can cover the plants with almost anything to help them to survive a mild frost: old bed sheets, straw mulch, plastic sheet, cardboard.

Pollination: Most tomato varieties are self-pollinated, so pollination isn't usually a problem. Often the first flowers fall off without bearing fruit, especially if temperatures go below 60°F, or above 90°F. In very hot weather you should water frequently to keep the plants cool. In cool weather you should put them under cloches.

Pests: When I said tomatoes are one of the easiest crops to grow, I could have added if you don't encounter a serious pest or disease problem. They have so many potential enemies, that it seems like it must be impossible to grow them at all. Potential pests include aphids, cutworms, Colorado potato beetles, flea beetles, leafhoppers, mites, nematodes, stink bugs, tomato fruitworms and of course slugs and snails.

Tomato hornworm: These huge caterpillars can do a lot of damage to tomato plants. I used to hand pick and kill them (usually with a stick as touching them didn't appeal to me). After a time I resorted to deportation from the garden because I found out that they turn into a spectacular moth (I know the deported caterpillars may well have died with no tomatoes to eat, but I can't think of everything!)

In recent years I haven't had to do anything, as trichogramma wasps do the dirty work for me. Their white cocoons can be seen on the motionless and unfortunate caterpillars - I almost feel sorry for them.

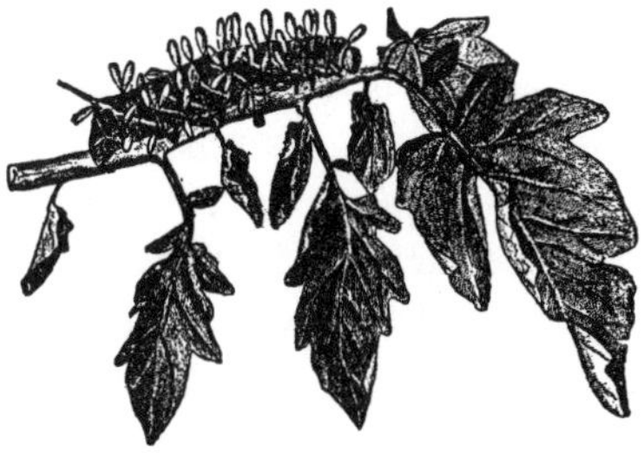

Disease: Tomatoes are also vulnerable to the host of diseases that affect members of the Solanum family. These include anthracnose, bacterial canker, bacterial spot, early blight, southern bacterial wilt, fusarium wilt, verticillium wilt.

You can help to keep some of these problems under control by rotation. Be careful when watering as many diseases can be spread on wet leaves (use drip irrigation). Many modern tomato varieties are resistant to verticillium wilt (V), fusarium wilt (F) and nematodes (N).

Tobacco Mosaic: This serious disease can be spread by smokers who handle the plant after smoking cigarettes. It may also be brought into the garden on seedling tomatoes. Prevent it by growing your own seedlings and not smoking.

Late Blight: This is the same killer that gets potatoes and is worse in cool humid weather. Spots appear on the leaves and then the whole plant turns black and dies (often overnight). You may be able to control it if you remove infected plants immediately, but it's an indication that the plants don't like the growing conditions. Up in western Washington I had whole beds of tomatoes and potatoes die almost overnight. They just didn't like the cool moist conditions (whereas the late blight did).

Other Tomato problems

Blossom end rot: Patches on the fruit turn black and rot. It most commonly affects the first few trusses of fruit. Remove any affected fruit immediately (they won't be any use anyway), to reduce stress on the plant. Pruning may make this problem worse. For some reason indeterminate varieties are less commonly affected.

Blossom end rot isn't a disease and is usually caused by lack of water during early fruit development, combined with a lack of calcium. The water shortage affects the transport of calcium in the plant, so the rot is caused by a local calcium deficiency.

Sunscald: This can occur when there isn't enough leaf cover to shade the fruits from direct sunlight and is most common on pruned plants. The simple way to avoid this is to stop pruning. Another simple answer is to put the plants closer together, so they shade each other.

Catfacing: This is caused by poor pollination and most often occurs in cool weather.

Splitting: This is caused by a sudden abundance of water, which causes the inside of the fruit to grow faster than the skin. In my garden this happens every year after the first fall rains. Cracked fruit are still perfectly edible, though they should be eaten quickly, as they won't keep for very long (they often go moldy).

Slugs and snails: If your tomatoes are unsupported and close to the soil, they may be damaged by slugs and snails. The best way to deal with these is to hand pick after dark.

Harvesting

When: The fruit will usually be ready to harvest 45 - 75 days after flowering (depending on variety). The fruit takes 30 - 45 days to reach full green size (where it will ripen off the plant) and a further 15 - 30 days to reach full ripeness. They are fully ripe about a week after they turn red. The fruit won't usually ripen below 55°F, or above 85°F.

Sunlight isn't necessary for ripening the fruits, only warmth, consequently they will ripen even in the dense shade in the middle of a plant.

I was going to write that you can recognize a ripe tomato because it is soft and red, but nowadays that is not necessarily true. They might also be yellow, green, purple, orange, white, pink or even black!

How: Gather the fruit when it comes away from the vine easily. Their flavor is at its peak when they are fully ripe. They can be gathered earlier however, as they will ripen off the vine.

If frost threatens, gather any fruits that are nearly full size, even if they are still green and ripen them indoors in a warm place. They won't be as good as fruit ripened on the vine (they will also have less vitamin C), but they'll probably be as good as anything you could buy.

Storage: Don't store tomatoes in the fridge, or below 55°F as it spoils their flavor. They should keep for a week or two at 55 - 65°F.

Tomatoes can be peeled and frozen for storage (peel by dipping in boiling water), or you can puree and freeze them. I put the whole fruit in a blender and puree them, skins and all.

Green tomatoes can be ripened in a warm dark place. Just make sure the fruit don't touch each other and remove any that start to rot (check them regularly). There are varieties (i.e. Burpees Long Keeper) that are intended for slow ripening indoors. If you have a lot of green fruit, keep them in a cool place and bring them into a warm room to ripen as needed (it takes about 2 weeks.)

Seed saving: Tomatoes are usually self-pollinated so saving seed is easy. A few varieties have a high degree of cross-pollination (these usually have long styles that stick out of the corolla) and should be isolated for purity, either by distance (25 ft and a barrier planting between them) or row covers. It doesn't hurt to separate the short style types by 10 ft and put another crop in between.

To get the seed, simply squeeze it from the ripe fruit (eat the rest), along with its juice (add a little water if it is dry) and let it ferment in a warm place for a few days. This will kill any disease organisms on the outside of the seed. Then scrape the scum from the top and rinse the seeds several times to remove bits of flesh. Strain the cleaned seed and dry it in a warm, dry place until you are sure it's dry.

Unusual growing ideas

Dry gardening: Tomatoes were once commonly dry farmed in California, where they received no irrigation water (or rainfall) at all. Such plants are markedly sweeter than conventionally grown plants. This is worth trying if you have a lot of space, but a limited amount of water for irrigation.

In a dry garden the plants must be spaced further apart than in a conventional irrigated garden. This eliminates competition with neighboring plants and gives their roots more space to forage for water. A mulch may also be helpful, as it conserves moisture and keeps down thirsty weeds.

Volunteers: Tomatoes are commonly found as volunteers in the garden. If these are not hybrids and you have the room, you might allow some of them to mature for a late crop.

Cool climate growing: To grow tomatoes outside in cooler climates, you have to use one of the fastest maturing and cold hardy varieties, such as the Sub-Arctics or Siberians (which may mean sacrificing some flavor). Start them inside early, warm the soil with plastic and cover the transplants with cloches. If you plan on using wire tunnels as supports, you can convert them into cloches by simply covering them with clear plastic. Some cool climate growers use black plastic mulch for the whole of the growing season, as it keeps the soil warmer.

Early crops: Getting an early crop of tomatoes means growing them in a cool climate for the first few months of their lives. See **Cool climate growing** above, for ways to do this.

Some people have part of their ego tied up in getting earlier tomatoes than their neighbors. If you are one of these people and do succeed in your quest to beat everyone else in your neighborhood, I prefer a subtle approach to letting everyone know about it. I just slip into the conversation that I am already getting sick of tomatoes. Of course the potential disadvantage of this approach is that you might be asked to give some away.

Containers: Some tomato varieties do well in containers, especially the smaller determinate cherry types (some of these even do okay in hanging baskets!) You can also grow the larger types too, though you will need a bigger container. You can also grow tomatoes in grow bags, which are simply large plastic sacks filled with a suitably fertile potting mix (see **Potatoes** for more on these).

Cuttings: You can get extra tomato plants by rooting suckers in water. This is a good way to multiply a single special plant you might have. It is also an easy way to grow your succession tomatoes.

Grafting: You can use this to grow a tasty heirloom tomato, while getting the advantage of a disease resistant variety by using it as a rootstock. I have never thought that this would be worth the effort, but it may be if you face big problems with disease.

Greenhouse: Tomatoes are a great greenhouse crop and in cooler climates this may be the only way you can grow them. They can be grown inside from early spring until late fall. In Europe there are varieties bred specifically for greenhouse growing.

Living mulch: I haven't tried it yet, but it is possible to grow tomatoes using living mulch. This means planting the transplants into an established bed of growing plants, which are usually some kind of annual nitrogen fixer, such as crimson clover or hairy vetch. This will require additional water, as you don't want the plants to compete. Yields may be somewhat later, but are often higher. Perhaps the biggest advantage is that it improves the soil while you are growing a crop.

Varieties

For a long time modern seed producers focused on the needs of commercial growers (understandably because they buy their seed by the pound rather than the gram). Their breeding work often concentrated on producing fruit that could withstand mechanical cultivation and harvesting. One of their achievements was the square tomato. This wasn't really square, but simply angular so it wouldn't roll off of conveyor belts.

The best tasting tomatoes

If you are going to grow tomatoes you may as well grow something that tastes good. Here are some varieties that commonly appear on lists of best tasting tomatoes.

Ananas Noir

Aunt Ruby's German Green

Better Boy F1

Black Krim

Black Plum

Brandywine

Carmello F1

Caspian Pink

Cherokee Purple

Momotaro

Mortgage Lifter

Sungold

Super 100's

Sweet million

Home gardeners were largely ignored by these seed companies, so many gardeners started to ignore them. They turned instead to the vast number of varieties that already existed; plants that have now come to be known as heirlooms. These are gifts to us from the gardeners of the past and are the common heritage of gardeners all around the world.

Probably no other crop has benefited as much from the recent interest in heirloom vegetables, as the tomato. We now have a mind boggling range of varieties, from 2-pound monsters down to the size of a pea. Determinate, indeterminate, climbing, early, mid-season, late, paste, black, green, purple, orange, yellow, striped and more. Ironically some of these are now finding their way on to supermarket shelves, alongside the descendants of those square tomatoes.

There is now so much choice of tomatoes it can be a problem knowing where to begin. You could grow 20 or 30 different varieties every year and not even begin to get through them all. In fact old varieties are probably reappearing faster than you could grow them.

The number of days to maturity mentioned on seed packets and in catalogs means from transplanting (so add 6 - 10 weeks to this).

There are also plenty of good hybrid varieties out there. I mostly avoid them though, simply because saving the seed of open pollinated varieties is so easy.

Taste: My first criteria in choosing a tomato is taste. The flavor of different varieties varies enormously, some are almost tasteless and others are delicious. I never could understand why anyone would want to grow a fruit that doesn't taste of anything. If I'm going to the trouble of raising a plant from seed, I want to have something special to show for it.

Climate also affects flavor, so a variety may taste good in one area, but not so good in another. For example in cool climates the large fruited types don't develop their best flavor. It really pays to experiment to find the best varieties for your area. This is fun too and every year I try some new varieties along with the old trusted friends.

The number of tomato varieties has exploded in recent years. Here is a tiny sampling of some of the best.

Early:
Glacier
Beaverlodge Slicer
Siberian
Stupice
Oregon Spring
Early Girl

Main
Beefsteak
Brandywine
Ponderosa
Marmande
Mortgage Lifter

Paste
Amish Paste
Principe Borghese
Roma
San Pablo

Cherry
Camp Joy
Chadwick Cherry
Gardeners Delight
Sungold

Unusual
Caro Red: Contains 10 times vitamin A of most tomatoes.

Kitchen use

Tomatoes are a tremendously versatile food. They are good raw or cooked and of course are a basic ingredient of Italian cooking.

Salsa

This is quick and easy to make and very satisfying. All the more so if you can gather all of the ingredients from your garden (except the salt).

8 tomatoes
1 medium onion
6 cloves garlic
½ cup cilantro
1 or 2 finely chopped jalapeno peppers
1 tbsp lime juice
½ tsp salt

Chop all the ingredients and mix together. Some people use a food processor, others prefer to hand chop. This is so good it is commonly eaten immediately, but it will be much better if left in the fridge overnight. This is only a basic recipe and can be altered in any way you like. You will probably want to vary the quantity of pepper you use, depending upon personal taste and how hot your peppers are.

Turnip

Brassica rapa

Introduction: It is probable that the turnip was domesticated independently in two different places. Somewhere in the vicinity of Afghanistan and in the Eastern Mediterranean. It has been grown in both those areas for several thousand years.

In Europe the large swollen roots have been grown for centuries as food for animals and poor humans. They were scorned by the better off classes as only fit for animals and still carry a slight stigma to this day.

In Asia the turnip is looked upon quite differently and is a very important crop in both China and Japan. In those countries a whole range of varieties exist.

Turnip is best known for its swollen root, but may also be grown for the tasty and nutritious leaves. Some varieties have been developed that produce an abundance of tender foliage.

Nutritional content: The roots contain vitamin C, complex carbohydrates, soluble fiber, calcium, magnesium, potassium, lysine and tryptophan. They contain around 130 calories per pound.

The leaves are rich in vitamins A, C and K, chlorophyll and some important phytochemicals (including isothiocyanates).

Crop value: Turnips are a fast growing (40 - 50 days), hardy and easily grown multi- purpose crop that is quite useful for the homesteader. The roots provide a substantial root vegetable, the leaves are nutritious greens, the flower buds can be used like broccoli (they are popular in Italy under the name broccoli raab) and the seeds can be sprouted like cress or alfalfa. It is also a good source of feed for livestock.

Ease of growing: Turnip is a cool season biennial and in a suitable climate it is pretty easy to grow.

Turnip is most satisfactory as a fall crop, as the swollen roots can mature in the cool weather which develops their best flavor. It is less useful in spring, as warm temperatures make the roots less palatable and can also cause them to bolt.

Climate: Turnip is happiest when growing in a cool (60 to 65°F) and humid climate. Older plants are quite hardy and many types can tolerate severe frost.

Soil

pH 6.0 (6.8) 7.5

Turnips need to grow quickly for best quality. This requires a rich, loose, well-drained, but moisture retentive soil. Brassicas in general do well on neutral, or even somewhat alkaline soil. If clubroot is a problem you should keep the soil pH above 6.5.

Like other Brassicas, turnips are vulnerable to boron deficiency, but this shouldn't be a problem if you add lots of organic matter.

Soil preparation: Like most root crops turnips prefer a loose soil. If the soil is heavy, or compacted, it can be loosened by incorporating 2″ of compost or aged manure. Double digging is also very beneficial. A good practice is to plant turnips on soil that was thoroughly dug and manured for a previous crop (such as potatoes).

About Turnip

Seed facts
Germ temp: 40 (60 - 85) 90°F
Germ time: 1 - 5 days
5 days at 50°F
3 days at 59°F
2 days at 68°F
1 day at 77°F * Optimum
Seed viability: 3 yrs
Germination percentage: 75%+

Planning facts
Hardiness: Hardy
Growing temp: 40 (60 - 65) 85°F
Plants per person: 5
Plants per sq ft: 9
Direct sow: 2 - 4 weeks before last frost
Fall crop: Plant 8 - 10 weeks before first fall frost
Height: 12″
Width: 8″

Harvest facts
Days to harvest: 40 - 80
Yield per plant: 3 - 16 oz
Yield per sq ft: 2 - 4 lb

Turnips don't require a lot of nitrogen (unless you are growing them for greens) as this encourages foliage growth rather than root growth. However if the soil is poor you may want to give them some fertilizer mix.

Turnips like lime, as it supplies calcium and decreases acidity.

Planning

Where: If you are growing turnips for their roots they will need full sun. Those grown for their leaves will do quite well in part shade.

Crop rotation: Don't plant turnips where another Brassica crop has grown in the last 3 years.

When: Turnip really needs cool nights to encourage it to store sugars in the root. If nights are too warm it will use those sugars for growth instead. This can make the roots pungent and quite unpleasant. Of course the only way you can get cool nights is by planting at the right time.

Spring: Biennial root crops store food in their roots as preparation for the coming winter. When you plant them in spring you are going against this natural inclination, so they tend not to do so well.

Spring isn't the ideal time to plant turnips because the weather gets warmer as they mature, which is the reverse of what you want. It's only worth planting them in spring if they have time to mature before the temperatures start to rise above 60 - 65°F (and nights are still cool).

Turnip can survive temperatures of 25°F and can be sown as soon as the soil can be worked in the spring (when it may only be 45°F). However it's generally better to wait until perhaps 4 weeks before the last spring frost. The first plantings may be grown under cloches to speed up their growth.

Fall Turnips do much better as a fall crop, as they have guaranteed cool weather when they are maturing and there are less problems with insect pests.

They are usually planted from late summer onward, maybe 8 - 10 weeks before the first fall frost date (the actual planting date depending upon when the weather starts to cool down). You want them to reach maturity just before it starts to get cold. Then it won't matter when growth starts to slow down. A few freezes will even improve their flavor.

Winter: In northern Europe fall planted turnips were once an important winter crop.

You can also plant turnips in the fall, for use the following spring as broccoli raab or spring greens.

Succession sowing: You don't need many turnip plants at one time. Sow a few seeds every 2 weeks, rather than a large number all at once. The exception to this would be a fall planting for storage, or over- wintering in the ground.

Planting

Direct sowing: Like most root crops, turnips don't transplant well, so they are almost always direct sown. The seed germinates easily at low temperatures and the hardy plants grows rapidly. They can be broadcast or sown in drills (shallow furrows). Sow the seeds ¼ - ½″ deep and 1″ apart.

Spacing:

Beds: Space the plants 4 - 6″ apart in the intensive beds.

Rows: If growing in rows, space the plants 3 - 6″ apart, with 18 - 24″ between the rows.

Care

The best turnips are those that have grown rapidly, which can only occur if the plants have everything they need in the way of nutrients, light and water.

Thinning: Like other direct sown root crops, they need careful thinning and weeding. Use the thinnings in the kitchen.

Fertilization: Give the plants a feed of compost tea, or liquid kelp, once they get going (remember, not too much nitrogen).

Water: Turnips don't need a lot of water, but it should be available constantly and not fluctuate too much. If the soil gets too dry, they can get woody and may even bolt. Irregular watering can cause the roots to crack.

Mulch: This is useful to prevent the soil drying out, to suppress weeds, to keep the soil cool and to supply nutrients.

A deep mulch of straw is helpful in winter to prevent the soil from freezing.

Bolting: Though the turnip is a biennial it will bolt in its first year in some circumstances.

The usual reason for bolting in turnips is stress caused by lack of water or nutrients, careless transplanting, or warm weather. It is natural for plants to bolt in the spring of their second year. It is what they are supposed to do.

Pests and disease: Turnips are close relatives of the cabbages and are vulnerable to the same pests and diseases (of which there are a considerable number.) Flea beetles and aphids have been the commonest problems for me, though usually there is no need to do anything about them, as these vigorous plants can handle them.

Harvesting

Roots: Spring roots should be harvested when they are still quite small, from 1½ - 3″ in diameter (this can sometimes be within a few weeks of sowing). When they get bigger than this they usually start to turn woody.

Winter roots can be harvested when somewhat larger, as they stay in much better condition in the cold weather. They are at their best after their tops have been killed by frost.

After pulling the root you should remove the tops (leave about 1″ of stem) so they don't draw moisture from the root. If the tops aren't too tough you can use them as a green vegetable.

Leaves: If you are growing turnips for the tender young foliage, it can be harvested as needed. As with the roots, the leaves also taste better in cool weather.

It is best to gather single leaves as they get large enough. Don't take them from the growing point and only take 1 or 2 leaves from a plant at one time, so it can continue to grow strongly.

Storage: In milder areas the roots can be left in the ground and harvested as needed (cover with mulch if it gets too cold). If the roots freeze you want them to stay frozen, so cover with thick mulch. Repeated freezing and thawing will cause them to rot.

Some people say leaving the roots in the ground through the winter is not a good idea as it may help Brassica pests to winter over. They advocate harvesting all of the roots in early winter and storing them in a root cellar at 34 - 40°F (if it's warmer than this they will eventually start growing). They can also be stored outside in a clamp (see **Potato**).

The root can be cut into cubes and frozen or canned (I can't say canned turnip has much appeal for me though). In the Middle East and Japan the roots are popular pickled.

Seed saving: Turnip is cross-pollinated by insects, so only one variety should be flowering at a time (or they should be caged or isolated by a half mile).

The usual method of obtaining seed is to plant it in late summer, protect it over the winter (inside or outside) and allow it to flower in spring. It should be planted in a block so insects are likely to visit many plants without going to other plants nearby. Collect the dry pods when they are ripe (they shatter easily so watch carefully), sift out the seeds, dry further and store.

In milder areas turnips may self-seed if given the opportunity.

Forcing: Any surplus roots can be potted up and forced like those of chicory, for winter greens.

Varieties

In England and Japan, where turnips are popular, they have different varieties for early and late planting, as well as some very dependable F1 hybrids.

Purple types

These are sometimes grown for greens as well as their roots.

Purple Top White Globe: The old standard (55 days).
Purple Top Milan - Italian heirloom with white flesh (50 days).
Snowball - Beautiful white roots (40 days).

Yellow types

These are prized for the edible root.
Yellow/Amber Globe - Heirloom from prior to 1840 (60 days)
Golden Ball - Outstanding flavor (50-60 days).

Oriental types

These grow fast and are almost like large radishes. They are quite good raw and are often steamed or stir fried. Good root types include: **Tokyo Market, Red Round, Komach F1, Tokyo Cross F1, Hakurei F1**

Nozawana is grown for its leaves.
Shogoin; A dual purpose crop grown for leafy greens or roots.

Leaf types

Seven Top: Important in the southeastern states for turnip greens. It can also be used for broccoli raab.

Tendergreen: This leaf variety is often thought of as a mustard and is grown like one, but it is actually a turnip.

Kitchen use

Small turnip roots (about 1½″ diameter) can be eaten raw as a substitute for radish. They are actually milder and better flavored than most radishes. Cooking turnip can be tricky, under-cooking is definitely better than over-cooking, which can turn them into watery mush.

The flowers and immature seedpods are a tasty minor additions to salads.

Broccoli Raab

In this country this Italian delicacy can be found in markets catering to Italian communities or foodies. The word raab means turnip, so the name means (logically enough) turnip broccoli. This is a pretty good description of the edible flower stalks it produces.

This isn't a highly productive crop, but it is a welcome one when it appears in early spring, when the garden often has little else to offer. It is grown in the same way as root turnip, with the aim of producing as big a root as possible (there is no worry about it getting tough).

Fall: The best time to plant broccoli raab is in late summer or fall, to mature the following spring. If it gets very cold, cover the plants with mulch to protect them, as they may die if it gets too cold. In early spring the plants bolt and send up slender flower stems. These aren't nearly as large as broccoli heads, but are used in much the same ways. The top 6 - 8″ of stem is cut before the flower buds open and is steamed or eaten raw. The plant will then produce more usable side shoots.

Spring: Broccoli raab can also be planted as a spring crop (it will act like an annual, rather than a biennial), started 4 weeks before the last frost date, though it doesn't usually do as well. When planted at the right time it will grow fast and mature in as little as 5 weeks. In cool climates it may be succession sown several times.

Varieties: There aren't many, though new ones are appearing.

Sessantina Grossa

Spring Raab

Watercress

Nasturtium officinale

Introduction: Watercress is native to Europe and adjacent parts of Asia and Africa. It is a highly nutritious plant and has been regarded as a special food for several thousand years. However for most of that time it has been gathered from the wild, rather than cultivated.

The cultivation of watercress is somewhat unusual, because of its specialized habitat requirements, but it grows easily enough if given the right conditions. Its native habitat is clean, slow flowing water in springs, ditches and shallow streams. In Europe it was grown commercially in special watercress beds, created beside streams to take advantage of the slowly flowing water. It will grow in any wet soil though, so long as it isn't stagnant (which can cause the plants to rot).

Growing your own watercress ensures that it is safe for use raw, which isn't always the case with plants gathered from the wild.

About Watercress

Perennial
Hardiness zones: 3 - 11
Germ temp: 45 (55 - 75) 85°F
Germination time: 8 - 12 days
Seed viability: 4 - 5 years
Days to harvest: 50 - 60 days
Growing temp: 45 (55 -75) 85°F
Perennial to zone 5

Nutritional content: Wild watercress spends it life bathed in nutrients and as a consequence it is very rich in minerals, including copper, iron, iodine (perhaps the richest source of any land plant), manganese and sulfur. It is also a good source of vitamins A, C and E. The cultivated plant will be somewhat less nutritious.

Watercress is related to the Brassica family and is rich in many of the same cancer fighting phytochemicals.

You don't eat watercress as a source of energy, in fact it may be the lowest calorie food in this book. With only about 50 calories to a pound, it makes cucumber (with 68) look positively fattening.

Watercress also contains the irritating mustard oil found in many members of the *Brassicaceae*, and can irritate the kidneys if eaten in excess.

Crop use: Watercress isn't a very important crop, even though it is quite nutritious.

Ease of growing: Watercress is easier to grow than people imagine, as it doesn't actually need clear running water, it just needs wet soil. It can even do well when grown in pots indoors.

Climate: This plant is native to cooler areas of northern Europe and Asia and prefers cool (55 - 75°F) weather. However it is quite adaptable and can take some heat (growing in water helps to keep it cool.)

Soil

pH 6.0 (7.2) 7.5

Watercress is accustomed to being bathed in nutrients and needs a fairly fertile soil for good growth. It does best if it is sightly alkaline.

Planning

Where: Watercress likes to grow anywhere the soil is naturally moist, but it can also be grown on dry land, if you take care to keep it moist. It just won't be as vigorous under these conditions.

When watercress is not growing in water it does better with some shade, especially in warmer areas. If it is growing in water then it will be most productive in full sun.

A good way to grow watercress is in shallow trenches (enrich the soil with lots of organic matter to slow down the rate at which it dries out). These are easier to keep moist.

Planting:

Seed: Watercress is easily grown from seed, either sown directly in the soil, or started inside and planted out as transplants. Seed is commonly used to start commercial plantings as it is sure to be virus free.

Cuttings: The fastest and easiest way to get watercress is to buy a bunch of fresh watercress from a market and root it in water (sometimes it already comes with roots).

Watercress roots very easily and this is actually one of the ways it propagates itself in the wild. Start by stripping the lower leaves from the cutting (if left on they may rot when submerged in water), then simply put the plants in a jar of water. Change the water regularly (every couple of days), otherwise it may start to smell and can cause the plants to rot. The plants should grow roots within a week or so.

When it comes time to plant, just use the ones that have the most roots. Plant them up to their leaves, so all of the stem is buried. Water well after planting and keep it well watered (maybe with well water.)

Watercress also transplants well, so you could take some from the wild and re-domesticate it.

Spacing: Space the plants 6 - 8″ apart. They are quite sprawling and the stems will root wherever they touch the soil. Eventually the plants will spread and fill in all the space in between them, to make a continuous carpet.

Care

Feeding: If the soil isn't very fertile you should give it an occasional feed of compost tea or liquid kelp.

Watering: For good growth the plants must have abundant moisture at all times. If they aren't growing in water they will need to be watered frequently (every day in dry weather). If they are growing in water you won't need to water them at all (which is nice).

Pests and disease: Commercial plantings are sometimes attacked by viruses, which is one of the best reasons for starting your plants from seed. Small home plantings may be attacked by slugs, snails, flea beetles, spider mites or whitefly.

Bolting: When watercress starts to bolt, its flavor deteriorates and can become bitter and / or very pungent (a trait it shares with most edible members of the *Brassica* family). Keeping the plants well watered and fed may slow this down, but it eventually happens every year (usually in late summer). You can remove flowers as they appear or you can let the plants produce seed for you.

Harvesting

When growing in water (with its temperature moderating influence) watercress can often be gathered year round. Gather the plants by pinching off the growing tips with your fingers (or by using scissors), leaving the roots and lower leaves to continue growing.

Seed saving: Watercress flowers are self-fertile and attractive to bees, so they produce seed easily. There aren't many varieties so you don't have to worry too much about keeping it pure.

Watercress will often self-sown if given the chance.

Unusual growing ideas

Given a suitable site, watercress is a reliable, hardy and easily maintained perennial crop. It could be a valuable part of a cultivated freshwater ecosystem, providing shelter and food for numerous organisms. These in turn provide food for fish, birds and small mammals.

Containers: Watercress grows well in containers, just use a wide pot, a fertile potting mix and keep it moist. If using seed just sow right into the pot. To minimize watering you can sit the contain in a larger container of water (make sure to change this regularly). Recently I have been experimenting with fiber pots sitting in a shallow pond and this seems to work well.

Pipe system. Get some 6″ diameter plastic pipe and cut it lengthwise into 2 halves (or use lengths of aluminum or plastic rain gutter). Then glue them together and put in the ground, so there is a very slight slope (¼″ in 12″) and the lip of the pipe is close to ground level. Put the end of the first section of pipe underneath an outdoor tap, so it can be watered easily. Almost fill it with gravel and then plant watercress in plastic containers filled with a mix of fertile soil and peat moss (and perhaps some dolomitic lime).

Waste-water: Watercress can help to purify gray water, though of course you wouldn't want to eat it from this source.

Ponds: Watercress will grow happily enough in a garden pond, though it doesn't like stagnant water. Algae can cause problems if it gets out of hand, as it can cover the watercress leaves in a green film that is hard to remove.

Bog: You can also create a watercress bog, which is basically a garden pond, lined with a rubber pond liner or sheet of heavy duty polyethylene (poke a few drainage holes in the sides of the liner) and then filled in with a suitable soil mix (equal parts sand, soil, and compost). You then sow seeds on the surface, or plant cuttings or transplants.

Harvesting

Gather the growing tips any time they are available and growing vigorously. This is a perennial so you don't want to take too much at one time.

Varieties

It is rumored that there are named varieties, though I have never seen any.

Kitchen use

Raw watercress is nice in salads, sandwiches and salad dressings. It is also good cooked as a potherb and in sauces, soups and stir-fries.

The seed is also edible and (if you can get enough of it to be worthwhile) can be used like mustard seed.

Watercress sandwiches

4 cups finely chopped cucumber
1 cup watercress
¼ cup butter, softened
1 tbsp chives
⅛ cup mayonnaise
½ teaspoon salt
⅛ teaspoon ground black pepper
Whole wheat bread

Put the salt on the cucumbers and leave for 15 minutes. Then mix them with the pepper, chopped chives and butter. Spread mayonnaise on 6 slices of bread and then a layer of chopped watercress. Spread the cucumber mixture on another 6 slices.
Put them together, trim off the crusts and cut into triangles. I suppose you could argue they are cucumber sandwiches as much as watercress. Either way they are very good

Watermelon

Citrullus vulgaris

Introduction: Watermelon is a famous treat for hot summer days. It is a member of the *Cucurbit* family and is grown in much the same way as the related melon.

This succulent tropical fruit originated in Africa and has been cultivated for at least 5000 years. It spread around the civilized world very early, apparently because it was carried on ships as a source of fresh water. It probably came to North America with African slaves.

Nutritional content: The fruit is mostly water, but also contains vitamin C, beta carotene, potassium, lycopene (a powerful antioxidant) and other important phytonutrients. As a source of energy it gives about 140 calories per pound.

Crop use: In nutritional terms watermelons aren't a very useful crop, giving a small amount of food value for the space they require.

Ease of growing: Watermelon is fairly easy to grow, so long as the climate is warm enough.

Climate: Watermelon is native to desert areas and does best with warm (at least 70°F and preferably 80°F or more), dry, sunny weather. If they don't get enough heat they won't be very sweet (heat = sweet).

The small types require 80 days of warm weather and larger types need as much as 120 days. They won't do well if the nights get too cold. High humidity can be a problem as it encourages disease.

About Watermelon

Seed facts
Germ temp: 65 (70 - 95) 100°F
Germ time: 3 - 10 days
8 days / 68°F
4 days / 77°F
3 days / 86°F * Optimum
Germination percentage: 80+
Viability: 2 - 4
Weeks to grow transplants: 3 - 4

Planning facts
Hardiness: Tender
Growing temp: 65 (75 - 85) 90°F
Plants per person: 4
Plants per sq ft: ¾

Transplants:
Start: on the last frost date
Plant out: 4 wks after last frost
Direct sow: 4 wks after last frost
Succession sow: 4 - 6 weeks after first sowing

Harvest facts
Days to harvest: 70 - 150 days
Harvest period: 12 weeks
Yield per plant: 2 lb (2 - 4 fruit)
Yield per sq ft: ½ - 1½ lb sq ft

If your climate isn't ideal for watermelons but you simply have to grow them, you should try the smaller varieties. You should also use row covers or black plastic mulch and try to find a warm south or west facing slope (or wall).

Soil

pH 6.0 to 7. 0
The ideal soil for watermelon is loose, moist, fertile, well-drained and fairly neutral, but it will grow okay in most kinds of soil. I have seen it producing fruit at the edge of a parking lot in Florida, no doubt from someones picnic.

Soil preparation: Watermelons are quite hungry plants so incorporate 2″ of compost or aged manure into the top 8″ of soil (they love old manure and can actually tolerate fresh manure better than most crops). They need nitrogen for early vegetative growth, and phosphorus (give them colloidal phosphate) and potassium (wood ashes) for fruiting. An organic fertilizer mix will also supply all of these.

Watermelons don't like very acid soil, so lime if necessary (ideally with dolomitic lime, which also adds magnesium).

Planning
Watermelons aren't difficult to grow, but they do need the right conditions, as well as plenty of room. In less than ideal conditions you may have to work to ensure they stay warm enough.

Where: Watermelons require a hot (ideally at least 80°F) sunny site. It should also have good air circulation to minimize disease problems.

Watermelons also require space of course. The bush varieties are fairly compact, but the bigger vining types are real space hogs. Plant these at the edge of the garden, where they can sprawl off in another direction. You could also trellis them, to reduce their garden footprint.

Crop rotation: Don't plant Cucurbits (melons, squash, cucumbers) in the same soil more frequently than every 3 or 4 years.

When: Watermelon needs warm weather and is one of the last crops to go out in spring. Don't plant it until at least 4 weeks after the last frost date, when all danger of frost is past and the soil temperature is at least 60°F.

If your growing season is short, you can speed up soil warming by using black plastic mulch. You can then simply plant through slits in the plastic. This will provide some extra heat in the summer.

Planting
You might want to pre-soak the seeds overnight before planting, especially if you are sowing directly outside in less than ideal conditions.

Transplants
Starting inside: If your growing season is short, you may have to start your watermelons indoors where it is a warm (+80°F). This isn't ideal though, because (like most Cucurbits) they dislike root disturbance.

Start the seeds in cell packs, soil blocks or individual pots. Plant 2 - 3 seeds to a block or cell and thin to the best one after all have emerged. The seedlings will be ready to plant out 3 - 4 weeks after sowing, when they have 3 or 4 true leaves.

Watermelons grow quickly, so it's not good to start them too early. You don't want them to get too big or root-bound. If it is too cold to transplant them out when they are ready, you will have to move them into larger pots.

There is little point in buying watermelon transplants, as it is so easy to grow your own from seed. This is not only cheaper, but they usually grow better too.

Planting out: Plant out the seedlings up to their first true leaves and water immediately. When they have recovered from transplanting, give them a liquid feed to get them growing again. In cool areas you might want to put them under row covers or cloches until the weather warms up.

Direct sowing: Watermelons do best when direct sown, so this is the way to go if your growing season is long and hot enou gh. They will germinate and grow rapidly in warm (75°F) soil. They may even out-perform transplants started several weeks earlier.

Usually you plant 2 seeds at each station (plant them 1″ deep) and remove the weakest one when they have both germinated.

Hills: Watermelons are often planted in hills (or ridges if you have a lot of them) as the raised soil warms up faster and ensures good drainage.

To make a hill remove 2 spade-fulls of soil, dump in 2 spade-fulls of compost or aged manure), then replace the soil. Mix it all together and shape it into a low mound with a depression on top. Plant the seeds on edge, ½ - 1″ deep, sowing 5 - 6 seeds on each mound. When these are growing well, pinch out (don't pull) the inferior seedlings, to leave the best 2 plants to grow on.

Succession sowing: If you have a long growing season you can get a continuous harvest by making several sowings, 3 - 4 weeks apart. You can also plant several varieties, with different maturation times.

Spacing: This will vary depending upon the variety you grow. There are large sprawling vines and compact bush vines.

Vines: These are often planted in hills, spaced 6 - 8 ft apart. with 2 plants to a hill.

If you intend to support the plants then it is good to plant in rows. If they grow vertically they take up a lot less space and can be spaced as close as 24 - 36″ apart.

Bush plants:
Rows: These may be spaced 24 - 36″ apart, in rows 48 - 60″ apart.

Beds: Plant them 15″ - 18″ - 24″ apart, depending upon the soil and variety.

Care

Watering: The plants will be most productive if they are watered deeply, a couple of times a week. However they are quite drought tolerant and if you need to minimize water use, they can just be watered when the fruits start to develop (or if it gets very dry).

The best way irrigate is with a drip system, as it doesn't wet the leaves (wet leaves encourages fungus diseases, such as mildew). Over watering is sometimes a problem with these desert plants, as it can lead to disease problems.

Mulch: Watermelons are planted quite far apart, so mulch is useful to help conserve moisture in the soil. Don't apply it until the soil has warmed up and the plants are big enough to tolerate slug damage. A mulch of compost or aged manure will also help to feed the plants.

Feeding: Watermelons are hungry plants and do best if fertilized regularly. Give them a feed of compost tea or liquid kelp every 2 - 3 weeks. Their main need for nitrogen is when they are young and growing rapidly. When they start to fruit they are more in need of phosphorus and potassium. Too much nitrogen at this stage may then simply encourage foliage growth at the expense of fruiting.

Weeding: Watermelon plants usually only need weeding when they are young. Once they get going they are vigorous enough to deal with most weeds. However if you are growing them in a very dry climate, weeds will compete for water, so it's best to remove them.

Protection: In cool climates the plants should be covered with cloches until the weather warms up. It is important that they gets lots of sun and heat, as this creates sugar and gives them good flavor. If cool weather threatens at any time you may want to use row covers.

Light frost won't damage the ripe fruit, but it will kill the plant and prevent any more fruit from ripening.

Pruning: The seedlings should be pinched back twice, so they produce four growing tips. These are then allowed to grow and flower. You can direct these vigorous shoots in the direction you want them to go (to vacant space).

Support: If space is very limited you can train the plants up trellis to save space, just as you would cucumbers. However the fruits are a lot heavier than cucumbers and will need support (slings made from old panty-hose work well.) You will also need a fairly substantial support structure.

Growing on a trellis only really practical with the smaller types. It isn't going to work with the 30 pounders.

Fruiting: The first flowers to appear are usually male and will eventually wither away (need I even say they can't produce fruit?) Female flowers will follow soon afterwards and if they are pollinated these will bear fruit. You can tell the difference because the female flowers are bigger and have a tiny "fruit" behind them.

If female flowers keep appearing, but no fruit develops, it usually means they aren't getting pollinated. Watch to see if there is bee activity around the flowers (of both sexes).

If you want to make sure your plants are pollinated, you can do it by hand, though this isn't normally necessary. Hand pollination is most often done in greenhouses or cloches, where insects may not be able to get to them easily.

The first fruit to be pollinated will be the best, so commercial growers often allow only one or two fruit to develop on each branch and then pinch off any others that form. The more fruit you allow to develop, the smaller they will all be.

Care of fruit: As the melon swells it can get quite heavy. If it is growing on a trellis it should be supported in a sling. If it is growing on the ground you can insert a piece of wood, plant pot, tile or stone underneath it, to get it off the soil (this will also prevent gophers tunnelling into them from underneath).

Pests: Watermelons suffer from many of the same afflictions as other Cucurbits. They are particularly vulnerable when small, so should be protected carefully at this time.

The various species of cucumber beetles are one of the worst pests, as they not only eat the plants, but can also spread diseases such as bacterial wilt.

Other insect pests include aphids, squash bugs, squash vine borers, mites, and more. Generally if your plants are healthy and growing rapidly, pests shouldn't be too much of a problem.

Rabbits, raccoons and birds may eat the ripe fruit.

Diseases: Powdery mildew is a common problem with watermelons (as it is with all the cucurbits), especially in humid conditions. It is important to keep the leaves as dry as possible, which is the main reason why drip irrigation is better than overhead watering. Good air circulation can also help minimize this and other disease problems.

Other diseases of watermelon include mosaic virus, downy mildew, alternaria leaf blight, anthracnose, fusarium wilt, curly top and bacterial wilt.

Harvesting

When: The first fruits will be ready to harvest in mid to late summer, about 35 - 45 days after pollination, which should be about 80 days after planting.

How: Cut the fruit from the plant, leaving a couple of inches of stem attached. Handle it carefully once it is harvested, as it will bruise easily.

When a Watermelon is ripe:

There are several ways to tell when the fruit is ripe, though not all of these indicators may be present at the same time.

The color of the skin becomes dull.

The fruit stops enlarging.

The tendril closest to the fruit usually turns brown and shrivels up (it should be dry and crisp).

The skin becomes so hard that a fingernail will barely dent it.

The spot where the melon was resting on the ground will turn from white to yellow or cream.

The traditional way to determine if a watermelon is ripe is to rap it with your knuckle and listen for a dull thud. There are problems with this though, one is that you need to know what to listen for. Another is that some watermelons don't always make the required sound.

Storage: The fruits taste best when eaten as soon as possible after picking. Otherwise whole fruit should be kept at room temperature or lower (ideally at 45 - 50°F). They can be stored in a fridge for a couple of weeks, but their flavor will slowly deteriorate. Once cut they deteriorate rapidly so cover with plastic wrap and use within a day or two.

Seed saving: If you grow an open pollinated variety and keep it pure, you can collect seed from the fruit for planting next year. I avoid hybrids simply because it seems a shame not to be able to use some of those seeds.

Watermelons are cross-pollinated by insects so you should grow only one variety at one time, isolate by a ½ mile, cage or hand pollinate. Hand pollinating watermelons isn't difficult, though the flowers are smaller than other cucurbits. The procedure is the same as described under **Melons.**

Unusual growing ideas

Short season growing: If you want to grow watermelons in areas with short growing seasons, use a small fruited variety, start the seed indoors and warm the soil with black plastic or cloches before planting.

Dry gardening: Watermelons can be grown without any irrigation at all. You will get fewer and smaller fruits, but they will be sweeter.

For this to work you have to space the plants further apart, so they have more volume of soil to extract water from. You should also remove weeds as they will compete for precious water in the soil.

Containers: Watermelon can be grown in a container, so long as it is big enough (5 gallon minimum for one plant) and you use a compact variety that produces small fruit. In a city you may also have to hand-pollinate, as often there aren't enough pollinating insects around.

Salad greens: You can get salad greens from melons, by sprouting the seeds like those of sunflower.

Varieties

Like most other Cucurbits watermelons come in bush or vining types.

When you get into the heirlooms you find that watermelons aren't always the conventional green with pink flesh. There are actually a wide array of colors, sizes and shapes. The best flavored types include:

Early (70 to 75 days to harvest)
Garden Baby - red flesh, 6 to 8 lb
Sugar Baby - red flesh, 6 to 10 lb
Yellow Baby - yellow flesh, 6 to 10 lb
Yellow Doll - yellow flesh 4 to 6 lb

Main Season (80 to 85 days)
Black Diamond - red flesh, 35-75 lb
Charleston Gray - red flesh, 20 to 30 lb
Crimson Sweet - red flesh, 20 to 25 lb
Calsweet - red flesh, 25 - 30 lb
Moon and Stars - Orange flesh 6 - 10 lb
Tender Sweet - Orange flesh 15 - 20 lb

There are also seedless hybrid varieties, which may be convenient, but the seed is expensive and obviously you can't save seed from them. They may also need another variety to be grown nearby as a pollinator.

Kitchen use

Watermelon is usually eaten fresh. Many Americans like to eat it ice cold, but it has more taste if it is eaten at room temperature (like red wine).

Pieces of watermelon flesh can be frozen for use in drinks.

You can also put the flesh in a blender and turn it into a drink.

Seeds: These are edible too and can be roasted like those of melon (see **Melons**).

Wheat

Triticum aestivum syn *T. vulgare*

Introduction: Wheat is thought to have originated in the Near East around 12,000 years ago and provided such a valuable source of nutrition that it quickly became an important crop and eventually revolutionized the way people lived.

The large scale cultivation of wheat was responsible for the start of civilization in that area. This happened because it provided such a surplus of food that some people could cease to be farmers and could go and build cities (the word civilized means living in cities). This eventually led to the creation of different classes of people: peasants, slaves, laborers, soldiers, craftsmen, traders, priests, generals, aristocrats and kings. In turn this led to centralized government, organized religion, taxes, tithes and the creation of professional armies and - err, maybe it wasn't such a great idea after all!

The cultivation of wheat was so successful that it spread to almost every area that was suitable for growing it (it was being grown as far away as England 5000 years ago). Wheat is a staple food for most of the people likely to read this book and is second only to rice in importance as a human food crop.

Nutritional content: Wheat seed is rich in protein, as well as complex carbohydrates and fiber. It also contains iron, manganese, selenium, zinc, niacin, riboflavin and thiamin. It is also a fantastic energy source, containing about 1500 calories per pound.

About Wheat
Germination time: 2 - 21 days
Germination temp 55 - 75°F
Growing temp: 55 (70 – 75) 85°F
Days to maturity: 110 - 170
Seed viability: 5 years
Yield: 1 lb in 10 sq ft

Crop use: Most gardening books don't even consider growing wheat as a garden crop and some of those that do reject the idea. Generally the reason for this is not that it's hard to grow, but rather that big Midwestern wheat growers are so efficient and have such an ideal climate that somehow we can't "compete" with them.

In fact home wheat growing can be quite practical and certainly isn't a competition. I'm not suggesting that you grow wheat instead of more conventional crops, but if you are already growing everything else you need and are looking for a new challenge (and if you have the space) then it could be an interesting and rewarding project. If you eat a lot of bread it would certainly be an important step towards food self-sufficiency.

An important bonus crop when growing wheat is the considerable amount of straw. This can be invaluable for building up the fertility of the soil.

Ease of growing: Wheat is a relatively easy crop to grow, but it requires a fair bit of processing to transform it into something edible. You need to be a little creative to use the wheat you grow.

The biggest problem with growing wheat is that it needs quite a lot of space to produce a worthwhile amount. This isn't a crop for the square foot garden.

Climate: Wheat prefers a fairly cool, moist climate for growth, but warm, dry weather is best for ripening the grain.

Soil

pH 5.5 (6.5) 7.0
To grow good wheat you need a good soil. It should be well-drained, fertile and moisture retentive. The type of soil doesn't matter too much, so long as it contains plenty of nutrients.

Bed preparation: Wheat has deep penetrating roots, so a thoroughly double dug bed is ideal for maximum yields. If you would rather have slightly lower yield and a lot less work you can just loosen the soil with a fork (it all depends upon how much effort you are prepared to make).

While cultivating the soil you should add a 2″ layer of compost or aged manure, as well as greensand or wood ashes (for potassium) and colloidal phosphate for phosphorus).

Planning

Finding seed: Wheat seed isn't found in your typical garden center vegetable seed display, so you may have to search to find a suitable type for planting. You can buy named varieties in small quantities from some mail order seed companies. If you live in a rural area you may be able to get wheat seed from a farm supply store (though it may be treated with fungicide). If all else fails you can simply plant winter wheat berries from a food store. The problem with this is that you won't know what variety it is.

Where: Wheat needs good soil and full sun for maximum productivity and of course enough space.

The biggest problem with growing wheat is the space it requires. Its been estimated that it takes 1000 sq ft to grow a bushel (60 lb) of wheat, so a family of 4 might need 4000 sq ft (an area 50 ft x 80 ft).

How practical this is will depend upon where you live. In urban areas few people have a spare thousand square feet of unused sunny space, though you might be able to plant a 100 sq ft wide growing bed and harvest up to 10 pounds of grain (there is probably no point growing much less than this, except perhaps as an experimental or seed crop). In many suburban and rural areas lawns often cover thousands of square feet and in such places growing wheat can be relatively practical.

Crop rotation: You should rotate your wheat crop annually (easier said than done if you need 4000 sq ft though), or only grow it once every three years.

When: Wheat prefers cool weather and in warmer areas it is most often planted in fall, to mature in early summer the following year. In colder areas you have to plant in spring.

Types of wheat

Winter wheat: This is the hardiest type. It is fall sown (September - October) in areas with fairly mild winters, where the temperature doesn't go much below 20°F. It needs to be well established with a good root system by the time cold weather arrives. The plants go dormant over the winter, but start growing again as soon as spring arrives and mature in early summer. The crop is out of the ground early enough that another crop can follow it.

Good timing is important with winter wheat, because you don't want the plants to be too advanced when cold weather arrives. If they have grown too big they may lodge (fall over) the following spring and won't yield well.

Winter wheat needs 4 - 6 weeks of cold temperatures (32 - 45°F) to vernalize it before it will flower and produce seed.

Spring wheat: This is generally grown where winters are too severe for winter wheat. It is planted in early spring as soon as the soil can be worked and matures in mid to late summer. It isn't as hardy or productive as winter wheat.

Spring wheat doesn't need to be vernalized before it can flower, it merely needs to get big enough.

In very mild winter areas spring wheat is sometimes planted in fall, so it can mature in early summer before the weather gets too hot.

Hard and soft: Both winter and spring wheat come in hard and soft types. Hard wheat is high in gluten and is preferred for baking bread. Soft wheat is lower in gluten and higher in starch and is commonly used for making pastry and crackers (though it can make good bread too).

Planting

Raising transplants: Some people actually grow wheat from transplants. Apparently it can increase yields by up to 50%, but it seems like a lot of work. I would only transplant if I had a small number of valuable seeds I wanted to multiply.

You can start the seed indoors in flats, about 6 weeks before the last frost. When the plants are about 2″ high they are transplanted outside. This should be about a month before the last frost date.

Direct sowing: This is the usual (more rational) way to plant wheat and is pretty easy (just like planting a green manure crop). Broadcasting the seed onto the prepared seedbed is the traditional and most picturesque method, but it is quite wasteful of seed unless you are good at it and can do it lightly. You certainly don't want to have to thin your wheat.

The most efficient way to plant is in rows with a seed drill, set to plant the seed to a depth of 1½ - 3″ (2″ typically). Cover with a couple of inches of straw mulch after planting to suppress weeds and reduce the need for watering.

Spacing: Wheat doesn't like to be crowded and can be planted a lot further apart than you might imagine. It was once said that you should be able to walk across a wheat field and only stand on one plant with each step. The reason that wider spacing works is because the plants tiller freely, which means they send out multiple stems. A spacing of 4 - 5″ is good when growing in wide beds (each plant will tiller, or send up multiple stems).

Researchers found that when wheat was sown in rows spaced 14″ apart, they only yielded 6% less than rows spaced 7″ apart (yet only required half as much seed for planting).

Conventional farmers aim for around 25 plants per square foot, which works out to be 5 - 6 sq inches per seed, or about 2 ½″ apart. They crowd their plants somewhat because it tends to increase uniformity of size and maturation time, which is good for machine harvesting.

Care

Water: Generally wheat doesn't require a lot of water, so it is only watered in very dry conditions. Too much water can cause lodging and disease problems.

Winter wheat will get most of its water from winter rains and will be almost done by the time the soil dries out in summer. Such a crop may not need watering at all, which can be a big deal in drier areas.

Spring wheat is more drought tolerant, but paradoxically is more likely to need watering because it is growing in the warmest and driest part of the year).

Weeds: Because of the relatively wide spacing and the sparseness of foliage on young plants, weeds were once a big problem for wheat farmers. Some weeds became synonymous with wheat fields (once known as corn), including corn spurrey, corn cockle, corn poppy and cornflower. Once the plants reach a certain size they are able to take care of themselves and crowd out weeds.

It is a lot easier to keep a small area of the young plants weeded if you plant them in beds with paths between them.

One problem is differentiating grassy weeds from your similar looking crop plants. This is one good reason to sow in rows, rather than broadcasting. Then if a plant isn't growing in a row then you can assume it's a weed.

Lodging: Lodging is another name for falling over and can be a problem when winter wheat is sown too early. If the over-wintering plants get taller than 6″ you should cut them back a little (it won't hurt them).

Pests: One advantage of small scale growing is that your plants are unlikely to be seriously bothered by pests or disease.

Birds and small mammals can be pests of wheat at both ends of the growing cycle. They will eat the grain and young plants when it is sown and they may eat the grain when it is ripening. Slugs and snails may eat young seedlings.

Hessian fly is a serious problem for wheat farmers in the east. You can avoid it by planting late (mid September to mid October).

Sawflies and chinch bug can also be problematic.

Disease: These include rust, bunt and mosaic virus.

Harvesting

When: Wheat is ready to harvest when the heads start to droop somewhat and the plants are turning yellow brown, but still have some green coloration. The seed should be quite hard and you should barely be able to dent it with your fingernail or teeth (it will harden even further as it dries out).

How: For centuries the wheat harvest was a major annual event for country people. It determined whether they lived well for the next year, or faced the prospect of hunger and possible starvation. No wonder the annual harvest festival was a time to give thanks for a good harvest.

Wheat should be harvested later in the day, after the dew has dried out. If you are working on a small scale, you can cut the seed heads with shears and then dry and thresh them.

On a bigger scale the whole plants can be cut with a sickle (remove any weeds as you harvest), propped upright and tied into a shock (or stook) to dry (a shock is a cluster of sheaves set upright and tied together with wheat stems). After the shocks had thoroughly dried, they were made into a stack and left until threshing time.

Threshing is the process of freeing the seeds from the hulls and the rest of the plant and was traditionally done with a flail (or failing that a piece of rubber hose will work). The seed heads are placed on a flat sheet and pounded energetically to loosen the grain from the husk.

The threshed seed is then winnowed to remove the chaff. This is done by tossing it into the air on a windy day (an electric fan is more reliable), so the light chaff was caught by the wind and blown away. The heavier seeds fall straight back down. A small quantity can be tossed in a flat basket to winnow. This was often done a small quantity at a time as needed.

The cleaned seed can be used immediately or dried further for storage. Drying is a critical step because if the grains aren't fully dry (less than 13% moisture) they will spoil in storage. A fully dry wheat kernel is hard and will shatter rather than dent.

The dry seed should be stored in an insect and vermin proof container such as a metal bin, in the usual cool dark place (40 - 60°F at less than 40% humidity). If moisture, heat or rodents don't get at the grain, it should remain edible for years (up to 10). Store your wheat as grain, not flour which is much more perishable (though you can store flour in the freezer).

Seed saving: Wheat is usually self-pollinated so it's easy to save the seed (you will be collecting it anyway). It isn't likely there will be many different wheat varieties growing around you, unless you live near a farm.

To improve your seed gather it from the healthiest and best plants in your planting. If you want to maximise genetic variability you could just take a portion of all of the wheat you just grew.

Your seed wheat should probably be stored separately from the bulk of the crop. It must be kept under optimum conditions if it is to remain viable for a long time.

Unusual growing ideas

Clover living mulch: Winter wheat can be under planted with a hardy annual clover, which covers the bed for the winter, suppresses weeds and supplies nitrogen. This improves the soil while growing a crop at the same time.

Cover crop: Winter wheat can provide the soil with many of the same benefits as a winter cover crop (and produce grain as a bonus).

Green manure: Wheat has also been grown as a winter cover crop or green manure.

Organic matter source: After you have harvested the grain crop, the straw is a valuable source of organic matter for enriching the soil (or for use as mulch). This is actually a significant bonus crop and makes wheat growing a more practical proposition.

Varieties: There aren't many varieties available in small quantities for the home gardener. Usually you just get winter wheat or spring wheat.

Winter Wheat: These tend to be higher yielding than spring wheat.

Spring Wheat: This is usually only grown if it's not possible to grow the winter types.

Kitchen use

Wheat is most often ground into flour for making breads, cakes, pastry, tortillas and pasta. It can also be cooked for making cereals and even be popped like popcorn.

Sprouted grain "bread"

Sprout 3 cups of wheat grains until they have shoots about ⅛th inch long. This takes from 12 hours to 2 days, depending upon how warm it is.

When the wheat is ready you put it in a food processor and process until it turns into a thick, sticky paste. There are two options for "baking".

One is to spread it out into a thin ¼" layer on a greased baking sheet and bake for 35 minutes at 325 F.

The alternative no-bake method is to spread it out into a thicker 1 ½" layer and "bake" it in the sun ideally as 80 F) for 12 hours.

Other grains

These are all grown in pretty much the same way as wheat.

Spelt (*Triticum aestivum ssp spelta*)
This subspecies of wheat and has become somewhat fashionable of late as a (yet another) superfood. It is said to be more nutritious and easier to digest than wheat.

Emmer (*Triticum dicoccum*)
Also known as farro, this is an ancient type of wheat noted for its ability to grow on poor soils. Like spelt it has become somewhat fashionable of late.

Rye (*Secale cereal*)
This is one of the easiest grains to grow because it does better on poor soil and in cold wet climates and is quite drought tolerant. It isn't as productive as wheat though and doesn't make such good bread.

Rye is grown in the same way as winter wheat and is usually planted in fall. It prefers a light acid soil.

Triticale (x *Triticosecale*)
This is a cross of rye and wheat, bred to give the high protein grain of wheat and the tolerance of poorer growing conditions of rye.

Barley (*Hordeum vulgare*)
This doesn't make as good bread as wheat, but it makes better beer.

Herbs

The aromatic culinary herbs ask so little and give so much, that they should be in every garden. If you don't have much space, herbs can even be planted around the garden as low maintenance ornamentals, groundcovers or foliage plants.

Basil

Ocimum basilicum
See **Basil**.

Bay

Laurus nobilis
A tree rather than a herb, but an important culinary flavoring nevertheless. A Mediterranean plant, it is drought tolerant, but not very cold hardy. In cool climates it is often grown in a container, so it can be taken indoors for the winter. In the right climate it can be very vigorous and one plant is enough to supply the kitchen.

Bay can be quite formal looking when clipped and a pair of potted plants can be quite ornamental.

Bay is one of the key flavorings of French cooking. The tough leaves are added to dishes while cooking to impart their flavor, but are removed before serving.

Chervil

Anthriscus cerefolium
This hardy annual is a cool weather plant and in warmer climates it can only be grown in spring or fall (in cooler climates it can be grown all summer).

Chervil doesn't like transplanting, so is usually direct sown. Start a spring crop no earlier than 3 weeks before the last frost. Start your fall crop after the hottest part of the summer is over, maybe 6 - 8 weeks before the first frost. It works best when sown thickly, so space the plants only 3 - 4″ apart. It is short lived so is often sown in succession every few weeks.

Chervil grows best in a typical rich garden soil and can tolerate quite a lot of shade (you are growing it for its leaves). Keep it well watered in warm weather to prevent premature bolting. When it eventually bolts you can collect the seed or allow it to self-sow. The seed isn't very long lived, so should be collected regularly.

Chervil tastes somewhat like anise and is one of the essential flavorings of French cooking (It is a traditional ingredient of "fines herbes").

The flavor of chervil is delicate and dissipates quickly when cooked, so should only be added at the last minute. It is mostly used for flavoring eggs, soups and salads where it won't get overpowered by stronger flavors. It doesn't dry well, so if you want to store it, freezing in ice cube trays works best (see **Basil** for more on this).

Chives

Allium schoenoprasum
This is one of the best onion flavored plants. It is often grown in herb gardens, but is so easy to grow and so pretty that it can be planted almost anywhere.

Chives will grow in almost any soil, but does best in a rich, moist one with lots of organic matter. Chives is easily grown from seed and will sometimes volunteer. It is often started indoors in flats or soil blocks and later transplanted outside. However it can also be direct sown too.

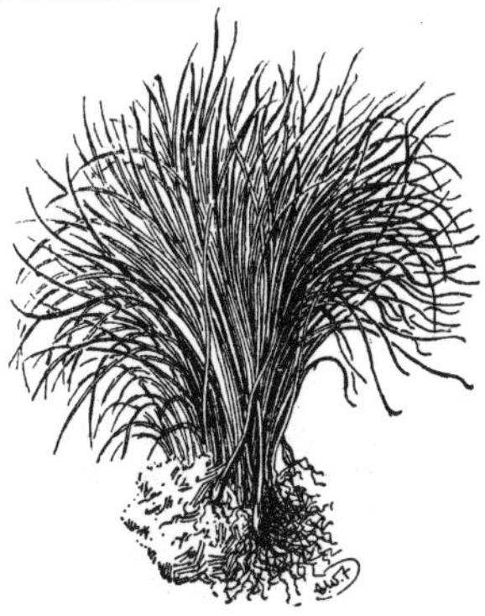

Once you have an established colony, chives can easily be propagated by division. The plants multiply quickly and may actually benefit from the occasional thinning.

Chives is pretty drought tolerant, so doesn't need a lot of watering. It is quite low growing and somewhat vulnerable to weeds, so weed regularly.

Remove the dead flowers to prevent the plant devoting energy to seed production (unless you want seed of course).

The leaves are at their best before the flowers appear, but can be used anytime they are available.

If you leave your chives alone for long enough, it will flower and make seeds. It won't cross-pollinate with anything.

Chives is used to add a delicate Onion flavor to soups, salads, salad dressings, eggs, dips, sauces and cheese dishes.

Coriander

Coriandrum sativum
See **Coriander**.

Cumin

Cuminum cyminum

This tender annual needs a long warm growing season to produce its aromatic edible seed. It is easily grown from seed, but in more northern areas it may have to be started indoors early.

Cumin needs a warm, sheltered location and a well-drained, fertile soil.

The seeds are an essential ingredient in curries, chili, soups and other dishes.

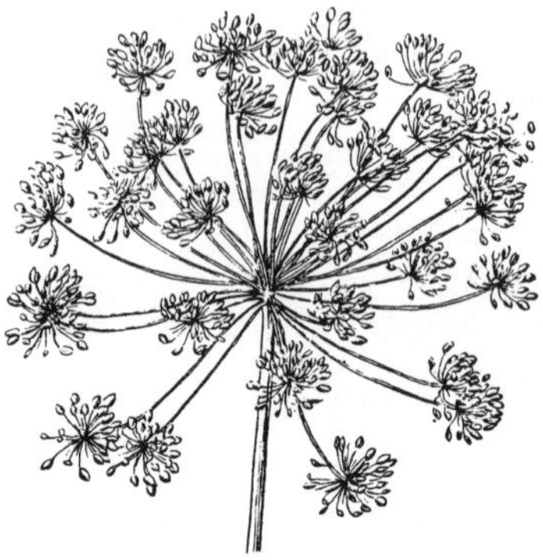

Dill

Anethum graveolens

This tender annual is a member of the celery family (*Apiaceae*) and like many of its cousins it has finely divided leaves and highly aromatic foliage. It is best known as the herb that gives pickled cucumbers their unique flavor.

Dill prefers full sun and well-drained, moisture retentive, fertile, slightly acidic soil, It can grow to 2 or 3 feet in height and needs shelter from strong winds.

It doesn't like transplanting, so is usually direct sown, starting around the last frost date. It is a short lived plant so if you want a continuous supply you will have to sow more seeds every few weeks Space the plants 12 - 18″ apart.

Both the leaves and the seeds can be used as flavoring (they taste the same). The flowers are edible too, though if you take them you won't get seeds.

Epazote

Dysphania ambrosioides

If you taste (or even smell) a fresh epazote leaf it has a decidedly aromatic hydrocarbon-like quality that many people find quite nauseating. However in Mexico it is an important flavoring for bean dishes and it definitely does add something nice to a pot of beans (it is also said to reduce their flatulence inducing effects).

.

Epazote is easy to grow from seed and self-sows in my garden. It is a short lived perennial in milder climates, but can't survive cold winters.

Garlic Chives

Allium tuberosum

This garlic flavored herb is grown and used in pretty much the same ways as chives. It is also quite commonly grown as an ornamental.

Ginger

Zingiber officinale

The easiest way to grow ginger is to get a piece of fresh (not dried) root from the market and plant it. Ginger isn't a very hardy plant and sometimes survives outdoors in my garden and sometimes not. In colder climates it must be grown in a pot, so you can take it indoors for the winter.

You can plant ginger in spring and harvest in fall, though it takes up to a year for the root to develop the best flavor. In the tropics they harvest the rhizome and immediately replant part of it Ginger may grow to four feet in height and is quite ornamental, especially if you can get it to produce flowers.

Lemongrass

Cymbopogon citratus

This subtropical grass is best known as a lemon-like flavoring for Thai food. It isn't very hardy, though it has survived the winter in my garden (including a few spells below freezing).

It can be grown from seed, but it is much faster and easier to grow from stem cuttings. Buy some lemongrass stalks from a market, root them in water and plant them out in a good garden soil.

Lovage

Levisticum officinale

Introduction: This uncommon perennial is one of my favorite salad plants. Its flavor is often compared to the related celery, but in my opinion it is much nicer.

Lovage does best in a rich moisture retentive soil with sun or part shade.

Lovage can be grown from seed, sown when it is ripe in summer or early autumn. It is an easy plant to grow and requires little attention. If you make sure the soil is kept fairly moist, that should be enough. The seedlings are quite vigorous, but will take several years to reach full size.

A mature plant can be quite enormous, sometimes reaching as much as 10 feet in height. They are attractive enough to be planted in the ornamental garden.

Lovage can be divided very easily. I initially bought a small plant, and as it got bigger I divided it. It also produced seed, which I used to grow more plants (I love lovage). Harvest the leaves, stems and seeds whenever you need them. I crave the young leaves and stems in salads, so rarely use them in any other way. They can also be used as a wonderful flavoring for soups and stews, in much the same way as celery.

Marjoram

Origanum majorana

Marjoram is a close relative of Oregano, but sweeter and more aromatic.

This native of the Mediterranean thrives in full sun and grows without any attention in my garden. It is a perennial, but not very hardy (only to zone 6).

Oregano grows well in relatively poor soils, so long as they are well-drained.

This species is easily grown from seed, but it is quite slow. It's quicker and easier to buy a plant and then divide it as necessary. You can also grow it from cuttings. Space the plants 12″ apart.

Marjoram is very drought tolerant (it grows completely independently in my garden), but will grow faster if watered occasionally. It isn't very hardy, so if winters are very cold you may want to pot it up and bring it inside for the winter. It does well on a kitchen windowsill.

Cut the tender shoots and leaves as you need them. They are best just before the flowers appear, so if you are going to preserve them, this is the time to harvest. They can be dried for winter use, or frozen in ice cube trays (see **Basil** for more on this).

Marjoram is great in soups, sauces and salad dressings.

Mints

Mentha species

The defining characteristic of most mints is their vigor; if given suitable growing conditions they will put on an amazing amount of growth in a season. There is a limit to how much growth you want from a plant though and the mints are happy to exceed that. They spread easily by means of creeping rhizomes and can be notoriously invasive. If your garden is big enough you might let them run free, but in most gardens it is necessary to confine them behind a barrier.

Mints are not very concerned about location and will do well in sun or part shade, so long as they get enough moisture. They grow best in a rich soil, though almost any moist soil will do. You can use quite a lot of mint if you dry it for winter use in tea.

Though mint is easily grown from seed, this isn't very desirable because the flavor of a seedling won't necessarily be the same as the parent plant. Some kinds are distinctly inferior and the last thing you want is to have your garden choked by one of these.

The mints are usually propagated vegetatively, as you can then be sure of what you are getting. The easiest way to do this is to dig up some of the spreading rhizomes and replant them. If you want a large number of plants you can cut them up into pieces and root them indoors.

Space the plants one foot apart and thin every few years as they get crowded. You should only need one plant (or bucket) of each variety.

It doesn't take a very talented gardener to grow mint, probably the hardest part is stopping it from taking over the garden entirely. The best way to grow it is in a 5-gallon bucket with the bottom cut out, sunk into the ground to within 2 - 3″ of the rim. This contains it very effectively. Don't think you can keep it under control by mowing, it will simply hug the ground and continue to spread.

When growing in confined spaces, mint should be divided regularly, to prevent it getting overcrowded. Replant a small part and discard the rest (or give it away). Be careful where, as it can re-root itself.

If mint does get out of hand it isn't usually that difficult to pull up the long runners. It only gets complicated when they get entangled in something.

This vigorous and independent plant doesn't need much attention. It does like moist soil however and won't be nearly so vigorous without it. In theory you could keep mint under control by not watering it very much, but drought stressed plants taste decidedly inferior to well watered ones.

Mint is best harvested just before it flowers. After it flowers you can encourage fresh new growth by cutting it down to the ground.

There are many different varieties and species of mint to choose from, each with a different flavor. The golden rule when buying any mint is to taste it before you buy.

Spearmint is the most useful as a culinary flavoring, but I much prefer peppermint as a tea. Apple mint with its soft fuzzy leaves is good raw in salads.

The use of mints as flavoring has extended beyond the kitchen and they are found in a variety of products.

Oregano, Greek

Origanum vulgare ssp hirtum Syn *O. heracleoticum*

Oregano, Italian

Origanum vulgare

These aromatic perennials are essential to Italian cooking. They both grow quite independently in my garden.

These species are native to the Mediterranean and love full sun. They don't need very fertile soil, but it should be well-drained. Space the plants 12″ apart.

These plants can be grown from seed, but it is better to use a superior cultivar. I bought a plant of each type and as they grew I divided them (they also self-sowed).

As Mediterranean plants they are as likely to suffer from too much water as from not enough. For maximum growth they do need occasional watering though.

If the plants start to get woody, cut them down to within a couple of inches of the ground. This will stimulate them to send up fresh new growth.

I have to admit to being completely oblivious as to whether it has any pests of not, I only pay it any attention when I am harvesting (it always looks healthy enough).

Cut the shoots and leaves as you need them. It can be dried for winter use but is better frozen (see **Chives**).

As with most herbs it is a good idea to smell and taste a variety before you buy it.

Oregano doesn't keep its flavor if cooked for too long, so should be added near the end of cooking. It's good with roast potatoes, as a topping for pizza and in sauces, stews, soups and vegetables.

Parsley

Petroselintum crispum

See **Hamburg Parsley**.

Rosemary

Rosmarinus officinalis

This evergreen shrub is native to the Mediterranean and is perfectly at home in my garden. In fact I don't really feel qualified to give you much advice about it, because it grows itself with no help from me. It grows into a medium sized bush that never needs irrigation and is one of the few plants that is never eaten by deer.

Rosemary likes a well-drained soil and a sheltered position with full sun. It doesn't like extreme cold and can be killed by temperatures of 5°F. In colder climates it is often grown in containers and brought inside for the winter.

I usually propagate rosemary by layering, as branches will root where they touch the ground. Just pin them down to the ground, cover with soil and keep them moist.

If you need a lot of plants, they can be propagated from softwood cuttings taken in late spring. These should be 3″ long and have a small heel of older wood attached. Root them in a plant pot filled with peat moss and covered with a clear plastic bag to increase the humidity. They should root within a month.

You can gather sprigs of this evergreen any time you need them, even in winter. The flavor of the fresh plants is best, but it can also be dried for later use.

In Mediterranean climates rosemary is a useful evergreen landscape shrub. Its blue flowers are a magnet for bees and positively hum on warm summer days, Of course this will give you far more rosemary than you could ever use.

There are quite a few varieties, but they differ more in their habit (upright, prostrate) than their flavor.

Use the fresh or dried leaves in stuffings, stews, soups (pea is good) and vegetables. Add a shoots to a barbecue, or remove the leaves and use them as skewers.

Saffron

Crocus sativus

This somewhat unusual plant is the source of the very expensive spice: saffron, which is important for its color as well as its distinctive flavor. It's expensive because each plant only produces a ridiculously tiny amount (the tiny styles of the flower are the saffron), I can't imagine who first though of using the styles of a flower as food but someone did (I can't imagine harvesting it for a living either).

Saffron is a pretty independent plant, I planted some about 5 years ago and then lost it (it is only visible above ground for a few months every year) yet it persisted with no care at all. It is propagated by means of offsets of the bulbs and is fairly easy to grow.

The narrow leaves resemble long narrow blades of grass and the plant is only really obvious when in bloom in autumn.

Saffron is easy enough to grow, if you can find some bulbs to plant (this is not so easy).

Sage

Salvia officinalis

Sage has been on the list of indispensable culinary herbs since medieval times and cooking just wouldn't be the same without it. You don't usually need more than 2 or 3 sage plants as it is quite strongly flavored. I have more than this because my son used to graze on it, sometimes defoliating whole bushes at one sitting (it never seemed to do him any harm).

It will grow in any well-drained soil, but prefers a light, slightly alkaline one.

Sage loves full sun, though in hot climates it will also grow in part shade. Like other Mediterranean herbs it is a very tough plant and once established it can be totally ignored, apart from harvesting. It is very drought tolerant and doesn't even need watering.

Sage is easily grown from seed in well-drained soil. The seedlings will taste as good as their parents, but you won't be able to start harvesting until their second year.

I initially bought a small plant (a rooted cutting) from a nursery. When that was big enough I divided it, layered it, collected the seed and took cuttings!

Sage layers well, just lay a branch down on the ground and cover it with soil. By the end of the summer it will have rooted and can be detached. You can also bury an entire plant (except the tips) in soil. The more vigorous branches will root easily.

Sage doesn't like very cold weather and in very cold areas it may not survive the winter outdoors. In which case it should be potted up and brought inside for winter use (or kept dormant in a cool garage).

Remove the flower stalks as they appear (unless you want seed) as this diverts energy from vegetative growth.

If a plant starts to get woody, cut it back hard, to encourage tender new growth. If a plant gets very woody dig it up, divide it, and replant the most vigorous parts (or just take cuttings).

Pick single leaves as you need them for cooking. They are evergreen and can be gathered year round in mild climates. In harsher climates you can pick whole branches just before they flower and dry them indoors (they dry well). Whole leaves can be frozen for winter use (but drying is easier and just as good).

Sage has pretty blue flowers and can be useful as a drought tolerant ornamental.

There are quite a few varieties out there: Golden, Tricolor, Berggarten (with big leaves). Unfortunately most of these look better than they taste.

Sage is best fresh, but is also good dried. It is good with cheese, beans, soups, pâté, eggs, pasta, cheeses, sauces, soups and various vegetables.

Shiso

Perilla frutescens

This tender annual is an important herb in its native Japan, where it is used in a wide variety of dishes (notably pickled umeboshi plums).

It is most familiar in the West from its use in sushi. It has an anise-like flavor, though this varies somewhat according to type. It is a member of the mint family (*Lamiaceae*).

Shiso is a warm climate plant and is grown in much the same way as basil, though it is bigger and more vigorous. It is easily grown from seed (this is said to need light to germinate, so keep on the surface), planted no earlier than 2 weeks after the last frost. Space the plants 6 - 12″ apart.

Pinch back the growing tips to harvest and make the plants bushier. It can grow quite tall (to 4 ft in height) so make sure it doesn't shade other plants.

This is quite an ornamental plant, especially those with red leaves. If allowed to flower and set seed it will self-sow vigorously.

The flowers and aromatic seeds are also edible.

Stevia

(*Stevia rebaudiana*)
Not a plant to drink by itself, but it is the best (pretty much the only) sweetener for any herbal tea. It can also be used as a sweetener in cooking. My children wrap a large spearmint leaf in a small stevia leaf for the ultimate in natural mint candies.

Stevia is a tender perennial, but it has survived in my garden for the last three winters (and at least 50 or more nights of freezing weather).

Stevia can be grown from seed, but I divide my plants in spring when they first start to emerge. By doing this I have all the plants I need.

Tarragon

Artemisia dracunculus
The importance of tarragon to some people is illustrated by this quote from James Beard:
"I believe that if ever I had to practice cannibalism, I might manage if there were enough tarragon around."

The only kind of tarragon you want is French tarragon, which can only be propagated from cuttings (you can't grow it from seed). This means you have to buy a plant to start with. Always smell and taste any herb before you buy it, to make sure it is a good cultivar. Don't buy tarragon seed as it will be the Russian type and inferior.
Tarragon prefers full sun, but in very hot climates it will also do well in part shade. It also likes well-drained soil.

Once you have your plant you can divide it in spring, or propagate it from stem cuttings.

Tarragon is an undemanding plant that requires little beyond an occasional watering. It is quite drought tolerant and can even go dormant in summer if it gets neglected too much. This is yet another herb I have planted and lost, only to find it several years later still hanging on.

Harvest the growing tips as you need them. If the plant gets woody then cut it down to within a couple of inches of the ground. It will send up vigorous new growth.

The leaves don't dry well, but can be frozen to preserve their fresh taste. See **Basil** for more on freezing herbs.

The leaves are used to flavor eggs, tomatoes, butters, vinegars, salads, mustards, sauces and soups (especially mushroom).

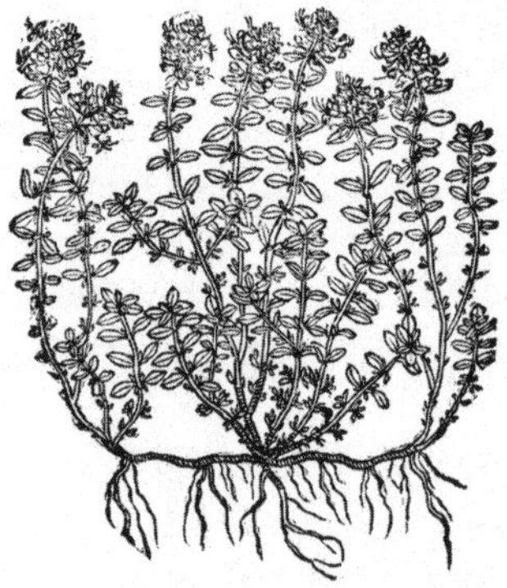

Thyme

Thymus vulgaris
Thyme is another essential herb in French cooking and one of the ingredient of "Fines Herbes" and Bouquet Garni".
Thyme will do well in almost any soil, so long as it is well-drained. It does best in full sun, but will tolerate some shade.

Thyme is usually grown from cuttings or division, though it can also be grown from seed quite satisfactorily. I bought a small plant and divided it as it grew. I also took cuttings.

Thyme is quite drought tolerant so only needs an occasional watering. If it starts to get woody cut it back to within a couple of inches of the ground and it will regenerate. You can also dig it up, divide it and replant the most vigorous pieces.

This low growing plant does well at the edge of paths.

Thyme is good fresh or dried. Its warming flavor goes well with winter squash, soft cheeses, pâté, vegetables, and tomato sauces.

Edible Weeds

There are a number of tasty and nutritious food plants already growing in your garden; the weeds. Some of these are as good as anything you can grow and I really urge you to try a few of them. As an added incentive using them can also help to keep them under control.

I like the edible weeds so much that I have been known to introduce them to the garden (In my present garden I had to do this with both purslane and dandelion).

As with any cultivated crop, these plants are only good to eat when gathered at the right stage of growth and prepared properly.

Annual weeds

Intensively fertilized and watered beds, with their disturbed soil are just made for annual garden weeds. Of thousands of plant species from all over the world, these are the plants that are best adapted to life in the garden. Many of the same weeds can be found in temperate gardens right around the world, because every gardener strives to create the same conditions (rich, moist, loose, bare soil). Disturb a patch of soil and leave it bare for a week and annual weeds will appear. Within a month they will have completely covered every inch of soil.

Many of the commonest annual weeds are edible to some degree and some are very good. If you gather these while they are young, you will have some of the most nutritious and vibrant foods to be found anywhere.

Pigweed

Amaranthus species

This is one of the commonest summer weeds and is probably in most peoples gardens by July. They produce an abundance of long-lived (up to forty years) seed and can out-compete almost any crop plants.

The pigweeds are close relatives of the amaranth I have already described as a crop (see **Amaranth**). The wild plants are just as nutritious and tasty and can be used in the same ways. The only significant difference is that you don't have to grow them.

Wintercress

Barbarea species

Wintercress gets its name because it is extremely hardy and can grow right through the winter in mild areas. It is at its best in cool temperatures and can get very pungent in warm weather. I use it like watercress, raw in salads or as a potherb. If it is too bitter to be palatable, the first cooking water can be thrown away and a lot of the bitterness will go with it. The unopened flower buds can be eaten raw, or cooked like miniature broccoli.

Some species (*B. vulgaris, B. verna*) are so good they are cultivated as minor crops. They are a good example of a no-work vegetable, that even self seeds itself.

Shepherds Purse

Capsella bursa pastoris

This opportunistic little annual is naturalized all around the world. It has been so successful because it sets seed abundantly (it pollinates its flowers before they even open) and its seed may remain viable for up to thirty years. It is also very hardy and can survive temperatures as low as 10°F.

Unlike many members of the mustard family, the leaves don't get very pungent or bitter, so can be used any time they are available. This plant is widely cultivated in Taiwan and China and can be found for sale in vegetable markets there. In moist fertile soil the leaves get much larger than in the wild, often several inches in length.

The leaves are at their best before the flowers appear. They can be used in salads, or cooked for a few minutes as a potherb. They are good sautéed with onion. The seed can be ground to flour and made into a condiment like mustard. It has also been sprouted like alfalfa *Medicago*).

Lambs Quarters

Chenopodium album

A single lambs quarters plant will produce about 4000 seeds on average. Some of these seeds are able to germinate immediately; others must lie dormant for several years (they are an insurance policy for the plant). This is one reason why it is such a formidable competitor as a weed.

The leaves contain large amounts of vitamins A, C and several B's, as well as calcium, iron and phosphorus.

Caution: It is often said that one should eat lambs quarters in moderation. This is because it contains oxalic acid, which can inhibit the absorption of calcium. The danger of oxalates in general is over-rated, as they pose little problem to a person with a healthy intake of calcium. They may be a problem for people with a history of kidney stones however.

A close relative of spinach, lambs quarters has been used as a salad or potherb for thousands of years. The young spring growth is good in salads, or as a potherb and is highly regarded by many wild food enthusiasts.

Mallows

Malva neglecta, M. rotundifolia
The Mallows are among the richest plant sources of carotene (which the body converts into vitamin A), containing as much as 16,000 i.u. per ounce. They also contain a lot of vitamin C and many minerals.

These hardy plants remain green all winter in mild climates, which makes them valuable winter greens in such areas. In China they are sometimes called winter amaranth, which gives an interesting insight into the importance of both species.

The tender young leaves can be used in salads, but are best boiled as greens. Older leaves can be chopped and cooked as a potherb, though you might want to change the cooking water once or twice. This is not necessary to remove any unpleasant taste, but to reduce their rather slimy quality.

The green seedpods have been peeled and used like okra (actually a relative) to thicken soups and as a cooked vegetable. Their unusual shape and texture makes them an interesting addition to salads. If you don't have them in your garden, but would like them, they are easily raised from seed. Once established they will self sow.

Miners Lettuce

Montia perfoliata
The plant got its common name because gold miners commonly ate it during the 1849 California gold rush. Before that event it was known as indian lettuce or Spanish lettuce for similar reasons.

Miners lettuce is a common weed on the west coast, where it grows in the cool weather of late winter and spring. It can be made into a weed elsewhere, as it is easily grown from seed and self-sows readily.

The mildly flavored and succulent leaves can be used as the base for a wild spring salad. They can also be used as a potherb, by steaming or boiling for a few minutes.

Peppergrass

Lepidium spp
All *Lepidium* species, native and exotic are edible and many are quite tasty. Like most members of the mustard family they are best in cool weather and becomes bitter and unpalatable in hot weather.

The leaves contain up to 10,000 i.u. of vitamin A per 100 grams.

The tender young plants are good in salads and some species have been cultivated for this. Older parts can be used raw if finely chopped. They can also be cooked as a potherb, though you may need to change the cooking water to reduce their strong flavor.

In Britain the seed has been sprouted indoors as micro-greens for as long as I can remember. Sprinkle a thin layer of seed on a wet paper towel and leave in a warm dark place for several days to sprout. When most of the seed has germinated bring them out into the light to turn green and grow. They are ready to eat when 2 - 3″ tall (in about a week).

If you can get enough of the seeds, they can be used to make a condiment like mustard (Brassica).

Lepidium sativum is cultivated as a dry land substitute for watercress and is known, appropriately enough, as garden cress. It is easily grown from seed in almost any soil, so long as the weather is cool. It bolts quickly in hot weather.

Purslane *Portulaca oleracea*

One of my favorite edible weeds, purslane is highly prized in Mexico (where it's known as verdolaga) and other countries. In fact it is so esteemed that several improved cultivars have been produced. The succulent leaves and tender growing tips are an excellent salad plant. They are also equally good as a potherb. This is a low growing plant and can get quite dirty in wet weather. It will stay cleaner if it is mulched.

Wild Radish

Raphanus sativus
This is the garden radish, escaped and reverted to its natural wild form. It is only of limited used as food as it doesn't normally produce a swollen root.

The young leaves can be used like the mustards (*Brassica*) as a tasty addition to salads, or as a potherb. In mild winter areas the whole plants can be eaten, cooked or raw, right through the winter. The flowers and unripe seedpods are also good in salads. The ripe seed can be sprouted like alfalfa, or used as a condiment like mustard.

Raphanus raphanistrum - **Wild Radish**
Used as above.

Chickweed

Stellaria media

One of the commonest plants in the world, chickweed is highly regarded as a source of wild greens. It is common, easily identified, mildly flavored, rich in vitamin C and in mild climates will provide food right through the winter. The tender growing tips can be used as a base for a salad, simply add pungent, sour and aromatic leaves to give more flavor. They are also an attractive garnish.

The young plants are a good potherb, though you will need to gather a lot, as it shrinks when cooked. The tops of older plants can be used in the same way, though you may need to discard the tougher stems.

Sow Thistle

Sonchus species

These useful food plants are more closely related to the lettuces (*Lactuca*) than to other Thistles. They are nutritious (rich in vitamins A and C) and no species is poisonous, so any with tender foliage can be eaten.

The mildly flavored young leaves are a good potherb and can even be used for salads if their spines are trimmed off. Older leaves are bitter, but have been eaten after cooking in several changes of water (I am not sure they have any nutrients left after this much cooking though). They can also be blanched to reduce their bitterness, by covering with a bucket (or board) for a few days to exclude light.

The succulent flower stalks can be eaten until the flowers appear. Peel and eat raw or cooked.

Perennial weeds

These weeds are more likely to be found in other parts of the garden, rather than the intensive beds, but they are worth knowing about.

Ground Elder

Aegopodium podagraria

This aggressive perennial spreads by means of creeping roots and by seed and is very invasive. It is also quite palatable, so if you can't beat it eat it.

The young leaves, picked while still young and tender can be eaten raw in salads. They can also be cooked for 10 minutes as a potherb, or added to soups. Ground elder leaves were once quite a popular food in parts of Northern Europe

Burdock

Arctium lappa

Even if you don't know this plant, you may be familiar with the hooked seed capsules. These cling to anything that passes by and were the inspiration for velcro.

The edible part is the long root, which is good enough that the plant is commonly cultivated in Japan

The roots of this biennial are best gathered in the middle of summer, when they first reach a useful size (12″ long and ½″ in diameter). They are scraped to remove the tough skin and chopped thin discs. These can be eaten raw in salads, baked or boiled. If their flavor is too strong, boil for 10 minutes with a little baking soda, then change the cooking water and boil a further 10 minutes.

Milkweed

Asclepias syriaca

This familiar weed contains a milky juice that is responsible for the common name milkweed. This juice is also responsible for the toxic and bitter flavor that pervades all parts of the plant.

The bitter toxins in milkweed are water soluble and can be removed by cooking them in at least one change of water. When prepared properly the plant is considered to be one of the best wild foods.

All parts must be carefully prepared before they can be eaten. The usual method of preparation is to drop the edible part in boiling water and simmer for a couple of minutes. This is then drained, more boiling water is added and it is simmered for another minute or two. You then drain them again, add more boiling water and simmer until cooked. Most of the bitter principle remains in the first two lots of water. Never put milkweed in cold water and bring to the boil, as this fixes the bitterness in the plant.

The tender spring shoots are used when 4 - 8″ high. They can be eaten like as a vegetable, added to soup or fried in tempura batter.

The young leaves can be gathered from the top of the plant until the flowers appear and prepared as above.

The immature seedpods are the best milkweed food. They are gathered when firm and only a couple of inches long and cooked as described above. They are mucilaginous (slimy) like okra pods and can be used in much the same ways.

The western species *A. speciosa* can be used in the same ways.

Chicory

Cicorium intybus

Chicory has a history of cultivation dating back to the ancient Egyptians. It was introduced into North America as a food plant by the first white settlers and is now widely naturalized.

Chicory leaves are as bitter as those of dandelion and almost as nutritious. They contain lots of vitamin A and C and many minerals including iron, potassium, calcium and phosphorus. The tender new spring leaves can be used in the same ways as the related dandelion), as salad greens, or as a potherb. As the plants mature they become impossibly bitter.

Blanching reduces their bitterness considerably (cover them with a plant pot or board) and this probably led to the forcing of the roots.

Thistles

Cirsium species

Thistles are available year round, are quite nutritious and are pretty good even when raw. The many species vary a great deal in habit and edibility so one must experiment with them to find the best.

The roots can be eaten year round but are best while dormant in winter. Locate them at this time by the rosette of leaves. I have dug roots in midsummer and found them tasty straight from the ground, however some species are bitter unless cooked in a change of water. They can be boiled, added to soup or baked.

The slow baked roots can be very sweet as their starch turns to sugar and were a favorite of Native Americans. Bake them in a 350ºF oven for 30 minutes. Native Americans dried and ground the baked roots to flour and baked a kind of bread with it.

The young spring leaves can be eaten as a salad plant if you trim off the spines and chop well. Older leaves can be cooked as a potherb for 15 minutes, though you might have to change the cooking water to reduce their bitterness.

The flower stems can be gathered before the flowers open, peeled of their tough skin and eaten raw or cooked (they are good in soup). For a quick snack, split the stems lengthwise and eat the succulent interior.

Evening Primrose

Oenothera biennis

The biennial roots are edible and can be gathered when dormant from fall to early spring. Locate them by finding the easily identifiable mature plants and then by searching for the leaf rosettes of young plants nearby. They are easy to recognize once you are familiar with them.

The palatability of the roots varies with stage of growth (generally younger plants are best). Some are good enough to eat raw; others must be cooked in a change of water to make them palatable (peeling also helps).

The young leaves and crowns can be used like those of dandelion (*Taraxacum*) and some species are even good raw. Older leaves are bitter, but can be eaten if treated like dandelions and boiled in a change of water.

This species has been cultivated in Europe as a root vegetable. It was once known as German rampion.

The western species *O. hookerii* can be used in the same ways as the above.

Great Plantain

Plantago major

Plantain is more often found in lawns and waste places, rather than garden beds (look for it on your paths). In spring the tender, newly emerged leaves can be used in sandwiches and salads, or boiled as a potherb for 10 to 15 minutes. They are rich in vitamins A and C and quite nutritious.

Older leaves tend to be hairy and somewhat tough, but can be used as a potherb if you strip off the tough veins. They are better used in soups and stews (it may help to put them in blender for a few seconds). They may be improved by blanching (just cover them with a board for a few days).

The related *P. coronopus* is sometimes cultivated as a salad plant.

Common Sorrel

Rumex acetosa

This species can be used in much the same ways as the cultivated French sorrel I have already described. This hardy plant often stays green all winter and doesn't get bitter in summer, so can be eaten any time it is available. The arrowhead shaped leaves are a good minor addition to salads and can even be used in salad dressings instead of lemon or vinegar.

Sorrel is also a fine potherb if you change the cooking water once or

twice, to reduce the sour flavor. See **French Sorrel** for more on this.

Sheep's Sorrel *(R. acetosella)*
This species is smaller than the common sorrel, but can be used in the same ways (the small leaves are a nice addition to salads).

Curled Dock

Rumex crispus
The docks are familiar to almost everyone, as they are among the commonest and most widespread of perennial weeds. No member of the *Rumex* genus is poisonous, though they do contain toxic oxalic acid (cooking reduces this considerably) and many species are too tough, bitter or astringent to be edible.

This species is very rich in vitamins A (up to 7000 i.u. per ounce) and C. It also contains many minerals and is one of the best plant sources of iron.

In mild climates this hardy plant grows right through the winter and at this time it can be good. The tender young leaves are a nice addition to salads, or may be boiled as a potherb for 5 to 10 minutes. Older leaves are bitter, but can be made more palatable by cooking in a change of water for 10 to 15 minutes. If they are astringent you might add a little milk to the cooking water. The leaves don't shrink much in cooking, so you don't need to gather a huge amount.

Patience Dock (*R. patienta*)
Red Dock (*R. sanguineus*)
These related species are sometimes cultivated as potherbs.

Dandelion

Taraxacum officinale
Dandelions are one of the commonest perennial weeds in many gardens. I considered including it in the crop section, as it is such as good food plant and there are improved varieties available. I didn't for the simple reason that in most areas people don't need to cultivate it, they already have it growing for free. In my case I had to introduce it into my garden initially, but it is now naturalized.

Dandelion leaves are more nutritious than most common vegetables. They contain up to 14,000 i.u. of vitamin A per hundred grams, along with lots of vitamin C and several B vitamins. They also contain many minerals, including calcium, chlorine, copper, iron, phosphorus, magnesium, silicon and sulfur. They are one of the richest plant sources of potassium.

Dandelion is only really good in cool weather and for most of the year it is too bitter for most palates. It is harvested in spring, from the time it first appears above ground, until the flowers stalks appear. It may also be good for a while in late autumn. In milder areas it may remain green and palatable all winter.

The young leaves can be used in salads, or cooked for 5 to 10 minutes as a potherb. If they get too bitter, change the cooking water at least once. Some people blanch the leaves by covering them with a box or a plank for a few days (just as they would with the related endive or chicory). This makes them less bitter and more tender.

Stinging Nettle

Urtica dioica
A weed of disturbed ground, rather than the vegetable garden, the nettle is famous (or infamous) for the sting in its leaves. It has a good reason for protecting itself as it does, as the young spring shoots are one of the most nutritious of all green plants. They contain more protein than almost any other green leaf, large amounts of chlorophyll, vitamin A, several B's, lots of C and D. They also contain an abundance of minerals including calcium, iron (one of the richest plant sources), manganese, phosphorus, potassium, silicon and sulfur.

The drawback to the use of Nettles as food is that they are only edible for a short time in spring. Not only does the plant get tough as summer progresses, but inedible crystal deposits form in the leaves.

Obviously this ferocious plant can't be eaten raw, you have to wear gloves to even handle it. However it only takes a few seconds of cooking to eliminate the sting and only a few minutes of boiling, steaming or stir-frying are necessary to produce an excellent potherb. The greens can be used as a substitute for Spinach in any recipe.

Other weeds

There are a lot more useful weeds out there. If you are interested in finding out more about them, I suggest you look at my book The Uses Of Wild Plants.

Index

Other books by Frank Tozer

The Organic Gardeners Handbook

This is is the essential companion to The New Vegetable Growers Handbook as it explains the basics of the craft of organic vegetable gardening: soil dynamics, soil management, fertilization, bed preparation, composting, mulching, crop planning, raising seedlings, direct sowing, watering, weeding, dealing with pests, harvesting, seed saving, season extensiongreenhouses and much more. A lot of the information in The Vegetable Growers Handbook will make more sense if you read this one too. Whether you are a complete novice and need your hand holding through every step, or a veteran gardener with a permanent layer of soil under your fingernails, this book can help you to become a better and more productive gardener. 248 pages.

ISBN: 978-0-9773489-1-6

$24.95

The New Food Garden

Subtitled "growing beyond the vegetable garden" this book expands the concept of food gardening to embrace the whole garden. The new food garden is centered around the intensive vegetable garden, but also puts hedges, ponds, pathways, arbors, lawns, roofs, and walls to work as additional growing space for food plants. Fruit and nut trees, bush fruit, edible vines, perennial vegetables, herbs, annual crops, aquatic plants, weeds, and edible wild plants are used to increase the quantity and variety of foods available with little extra work. The author doesn't just look upon the garden as a place to grow food, however; it is also a place to be lived in and used, so he also concentrates on making it beautiful, comfortable, and efficient. He also describes practical ways in which the garden can help us to reduce our impact on the earth. The ultimate aim of the book is to change the way you think of the garden and make producing food an integral part of the home and everyday life. 360 pages.

ISBN 978-0-9773489-4-7

$29.95

The Uses Of Wild Plants

This unique guide to the wild plants of North America describes the uses and cultivation of more than 1200 species in over 500 genera. A treasury of information on edible plants, as well as every other aspect of plant use, it describes how wild plants were used in the past, how they can be used today and how they might be used in the future. It discusses how plants have been used to treat sickness and how they can help to enhance health by providing superior nutrition. It also describes how they can be used for dyes, cosmetics, soap, paper, fuel, clothing, perfumes, glues, craft materials, and many other home, commercial and industrial uses. Looking to the future, it shows how wild plants could help us to create an ecologically sustainable society, by providing new crops for food, medicine, fuels, renewable energy, chemicals and building materials. How they could help to clean our rivers and lakes, desalinate soil, remove toxic chemicals from polluted groundwater, recover valuable nutrients from waste, and maybe even reduce global warming. It also discusses the cultivation of these plants and their uses around the garden, homestead and farm. 264 pages.

ISBN 0-9773489-0-3

$24.95